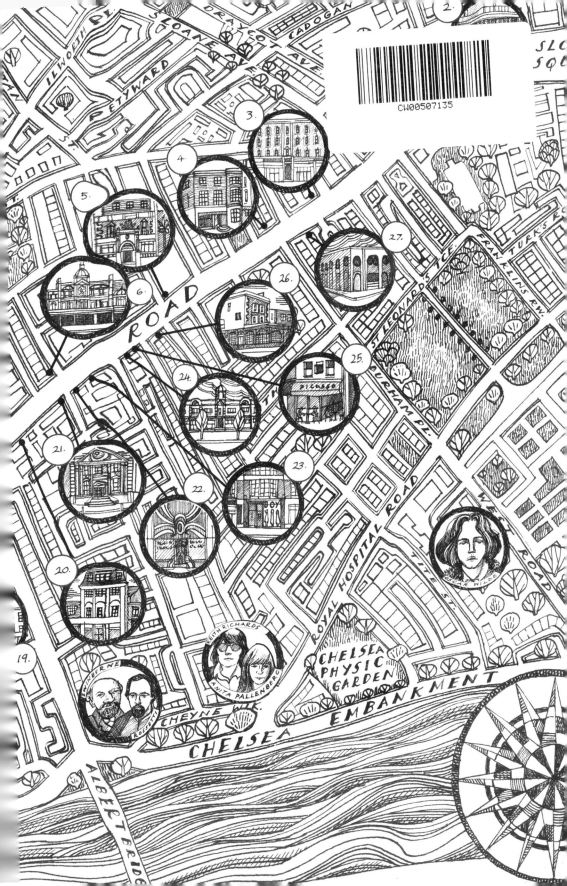

KING'S ROAD

To my aunt Zola, skipping off school to see Bill Haley in 1957; my uncle Edmund, singing Elvis songs in the Slough pubs of the fifties; my father John, with his BSA Gold Star; my brother Derek, hitching across the country to see the Ramones; and to John Peel, who changed the world.

Contents

Introduction to the revised edition

This is a new and considerably expanded version of a book I originally wrote in 2004–5. Its inspiration, one afternoon at the Berlin flat where I was then living, was simply that two of the most important bands to have emerged from England – the Rolling Stones and the Sex Pistols – began life along that one short stretch of tarmac, the King's Road. From that starting point followed a growing awareness of the avalanche of significant cultural developments and events with direct links to the neighbourhood, although many of the original individual shops, cafes and restaurants which had made the road unique were already long gone, and it was now home to four separate branches of Starbucks.

Peel back the façade, however, and the effects left by the former residents, tenants and habitués of Chelsea's chequered past on the life and history of the nation and the wider world are unmistakeable. A volatile mixture of high culture and low culture, the King's Road and its environs spent several centuries regularly throwing out sparks in all directions: from landmark musical performances by Mozart and Billie Holiday all the way through to the earliest sightings of X-Ray Spex; from Aleister Crowley's 1922 novel *Diary of a Drug Fiend* to the Rolling Stones' 'Sympathy for the Devil'; from James Bond to bondage trousers; and from *Look Back in Anger* to the *Rocky Horror Show* – both products of the Royal Court Theatre.

For this new edition, I had no interest in changing the original cut-off date of 1979 – the end of the last decade when there was anything remotely inexpensive and alternative about the King's Road. Coincidentally, that was also the year that Margaret Thatcher moved from her home in one of the more well-heeled parts of Chelsea to 10 Downing Street. The number of unemployed when she came to power was around 1.5 million, and by 1983 had risen to more than double that figure – a 12 per cent unemployment rate for people over the age of sixteen, the worst since the 1930s.

Between 1981 and 1983, I also became a dole statistic, living just across the river in Battersea. Those were the years I started regularly walking around Chelsea: up the side of Battersea Park, across the Albert Bridge, along Oakley Street where both Bowie and Scott of the Antarctic had lived – over half a century apart – to hit the King's Road at the corner near the spot where the pre-Rotten Sex Pistols made their first brief appearance at a private party. Exploring the side streets with no particular aim, I'd occasionally stop to look at whichever houses had blue plaques commemorating illustrious former residents. There was one on Cheyne Walk for George Eliot, but no indication that Keith Richards and Anita Pallenberg had lived next door in the late sixties. Turn around and face the river with the Albert Bridge on your right, and there was also nothing to let you know that Malcolm McDowell's Alex the droog character had received a thorough kicking in *A Clockwork Orange* from a group of tramps in the underpass beneath its northern end, or that the Clash had played on a pontoon moored at the southern end when filming the video for 'London Calling'. These things, and a great deal more besides, eventually resulted years later in the writing of this book.

A lot has changed in the almost two decades since *King's Road* was first published, and among the many people who kindly agreed to speak to me for the original edition, there are those who are sadly no longer with us. My friend Nikki Sudden – the first person I interviewed for it – died tragic-ally early at the age of forty-nine, less than four months after the book appeared, while the great John Peel, who invited me for Sunday lunch at Peel Acres in 2004 before settling down for a lengthy afternoon chat running to nearly 14,000 words, passed away equally unexpectedly before that year was out. The years since have seen the loss of key cultural figures I had interviewed such as Mick Farren, Christopher Lee and Colin Wilson, and while I was working on the revised edition, I was saddened to hear of the death of Cynthia Plaster Caster, who had been a friend for the last thirty years. The King's Road of this book has slowly slipped into history, along with many of those who knew it well in its great days, and I'm deeply grateful for the insights and memories these people shared.

I'd like to say a big thank you to David Barraclough and everyone at Omnibus Press for commissioning the new edition and giving me the chance to revisit and expand this book a decade and a half after its first appear-ance, and to my good friend and literary agent Caroline Montgomery at Rupert Crew Limited for her invaluable help in making it happen. Much love and heartfelt thanks to Katja Klier, always the first person to read my manuscripts, for her fine suggestions, criticisms and insights, unfailingly improving the end result.

When the first edition appeared in November 2005, it received what is sometimes referred to as a blizzard of publicity. The book got me on television, on radio chat shows, and also in most of the glossy magazines and almost all of the national press. It had its share of good reviews, and a few bad ones – in fact, more press attention than anything I have ever written. The Saturday edition of one national newspaper devoted most of a page to a full-on hatchet job, but then the following day's Sunday edition of the same title ran an equally large and very positive review by a different writer. All of which, once the smoke clears, counts for not very much at all in the real world. A month or so later, I received a hand-written letter from Mary Quant, very kindly saying that she had enjoyed the book. That'll do me, thank you.

Max Décharné
London, 2022

Snapshot 1966

'Swinging where, and in what direction?'

'The King's Road was somewhere "cool", and the centre of "Swinging" London – at least, that's what the media told us. Swinging where, and in what direction?'

Christopher Lee

If it's not for sale, you shouldn't put it in the window

It was April 15, 1966, and the new edition of *TIME* magazine arrived on breakfast tables across America. The cover feature by Piri Halasz, 'London: The Swinging City', informed the magazine's largely conservative readership that 'in a once sedate world of faded splendour, everything new, uninhibited and kinky is blooming at the top of London life.'

Splashed across the front page was a painting by Geoffrey Dickinson which must have seemed to people in Texas, Ohio or Utah like a window into an alien world: the cartoon red London bus decorated with the then-current advertising slogan 'Join the Tea Set'; a bingo hall; a long-haired singer wearing Union Jack shades and a Who T-shirt; John and Ringo from the Beatles driving a Rolls-Royce; newly elected prime minister Harold Wilson with his mac and pipe; a 'dolly bird' in a black-and-white op art dress; Big Ben; a David Bailey-type taking a photo; a neon sign reading 'ALFIE' in honour of Michael Caine's current hit film; some upper-class gamblers around a roulette wheel; an E-type Jag; several guardsmen in busbies; a discotheque; a blue-and-white Mini car.

Prior to making the cover painting, said *TIME*'s editorial, artist Dickinson 'prowled from Carnaby Street to King's Road, slipping in and out of boutiques and coffee houses, among other places, and summed up the scene in a collage technique that includes, as he put it, "bits of just about everything – acrylics, watercolour, chalk, pen and ink, labels".' At that time Carnaby Street was by far the more famous across the world, but it was already on the slide, fast turning into the theme park it remains to this day. As George Melly pointed out in his landmark 1970 book *Revolt into Style*, 'the "in" group wouldn't have been seen dead in Carnaby Street by 1966. Chelsea, after a period of decline, reasserted its role as the stage of fashion, and so it has remained ever since.'

Credit: author's collection

Movie edition of Bill Naughton's novel Alfie, February 1966

The hip crowd which had colonised the King's Road by 1966 were at the forefront of much that was new in theatre, fashion, art, music and photography – a situation which had been building for over a decade – but the fact that *TIME*'s article specifically singled out the road on several occasions in pictures and text helped ensure that, from then on, tourists flying in from other parts of the globe would be heading to Chelsea in search of 'the scene': 'Now, as if by common instinct, the whole flock homes in on King's Road, site of such bird boutiques as Bazaar and Granny Takes a Trip, as well as Hung On You, the "kinkiest" (wildest) men's shop.'

Soon local residents, long-time Chelsea groovers and ordinary Londoners could barely push their way along the crowded pavements between Sloane Square and World's End because of all the sightseers, film crews and media pundits. Mary Quant told me that at the height of the hysteria, 'American news magazines and TV were often filming both sides of the King's Road at the same time.' It became one of the great catwalks of the world – a place to see and be seen. As Milton Shulman wrote in a 1967 guidebook:

In Chelsea, the girls in their breathtaking short skirts, their outrageous dresses inspired by anything from *art nouveau* to the Union Jack, their mad stockings and kinky boots, their obvious acceptance of the stares of stunned, gasping males, are so tantalising and so beautiful that any account of entertainment in London must inevitably give them pride of place.

Even Michael Caine's mother was aware of the fuss, as he recalled on BBC TV's *Parkinson* talk show in 2002:

In the sixties, she said, 'What's all this about mini-skirts, what's going on?' I said, 'Have you seen a mini-skirt?' She said, 'No.' So I said, 'Saturday, I'll take you down the King's Road.' And we're walking down the King's Road – I said, 'Here's one now,' and this girl walked by with a mini up to *here*. She goes by and my mother looked at her. So, we walk on a bit. She never said a word. So I said, 'What do you think, Mum?' She said, 'If it's not for sale, you shouldn't put it in the window.'

When We Say 'Peace,' We Mean 'Peace'

Clearly, in running a cover feature about swinging London – 'Miniskirts are for dancing, walking and girl watching. Sitting in them takes practice. [. . .] The guards now change at Buckingham Palace to a Lennon and McCartney tune, and Prince Charles is firmly in the long-hair set.' – it was not *TIME*'s intention to compete with the likes of the *NME* or *Vogue*. Indeed, until that point, the magazine's 1966 covers had been mostly devoted to weightier matters. The previous week's had been a sombre, all-black affair posing the question 'Is God Dead?', sparking a furious debate on the letters pages from readers such as the retired colonel from California who wrote in to call the story 'biased, pro-atheist and pro-Communist, shocking and entirely un-American'. Presumably that same colonel would have been equally unhappy with *TIME*'s March 18 cover story ('Eastern Europe: Life under a Relaxed Communism' with a winsome portrait of 'Rumania's Party Boss Ceausescu'), but probably approved of the bronze bust adorning the January 7 issue, showing their Man of the Year for 1965, General William Childs Westmoreland, 'commander of all US forces in South Viet Nam'. Although Man of the Year status did not necessarily convey unqualified approval – as the 1938 winner Adolf Hitler presumably discovered – in this particular case the accompanying article was full of praise for Westmoreland: 'the sinewy personification of the American fighting man in 1965 who, through the monsoon mud of nameless hamlets, amidst the swirling sands of seagirt enclaves, atop the jungled mountains of the Annamese Cordillera, served as the instrument of US policy'.

The rights and wrongs of the Vietnam War provoked many letters to the editor of *TIME* during 1966 – including a fine piece of sarcasm from one Sidney L. Sincoff of New York, calling for the whole country to be nuked so that 'then we could send in bulldozers and florists to make a garden where Viet Nam once stood. We could do this in other trouble spots to teach the population that when we say "peace," we mean "peace".' – and yet, in a year filled with political and social upheavals of all kinds, Piri Halasz's 'London: The Swinging City' cover feature had an impact far greater than anyone could possibly have imagined, as she told me:

> It is a source of great pleasure to me that the cover should still be of interest so many years later. My research indicates that it's been mentioned and/or quoted in more books and articles than any other cover story in *TIME* that I know about. This may be a dubious distinction, given the fact that a lot of the references are negative, and that *TIME* itself was disliked by a lot of people, but it's a distinction nonetheless.

According to that week's editorial by *TIME*'s publisher Bernhard M. Auer, Piri based her article on personal experience, and also drew on the work of 'seven staffers in our London bureau, as well as five U.S. and British photographers' who sent over to New York the results of 'four days of the most concentrated swinging – discothèques, restaurants, art gallery and private parties, gambling, pub crawling – that any group of individuals has ever enjoyed or suffered, depending on your point of view.'

'The London cover was not my idea,' says Piri. 'I was told that it had first been discussed in London in January when a senior editor from the New York office was visiting and the whole bureau had gone out to lunch with him. The original idea was that the cover should run in the "Modern Living" section instead of "World" and be a spring "travel" cover, all about what a great place London would be for *TIME*'s predominantly American readers to visit that summer, where to eat and drink, how to amuse oneself, what to buy, etc. Then on March 31, for reasons best known to himself, the managing editor [Otto Fuerbringer] decided that he wanted to run the cover in "World" instead of "Modern Living" and asked if I'd write it. This was only nine days before the cover actually went to press, so there was no time for me to go over to London myself.'

Mini-Skirted! Self-Asserted! Ring-a-Ding-Dinger!

TIME's instincts were sound, but they were hardly blazing a new trail. 'Swingers' seemed to be everywhere that year, if the press and the advertising people were to be believed. In January 1966, *TIME* themselves, profiling hip young film composer John Barry, described him as 'a swinger in the Bond mould – clothes with an Edwardian flair, fashionable Chelsea apartment, Pickwick Club, E-type Jaguar (white, XK), E-type wife (brunette actress Jane Birkin).' American singer Roger Miller, whose previous records included 'Dang Me' and 'You Can't Roller Skate in a Buffalo Herd', began the year by reaching the Top Twenty on both sides of the Atlantic with a song entitled 'England Swings', but this turned out to be something of a red herring, since the lyrics dealt solely with an old-fashioned London full of obvious tourist landmarks, bowler hats and walking canes.

Heedless of Miller's advice, in February another major US magazine, the *Saturday Evening Post*, ran an article telling its readers in no uncertain terms that 'Miami Beach swings', but this failed to start a trend. In March, the British Triumph car firm advertised their Spitfire Mk 2 in the US magazine *Evergreen Review* with the slogan 'Longer, lower, wider, faster, swinger', while back in the UK, Warren Beatty and Susannah York were making a US-financed film at Pinewood called *Kaleidoscope*, described by producer Elliott Kastner as a 'swinging comedy-suspense-action picture'. Susannah York's character was billed as 'a kookie young Londoner who runs a Chelsea boutique and has a Scotland Yard inspector for a father.' Over in Hollywood, Ann-Margret was shooting a movie entitled – yes, you've guessed it – *The Swinger*. 'Mini-skirted! Self-asserted! Ring-a-ding-dinger! that's The Swinger' said the adverts: 'A hectically saucy mixture of lechery, depravity, perversion, voyeurism and girlie magazines [. . .] a heavy, witless pudding,' said the *Monthly Film Bulletin*. Not to be outdone, Polaroid announced their new Land Camera, the Swinger Model 20: 'Give the Swinger – $19.95.'

The Swinger advert, December 23, 1966

Even the normally conservative British tourist agencies, long used to peddling a cosy image of Sherlock Holmes, ancient castles and thick London fog, placed adverts in America's upmarket *Harper's* magazine during the same month as *TIME*'s cover feature with the tagline 'Come to Britain – ancient & mod':

> Explore Britain. Browse its meandering lanes. Sample its inns, with their old-worldly charm and unworldly prices. Slow down. Restore yourself. For what? For London's swinging world! There's the *Showboat* for music, *Annabel's Discothèque* for dancing. Or make the scene at the glittering *Talk of the Town*, where the show goes on as you dine. Go from gamboling to gambling in the world's most aristocratic old gaming clubs. And the most 'with it' new ones.

Painted Ties, Kinky Boots and PVC Underwear

London appeared to be in the grip of a powerful artistic upheaval: Michelangelo Antonioni was wandering around town that month shooting material for his own take on the emerging scene, a movie called *Blow-Up*. Miles, the counterculture lynchpin from the Indica bookshop who had helped organise the pivotal 1965 Albert Hall *Wholly Communion* poetry reading, recalls being interviewed twice at the start of the year by major US magazines: 'I had an interview with the *New York Herald Tribune* about the shop, and the previous week *Time-Life* had taken me for an £8 lunch – more than half my weekly wage at Better Books – because *LIFE* was planning an underground issue and wanted information on the English scene.' As Simon Napier-Bell, the then-manager of the Yardbirds and Marc Bolan, later remarked: 'London didn't start swinging immediately it hit the sixties. In fact, London didn't even know it was swinging till some overseas journalists turned up around the middle of the decade and told us what was going on.'

The satirists at *Private Eye* responded to this flurry of activity by printing their own 'Swinging England All-Purpose Titillation Supplement' to assist the 'very small number of American periodicals which have not yet produced their twenty-four-page survey of the Swinging, Vibrant, Thrusting New England Where Even the Hovercraft Wear Mini-Skirts etc. etc.' Pictured inside was 'mini-skirted Helen Kray . . . one of the swinging, way-out, ahead-of-the-crowd Kray twins who have set London's "Up" crowd by the ears'. The magazine already had a history of gleefully poking fun at the increasing trendiness of the King's Road, something its proprietor, the comedian Peter Cook, seemed to find particularly amusing. In May 1966 they took a swipe at shops like Granny Takes a Trip – 'Old clothes, cast-offs desperately wanted. Send: Cookieboutique, King's Road. S.W.3.' – while on television, together with Dudley Moore on the BBC TV show *Not Only But Also*, Cook performed a sketch entitled 'Father and Son', in which Dudley as the working-class father berates his middle-class son, the owner of a boutique selling 'painted ties, kinky boots and PVC underwear'. (Dudley: 'You used to say, "Daddy, what's that?" I used to say, "It's a ship." You never ask me that anymore, do you? You don't have to ask me anything. Do you, eh? Fancy pants. All you need to do is go strutting down the King's Road every Saturday afternoon, showing off to your friends.')

TIME may not have been breaking new ground with the idea for their feature, but in other respects they were behaving quite out of character. As Piri Halasz says:

> It was unusual for *TIME* to employ women writers, period. I was not a feature writer, I was a regular staff writer, just like all the men. I got a monthly wage and wrote about whatever they assigned me to. I had been a passionate Anglophile since adolescence, however, studied UK government and literature in college, and had seen many British plays and movies in New York. My mother, an advertising copywriter, had recently spent a couple of years working for London ad agencies, and I'd also had two English roommates in New York, so I had plenty of contacts there. Finally, I'd been in London in the spring of '65 for about a week. I was really much more interested in writing about politics and had no interest in writing about fads or fashions, so I did my best to get the bureau to show and tell me more about Harold Wilson et al., but they seemed to prefer taking me to trattorias and the Ad Lib.

We May Be Broke, But At Least We're Swinging

From the response in *TIME*'s letters pages over the following weeks, however, it seemed that people were determined to judge the article in terms of its depiction of the fads and fashions:

> That's a hell of a test by which to measure a city's greatness: its ability to appeal to the moronic fringe, the smart alecks and the social climbers.

> As a dolly from the scene, I say cheers for your gear article on the swinging, switched-on city of London and boo to all the American geese who call it humbug.

Your article provided Londoners with a good laugh, but it was hardly realistic. Visitors find the same old dingy streets and grimy restaurants, and while there are youths going about with girlish hair styles and outlandish clothes, you can hardly expect us to be proud of such weirdies.

For the year's most ridiculous generalizations, you deserve to swing indeed. All of you. And not in London either.

The predictable result of all this worldwide attention was that the locals soon started to feel like tourists in their own hometown, a feeling perhaps best summed up by an opinion piece Godfrey Hodgson wrote for the November 1966 edition of *Town* magazine, entitled 'Babylon '66':

The only impact this whole swinging London thing has had on me is that I can't get up the King's Road on a Saturday lunchtime to buy a piece of steak. It's too choked with Americans hurrying on down for a piece of the action. Never mind. We ought to be proud of them. Because now, they say, this great grey gloomy water-colour city of ours, that used to be the nub of the empire and the blue-nose capital of the universe, has been transformed by the wand of the Bad Fairy – and there are some shocking fairies around – into Babylon 1966. Paris, 1900. Berlin, 1920. New York under Prohibition. Tum-tum-tum *Charleston, Charleston* . . . Bathtub gin and 'Brother, can you spare a dime.' It looks as if we may have the unemployment to match by Xmas, too. We may be broke, but at least we're swinging. *TIME* magazine says so, and I always believe what I read in *TIME* magazine . . .

How, then, had it come to this?

Part One

Lost Highway

1

'Treading on a Prince of Wales'

Punk Rock Rotten Razored

June 12, 1977, and the writer Kris Needs is walking along the King's Road towards Malcolm McLaren and Vivienne Westwood's Seditionaries shop at number 430, wearing one of their Sex Pistols T-shirts featuring Jamie Reid's collage of Queen Elizabeth II sporting a rather fetching safety pin through her lip. It is one week after the monarch's Silver Jubilee celebrations, and that image of a punk-friendly Liz also stares out from the picture sleeve of the new Pistols single, 'God Save the Queen'. The previous day Needs had interviewed the band for an upcoming article in the rock magazine *Zigzag*, and found them to be a pretty friendly bunch, as groups go. By chance, he runs into Pistols guitarist Steve Jones in the King's Road, who asks him if he's seen that morning's front-page headline on the *Daily Mirror*, which reads:

> PUNK ROCK JUBILEE SHOCKER
> Today, after a Jubilee week in which the Queen's popularity has never been higher, she is the subject of attack by a punk rock group. The Sex Pistols have burst into the Top Ten with a record which calls the Queen a 'moron'.

Jones and Needs laugh about this, and agree that this is more than likely to help send the single to number one. Shortly afterwards, as the writer nears World's End, he is yelled at by a complete stranger who tells him loudly to piss off. As Needs recalled in the following month's edition of *Zigzag*:

'I saw a bloke in his mid-thirties standing there looking at me with utter contempt. He stared at my "God Save the Queen" T-shirt (same as that advert) and shouted "Bastard!" He didn't look like one of those loonies either. Patriotism lives. I just told him to fuck off. God save the Pistols.'

Ever since the infamous Bill Grundy Thames TV appearance on December 1, 1976 and the tabloid feeding frenzy which it had provoked – 'TV FURY AT ROCK CULT FILTH' – it had become ever-more dangerous to walk the streets in anything resembling punk gear. Provincial towns up and down the UK that summer featured the now-popular national sport of punk-bashing, as spiky-haired teens ran the gauntlet of generally older and more numerous gangs of beer-boys, casuals, Teddy boys and offended 'patriots'. The tabloids had been running a string of articles about 'offensive' punk rockers, and in the wake of the Jubilee, the *Daily Mirror* was able to report that designer Jamie Reid had been attacked by a gang, and that Johnny Rotten had been set on in a Hampstead pub car park by a knife-wielding group of men in their thirties:

PUNK ROCK ROTTEN RAZORED

A spokesman for Virgin Records, who issued the controversial 'Queen' disc, said, 'It looks as if the punk rockers are in for a hard time. [. . .] A lot of people were upset at the record about the Queen, and that could be part of the problem.'

That same day's papers reported that another member of the band, drummer Paul Cook, had been beaten over the head with an iron bar in Shepherd's Bush, requiring fifteen stitches. John Blake, writing the front-page article in the London *Evening News*, highlighted the rivalry between Teds and punks, quoting a police officer who said: 'If it carries on at the present rate I would not be surprised to see pitched battles like those at Hastings and Brighton in the sixties.'

Small wonder then that when the German film-maker Wolfgang Büld came to town in September 1977 to shoot the documentary *Punk in London*, he had difficulty even finding enough punks down the King's Road to fill the screen. As he told me: 'I had to bribe a bunch of them with beer to stand outside Town Records, near the Seditionaries shop, for those scenes in the opening titles of my film. We'd been told there would be lots of punks down the King's Road, but they were really hard to find.'

Even at the high-water mark of UK punk in the summer of 1977, in the very street where the Sex Pistols had formed and in which Westwood and McLaren had invented the classic punk look, it was still sometimes a risky business to walk the King's Road in safety pins and a 'God Save the Queen' T-shirt.

Boring Old Gits to Wed

In some ways, this is strange, given that the area had long been a fashion catwalk for some of the world's most extreme trends, and Chelsea in general had a history of tolerance towards artists and bohemians of all kinds. Yet the land surrounding this short stretch of road in which key elements of the UK punk movement developed had at one time been owned by Henry VIII, and was at various times home to the likes of Catherine Parr, Anne of Cleves, Elizabeth I and Edward VI. Offending royalist sensibilities in 1977 was still a risky business and exposed the punks to the wrath of the tabloids, who were some years away from their later incarnation in which the phone-tapped private conversations between members of the Royal Family would be printed verbatim in the press, Prince Charles's wedding in 2005 announced by the *Daily Star* with the headline 'Boring Old Gits To Wed', and the *Daily Mirror* – so concerned in 1977 about the Sex Pistols' 'God Save the Queen' single – would happily print a poem by Brian Reade to mark the occasion entitled *Ode to a Royal Engagement* which said 'let the kingdom yell and roar, "hurrah for the whorer and his whore".' Times change.

Back in 1536, it would have been a brave act indeed to publicly refer to one of the Royal Family as a 'whorer', when insults were generally countered not with a libel writ but with a masked gentleman swinging an axe. This was the year in which Henry VIII acquired Chelsea Manor on the banks of the Thames from Sir William Sandys, exchanging it for some property in Hampshire, by which time the king had already sent a number of his critics to the executioner's block. Henry turned out to be about as satisfied with his house as he was with most of his wives, and promptly built a new Chelsea Manor near the original one, on ground which is now part of Cheyne Walk. This would have made the king a near neighbour of Sir Thomas More, former Speaker of the House of Commons and author of *Utopia*, had Henry not indulged in one of the other sports of kings and executed his former friend the previous year. Until then, Sir Thomas had been one of the most famous residents of the small village known as Chelsey or Chels-hithe, having built himself a house on land he had acquired in the early 1520s. The painter Hans Holbein, who knew both More and his much-married friend, recorded the scene of riverside domesticity in a famous group portrait of Sir Thomas at home surrounded by his family. More's house and grounds, with gardens sweeping down to the river where Battersea Bridge now stands, included the spot where 350 years later McLaren and Westwood's King's Road shop would sell anarchy and revolution to the passing trade.

The friendship between Sir Thomas More and Henry VIII came to an abrupt end in 1534 when More refused to sanction the king's repudiation of the ecclesiastical authority of the Pope in England. In order to dissolve his marriage to Catherine of Aragon and marry Anne Boleyn, Henry had declared himself head of the Church of England, an act which reads somewhat like a potential Westwood/McLaren T-shirt slogan: 'When in doubt, start your own religion'. Refusing to play along with the king's latest adjustment to the constitution, Sir Thomas was arrested at his house in Chelsea on April 17, 1534, and conveyed by boat along the Thames to the Tower, charged with high treason. As an old friend of the king, on the sovereign's insistence, he was given the pleasure of beheading, rather than the more 'common' fate of hanging, a favour also bestowed on several others among Henry's nearest and dearest, such as Anne Boleyn, Catherine Howard, and Thomas Cromwell, the Lord Great Chamberlain – just a small selection of the estimated 50,000–70,000 people he had executed during his singularly bloodthirsty reign, at a time when the total population of the country was only 400,000.

Looking as Cheerful as
Any Man Could Do in That Condition

Chelsea, even in these early days, was something of a contradiction. Home of the king, yet also the home of the man who had spoken out most publicly against him. A favourite dwelling place of the rich, for hundreds of years it was also a magnet for artists, misfits and bohemians, and it was not until the 1980s that rising rents and house prices largely drove out the latter. Of course, in the days of Henry VIII, as far as Londoners were concerned, Chelsea was some distance outside town – a small village with only a few scattered houses and plentiful greenery.

Henry died in 1547, and although various of his children, ex-wives and dependants lived in the area during the rest of the 16th century, Chelsea had to wait until the Restoration in 1660 for the monarch who literally put the King's Road on the map: Charles II. He had it constructed as a private thoroughfare to smooth the journey between his palaces at Hampton Court and Whitehall. Privileged individuals could also use it, and were issued with special copper passes with the royal monogram on one side and the words 'The King's Private Roads' on the other. Some people claim that Charles had it built in order to visit his mistress Nell Gwyn at her house in Fulham. That may perhaps be the case, but given that the king was also carrying on affairs with Lucy Walters and the duchesses of Portsmouth and Cleveland, among others – by whom he had children such as the dukes of Southampton, Richmond, Grafton, Monmouth and St Albans, and the countesses of Tamworth, Lichfield, Sussex and Derwentwater – it is a wonder he didn't pre-empt half the motorway systems of southern England.

Charles II was in some circles a popular king, though less so with the likes of the Irish landowner Thomas Blood, the Crown Jewel thief, who once lay in wait among the reeds near where the Albert Bridge now stands, planning to shoot the monarch as he swam in the river by Battersea Fields. Another group with less than brotherly feelings towards Charles were the regicides who had signed the death warrant of his father, Charles I. Some, like Oliver Cromwell, were long dead (although just to be on the safe side the authorities dug him up, hanged his corpse at Tyburn, then stuck his head on a pole above Westminster Hall, from where after some years it was eventually stolen), but after the restoration of the monarchy, the surviving regicides were arrested and tried for treason. The diarist Samuel Pepys, who had witnessed the execution of Charles I at Whitehall, records going to see the first of the regicides meet his fate on October 13, 1660: 'to Charing Cross to see Major-general Harrison hanged, drawn and quartered; which was done there, he looking as cheerful as any man could do in that condition'.

Just over a decade later, in 1673, in a city still reeling from the effects of the plague that had killed 70,000 of its inhabitants, the Society of Apothecaries founded the Chelsea Physic Garden on land between the King's Road and the river. Then, in 1682, construction work began next door to the Physic Garden on that other great Chelsea institution, the Royal Hospital. Founded by Charles II, and built to designs by Sir Christopher Wren, it opened its doors to the first 476 Chelsea Pensioners on March 28, 1689. Adding to the construction work, between 1690 and 1691, Richard Jones, 3rd Viscount and 1st Earl of Ranelagh, built himself a house surrounded by twenty acres of gardens just east of Chelsea Hospital. He had been Paymaster General of the Hospital since 1685 – a title which he apparently interpreted in a somewhat personal fashion, since he was later sacked for having managed to illegally pay the then colossal sum of £72,000 into his own bank account. After his death, the grounds of his house were to become famous as Ranelagh, one of the great pleasure gardens of

London and one of the main reasons why fashionable society in the 18th century would make the journey out to Chelsea.

Someone who would have been able to watch all this building work taking place in the area of the Royal Hospital was the writer Mary Astell, who had lived in Swan Walk, next to the Physic Garden, since the 1680s, and who in 1694 published *A Serious Proposal to Ladies for the Advancement of Their True and Greatest Interest*, a landmark in early feminist writing. Some 275 years later, another woman living just a few hundred yards away on the King's Road in a building called the Pheasantry was to publish an even more influential book entitled *The Female Eunuch*.

Another local resident of that time whose literary efforts would have parallels in the upheavals of the Chelsea of the late 20th century was the man who lived a short distance along the river to the west, on land which once formed part of Sir Thomas More's Chelsea estate. Here stood the Palladian mansion known as Danvers House, which, sometime in the 1690s, became the home of a man chiefly known as a hellraiser and libertine, who had recently written the lyrics of a song which was said to have had enormous political repercussions. 'God Save the Queen' by the Sex Pistols may have been the opening shot in a general lessening of deference towards the monarchy in the UK in recent times, but its effects were trivial compared to the impact on the monarch James II ascribed to a song of 1688 entitled 'Lillibuléro', written and published anonymously by Thomas, Marquis of Wharton, once described by his fellow Dubliner Jonathan Swift as 'the most universal villain that ever I knew'.

Concocted by the Protestant Wharton in mock-Irish dialect, the song's title was apparently based on the Gaelic rallying cry celebrating the Catholic uprising of 1641 in which many Protestants died – *An lile bá léir é, ba linne an lá* ('The lily prevailed; the day was ours') – and it was written to discredit the Catholic King James of England, who was mocked by name in the final verse. By the time of the song's publication, James II was struggling to hold on to his throne, and the song was said to be popular with the king's standing army, many of whom turned against him, as did much of the public. James eventually lost his crown – more as a result of his defeat by the Protestant forces of William of Orange at the Battle of the Boyne and the siege of Limerick than the effects of a satirical ballad – but Wharton was happy to take some of the credit. According to a pamphlet published in London in 1712, entitled *A true relation of the several facts and circumstances of the intended riot and tumult on Q. Elizabeth's birth-day, &c.*, the Marquis was given to boasting that he had 'sung a deluded Prince out of Three Kingdoms'. Wharton himself went on to become Lord Lieutenant of Ireland.

You Would Not Go Alone to the World's End

With the coming of the 18th century, the literary, artistic and recreational side of Chelsea began to flourish, in part because the population was rising and the number of watering holes increasing. William Congreve, in his play *Love for Love* (1695), mentioned the King's Road tavern the World's End – a pub which survives to this day and gave its name to that district. The play's characters Mrs Foresight and Mrs Frail engage in a dialogue in which the former accuses the latter of immodest behaviour for having been seen in a coach driving through Covent Garden with a strange man ('the place is public, and to be seen with a man in a hackney coach is scandalous'). Mrs Frail argues that this is entirely innocent, but 'If I had gone to Knight's Bridge, or to Chelsea, or to Spring Garden, or Barn Elms with a man alone, something might have been said.' Chelsea, it is clear, already had something of a reputation:

MRS FORESIGHT You have been at a worse place.

MRS FRAIL I at a worse place, and with a man!

MRS FORESIGHT I suppose you would not go alone to the World's End.

MRS FRAIL The World's End! What, do you mean to banter me?

MRS FORESIGHT Poor innocent! You don't know that there's a place called the World's End? I'll swear you can keep your countenance purely: you'd make an admirable player.

Jonathan Swift lodged for a while in Old Church Street, shortly before his return to Ireland upon accepting the Deanship of St Patrick's Cathedral, Dublin. He discussed his reasons for moving to Chelsea in one of his *Letters to Stella*, written on April 24, 1711: 'I design in two days, if possible, to go lodge at Chelsea for the air, and put myself under a necessity of walking to and from London every day.' His first impressions upon arrival were not particularly favourable: 'I got here in the stage-coach with Patrick and my portmanteau for sixpence, and pay six shillings a week for one silly room with confounded coarse sheets. We have had such a horrible deal of rain, that there is no walking to London, and I must go as I came until it mends.'

Having tried both the bedding and the weather and found them wanting, Swift left Chelsea after a few months, but would often return to the district to visit friends on various occasions in later life, and when he published *Gulliver's Travels* in 1726, he included at least one memorial to his time in the area: a crying infant who lets out 'a Squall that you might have heard from *London-Bridge* to *Chelsea*'.

Another of the literary and artistic figures who came to the area in Swift's day was the playwright John Gay, who lived at number 16 Lawrence Street from 1712 to 1714. Two of his plays, *The Beggar's Opera* and its banned sequel, *Polly*, later formed the basis for Brecht's *The Threepenny Opera*, the text of which, like several of the latter's key works, was largely written by his unacknowledged collaborator Elisabeth Hauptmann.

Chelsea at that time was still a relatively small, self-contained community in which most people would have known the other residents, either to converse with, or at least raise a hand to in polite greeting when encountering them in the leafy paths and lanes. The population of the parish in the 1720s was recorded as consisting of 461 families, plus a further 20 at the Royal Hospital. As the village grew in size and artists moved in, so did the publicans and the cafe proprietors. If you were planning on residing there and had more than the average amount of money to spare, the following advertisement in the *Daily Journal* from June 26, 1728 might possibly have been of interest:

> *To be Lett,*
> *At CHELSEA,*
> *A Fine large House, pleasantly situated on the Bank of the River Thames, near the Swan, with 2 Coach Houses, Stables, and other Out Offices; and 2 convenient handsome Gardens, wall'd in, well stock'd with Wall and other Fruit trees, lately inhabited by the Right Hon. the Earl of SUFFOLK, built by Mr VANHALSE. Inquire of CHARLES WALLER, Esq; on Swan Row at Chelsea, or of Mr HEASMAN, Upholder, in Bedford-street, Covent-Garden.*

The fashionable Don Saltero's Coffee House opened at 18 Cheyne Walk sometime around 1718, as did the Six Bells at 197 King's Road, a pub which survives to this day. Smart houses sprung up along the road itself, such as the one at number 211, built in 1723 for a man named John Perrin by the architect Giacomo Leoni, which is now known as Argyll House, having been briefly owned by the Duke of Argyll. Sir Hans Sloane – who was to stamp his influence and his name firmly all over the street names of the district – acquired Henry VIII's former home, Chelsea Manor, as his own residence. By an odd twist of fate, he also purchased (and promptly demolished) the old house of Sir Thomas More, adding the grounds to his estate. The extensive collection of antiquities which Sloane kept in his Chelsea house eventually helped form the basis of the British Museum. He also contributed greatly to the development of the Chelsea Physic Garden and its assortment of plants from all over the world, and it was he who first sent cotton seeds from that garden – said to have come originally from the islands in the Pacific – across the Atlantic to be planted in Georgia, giving rise to the entire cotton industry in the southern states of America.

Eating, Drinking, Staring or Crowding

At the river's edge alongside the Physic Garden, Ranelagh pleasure gardens opened to the public in 1742, and proved to be a major attraction in the social life of London for the next sixty years – the foundation stone of Chelsea's reputation as a centre of fashionable amusements. These were the grounds of the former home of the Earl of Ranelagh, in the shadow of the Royal Hospital, and had played host to notable entertainments in the past. Some twenty years earlier the German composer Handel performed his *Water Music* at Ranelagh in front of his fellow countryman, the Elector of Hanover – now King of England – George I. The choice of performer was not surprising, since Handel had been George's concert master back in his Hanover days.

The chief attraction of the new pleasure garden was the Rotunda, a huge structure nearly two hundred feet in diameter, resembling the dome that was later built over the British Museum reading room. The novelist Horace Walpole, author of gothic landmark *The Castle of Otranto*, reported on April 22 that it was already drawing crowds before it had even opened officially:

I have been breakfasting this morning at Ranelagh-garden: they have built an immense amphitheatre, with balconies full of little ale-houses; it is in rivalry to Vauxhall, and costs above twelve thousand pounds. The building is not finished, but, they get great sums by people going to see it and breakfasting in the house: there were yesterday no less than three hundred and eighty persons, at eighteen pence a-piece.

Of the official opening ceremony on May 24, Walpole commented: 'the Prince, Princess, Duke, much nobility, and much mob besides, were there. There is a vast amphitheatre, finely gilt, painted, and illuminated, into which every body that loves eating, drinking, staring, or crowding, is admitted for twelvepence.' This occasion had been advertised two days earlier in the *Daily Post*, as follows:

> *RANELAGH HOUSE, Chelsea.*
> *On Monday next the Musical Entertainment will be open'd for the Season, and on Wednesday will be a Ridotto.*
> *Tickets for the Ridotto will be deliver'd at White's Chocolate-House, St James's-Street; at Tom's Coffee-House in Cornhill; and at Ranelagh House.*

Given that the above-named Chocolate House exists to this day simply as White's, the oldest-established gentlemen's club in London, and Tom's Coffee House was the actor Garrick's usual haunt, it is indicative of the kind of patrons the new pleasure garden's owners were seeking to reach, and although Walpole initially compared Ranelagh unfavourably to the rival Vauxhall, it soon became a favourite of the fashionable set, and a couple of months later he wrote of his intention to see a masquerade there, because 'the King is fond of it, and has pressed people to go'. By 1744, despite his earlier reservations, Walpole concluded that Ranelagh 'has totally beat Vauxhall. Nobody goes any where else – every body goes there. My Lord Chesterfield is so fond of it, that he says he has ordered all his letters to be directed thither. [. . .] the floor is all of beaten prince – you can't set your foot without treading on a Prince of Wales or Duke of Cumberland.'

Over the following decades, the attractions at Ranelagh included spectacular firework displays, shooting competitions, a purpose-built canal with a gondola, pagodas, and even a working model of Mount Etna. Perhaps chief among Ranelagh's claims to fame is that the eight-year-old Mozart gave a concert there on June 29, 1764, during a tour of much of Western Europe which found him performing in front of a variety of monarchs including George III and Louis XV of France. He then lived for short a time with his family in nearby Ebury Street, where he wrote his symphonies K16 and K19. A prominent advert appeared in the *Public Advertiser* on June 26, 1764, giving details of Wolfgang's upcoming Chelsea performance:

> *For the Benefit of a Public useful Charity.*
> *AT RANELAGH HOUSE, on Friday next, will be performed beside the usual Entertainments of Music and Singing.*
> *At the End of the third Act, a very favourite Chorus in ACIS and GALATEA: Oh the Pleasures of the Plains, &c. End of Act Four, The Song and Chorus in ALEXANDER'S FEAST. Happy Pair, &c. To conclude with the*

Coronation Anthem, God Save the King, &c. In the Course of the Evening's Entertainments, the celebrated and astonishing Master MOZART, lately arrived, a Child of 7 years of Age, will perform several fine select Pieces of his own Composition on the Harpsichord and on the Organ, which has already given the highest Pleasure, Delight, and Surprize to the greatest Judges of Music in England or Italy, and is justly esteemed the most extraordinary Prodigy, and most amazing Genius that has appeared in any Age.

For once, the language used by the promoters was completely justified, although in true showbusiness fashion, they did manage to shave a year off his true age.

The young James Boswell was based in London the year prior to Mozart's visit, and a frequent visitor to Ranelagh. He recorded in his *London Journal* that one day, feeling depressed after viewing a hanging at Tyburn, 'I went to Lord Eglinton and begged he would try to relieve me. He made me dress and dine with him, and said he would take me at night to Ranelagh and introduce me to some pretty women.' On another occasion he went there to see a famous equestrian perform 'standing upon one and then two horses at full gallop, with all his feats of agility. It was a true English entertainment. The horses moved about to the tune of "Shilinagarie".' ('Síle ne Gadra' – an Irish Jacobite song by Timothy O'Sullivan.) Coincidentally, the talented equestrian's name happened to be Johnson.

Located just near Ranelagh was the Chelsea Porcelain Manufactuary, established in the early 1740s, which would inspire the name of one of the finest King's Road pubs, the Chelsea Potter. Their products were highlighted in the following notice which appeared in the December 12, 1752 issue of the *London Daily Advertiser*:

CHINA KNIVES AND FORKS
Of the CHELSEA MANUFACTUARY
In the greatest variety of the Most Beautiful DRESDEN PATTERNS
Mounted and SOLD by
NATHANIEL JEFFERYS,
CUTLER to His MAJESTY, their Royal Highnesses
the PRINCE of WALES, and the DUKE.

The fashionable also came to Chelsea to patronise the Cheyne Walk establishment of an Italian doctor called Dominiceti, who offered supposedly health-giving bathing treatments at number 6 during the 1770s. He took out the following illuminating advert on February 25, 1773 in the pages of a London newspaper called *The Public Hue and Cry, or, Sir John Fielding's General Preventative Plan* (which sometime later evolved into the more concisely titled *Police Gazette*):

> About eleven months ago, a Gentleman, who had been most afflicted for near two years with the most excruciating rheumatic pains all over his body, and in spite of the best remedies, and the power of opium, could not enjoy a moment of rest neither day nor night, and often to safe his pains was obliged to drink above a pint of brandy, and other spiritoas [sic] liquors at a time; was in this extremity brought to Chelsea, where by the use of my baths, stoves, and fumigations, he was, in the space of a fortnight, entirely recovered, and continues to enjoy perfect health. His name, and the names of the Gentlemen of the facility who attended him, previous to his use of my baths, &c. may be known by an application to my books.
>
> B. DE DOMINICETI, M.D.

Directly below this was printed a testimonial for Sir John Fielding himself – the legendary magistrate at Bow Street and brother of novelist Henry Fielding – who wrote that he had investigated this case and fully approved Dominiceti's claims.

A doctor of a different kind lived at 215 King's Road during that decade, Thomas Arne, probably most famous as the composer of the song 'Rule Britannia', later regularly sung by intoxicated flag-waving Prom-goers just up the road at the Albert Hall.

Anyone walking east from Dr Arne's house down the King's Road at this time would have passed an impressive building on the northern side which later came to be known as the Pheasantry – destined to have a long and colourful history – and would eventually reach Sloane Square, first enclosed in 1771. That was also the year the new Battersea Bridge opened, but only for pedestrians at first. Vehicles had to wait until the following year, and by the end of the decade it became the first wooden bridge across the Thames to be lit by oil lamps. Modern Chelsea was taking shape, although for all the progress, some local businesses foundered, such as that of Chelsea brewer Richard Green, who went bankrupt in 1772, his premises and home being then offered for sale and described in the auctioneer's particulars as follows:

> All the Plant or spacious Leasehold Brewhouse, Dwelling-house, roomy Store-houses, Cellars, &c., the Whole so judiciously constructed as to be capable of being worked with half the usual Number of Assistants,

being one of the completest Brewhouses in the Kingdom, and desirably situate near the King's Road, CHELSEA CREEK, that abuts on the Premises; the Advantage of which is a Saving in Carriage from 200 to 300l. yearly. The Whole held on Lease, upwards of 60 Years unexpired, subject to a Ground rent of 15l. and in the most substantial Repair.

Dinners, Balls and Music, Especially the Bagpipes

In August 1788, a highwayman named Thomas Hogg was hanged at Chelmsford, and when speaking to a priest on the scaffold in his last minutes, confessed to several unsolved crimes which he had on his conscience, as was reported in the news-sheet *The World* several days later:

> [Hogg said] that he could not die in peace, if he did not disclose some particulars of his life, which hitherto he had concealed: one was, that about twelve or thirteen years ago, he shot a Gentleman dead at Tunbridge, on the highway, whom he robbed: that not long after, he also shot another gentleman at Chelsea, on the highway, whom he left for dead, but who, he was afterwards informed, is still alive.

Life in Chelsea clearly sometimes had its dangers, but despite the popular image of highwaymen of someone lurking in a deserted forest or on a moorland path, in the London of those days it was equally possible to be robbed by one when attempting to cross a square in the West End. The king himself had survived a knife attack two years earlier when emerging from his carriage outside St James's Palace, and had another close call in 1800 when someone took a shot at him inside the Theatre Royal, Drury Lane. Although these were attempted assassinations rather than robberies, it is not for nothing that the long canes carried by Regency dandies were often made of a thick outer casing of wood around an inner core of iron or lead and could break an assailant's leg in one quick movement.

Even though relatively few people lived along the King's Road at the close of the 18th century, it was the scene of two separate attempts in 1792 to foment unrest, one at each end of the street. An organisation called the Free and Easy or Arthurian Society met in the agreeable surroundings of the Star and Garter pub in order to plot a violent uprising to have taken place in Sloane Square, but the authorities were given warning and the predicted mayhem never happened. Further west, down towards World's End, there were plans to burn an effigy of Tom Paine, who had just been indicted and fled from England to France that year following the publication of part one of his work *The Rights of Man*. These were fearful times – across the channel Louis XVI and Marie Antoinette were already under arrest, and eventually they and many of those who had unleashed the Reign of Terror, including Robespierre and Danton, would also have their height arbitrarily reduced in the Place de la Concorde. Indeed, when Paine reached Paris, he quickly went from being enthusiastically received to narrowly escaping the guillotine.

The French Revolution was much in Londoners' minds, especially since a decade earlier they had witnessed a 60,000-strong mob led by Lord George Gordon in June 1780 engaging in citywide scenes of prison-burning, distillery-looting and the storming of Parliament, during which frightened MPs were forced to chant 'No Popery'. This event, popularly known as the Gordon Riots, was later re-enacted by film-maker Julien Temple with the aid of some dummies of the Sex Pistols and about fifty extras dressed as punks at the start of his 1979 feature-length love letter to Malcolm McLaren, *The Great Rock'n'Roll Swindle*. Lord George Gordon, tried and acquitted of high treason, spent the rest of his life in Newgate jail 'solacing himself with dinners, balls, and music, especially the bagpipes'.

One part of London society spent much of this time pretending that such matters as the French Revolution were a mere sideshow and that the burning questions of the day consisted of the cut of a jacket, the complexity of a cravat and the correct establishment at which to go dining or dancing. Fashion dominated the thinking of the elite circle around the Prince of Wales, and chief among the arbiters of taste was George Brummell, who inherited his patrimony under the terms of his father's will on turning twenty-one, gradually establishing himself as the premier dandy of the age, and profoundly influencing the way that men dress from that day to the present. When Brummell first arrived on the scene, Ranelagh pleasure gardens were still a regular destination in fashionable circles, and he would have spent time there, but their reputation was fading and they closed in 1803.

As Regency dandies go, Brummell certainly wasn't the most ostentatious – that honour probably belonged to the Green Man of Brighton, whose possessions, servants, clothes and vehicles were all of the same harmonious shade as his dyed green hair, which he adopted fifty years before Baudelaire and almost two hundred years before Johnny Rotten did the same. Even Brummell's nickname of 'Beau' was understated compared to those of his contemporaries such as 'Poodle' Byng, 'Teapot' Crawfurd and 'Kangaroo' Cooke.

Brummell's importance derives from two simple facts. Firstly, after centuries of male fashions which had run the gamut from the primitive to the ridiculous, he introduced a basic style of well-cut jacket, waistcoat and trousers which with small variations evolved into the modern suit that has prevailed ever since. Secondly, and more importantly from the point of view of future Chelsea residents such as Oscar Wilde or the late 20th-century King's Road fashion trailblazers, he demonstrated the importance of the correct clothes-wearing attitude – the confidence and the attention to detail which would be so important to the *fin de siècle* aesthetes, early Teddy boys, mods like the youthful Marc Bolan, first-generation skinheads or the original 1976 punks drinking at the Roebuck on the King's Road. In short, Brummell, like Mary Quant or Vivienne Westwood, helped change the way the world dresses. It is no surprise that one of the sixties boutiques down the King's Road was called Dandie Fashions.

2

'Demure immorality in silk and fine linen'

Village People

Chelsea began the 19th century still a separate community, but gradually became part of London itself as the decades passed. In the midst of all the building projects and changing times, some local traditions continued, such as the making of local pottery, and the usual futile attempts to assassinate the king and steal the Crown Jewels. This time it was a certain Colonel Despard and his followers who in 1803 discussed their plans to do away with George III and rob the Tower over quiet pints of ale in the Magpie and Stump down by the river on what is now Cheyne Walk. Three years earlier, all they might have needed to do would be to position him in the right place in the right part of the parish and wait hopefully for him to be felled by airborne metal during the particularly violent storm which destroyed roofs and blew down entire houses across London in November 1800, as described in William Cobbett's newspaper *The Porcupine*: 'The lead upon the chapel and other apartments of Chelsea Hospital was rolled up by the violence of the wind like a piece of cloth.'

On a less insurrectionary note, the area also saw many current and future notables in residence: engineers Marc Brunel and his son Isambard Kingdom Brunel lived at 98 Cheyne Walk from 1808 to around 1825; the novelist Elizabeth Gaskell was born at what is now 93 Cheyne Walk in 1810, and then returned to live at 7 Beaufort Street in the 1820s; Jane Austen corrected the proofs of her first novel, *Sense and Sensibility*, while staying at her brother Henry's house at 64 Sloane Street in March 1811; the seven-year-old Edgar Allan Poe – some 150 years prior to his unpaid walk-on part in the lyrics of

'I Am the Walrus' – learnt spelling, geography and catechism while attending a boarding school run by the Misses Dubourg at 146 Sloane Street between 1816 and 1818; Percy Bysshe Shelley and Mary Wollstonecraft were at 41 Hans Place for some of 1817, the year he wrote 'Ozymandias'. This represented an impressive amount of culturally significant activity in what was still a village, albeit a rapidly expanding one. The population of the parish in 1801 was recorded as 11,604, and ten years later had risen to 18,262.

Let's Get Physical

The Chelsea Physic Garden continued to have a radical effect upon the plant life and crops of the wider world, largely because of what came to be known as the Wardian Case. Although sounding suspiciously like a tale by Poe, this was actually an item of botanical equipment roughly resembling a modern greenhouse or garden shed, invented accidentally in 1829 by the Garden's Dr Nathaniel Ward. By means of the case, plant samples could for the first time be safely packaged and kept alive during long sea voyages. As a direct result of this, quite apart from the craze for orchid-rearing and potted ferns which then developed in Victorian households, over the next twenty years Wardian Cases were used to introduce rubber trees from Brazil into Sri Lanka and Malaya for the first time, and smuggled the first tea plants from China into Assam in India, giving rise to whole new national industries in those countries. A sense of the range of flora being grown in Chelsea can be gained from this short news item published in *The Standard* – later the *London Evening Standard* – on August 8, 1827: 'In the Botanic Gardens at Chelsea, there are no less than 330 species of foreign wheat at this time ripening, besides 40 sorts of oats, and 18 varieties of barley.'

If you stood in the Physic Garden in the year of Dr Ward's discovery and looked across the river to the opposite bank, you would see Battersea Fields, now Battersea Park, the site of a notorious tavern called the Red House. Shooting competitions, gambling and a selection of local prostitutes drew people to the weekly fairs held there, who travelled there by boat, alighting at a jetty near where the present Chelsea Bridge stands. However, when prime minister the Duke of Wellington, victor of Waterloo, came to Battersea Fields on March 21, 1829, it was for marksmanship of a different kind. He was there to fight a duel with the 10th Earl of Winchilsea over the issue of Catholic emancipation, but both men deliberately aimed wide, and honour was satisfied in a swift and business-like fashion, as the papers reported: 'His Grace was seen riding through the Horse-Guards at six o'clock on Saturday morning, and returned to Downing-street at eight.' Duelling was already illegal at that time in England, and a Major Campbell had been hanged in 1808 for killing a Captain Boyd during one such showdown, but in Wellington's case charges were much less likely because no blood was spilt, and the fact that he was the head of the government probably also helped. In the unlikely event of a fatal wound and either participant requiring the last rites, the rector of Chelsea would have been close at hand, just across the bridge. His name was Dr Wellesley, the Duke's brother.

Several months later, Wellington's government introduced the Metropolitan Police, under Home Secretary Robert Peel, whose first 895 constables began patrolling London on September 29, immediately becoming a talking point, as this report from *The Standard* published on October 1 makes clear:

NEW POLICE – A correspondent informs us, that in passing from the City to Chelsea at a late hour last evening, he found that the new police had extended themselves westward as far as Smith-street, King's-road. He adds, that they appeared to be more fond of talking than watching – as he found them in groups of three and four, leaving wide spaces of the road completely unguarded.

In the following year, 1830, the hitherto private King's Road was finally opened up to the public. This in turn helped promote house-building in the area, which by now had an extreme mixture of dwellings, from mansions to slums, and the neighbourhood continued to attract writers and artists. Historian Thomas Carlyle and his wife set up home at 5 Cheyne Row (now number 24) in 1834, where they remained all their lives, and in which he wrote his classic history *The French Revolution* (1837), having soundproofed his workroom to guard against street noise. Another giant figure of the coming Victorian age, Charles Dickens, married Catherine Hogarth in 1836 at St Luke's church, Sydney Street, a few steps north of the King's Road. In his younger days, he was often to be seen at the fashionable Kensington Gore salon of the writer Lady Blessington, whose other regular guests included former-dandy-novelist-and-future-bastion-of-the-Empire Edward Bulwer Lytton, dandy-novelist-and-future-prime-minister Benjamin Disraeli, and nephew-of-Napoleon-and-future-emperor-of-France Louis Napoleon Bonaparte. Despite such an illustrious roll call of visitors, Lady Blessington's home, Gore House, was later knocked down and a more grand establishment known as the Royal Albert Hall built on the site.

Proper pavements were laid along the King's Road for the first time in 1845, and the following year parliament passed an Act for the draining and levelling of a portion of Battersea Fields in order to create a new royal park, measuring some 320 acres. Just across the river, a man calling himself Admiral Booth took up residence at 6 Davis Place (now 119 Cheyne Walk), looking to enjoy a long and happy retirement. He managed five years in this peaceful spot, with few being aware that his real name was Joseph Mallord William Turner, one of the greatest painters of that or any other age, who had adopted the name 'Booth' from the landlady of the pub on the corner, the Aquatic Stores. The boat builder Charles Greaves had a yard in Cheyne Walk and occasionally rented out boats to Turner. Greaves's son Walter, born in 1846, later also become a painter, much influenced by another local resident, Whistler.

Graphic Delineations in Song and Dance

Turner had come to that riverside corner of Chelsea in search of the quiet life, but practically on his doorstep a new pleasure garden opened for business, promising to be everything that Ranelagh had been and more. It was centred around a mansion in twelve acres of ground between the King's Road and the river, called Cremorne, which derived its name from a former owner in the late 18th century, Viscount Cremorne. This new public attraction seemed determined to offer a little something of everything, as seen in this advert from 1843 for an event promoted by its owner, Renton Nicholson:

Credit: Hulton Fine Art Collection/ Getty Images

The Dancing Platform at Cremorne Gardens, 1864

NICHOLSON'S
1000 GUINEA FETE!!!
CREMORNE HOUSE,
KING'S ROAD, CHELSEA.
MR. NICHOLSON, of the 'Garrick's Head' Hotel, Bow Street,

LORD CHIEF BARON
OF THE JUDGE AND JURY SOCIETY,
And Editor of the
ILLUSTRATED LONDON LIFE WEEKLY NEWSPAPER,
Has the honour to announce to his best Friends, the Public, that he
will offer to their patronage a
THREE DAYS' FETE!
On a Scale of UNMATCHED SPLENDOUR,
in the Park and Grounds attached to the above-named
NOBLE MANSION, on
MONDAY, TUESDAY, & WEDNESDAY,
July 31st & August 1st & 2nd.
Amongst the Thousand and One Entertainments provided by
MR. NICHOLSON, are a
MOCK TOURNAMENT!
RACING, OLD ENGLISH SPORTS,
MINSTRELSY, MUSIC, DANCING,
Embracing the attractive Impersonations of more than 100 Eminent
Pantomimic and Comic Actors, Posturers, Dancers, Conjurors, &c.,
with Graphic Delineations, in Song and Dance, of the far-famed
TOM MATHEWS,
The Immortal Clown, the Joey Grimaldi of Modern Times.
MR. GREEN, THE CELEBRATED AERONAUT,
Will ascend from the Lawn, in his
MAJESTIC BALLOON.
Taking up with him, and liberating experimentally, an extensive
AERIAL TRANSIT SHIP.
MR. ALEXANDER BURKE'S
CELEBRATED PONEY, BOBBY,
Will trot seven miles and a half in 30 minutes,
WITH A MONKEY ON HIS BACK,
Attired *à la* CHIFNEY, in Jockey Cap, Jacket, Top Boots and Spurs,
and carrying a Whip in his hand.
The Amusements of each Day to conclude with a
GRAND BALL & CONCERT
In the Illuminated Gardens.
ADMISSION ONLY ONE SHILLING.
~ Cremorne House can be reached from any part of the
Metropolis by Omnibus, for 6d., and by Steam Boat for 4d.
CROKER, PRINTER, 199 STRAND.

What with all the balloons ascending and parties arriving by steam boat, to say nothing of the noise of the dancing and the crowds applauding equestrian monkeys, it is hardly surprising that Carlyle soundproofed his room, and a wonder that Turner got any sleep at all.

The adventurous Mr Renton Nicholson appears to have had something of a short-lived relationship with 'his best Friends, the Public', since by 1846 he was gone, and Cremorne passed into the hands of Thomas Bartlett Simpson, who set out to make the place even more of a sensation and to beat Vauxhall Gardens at its own game. In this, it seems he succeeded, since the latter was auctioned off in 1859; indeed, the pictures which had once hung on its walls wound up in the banquet hall at Cremorne.

As the fireworks lit up the night, balloonists ascended, often taking a bizarre selection of wildlife and farm animals up with them for no apparent reason. Novelty was everything: the latest dances, the fastest horses, and, after dark, faster women. Dr William Acton, in his snappily titled 1857 publication *Prostitution Considered in its Moral, Social, and Sanitary Aspects in London and Other Large Cities and Garrison Towns*, remarked that although during the day Cremorne was frequented by reasonably moderate and well-behaved people, when the evening arrived, one crowd was replaced by another of a different kind, and 'as calico and merry respectability tailed off eastward by penny steamers, the setting sun brought westward Hansoms freighted with demure immorality in silk and fine linen. By about ten o'clock, age and innocence [. . .] had seemingly all retired.' According to an altogether more scandal-hungry memoir of the time, the anonymously published *London in the Sixties*, Cremorne was also a reliable destination for anyone in search of a good punch-up: 'A Derby night without a row [. . .] was, in those days, an impossibility,' and 'to pass the private boxes was to run the gauntlet of a quartern loaf or a dish of cutlets at one's head'. A hundred years before the running battles between rival football mobs or punks and Teddy boys, people could already be seen fleeing down the King's Road attempting to escape from the drunken fistfights at Cremorne.

You Know How to Whistle, Don't You Steve?

One man who found the atmosphere at the pleasure gardens much to his taste was the painter James Abbott McNeill Whistler. He had his first glimpse of Chelsea when staying with his sister in Sloane Street in 1848 as a four-teen-year-old, and twenty years later came to live very near to Cremorne and Battersea Bridge in a house that is now 96 Cheyne Walk. The year after the teenage Whistler visited the area, a man with considerably more facial hair but a less finely developed sense of humour moved to number 4 Anderson Street, which runs north off the King's Road. The Europe-wide political disturbances of 1848 had prompted Karl Marx and his family to come to London, seeking a more tranquil place in which to inspire the future architects of the Gulag Archipelago and the Cultural Revolution. They remained in Anderson Street for half a year until being evicted by running-dog lackeys of bourgeois imperialism for non-payment of rent. Karl wasn't to know that in 1976, a few hundred yards down the King's Road from his former lodgings, McLaren and Westwood's SEX emporium would be selling several varieties of shirt emblazoned with his picture, front and back, accompanied by stencilled phrases such as 'Try Subversion' and 'Only Anarchists Are Pretty', cunningly priced at eye-wateringly high rates that any venture capitalist might admire. He might, however, have been amused to discover that Johnny Rotten and Sid Vicious were also evicted by the bailiffs from their Chelsea flat in 1977 because a certain Sex Pistols manager had apparently failed to pay the rent. No-one said the revolution would be easy.

Someone who could easily have afforded to pay the Marx family's bed and board, but would probably have resented the expense, was a Chelsea resident who died a couple of years later in 1852. James Camden Neild, of 5 Cheyne Walk, had been a thoroughgoing miser during his lifetime, and in death left £500,000 to Queen Victoria – roughly equivalent to £70 million in today's money, which presumably helped her keep the wolf from the door for a little while longer. Other deaths that year included the Duke of Wellington, aged eighty-three, whose body lay in state on the King's Road at the Royal Hospital, and also two mourners, crushed to death in the crowds attempting to file past his coffin.

I Believe He Once Kept a Gorilla

In 1858 the first incarnation of Chelsea Bridge opened to the public, and construction work also began on the first version of the town hall in the King's Road, then known as Chelsea Vestry Hall. Two years later, Mr Dench, described as a King's Road hot-house builder, let part of his premises facing the street for use as a very early photographic studio – a century before Michael Cooper had his own just nearby, in which he took some key portraits and record covers of the 1960s.

William Holman Hunt, who had founded the Pre-Raphaelite Brotherhood in 1848, lived at 59 Cheyne Walk between 1850 and 1853, paving the way for perhaps the movement's most famous member, Dante Gabriel Rossetti, who in 1862 moved to 16 Cheyne Walk, near the site where the Albert Bridge would soon be built. Rossetti rented rooms out to the poet Algernon Charles Swinburne, and visitors to the house included Whistler, William Morris, Burne-Jones, John Ruskin and the painter Simeon Solomon, the latter of whom later claimed to have chased Swinburne around the house, both of them naked. As F. Locker-Lampson recalled in his memoirs, *My Confidences* (1896):

> I have been at Rossetti's house at Cheyne Walk, and he has been to me in Victoria Street. I liked him on both occasions, but from what I hear he could hardly have been a comfortable man to abide with. He collected Oriental china and bric-à-brac, and had a congregation of queer creatures – a raven, and marmots or wombats, &c. – all in the garden behind his house. I believe he once kept a gorilla. He was much self-absorbed.

Dante Gabriel Rossetti, Christina Rossetti and William Michael Rossetti with their mother Frances in the garden at Cheyne Walk, photographed by Lewis Carroll

If anything, Locker-Lampson seems to have underplayed the size of Rossetti's menagerie: Jean Overton Fuller fails to mention the gorilla, but goes on to list 'armadillos, hedgehogs, mice and dormice, a Canadian marmot, an ordinary marmot, a racoon, squirrels, wombats, wallabies, kangaroos, two owls (named Jessie and Bobbie), and peacocks.' The shrieking of the peacocks drove the neighbours to distraction, as did the tunnelling of the armadillos. There is no mention of pheasants in either of these lists, but had Rossetti felt the need for some, the firm of Messrs Baker at 152 King's Road was now in business offering several varieties of these birds for sale, since which time the building itself has been known as the

Pheasantry. Their stock would mostly have been bred for a short life and a violent end at the hands of the blood sports brigade, but daily existence for the animals at Cheyne Walk could also be hazardous: Whistler noted in his diary, after visiting Rossetti and Swinburne for dinner, that one of the wombats accidentally suffocated at the table while he was there, having become trapped unnoticed in a large box of cigars.

Venturing out of the house, Rossetti and his friends often drank in the Six Bells just around the corner on the King's Road, although they would have had to wait until 1865 if they wanted to walk there by means of Oakley Street, since that thoroughfare was not laid out until then. Had they been looking for rowdier entertainment, nearby Cremorne was still in business, but its reputation sank ever lower during its last decade. Nevertheless, one night's entertainment in the early 1860s promised 'The brilliant, matchless, and unparalleled performances of THE WONDROUS LEOTARD, MR. D'ALBERTE, The English Rope-Walker, and Blondin's Challenger, who will go through his extraordinary and incredible performances on the ILLUMINATED ROPE', equestrian events, various orchestral and vocal and ballet interludes, 'SIGNOR BUONO CORE, The Italian Salamander, or Fire King', and, perhaps for the benefit of Rossetti, 'MR. HENRY COOKE's celebrated Circus Troupe of EDUCATED DOGS AND MONKEYS' – all for a shilling.

Chelsea is Radical

Dogs were also of interest to other residents of Chelsea at this time, according to Henry Mayhew, who published the fourth volume of his monumental social study, *London Labour and the London Poor* in 1862. This instalment concerned itself with London's underworld, and when dealing with crimes of theft, he included a section entitled 'Dog Stealing', which he said was 'very prevalent, particularly in the West End of the metropolis, and it is a rather profitable class of felony'. Dogs would be seized by the kidnappers, and the owner sent a message telling him to pay up or it would be killed. According to Mayhew, 'these thieves reside at the Seven Dials, in the neighbourhood of Belgravia, Chelsea, Knightsbridge, and low neighbourhoods, some of them men of mature years'.

In an early sign of the street's future reputation as a centre of fashion, readers of the newly established *Chelsea News and General Advertiser* might have noticed the following advert placed by a local trader in the July 29, 1865 edition:

Robert Gornall,
TAILOR AND TROUSERS MAKER,
(FROM BUCKMASTER'S),
61, King's Road, Chelsea, opposite the Man-in-the-Moon.
*R.G. begs respectively to return his sincere thanks to the inhabitants of Chelsea
and its vicinity for the liberal patronage he has received for the past four years,
and hopes by punctuality and strict attention to business, combined with a
superior cut and fit, to merit the continuance of their kind favours.
Coats from 26s., Trousers and Waistcoats from 22s., Black Cloth Coats from
30s., ditto Trousers and Waistcoats from 28s., Youths' Suits 21s.
Mourning orders executed with facility. Riding Habits, Liveries, &c.*
CLEANING AND DRYING

Appropriately enough, this appeared directly below an advert for H. Cocks Pianoforte Warehouse at 39 King's Road, so the musical side of the area was also represented.

Over at the very eastern end of the King's Road, two major developments occurred within a little over a year – Sloane Square underground station came into operation on Christmas Eve 1868, then on April 16, 1870, the New Theatre, Chelsea, opened up for business nearby in Lower George Street, just off Sloane Square, on the site of the former Ranelagh Chapel. After several changes of name and one minor change of location – to a position right next door to the Underground – this eventually became the Royal Court Theatre.

Many other local landmarks also date from around this time: the Royal Albert Hall was completed in 1871; Chelsea Embankment was built between 1871 and 1874; the Albert Bridge – constructed by the local Chelsea firm Holbrook – opened for pedestrian traffic on New Year's Eve 1872 and then fully in August 1873; a draper by the name of Peter Jones began trading at numbers 4 to 6 King's Road in 1877, gradually expanding by buying several of the surrounding buildings; Trafalgar Studios and Wentworth Studios, the first purpose-built artists' studios in Chelsea, were constructed by John Brass in 1878 to form what became known as the Manresa Road artists' colony. By contrast, whatever pleasure was to be had at Cremorne Gardens was deemed to be long since gone and the place was sold for property development in 1877, presumably leaving anyone wishing to ascend in a balloon while sitting on a cow to look elsewhere.

Not everyone in the district necessarily had the time or the money for such entertainments. Dickens, writing in his 1879 *Dictionary of London*, said that 'Chelsea contains a great population of the working class. Chelsea is Radical, while Kensington may be looked upon as Conservative.' These days Cheyne Walk has long been an exclusive address, but in the early 1870s number 46 still housed an establishment called the 'Home for Destitute and Friendless Girls'. Even so, the fine house at 4 Cheyne Row into which George Eliot moved in 1880 was certainly impressive, although she was only able to enjoy it for a few short weeks, dying very soon afterwards, having been prescribed regular quantities of champagne by her physician to ease her last illness.

Liberal supplies of champagne or other intoxicating beverages might have been useful to anyone needing the attentions of a dentist in those days. William Gregory, at 153 King's Road, who advertised himself forbiddingly as a 'Surgical and Mechanical Dentist', was particularly keen to stress his skill in the field of artificial teeth:

> *May be consulted daily from 10 to 7. Free of charge. Specimens of mechanical Dentistry for inspection.*
> *His PRIZE MEDAL TEETH, so natural in appearance, defy detection: they restore mastication and articulation and last a lifetime.*
> *A set of Artificial Teeth from £1 to £15. Repairing, Enlarging, or Re-Modelling old Sets, receive the greatest care and dispatch.*
> *New springs fitted in minutes.*
> *Teeth extracted on the most approved principles, and the purest amalgams used for stopping. Scaling conducted with care.*

If something stronger than champagne was needed to fortify the nerve before visiting Mr Gregory, then residents might be well advised to pick up a bottle of Burrough's Ozone Whiskey, available from local suppliers such as C. A. Bignell at 440 King's Road, or J. F. Seymour of 126 King's Road, advertised under the slogan 'Ozone is necessary to health'.

Cockney Impudence

Whistler, the painter who did more than anyone to immortalise the river at Chelsea, took possession of his new, purpose-built studio, the White House, in Tite Street in October 1878, but within six months was declared bankrupt as a result of his ruinous libel action against Ruskin. The cause of their dispute was a painting which attempted to capture the essence of a moment Whistler had experienced while watching a firework display at Cremorne. Ruskin, reviewing it alongside other works by the same artist exhibited at the Grosvenor Gallery, trotted out the customary abuse that is often reserved for anything new:

For Mr Whistler's own sake, no less than for the protection of the purchaser, Sir Coutts Lindsay ought not to have admitted works into the gallery in which the ill-educated conceit of the artist so nearly approached the aspect of wilful imposture. I have seen and heard much of cockney impudence before now, but never expected to hear a coxcomb ask two hundred guineas for flinging a pot of paint in the public's face.

While it is entertaining to imagine what Ruskin might have made of the work of Jackson Pollock, he was hardly alone in his views. Across the Channel, much the same things were being said about the first impressionist shows in Paris. As the critic Albert Wolf wrote in *Figaro*, reviewing the group's second exhibition in 1876 at a gallery in Rue Le Peletier which included works by Degas, Monet, Morisot, Pissarro, Renoir and Sisley, 'Rue Le Peletier is unlucky. After the fire at the Opera, here is a new disaster befalling the district.' Of course, critical opinion is just an opinion, but it helps shape public perceptions, and as a partial result of years of negative publicity, when the fine painter and collector Gustave Caillebotte died in 1894, leaving his unparalleled personal trove of paintings by the leading impressionists to the French nation, there were many complaints in 'respectable' art circles, and the state accordingly refused to accept some of them, taking, for instance, only eight out of the sixteen Monets offered to them in the bequest, which now form the basis of one of the most popular art collections in the world. Similarly, in 1912, when former Chelsea resident Oscar Wilde was included in a mural depicting famous local figures decorating Chelsea Town Hall, the council voted in 1914 to have it removed, so scandalous was his name then supposed to be following years of virulent public abuse. Oscar had been dead for over a decade by then, but they were still frightened of displaying even a picture of him. As luck would have it, the council was distracted by an event known as the Great War, and the mural remains.

Bela Lugosi's Dad

Following his bankruptcy, Whistler lost his purpose-built studio, the White House, but by 1881 he was able to move into a new studio a few doors away at 13 Tite Street, the same year in which Oscar Wilde took up lodgings with his old Oxford friend, the painter Frank Miles, at 1 Tite Street (later renumbered 44). Wilde had lived in Chelsea before in 1876 – at his mother's house, 87 Oakley Street – and returned to Tite Street following his marriage in 1884, taking a house at number 16. He lived and worked there throughout the years of his fame, until the same supposedly polite society that had heaped approval upon him switched around abruptly in 1895 and ate him for breakfast, at which point his house was ransacked by the public, numerous personal belongings were stolen, and the remaining contents then auctioned off. A blue plaque recording Oscar's residency in Tite Street was placed on the outside of the house in October 1954, which, so far, has escaped the souvenir hunters.

In the days when his plays and books were still the height of fashion, many distinguished visitors came to call on Wilde and his wife Constance, including Sarah Bernhardt, John Singer Sargent, Mark Twain, Lily Langtree, Robert Browning, Swinburne and mister 'pot of paint' himself, John Ruskin. Some mornings Oscar would notice a carriage drawing up in Tite Street a few yards from his door, out of which would step a woman dressed in full medieval costume, with a gold crown on her head. The two of them would then wave at each other. It was his good friend, the actress Ellen Terry, arriving at the studio across the road to have a portrait painted of herself in the role of Lady Macbeth. Terry had appeared to great acclaim at the Belgravia Theatre – forerunner of the Royal Court – in 1876, and later lived at 215 King's Road between 1904 and 1920.

Another friend of Wilde's whose principal career was in the theatre, but who is chiefly remembered for a single novel, lived around the corner at 27 Cheyne Walk. He spent a great deal of his career working for the actor Henry Irving but made headlines one day after diving into the river from a Thames steamer in an attempt to rescue an apparently suicidal man who had jumped from the boat. He succeeded in retrieving the jumper from the river and taking him back to number 27, but the person had died. For his courageous actions, Bram Stoker was subsequently awarded the bronze medal of the Royal Humane Society. He later caused a far greater sensation in 1896 with the publication of *Dracula*, a character whose most illustrious interpreter, Christopher Lee, also lived in Chelsea for much of his life, just north of Sloane Square. Stoker's next novel, published the year after *Dracula*, was a sentimental tale called *Miss Betty*, set in the Cheyne Walk of the 18th century.

Paraded Around Town in a Bag

The 1880s saw further changes to the district. The old wooden Battersea Bridge, immortalised in Whistler's paintings, was finally declared unsafe except for foot passengers in 1883 and taken down in 1887. In Lower George Street, off Sloane Square, the Belgravia Theatre became the Court

Theatre, was extensively remodelled in 1882, then completely demolished in 1887. It then reopened as the Court Theatre with a production of Sydney Grundy's farce *Mamma* in a new building in Sloane Square itself, designed by Walter Emden and W. R. Crewe.

Another famous Chelsea resident who lived in Beaufort Street, just south of the King's Road, met a grisly and futile end in January 1885. Colonel Charles George Gordon, unarmed and with no troops, had travelled to Khartoum in the Sudan partly at the suggestion of the *Pall Mall Gazette* in order to help evacuate a garrison of Egyptian troops. Ranged against him were the armies of the Mahdi, who offered him a safe passage out of the town, which he refused. A British column of troops, belatedly sent to rescue him, eventually arrived two days after his severed head had been paraded around town in a bag. In death, he became even more of a national hero: a 1921 British encyclopaedia entry about Gordon's death calls him a 'true heroic type, a medieval warrior saint, a puritan mystic in the midst of 19th century materialism, a man who lived by the Faith that can move mountains'. Somewhat shorter and more prosaic was Gordon's last letter to the British government, appealing for help: 'You send me no information though you have lots of money. C.G.G.'

Back in Chelsea in 1889, Jerome Klapka Jerome, who lived near the river at Flat 104, 91–104 Chelsea Gardens, Chelsea Bridge Road, and had recently returned from a honeymoon spent on the Thames, wrote and published one of the all-time classics of life on the water, *Three Men in a Boat* (1889). He had been named by his father in honour of the Hungarian General Georg Klapka, a hero of the 1849 Hungarian uprising, who had later come to Britain and lodged with the family, thereby becoming a friend. Jerome's parents obviously enjoyed themselves when picking names: his sisters were Paulina Deodata and Blandina Dominica, and he also had a short-lived brother called Milton Melancthon.

Any number of men in boats passing down the river could not fail to notice the opening in 1890 of the new Battersea Bridge, designed by Joseph Bazalgette, even if it did lack the ramshackle charm of the wooden construction which it replaced, but a certain Charles Augustus Howell would not live to make use of it. He had been an art agent, wheeler-dealer, friend of the Pre-Raphaelites, one-time secretary to Ruskin, and the man who boasted of having recovered Rossetti's poems – seven years after the burial – from inside the coffin of Rossetti's wife Lizzie Siddal. Howell was described in Hall Caine's memoirs as 'a somewhat battered person, with the face of a whipped cab-horse', but in 1890 his luck ran out for good and he was discovered lying dead in the street outside a Chelsea pub with a gold coin between his teeth.

A mysterious death, but understandably overshadowed in notoriety by the string of grisly homicides perpetrated by the killer who called himself Jack the Ripper during the second half of 1888 in the East End. Many theories were put forward at the time as to Jack's identity, and still more have followed every decade since, including the assertion of crime novelist Patricia Cornwell, who spent £2,000,000 buying up paintings and artefacts of the Chelsea artist Walter Sickert, convinced that he was the Ripper. In 2001 she was accused of 'monstrous stupidity' by art historians after it was alleged that she had destroyed one of the paintings in the search for clues. It may well be the case that Sickert is being targeted simply because of his choice of subject matter and taste for the low life. As Sir William Rothenstein later recalled:

> He had a small room where he worked, at the end – the shabby end – of the Chelsea Embankment west of Beaufort Street. Needless to say, this room was in one of the few ugly houses to be found along Cheyne Walk. [. . .] Every man to his taste, I thought; but had I a little of your charm, your finished manners, your wit and good looks, I should not be painting in a dusty room in the squalidest corner of Chelsea. Nor, for that matter, should I be laboriously matching the dingy tones of women lying on unwashed sheets, upon cast-iron bedsteads.

Yellow Fever

When not painting in 'the squalidest corner of Chelsea', Sickert could hardly have been spending all of his spare time in the East End, since he had space enough in his diary in 1891 to band together with fellow artists such as Whistler and George Clausen to found the Chelsea Arts Club, which met originally at 181 King's Road, home of the painter James Christie. Sickert also contributed to issue number one of a new periodical which, for a few brief months, became the epitome of 1890s taste, *The Yellow Book*. Published in April 1894 (or Aprtl, as the first edition mis-spelled it), it was a magazine in hardback book format, with a stunning cover design and illustrations by Aubrey Beardsley and a selection of literary and artistic contributions, many of them from people who clearly knew Chelsea well: in Henry Harland's short story *A Broken Looking Glass*, the protagonist returns home after having dined with a friend at Cheyne Walk; in George Egerton's short story *A Lost Masterpiece*, the narrator boards a river steamer at Chelsea, bound for London Bridge; Walter Sickert's illustration, *A Lady Reading*, is signed simply 'Sickert, Chelsea'.

It had been named *The Yellow Book* at Beardsley's suggestion, since novels imported from France at that time tended to have yellow jackets, and their contents had a reputation for being somewhat more liberal or shocking than their counterparts in England. In short, the name had a subtle hint of scandal. What was found between the covers was simply some of the best material of the age – stories and poems from the likes of Max Beerbohm, Henry James or Arthur Symons, and pictures from people like Beardsley, Will Rothenstein or Laurence Houseman.

However, when Oscar Wilde's criminal libel action against illiterate bully the Marquess of Queensberry collapsed in 1895 and Wilde was prosecuted in turn following his arrest at the Cadogan Hotel in Sloane Street, it was widely reported in the press that he had been carrying in his hand 'a yellow book'. In actual fact, this turned out to be a yellow-bound copy of a French novel, *Aphrodite* by Pierre Louÿs. Not wishing to let the truth get in the way of a good story, readers of newspapers in 1895 proved every bit as eager to take up the cudgels as the punk-bashing tabloid-buyers of 1977, and immediately an angry mob attacked the office of *The Yellow Book* on Vigo Street, smashing the elegant bow window with rocks. Blissfully ignoring the fact that Wilde had no connection with *The Yellow Book*, their argument was simple – Oscar was poison, and anything he touched must be shunned. Beardsley had provided illustrations for the book of Wilde's *Salome*, among scores of other literary commissions in his all-too-brief career, but the two of them could barely stand to be in the same room as each other. Oscar's opinion of volume one of *The Yellow Book*, expressed in a letter to Bosie Douglas, was very clear, and singularly mean-spirited: 'It is dull and loathsome, a great failure. I am so glad.' Publisher John Lane was assailed on one side by the public and on the other by the more straight-laced and hypocritical of his authors, including Mrs Humphrey Ward, who recoiled from sharing an imprint with such sordid products and demanded action (in much the same way as musicians like Rick Wakeman are supposed to have done upon discovering that their record label, A&M, had signed the Sex Pistols). Lane could hardly sack Wilde, because he did not work there anyway, so he did the next best thing and sacked Beardsley – a catastrophically stupid move from which the magazine never recovered.

3

'Two world wars and no world cup'

Amazing Stunts with a Grapefruit

As the 20th century began, the Victorian age seemed almost in a hurry to slip away. Wilde was dead, and so was Beardsley, aged just twenty-five, as were Burne-Jones, William Morris and Ruskin. Whistler only lasted until 1903, and even the woman who had given her name to the entire previous era – and also bestowed it on a museum, a waterfall, an island in Canada, a state in Australia, a railway station, a medal for bravery, a horse-drawn carriage, a dockyard, a port in Brazil, a battleship that sank with all hands having been rammed by its own side, and even on a giant water lily up the Amazon – hung on just long enough to find herself less than amused with the new century, then packed it all in, giving rise to one of the biggest royal funerals of them all. Electric light, tube trains, motor cars, typewriters and telephones had all become an established part of the scene. Modern life may or may not be rubbish, but it is interesting to note how old-fashioned so much of it really is.

Chelsea was well established by 1900 as a favourite haunt of writers and artists, and the final decade of the previous century had seen the founding of the South Western Polytechnic in Manresa Road, which would eventually evolve into Chelsea Polytechnic, and later still, Chelsea College of Art. To give just two examples from many, in 1898 the painter Philip Wilson Steer had moved to 109 Cheyne Walk, which remained his home until his death in 1942, while Bertrand Russell, another person with strong ties to the area who later ran for local MP, set up house with his first wife Alys at 14 Cheyne Walk in 1902. If either were fans of old-style, elbow-in-the-ribs musical-hall entertainment – in the immortal words of the Goodies, 'A Song, a Smile and Amazing Stunts With a Grapefruit' – then their timing was perfect, since the Chelsea Palace of Varieties threw open its doors in 1903. Located at 232–242 King's Road, on the corner of Sydney Street opposite the Town Hall, it had space for 2,524 people.

Theatrical entertainment of a different kind was on offer at the Court Theatre down the road in Sloane Square. 1904 saw a visit from the world-class Abbey Theatre Company from Dublin presenting a series of Irish plays, and that year also marked the start of a new management regime under the control of Harley Granville-Barker and J. E. Vedrenne, who provided a home at the Court for a succession of eleven important plays by George Bernard Shaw, many of which premiered there. Granville-Barker – a young actor and author of the play *The Voysey Inheritance*, which is regularly revived to this day – was still in his twenties, and had impressed Shaw several years previously when acting in a play called *The Coming of Peace*, an adaptation of a German play by Gerhart Hauptmann.

Granville-Barker first came to the Court in 1904 to produce and act in *Two Gentlemen of Verona*, part of a Shakespeare season then in progress, as a result of which he was offered the chance to co-manage the theatre by the new leaseholder, John Highfield Leigh, and his business manager, J. E. Vedrenne. That same April, they staged their first Shaw adaptation, *Candida*, and over the next three years, with Shaw as director, the Court devoted the majority of its time to presenting his plays, including *Man and Superman, Major Barbara, John Bull's Other Island, The Doctor's Dilemma* and *You Never Can Tell*. The rest of their repertoire also featured translations of works by many important contemporary European dramatists, a tradition later renewed when the English Stage Company began its presentations at the Royal Court from 1956 onwards. Granville-Barker left the Court for the Savoy Theatre after the 1907 season, but his three-year partnership there with Vedrenne had a made a significant impact on the staging of modern drama in England.

Blind and Leprous in Tahiti

Next door to the Town Hall, just across the road from the newly opened Chelsea Palace, a collection of rooms at 181–183 King's Road known as the Chenil Galleries began showing artworks in 1905, quickly achieving a reputation for championing the productions of modern artists. Some criticised their 1910 exhibition of paintings by Augustus John – who moved to the area four years later and remained for over fifty years – on the grounds that it was too avant-garde, but the gallery was undeterred, and the following year hosted the debut one-man exhibition of Eric Gill, who went on to design landmark print typefaces such as Gill Sans and Perpetua, as well as sculpting the figures that adorn BBC Broadcasting House. Whether the proprietors or the BBC would have been quite so keen had they known that Gill was a serial sexual abuser of his own young daughters, and even the family dog, is another question entirely.

Novelist and playwright W. Somerset Maugham lived at 27 Carlyle Mansions, Cheyne Walk, from 1904. He went on to pay tribute to the area's reputation in his novel *The Moon and Sixpence* (1919), the story of one man's attempts to lead the 'artistic' life, in which the hero is given dinner by a would-be patron, one of 'the most harmless of all the lion-hunters that pursue their quarry from the rarefied heights of Hampstead to the nethermost studios of Cheyne Walk'. As the reviewer from the *Manchester Guardian* helpfully explained:

> Mr. Maugham's story is that of a respectable stockbroker who deserts his wife after seventeen years of marriage and goes alone to Paris to follow a new ideal – the ideal of great and for a time unrecognisable art. The break is succeeded by privation and industry, by long periods of work and outbursts of savage sexual conquest; and the artist at length dies, blind and leprous, in Tahiti.

Antarctic explorer Robert Falcon Scott, who met an equally unpleasant end in somewhat colder regions, came to live at 56 Oakley Street in 1905 on returning from his marathon voyage in the ship *Discovery* as leader of the National Antarctic Expedition (1901–04), during which he established the true position of the south magnetic pole. Scott gave up his house in Oakley Street in 1908, on the occasion of his marriage, dying four years later on another expedition, shortly after reaching the pole.

Credit: Daily Mirror/Mirrorpix

Chelsea painter, Mrs Fagan, arriving at the Chelsea Arts Ball in a sedan chair carried by fellow artists Mr Jack and Mr Macbeth, March 1910

The Chelsea Arts Ball was first staged in 1908, organised by the Chelsea Arts Club. Generally held at the Albert Hall, it was a suitably uninhibited occasion which ran annually until being banned in 1959, so that historians of the sixties could pretend that everything was really strait-laced until the Beatles came along. Somewhat more restrained, and certainly with less revealing costumes, was the annual Chelsea Flower Show, which began in May 1913 in the grounds of the Royal Hospital and continues to this day.

In the Realm of the Census

It is probably worth pausing at this point to examine the 1913 Ordnance Survey Map of Chelsea, to give a flavour of the area around the King's Road just before the war broke out. At first glance, it appears vaguely similar to the Chelsea of today, but on closer inspection the building usage has changed considerably. The King's Road of that time was still a place full of local shops which would mostly be swept away with the advent of rock'n'roll, high fashion and all-purpose 'swinging': number 128, site of the mid-fifties Fantasie coffee bar started by Mary Quant's business partner Archie McNair, was then home to Frederick Harding & Sons, Bootmakers; at number 124, Alvaro's, the ultra-hip sixties restaurant patronised by the likes of Michael Caine and Keith Richards, was Webb, Sons & Clarke Ltd, Wholesale Cheesemongers; at number 196, early seventies cowboy outfitters the Emperor of Wyoming was simply Walter Brazil, Pork Butcher; number 488, sixties boutique supreme Granny Takes a Trip was known less controversially as Theodore Matthiae, Baker; and, perhaps appropriately, number 430, the shop from which McLaren and Westwood unleashed the Sex Pistols, was in 1913 the premises of Joseph Thorn, Pawnbroker.

Walking along the King's Road that year you would certainly encounter drapers, hosiers, tailors, dressmakers, bootmakers and shoemakers in considerable numbers, but alongside them were tobacconists, grocers, ball-bearing suppliers, laundries, dairymen, gasfitters, oilmen, carpenters, fried-fish dealers, coal merchants, plumbers, fruiterers, ironmongers, servants' registry offices and several artificial teeth manufacturers. Compared to today, however, restaurants and cafes were in extremely short supply: Alice Kohl's tearooms were at number 163; John Woodward's coffee tavern at number 156; Florence Trethewy's coffee rooms at number 281; Ernest Harrington's coffee rooms at number 513; Helen B. Derby's restaurant at 12 Vale Terrace; Alfred Hawkins' dining rooms at number 57; Frederick Howell's dining rooms at number 377; and Alfred John Moore's dining rooms at number 494, and that was it. One tearoom, but three artificial teeth manufacturers; one restaurant, but four ironmongers; three apiece of coffee houses and dining rooms, but twelve grocers and eighteen butchers. There was still a cart works (Thomas Blanch at number 289), but the changing times had already given rise to Hooper & Co., Motor Body Builders at number 77a and the motor garage Ormerod & Co. at number 85. The legendary Thomas Crapper & Co. Ltd, Sanitary Engineers were at number 120, where they proudly remained until the sixties, eventually undergoing a metamorphosis into a branch of Laura Ashley that itself, these days, is no more.

Overwhelmingly then, the King's Road in that last year before the outbreak of the First World War was still a local high street offering basic services to the community, albeit with a higher than usual concentration of clothing and footwear outlets. Numerous residents of Cheyne Row and Cheyne Walk were listed simply as 'artist' or 'sculptor'; some of lasting fame, such as Jacob Epstein (72 Cheyne Walk), many of them not. As for cinemas, even though 1913 was relatively early days for the silver screen, and D. W. Griffith over in Hollywood had not yet made his three-hour hymn of praise to the Ku Klux Klan, *Birth of a Nation* (1915), there were already several cinemas in evidence: London & Provincial Electric Theatres Ltd at numbers 148–150 (which later became the Classic); the Chelsea Picture Palace at number 182; and Popular Entertainments Ltd at number 281 (later the Essoldo, then the King's Road Theatre, now the Everyman Cinema). The King's Road pubs of 1913, up until at least the seventies, would have provided a welcome set of fixed points by which to navigate, but since then far too many, like the Man in the Moon, the Roebuck and the Six Bells have either been turned into expensive wine bars or had their names changed and the heart taken out of them. Interestingly, the finest surviving King's Road watering-hole, the Chelsea Potter, is not listed in 1913 under that name – the entry simply reads 'Commercial tavern', with Arthur Frederick Loveridge as the landlord.

The Haunt of the Sage and the Seagull

In the run-up to the First World War, writers came and went: Radclyffe Hall moved to Tite Street, to 39 Cadogan Square in 1911, and then to a succession of Chelsea addresses until 1920, although by the time of the scandal surrounding her novel *The Well of Loneliness* (1928) she had moved to Brompton; Bram Stoker and his wife Florence left Chelsea for good in 1910, relocating from Durham Place to St George's Square in Pimlico, where he wrote one final novel, *The Lair of the White Worm*, before dying of Bright's disease in April 1912; a fourteen-year-old schoolboy from across the river called Noel

Coward would often come to have tea with Chelsea artist Philip Streatfield in 1914 as he painted a nude portrait of a model called Doris; in January 1913, after ten years of living at the Reform Club, Henry James finally settled in Chelsea at 21 Carlyle Mansions, Cheyne Walk, where he remained until his death in 1916. 'This Chelsea perch, the haunt of the sage and the seagull proved, even after a brief experiment, just the thing for me.'

What preoccupied James most during these last years was the progress of the First World War, which formed the subject of many of the letters and pamphlets he wrote during that time: 'the destruction of such masses, on such a scale, of the magnificent young life that was to have been productive and prolific, bears down any faith, any patience, all argument and all hope.' He visited wounded soldiers in hospital in London and helped raise money for an organisation in Chelsea catering for Belgian refugees who had settled in the district. James would also have been able to witness another side of the war merely by standing outside his house and looking across the river, as a Zeppelin hovered over Battersea Park during one of the early bombing raids, but he did not live to see the end of this conflict which he had followed so closely. He died on February 28, 1916, and his funeral was held at Chelsea Old Church.

As Henry James was taking leave of his home, one of the other great Anglophiles from America, T. S. Eliot, was moving in upstairs at the same building. He arrived at 19 Carlyle Mansions, Cheyne Walk in 1915, and was still there when *TIME* magazine profiled him as an elder literary statesman in 1950, in which they described him leaving his flat after a hearty breakfast dressed in 'an impeccable dark blue suit and carrying a tightly rolled umbrella', on his way to catch the number 49 bus to his day job at Faber and Faber. The transatlantic traffic sometimes worked both ways – in 1914 a man who lived in a studio in the Fulham Road but was later to set up home off the King's Road visited America, during which trip a magazine called *This World* printed a lurid account of the orgies alleged to have taken place at his studio back home. This was the first, but perhaps not the last, that many people would have heard of Aleister Crowley.

Ecstasy in the Brompton Road

Crossing the Atlantic in wartime was a hazardous business, and in 1915 a woman who lived at the Pheasantry, 152 King's Road, was killed when the ship on which she was travelling was torpedoed by a U-boat. Her name was Eleanor Thornton, and she had posed for numerous paintings and sculptures during the preceding decade – many of them the work of Charles

Robinson Sykes, a graduate of the Royal College of Art in South Kensington, who in 1910 designed the famous winged Rolls-Royce radiator mascot the Spirit of Ecstasy in his studio at 193 Brompton Road. Eleanor Thornton was said by some to have been the model for this figure, although this has been disputed.

The only listed business at the Pheasantry in 1913 had been that of Amédee Joubert & Son, Upholsterers, but in 1916 a Russian dancing academy was started there by a former member of Diaghilev's Ballets Russes, Princess Serafina Astafieva. Shortly after the war's end, a nine-year-old girl from Muswell Hill named Lilian Alicia Marks was brought to her, fresh from a triumphant appearance in a version of *Dick Whittington* in Kennington. This pupil, now renamed Alicia Markova, was spotted by Diaghilev on a visit to the Pheasantry in 1921, as a result of which he eventually offered her a position in his ballet company. Margot Fonteyn (Margaret Evelyn Hookham) and Anton Dolin (Sydney Francis Patrick Chippendall Healey-Kay) were two of the other famous dancers who trained at Astafieva's academy.

The New Zealand writer Katherine Mansfield lived for a while in 1917 at 141a Old Church Street, having been familiar with Chelsea for some years. She had met Aleister Crowley in the years before the war at the parties of Chelsea hostess Gwendoline Otter (who was for some time a member of Crowley's Order of the Brothers of the A. ∴A. ∴), during which Aleister introduced Mansfield to the drug anhalonium, derived from peyote, inducing similar symptoms to those experienced fifty years later at certain fashionable parties in the area. The three-bedroom house in Old Church Street in which Mansfield lived in 1917 came on the market in 2004 for £1,450,000, a price which would have amazed its early 20th-century occupants, but even that would have been a bargain compared to 2016, when the same property sold for £7,550,000. Also in Old Church Street in 1917, at number 53, was an eleven-year-old who would later call for the wholesale bombing of some real-estate to the west of London, but would then be instrumental in helping to save the Albert Bridge from demolition, the future Poet Laureate John Betjeman.

Edith's Grove

With the war's end, a new influx of writers and artists began, and the first wave of jazz music and jazz dancing hit London in 1918. The twenty-year-old Vladimir Nabokov – having narrowly escaped a grisly fate at the hands of disciples of ex-Chelsea resident Karl Marx during the Russian Revolution – moved with his parents and other relatives into a rented house at 6 Elm Park Gardens, between the King's Road and Fulham Road. While living there, he translated the work of several English-language poets, and also experimented with writing poems in English himself, before going up to study at Cambridge University in October 1919. It is not hard to imagine what this refugee from the revolution would have made of the 1919 pro-Bolshevik 'Keep-hands-off-Russia' rally held up the road at the Albert Hall, at which a sixpenny book of poems entitled *The Winstonburg Line* was available, written by an ex-soldier named Osbert Sitwell.

The month after Nabokov moved out of Chelsea, Osbert and Sacheverell Sitwell, together with the composer William Walton, moved into number 2 Carlyle Square, off the King's Road, from which base they and their sister Edith Sitwell would exert a powerful influence over the cultural life of the twenties and thirties. The first, and possibly most famous example of this came in 1921 when Edith and Walton worked together in the house at Carlyle Square setting some of her poems to his music, resulting in a piece they named *Façade*. It was premiered at their home on January 24, 1922, with Edith reading her poems, accompanied by an ensemble conducted by Walton. A more public Chelsea performance was given four years later in 1926, when *Façade* was presented in a revised and expanded version at the Chenil Galleries in the King's Road, and Diaghilev was among the celebrities in the audience.

Chelsea was not entirely unknown territory for the Sitwells even before the Carlyle Square days. Just before the war, Edith's aunt, Mrs George Swinton, was having an affair with the painter Walter Sickert and had arranged for her to meet the great man. Osbert, meanwhile, was stationed at Chelsea Barracks after the outbreak of hostilities before being sent over to France, and was returned there in 1916, having sustained a leg injury. Securing a house in Swan Walk, near the Chelsea Physic Garden, he and Edith scored an early success at a 1917 literary evening in the home of renowned hostess Lady Sybil Colefax, at which T. S. Eliot also read a religious poem of his entitled *The Hippopotamus*. The highlight of the Sitwells' time at Swan Walk was a party they threw there for the Ballets Russes on October 12, 1918, a month before the war's end. Among those present were D. H. Lawrence, Lytton Strachey, Ottoline Morell, Roger Fry, Maynard Keynes, Clive Bell and Mark Gertler. Following their move to Carlyle Square, the parade of illustrious guests continued, with one dinner party alone including Virginia Woolf, Aldous Huxley, Arnold Bennett and Siegfried Sassoon. The Sitwells' circle ranged from surviving friends of Oscar Wilde such as Robert Ross to the likes of Pablo Picasso and Jean Cocteau.

Lady Sybil Colefax herself moved in 1922 to Argyll House, 211 King's Road – a stone's throw away from the Sitwells in Carlyle Square – where she remained until 1937, presiding over one of the great salons of the age, entertaining a stream of celebrities from Churchill to Cole Porter. Between the drawing room of the Sitwells and the salon of Lady Sybil Colefax, some of the most well-known cultural figures of the twenties were passing through the King's Road.

The Wickedest Man in the World

A few hundred yards west of Lady Sybil's home, a man who had recently returned from living abroad and wanted to settle in Chelsea discovered what he was looking for while walking down the King's Road in 1922. Seeing a removal van parked outside number 31 Wellington Square, he concluded that there might be rooms available. It turned out that the landlady herself was just moving in, and there was indeed other space on offer. This probably came as little surprise to the man in question, because he had been searching for anything to do with the number 31, which he considered significant as the Sacred Key to the *Book of the Law*. 'The bow drawn at venture had hit the ideal at the first twang of the string,' Aleister Crowley recalled, and so the man who sometimes called himself The Great Beast 666, and whom a newspaper once described as 'The Wickedest Man in the World', settled on the King's Road. While living there, he wrote his most famous book, *Diary of a Drug Fiend*, for which he was paid a £60 advance by the publisher Collins. Some forty-five years later, his photograph would appear alongside various others in an assemblage of images and floral displays put together just around the corner in a photographer's studio in Flood Street as a cover illustration for a collection of songs apparently concerning a character called Sergeant Pepper.

Crowley's circle of acquaintances included the writer Ronald Firbank, author of novels such as *The Flower Beneath the Foot*, who was also a friend of Osbert Sitwell's. Firbank did not live in London, but would come to stay each summer during the twenties, ritually announcing the fact via the classified section of *The Times* or the *Morning Post*. One summer his choice of temporary residence was a flat in Sloane Square, despite the fact that a character in his 1915 novel *Vainglory* had once remarked, 'I can imagine her asleep in a rather boring Louis XVI bedroom with a window on Sloane Square.' By way of making himself feel at home, Firbank installed a potted palm tree and made arrangements for a florist in the square to send over a gardener twice a day in order to minister to its needs. According to Osbert Sitwell, 'Ronald was much pleased with this man, for he wore a green baize apron, and had a rustic way of speaking, so that it was "just like being in the country".' When

Firbank then decided to relocate to a flat in Piccadilly, he made arrangements that the same man should walk there twice a day from Sloane Square, carrying his watering can, in order to continue the valuable work.

A selection of more permanent residents came to settle in Chelsea, such as the actress Sybil Thorndike (who become a neighbour of the Sitwells by moving to 6 Carlyle Square in 1921), Bertrand Russell and his second wife Dora (setting up home at 31 Sydney Street in 1921), Arnold Bennett (at number 75 Cadogan Square from 1922) and A. A. Milne, who arrived at 11 Mallord Street in 1920, a few yards north of the King's Road towards World's End, making him a neighbour of the painter Augustus John. In 1925 Milne relocated, but the journey could not have been particularly traumatic, since he only shifted as far as number 13 in the same road. During the time of his residence in Mallord Street, he produced books which were somewhat different in intent and projected audience than those Mr Crowley was writing along the road nearer Sloane Square, but they served to make him equally well known: *When We Were Very Young* (1924), *Winnie the Pooh* (1926), *Now We Are Six* (1927) and *The House at Pooh Corner* (1928). However, during the first two years that Milne spent at Mallord Street, he wrote a very fine book of a different kind, a country house detective novel called *The Red House Mystery* (1922), later singled out for consideration by Raymond Chandler in his landmark 1944 essay, *The Simple Art of Murder*. When I was first researching this book in 2004, Milne's house at number 13 – five bedrooms, three reception rooms, four bathrooms – was being offered for sale by an estate agent in Sloane Avenue with an asking price of £3,250,000, and in 2022 the figure would be closer to £10 million, which rather suggests that it requires a wallet of heroic proportions to live at Pooh Corner these days.

At number 65 Cheyne Walk at this time there was a bookshop with the same sense of adventure and respect for the avant-garde that would later be shown in the sixties and seventies by London shops such as Better Books, Indica and Compendium. Its name was the Chelsea Book Club, and in addition to holding art exhibitions, it was also known as the place in 1922 where a virtually unobtainable novel called *Ulysses* by James Joyce could be found. The usual guardians of morality were doing their best to protect the public from this supposed filth, prior of course to its elevation to classic status once the author was safely dead and unlikely to have much further use for the royalty cheques. Among those perhaps less likely to be corrupted by the varieties of the English language demonstrated in *Ulysses* were the short-skirted, jazz-age patrons of that year's Chelsea Arts Ball, who were captured in one of the regular *Topical Budget* newsreel films for cinemas in a sequence entitled 'Bohemia's "Brighter London" at Chelsea Arts Ball'.

Someone a little too young to yet be indulging such bohemian rhapsodies
was the eleven-year-old Eton schoolboy who moved with his mother into
Turner's old house at 119 Cheyne Walk in 1923, but Ian Fleming would
stamp his influence on a later generation of bright young things worldwide
by means of a fictional character named Bond who lived in an unnamed
square just off the King's Road.

Hernia, Gob and Sago Whittlebot

In the 1923 general election, Sydney Street resident Bertrand Russell stood
as Labour Party candidate for Chelsea but failed to win, while a man with
a considerably better track record in attracting the voters, ex-prime minister
David Lloyd George, came to live at 10 Cheyne Walk in 1924. These days
that would be a very expensive address, but even in those days, Britain's
wartime leader was hardly short of money, having fallen from power two
years earlier after being accused in the House of Lords of systematically
handing out peerages and knighthoods in return for cash during his term in
office. Standing at the door of his new house, Lloyd George would have been
able, if the mood took him, to wave in a neighbourly fashion in the direction
of the new tenant of number 2 Cheyne Walk, the actor John Barrymore.

In June 1923, the press had another chance to sneer at one of Chelsea's
artistic products when Sitwell and Walton's *Façade* was given a public
performance at the Aeolian Hall in Bond Street in the presence of luminaries such as Virginia Woolf and Evelyn Waugh, giving rise to the following
encouraging headline, which would also make an excellent title for most
live LPs: 'DRIVEL THEY PAID TO HEAR'.

Someone reputed to have walked out of the performance was an
acquaintance of Osbert Sitwell's called Noel Coward. He had originally
gone to school in Battersea, before moving across the river to Ebury Street
when his family opened a guest house there, where he began composing
songs on a second-hand piano purchased from Harrods. The adult Noel
used the experiences of that evening watching *Façade* as raw material when
writing his new show which was produced later that year at the Duke of
York's Theatre, entitled *London Calling!* When the Clash adopted the same
title fifty-six years later – minus the exclamation mark – for a single and
for their third album, Joe Strummer was living on the King's Road at the
World's End estate, and they shot the video for the song out on the river
in torrential rain in the shadow of the Albert Bridge.

In Coward's show of that name, the Sitwells were ridiculed in a sketch
called 'The Swiss Family Whittlebot' under the thinly disguised names

of Hernia, Gob and Sago Whittlebot, which prompted a bitter and long-running feud between the author and his former friends.

Theatregoers in London could still drive into town in those days and expect to find parking spaces, although the number of cars on the roads was obviously increasing. In order to cater for the upper end of the carriage trade, the Blue Bird Garage opened at 350 King's Road in 1924, near World's End – a select destination for the motoring set with considerable amounts of space and special rooms for customers and their chauffeurs.

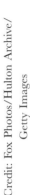

The Bluebird Garage, Chelsea, April 1929

At the Chenil Galleries, 181–183 King's Road, on April 27, 1926, *Façade* received its second public outing, and now the press reception was much more favourable, with the *Sunday Times* calling it 'the jolliest entertainment of the season'. Another notable event at the same venue that summer was the twin solo exhibitions in adjoining rooms by the painters Gwen and Augustus John – a pairing not repeated until their 2004 joint show at the Tate Britain – and Mary Chamot wrote about both painters in turn over two successive issues of *Country Life*. Augustus had for some time maintained a studio of his own at the Chenil, but although the place was clearly an important part of the art scene during the twenties, hosting avant-garde exhibitions eventually proved insufficient to pay the rent. At the start of the thirties, it diversified in the service of a new art form, jazz music, which began to be recorded there when part of the Chenil Galleries was rented out to the Decca label.

Bandleader Spike Hughes began cutting jazz sides for Decca at the Chenil Galleries in 1930, and he and his combo the Three Blind Mice accompanied US visitor Jimmy Dorsey at a session there that April. Hughes is generally regarded as one of the first people to actually try to play and record authentic jazz in the UK, and he also wrote some of his own material, including one piece called 'Six Bells Stampede', which, when you're recording at the Chenil Galleries – a mere fifty-yard dash for a thirsty musician from a pub called the Six Bells – is not particularly surprising. The label advertised him that year as follows:

> *There is a young man – Spike Hughes,*
> *He holds most original views,*
> *He's the dancing fan's Mecca,*
> *You must hear him on Decca,*
> *In 'hot' choruses, foxtrots and blues.*

Sales were apparently not that good, despite Decca's full-page adverts, and so most other home-grown outfits stuck to a more crowd-pleasing mainstream kind of dance music. The bandleader Roy Fox, who also recorded at the Chenil Galleries studio around that time, complained about the acoustic qualities of the set-up, but Decca was still using the place on July 13, 1933, when one of the all-time greats came to the King's Road to record. Backed by some of the best jazz musicians in the world, and billed on record as Duke Ellington and His Famous Orchestra (to be specific: Freddy Jenkins, Arthur Whetsel, Cootie Williams, t; Lawrence Brown, Joe Nanton, tb; Juan Tizol, vtb; Barney Bigard, cl, ts; Johnny Hodges, cl, ss, as; Otto Hardwick, as, bsx; Harry Carney, cl, as, bs; Duke Ellington, p; Fred Guy, g; Wellman Braud, b; Sonny Greer, d), the Duke laid down versions of his own compositions 'Hyde Park' and 'Harlem Speaks', plus 'Ain't Misbehavin'' (Waller-Razaf-Brooks) and 'Chicago' (Fisher). It had been a long time since Mozart played a show in the neighbourhood, but the King's Road was once more firmly back in the musical big league. This was Ellington's first tour of England of many that were to follow over the decades, and he understandably made a huge impression on the assembled local jazz musicians of London who caught his historic two-week run of shows at the Palladium and took inspiration away with them which then fed into their own playing and songwriting.

A Huge Quantity of Medicinal Drugs of All Sorts

In the October 1930 issue of a relatively new magazine aimed at dance band musicians which was still known as the *Melody Maker and British Metronome* – and which had helped organise the Ellington tour – there was an advert placed by the Cavendish Music Co., Regent Street, advertising the sheet music for a new song apparently designed to capitalise on a new invention, entitled 'I Don't Need a Television'. That same month, next door to the Chenil Galleries, they were holding the Fifth Annual Chelsea Dance Band Contest at Chelsea Town Hall: 'Organiser: Mr F Garganico, The Knightsbridge Rooms, 58a Brompton Road, SW3. Open for competitors up to eight pieces.' *Melody Maker* recommended – in language which in later years could have come straight from a cheaply printed card in a phone box – that 'Dance musicians without "dates" [. . .] should drop in for an exciting and instructive time.'

Across the river next to the park, red-telephone-box designer Sir Giles Gilbert Scott's iconic art deco landmark Battersea Power Station had been under construction since 1929. It would eventually open in 1935, and its four chimneys (three working, one false, to make up the numbers) subsequently had a walk-on part in rock history. It can be seen in *The Great Rock'n'Roll Swindle* as the Sex Pistols 1977 Jubilee boat trip goes down the river; Pink Floyd put it on the cover of their *Animals* album next to an inflatable pig; and the Jam shot the video for their 1978 single 'News of the World' up on top of the building in their full, two-tone shoe, *All Mod Cons* gear. And then? Following its decommissioning as a working power station in 1983, it was sold off amid much local protest in 1987 to developers who tore off the roof of the Grade II* listed building and demolished the west wall in a failed attempt to turn the place into a theme park, leaving it open to the elements and rotting away – a sad contrast to the fate of Bankside Power Station, which was sympathetically adapted to become the Tate Modern. In the event, it took much wrangling and the best part of four more decades before the ravaged building and its surrounding spaces were eventually converted into an upmarket shopping mall, office space and bar/restaurant area at a cost of £9 billion, designed to appeal to anyone with a spare £18 million to spend on a penthouse flat. Meanwhile, as of 2022, Gilbert Scott's iconic building itself is now hidden from most landward views by the enveloping modern apartment buildings which have been constructed in a ring around it, whose design style clashes jarringly next to his classic 1920s deco lines.

Back in 1932, as Battersea Power Station was still under construction, the six-year-old John Osborne was living with his family across the river in Fulham at 2 Crookham Road, an area he would later recall as 'gloomy and uninteresting', very likely neither knowing nor caring that a theatre in Sloane Square called the Court had just closed down after a chequered history going back fifty years. Almost a quarter of a century later, having survived stints as a cinema, years of lying empty, and the occasional attentions of the Luftwaffe, it would reopen with a season of plays which included one by that Fulham resident which would help establish its reputation and ensure its survival.

As the Court Theatre shuttered its doors in 1932, a few hundred yards away at the Pheasantry, a club and restaurant opened for business which would later attract some very famous names, including Humphrey Bogart, Dylan Thomas, Augustus John, Francis Bacon and Sigmund Freud. Run by an Italian called Réné de Meo, it was named, not entirely surprisingly, the Pheasantry, and became a fixture on the Chelsea scene until the mid-sixties.

In 1934, the artists' materials and picture-framing specialists Green & Stone moved from rooms in the Chenil Galleries to their own site at 259 King's Road; the new Chelsea Bridge opened, not as elegant as the Albert Bridge, but it managed to provide a convenient location at its southern end for the pie stall which would become a magnet for successive generations of bikers; and a certain Mary Quant was born, on February 11, in the South East London district of Blackheath. At that point, future James Bond author Ian Fleming was living in Cheyne Walk, aged twenty-six, and then moved a short distance in 1936 to 22a Ebury Street. The sixties were closing in.

In Sloane Square, the disused Court Theatre was converted into a cinema in 1935, and around the same time number 206 King's Road – which in 1913 had been the premises of William Edward Robinson, Surgeon & Physician – became the Gaumont Cinema, part of which survives today as the Chelsea Cinema. On Sloane Avenue, running north off the King's Road, a new apartment block called Chelsea Cloisters opened in 1938, which for a while in the seventies would be home to a post-Floyd Syd Barrett, and then to public enemies numbers one and two Johnny Rotten and Sid Vicious. It was also the last residence of Roberto Calvi, the disgraced president of the Banco Ambrosiano, known as 'God's Banker', whose body was found hanging beneath Blackfriars Bridge on the morning of June 18, 1982. Calvi had flown to the UK, shaved off his moustache in an apparent attempt to disguise himself, and remained in his eighth-floor flat at Chelsea Cloisters, running up a serious phone bill, terrified of opening the door and in possession of what the coroner later described as 'a huge quantity of medicinal drugs of all sorts'. He last used his home phone shortly before midnight, some eight or nine hours before his body was found at Blackfriars.

Strip Strip Hooray!

In the years immediately prior to the Second World War, removal firms in Chelsea were kept as busy as ever: Wyndham Lewis moved into 21 Cheyne

Walk in 1935, then out again in 1936; Augustus John relocated from his home of many years at Mallord Street to 49 Glebe Place in 1935; Cecil Beaton's mother found a house at 8 Pelham Place, near South Kensington tube, which became Cecil's London base until 1974; and Joyce Grenfell settled at 149 King's Road. A young woman called Mollie Craven who moved into a basement flat at 1 Glebe Place in 1937 found that her new landlord, an artist whose studio was on the top floor, was a man named Francis Bacon. He had been in the area for some years, originally renting a studio at 7 Queensbury Mews, South Kensington, in 1929, in the days when he intended to become a furniture designer. From the window of his studio in Glebe Place, he could watch the former Pheasantry ballet student Anton Dolin practising his dance moves in his room across the street.

The Chelsea Palace, in common with most British music halls, was finding that the audience for traditional variety shows was declining, and that it paid to include some jazz and dance bands on the bill if you wanted to pull the crowds. In the same way that late fifties and early sixties rock'n'roll and beat group outfits would play the old variety and cinema circuits up and down the UK, acts like Nat Gonella and his Georgians were booked into the Chelsea Palace in the late thirties, in contrast to its more traditional fare of Gracie Fields and the 'Prime Minister of Mirth', George Robey. The two strands of entertainment existed in a kind of uneasy truce throughout the following decade, and were also joined by skin shows of varying degrees of exposure. Some said that the latter kinds of show around town – with titles like *Eve On Parade, Strip Strip Hooray!* or *Don't Blush Girls* – were signs of increasing desperation on the part of the theatre managers, which is probably true, but it is also fair to say that attitudes to casual sex and all kinds of suggestiveness became far more tolerant during the Blitz. The dark streets of the blackout provided numerous opportunities, and the prospect of random sudden death from the thousands of tons of high explosives being dropped nightly on London during 1940 understandably led many people to discard the strait-laced moral standards of certain members of the previous generation and behave as if each day might well be their last.

Anyone labouring under the mistaken impression that the sixties generation were the first to experiment with some kind of liberated lifestyle might perhaps try reading *Love Lessons*, Joan Wyndham's excellent wartime diary of her experiences among the Chelsea art community during the years of the Blitz. Aged seventeen, she rented an artist's studio in Redcliffe Road and signed up for art school at what was then still known as Chelsea Polytechnic in Manresa Road, where Henry Moore and Graham Sutherland were both on the teaching staff. Intermingled with her studies, she also worked at the first-aid post at St Mark's College in the King's Road. In Joan's entry for September 9, 1940, she describes hearing a bomb fall nearby and going with her friends to look for the crater: 'It was in Bramerton Street, a whole house destroyed, the air full of smoke and dust, and all the inhabitants of that part of Chelsea beetling around the barricades like insects disturbed, pansies and lesbians and all.'

The bomb appears to have landed just near a club called the Gateways, which had been founded in the thirties and remained there until 1985, making it what is claimed to be the longest-running lesbian club in the world. Dylan Thomas and Quentin Crisp were also among its visitors, and the club and its patrons even briefly became Hollywood film stars in 1968. Wyndham's own studio was destroyed by a bomb two days after the Bramerton street blast. Luckily, she was elsewhere at the time, and she records in her diary that by that stage roughly a quarter of Redcliffe Road was in ruins, and most of the rest of the houses had been evacuated.

Sloane Square Underground Station, which had only just been repaired following a previous bombing raid, was completely destroyed by a direct hit on November 12, 1940, and seventy-nine people were injured as part of the roof collapsed onto a train. The Court Theatre, still operating as a cinema, was also damaged. On April 16 the following year, Chelsea Old Church, the burial place of Sir Thomas More and Sir Hans Sloane, with a history stretching back to the 12th century, was almost totally destroyed during a huge night raid of indiscriminate bombing on London by the Luftwaffe. Before the year was through, Gollancz published the writer John Strachey's book about his work as an air-raid warden in Chelsea during those times under the title *Post D*. Francis Bacon's response to his country's call-up was somewhat more direct. An asthma sufferer, he went to Harrods, hired an Alsatian and slept alongside it the night before his army medical. The proximity of the dog left Bacon in a terrible state, and he was promptly turned down on medical grounds.

Chelsea, Eh? Bet You're Hot Stuff

Life carried on amid the explosions and the rubble, and the Chelsea Palace remained open for business. At the height of the Blitz in September 1940, a sixteen-year-old Max Miller fan and would-be comedian called Alfred Hawthorne Hill arrived at its stage door, having given up his milk round and sold his drum kit for £8 to finance the venture, travelling up from Southampton armed only with the addresses of three variety theatres at which to look for work. He set out determined to try his luck at the Metropolitan, Edgware Road, the Empress, Brixton and the Chelsea Palace in the King's Road. As he recalled in 1955: 'At the Chiswick Empire they did not want to know about Alf Hill. I had much the same reception at the "Met", but at the Chelsea Palace I was lucky enough to arrange to see Harry Benet at his office the next morning.'

Following a night spent sleeping rough on Streatham Common to save money, he went along to see the impresario and was offered a part in a revue starting in East Ham a few days hence. And so the teenager who changed his first name a few years later in honour of his hero Jack Benny, became a worldwide television comedy star and knocked Slade's 'Coz I Luv You' off the number one spot in 1971 with a song called 'Ernie (The Fastest Milkman in the West)', gained his first big break in show business by banging on a door in the King's Road.

Benny Hill was not the only person drawn to the Chelsea Palace during the war. The Southern Crusaders band of the 57th Regiment Royal Armoured Corps, featuring former musicians from the famous orchestras of Harry Roy and Billy Cotton, gave a show there in December 1941, becoming the first army band to play at a music hall. Some weeks the variety bill at the Palace featured a selection of run-of-the-mill acts – such a line-up from August 1942 in which their top attractions were Radio Fun Fair with Suzette Tarri, the Two Leslies, plus Renara and Joe Peterson, which seems somewhat short on household names compared to other London halls that week that boasted much bigger stars like Sid Field or Charlie Kunz – yet in March 1943, for instance, the venue played host to the nationally known Henry Hall and his Band, a man familiar to all radio listeners as the leader of the BBC Dance Orchestra. Meanwhile comedy at the Palace that month came in the guise of a show entitled *Get Up Them Stairs*, starring British film stars Hal Monty and Bunny Doyle.

An item in the obituary column of the December 17, 1943 edition of the *West London Press & Chelsea News* recorded the death at 430 King's Road of the pawnbroking shop's long-time proprietor, Joseph Edward Thorne, aged sixty-eight, 'a prominent member of Chelsea Conservative Club and a former president of Chelsea Bowling Club'. Three decades later, his premises would be taken over by Malcolm McLaren and Vivienne Westwood.

By this stage of the war, Joan Wyndham was nineteen and serving in the WAAFs, mostly up north and in Scotland, having discovered that her place of origin often prompted the following response among RAF pilots:

'Where do you come from? Chelsea, eh? Coo-er! Bet you're hot stuff, have you got a beard?' Back in town that same July on leave, after a hard evening fending off an overly amorous Dylan Thomas, she went to play billiards with her friends at the Six Bells on the King's Road, 'then we all went off to the Cafe Bleu for dinner with Quentin Crisp, our divine, red-headed neighbourhood pansy.' Quentin, who, as George Melly later remarked, must have had 'the courage of a lioness' to walk the streets dressed as he did, had arrived a couple of years earlier, and found the area to be a slightly more tolerant place where he could mostly be himself without the usual threats and intimidation that followed him when venturing into other parts of town. As he himself said in the publicity material for his 1976 one-man show, *An Evening With Quentin Crisp – Straight Talk from a Bent Speaker*:

> Quentin Crisp has lived for Thirty Five years in Chelsea in one room without ever cleaning it. Now in the winter of his life he describes himself on his Income Tax forms as a retired waif. In the past he has been unsuccessfully an illustrator, a writer, a televisionary and is currently an artists' model. His hobby is taking the blame. In spite of all this, he has the nerve to preach on the subject of life-style and claims by means of it to cure you of your freedom!

Just as the Rolling Stones in the early sixties would encounter hostility over the length of their hair, or the punks in the mid-seventies over the colour of theirs, Crisp set out to look exactly the way he wanted, and if that caused problems on the streets, then the last thing he intended to do was change his appearance. Unlike Oscar Wilde, he survived long enough to outlive most of the prejudice and eventually found himself declared something of a national hero, but in the forties and fifties, there were few other places in the country where he could have experienced anything like the casual and friendly acceptance that he found in the bohemian community of Chelsea.

A Rather Disgusting Little Restaurant

Francis Bacon changed locations in 1943, but did not go far, occupying Sir John Everett Millais' old studio at 7 Cromwell Place, near South Kensington tube, where he was to remain until 1950. It was here that he painted the triptych entitled *The Studies for the Three Figures at the Base of the Crucifixion*, which caused a sensation when shown at the Lefevre Gallery in April 1945.

As the war finally drew to a close, with the local authorities still some years away from putting up a blue plaque to mark Oscar Wilde's former house in Tite Street, his surviving son, Vyvyan Holland, lived a short distance away in a flat on Sloane Street. He was visited there in 1945 by Cecil Beaton, then in the process of designing sets and costumes for a revival of *Lady Windermere's Fan*, to be directed by John Gielgud. Holland reminisced about the original production of the play, and how shocking it had been to the family to become complete pariahs after Wilde's court case and sentence. He told Beaton that he and his mother had been forced by the management to leave a hotel at which they had been staying under an assumed name once their true identity was revealed, and that even people who had dogs named Oscar would change it to something else. A few days later, catching the train up to Manchester with the play's backer, Binkie Beaumont, for the first out-of-town preview, Cecil had intended to discuss his costume designs on the journey, but on opening the daily paper found news that the atomic bomb had been dropped on Hiroshima. He recorded in his diary that he then felt incapable of discussing 'theatrical trivialities'.

At the end of the war a young able seaman – not yet demobbed, but with a keen interest in jazz, anarchism and surrealism – ventured up to town to visit the wilds of Chelsea for the first time, following an exploratory letter directed at the Surrealist Group of England, headed by Magritte's friend E. L. T. Mesens. Having received an encouraging response from the group's secretary, Simon Watson Taylor, George Melly found himself knocking on the door of a flat in Markham Square. He and Watson Taylor promptly went off in search of lunch 'along King's Road to a rather disgusting little restaurant (even by the standards of the time) called the Bar-B-Cue where we ate Spanish omelettes under a poor mural of cowboys roping steers.' Holding court in that same restaurant was Quentin Crisp – with hair hennaed red, nail varnish, mascara and lipstick – whose attention was caught by Melly's naval uniform. As Melly later wrote:

> He lived and lives in an amazingly squalid room somewhere off King's Road and in the quarter saw no reason to do more than slap cosmetics over the grime. [. . .] When Simon left for his appointment, Quentin suggested we went to the cinema to see 'One of Miss Hayworth's films'. And so we did, arousing many a curious glance.

Later that year, while Melly was staying the night at a house in Oakley Street into which he was later to move for most of the fifties, he encountered Crisp again, who was taking advantage of the landlord's hospitality in order to have a bath, since his own room had no washing facilities.

George Melly was hardly the only member of the services drifting into Chelsea. In 1946, a newly demobbed Peter Sellers, fresh from the RAF, briefly worked in WAAF headquarters in Cadogan Square. As part of his gradual move into the world of show business, he was assisting Ralph Reader in his plans for women-only Gang Shows. Meanwhile, over in Neville Street, off the Fulham Road, young Virginia Ironside was attending a school run by her aunt. Among the other pupils were future actresses Jane Birkin and Juliet Mills (daughter of Sir John), as well as future IRA art thief Rose Dugdale.

Somewhat removed from all this glamour, 1947 saw the eighteen-year-old John Osborne working as an assistant on a magazine called *Gas World,* and another called *Nursery World.* Just in case this proved somewhat over-stimulating, the powers that be then transferred him to another publication called *The Miller,* which concerned itself exclusively, and perhaps not entirely surprisingly, with milling. His editor on this new publication, Arnold Running, lived in a mansion block between Cheyne Walk and the King's Road, giving the Fulham teenager a glimpse of the area in which he was to live and achieve such success, ten years hence.

I Make Whoopee at Seventeen

Diana Dors, another teenager on the way up (from Swindon, rather than *Gas World*), having recently finished shooting a feature film called *A Boy, a Girl and a Bike*, celebrated by moving out of the YWCA and renting a small flat near World's End in 1949 for the princely sum of six guineas a week. It was not yet the sixties, but Diana was swinging already, as she recalled in her first autobiography, in a chapter entitled 'I Make Whoopee At Seventeen':'I didn't realize it but the cute flat was slap dab in the middle of one of the worst areas I could have established myself in, for Chelsea in those days, just after the war, was much wilder than it is today [1960].'

Diana had already seduced her film's co-star, the young and completely inexperienced Anthony Newley, in a borrowed Chelsea bedsit some months before, but now her endless parties, late nights and loud music ensured that she was thrown out of her new place after six months owing to complaints from the neighbours. She moved on to Jermyn Street, but it was far from the last that Chelsea would see of her. The title of her 1960 autobiography, recalling her wild life in the fifties, used a word which would come to be most closely associated with the decade that came after. However, as *Swingin' Dors* suggests – with its stories of wild parties with two-way mirrors on the ceiling of her Chelsea home so that guests could spy on people having sex in the bedrooms – although the rest of the country may have woken up out of its stupor 'between the Lady Chatterley trial and the first Beatles LP', down on the King's Road in the fifties, the blue touch paper had already been lit and the fireworks were going off in all directions.

Forget about the sixties for the moment: the fifties was the decade in which Michael Caine, Albert Finney and Sean Connery started acting; Keith Richards, Brian Jones, John Lennon and the rest first picked up instruments and tried to become rock'n'rollers, Karel Reisz, Lindsay Anderson and Tony Richardson first made films, David Bailey took up the camera professionally; and a woman called Mary Quant, living in a bedsit in Oakley Street, opened her first boutique on the King's Road . . .

Part Two

Everything
but the Kitchen Sink

4

'Edwardian suits,
dance music and a dagger'

The Goat-Between

It is a favourite trick of most people who write books about the pop culture revolution of the sixties to characterise England in the fifties as some kind of utter wasteland where everyone hung around buttoned up to the neck in shapeless raincoats waiting for the Beatles to come along so that they could throw off their shackles and start having sex. Perhaps it was, if you were a small child at the time, whose life was utterly blighted by the continuation of sweet rationing, or if you lived in one of the soulless New Towns that the Le Corbusier fans were spreading across the country like acne, but if you were old enough to drink, go out dancing or generally get yourself into trouble, then round about the middle of the decade the action started in no uncertain terms. Furthermore, if you were in the vicinity of the King's Road, then your version of the fifties would no more resemble that of someone in Cheltenham or Dundee than the life of a goat farmer on the small Greek island of Nisyros today resembles that of someone in Athens.

Grim, grey, depressing; England in the fifties could plead guilty to all of those on occasion, but it is worth remembering that a significant proportion of the country was still like that all the way through the 'swinging' sixties, and you would have no trouble finding uncleared bomb sites full of rubble all over London way past the point when it was being hailed by *TIME* and other magazines as the most happening city in the world. As the director Ken Loach showed in the 1966 BBC TV drama *Cathy Come Home*, not everyone in town was burning up and down the street in a convertible E-type

Jag and sipping cocktails with Brigitte Bardot. However, the King's Road had a significant head start on the sixties, and as 1950 rolled into view, the decade finally arrived in which this short stretch of pavement really began to stamp its imprint on the culture and fashions of the world.

Be Careful, They're Dangerous

Diana Dors celebrated the New Year's Eve that rung in the fifties in the Cross Keys pub in Lawrence Street, down near the river between the Albert Bridge and Battersea. That night she met a smooth-talking member of what was to become famous as the Chelsea Set, whose full name was Michael Caborn-Waterfield, later known to his friends, the press and public alike as Dandy Kim. Through Kim, a year later, Diana met the man with the taste for two-way mirrors who was to become her first husband: Dennis Hamilton. Dors, a product of the legendary Rank Charm School, had already made a string of relatively forgettable British pictures, and had a habit of showing up in the daily papers as often for what she was wearing or for something she had said, rather than for any acting she might have done on the screen. For a teenager to be leading such an allegedly 'fast' Chelsea lifestyle in a country still in the grip of rationing and deprivation was a godsend for the tabloids. Something else they developed a fascination with was the recently invented social class 'teen-agers', and their darker flipside: cosh boys, razor boys, and then – a capital letter, if you please, for the new thing – Teddy boys.

Admittedly, societies have been getting uptight about youth behaviour and youth fashions and dances for centuries, so this was in many ways nothing new. The waltz, after all, had been denounced as obscene and immoral in its day, and was itself only the latest in a wearily predictable list of dances to be attacked on these grounds. However, with the teenager firmly labelled and located in the crosshairs where no tabloid journalist or amateur pulpit preacher could miss them – and the added visual impact that television was to bring to the witch-hunt as the decade went on – the message could be put forth effectively and nationwide: 'One of the gravest problems now facing this country is how to curb the wave of violent crimes by "cosh kids" and other young thugs who have roused the nation to a fever of indignation.' Thus spake the cover article of the tabloid *Sunday Pictorial* on March 19, 1950. You might think that the 'grave problems' confronting the nation at the time might include the business of developing the newly established National Health Service, or rebuilding Britain's shattered, war-damaged cities, or even just the business of providing decent-quality food for people after years of deprivation, but you would be wrong. The nation was apparently in 'a fever of indignation', and it is an even bet that if they were, the *Sunday Pictorial* helped them get that way. The article continued, under the suitably non-judgemental title *A Boy Thug Talks*: 'Who are these teen-age hooligans? What is behind the warfare between gangs armed with razors and sharpened bicycle chains? How does a boy grow into one of these brutes, terrorising peaceful citizens?' The sixteen-year-old 'boy thug' in question – an ex-approved school inmate who had, of course, seen the light and gone straight, stopping only to unburden himself to a national newspaper on the way – told of the bad company he got into, and of the strangely fashionable way in which they were dressed: 'They were all older than us, about twenty or twenty-two, and very smart in their birds-eye suits and long draped jackets. Duke nearly busted with pride when they showed us a couple of new guns he had got for a stick-up. Lugers they were.'

So there you have it – long draped jackets and packing weapons. Only three months into 1950 and the pattern was already set, with the message loud and clear; that you should watch out for these strangely dressed young people because they are bound to be tooled-up and looking for trouble. A quarter of a century later the press were sending out the same message about these funnily dressed punk rockers; 'Here's how to recognise them; be careful, they're dangerous.'

Jaunty-Thonged

Of course, there were plenty of other people in the newspapers doing their best to scare the hell out of the public. Consider for example this toothpaste advert from the same year: 'Would you believe it! He's liable to lose half his teeth by the time he's forty, because of MOUTH ACID.' Even the government was at it, trying to put a stop to one of the only things that was free. During the spring of 1950 the Ministry of Health and the Central Council for Health Education ran a series of adverts in the press, telling people off in language more likely to be encountered these days in the broadcasts of US Christian fundamentalist preachers: 'VD . . . Syphilis . . . Gonorrhoea . . . How can these diseases be avoided? By not running the risk. Clean living is the real safeguard. Contraceptives cannot rule out the risk of infection.'

So, to recap: don't wear a draped jacket, because that will label you as a gun-toting berserker, and handfuls of your teeth are due to fall out very soon but don't worry, you will not need to be attractive to the opposite sex anyway because any kind of bodily contact will almost inevitably lead to a slow and painful death from syphilis. Come to think of it, no wonder the country was in a 'fever of indignation'.

But it was not all doom and gloom. Over in America, Hollywood was still working hard to entertain the world, and two of its latest products were about to hit Britain's shores. UK film magazine *Picturegoer* managed to write off one of the great post-war pictures, *White Heat* ('Cagney not at his best in a familiar type of gangster melodrama'), but they were right on the money the following year when future US president Ronald Reagan and a supposedly 'loveable' chimp both had their finest hours in the immortal *Bedtime for Bonzo*: 'Looking back on many, many years of picturegoing,' said reviewer Lionel Collier, 'it's hard to recall a film that has irritated me quite as much as this one.'

Still, at least that percentage of young people not busy dying of VD, coshing old ladies or chewing the furniture in frustration while watching Ron and the chimp were finding an ever-increasing selection of things on which to spend their money: jazz records, perhaps, or fashionable shoes. 'Teen-agers', shrieked an advert in October 1950, 'here's a shoe twosome from the *Easy Goer* range that will solve your foot fashion problems this winter. [. . .] It's a jaunty-thonged tie-shoe with a neat wedge-heel and cunning "mud-guard".' Clearly, by this stage, teenagers (with a hyphen or without) had become a target group as far as the advertising industry was concerned, and if they weren't 'jaunty-thonged' already, then by God they should be made to feel very unhip and old-fashioned.

Meanwhile, some distance away from the pressure-cooker atmosphere of advertising copywriters' offices in the teeming metropolis – well, in Ilfracombe, to be exact – a young actor named John Osborne was working with a theatre company called the Saga Repertory Company. Eventually, they set off in search of London and the bright lights, but wound up on a disastrous tour of the south. 'In Hartley Witney eight people turned up,' Osborne recalled, 'and in East Grinstead none at all.' Perhaps he should have tried wearing a 'neat wedge-heel and cunning "mud-guard".'

Hungry World's End shoppers or residents in September 1950 may have been drawn to the following announcement in the West London Press of a new business which had started at the future home of Westwood and McLaren's 1970s empire:

NOW OPEN!
CAFÉ EDEN
THE WORKING MAN'S CAFÉ
430 KING'S ROAD, S.W.10
(Opposite World's End Police Station)
Open from 6.30a.m.–11.30p.m.
BREAKFASTS-DINNERS-TEAS-SUPPERS

AFTER THE CINEMA
Why not call for a nice
APPETISING SUPPER?
We are open to 11.30p.m.
Always a good cup of freshly-made tea

A month later, they had a new advert, advertising lunch ('main dish and two vegetables') for one shilling and sixpence, and had also rolled out the following enticements, which highlight the fact that this end of the King's Road was still mostly a working-class district:

Credit: author's collection

Never Mind the Bollocks, Here's the Jellied Eels
– Café Eden advert, October 1950

On the playing fields of Eton, however – and presumably, the dining rooms and most other places around the grounds – were a couple of schoolboys called Robert Fraser and Christopher Gibbs, the former of whom was to be arrested with Mick Jagger in 1967 and became one of the most important people in the London art scene of the sixties, while the latter, during that same decade, was often to be known simply as the 'King of the King's Road'. George Melly, however, was already right in the thick of things. He had settled in a cheerfully bohemian shared house in Margaretta Terrace, built in 1851, which, he later wrote, had been a favourite street in which Victorian members of parliament would install their mistresses, it being a short and presumably breathless hansom cab ride away from the House of Commons. Securing a job working for E. T. Mesens, while at the same time establishing himself as a jazz vocalist with the Mick Mulligan Band, he lived a short walk from the King's Road, his walls hung with surrealist pictures.

George's favourite drinking spot in those days was the Cross Keys – the same friendly pub where Diana Dors first met Dandy Kim – which was a favourite jamming spot for jazz musicians. Billy Jones, the landlord, played piano, and was renowned for having once sat in with the Original Dixieland Jazz Band when they came to England in 1920. Friends and fellow jazzers from all over would habitually crash out in George's room after a late session, having long since missed the last tube home. Although the Mulligan band trailed up and down the length of pre-motorway Britain in a small van, sometimes their shows were much closer to home, such as appearances at the Royal College of Art in South Kensington, where they would cart the gear up flights of stairs decorated with 'huge canvasses of babies in sinks and kitchen tables covered with cornflake packets and cheesegraters'.

Intimate Surroundings, Reasonable Prices

When not warning of the dangers of VD, the government was simultaneously doing its best to convince everyone that the UK was a happening kind of place, had thrown off the deprivations of the war years, and was positively bursting at the seams with culture. To this end, they inaugurated the Festival of Britain in 1951, which – aside from turning some land on the South Bank into the skateboarder's paradise it is today – also had serious designs on Battersea Park. In an echo of Cremorne and Ranelagh, something known as the Festival Pleasure Gardens was laid out and a fun fair built. As the press reported, in contrast to the activities on the South Bank, Battersea Park's job was to 'present the lighter side of the Festival of Britain. [. . .] Features include a miniature railway, a Grotto, the Riverside Theatre, the Amphitheatre and a Punch and Judy Theatre.' In other words, no balloon ascents with wild animals, and no fatal attempts at solo flight in the manner of Vincent de Groof – who died after jumping from a balloon over Cremorne in 1874 – but at least they had Punch and Judy.

Another side effect of the Festival of Britain was the July 1951 jazz concert held up the road at the Albert Hall in the presence of Princess Margaret, from which several live recordings were released as 78s, including 'I'm Travellin'' by Ken Colyer's outfit, the Crane River Jazz Band. Also recorded, but not released at the time, was a vocal number by local resident George Melly with the Mick Mulligan Band. As Chas McDevitt has pointed out, had this performance of 'Rock Island Line' seen the light of day, it would have appeared a full four years before Lonnie Donegan's breakthrough hit version.

Along the King's Road, it was still business as usual at the Chelsea Palace. Later that decade rock'n'roll would eventually finish what the dance bands had started, closing the Palace and most of the other music halls down, but the listing for June 1951 still featured the kind of variety-based girlie shows they had been presenting since the war: nightly at 6.30 and 8.40, a revue called *Let's Go Gaye*, and another the following week entitled *Copacabana*.

Though food rationing was still in place and dining out an extravagance for many, the restaurant section in listings magazine *What's On in London* was to quadruple in size during the first half of the decade as new eateries opened up. Even so, places like the Unity restaurant at 91 King's Road still felt the need to spell out in their 1951 adverts that they were 'licensed to sell wines', as if this was something not to be taken for granted, and by 1953 they had made the giant leap of being able to claim 'licensed for beers and wines'. This might sound quite tame, but it is worth remembering that a decade later legendary sixties all-night clubs like the Flamingo in Wardour Street had no drinks license at all, which they circumvented by having bottles of whiskey under the counter, thus making their sales figures for suitably fortified 'orange juice' extremely impressive.

Some King's Road restaurants offered other inducements for the discerning diner, such as those at the Bar-B-Q, which in January 1951 presented an exhibition of paintings by Countess Lina Monici, a former opera singer and friend of Aleister Crowley, glowingly reviewed in the *West London Press* under the headline, 'PAINTS WITH HER THUMB':

> The exhibition, consisting of some 12 pictures – mainly flower studies – is valued, so the countess tells me, at £1,500. It was arranged with the help of the proprietor of the Bar-B-Q, Mr Drueff, who took the onslaught very calmly. 'This is Chelsea,' he said, 'and in Chelsea you've got to expect things like this. The countess is up against it, so we're doing what we can to help out.' [. . .] One of the pictures was still wet and the countess used it to demonstrate her method of painting – with her thumb because her hand is partly paralysed. Then she caught sight of a plate of gorgonzola cheese, and insisted on having it placed next to one of the pictures. 'It's so poetic,' she declared.

Down on Cheyne Row, and most definitely in possession of a license to sell adult beverages, was a pub called the King's Head and Eight Bells, which the 1951 guidebook *London Night and Day* referred to as a 'favourite scenic background of *Picture Post*'s "film star with pint" features', its regulars said to include 'Chelsea artists and intellectuals'. Over at the Pheasantry, another film star, Humphrey Bogart – with or without pint, but usually with Lauren Bacall – would stop by for a meal when in town, although the restaurant in those days did not advertise itself in quite the same strident manner favoured by a new arrival at 124 King's Road, the Magic Carpet Inn. The Inn's 1952 adverts spoke of 'Superb Food – Superb Wines – Intimate Surroundings. Reasonable prices', then moved into capital letters to describe it as 'CHELSEA'S SUPERIOR AND LOVELY RESTAURANT'. Obviously not satisfied with this state of affairs, by 1954 their advertising copy contained all of the aforementioned, followed by the words 'Intimate and Floral Surroundings. Famous Paintings. Reservations Strongly Advised', and then with a megaphone, 'FAMOUS THROUGHOUT THE WORLD'. In the mid-sixties, the restaurant at 124 was certainly world famous, but not for its paintings or even, sadly, for its 'floral atmosphere'. By then it had changed hands and become Alvaro's, whose renown came partly from the food but mostly from the fact that people such as Michael Caine, Jean Shrimpton, Terence Stamp and various Rolling Stones were often to be seen dining there.

Keep Premature Wrinkles at Bay

This, then, was the King's Road at the start of the fifties, coming back to life after the worst years of post-war austerity, with new shops, restaurants and bars opening up and a certain amount of glamour returning.

If you were a seventeen-year-old art student getting to know the area, what could you do for entertainment in June 1951? For a night at the flicks on the King's Road itself, there was the arty option – Jean Marais in *Le Secret de Mayerling* at the Chelsea Classic; downmarket slapstick with *Abbott and Costello Meet the Invisible Man* at the Gaumont; or how about a revival of Edward G. Robinson's courtroom drama *I Am the Law* at the Essoldo? You might want to check the details in that week's edition of *Picturegoer*, at which point it would be strange to see your own name staring back at you:

> Mother raves about fragrant, refreshing Quants. She says there's nothing like it to keep premature wrinkles at bay, and free the complexion from spots and other unattractive blemishes. She finds Quants ideal for mouth and throat hygiene too, and uses it as the 'natural' deodorant to protect her 'all-day' freshness. Father soothes annoying after-shave irritations with Quants. Its comforting coolness brings speedy relief. While the family stands by Quants as the best treatment for minor abrasions and burns, bruises, sprains, stings etc., and as an excellent rub-down for tired, aching limbs.

By the middle of the following decade, that name would mean only one thing across the world, and the makers of ointments guarding against 'annoying after-shave irritations' presumably had to go in for some rebranding.

Credit: Fred Ramage/Keystone/Hulton Archive/Getty Images

Mary Quant aged 16, helping with preparations for the Chelsea Arts Ball at the Royal Albert Hall, December 30, 1949

The woman whose fame was to grow to such an extent that her 1966 autobiography would be titled simply *Quant by Quant* was at that time a Goldsmiths College student for whom the Chelsea world was just opening up. She met a young man called Alexander Plunket Greene, currently occupying the otherwise empty Chelsea house of his mother who was living elsewhere in the country. Left to himself, Alexander had gradually moved his sleeping quarters from room to room, changing whenever the previous bedroom had become uninhabitable even for a teenager, and displaying a heroic disregard for such trivialities as hoovering, laundry and doing the dishes. As Mary later recalled in her autobiography, she found this behaviour 'distinctly cosmopolitan and exciting'. It was the beginning of a relationship which would endure right up until Alexander's death in 1990. He was also a Goldsmiths College student, and then went on to work as 'a sort of photographer' in the King's Road. When not occupied with this or with student life, Mary and Alexander also found time to stage a fake kidnapping outside South Kensington tube station, just for the hell of it, which attracted immediate attention from passers-by, with several of what the tabloids enjoy terming 'have-a-go-heroes' attempting to come to the aid of the kidnap victim (in reality, the girlfriend of a sculptor whom they knew). Narrowly escaping the angry mob courtesy of some skilful getaway driving, they hid out in a local cincma for most of the day until it seemed safe to emerge.

Ladies Night in a Turkish Bath

Just as Mary Quant was getting to know the area, another crucial player in the King's Road's mid-fifties creative explosion was stepping cautiously back into the limelight after over a decade out of the picture. In the April 4, 1952 edition of *What's On in London*, a news item in Frederick Deeps and Peter Noble's 'Show Talk' column announced:

> Re-opening next month is the Royal Court Theatre, Sloane Square, bomb-damaged during the early part of the war. Alfred Esdaile, who owns the Court, will run it as a club theatre (along the lines of the Arts). It seats 550, will open with a new play *The Bride of Denmark Hill*, by Lawrence Williams and Nell O'Day. On the advisory committee of the Court are Dame Sybil Thorndike, Sir Lewis Casson, Joyce Grenfell, Ellen Pollock and Giles Playfair.

This was in many ways a false dawn, and the Royal Court would have to wait another four years until the arrival of George Devine and the English Stage Company for its great days to begin, although the 1952 reopening seems to have begun with the best of intentions. The theatre's new leaseholder was a former music hall comedian called Alfred Esdaile – who before the war had run lavish girlie shows inspired by the Folies Bergère at the Prince of Wales Theatre on Coventry Street and was also the inventor of the microphone which comes up out of the stage floor. Their debut offering, *The Bride of Denmark Hill*, described in the publicity as a 'new play based on the life of Ruskin', sounds as if it might well have been at home among the late fifties seasons at the Court, but it sank like a stone.

Before long, the theatre went over to more populist fare, apparently in search of an audience in a King's Road where the Classic Cinema was busy advertising an X-rated French film called *The Isle of Sinners* and the Chelsea Palace music hall was presenting shows such as the farce *A Ladies Night in a Turkish Bath* or the revues *Forces in Petticoats* and *Here Come the Girls*. In the face of such competition, it is not surprising that by September 1952 the Royal Court's new offering was a comedy by Frank Baker called *Miss Hargreaves*, based on a successful TV show and starring the very popular Margaret Rutherford. Things stayed on the lighter side as the year progressed, with an adaptation in October of Oscar Wilde's *Lord Arthur Saville's Crime* – a short story written just up the road in Tite Street and published in 1891. Constance Cox, who adapted the work for the stage, had, wrote one reviewer, used Wilde's story as 'a springboard into drawing-room farce [. . .] making its hero – as practically everyone has remarked – into a Victorian edition of Bertie Wooster.'

The theatre was also branching out in other ways, as the press adverts for the Wilde play show. It was now offering 'Dancing Nightly at 11.00pm' with an appearance by French cabaret singer Zaza Bartira, whose repertoire was described by a journalist from trade paper *The Stage* as 'not confined to the saucy and sentimental', and also containing 'graphic sequences of mime'. These were the beginnings of the Royal Court Club, at this point under the auspices of future Liberal MP and sometime TV dogfood advertiser Clement Freud, which survived well into the sixties. After a year of casting around for a hit, the reopened Royal Court appeared to have found one in the autumn of 1953 with a production first premiered in Edinburgh, entitled *Airs on a Shoestring* – billed as an 'intimate revue, devised and directed by Laurier ("Penny Plain") Lister' – which ran there continuously until March 1955. It pulled in crowds, but it was a long way from there to *Look Back in Anger*.

Turn a Knob for an Evening's Entertainment

Just as the Royal Court was coming back to life, there were further tentative signs, both nationally and locally, of the approaching pop-culture storm. At the still bomb-damaged Chelsea Old Church, on August 12, 1952, the baptism took place of Caspar Robert Fleming, whose father Ian's debut novel, *Casino Royale* – written in January and February of that year – had just been accepted for publication by Jonathan Cape. The novel's protagonist was described as living in a flat in a quiet, unspecified square off the King's Road, not far from where the author himself lived, and also near to the cheap accommodation of a young Edinburgh body-builder who was destined to play the part of that character on the big screen some ten years later.

As far as the rest of the country was concerned, SW3's bohemian reputation as a place where people of an artistic persuasion were probably having a fair amount more fun than you would only have been confirmed by an article in the August 22 edition of the *New Musical Express*, published under the unpromising headline 'Accordion Used On Society Dates', and giving details of 'a most interesting function' which 'made a few hardened musicians' eyes pop:

> Occasion was the party flung at the Old Church Street premises of the Chelsea Arts Society, with the band provided as usual by tenor/ clarinettist Phil Kirkby released for the evening from his wonted spot in the Hungarian Oscar Grasso Intimate Music Outfit. Nothing more Chelsea than the costume – or lack of it! – of the artists' models can, according to report, be imagined. That includes the young lady dressed as Crystal Palace in a transparent mac and apparently little else, although the special murals depicting Bacchanalian scenes had a fair degree of attention.

Television was creeping slowly into the everyday life of the nation. It helped if you lived in London, because many parts of the country still could not receive a signal, and also if you had money, as it was not a cheap option by any means. Nevertheless, although there was still only one channel, run by the BBC, the new medium was beginning to make itself felt. In February 1952 they began broadcasting a weekly show called *Current Release*, the first programme devoted to previewing new cinema films, prompting *Picturegoer* reader Joyce Clegg to write in that month asking whether watching the television was likely to become a popular way of spending the evening: 'If the cinema's counter-attraction is not strong enough, I feel that to sit by the fire and turn a knob for an evening's entertainment may well become a national habit.'

Someone who might have agreed with Joyce was a 24-year-old television director called Tony Richardson, who tracked down the phone number of theatre director and actor George Devine to ask him to appear in a TV adaptation of a Chekhov short story. 'I can't be bothered,' replied Devine, 'the thing bores me to hell.' Richardson rang him back and asked him out for a drink. The upshot was that they got on well, Devine agreed to act in the play, and this marked the start of the friendship between the two key directors who, together with Richardson's then partner George Goetschius, were to launch the ground-breaking 1956 English Stage Company season at the Royal Court.

Jazz music fans browsing the small ads pages at the back of the *NME* that autumn might possibly have been drawn to Chelsea by the following advert:

LEARN TO DANCE JIVE, FREE STYLE instruction Monday, Wednesday and Saturday, 8 till 11 p.m., 2s. 6d. Sunday Afternoon Club, 3 till 5.30p.m., 2s. 6d. – Delaney's School for Jive, 143, King's Road, Chelsea, S.W.3 (entrance in Flood Street).

Some of those taking advantage of this might well have been teenagers wearing narrow trousers and longer draped jackets, because out in the streets of London, Teddy boy fashions were there in all but name by the end of 1952 – although it would be the following year before the name became common currency among the press – and they danced to jazz before rock'n'roll became available in the UK. However, when a policeman was shot and killed in Croydon in November 1952 during a warehouse burglary, the press noted the fashionable dress of the two teenagers involved, Christopher Craig and Derek Bentley: finger-tip draped jackets, crepe-soled shoes. Youth culture was starting to develop its own dress codes, and if anyone from the younger generation was involved in any trouble, serious or otherwise, their mode of dress was often highlighted in the newspaper reports, such as in the 1953 *Daily Mirror* headline about a London murder, 'Edwardian Suits, Dance Music and a Dagger'. Of course, this style was not the only option for with-it kids: a company called Lily Shoes, ignoring the word 'teenager' and opting instead for the phrase 'fashion conscious young timers', ran a series of adverts in the summer of 1952 highlighting their new 'saucy boy' shoe, but it seems that brothel-creepers and winkle-pickers eventually won that particular battle for hearts and minds.

Diana Dors had by now married Dennis Hamilton, a very saucy boy indeed, and was living in the latest of a series of Chelsea apartments she had occupied over the past couple of years. Her current home was the one in which parties were held regularly featuring amyl nitrate, stag films, prostitutes, and the famous two-way mirror on the bedroom ceiling. Diana's biographer Damon Wise reports that the happy couple were in the habit of driving up and down the King's Road with their actor friend Victor Spinetti in a powder-blue Cadillac, occasionally stopping off outside Peter Jones department store on Sloane Square in order to torment the commissionaire – 'Can I help you sir?' 'Yes. I want to buy a ribbon . . . to match the colour of your eyes!' – after which they would floor the accelerator and drive off laughing.

Officer, Could I Speak to You for a Moment?

Chelsea stores could also prove to be dangerous places, at least according to a 1953 crime novel by Jane Boyd entitled – with commendable directness

– *Murder in the King's Road*, whose dust jacket showed a colour illustration of the victim lying dead in the middle of a shop window display. The publisher's blurb on the inside flap set the scene:

> Exercising her dog at an early hour in the King's Road, Miss Arbutus, a respectable, middle-aged spinster, pauses to look into an antique-dealer's window and on a Regency couch sees a reclining figure. Little did she know what she was involving herself in when she ran after a policeman and reported that in her conviction the figure was a corpse. [. . .] From film actress's drawing room to country cottage, from Chelsea studio to consulting room, the investigation pursues its course to its unexpected conclusion.

This novel depicts a very polite, well-heeled world in which Miss Arbutus reports the crime with the words 'Officer, could I speak to you for a moment? There is something very odd in Dedham's shop in the King's Road.' She is met with an equally decorous response from the seemingly unflappable PC Jones, who merely says, 'I'll go with you, Madam, and you can show me what you've seen.' All of which is a far cry from some of the phrases employed twenty years later by the London coppers played by John Thaw and Dennis Waterman when encountering crimes in the 1970s TV series *The Sweeney*, such as the immortal 'Get yer trousers on, you're nicked' or 'I hate this bastard place. It's a bloody holiday camp for thieves and weirdoes, all the rubbish.'

The publisher of *Murder in the King's Road* claimed that the name 'Jane Boyd' was a pseudonym for a 'crime writer of distinction', but the real identity of the author has managed to remain a mystery throughout the seven decades since its publication, despite the fact that copies of the first edition now fetch almost £200. By contrast, another crime writer of distinction, Gold Dagger Award-winner Lionel Davidson, also put the district at the heart of his highly entertaining 1978 crime novel *The Chelsea Murders*, whose plot at various points takes in places such as the Chelsea Art School, Sloane Square, the Royal Hospital, the Albert Bridge, Margaret Thatcher's then home in Flood Street, the Chelsea Potter and Markham Arms pubs, and the mansions along Cheyne Walk, with clues to the murders that reference famous former residents of the area such as Whistler, Swinburne, Rossetti, A. A. Milne and Oscar Wilde. Several of the main characters work in a King's Road denim clothes shop called Blue Stuff run by a proprietor solely interested in the money, and who will happily tell prospective customers that whatever they have optimistically tried on looks wonderful. Quite what Jane Boyd would have made of any of it is hard to say.

Swarthy and Amorous

As 1953 progressed, restaurants continued to spring up along the King's Road, including one at number 172 called Chez Michael which offered a set lunch for three shillings and sixpence. 'Bijou Restaurant with Intimate Atmosphere. Between the Classic and Gaumont Cinemas', said their adverts. (In 1913 this building had been the premises of a butcher with the strangely evocative name of John Osborn.) Nearby at the Chelsea Palace, old-style music hall was slowly fading away, but some of their variety bills on offer in 1952 and '53 still featured big names such as Wilson, Kepple & Betty, Max Wall or the Beverley Sisters, as well as rising star Benny Hill. There were also top-of-the-range revues, like *Randle's Scandals for 1953*, starring Frank Randle and Jack Doyle, mixed in with the usual girlie shows, although the adverts which read '*Call Me Mister* – starring Louis Hayden, Norman Yeoman and All-Male Cast' perhaps had a different clientele in mind.

Entertainment aimed at a slightly younger audience was also becoming available. Groups such as the Original Crane River Jazz Band had been including skiffle interludes in their otherwise traditional New Orleans jazz material at gigs – using a stripped-down proto-rockabilly line-up such as acoustic guitar or banjo, stand-up bass and washboard or snare – and this had gained in popularity until in 1954 it collided head-on with another key cultural development: the rise of the coffee bar. Enough of them sprang up during that year to prompt an article in *What's On in London* by Frank Jackson on this new phenomenon, entitled *The Return of the Coffee House*, a headline which conjured up images of 18th-century literary men such as Addison and Steele or Dr Johnson engaging in learned conversation and society gossip. Chelsea in those days had boasted one of the famous haunts of such men, Don Saltero's Coffee House, but the 1954 version that came to the King's Road, just as such establishments were also proliferating in Soho, was a different beast entirely. 'Londoners are acquiring an old habit in a new style', wrote Frank Jackson, and this kind of coffee bar was evidently novel enough that he felt the need to explain the sort of thing that might be encountered in one of them: 'The coffee is standardised. It comes out of those Italian-made "espresso" machines, which look like outsize chromium-plated table radios. But the customers are far from standardised, and each coffee house has an atmosphere all its own.'

This was the last full year before rock'n'roll hit Britain – Bill Haley's first UK chart single, 'Shake, Rattle and Roll' arrived on December 17, 1954, eventually reaching number four – and although coffee bars were generally designed as teenage hangouts, some of them looked more to the French Existentialist scene than to America for inspiration. One such mentioned by Jackson was the Chiquito, near Tottenham Court Road:

> Here you could easily imagine you were in a cafe on the Left Bank in Paris. French is spoken by most of the customers, whose average age is the late teens. The girls have long hair tied in horse's tails, wide skirts, tight blouses. The boys are swarthy and amorous. The radiogram plays records of French cabaret stars or of calypsos full of sexy innu-endos. There are mysterious, but obviously quite innocent comings and goings to the cellar.

Other coffee bars favoured live entertainment, and here the emerging skiffle outfits came into their own. With minimal, generally unamplified equipment, they could squeeze into the smallest basement and cause a stir with their up-tempo, folk, blues and country-based material. A key part of the success of such places was due to the fact that they provided somewhere teenagers could meet, as opposed to pubs and clubs selling alcohol, which were generally inaccessible due to the age restrictions in the licensing laws.

The Lad's Foolish but He's Not Vicious

It was not just age that could see you barred from certain premises – some-times it was simply what you were wearing. One of the major trends in 1954 was for dancehalls, cinemas and similar public places to introduce outright bans on the admittance of anyone wearing 'Edwardian' or draped clothing. Teddy boys now had an established name and had appeared in a fair number of front-page newspaper headlines, usually in connection with muggings, gang fights and even post-office robberies. In the army, compulsory National Service was still in force for teenagers, and because so many new recruits were partial to wearing drapes and drainpipe trousers on their evenings off in town, regulations were altered in many regiments, banning soldiers from appearing in public in such clothes, on the grounds that they were bringing the services into disrepute.

In these last years before rock'n'roll, the Teds were already being classed as pariahs, so that when proper outlaw music arrived, they were ready and waiting. John Peel, still a schoolboy at the time, was fully aware of the shock value of this kind of clothing, as he told me: 'I had a pair of drainpipe trousers, and I'm a nice middle-class boy, you know, but I had a pair of drainpipe trousers in the cupboard that I bought in Liverpool, and I never dared wear them, but just the knowledge that they were there was enough to make me feel, *I am one hell of a guy . . .*'

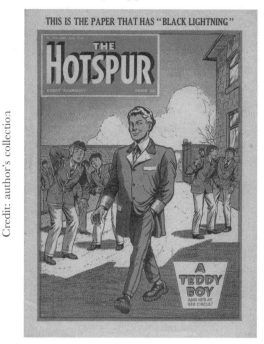

Credit: author's collection

Teds in the playground, December 1954

To give some idea of the avalanche of press that the Teds had been attracting in the immediate pre-rock'n'roll era, it is instructive to note that on December 11, 1954 – one week *before* Bill Haley and His Comets' first UK chart entry – as a subculture, they were well-known enough that one of the main weekly children's comics, *The Hotspur,* devoted its entire front page to a drawing of a pupil in full drape jacket, creepers and drainpipes, with the caption 'A Teddy Boy – and he's at Red Circle!' The target audience for this comic would have been maybe seven to twelve years old, and yet the paper's editors obviously thought that their readers would not only know what a Teddy boy was, but also have a fair amount of background informa-tion about their supposed anti-social habits. The comic character in question is a boy called Edward Brown (aka Teddy), who is temporarily diverted to a public school called Red Circle because there is no room at the approved school down the road to which he's been sentenced. 'The lad's foolish but he's not vicious,' says the officer who delivers him. 'He's an orphan who's always had to live on his wits, and he got into the wrong company.' Asked what he thinks of his new school, Teddy Brown's rather astute first comment is that it 'looks like the world's only illuminated cemetery to me', and as for his appearance, it is clear that by this time the classic Ted look was well known enough that even comic story writers could get it right:

> His long hair was waved and oiled, with two wings brushed back over his ears and round the back of his head . . . He was about the same age as the Red Circle Fourth Formers, and he was a well-built lad, but there the resemblance ended. He wore a white shirt, a brightly coloured waistcoat, and a bootlace tie. Over this he had a jacket of expensive material, cut long, with velvet collar, and trimmings to the cuffs and pocket flaps, and a pair of narrow trousers. The picture was completed by a pair of thick-soled shoes.

If children of primary school age were supposed to be hip enough to recognise a Ted when they saw one, it seems logical that the BBC had just started a weekly television variety show called *Teleclub* aimed specifically at teenagers, showcasing acts who were sometimes themselves the same age as the target audience, as were the programme's two presenters: Howard Williams, 'a young actor from Sidmouth repertory', and the 'eighteen-year-old blonde from variety and films', Shirley Eaton, some ten years prior to her famous all-over paintjob in *Goldfinger*. Still living in Chelsea, but probably not tuning into *Teleclub* every Tuesday, Ian Fleming was continuing to write novels featuring James Bond – that year's entry in the series being *Live and Let Die*. As it happened, a letter to the *New Musical Express* back in January from a reader had praised a singer making their variety debut at the Chelsea Palace music hall, saying, 'I found his performance far more satisfying than that of any visiting American I have seen treading the Palladium boards.' The artist in question was Monty Norman, just under a decade before he wrote the score for the first Bond film, *Dr No*.

Look Back in Morecambe

As it happened, the man who was to star opposite Shirley as Fleming's most famous creation was currently doing part-time modelling work, and over the next couple of years some of it would be for a Soho shop which opened in 1954 and would help initiate the men's fashion revolution of the next decade, having a significant influence on many King's Road boutiques. Vince Man's Shop was situated in Newburgh Street, a quiet backwater off the equally unknown Carnaby Street. Owned by Bill Green, it catered mostly to the gay trade, and Sean Connery was to model shirts, sweaters and jeans for their catalogues and adverts in the mid-fifties. Crucially, however, it was a salesman called John Stephen, who worked at Vince's for a short while, who went on to revolutionise Carnaby Street and turn it into the international brand name which it became by 1966.

If the two words 'Carnaby Street' were yet to have any wide currency, the same could also be said for the phrase 'pop art', coined in 1954 by the critic Lawrence Alloway after a meeting at the ICA of a small circle of people to which he belonged, who called themselves the Independent Group. They included artists such as Richard Hamilton and Eduardo Paolozzi and architects like James Stirling, and had been in existence for two years. Like John Stephen's vision for Carnaby Street or Sean Connery's portrayal of Fleming's character James Bond, the Independent Group's theories of pop art – and Hamilton's pictures in particular – would eventually help shape the look and fabric of the sixties London scene.

For the moment, as 1954 drew to a close, Chelsea life went on much the same as ever: at the Chelsea Palace there was a variety bill, 'Lee Lawrence, Harry Bailey, Three Indriksons, etc (till Oct 16)', followed by a revival of Hugh Hastings' enormously popular comedy *Seagulls Over Sorrento*. The latter play seemed to show up everywhere, including a version on the BBC the following year starring a pre-Hammer Films Peter Cushing, and a provincial production up at Morecambe in May in which young actor and would-be playwright John Osborne accepted a bit-part, using his free time during the days to continue writing his own play, *Look Back in Anger*.

On the last night of 1954, the Chelsea Arts Ball took place once more, as it had done for half a century. This year's event was again held at the Royal Albert Hall, with swing and Latin music courtesy of Jack Parnell, Edmundo Ros and Ted Heath – the bandleader, not the amateur conductor and future prime minister. Always an occasion for outlandish costumes and fancy dress, the theme this time was 'The Seven Seas', with decor by *St Trinian's* creator Ronald Searle. Ordinary tickets were £3.10s each, including supper, but you could also hire private boxes for £12, £25 or £40. Obviously, boxes could accommodate several people, while privacy at the Arts Ball often meant that people could indulge in all sorts of behaviour not normally allowed in public, but even so, in a year when six or seven shillings would buy you a decent meal with wine in a King's Road restaurant, and in which the Society for Cultural Relations with the USSR was holding its New Year's Eve party in Kensington at five shillings a head, £40 was serious money indeed.

The coming year was to bring rock'n'roll, commercial television, the writing of *Look Back in Anger* and the opening of a boutique at 138a King's Road called Bazaar. The revolution starts here.

5

'Quantum leap'

Socialites, Actors, Con-Men, and Superior Tarts

At the start of 1955, Winston Churchill was still prime minister, *Airs on a Shoestring* was *still* running at the Royal Court and the BBC still had a monopoly on UK television broadcasting, but none of these situations would last the year.

Youth culture – which would have been an alien concept a decade earlier – slowly began to assert itself, and Bill Haley started 1955 at number four in the charts with a cover of Joe Turner's *Shake, Rattle and Roll,* just as he was to finish the year with the big one, *Rock Around the Clock*. On the other hand, a couple of places higher in the listings was the former Ted Heath singer Dickie Valentine, known to his mother as Richard Bryce – 'dislikes: dirty ashtrays, women with too much make-up and smoked salmon', which prompts the question just how much smoked salmon the women of his acquaintance were supposed to be permitted. Dickie's audience mostly consisted of screaming twelve-year-old girls. He was a big hit with the *New Musical Express*, topped the bill at the Palladium that year and even made it across the pond to appear on the *Ed Sullivan Show,* but he was strictly old-school, as was 'another young man who, surprisingly enough, never thought of himself as a popular singer', Max Bygraves, who also went the Ed Sullivan route that year. Both of them chalked up huge record sales in Britain in 1955, but the kids were soon going to be looking for something a little more dangerous than 'Gilly Gilly Ossenfeffer', 'Christmas Alphabet' or 'You're a Pink Toothbrush'. As to where to buy any of these songs, or indeed something on which to play them, an advert in the February 12 edition of the *Record Mirror* read as follows:

ELECTROLA
for all the latest in
RECORDS, TAPE RECORDERS,
PLAYERS, RADIO AND
TELEVISION
and all electrical appliances.
Terms available
106 KING'S ROAD, CHELSEA,
LONDON, S.W.3.

Those in search of even more action could now find it at a new coffee bar
called the Fantasie which had just opened at number 128 King's Road. It was
owned and run by a former solicitor named Archie McNair, who lived upstairs
and also ran a photographer's business from the same building. When not at
the Fantasie, he used to drink at a pub called Finch's in the Fulham Road,
where he had recently met a young couple who were also regulars, Mary Quant
and Alexander Plunket Greene. In fact, he had asked them to go into business
with him when he'd started up the Fantasie, but they had declined, thinking
that coffee bars had an uncertain future. However, the friendship between them
flourished, and in this bohemian world of 'painters, photographers, architects,
writers, socialites, actors, con-men, and superior tarts', as Mary later described
it, the three of them cast around for a suitable joint business venture into which
they could invest their time and energy. For the moment, the Fantasie coffee
bar was proving to be a big success with the younger King's Road crowd.
Up-and-coming proto-rock bands like the Chas McDevitt Skiffle Group played
there regularly that year, not least because most of them lived nearby, and if
you were too young to legally hang out in pubs, there was also an added
attraction, as Mary Quant explained to me: 'Some nights at the Fantasie the
espresso coffee was laced with vodka. The Fantasie belonged to our partner
Archie McNair. He also had a team of photographers working in a studio
above the Fantasie. They included Armstrong-Jones.'

Antony Armstrong-Jones was a young photographer with a growing reputation – who famously went on to marry Princess Margaret and become
Lord Snowden, uttering the memorable one-liner, 'Inigo Jones, out-'e-come
Snowden' – while Mary Quant's partner Alexander had also briefly worked
as a photographer in the King's Road after leaving college. When not drinking
the fortified coffee at the Fantasie or mingling with the crowd at Finch's in
the Fulham Road, Mary and Alexander would also visit the music hall shows
at the Chelsea Palace, which, having seen in the year with the pantomime
Aladdin, by the spring was offering such delights as *Fanny Get Your Fun*, or the

revue *Montmartre*. The programmes would change every few days, so there was always something new to see. 'We went once a week,' Mary told me. 'The Chelsea Palace chorus girls wore very naughty fur bikini knickers.'

Incomprehensible and Pretentious

Meanwhile, somewhere in South London, a young man from Leicester called Colin Wilson was developing a book idea that had occurred to him over the Christmas holidays, tentatively entitled *The Pain Threshold*, eventually published in 1956 as *The Outsider*. Such was his enthusiasm, he had temporarily put aside his previous project, a book about Jack the Ripper. The work progressed well, mostly in the reading room of the British Museum, where he was encouraged by one of the staff, the writer Angus Wilson.

As *The Outsider* took shape, the actor John Osborne was mulling over an idea for a play that spring, which led eventually to his diary entry for May 4, 1955, which said: 'Began writing *Look Back in Anger*'. Two days later, he had already finished Act One, and during the next ten days he worked at it steadily, taking time off to note that his dog had died, and also to visit the theatre: firstly a production of Sandy Wilson's jazz-age romp *The Boy Friend* (later filmed by Ken Russell, starring Twiggy), secondly Ibsen's *Hedda Gabler* at the Lyric, Hammersmith, which gave Osborne his first sight of George Devine, the man who, a year later, was to revolutionise the Royal Court.

Devine had become friends with the young Tony Richardson following their meeting in 1952, and the two had already made attempts to negotiate with Alfred Esdaile at the Royal Court with a view to setting up a company there. The Arts Council expressed their willingness to back the scheme, but then Esdaile – enjoying the success of *Airs on a Shoestring* – asked for a considerable sum of money for the sub-lease of the theatre and the scheme was abandoned. Devine and Richardson then looked into the idea of leasing the Kingsway Theatre instead. Since this was also one of Esdaile's buildings, the whole charade began again, but this time with the involvement of a group from Devon including Ronald Duncan, J. E. Blacksell and Lord Harewood, who were attempting to establish something known as the English Stage Company under the chairmanship of Neville Blond. By the end of 1954 they had reached some sort of agreement with Esdaile, and in March 1955 Devine was appointed artistic director of the new company, with Richardson as his associate. For the moment, however, the plan was still to establish the new company at the Kingsway Theatre.

Over at the Royal Court itself, *Airs on a Shoestring* finally sailed off into the sunset, to be replaced at the beginning of April by the well-intentioned but critically savaged play *Uncertain Joy* by Charlotte Hastings, starring Roger Livesey and Ursula Jeans. The play, said reviewer Kenneth A. Hurren in *What's On in London,* 'takes its title from a Danish proverb, "Children are certain sorrow and uncertain joy", and is intended, I suspect, as an argument in favour of "understanding" difficult children rather than belting them with a razor strop.' Despite its good intentions, he found the characters 'overdrawn', the dialogue 'infested with dull clichés' and the plot 'disastrously melodramatic'. Still, the playwright could perhaps have taken some comfort from a review of a different work in the *Guardian* the following month: '*Waiting for Godot* at the Arts Theatre Club,' wrote Peter Hope-Wallace, 'is a play to send the rationalist out of his mind and induce tooth-gnashing among people who would take Lewis Carroll's Red Queen and Lear's nonsense exchanges with the fool as the easiest stuff in the world.' Praising both the acting and Peter Hall's production, Hope-Wallace nevertheless wrote that 'the language, however is flat and feeble in the extreme' but concluded that 'it is good to find that plays at once dubbed "incomprehensible and pretentious" can still get a staging'. The Royal Court's 1956 revolution was still a year away, but the stage was being set.

Bicycle Chains, Knuckle-Dusters, and Razors

At 28 Mallord Street, SW3, Francis Bacon was painting a portrait of one of his chief patrons, Robert Sainsbury, which had been commissioned by the sitter's wife, Lisa. The house in question had been lent to them for the purpose by the Honourable Michael Astor, but Bacon was frequently unhappy with the progress of his own work, and had a habit of destroying his own canvasses with razor blades.

In April 1955, Winston Churchill – who back in 1898 had taken part in what is often mistakenly referred to as the British Army's last ever cavalry charge when riding with the 21st Lancers at the Battle of Omdurman – stepped aside as prime minister for the last time following a series of heart attacks. His successor, Sir Anthony Eden, would shortly attempt to relive the buccaneering days of the British Empire with a disastrous military intervention in Suez, but for the moment was managing to restrain his warlike impulses. Anyone reading the newspapers around the time of Eden's appointment as prime minister, however, could have been forgiven for thinking that the main threat of violence came not from anywhere abroad, but from these young people in Edwardian clothes who were starting to identify themselves with the burgeoning rock'n'roll scene. The main headline on the front of the *Oxford Mail* in September read:

ARMED 'TEDDY BOYS' HOLD UP AMERICANS

The front page of the *Sunday Dispatch* in June had been a little more hopeful in its reporting of this apparent threat to civilised society:

WAR ON TEDDY BOYS
Menace In The Streets Of
Britain's Cities Is Being
Cleaned Up At Last

Describing the wave of bans and even vigilante groups designed to counter the perceived problem, the newspaper reported that:

The menace of the Teddy Boys is being broken by the concerted action of police and public and by the firm stand taken by many dance-hall and cinema managers. In some places groups of 'vigilantes' have been formed to combat the thugs in Edwardian dress who, often armed with bicycle chains, knuckle-dusters, and razors, have terrorised peace-loving citizens for two years. Tonight many of these long-haired youths in fancy waistcoats, long velvet-faced jackets and drainpipe trousers will find the doors of cinemas, dance-halls, cafes, pubs and clubs barred against them.

It was all very well people writing to the papers saying that a dose of National Service would sort them out, but the services were full of them anyway, and the Army was busy devising new regulations to prevent its members wearing Edwardian gear while on leaves and pass-outs. Teenagers had discovered that their new clothes and hairstyles could scare the hell out of ordinary society, and from here on, there was no going back. All they needed was the right soundtrack for that lifestyle.

Bill Haley was already known in Britain, and was stirring things up pretty well, but the man who was really going to cause mayhem had just turned twenty in 1955. Already popular from a year of touring in the southern states of America, Elvis Presley had recently watched his new pink Cadillac catch fire and burn itself out on the highway, but that did not stop him; he simply bought another one. He cut his final single for the Sun label in Memphis that June – a flat-out rockabilly masterpiece by the name of 'Mystery Train' – and was lined up that summer as the support act for Bill Haley and Hank Snow on an even bigger US tour. Word had it that RCA records were sniffing around, thinking of buying his contract, while a fake colonel with a criminal past and dollar signs for eyes moved in to take care of business, and would eventually ensure that Elvis would never come over to play in front of all those Teds in Britain who had helped lay the groundwork for the coming revolution.

In terms of men's fashion, Elvis and the Teds had an awful lot in common, and what outraged the detractors of both was that they dressed in such a way that made everyone else on the street look like they existed only in monochrome. These people looked seriously sharp – it is not for nothing that one of Presley's early nicknames was the Memphis Flash. The Teds had their own style firmly in place long before rock'n'roll, but the two came together in the mid-fifties, and although rock'n'roll street style has long since become an international language, other countries have never managed to properly imitate the Teds. However, new subcultures were to follow every few years, and from then on, it was not too many years before young people around the world were starting to dress the way they did in London.

Bedsit Revolution

John Osborne on his houseboat, June 1956

In the summer of 1955, a reviewer in the *New Statesman* called novelist Kingsley Amis a 'literary Teddy Boy,' but up on the pier at Morecambe at the end of May, it was jazz, not rock'n'roll, that provided the background to the play which the supposedly angry young John Osborne was writing, whose lead character, Jimmy Porter, was an amateur trumpet player. John finished writing it on June 3 back in London, where he lived on a Thames houseboat called the *M/Y Egret* in the Cubitt Yacht Basin near Chiswick

Bridge. Two months later, while lying on the deck and reading a copy of trade paper *The Stage*, he noticed an advert for a new theatre group called the English Stage Company, and decided that it might be worth sending them his new play, *Look Back in Anger*. Anticipating a lengthy wait for any response, he was shocked to receive an answer virtually by return of post, offering him an initial £25 for an option on the play and a request for a meeting with a certain George Devine. Things were falling into place.

Back in the Fantasie coffee bar, Mary Quant, Alexander Plunket Greene and Archie McNair had finally hit upon a plan: they would pool their resources and open a boutique on the King's Road selling clothes under Mary's name. The idea of starting a clothes shop in that area might seem like an obvious one in the light of what was to follow in the sixties, but for its time, it was radical. High fashion in the mid-fifties was presumed to be something which emerged fully formed from across the Channel, at the whim of someone French or Italian whose designs were then faithfully passed on to the British through the medium of magazines like *Vogue* and the national newspapers. Designing your own clothes from a bedsit in Oakley Street and selling them around the corner was hardly a well-trodden path to success in 1955. Nevertheless, that was their intention.

With an idea like that, you need luck on your side, and a little bit of money certainly does not go amiss. Alexander put up £5,000 he'd just received upon turning twenty-one, which Archie matched with £5,000 of his own. With this, they were able to buy a building at 138a King's Road on the corner of Markham Square, next door to a pub called the Markham Arms. This provided a good start, but without enormous amounts of hard work, and their trump card, Mary's designs, their success was hardly guaranteed. Plenty of people have a little money now and then, but what the three of them built on this foundation in over the next decade was nothing short of astonishing.

As the Teds were readying themselves for rock'n'roll, Mary Quant and her partners for the launch of their boutique, and the English Stage Company for their takeover of the Royal Court, another part of the modern landscape was coming into view – commercial television, in the shape of the ITV network. The BBC had enjoyed a monopoly on UK TV broadcasting for three and a half decades, but all that was due to change on September 22, 1955. The government appointed Sir Kenneth Clark, former director of the National Gallery and chairman of the Arts Council, to be chairman of the new Independent Broadcasting Authority, widely regarded as a safe pair of hands. However, there was much discussion in the press about the likely effects of this new channel on everyday life. *Films and Filming* magazine commented in August:

September 22 – D-Day for Britain's commercial television programmes and an H-Bomb day for the British entertainment industry. If the plans of the programme-contractors materialise in anything like the way they promise, then it will bring about just as big a revolution as the birth of talking pictures did in 1928 with *The Jazz Singer*.

ITV's programmes ranged from the popular quiz *Double Your Money*, presented by future *Opportunity Knocks* supremo Hughie Green, to more highbrow items featuring the works of Noel Coward or Chelsea's formerly unmentionable son, Oscar Wilde. Casting his eye over the new channel for what was still known as the *Manchester Guardian*, Bernard Levin set the programmes to one side and reviewed that new innovation for Britain, the adverts: 'Is any general pattern discernible, and, if so, should we be disturbed by it?' he asked. 'My immediate reaction, goaded into incivility by several days of the most idiotic verse imaginable – and in many cases unimaginable – is to answer with an emphatic affirmative to both questions.' Punch-drunk from several days of listening to the chirpy jingles poured forth by the likes of Remington, Esso, Cadbury's and Kleenex, he had the air of a man who has seen the future, and found it somewhat vulgar. Advertising, though, did not necessarily look bad to everyone, especially if you had ambitions to be in the film trade.

The Independent Group at the ICA had arrived at the term 'Pop Art' the previous year after viewing a selection of blow-ups of adverts, while the same issue of *Films and Filming* which noted the dawn of commercial television also carried the following news item: 'I hear of changes at the National Film Theatre. Karel Reisz, the theatre's immensely successful programme organiser and press officer, leaves to become Films Officer to the Ford Motor Company.' Reisz, like several of the future film directors who would shape the kitchen-sink boom of the early sixties, was happy to link up in his early days with big business, and Lindsay Anderson's 1957 documentary about Covent Garden fruit market was also sponsored by Ford.

Naturally, some future kitchen-sink directors were also coming up via the medium of television, in particular Tony Richardson, who – in addition to earning £14 a week helping to make things ready for the English Stage Company's opening season as George Devine's assistant – was also directing a BBC crime series called *Tales From Soho*, in which he found room for the odd bit-part acting role for John Osborne. As the autumn of 1955 approached, Devine and Richardson continued their search for suitable plays for the following year's opening season, and it was also becoming clear that the Kingsway Theatre was in poor condition and in need of too many expensive repairs to be a viable home for the company. Once again, attention returned to the Royal Court, and the last of the red tape and objections were eventually dealt with, leaving the English Stage Company free to concentrate on its main objective of launching a writer's theatre in Sloane Square that could compete with the best of the West End.

Bazaar Goings-on

A few hundred yards along the King's Road at number 138a, otherwise known as Markham House, the triumvirate of Mary Quant, Alexander Plunket Greene and Archie McNair were working to make the premises ready for the opening of their boutique. Prior to their takeover, the building had been home to a firm of solicitors. One major reason for having bought the property was the basement, which Alexander hoped to turn into a jazz club, with the boutique at ground-floor level. In the end, their application for a nightclub licence was refused by the local authority, so they opted to make the basement a restaurant instead, named Alexander's, while the boutique was called Bazaar. They acquired the building in the spring, and spent the summer on alterations to the ground floor and basement so that they could be used as commercial premises. Mary moved into a bedsit in Oakley Street which was also to serve as her work-room, and began developing contacts with clothing wholesalers, since the initial idea was to sell items from a wide range of sources. As Mary explained: 'It was to be a bouillabaisse of clothes and accessories . . . sweaters, scarves, shifts, hats, jewellery and peculiar odds and ends.'

Credit: Evening Standard/ Hulton Archive/Getty Images

Mary Quant and her husband Alexander Plunkett Greene
at Bazaar, 138a King's Road, 29 December, 1956

Bazaar opened its doors in November 1955, a couple of weeks after the downstairs restaurant, Alexander's. They threw an opening-day party, with a striped marquee in the forecourt, free food and drink, and sent out invitations to the press, nearly all of which were ignored. Being new to the game, they had only the sketchiest idea of how to set about contacting the press in the first place. They were also charging an insufficient mark-up on wholesale prices, so that for a few weeks they were actually losing money on items which they sold, while at the same time alienating their suppliers and indeed other shops in the area, since they were inadvertently under-cutting the fixed retail prices. This was unfortunate, but the good news was that the stock was mostly flying out of the door.

For the opening, Mary had designed some hats, and also 'a pair of mad house-pyjamas'. The latter were noticed by *Harper's Bazaar*, which then featured them in their magazine. A sign of things to come was that an American customer bought the same pair of house-pyjamas a few days later, explaining that he was a clothing manufacturer, and he intended to go back to the US, copy the design and mass-market them. Wholesale theft of ideas has always been rife in the fashion business, but it graphically demonstrated that even in their opening weeks in 1955, the designs that Mary was creating in her Chelsea bedsit had the potential to reach out across the world.

Rebel Music

In the same month that Bazaar opened – after a year in which the Top Twenty had featured such decidedly middle-of-the-road number one hits as 'Softly Softly' by Ruby Murray, show tunes like 'Hernando's Hideaway' by the Johnston Brothers, and religious songs like 'I'll Walk With God' by Mario Lanza – Bill Haley and His Comets finally made it to the very top of the heap in the UK with their worldwide smash, 'Rock Around the Clock'. Recorded in 1954, but currently riding an unstoppable wave courtesy of its use in the upmarket juvenile delinquent film *Blackboard Jungle*, the Comets' mixture of slapping upright bass, a fearsomely amplified pistol-crack snare and one of the first great electric guitar solos to hit the UK mainstream was sending out a message that definitely seemed to be getting through to the kids. Even adults for whom the charts meant less than nothing could hardly have failed to notice the changes.

On November 23, two days before Haley's record hit the number one slot, BBC Radio's Light Programme broadcast a new episode of the comedy show *Hancock's Half Hour* entitled 'The Blackboard Jungle', sending up the new phenomenon of disaffected youth. Another person helping to put the subject firmly on the map was already dead, but only just starting to make an impact in Britain. James Dean's debut starring role in the film *East of Eden* had been shot in 1954, but only reached UK cinemas in August 1955, one month before a student called Donald Turnupseed pulled out onto the highway in the path of Dean's Porsche Spyder, resulting in the star's death on September 30, aged twenty-four. Donald suffered a bruised nose, followed by a lifetime as a virtual recluse, hiding from enraged Dean fans. *East of Eden* received fine reviews in the UK, with Dean singled out for his portrayal of the character Cal Trask. He had spent 1955 shooting two further films, *Rebel Without a Cause* and *Giant*, both of which were not released in the UK until 1956, just as rock'n'roll was really taking hold: the latter film was a flabby three-hour George Stevens soap opera with way too much Rock Hudson and a bare twenty minutes of Dean, but the former, made by a much finer director, Nicholas Ray, helped define the era and set the pattern for much of what was to follow.

As the year came to a close, the new medium of commercial television took a chance on a one-off entertainment programme broadcast on December 23 featuring a young expatriate American who sang, told jokes and played various instruments. It was not a success, and its star later described it as 'puerile', but *The Dick Lester Show* gave the British public a brief chance to see the man who would later direct quintessential sixties feature films such as *A Hard Day's Night*, *The Knack* and *Help!*

In the charts that Christmas, Dickie Valentine was back at number one, but 'Rock Around the Clock' clawed its way to the top again in January. During the coming year, rock'n'roll would make a serious impression on the UK scene for the first time, Mary Quant's boutique consolidated its position and began attracting customers from an ever-widening area, and the English Stage Company finally opened up for business at the Royal Court Theatre. All the pieces were very nearly in place, and from now on, the King's Road was moving to a position at the forefront of the emerging youth culture.

6

'Anger is an energy'

This is Tomorrow

In England, 1956 was when the bomb really went off. The shock waves rippled down through popular culture for at least the next quarter of a century, but if you are looking for a time when things reached critical mass and threw out sparks in all directions, this is the only place to start.

Clothes? Mary Quant's Bazaar began opening up the King's Road, watched closely by a young man called John Stephen, who would go on to turn a back alley called Carnaby Street into a worldwide brand name before it burnt out into a tourist trap in a few short years.

Theatre? John Osborne and the English Stage Company at the Royal Court disturbed some of the long-established conventions of polite drama, clearing the field for playwrights such as John Arden, Ann Jellicoe, Arnold Wesker and Edward Bond, and setting the scene for the kitchen-sink realism of British cinema over the next few years. The media found themselves a new stereotype this year – the Angry Young Man.

Art? An exhibition at the Whitechapel Gallery called *This Is Tomorrow* included a painting by Patrick Hamilton entitled *Just what is it that makes today's homes so different, so appealing?*, generally held to be the first true example of pop art.

Film? Both *Rebel Without a Cause* and *Rock Around the Clock* hit British cinemas this year, prompting stories of rioting and hysteria, while at the same time boosting sales of rock'n'roll records, jeans, red bomber jackets and motorbike boots.

Music? Rock'n'roll – a mixture of styles incorporating anything from R&B, rockabilly, doo-wop, jump blues, hillbilly boogie and hopped-up country and western – became the new press whipping boy, while simultaneously sweeping away almost everything in its path. At the start of the year, it was a developing trend; by December, it had brought the opposition to its knees. For the purposes of our discussion, rock'n'roll can be summed up in one record, which was cut in New York on January 10, 1956. It was called 'Heartbreak Hotel', and it hit the UK like an express train.

Two-Way Family Favourites

Elvis recorded 'Heartbreak Hotel' on January 10, 1956, during his first session for his new label, RCA. In the face of competition from other major labels, they'd managed to lure him away from Sam Phillips's legendary Sun label in Memphis, as their A&R man memorably commented, 'because RCA's money is so much greener than everybody else's'. Elvis had released five singles for Sam's label which will stand among the best 45s ever issued, but he never had the muscle of a big company behind him until 'Heartbreak Hotel', and as far as the UK was concerned, the Sun material didn't exist at that point. As John Peel told me: 'Nobody had any idea about any of that other stuff,' so the impact of that first RCA single was even more astonishing than it would have been for the Memphis crowd who had been watching Presley's career develop since 1954. 'I first heard it on the *Two-Way Family Favourites* programme', said John. 'You used to listen to that, to request programmes, basically, in the hope of hearing one record or so that you liked.'

For the moment, though, in January 1956, Elvis was unknown to BBC radio listeners, and although Bill Haley was topping the charts with 'Rock Around the Clock', the film of the same name would not arrive in British cinemas until the summer. Right now, the new music sensation came from somewhere much closer to home, and he sang with a Cockney accent.

Lonnie Donegan – the man whom *Melody Maker* called the 'Scots-Born Irish Hill-Billy From London' – first hit the charts with a single called 'Rock Island Line' on January 6, 1956, and soon it seemed as if half the country was cannibalising old washboards and tea chests in order to have a go at this thing known as 'skiffle'. No matter that the song itself was a cover of a decades-old Lead Belly performance, or even that Donegan's version had actually been recorded in 1954 as part of a Chris Barber Jazz Band album – as far as teenagers were concerned this was the very latest thing, and just as punk was to do twenty years later, skiffle inspired great numbers of them to pick up some sort of instrument for the first time and have a go at making music. By the close of the 1950s Lonnie would be doing end-of-the-pier-style Cocker-ney knees-ups like 'Does Your Chewing Gum Lose Its Flavour' and 'My Old Man's a Dustman', but for a while there, he was red-hot and stoking a revolution. As John Peel explained to me: 'Lonnie was our Elvis really, you know, and he got side-tracked into a lot of bollocks, in the same way that Gene Vincent did. But, of course in those days, people used to talk about becoming an *all-round entertainer*. Peter Sellers did that piss-take of it, but that was what everybody aspired to.'

Vic Flick – who in a couple of years' time would be the lead guitarist with the John Barry Seven, playing the iconic riff that drives the original main title theme of the James Bond films, not to mention the equally fine title music for the 1960 cult film *Beat Girl* – also started out in the skiffle game in the mid-fifties, as he told me:

> I was gigging around town, and I met this bass player called George Jennings, and we worked together a bit and he said 'Do you want a job with Bob Cort's Skiffle Group?' I was just a freelance professional musician looking for any job that came along. I was kind of influenced a bit by American guitar players at the time – not too many English guitar players – by people like Tal Farlow, and the guy with the Count Basie Orchestra, more so than the English people. But it was a good time to be in the music business.

Meanwhile, down in the Fantasie coffee bar, Chelsea's own Chas McDevitt group were already preaching the skiffle gospel to the King's Road crowd, but would have to wait until the following year for their own taste of Donegan-style stardom.

Excruciating Discomfort on Foot-High Stools

By 1956, coffee bars were enough a part of the scene that they were made the subject of one of the BBC TV *Panorama* programme's 'human interest' stories – other hot topics covered that year included 'Father Christmas', 'Smoking and Lung Cancer' and 'Italians in Bedford' – and one such place also appeared in Roger Longrigg's fine Chelsea novel of the young advertising set, *A High-Pitched Buzz*. Henry, the narrator of the book, lives in Pont Street, his best friend in Cadogan Gardens, and he works at an advertising agency alongside two characters whose nicknames reflect the King's Road setting: a Mr Egerton (known as Egerton Crescent) and Miss Markham (known as Markham Square). Towards the end of a Chelsea night out, Henry and his friends visit a coffee bar:

[. . .] one of the still-nearly-new ones that had recently appeared, like
a disease, all over west London. This one was called *La Guitarra*, and it
had indeed a Basque-shirted youth playing indifferent Flamenco in a
corner. In other respects it was less consistent with its chosen character.
The lanterns were Japanese; the cups were Italian; the clothes showed
a strong American influence; the clientele was irrevocably English. It
was crowded, dark, noisy, and rather gay. We arranged ourselves round
a foot-high table painted in bold primary colours, and sat in excruciating
discomfort on foot-high stools of wrought iron. [. . .] Sweatered figures
pressed round us; girls with loose dark hair and tight dark trousers called
to each other in slight but perceptibly cockney accents.

Coffee bars were just one of the forms of entertainment that year which
were aimed mainly at teenagers. When not hanging around in basements
drinking espressos, young Londoners now also had the option of seeing *Rebel
Without a Cause*, which opened in January ('It's brilliant – but a brute of a
picture,' said reviewer Margaret Hinxman), but other doors were being barred
against them. *Picturegoer* journalist Laurie Henshaw, writing in his column
'Down Tin Pan Alley', reported 'Oh dear, those ballroom bosses are at it
again. One hall recently banned Teddy Boys. Now another has banned jiving.
The excuse? "An attempt to raise the standard of dancing".' However, a few
pages later in the same magazine, there was an interview with a man called
Maurice Cheepen, manager of the Troxy, a 3,000-seat Gaumont cinema in
Stepney, who reckoned that the threat from juvenile delinquents had been
much exaggerated in the press, and that pre-war cinemagoers were much
rougher: '"Drunks used to slash seats – and the doormen had to be six-foot
ex-Guardsmen to keep order. [. . .] But nowadays, not even the Teddy Boys
cause much bother. They wear queer clothes and I kid them about their
get-up," Mr Cheepen said. "But, generally, they're quiet and polite and a
word from the usherette is enough to silence any noise."'
Just as Mr Cheepen was all but ruining the newly established fearsome
reputation of modern youth, over in Sloane Square at the recently occupied
offices of the English Stage Company, the search was on to locate an
archetypal troublemaker, a suitably angry young man.
Finding the right actor to play the part of Jimmy Porter in Osborne's
Look Back in Anger was just one of the tasks facing George Devine and Tony
Richardson. With only a few months left before their debut season's opening
date of April 2, they settled on Kenneth Haigh for the role, apparently at
Richardson's suggestion. According to Osborne's somewhat dismissive later
account, 'The part claimed Kenneth like a stray dog. But then, there were

no other takers,' and he also credited Richardson with the choice of Mary Ure for the part of Jimmy's long-suffering girlfriend Alison.

The play itself was not regarded by the company as the great new hope of their opening season, which also included works by established writers such as Arthur Miller and Angus Wilson; that honour probably belonged to *Cards of Identity* by Nigel Dennis, based on his own successful 1955 novel of the same name. As the English Stage Company's group of actors were assembled – including Robert Stephens, Joan Plowright, John Welsh, Rosalie Crutchley, Michael Gwynne, Alan Bates and Osborne himself – rehearsals began in a church hall near Peter Jones for the opening play, *The Mulberry Bush* by Angus Wilson. Members of the company not immediately occupied with rehearsals were sent for training sessions with Yat Malmgren, which, as Osborne recalled, involved 'lying on the floor and having your character analysed from your choice of movements'.

We Wanted to Shock People

While the Royal Court's finest were writhing about on floors, a few hundred yards further west, outraged members of the public were occasionally to be seen indulging in that time-honoured ritual, the futile protest, outside the new boutique at 138a King's Road. According to Mary Quant, 'In the early days, businessmen in bowler hats and rolled umbrellas used to beat on the Bazaar shop window as they were so shocked by the clothes.' It had always been the intention to make the place look different from everywhere else, and their window arrangements were intentionally provocative, with special display figures which had been custom-made in imitation of the poses adopted by models in contemporary fashion photographs. 'We wanted people to stop and look,' said Quant. 'We wanted to shock people.'

Despite the attentions of the bowler-hat brigade, after a few shaky weeks in which they were under-charging for items they had ordered from suppliers, the main problem Quant, Plunket Greene and McNair were facing was simply keeping up with demand, and sometimes stock ran so low that even sparing enough items to dress the window was a problem. It was partly frustration at not being able to find suitable garments that inspired Mary to turn increasingly to creating her own designs. Working in her bedsit in Oakley Street, she would buy readymade paper patterns from Butterick and adapt them, producing something new in the process.

At this stage, Mary was still buying her dress material over the counter at Harrods, since she was not yet aware that it could be bought wholesale.

Demand was growing to such an extent that soon a woman was employed at the bedsitter to help with the sewing, swiftly to be followed by several others. The results of the day's work would be taken along the road to Bazaar where they would be snapped up by waiting customers, enabling Mary to visit Harrods again the following morning to buy more material, and so it went on. Meanwhile, the downstairs restaurant, Alexander's, was doing equally well, quickly establishing itself, Mary told me, as 'the most fashionable restaurant in Chelsea if not London, for some years. All the film and fashion photographers came there. Also actors and film stars – Grace Kelly, Audrey Hepburn, Bardot, Rex Harrison, Leslie Caron, Joe Losey, Kubrick, Antonioni, Simone Signoret . . .'

Bazaar and Alexander's would soon prove popular with the actors and company of the Royal Court, but in these last weeks before the opening of the theatre's first season, there were many things to be attended to, such as publicity. John Osborne later wrote of his first meeting that spring with the English Stage Company's part-time publicist, George Fearon, and claimed that it was this man who, having read an advance copy of *Look Back in Anger*, called him to his face an 'angry young man'. This phrase duly found its way into their promotional material and hung a label on the emerging movement from which it is still struggling to escape. Certainly, as early as July of that year the *Evening Standard* would use that phrase as the headline of an article about Osborne, which may well have been prompted by Fearon's press handouts. *Angry Young Man*, as Kenneth Allsop pointed out, had already been the title of Leslie Allen Paul's 1951 autobiography, but this 'story of a Marxist's personal class-warfare during the Twenties and Thirties and eventual conversion to Christianity' failed to bring the phrase into the everyday repertoire of tabloid headline-writers in the same way that the class of '56 were to achieve.

Momma Don't Allow

Youth, angry or otherwise, was certainly kicking up a fuss that spring. Teenage record-buyers had put another Bill Haley disc, 'Rock-a-Beatin' Boogie', up high in the charts close on the heels of 'Rock Around the Clock', while Lonnie Donegan's 'Rock Island Line' was selling so strongly that he announced his decision to quit Chris Barber's Jazz Band and go it alone with his own skiffle outfit. James Dean's *Rebel Without a Cause* was doing phenomenal business in UK cinemas, and over at Warner Brothers in Hollywood the dead star was still receiving more fan mail per week than any living actor.

In this atmosphere charged with teenage exuberance, the English Stage Company finally opened up for business at the Royal Court on April 2, 1956, with Angus Wilson's *The Mulberry Bush* – a damp squib of a production that failed to pull much of a crowd, and which in any case had already been seen by theatregoers in Bristol. As a calling card for the new company, it was hardly a radical choice, and although it gave young actors such as Kenneth Haigh and Alan Bates their first taste of the Court's stage, in the main the reviews were not kind.

The second offering of the season, Arthur Miller's *The Crucible*, opened on April 9, but director George Devine had for some reason made the decision to cut one of the characters, Giles Corey, from the play completely, without asking Miller's permission – a strange move from a company which had been specifically founded as a writers' theatre. This prompted an understandably threatening telegram from the author to the effect that they could either reinstate the character or close the play immediately, at which point Devine restored the part. In the event, regardless of the varying numbers of people in the cast – which included all five actors shortly to open in *Look Back in Anger* – *The Crucible* failed to draw much in the way of a crowd, perhaps because this production had also been previewed some weeks before in Bristol. So far, there was little sign that the Royal Court was about to be any more successful than it had been in the wake of its 1952 reopening, and, in terms of ticket sales, the extended run of the musical revue *Airs on a Shoestring* might have looked to the accountants like some kind of long-lost golden age.

As *The Mulberry Bush* and *The Crucible* struggled to attract the crowds away from the West End to Sloane Square, venerable British jazz bible the *Melody Maker* (founded 1926) was congratulating itself on printing its first ever 'popular' charts. A front-page article with the prophetic headline 'Top of the Pops' explained: 'Despite many requests in the past from all branches of the British music industry we have refused to jeopardise the integrity of the *Melody Maker* by publishing any list of which we could not be assured of the complete and utter integrity.'

The slight drawback with all this was that, as the year progressed, much of what was to appear in those charts filled the paper's staff and a good many of their readership with horror. Even during that first week, the signs were there: 'See You Later, Alligator' by Bill Haley and His Comets was at number seven in the UK, with 'Rock Island Line' by Lonnie Donegan at number fourteen. Meanwhile, in the separate chart labelled 'America's Top Discs', a certain Elvis Presley was currently at number ten with a song called 'Heartbreak Hotel'. Within a month, he would also be a household name in Britain.

Elsewhere in that same issue of *Melody Maker*, their finest and probably most open-minded writer, Max Jones, was reviewing a jazz documentary which had been shown in February 1956 as part of the National Film Theatre's new 'Free Cinema' presentations:

> Karel Reisz and Tony Richardson have filmed a Chris Barber evening at the Wood Green Jazz Club, and called the picture, *Momma Don't Allow*. [. . .] In one respect, the film is remarkable: it ignores the drug and delinquency prejudices which have become inseparable from jazz in the average editorial mind. It doesn't assume that the young man in Edwardian clothes has a bicycle chain in one pocket and a drum of pepper in the other. In fact, it doesn't moralise at all.

This report is interesting for several reasons: for one thing, it is probably one of the last occasions in which young people in Teddy boy clothing might have been assumed to be jazz fans rather than rock'n'rollers; secondly, the Tony Richardson here referred to is indeed the same person who was currently at the Royal Court, busily working as director to make sure that *Look Back in Anger* was ready for its opening the following month.

The footage of Chris Barber's band had been shot in the winter of 1954–5, when a pre-fame Lonnie Donegan was still playing with them. Because of rapid changes in the music scene, by the time the film was seen, it was already something of a period piece. Karel Reisz had been a BFI employee when shooting it, but he was now working for the Ford Motor Company, and both he and Richardson – together with another Royal Court and Free Cinema director, Lindsay Anderson – would in the next few years be at the forefront of the emerging kitchen-sink school of British film-making. Here, in one simply plotted twenty-minute 16mm film, the careers of key people who were to have a revolutionary effect on the worlds of theatre, music and cinema came together to make a few points about contemporary youth culture and the class differences between local Wood Green Teddy boys and a group of more affluent visiting jazz fans.

Solid Gold Lavatory Railings

Whether you were into jazz, blues or rock, the main problem with being in Britain for many years was that the Musicians' Union had long ago quarrelled with its opposite number in the US, resulting in a ban on visiting artists from America which, incredibly, lasted from the mid-thirties to the mid-fifties. Because of this, although earlier generations of British jazz fans had been able to watch the likes of Fats Waller, Louis Armstrong, Cab Calloway and Duke Ellington in the flesh back in the late twenties and early thirties, if you had the misfortune to grow up in the forties and were out in the clubs of London looking for American artists, because of the MU, there were none to be found. By 1956, this restriction had been lifted, and Louis Armstrong was to make a triumphant return in May, playing in front of hugely enthusiastic crowds, including Princess Margaret, who received the following onstage dedication from Satchmo: 'Now we are going to jump one for one of our special fans. We're gonna lay one on for the Princess.' George Melly, still living in Margaretta Terrace, recalled his incredible excitement at the prospect of finally seeing one of his real jazz heroes in the flesh, and that as he walked from his home up the King's Road on the way to Earl's Court where the show was due to take place, 'even the railings of the Gents at the World's End seemed made of gold'.

In April, up at the Albert Hall, jazz fans also had the opportunity to enjoy what was advertised as 'The Greatest Musical Thrill of the Century' – a performance by another American import, Stan Kenton and His Orchestra – with a top ticket price of 25 shillings. However, *Melody Maker* readers may have noticed in the April 21 issue that the transatlantic trend was now apparently also working in the other direction, as the US charts showed: at number two, 'Heartbreak Hotel' by Elvis Presley; at number seven, 'Blue Suede Shoes' by Carl Perkins; and close behind at number eleven, 'Rock Island Line' by Lonnie Donegan. A full six years before the 'British Invasion', Lonnie was climbing up the American charts, selling US music back to them with a song he had recorded in London in July 1954, the same month that Elvis cut his first Sun single. On April 30, readers of the *Daily Mirror* woke up to find an article called 'Rock Age Idol' about this young man who was stirring things up across the pond. 'He's Riding the Crest of a Teenage Tidal Wave', ran the headline, and that wave was only a couple of weeks away from hitting Britain.

Cross-cultural exchange was certainly in the air, and in a spirit of friendship, Soviet premier Mr Khrushchev, when visiting some Oxford colleges in April, was shown sometime Chelsea resident Jacob Epstein's sculpture of Lazarus in New College Chapel. His verdict? 'Decadent rubbish.' Judging by what was to come in the next few months, he could probably have got a job as a record reviewer at the *Melody Maker*.

Leading the pack at that paper, in a column published on May 5, 1956, was Steve Race, who did not seem to know or care that he was throwing all the same witless insults in the direction of rock'n'roll that the small-minded detractors of jazz had used in previous years:

Viewed as a social phenomenon, the current craze for Rock-and-Roll material is one of the most terrifying things ever to have happened to popular music. [. . .] I hope the gimlet-eyed men of commerce who are at present trying to bring about a Rock-and-Roll boom in this country are aware of what they're doing. I also hope that the BBC Song Committee will be more vigilant than ever when vetting the cheap, nasty lyrics on which the Rock-and-Roll movement thrives. [. . .] It is a monstrous threat, both to the moral acceptance and the artistic emancipation of jazz. Let us oppose it to the end.

On the page opposite this pro-censorship rant, there was an advert from the BF Wood Music Co. Ltd, Denmark Street, London, which simply read:

INVITING YOU TO
HEARTBREAK HOTEL
HOST: ELVIS PRESLEY
HMV POP 182
ADDRESS: No 1 AMERICAN HIT PARADE

Anger Management

Two days after publication of the issue of *Melody Maker* in which Steve Race was calling down fire and brimstone upon the heads of rock'n'rollers, *Look Back in Anger* was previewed at the Royal Court, prior to its official opening night the next evening on May 8, 1956.

> **LOOK BACK IN ANGER.** Play by John Osborne about a disagreeable young man who is at odds with the world, his generation and practically everything, and voices his complaints with tireless ferocity. Kenneth Haigh, Mary Ure, Alan Bates, Helena Hughes. O.—May 8. Rev. 1070—7. ROYAL COURT, Sloane Sq., S.W.1 (SLO 1745). U.: Sloane Sq. **See Theatre List for dates of performances.**

Like the Sex Pistols shows at the 100 Club in 1976, so many myths have built up around the first night of *Look Back in Anger* that it is hard to sift out anything vaguely resembling the truth from among it all. Memory is a tricky thing at the best of times, but in this case one of the key figures who actually *was* in the audience that night, Kenneth Tynan, gleefully admitted in his diaries that he deliberately spread all sorts of fake stories about this night. When interviewed about it by Robert Cushman in August 1976, he said that he concocted them with the help of Kingsley Amis and Tom Stoppard, claiming that Evelyn Waugh was in the audience, or that West End impresario Binkie Beaumont was supposedly in despair, seeing the whole of his livelihood in ruins. Other people, Osborne included, seem happy to have spread the story that the reviews were generally bad, recalling that George Devine was very depressed with the following day's papers, and that Tony Richardson had asked them both: 'But what on earth did you expect? You didn't expect them to *like* it did you?'

In reality, the overall result seems to have been neither disaster nor triumph, and the critics appear to have had a higher opinion of the author than of the play itself. The *Manchester Guardian* called it a 'strongly felt but rather muddled first drama', while the *New Statesman* thought that Osborne spoke with 'the authentic new tone of the Nineteen-Fifties, desperate, savage, resentful and, at times, very funny' and concluded that 'this is the kind of play which, for all its imperfections, the English Stage Company ought to be doing.' The *Daily Mail* felt that the play was no masterpiece but called Osborne 'a dramatist of outstanding promise: a man who can write with a searing passion, but happens in this case to have lavished it on the wrong play', while the *Financial Times* went even further, calling *Look Back in Anger* 'a play of extraordinary importance' and predicting that 'its influence should go far beyond such an eccentric and contorted one-man turn as the controversial *Waiting for Godot*'. These are hardly the worst notices a fledgling playwright will have ever received. Perhaps Osborne was thinking more of the verdict of the *Birmingham Post*, who said: 'We shall be very frank about this. If more plays like tonight's *Look Back in Anger* are produced, the "Writer's Theatre" at the Royal Court must surely sink. I look back in anger upon a night misconceived and misspent.'

While the overnight reviews may not necessarily have been to the English Stage Company's taste, the Sunday papers printed at the end of that week brought better news. Harold Hobson in the *Sunday Times* echoed the cautiously favourable line of some of the midweek critics – 'Mr John Osborne is a writer who at present does not know what he is doing. [. . .] Though the blinkers still obscure his vision, he is a writer of outstanding promise, and the English Stage Company is to be congratulated on discovering him' – but it was the influential critic from the *Observer*, Kenneth Tynan, who pushed the boat out in no uncertain fashion:

Look Back in Anger presents post-war youth as it really is. [. . .] To have done this at all would be a signal achievement; to have done it with a first play is a minor miracle. All the qualities are there, qualities which one had despaired of ever seeing on the stage – the drift towards anarchy, the instinctive leftishness, the automatic rejection of 'official' attitudes, the surrealist sense of humour [. . .] the casual promiscuity, the sense of lacking a crusade worth fighting for. [. . .] The Porters of our time deplore the tyranny of 'good taste' and refuse to accept 'emotional' as a term of abuse; they are classless, and they are also leaderless. Mr Osborne is their first spokesman in the London theatre. [. . .] That the play needs changes I do not deny: it is twenty minutes too long and not even Mr Haigh's bravura could blind me to the painful whimsy of the final reconciliation scene. [. . .] I doubt if I could love anyone who did not wish to see *Look Back in Anger*. It is the best young play of its decade.

With the foremost drama critic of the age on his side, Osborne had certainly made the beginnings of a reputation during that opening week. However, the box-office returns were nothing much to write home about, and the play was very far from being an overnight success. One person who went along to see it that month was Colin Wilson, whose first book, *The Outsider*, was also published in May, and who had been encouraged in his work by the man who had written the Royal Court's opening play of the season, Angus Wilson. 'Dan Farson took me along,' Colin Wilson told me. 'It was about two weeks after *Look Back in Anger* had been reviewed, just around the time when *The Outsider* came out. I didn't like it at all. In particular, the constant attacking of the girl, played by Mary Ure, who just stands there ironing. Now what most of the audience didn't know was that Osborne's wife Pamela had treated him badly, and so there was some cause for this anger, but in the play, all the girl has done is to stand there ironing, so it doesn't make sense. Ken Tynan helped make that play popular.'

Idiotic Howling

During those brief few weeks between the opening night of *Look Back in Anger* on May 8 and the publication of Wilson's *The Outsider* on May 28, things were moving at quite a pace. On the same day that Ken Tynan was singing Osborne's praises in the *Observer*, Jack Jackson's national UK TV show that Sunday evening plugged Elvis Presley's 'Heartbreak Hotel', which will have been the first exposure for many British people to this new phenomenon. The following day, across the pond, *TIME* magazine ran its debut profile of Elvis for the benefit of their huge mainstream readership, giving them a few salient facts about this 'drape-suited, tight-trousered young man of 21' currently occupying the number one slot in the charts:

All through the South and West, Elvis is packing theatres, fighting off shrieking admirers, disturbing parents, puckering the brows of psychologists, and filling letters-to-the-editor columns with cries of alarm and, from adolescents, counter-cries of adulation. [. . .] In Fort Worth 16-year-olds have carved his name into their forearms with clasp-knives (one did it four times). [. . .] In Amarillo, when asked if he intended to marry, Elvis answered: 'Why buy a cow when you can get milk through a fence?'

Seemingly unimpressed with such thorny questions of farming and philosophy, *TIME*'s readers responded mostly with scorn in the next few issues – 'There must be some error, since in your May 14 issue I find Elvis Presley in the Music section. What does that idiotic howling have to do with music?' Someone else lining up to condemn rock'n'roll that month was a certain Asa Carter from Alabama. Asa's qualifications as a music critic seem to have been absolutely non-existent, but his bigoted, white-supremacist views were duly quoted in the pages of *Melody Maker*:

JIM CROW CHIEF HITS AT ROCK AND ROLL – Asa Carter, secretary of the North Alabama White Citizens Committee, has condemned rock'n'roll music, stating that it is being encouraged 'as a means of pulling down the white man to the level of the negro. It is part of a plot to undermine the morals of the youth of our nation,' says Carter. 'It is sexualistic, unmoralistic and the best way to bring people of both races together. If jukebox operators want to stay in business they had better get rid of these smutty records with their dirty lyrics.'

Despite all this, 'Heartbreak Hotel' remained at number one in the US that month – with Lonnie Donegan's 'Rock Island Line' just a few places behind – and Elvis had finally started climbing the UK charts as well. The *Melody Maker* charts for May 19 showed no fewer than *five* songs in a tie at number eighteen, including 'Rock Island Line', which had been in and out of the listings since January, and two new entries, 'Heartbreak Hotel' and Carl Perkins' 'Blue Suede Shoes'. Rock'n'roll – played by sharp-dressed Memphis musicians wearing suitably flash clothes from their hometown's finest tailor, Lansky's on Beale Street – had definitely arrived as far as Britain's teenagers were concerned, and young people like Malcolm McLaren, John Lennon and Marc Bolan were wising up and taking notes.

Like a Vulture in Sudden Song

On May 15 at the Royal Court, with *Look Back in Anger* still running, Ronald Duncan's double bill of short 'poetic dramas', *Don Juan* and *The Death of Satan*, opened, cut down by Devine despite the author's misgivings from two full-length plays. The cast for the productions included Nigel Davenport, Rachel Kempson, Joan Plowright, Robert Stephens, and also John Osborne in a minor role. Set design and costumes were by the major British painter and book illustrator, John Minton, who had previously worked in this capacity on John Gielgud's 1941 production of *Macbeth*. Despite all this, the public stayed away, and it was withdrawn after eight poorly attended performances. Over in the East End of London, a fine play called *The Quare Fellow* by Brendan Behan opened on May 24 at the Theatre Royal, Stratford East, under the direction of Joan Littlewood. It was enthusiastically received in the press, including a review in *What's On in London* from Kenneth A. Hurren which bizarrely claimed that it 'soars on the wings of language like a vulture in sudden song' – not an image that most metropolitan readers would have had a chance to compare in real life. Soon the same magazine was saying of Behan that he had 'become the theatrical personality of the year. With his ambling gait, his love of good liquor and ribald humour, he remains something of an enigma.'

May 26 brought about a leader column in *The Times* entitled 'Wrath at the Helm', which stated:

> People who like to leave the theatre in an argumentative mood will go to see Mr John Osborne's play *Look Back in Anger*. They will not necessarily argue about the merits of the piece, but they will remember those reviews in which it has been put forward as an expression of opinion valid for the generation of those in their late twenties. They will see a thoroughly cross young man, caught into an emotional situation where crossness avails nothing.

That same day's papers also included a profile in the London *Evening News* of Colin Wilson, under the headline, 'A Major Writer – And He's 24'. Wilson's book, *The Outsider*, was due to be published two days later, and in between, on May 27, it received the seal of approval from Cyril Connolly in the *Sunday Times* ('one of the most remarkable first books I have read for a long time') and from Philip Toynbee in the *Observer* ('a remarkable book'). The author himself was younger than Osborne, and certainly no less confident: 'My hopes for the future are, as a writer, to leave a mark as deep as that left by Plato or Goethe, and, as a member of the human race, for a higher type of man.' On publication day, the first printing sold out immediately.

Colin Wilson had friends who lived in World's End at this time, so would often visit places such as the Chelsea Arts Club, where Augustus John was still to be seen on occasion, and the Pheasantry, where he would drink with the painter Pietro Annigoni. He also recalls visiting Clement Freud's Royal Court Club, located above the theatre, as he told me: 'I only went up there once – it was with Samuel Beckett. That was when he was presenting *Endgame*. I never liked his stuff, I always wanted to say to him, "Come on, what is all this?" you know, but he was a such a pleasant person, I couldn't bring myself to say it.'

Sombreros, Banjos and Nude Paintings of Herself

Someone else experiencing the Chelsea life was 21-year-old actress Joy Webster, profiled in that month's issue of the film magazine *Photoplay*, who had come to town from Birmingham but seemed to be learning the bohemian ropes quickly enough: 'I believe in realism. Realism in acting; realism in photography. If you want to take a front cover of me, put me in a man's shirt and let me stand under a waterfall. It'll look alright, I promise you.' Her home decor seems to have been a textbook case of late-night existentialist *moderne:* 'Joy lives in Chelsea, in a flat decorated with chianti bottles, sombreros, banjos and nude paintings of herself. And she plays the bongo drums. Of course.'

7

'Cherry red, teak, or mint green goat'

Bad Champagne and Dubious Caviar

It was not just the bohemian set who were cutting loose in 1956. Over a decade after the end of the Second World War, the country was finally showing signs of escaping austerity conditions, and the social 'season' returned with a vengeance that year. In early June, the *New Statesman* reported:

> The British upper class has got the bit between its teeth. Not since the 30s has it consumed so much bad champagne and dubious caviar, trampled so much broken glass underfoot, and driven so many village dressmakers to profitable distraction. Society is scrambling shakily to its feet again and cocking a tentative snook at the masses.

Some aspects of the class war were being re-enacted onstage in *Look Back in Anger*, as 'posh' Alison told stories about how Jimmy and his mate Hugh used to conduct 'guerrilla raids' from their base in working-class Poplar on the parties of the rich folk in 'W1, SW1, SW3 and W8', watched by the audiences every night at the Royal Court, SW3. Box-office figures for the play were still unremarkable, and when *Cards of Identity* by Nigel Dennis joined it in repertory from June 26 onwards it was felt in some quarters that perhaps the latter would be the play to bring the English Stage Company their first much-needed success. Colin Wilson, a friend of Dennis's, was certainly of that opinion: 'I thought it was very good, much better than *Look Back in Anger*.' It seems that *Cards of Identity* caused a more hostile audience reaction at the Court than *Anger*. Irving Wardle spoke to

Alan Bates, who acted in both productions, and concluded that 'where there would be individual reactions to the Osborne, Dennis's play used to excite group protests, usually from the best-dressed sections of the house.'

Colin Wilson and John Osborne themselves were both attracting regular press attention. On June 12, the 'literary Teddy Boy' himself, Kingsley Amis, reviewed *The Outsider* in the *Spectator*, calling it 'more compilation than original work', while on July 2, a much more favourable and lengthy profile of Wilson appeared in *TIME* magazine, under the headline 'Intellectual Thriller', despite the fact that the book wasn't even available in the US at that stage. Then, on July 7, the *Evening Standard* ran a piece about John Osborne entitled, perhaps inevitably, 'Angry Young Man'.

If He Did That in the Street We'd Arrest Him

In addition to keeping their readers up to date about the new generation of supposedly angry writers, the press continued to paint a picture of the emerging rock'n'roll scene in terms which would probably have had Attila the Hun reaching for the address of a good libel lawyer. An American policeman who had witnessed an Elvis concert was reported as saying, 'If he did that in the street, we'd arrest him', and comparisons were drawn between the crowd response for Presley and those at any of Hitler's rallies. Nothing like keeping a bit of perspective.

Of course, jazz music had been decried in equally ridiculous terms in the past, and according to *Melody Maker*, it was still subject to prejudice from the tabloid press. In an article which prefigured much of the 1960s media hysteria about drugs, Mike Nevard laid it on the line about the evils of marijuana in the June 30 edition of the paper. 'Because I like jazz', he wrote, 'I have to make it clear that I do not use marijuana, heroin, morphine, cocaine, opium, dilaudid, dionin or cider.' Having established that in all his years of attending jazz clubs in town, he had seen absolutely no sign of 'reefers', he then quoted extensively from a 336-page report by the US Commissioner of Narcotics, in relation to marijuana: 'One man, under the influence of the drug, killed two women, then sliced himself to pieces across the abdomen, heart and throat and roamed about for hours, unable to feel the pain. Another smoked his first marijuana cigarette, leaped thirty feet out of a window, and battered his neighbour to death, screaming: "God sent me to kill this man!"'

These same stories, almost word for word, would later show up in 1966 articles about the new drug LSD. Nevard concluded by asking the following tricky question: 'Is the public to believe that because Princess Margaret likes jazz she smokes a hokum pipe? Or that Clarence House is an opium den?' Sadly, like *Melody Maker*, the *Evening Standard* was not offering to clear up this particular point either, but it at least managed to inform its readers in July that the Duke of Edinburgh had invented a 58ft electric tablecloth for the Royal Yacht Britannia, containing 'hundreds of yards of wire sandwiched between layers of felt and latex', so that candlesticks would light up when placed anywhere upon it. Perhaps he should have entered it into the following month's *This is Tomorrow* exhibition at the Whitechapel Art Gallery, alongside Patrick Hamilton's *Just what is it that makes today's homes so different, so appealing?*

On July 9, John Osborne – who was definitely not a fan of the Royal Family – gained his most significant piece of national publicity to date when interviewed by Malcolm Muggeridge on BBC TV's *Panorama* programme. Three days later, in a *Daily Mail* piece about the Angry Young Men, Daniel Farson made a specific comparison of Osborne's Jimmy Porter to James Dean in *Rebel Without a Cause*, who seemed to many in the press to have come from the same mould. Certainly, they were both jazz fans – Porter played a little trumpet, Dean was memorably photographed hiking around the late-night streets of New York with a drum on his back, and quoted by journalists as saying 'I'm playing the damn bongos and the world can go to hell.'

In 1956, less than a year after his death, the first of what has proved to be a virtually inexhaustible stream of books about James Dean appeared. This one, at least, had the benefit of first-hand knowledge, since it was written by Dean's former roommate, Bill Bast, who then visited England and became friendly with Colin Wilson. 'He came to stay with us down here in Cornwall,' Wilson told me. In July, *Photoplay* magazine printed an article about Dean by Eric Random entitled 'I Call This Cult Dangerous', which argued that 'a cult dedicated to a dead boy is a fearsome, frightening thing. It should be brought to an end. NOW!' By November, the same magazine was running a monthly Dean feature series, written by Bill Bast. Seventeen years later, Vivienne Westwood and Malcolm McLaren's rock'n'roll clothing emporium Let it Rock, at 430 King's Road, was renamed Too Fast To Live Too Young To Die, after the famous fifties slogan about James Dean.

Lamentably Contrived Cod-Jazz

While John Osborne was hitting the headlines in Britain, another Royal Court author was attracting attention for different reasons. On June 21, Arthur Miller appeared before the House Un-American Activities committee – a contradictory bunch of people who attempted to deal with the Communist threat by holding show trials in a manner of which even Stalin would have been proud. To his credit, Miller refused to play the game and name names – 'I will tell you anything about myself, but I cannot take responsibility for another human being.' He married Marilyn Monroe on June 29, 1956, and had recently applied for a passport so that he could join her in a trip to England, where she was due to film *The Prince and the Showgirl* with Laurence Olivier. In this, he was successful, as *TIME* reported on July 16:

> At week's end Miller, having filed 'further evidence of anti-Communism' with the State Department, got the passport for which he applied last May. State cautiously made it valid for only six months instead of the usual two-year period, but it freed Miller to wing to England this week with Mrs Miller.

Arthur Miller and Marilyn Monroe arrived in London coincidentally just as the Bill Haley film *Rock Around the Clock* hit the cinemas, to the accompaniment of scare stories in the press about rioting and seat-slashing during showings. *Melody Maker* kept giving the new music both barrels, week after week, enthusiastically reporting any attempts to ban rock'n'roll, while deploring the music ('cod-jazz'), the taste of the public ('It is one of the embarrassments of democracy that this is the age of the common man') and newcomers like Gene Vincent ('almost lamentably contrived'). During the month of July, though, there were signs that despite all the whining and expressions of horror, things were beginning to change. *What's On in London*'s resident film critic F. Maurice Speed admitted to his readers that he did not feel qualified to talk about *Rock Around the Clock* – 'which is I understand currently knocking and kniving the jazzters at the London Pavilion' – so he sent along a younger member of staff, who was suitably breathless: 'Oh brother, if you don't rock an' roll after this movie, visit a psychiatrist.'

A Country Inn Infested with Wood Fungi

In that same issue of the magazine, coffee bars were proving enough of a phenomenon that they now had their own separate listings page – including the 2 I's at 59 Old Compton Street, which was to play a key role in the emerging British rock scene – while the adverts for the Pheasantry Club at 152 King's Road were boasting that 'Peter Ustinov met Suzanne Cloutier at The Pheasantry . . . Mario will be pleased to meet YOU'. Both *Look Back in Anger* and *Cards of Identity* were still running at the Royal Court, and at this stage, Osborne's play had yet to set the box office alight, as might possibly be deduced from *What's On*'s terse review:

LOOK BACK IN ANGER. Play by John Osborne about a disagreeable young man who is at odds with the world, his generation and practically everything, and voices his complaints with tireless ferocity. Kenneth Haigh, Mary Ure, Alan Bates, Helena Hughes.

By comparison, the magazine seemed a little more enthusiastic about Nigel Dennis's offering:

CARDS OF IDENTITY. Nigel Dennis's adaptation of his own novel. A fantastic farce concerning the activities of an advanced group of psychiatrists who hold that the experiences and accidents of life that make us what we are can be expunged from the consciousness and an alternative 'past' substituted, thus changing both character and personality! Michael Gwynn, Joan Greenwood, George Devine, Kenneth Haigh.

Among the other delights on offer that week to the dedicated London theatregoer were shows such as *Dry Rot* with Brian Rix at the Whitehall Theatre (described as a 'farce by John Chapman about the switching of racehorses, set in a country inn infested with wood fungi'), *Gigi*, with Leslie Caron at the New Theatre, and the mother-in-law comedy *Sailor Beware* starring Peggy Mount at the Strand Theatre – a film adaptation of which would be released that September, which included Chelsea's own bongo-playing bohemian Joy Webster as a character named Daphne Pink, and also much further down the cast list in an uncredited role, 23-year-old Michael Caine playing a sailor. Of course, there was also Agatha Christie's *The Mousetrap* at the Ambassadors, which had been there for almost four years and was already billed as the longest run in town. Even the Chelsea Palace on the King's Road was having a go at presenting a play for a few days – *Bad Girl*, with Simone Silva – before reverting to one of its more customary revues, entitled *Nite Life USA*.

At the start of this week in question, July 26, 1956, *Look Back in Anger* had received something of a publicity boost when the *Daily Express* ran an article by John Barber entitled 'Today's Angry Young Men and How They Differ From Shaw'. Presumably, one of the most obvious differences in a year when youth was at a premium would have been that Shaw had been born in 1856, five months after the end of the Crimean War, but even if the crowds were not yet besieging the ticket office at Sloane Square, it all helped to save the play from the fate of previous entries in the season, and it ran steadily though unspectacularly through the summer.

Skiffle or Piffle?

Over in Egypt on July 25, President Gamal Abdel Nasser's government nationalised the Suez Canal – much to the annoyance of the British prime minister Sir Anthony Eden – while back at the *Melody Maker*, musician Alexis Korner was writing a somewhat tongue-in-cheek article about the DIY music craze sweeping Britain, under the title 'Skiffle or Piffle?': 'It is with shame, and considerable regret, that I have to admit my part as one of the originators of the movement; a movement that has become the joy of community songsters and a fair source of income for half the dilettante three-chord guitar-thumpers in London.'

Skiffle was definitely enthusing the young, but by August there was a new trend emerging, that of former UK jazz players jumping ship and emerging as born-again rock'n'rollers just as the cash registers started ringing. No US rockers had yet toured Britain, and the stream of home-grown Larry Parnes discoveries from the 2 I's coffee bar were still a month or two away, so for the moment, there was a definite gap in the market. First in with a band was former Ronnie Scott sideman and jazz drummer Tony Crombie, whose decision to switch sides made him the front-page lead in the August 4 edition of *Melody Maker*: 'CROMBIE FORMS ROCK-AND-ROLL OUTFIT: Britain's first full-time rock-and-roll group hits the road at the end of this month.' After Tony came the deluge, as everyone and his grandmother formed a band, preferably with the words 'Rock' or 'Rockin'n'Rollin'' as part of their name, but the kids could usually tell the real thing from the bandwagon-jumpers anyway, as John Peel told me:

It was such a good time to live through, because you just knew at the time that it was shite. That it was opportunist – you wouldn't have known the word opportunist – but you kind of knew that Gene Vincent was right and that all of this other stuff was wrong. It was exactly that: Musicians' Union people and jazzers thinking, 'Fuck me, we'd better get into this . . .'

The Chelsea Palace went on presenting its regular programmes of girl shows, with imaginative titles like *Folies Can-Can* and *Paris After Dark*, based on the persistent theory that folks across the Channel were enjoying a defiantly smuttier lifestyle than anyone in Blighty, but the real action that summer was at showings of *Rock Around the Clock*. Film trade journal *Kinematograph Weekly* felt the need to address cinema managers directly in its September 5 issue with an article entitled 'Face Up to the "Rough Stuff" Problem':

> Rowdyism in the cinema has hit the headlines again in the national press. This time, Mr John Pound, assistant manager of the Prince of Wales cinema, Harrow Road, London, was slashed and assaulted by hooligans who, it is alleged, were incited by the film *Rock Around the Clock*. [. . .] At Teddington, ten youths causing a disturbance near the Gaumont were arrested; eight of them were under 17. At the Gaumont, Chadwell Heath, Essex, 30 Teddy Boys were thrown out by the police after damaging seats; one was charged with assaulting a constable. At the West Ham Gaumont scores of youths and girls were ejected by the police and one is to be charged. More hooligans were arrested at the Dagenham Gaumont.

The fuss about cinema showings of *Rock Around the Clock* was such that it even prompted *TIME* magazine to run an article in late September about this strangely dressed group of people from England called 'The Teds', complete with a photo of a likely group of velvet-collared lads hanging around on a street corner, one of whom looks disturbingly like a younger version of Joe Strummer. Violence was the main focus of the piece, but it also had the novelty of attempting to introduce American readers to various bits of Cockney rhyming slang: 'a road is a "frog" (from the phrase frog-and-toad, which rhymes with road)', they explained, 'a suit is a "whistle" (from whistle-and-flute), and a girl is a "bird". Whistles and birds are a Teddy boy's major hobbies.' Presumably, not many people were paying attention, because a decade later when the same magazine printed their legendary 1966 Swinging London cover feature, they were still having to explain that girls were called 'birds', but what with Lonnie Donegan hitting the US charts and his recording being covered by seven different American artists, this first recognition of London youth culture and clothing marks the point at which the rest of the world was slowly beginning to take notice.

In Britain, the Teds even had an ITV documentary made about them that year, when as part of producer Caryl Churchill's Associated Rediffusion series *Big City* some Teds from the Elephant and Castle were filmed in and around the streets and bomb sites of their local turf.

Hello Norma Jean

Marilyn Monroe had been in London since July filming *The Prince and the Showgirl*, and caused a sensation on October 11 when she and her new husband Arthur Miller attended the first night of his play *A View from the Bridge* at the Comedy Theatre. Miller – who had been convicted of contempt of Congress after his HUAC appearances, but cleared on a technicality – had revised and expanded his play from the one-act version which appeared in New York the previous year, and this new incarnation directed by Peter Brook starred Anthony Quayle, Richard Harris and, fresh from the Royal Court production of *Look Back in Anger*, Mary Ure. By this time, Ure and John Osborne had become a couple, and they moved into a house just south of the King's Road in Woodfall Street. This short stretch of road comprising only a handful of dwellings was to lend its name to the film company formed by Osborne and Tony Richardson that helped revolutionise British cinema in the coming years.

Credit: R Powell/Daily Herald/Mirrorpix

Marilyn Monroe at the Royal Court watching her husband Arthur Miller,
18 November 1956

At the opening of *A View from the Bridge* at the Comedy Theatre, perhaps unsurprisingly, Marilyn drew all the press attention, and it was a similar story when Arthur Miller appeared in a panel discussion onstage at the Royal Court for a symposium entitled *Cause Without a Rebel*. Marilyn was sitting in the stalls, and as far as the fans outside in Sloane Square were concerned, she might as well have been the only person in the building. Colin Wilson was also onstage taking part in the panel with Miller, as he told me:

> There was discussion at the Royal Court, with me, Arthur Miller and also Wolf Mankowitz. Miller was over for *A View from the Bridge*, and Marilyn was in the audience. When we left, we had to go out the back way, because of the crowds, and there was Arthur Miller, then Marilyn, then me, and when she saw the crowds, it was my hand she instinctively reached for. I honestly think there was an attraction there.

Luckily, it was not only Marilyn by that stage who was drawing people to the Royal Court. In a hugely beneficial publicity move, BBC television broadcast a short excerpt from *Look Back in Anger* on October 16, 1956, introduced by Lord Harewood, and the impact on attendances was immediate. Within two weeks takings had nearly doubled, so that when Osborne's play had to be taken off in order that the next item in the season, Brecht's *The Good Woman of Setzuan*, could be staged, Osborne's play successfully transferred to the Lyric, Hammersmith. At last, the English Stage Company had a genuine hit on their hands.

George Devine had been very keen to present one of Brecht's plays as part of the Royal Court's opening season. Brecht himself had died earlier in the year, but in September 1955, Devine, touring in a production of *King Lear*, had met Brecht and his wife Helene Weigel when appearing at the Hebbel Theatre in Berlin. Over drinks, Devine and Peggy Ashcroft had secured Brecht's approval for a London production of *The Good Woman of Setzuan*. There had already been a number of Brecht productions at other London theatres during the earlier part of the fifties, but his work was regarded by many at the English Stage Company as something of an inspiration for what they were trying to achieve at the Royal Court, both in terms of content and staging. What they were not to know at the time was that much of what they admired in Brecht's plays was actually written over the years by a selection of women, such as Elizabeth Hauptmann, Ruth Berlau and Grete Steffin, who, according to leading Brecht scholar John Fuegi, were consistently denied both written credit and financial reward for their work. *The Threepenny Opera*, perhaps his most famous play, is estimated by Fuegi to be 80 to 90 per cent the work of Elizabeth Hauptmann, and by the same token a fair amount of the credit for *The Good Woman of Setzuan* should apparently go to Grete Steffin.

Regardless of its authorship, and despite George Devine's hopes for the production and a cast which included Peggy Ashcroft, Nigel Davenport, Joan Plowright and even future *Department S* late-sixties cult TV smoothie Peter Wyngarde, it was largely seen as an experiment that failed. Reviewing the play in the pages of *What's On in London*, Kenneth A. Hurren felt that in tackling 'the old theatrical cliché concerning the prostitute with a heart of gold', Brecht had 'expressed himself [. . .] in an inordinately repetitious and tiresome fashion and I can't help feeling that the well-meaning people who are bringing his works to London are grievously misguided.' In the event, the production stuck it out until December 8, after which it was replaced by the somewhat more entertaining prospect of a revival of William Wycherley's comedy from 1675, *The Country Wife*, which did extremely good business, and helped make a star out of Joan Plowright before transferring successfully to the Adelphi. Meanwhile, *Look Back in Anger*'s own transfer at the Lyric, Hammersmith, was still doing very well, and on November 28, Granada Television broadcast a complete performance of the play on the ITV network. John Osborne, currently settling into his new home at 15 Woodfall Street, a short walk from the Royal Court, had come a long way in the few months since *Look Back in Anger*'s opening night, and would no longer have to rely on the bit-part actor's wages he was receiving from the company – such as his small role in *The Good Woman of Setzuan* – in order to pay the rent.

A Swiss Yodeller Struggling Against Croup

In a year when Osborne and others were classified as Angry Young Men, and rock'n'roll and the Teddy boy 'riots' at cinemas were demonised in the press, it turned out that all of them were amateurs when it came to starting trouble: the real thing was kicked off by a collection of genuine Edwardians – prime minister Anthony Eden and his cabinet, who on November 4 voted sixteen to six in favour of an airborne invasion of Egypt, despite 30,000 people opposed to military action demonstrating in Trafalgar Square that day.

The international situation had been growing ever more tense since the Suez Canal had been nationalised by the Egyptians earlier in the year, and war was certainly in the air – Israel had attacked Egypt on October 30, and in a different conflict, Russian tanks rolled into Budapest on November 3. Britain sent the troops into Suez on November 5, bombing Cairo and the surrounding area. The end result was huge condemnation, both in the UK and abroad, particularly from the US and the United Nations. By November 8, Eden's government had declared a ceasefire, and the whole affair pretty much finished his career.

Becoming a focus for popular protest, the Suez crisis acted as a forerunner of the emerging CND campaigns and the sixties anti-Vietnam demonstrations – the younger generation, in particular, had seen the government in a new and more fallible light. As Bernard Levin later wrote when discussing Jimmy Porter's most famous line from *Look Back in Anger*:

> 'There aren't any big, brave causes left' – no slogan has ever been so entirely falsified so quickly. In the sixties, indeed, there were so many big brave causes that disillusion (the ultimate repository of all hopes for such causes) rarely had time to set in properly over one cause before a new fashion in causes had sprung up.

Back at home, while rock'n'roll was being denounced in many quarters as the Devil's music, it was nevertheless having a colossal effect on the entertainment business in general. There had been talk of one of disc jockey Alan Freed's US rock'n'roll package shows playing at the Albert Hall in November, of the kind which he had been promoting with great success at the New York Paramount Theatre. This would have been a huge breakthrough, since his bills that year featured the likes of Gene Vincent, Frankie Lymon, Jerry Lee Lewis and Screamin' Jay Hawkins, but although Freed's lawyer Warren Troob had flown over during the summer to negotiate the details, for some reason it fell through.

If rock'n'roll was yet to come to the Albert Hall, it was nevertheless proving a crowd-puller during the last days of the King's Road's increasingly troubled music hall, the Chelsea Palace. During the second week of November, the Palace had been presenting a rock show headlined by Art Baxter and His Rock'n'Roll Sinners – a London outfit formed by an ex-Ronnie Scott jazz vocalist who had only been gigging a month but shot to short-lived overnight fame by riding the rock bandwagon. The following week saw the music hall reverting to one of its more usual skin shows, *La Revue des Filles*, but all through November and December they were also running a talent competition in conjunction with Radio Luxembourg, which was won four weeks in a row by Chelsea's own Chas McDevitt Skiffle Group. This not only gave these Fantasie coffee bar regulars a chance to play in front of a much bigger audience, but it was also here that they became friendly with another act who had entered the competition, a young singer who called herself Nancy Whiskey, with the result that she joined the McDevitt group. Within six months, their single 'Freight Train' would be in the charts on both sides of the Atlantic, and they appeared alongside the Everly Brothers on the *Ed Sullivan Show*. Nancy left the group a couple of months later, claiming that she had never much liked skiffle in the first place, but even so, their rise from a King's Road coffee bar to international fame made a huge impression on other young UK musicians, as did Donegan's success.

The likes of Lonnie might have had some reviewers perplexed – 'He sings like a Swiss yodeller struggling against croup and St Vitus's Dance' – yet all over the country, the coming sixties generation of musicians were picking up cheap instruments, washboards and tea chests and trying to figure out how to make some noise. The do-it-yourself spirit was very much like that which arrived again in 1976 with UK punk, where Pete Shelley from the Buzzcocks used a guitar whose body had been broken in half, and the drummer from the Worst beat out the rhythm on a plastic kids' kit he had bought in Woolworth's. 'Here's one chord, here's another, now go and form a band' was the message, and as 1956 drew to a close, the possibility of actually getting up and performing in front of people, or maybe even making a record, had been very healthily demystified for large numbers of young people.

Of course, you cannot please everybody: Laurie Henshaw at the *Melody Maker* wrote a virtual end-of-year obituary for the business entitled 'Rock'n'Roll Swamps '56 Music Scene' in which – having quoted a Nottingham clergyman who had been specially wheeled out to call rock'n'roll 'a revival of devil-dancing . . . the same sort of thing that is done in the black magic ritual' – he then despairingly asked: 'Should we pack our portable typewriters and steal away into the night? A thousand times no. While there are musical standards to be upheld, then let the critic shout them above the crowd. Otherwise, abject surrender to the lumbering dictates of the masses and grim prospects of a musical 1984.'

All of which probably made the average sixteen-year-old like rock'n'roll even more. Let's face it, if you were that age in 1956, which type would you prefer: the parent-friendly bowdlerised version of rock presented by Pat Boone – 'I am a religious man', Pat told the press, 'the teenagers showed that they don't want smutty lyrics' – or the one summed up in the hysterical article about the James Dean 'cult' in October's *Picture Post*: 'America has known many rebellions – but never one like this: millions of teenage rebels heading for nowhere, some in "hot-rod" cars, others on the blare of rock'n'roll music, some with guns in their hands. And at their head – a dead leader.'

Still, not everyone in the public eye tarred young people with the same brush. An advert in the October 20, 1956 issue of *Picturegoer* showed a wholesome group of kids who would have been a credit to any Enid Blyton novel advertising a new range of shoes called Clark's Teenagers, available in 'Cherry Red, Teak, or Mint Green Goat'. If only Carl Perkins had run into a pair of the latter before writing his million-seller.

Candles Stuck in Chianti Bottles

The Pheasantry Club at 152 King's Road was the subject of a glowing article in the November 2 edition of *What's On in London*, which gives an evocative picture of Chelsea restaurant life at the time:

> Today the Pheasantry Club is one of the showplaces of Chelsea, right in the heart of the Greenwich Village of London. In a district which is to the West End what the Left Bank of Paris is to the Champs Elysées, the Pheasantry holds sway as a meeting place of the famous. You enter through that remarkable archway, through the charming garden (where, on hot nights, club members take the night air with their Pernods and Camparis), and proceed down the stairs to the quaint bar. This leads, in turn, to the gay, Italianesque restaurant where proprietor Mario Cazzani is waiting to guide you through his French and Italian menu. Here, with candles stuck in Chianti bottles, an accordion trio playing discreetly in the background, gay checked table-cloths on the tables ranged around the walls, the gri-sticks pointing heavenwards – here we are in a distinctive 'atmosphere' duplicated nowhere else in London. [. . .] The spaghetti and tagliatelli here are great. The Shasklik, served on a flaming sword in a darkened restaurant, is superb. The Steak Diane is more than distinctive. Average price of a dish is 8/6d. Membership is only 10/6d. a year. A carafe of Chianti is £1. [. . .] Rossano Brazzi eats here when in London. So do Valentina Cortese and Richard Basehart, Humphrey Bogart and Lauren Bacall. Annigoni, the fashionable portrait painter, always makes his own spaghetti in the huge and spotless kitchens here!

The Chelsea Palace finally closed up shop at the end of December after fifty-three years as a music hall. It saw out its last months with an uneasy mixture of traditional variety acts, leg shows and straightforward music performances. Indeed, the edition of the *Record Mirror* published three days before Christmas contained a half-page picture of home-grown rock outfit Art Baxter and His Rock'n'Roll Sinners posing specially for the paper's cameras on the stage of the Palace, accompanied by a breathless description of Art which revealed that 'he pitches into his act with such furious, knock-about energy, he has to pad himself heavily to avoid serious injury'. One lasting benefit to come from these final bookings was that one night in early October, while Mary Ure was in rehearsals for *A View from the Bridge*, John Osborne had walked up the road from Woodfall Street to catch comic legend Max Miller headline a variety at the Palace. By chance, an earlier act on the bill performed an impression – which Osborne had seen before, of Charles Laughton in the role of Quasimodo – and the seeds of the idea for his next play, *The Entertainer*, were planted. John later wrote: 'A smoky green light swirled over the stage and an awesome banality prevailed for some theatrical seconds, the drama and poetry, the belt and braces of music hall holding up an epic.'

Credit: author's collection

Sean Connery modelling clothes for Vince Man's Shop, July 1957

While Osborne was watching Quasimodo at the Palace, a potential break came through for another Chelsea resident who was still subsisting as a male clothing model for Vince Man's Shop near Carnaby Street ('Pink Shirts For Pale People'), as was duly reported in the Show Talk column of *What's On in London* for November 9: 'Sean Connery, the husky young actor who I mentioned the other week, gets a test for an important role in *The Death of Uncle George*, Nigel Patrick's first film directing chore and starring Charles Coburn.'

At this stage, Ian Fleming had just finished writing a book called *From Russia with Love*, due to be published in 1957, but it was still some years before Connery and Bond would have their mutually beneficial meeting.

The year ended, as ever, with the Chelsea Arts Ball at the Royal Albert Hall. Jazz bands, not rock, were the order of the day, and for a top price of £35 for a box, people could dance from 10pm to 5am to the music of Ted Heath, Ivy Benson, Sid Phillips and Humphrey Lyttelton. On December 22, the last British troops pulled out of Suez, the prime minster took a holiday on medical grounds, and television critic Kenneth Baily was looking back at the first full year of commercial TV in Britain, lamenting ITV's 'deadly repetition, abysmal humour and cheapjack appeal'.

One way or another, it had been quite a year.

8

'A gold filling in a mouthful of decay'

The World's Greatest Song-and-Dance Spoons Man

At the start of 1957, activities in various parts of the King's Road were beginning to make an impression on popular culture: the 'angries' from the Royal Court were a household name, and Mary Quant's designs at Bazaar were steadily building a reputation. After theatre and fashion, the new year added a further sphere of influence – television. The former music hall at 232–242 King's Road, the Chelsea Palace, was converted into a studio by one of the new ITV companies, Granada TV, from which it broadcast each week a stream of live entertainment shows to the nation, featuring some of the biggest names in the business. Bruce Grimes became a production designer for Granada at the new studio when it opened up for business that year, and he lived for much of the time just across the road in Flood Street, as he told me:

Credit: Stan Phillips/Fox Photos/Hulton Archive/ Getty Images

King's Road, June 1958, with Granada TV
(formerly Chelsea Palace music hall) on the right

I used to work at the Chelsea Palace, and we had offices in Flood Street – the art department, you know. We used to do several shows a week: things like *The Army Game*, and there was a horrible programme called *Spot the Tune*. It was black and white television. They were live, nothing recorded, which made it very exciting, particularly on the variety show, *Chelsea at Nine*.

In an era when the nation had only two television channels, *Chelsea at Nine* commanded a huge audience, so that these performances from the King's Road were seen in homes wherever the still-expanding TV network had reached. It began in September 1957, and its musical director, George Melachrino – who, like Bruce, also lived in Flood Street – told the *West London Press*: 'A big new family is coming to work in Chelsea, including two American television experts, a number of British experts, 20 of the most talented singers and dancers in show business, about the same number of musicians and scores of technicians.'

It was also announced that some rehearsals would take place across the road at the Six Bells pub. The assembled cast and crew of the new programme must have therefore been delighted to see it greeted by the *News Chronicle*'s regular TV reviewer James Thomas with the pronouncement that 'it had all the atmosphere of entertainment at Wormwood Scrubs', but just a month later they were already able to present a line-up for one broadcast that featured Charles Laughton, Peter Sellers, Yehudi Menuhin, Anton Dolin and Petula Clark.

A classic weekend variety show, it rounded up anyone interesting who might be passing through town, giving space in particular to some of the finest jazz performers of the age, mixed in on occasion with some other acts who would have had trouble impressing an end-of-the-pier audience at Clacton, as Bruce explained to me:

We did other shows during the week, but *Chelsea at Nine* was weekly, so we used to start on the Monday getting the acts in, and sometimes we wouldn't get the last act until the day before or even on the day, and we had to rustle stuff up for it. The audience was the circle. The stalls down below was all camera tracks and so on, because in those days it was very heavy equipment, and masses of lights and stuff. You were working with three cameras, and you'd be ten minutes into air time – a live show – and one of the cameras would go on the blink, and then you had to wing it. It was hairy, but it was wonderful, because the adrenalin was really pumping and any mistakes were going to be seen by millions of viewers, and that really was exciting.

There were resident dancers – The Grenadiers – and they did two numbers, one dance and one song. There were stand-up comics, there was ballet, there was opera, there were excerpts from all sorts of things. We had Ella Fitzgerald – this was later, when they *were* recording it – and she had to introduce the next act as 'the world's greatest song-and-dance spoons man', and she couldn't do it. I mean, she just cracked up every time, saying this nonsense, and finally they said, look, forget it, we'll do it another way. You know, she just couldn't introduce this *berk* as 'the world's greatest song-and-dance spoons man'.

Omit 'Balls'

Dodgy cutlery players and other failed variety performers were exactly what were occupying the mind of John Osborne that spring as he was writing *The Entertainer* in his new home in Woodfall Street, partially inspired by the Quasimodo impression at the Chelsea Palace the previous autumn. In those days, theatrical works were still subject to censorship by the Lord Chamberlain, and in due course, Osborne submitted his play to the appropriate authorities for vetting, prompting the following reply on March 20: 'Act II: Page 27 alter "pouf", (twice) [. . .] Page 30, alter "shagged" [. . .] Page 43, omit "rogered" (twice) [. . .] Page 44, omit "I always needed a jump at the end of the day – and at the beginning too usually." [. . .] Act III: Page 21, omit "balls".'

While the shrinking violets at the Lord Chamberlain's office were working tirelessly to protect London's theatregoers from everyday life, Osborne's previous opus had been given the honour of being parodied on the BBC Light Programme's *Hancock's Half Hour*, which featured an 'East Cheam Drama Festival' production of a play called *Look Back in Hunger*. Perhaps coincidentally, another *Hancock* episode, broadcast on January 13, 1957, was entitled *Almost a Gentleman*, which many years later became the title for the second volume of John Osborne's autobiography. *The Entertainer* was scheduled for an April premiere at the Royal Court, but before that came a play by Carson McCullers, *The Member of the Wedding*, which opened on February 5. Directed by Tony Richardson and starring Richard Pasco and Geraldine McEwan, it also featured the legendary blues singer Beatrice Reading in an acting role – an early example of the English Stage Company's links to the music world, which proved to be a recurrent theme in the years to come.

That same week, a different kind of music was on offer in London for the first time, as Bill Haley and His Comets began their debut UK tour, amid scenes of good-natured mayhem and massive tabloid press interest. As the first US representatives of the new music to make the journey across the Atlantic, the stakes were high, and everyone, pro and anti, seemed to have an opinion on the matter. 'Haley's No Jumped-Up Jazzman', Cyril Bennett told readers of *Picturegoer*, while 400 fans were taken down on a special train organised by the *Daily Mirror* to meet Haley's boat when it docked at Southampton. The press were waiting for riots at his opening shows at the Dominion, Tottenham Court Road, but, although the crowd response was hugely enthusiastic, the main thing likely to have started trouble was the band's refusal to play more than a half-hour set.

Will Stimulate Rather Than Stun

On February 18, the BBC launched a new current affairs programme called *Tonight;* as Christopher Booker later wrote, 'It was symbolic that the new programme, with its earnest lack of respect and "satirical" interludes, should originally have been put out from a tiny studio in Kensington, far from the centres of the BBC empire.' Although many of the leading lights of the early sixties satire boom were still at university in those days, there were already tell-tale signs appearing. Bernard Levin, later a mainstay of *That Was the Week That Was*, became an early contributor to *Tonight*, while 1957 also saw the opening of the Satire Club in Duke of York Street – whose adverts read: 'Will stimulate rather than stun your intelligence. Food with a political flavour' – some five years ahead of Peter Cook's Soho club The Establishment.

Meanwhile, despite Bill Haley's hugely successful UK tour, the press were gleefully forecasting that rock'n'roll was already on its last legs and due for the scrapyard: 'There will be a need to replace it with a new craze,' *Picturegoer* told its readers in March, 'and the indication from America is that calypso is the answer.' John Peel remembered the attitude of the mid-fifties music papers: 'They were desperate. When people started doing calypso they said, "Ah! Calypso is gonna sweep rock'n'roll away . . ." I remember that. Harry Belafonte, they thought. You could tell the jubilation.'

Just to further emphasise the fact that the squares were attempting to bail out the *Titanic* with a bucket, the finest rock'n'roll film of them all, *The Girl Can't Help It*, opened in London on March 18, featuring the likes of Little Richard, Gene Vincent and Eddie Cochran in glorious Technicolor. Even the BBC TV were at last trying to get in on the act, having launched a music show in February called the *Six-Five Special*, produced by a far-sighted man called Jack Good. For a dying movement, rock'n'roll was looking remarkably healthy.

John Osborne's new play was still tied up in rehearsals and censorship arguments, but on March 11 *Look Back in Anger* returned to the Royal Court, and the English Stage Company was now fielding offers from abroad, which would see it opening later in the year on Broadway and also being presented at the Moscow Youth Festival – although whether Khrushchev also judged this to be 'decadent rubbish', history does not record. Osborne, however, also had his mind on other mediums than theatre. He was interviewed at the Royal Court in late March by the magazine *Films and Filming* about his plans to move into the world of cinema. In an article headed, with wearying predictability, 'Angry Young Film Man', they wrote:

> Playwright John Osborne, who was watching final rehearsals of his new play *The Entertainer* [. . .] told me he is going into films. In fact, right through the hectic days of writing his new play he was preparing a film script of his headline-hitting *Look Back in Anger*. He expects it to go into production this summer, with Tony Richardson (the director of the original stage production) directing the film. Richardson's previous film directing chore was *Momma Don't Allow*, which was shown at the National Film Theatre in the Free Cinema programme.

Osborne and Richardson's new company, in partnership with seasoned movie producer Harry Saltzman, was Woodfall Films – named after the tiny road in which John lived with Mary Ure, just south of King's Road. In actual fact, the film of *Look Back in Anger* finally went into production over a year after the predicted time, largely because of difficulties in raising finance. Although backers were keen to invest in a film of the controversial play, Osborne insisted that Tony Richardson be allowed to direct, and few people wanted to risk money on a man whose previous film experience was limited to having co-directed a twenty-minute 16mm documentary. Because of this delay, Woodfall's debut feature was to be pre-empted in the cinemas as the first of the kitchen-sink dramas by the film adaptation of John Braine's novel *Room at the Top*, which had been published in early March 1957 to generally very favourable reviews, prompting the *Daily Express* to buy the serial rights. The 'angries' were seemingly everywhere that month, and the actor who had originated the part of Jimmy Porter, Kenneth Haigh, was duly profiled in *Picturegoer* magazine under the devastatingly original headline 'He's Looking Around in Anger':

> It looked as though Kenneth Haigh was going to play the British version of America's rebels without a cause – a sort of coffee-bar neurotic. He played that kind of nasty young man in *My Teenage Daughter* and in the sizzling, controversial play *Look Back in Anger*. All of which made Kenneth Haigh ANGRY. [. . .] Though 'classically' trained – Central School of

Drama – he is a firm believer in the Lee Strasberg Method school of acting. He's ANGRY with the actor who can't say 'Pussycat, pussycat, where have you been?' as though it contained a great truth.

Gin and Misery in a Showbusiness Setting

Elsewhere in the same magazine there was also a short piece about another Royal Court actor, 23-year-old Sean Kelly – who had appeared in their autumn production of *The Good Woman of Setzuan* and had since landed a contract with Warwick Films – making a bid for the James-Dean-misunderstood-rebel image: 'Me? I may seem a bit wild. Sometimes I like to look like a Teddy boy. But there's plenty of room for eccentricity in this world.'

Someone else who was breaking into films that month was Tommy Steele, the coffee bar sensation from the 2 I's in Soho, whose debut disc *Rock with the Caveman* first hit the charts at the end of October 1956. Eyebrows were raised in the press and elsewhere, perhaps understandably, that a mere six months later at the ripe old age of twenty he was shooting an autobiographical feature film entitled *The Tommy Steele Story*. By the end of 1957, he was well onto his second film, already shifting his rebellious image in the direction of becoming 'an all-round family entertainer', and within three years would be singing kiddie's songs about a 'Little White Bull'.

An entertainer of a slightly different kind was now limbering up for action at the Royal Court. The English Stage Company had secured a huge publicity coup in obtaining Sir Laurence Olivier for the title role of Archie Rice in Osborne's play. Since Olivier had a crowded schedule and was already committed to opening in a production of *Titus Andronicus* elsewhere during the summer, no time could be spared for lengthy censorship arguments with the Lord Chamberlain's office or the April opening date would be missed. Hence, Osborne gave in to their various petty demands and *The Entertainer* premiered on its intended date of April 10, with every seat already sold out, mostly in tribute to Olivier's pulling power.

When it came to the big day, John had other things on his mind, since he also had to make an earlier appearance at the law courts in the Strand where the divorce case between him and his first wife Pamela was being heard. Admitting adultery, he was granted a decree nisi without costs, whereupon the attendant press headed for the Royal Court to deliver their own judgement on his latest work. In the event, the praise was more for Olivier's acting than for the play itself. The *Observer* called it 'one of the great acting parts of our age' and the *Daily Telegraph* spoke of 'a tour de force of impersonation and disguise', but the *Daily Herald* threw a bucket of cold water over the whole thing, saying, 'For long stabs it was gin and misery in a showbusiness setting, with no hope in sight for anybody. It's so darned depressing.'

After the audience had gone, the cast and crew held an opening-night celebration on the stage of the theatre with impromptu songs from Mary Ure, Osborne, Richard Pasco and Olivier's wife, Vivien Leigh. The great actor himself reprised some of his music hall sketches from the play. As Osborne later remembered the evening: 'Olivier's presence and the sense of occasion prompted the notoriously mean management of the Court to allow us the stage and a few bottles of extremely cheap wine for a party. The band played, stage-hands and actors danced and drank.'

Mary Quant told me: 'Every new production at the Royal Court was greeted with huge excitement and interest. The actors and writers and producers all came to Bazaar. The men brought their girlfriends and very much promoted the clothes at Bazaar. John Osborne and Mary Ure became friends and we spent some weekends together in Oxford.'

A Good Line in Making His Farts Explode

In addition to *The Entertainer*, the Royal Court held a 'French Fortnight' which included the premiere, in French, of Samuel Beckett's new play, *Fin de partie* – a prestigious occasion attended by that country's ambassador. With the new theatre company's reputation established, the plays at Sloane Square followed on at roughly monthly intervals: May 14 saw the opening of the English-language premiere of *The Chairs* by Eugène Ionesco, together with *The Apollo de Bellac* by Jean Giraudoux, adapted by Ronald Duncan, both directed by Tony Richardson; from June 9 it was *Yes, and After* by Michael Hastings, directed by Osborne's old friend John Dexter; then on June 26 *The Making of Moo*, 'A History of Religion in Three Acts' by Nigel Dennis, specially written for the Royal Court. Both John Osborne and George Devine acted in the latter, which starred English Stage Company regular Robert Stephens, who lived nearby in Glebe Place with his wife Tarn. Osborne and Mary Ure socialised frequently with the Stephens, as John later wrote:

> We spent many evenings together eating heartily at the cheap Indian restaurants at the World's End and drinking late into the night. Robert was a rumbustious jokesmith and had a good line in making his farts explode when exposed to a naked match. Actors from the Court, employed or out of work, dropped in at almost any hour at the Stephens' house in Glebe Place.

Another occasion for the Court company to get together presented itself around this time when Osborne, newly divorced from Pamela, married Mary Ure at Chelsea Registry Office on the King's Road. They chose a Sunday morning, hoping to avoid any publicity, but the newsmen showed up anyway. The witnesses were Tony Richardson and the actress Vivienne Drummond – who had lately been appearing in the revised cast of *Look Back in Anger* – and the reception took place around the corner at Au Père de Nico in Lincoln Street, with guests including George Devine and Robert and Tarn Stephens.

Over at the National Film Theatre, the third evening of films presented under the Free Cinema banner had taken place in May. Two of the four were directed by Lindsay Anderson, a friend of Tony Richardson's, who was soon to begin working at the Royal Court. Anderson's two films were *Wakefield Express* and *Every Day Except Christmas* – the latter a documentary about the porters at Covent Garden market. Another of the entries, *Nice Time* by Claude Goretta and Alain Tanner, focused on Piccadilly Circus 'equated with contemporary industrialised culture', featuring those newly successful graduates of the Fantasie coffee bar, the Chas McDevitt Skiffle Group, who hit the charts for the first time the previous month with a song called 'Freight Train'.

Some critics were moved to ask exactly what these documentaries did that had not already been done years before by the old GPO film unit, but nevertheless the Free Cinema movement laid some of the ground rules for the coming kitchen-sink approach. Their 1957 promotional material asked viewers to watch their work 'in direct relation to a British cinema still obstinately class-bound; still reflecting a metropolitan, Southern English culture which excludes the rich diversity of tradition and personality which is the whole of Britain.' The fact that the likes of Anderson had come up from wealthy homes via public school and Oxford University was largely overlooked. For its part, the growing artistic staff of the Royal Court, which Anderson joined that year, also consisted largely of people from an Oxbridge background, such as Richardson, Devine and Anthony Page. Nevertheless, they were instrumental in putting forward working-class subjects and breaking away from the stultifying, drawing-room country house atmosphere of much of the English drama of the preceding years, giving space to new dramatists such as Arnold Wesker, Ann Jellicoe and John Arden.

An innovation at the Royal Court that May, designed to give as many new plays a start as possible under the limited financial circumstances, was the concept of staging one-off performances of rehearsed plays 'without decor' on Sunday evenings. If well-received, they could then be added to the repertoire, but at the very least, the authors would have seen their work presented to the public. The first of these was *The Correspondence Course*, by Charles Robinson, and the idea proved successful enough that 'without decor' presentations on Sunday evenings became a regular part of the theatre's activities.

Your Coffee on a Coffin

By the summer of 1957, coffee-bar culture had thoroughly established itself in London, with new cafes seemingly opening by the week. Themes were becoming more outrageous, perhaps the winner in this category being Le Macabre in Meard Street, whose adverts featured a frisky-looking skeleton chasing a nude woman, accompanied by the slogan 'Your Coffee on a Coffin'. True to their word, the tables were the appropriate shape, with what appeared to be hollowed-out skulls serving as sugar bowls. The proprietor of a new establishment, the Nucleus in Monmouth Street, showed a fine sense of surrealist *élan* when describing his premises to the press in June: 'Its interior is really a reproduction of ideas invented by people whose yearning to create has overcome their mental stability.'

This significant growth in the available number of establishments for eating or drinking was also evident in the King's Road itself, as *What's On in London*'s restaurant critic noted: 'Kensington and Chelsea are nowadays rich in places to eat, Continental restaurants, espresso bars where French food is also served, bars and eating houses colourful, friendly and not expensive.'

In addition to established restaurants such as the Magic Carpet Inn, the Pheasantry and Au Père de Nico, there was now Choys, a Chinese restaurant, at 172 King's Road, while at 44 Old Church Street there was L'Aiglon, which advertised itself as 'Chelsea's Theatre Restaurant'. These were all fine locations in which to entertain friends, and for those larger occasions, well, just across the river there was always Battersea Park. Presumably sensing that its wide-open spaces had a certain something that the average trattoria just couldn't handle, movie mogul Mike Todd (aka Mr Elizabeth Taylor) invited 1,500 'personal guests' to a midnight party in the Battersea Festival Gardens after the premiere of his film *Around the World in 80 Days*, ferrying most of them up the river from Charing Cross. Had they been paying close attention, they would have noticed during the film a scene in which the comedian Cantinflas rides a penny farthing along Upper Cheyne Row.

In September, Osborne's *The Entertainer* was revived at the Palace Theatre, shortly after *Look Back in Anger* had itself returned once more to the Royal Court. This was followed on September 17 by a presentation of *Nekrassov* by Jean-Paul Sartre, starring Robert Helpmann and Margot Cunningham – continuing the English Stage Company's policy of presenting modern European drama in translation. Then, on October 1, the King's Road theatre revolution finally had its first international impact when *Look Back in Anger* opened on Broadway, with Tony Richardson directing the original 1956 London cast. Opening reviews were very good, and within a fortnight they had the benefit of almost two whole pages in *TIME* magazine:

> Jimmy Porter looses his bilious scorn, like a revolving gun turret, on everything within range: art, religion, radio, Sunday, England and, again and again, his wife and mother-in-law. As minutely venomous as a wasp, as sweepingly violent as a whirlwind, his mockery sauced with self-pity, his growl subsiding in a whine, he brings to a vast repository of grievances a commensurate repertory of abuse.

The play hopefully posted to Sloane Square some two years before in response to an advert in *The Stage* by a jobbing repertory actor living on a leaky Thames barge was now receiving national publicity all across America. While not entirely complimentary – the reviewer pointed out, as several English critics had done, that the play essentially runs out of steam after the first act – the article praised both Kenneth Haigh's acting and also Osborne's depiction of 'a gray-as-ashes England where upper-class loss has not meant lower-class gain', concluding that 'not for a good many years has anyone come out of England with playwright Osborne's verbal talent for throwing stones'. Tony Richardson later recalled that he felt Haigh was not pulling his weight, and was even cutting some of his own speeches at will, but that the problem was solved by the play's US promoter, David Merrick, who hired a young woman to jump onstage one night and hit Haigh in the face, ostensibly as a protest against Jimmy Porter's treatment of women. The stunt worked, press reaction was instantaneous, and the play sold out for months on end.

Prances Forward and Slaps the Cheeks

Back at home, John Osborne's talent for throwing stones had certainly not deserted him, as the October publication of a book called *Declaration* proved all too well. Intended as a collection of pieces by some of the new writers and thinkers who had appeared in recent years – many of whom had been labelled Angry Young Men – it received a great deal of press coverage, mostly due to the fact that it contained a piece by Osborne in which he wrote, 'My objection to the Royalty symbol is that it is dead: it is a gold filling in a mouthful of decay.' The response, predictably, was much the same as it would be in 1977 when the Sex Pistols released their 'God Save the Queen' single at the height of Elizabeth II's Silver Jubilee celebrations. *Declaration* had been put together by Tom Maschler with contributions from John Osborne, Colin Wilson, Doris Lessing, Lindsay Anderson, Kenneth Tynan and John Wain, among others. Kingsley Amis had also been approached, but had turned down the offer. An interesting selection of contributors, but as soon as word of John Osborne's comments about the Royal Family were made public, there was trouble, and some of it came from right at home in Sloane Square, as the *Daily Herald* pointed out on October 15:

> A cocktail party for the publication of *Declaration* was banned from London's Royal Court theatre over criticism of Royalty by the Angry Young Man author John Osborne. Mr Reginald Poynter got a telegram from Mr Neville Blond, chairman of the English Stage Company, saying: 'We will not permit the party to be held in any part of the theatre.' He also got a call from Mr George Devine who said, 'Members of the Council are shocked at the John Osborne piece and in particular at the references to royalty. They wish to be disassociated from the book in every way.'

Denied the hospitality of the Court, the launch was instead held further up the King's Road at the Pheasantry, where the guests included the actor Rod Steiger and politicians Michael Foot and Aneurin Bevan, but not Colin Wilson. 'No, I didn't go to the *Declaration* launch party,' he explained, 'although Doris Lessing told me just the other day that it had sold rather well, and helped to launch Tom Maschler's career.'

L-R: Bill Hopkins, John Wain, Lindsay Anderson, Tom Maschler, Doris Lessing and Kenneth Tynan at the *Declaration* launch party, October 14, 1957

The author Kenneth Allsop – writing about *Declaration* only a few months after publication in his entertaining book-length study of the new movement, *The Angry Decade* (1958) – was far less concerned with Osborne's views about the Queen than about Lindsay Anderson's contribution, entitled 'Get Out and Push', in which he 'prances forward and slaps the cheeks of lots of people he thinks haven't enough contact with the worker':

> Anderson makes documentary films and, staunchly uninfluenced by the fact that he has also made *The Adventures of Robin Hood* for Independent Television, here denounces the British cinema industry as commercial and corrupt. [. . .] This phoney idealism, this bogus 'common man' identification done in a corduroy cap and with a private income, is exactly the sort of 'sincerity' George Orwell loathed, for it has all the stink of that guilt-ridden period of cocktail party Communists and Mass Observation Balliol men with an uneasy 'pleb' accent.

It was not only the *Declaration* launch party that was being given the cold shoulder by the Royal Court that autumn. Colin Wilson had written a play for the English Stage Company called *The Death of God*, as he explained to me: 'I had a meeting with George Devine and he said, well send it in, maybe we can do it as a Sunday-night performance [without decor] and then if it's a success then we could stage it properly. I sent it in, and it was eventually returned to me just with a rejection slip.'

The *Daily Mail* got wind of the story, and published an article which was headlined 'Outsider's Play Thrown Out', in response to which Ronald Duncan from the Royal Court was quoted as saying: 'The play was bad. [. . .] You can detect the influence of *Arms and the Man*, but the main inspiration seems to be a TV children's serial.' By contrast, a writer who did succeed in making it through the Court's selection process that October was John Arden, whose play *The Waters of Babylon* was given a Sunday night performance, marking the start of his long association with the English Stage Company.

Lizzie Strarta and the Aristo-Fannies

On October 21, 1957, an article in *The Times* mentioned the unfamiliar word 'boutique' in relation to the selling of clothes, while John Francis Lane of *Films and Filming* magazine casually let drop that month that he had been dining out in Chelsea with Luchino Visconti and Marcello Mastroianni, whose film *White Nights* was currently appearing at the London

Film Festival. Meanwhile, over in an obscure part of Soho, a former employee of Vince Man's Shop had now set up under his own name and was advertising as 'John Stephen of London, 5 Carnaby Street – Contemporary Clothes in an Edwardian Atmosphere'. His first shop had opened earlier in the year around the corner in Beak Street, but he had recently moved due to a fire. John's parents had attended the opening night of Bazaar in the King's Road some two years previously, and Mary Quant spotted them taking notes.

Still on the subject of fashion, in a year when many teenagers were attempting to dress like James Dean, it is interesting to see John Taylor, editor of *Tailor and Cutter* and *Man About Town*, solemnly warning readers of the December 7, 1957 issue of *Picturegoer* against that degenerate item of clothing, blue jeans, using the kind of patronising language that less house-trained members of the landed gentry might reserve for dealings with their servants: 'Stop making yourselves ridiculous. I mean you kids. [. . .] When you cram yourself into a pair of jeans just because Elvis, Terry or Tommy wears them, you're acting like a child with a Lone Ranger set. [. . .] My mother and father were mad about Al Jolson. But they didn't go around all blacked-up . . .'

In the November 22 edition of *What's On in London* there seem to have been enough Chelsea restaurants for the district to merit its own page of adverts for the first time. Alongside the usual suspects, there were also newer ones such as the John-dory, a seafood restaurant at 144 King's Road ('Unlicensed. You are welcome to bring your own wines'), and also the Blue Cockatoo, which billed itself as being in 'Old Chelsea. Wine and dine by candlelight, 35 Cheyne Walk'. The 'Night Life' column in the same copy of *What's On in London* carried the following news item:

> Last minute change at the Embassy Club [6 Old Bond Street] this week means that blues singer Beatrice Reading is topping the bill there. Beatrice, who made a big hit as a straight actress in *The Member of the Wedding*, has another acting role in *Requiem for a Nun* which opens next week at the Royal Court Theatre.

The play in question was written by William Faulkner, and had already been produced in New York. American actress Ruth, who starred in the Court production with her husband Zachary Scott, also owned the UK rights to the play. It opened on November 26, following on from the still-popular *Look Back in Anger*. However, just as the previous year at this 'writer's theatre' had ended not with work by a new playwright but with a

revival of a 17th-century comedy, the Royal Court saw out 1957 with
something that made the author of *The Country Wife* look positively youthful,
opting for a work written sometime around the 4th century BC: the anti-war
comedy *Lysistrata* by Aristophanes. Kenneth A. Hurren in *What's On in
London* was less than impressed: 'Not even the elaborately stylised frivolities
and interminable choral chants with which Minos Volanakis tediously
embellishes his production at the Royal Court can extend the playing time
of *Lysistrata* (here pronounced 'Lizzie Strarta') by Aristophanes (presumably
'Aristo-fannies').'

The annual Chelsea Arts Ball saw out the year, although as an institution,
because of the killjoys, it would not see out the decade. Margery Sharp's
new novel, *The Eye of Love*, featured a hero and heroine who first meet at
this event in the Albert Hall: 'He went as a paper parcel, and she as a
Spanish dancer'. Bruce Grimes, then working for Granada TV at the old
Chelsea Palace, remembers going to the Arts Ball:

> I used to go there in the late fifties, the last couple of years before it
> packed up. It was all kind of fancy dress stuff, but you know, it was
> a pretty wild party, and it went on upstairs, in all the galleries and
> boxes. There's a tale or two there . . . Then it used to split up into
> parties and moved on. It went through the next day, mostly. You kind
> of crashed out the following night.

Of course, events like these would not have gone down well with the
authorities in North Carolina, where, as *LIFE* magazine reported in December,
the state Baptist convention on dancing had just renewed a ban on the practice which had been in place since 1937: 'An anti-dance delegate said,
"Dancing deteriorates the spiritual atmosphere, wherever it takes place".'

Well, as the old saying goes, it does if you're doing it right.

9

'Indefensible drivel'

An Ineffably Vulgar Comedian

For all those who were not yet heartily sick of hearing about John Osborne by this stage, the news was looking pretty favourable: the January 1958 edition of *Good Housekeeping* magazine ran an article entitled 'A short directory to Angry Young Men', profiling the playwright alongside Colin Wilson, Kingsley Amis and the usual suspects, while *What's On in London* reported the triumphal progress of his newest work: '*The Entertainer*: now a hit in London and soon to open in New York, will shortly open in Paris, with Eddie Constantine in the Olivier role.' Not bad for a show the same magazine had summed up elsewhere with the words 'Laurence Olivier as an ineffably vulgar comedian reduced to presenting himself in tenth-rate girls shows.'

An actor now living around the corner from the Royal Court who was achieving worldwide recognition around the same time as John Osborne was Christopher Lee, having completed filming his definitive performance in the title role of *Dracula* for Hammer on January 3, 1958, which would cause a sensation when released in May. His previous role, that of the Creature in Hammer's *The Curse of Frankenstein* (1957), made Lee's name but not his face famous, since that had been almost completely hidden under all the make-up, but it was his suave and urbane portrayal of the Count which elevated him to international stardom.

Christopher Lee told me that he would attend productions at the Royal Court at this time: 'I saw some of them, naturally. There were some very fine actors for the *type* of play that was written. Some of them were remarkable plays with some remarkable actors.' As for the production of *The Entertainer* with Laurence Olivier, 'I thought that was a superb play, superbly acted. Of course, they didn't pick on an unknown actor.'

John Osborne himself travelled over to New York for *The Entertainer*'s New York debut – it had opened in Boston, and then moved on to Broadway, close by the theatre in which *Look Back in Anger* was still running – having taken along with him a present for his wife Mary Ure which he had purchased at Bazaar in the King's Road. He later recalled: 'I went to pick up Mary. She had discarded the Mary Quant dress I had brought back for her and was wearing a middle-aged, flouncy black number from Saks, topped by one of those skull-cap ornaments favoured by American ladies-who-lunch.' She might have been worried that Quant designs at that stage would have been a little too radical or youth-orientated for American tastes, since it was not until the following year that Mary Quant and Alexander really made headway in the US market with their trips to New York. Still, it was an interesting example of two strands of the emerging King's Road popular culture meeting as they began to gain recognition in places a long way away from Chelsea.

An Angry Young Brawl

While other parts of the world were just about to have a taste of Royal Court action, back at home long-time Chelsea resident George Melly was appearing with the Mick Mulligan band and a stellar cast of British jazz performers in the Albert Hall at what was billed as an 'All Night Carnival of Jazz' on January 17. For those who think late-night club gigs are a relatively recent phenomenon in London, it is worth pointing out that the event was scheduled to run from 10.30pm to 7am, and the bars were licensed till 1.45am, a good three hours later than normal.

February 1958 brought a hugely influential US rock'n'roll act to Britain, the Crickets, who since the autumn of 1957 had been releasing so many hit records that their record label had begun issuing some under the band name and some under the name of their singer, Buddy Holly. Hence, 'That'll Be the Day' had charted in September 1957 as a Crickets single, 'Peggy Sue' as a Holly single in December, followed a couple of weeks later by 'Oh Boy' as the Crickets, then another two hits in March 1958 with 'Listen to Me' (Holly) and 'Maybe Baby' (Crickets). These were all written and recorded by the same band, and it was their line-up – two guitars, bass, drums – which went on to be copied by the Beatles and just about every other UK rock act. Holly's subsequent fame has obscured the fact that this was a group act, and was seen as such by the British teenagers who watched that February UK tour and went off looking to buy red Fender Stratocasters just like Holly's, and to form groups of their own. Mick Jagger's first ever experience of live rock music was a Crickets show at Woolwich Granada, while a young Malcolm Edwards, later known as McLaren, saw the same tour at the Finsbury Park Astoria. Elvis was always huge in Britain, but it was the Crickets who taught many future UK rock musicians what a band should look like and that maybe you should think about writing your own material.

Down on the King's Road, the Classic Cinema at number 148, which dated back before the First World War, was being given what was in all likelihood a much-needed overhaul: 'The little Classic Cinema in King's Road, Chelsea, neighbour of the new coffee bars, the Greek, Italian, Chinese and Indian restaurants, and old antique shops, is rapidly taking on a New Look to suit the changing times. Eventually it will emerge as a place of entertainment of which the borough can be proud.' Across the road from the Classic, a cafe which was to become a Chelsea institution was advertising itself that February in these words: 'The Place to meet your friends is PICASSO RESTAURANT AND COFFEE BAR. Snacks and all Meals available at all Times'. By now, the coffee-hungry masses had a formidable choice available to them on the King's Road: the Fantasie at number 128; Hernando's Hideaway at number 229; the Orrery at number 355; Picasso at number 127 and Sa Tortuga at number 51.

Meanwhile, in Sloane Square, John Osborne's past was coming back to haunt him, as his pre-*Look Back in Anger* play *Epitaph for George Dillon* – co-written with Anthony Creighton – was finally given an outing at the Royal Court, directed by William Gaskill, with Yvonne Mitchell, Robert Stephens and Wendy Craig among the cast. Osborne had originally dug out the script the previous year in response to a request from the Oxford Experimental Theatre Club, who had mounted a production of it. According to his version of events, this had encouraged George Devine to think about bringing it to the Court, despite the fact that Devine himself felt it to be 'an apprentice work unwisely resurrected'.

Running in parallel with Osborne's play was *The Sport of My Mad Mother*, featuring a group of violent Teddy boys and the Indian goddess of destruc-tion, which opened on February 28. This was the debut work by Ann Jellicoe, who had come to attention via a play-writing competition run by the *Observer*, and whose 1961 play, *The Knack*, was to become, in Richard Lester's hands, one of the films most associated with the thing which became known as 'Swinging' London.

Other developments that February included a new arts programme on
BBC TV called *Monitor*, presented by Huw Wheldon – which proved influential, not least in that it gave the young Ken Russell a platform to begin
making short films   and also the launch meeting at Conway Hall of an
organisation called the Campaign for Nuclear Disarmament, which staged
the first of its Aldermaston marches that Easter.

According to the press, peace campaigners might also have been required
in Sloane Square, as they gleefully reported that the Young Men had indeed
become even more Angry than usual. The occasion was the Sunday night
without decor staging at the Royal Court of a play called *The Tenth Chance*
written by Stuart Holroyd, a friend of Colin Wilson and fellow *Declaration*
contributor. It was directed by John Osborne's *George Dillon* co-author
Anthony Creighton, with a cast including James Villiers, Ronald Fraser,
and, according to Osborne, 'the daily who cleaned Woodfall Street'. There
were disturbances in the theatre during the performance, and then later,
in the pub next door, Osborne writes that Colin Wilson kicked over the
critic Kenneth Tynan's chair, because he had noisily walked out of the play
before the performance was over. 'The following morning,' said Osborne,
'I read that I had been at the centre of "an angry young brawl" in a
Chelsea pub.' Colin Wilson, who attended the play with its author Stuart
Holroyd and their mutual friend, the writer Bill Hopkins, gave me his
memories of the evening:

> My friend Stuart Holroyd had written a play, and Christopher Logue
> and Ken Tynan were in the audience. During the performance, Logue
> stood up and shouted 'Rubbish!' and then walked out. Tynan walked
> out as well. I was sitting in the stalls near the front and when he
> walked past me I said, 'Look, if your friend wants to criticise the play,
> why doesn't he do it in the proper place, like a newspaper?' Tynan
> just said 'G-g-g-g-get out of my way.' Anyway, we were all standing
> outside, me and Bill Hopkins and Stuart Holroyd and various wives
> and so on, and we decided to go next door to the pub for a drink.
> Christopher Logue was in there, leaning back on one chair with his
> feet on another, and Stuart's wife went up and just started screaming
> at him, and he fell off his chair. I went up to him while he was lying
> there and he looked up and obviously thought I was going to kick
> him in the head.
>
> We all went on to a friend's flat which was around the corner in
> Sloane Street for another drink, and after a while, I was going down
> the corridor and I heard Bill in another room calling up one of the

papers and going, 'Is that the *Daily Express*? Did you know there was a fight with the Angry Young Men tonight in a bar next to the Royal Court? Yes, Osborne was there, but he wasn't directly involved. And Bill Hopkins, that's B . . .I . . .L . . .L . . .' That's how that got into the papers.

It Doesn't Bark, and It Knows the Secrets of the Sea

Another way to appear in the press that year was to run a restaurant, a coffee bar or a nightclub. London had woken up with a vengeance in the previous two years, and in the Chelsea area it seemed as if new places were opening virtually every few days. As a measure of how profitable these ventures could be, April 21 saw the extremely expensive relaunch of the Casino de Paris in Denman Street as an upmarket strip joint, with a show allegedly costing £30,000 to stage. The two men responsible for this, Eric Lindsay and Ray Jackson, had both been out-of-work actors in 1956 when they decided to open a coffee bar called Heaven and Hell at 57 Old Compton Street. Riding the coffee bar craze with a good gimmick – upstairs was heaven, downstairs was hell – they made money hand over fist and were in a position a mere two years later to also take on the much larger Casino de Paris. Lindsay and Jackson were profiled admiringly just before the launch in *What's On in London*, and the same issue also featured an interview with the man who was probably the most successful restaurateur on the King's Road in those days, George Brampton from the Magic Carpet Inn at number 124:

> When ex-RAF photographer George Brampton and his pretty wife Gwen took over this charming eating house twelve years ago it was a derelict shop formerly a butcher's. Now it is a veritable wonderland, full of red leather, discreet lamps, coloured lights and wall after wall covered with modern paintings, most of them by Chelsea artist Robin Goodwin (whose nudes manage to create quite an appetite for dinner!). [. . .] The waiters wear bright red waistcoats. Candles glow in Chianti bottles. Multi-coloured glass lamps swing from the ceiling. The wall settees are enticing. And pretty Pat Honni plays discreet accordion music in the background.

The secret of Brampton's success had been to hire a decent French chef, and then also to employ Italian and Turkish chefs as well, initially making his restaurant something relatively exotic in the austere culinary atmosphere of early-fifties London. 'You must remember that I was something of a pioneer in opening an eating house in Chelsea on Continental lines,' Brampton claimed. 'Now, of course, there are many similar establishments in Chelsea and Kensington.'

By this time, Mary Quant had moved from her bedsit in Oakley Street and was living in the building that Archie McNair owned, directly above the Fantasie coffee bar. Their business kept taking on more employees – in addition to the women working the sewing machines, they had also recruited a cutter – and as space became more of a problem, Archie's front room was turned into a workplace. In response to great demand, they opened a second branch in Knightsbridge, but this did not solve their basic manu-facturing space problems, and so McNair walked around the area between the King's Road and their new store, eventually finding a building roughly midway between the two, in Ives Street, which they could use as a head-quarters for the business and a workshop. The partnership of Quant, Plunket Greene and McNair purchased the building, which became a permanent base for Mary Quant Limited for the immensely successful years to come.

Bazaar in the King's Road dressed its shop window to lure in or merely just to entertain passers-by, and sometimes Quant and Plunket Greene would hide nearby in order to listen to people's reactions to the various displays. On one occasion the window was completely filled with empty milk bottles, with just a single tailor's figure disappearing out of view and a sign saying 'Gone Fishing'; at other times figures were suspended upside-down from the ceiling. The main thing was to get a reaction. They once stood a figure in the window, leading a large lobster (deceased) on a gold chain – a move reminiscent of the actions of the 19th-century French poet Gérard de Nerval who had walked through the Jardin des Tuileries with a live lobster on a silk ribbon instead of a dog. When asked why, he replied 'Because it doesn't bark, and it knows the secrets of the sea.'

Resounding Tinkles and Mad Passionate Love

Such proto-surrealist sentiments would have probably been very much to the taste of the next writer whose work was presented at the Royal Court, N. F. Simpson, who, like Ann Jellicoe, had come to the attention of the English Stage Company by way of the play-writing competition run by the *Observer*. A double bill of his works consisting of *A Resounding Tinkle* and *The Hole* opened on April 2 – the former being the everyday tale of a suburban couple who keep an elephant in their back garden. In fact, the

Court performed only the first part of *A Resounding Tinkle*, and a little later, when an undergraduate called John Bird at the Cambridge Amateur Dramatic Society managed to organise a performance of the reputedly unstageable complete version, with a cast including a pre-*Beyond the Fringe* Peter Cook, he was offered a job at the Royal Court as a result.

The play that followed the Simpson double bill was *Flesh to a Tiger* by Barry Reckord, a Jamaica-set piece featuring an almost entirely black cast. 'Vividly conveys the chanting, writhing, drum-throbbing, candle-lit fervour of semi-pagan rites', said the *Daily Mail*, but although the performance of Cleo Laine was widely praised, the play itself was generally held to be confused at best, and at a time when vicious race riots were about to break out in Notting Hill, it may well have seemed to have had only a slim connection to anything approaching real life. The English Stage Company also ended the year with its second production of 1958 to feature a largely black cast; in this case, a work by the West Indian playwright Errol John entitled *Moon on a Rainbow Shawl*, which had also come to the Court's attention when it was entered in the same *Observer* play-writing competition that had produced Ann Jellicoe and N. F. Simpson. Over at Joan Littlewood's Theatre Royal, Stratford East, another part of the upcoming kitchen-sink scene was falling into place with the opening in May of nineteen-year-old dramatist Shelagh Delaney's debut play *A Taste of Honey*.

One of the biggest successes among the programmes regularly broadcast from the old Chelsea Palace by Granada TV was the sitcom *The Army Game*, which had made stars of performers like Bernard Bresslaw and Alfie Bass. Its popularity was such that four of the cast reached the Top Five of the charts in May with the imaginatively titled single 'The Signature Tune of The Army Game'. Just to prove that this was no fluke, Bresslaw then released a very successful solo record, sung in character, titled 'Mad Passionate Love', which even scored some US sales. The series spawned a sequel series named after two of the characters, *Bootsy and Snudge*, also made by Granada at the Chelsea Palace. Then the newly successful Hammer Film Productions – currently engaged in making *The Revenge of Frankenstein* starring Peter Cushing – announced to the press in May that they were about to begin filming a big-screen version of *The Army Game*. This duly appeared in London cinemas in November, under the title *I Only Arsked* (a deliberately mis-spelled catch-phrase of Bresslaw's from the show), and featuring many of the King's Road regulars in the cast. The success of this film prompted Hammer to then star Bresslaw in their rock'n'roll-themed Jekyll and Hyde comedy, *The Ugly Duckling*, in which Bresslaw's mild-mannered character turns into a smooth-talking Teddy boy at the local Palais after drinking a potion.

Granada continued to bring an impressive mixture of talent to the King's Road for their weekly variety show, *Chelsea at Nine*, and some of the finest names in jazz performed on the show at one time or another, as Bruce Grimes told me: 'I was there when Duke Ellington appeared, that was great. We also had Erroll Garner, on the piano, we had Oscar Peterson . . . I'm pretty sure we also had Louis Armstrong, in fact, I'm positive we had Louis Armstrong.'

In March 1958, *Chelsea at Nine* featured the great early rock pioneer and inspirational electric guitarist Sister Rosetta Tharpe, who had been touring the UK with the Chris Barber Band. Mixed in with music performers of this calibre, there were also entertainers who, despite the efforts of certain un-named spoons players, succeeded in giving the show a deserved reputation for quality comedy. Although the Goons were exclusively a BBC phenomenon, Bruce Grimes remembers Spike Milligan appearing on the show around this time, as well as another comedian who had been a Goon in former years:

> We had Mike Bentine, he used to do skits there. He was crazy. I did a Flea Race for him. We rigged it all up in the art department and he came to see how it all worked and have a little rehearsal on it, and he came round in full Ascot kit – the grey felt hat, you know, the works. He was absolutely insane, walking around the table with his binoculars on looking at this flea table and giving a commentary, it was hilarious. Bruce Lacey was another guy we had. He used to turn up in the King's Road in full safari outfit, complete with gun stuck in a Sam Browne belt and all the rest of it, or Chinese armour.

Artistic Suicide

While Granada was entertaining the nation on ITV, the only other TV channel, BBC, had been running a show since the previous year called *Six-Five Special*, aimed squarely at its teenagers and produced by a forward-thinking man from the Home Counties called Jack Good who was to revolutionise music television coverage in both the UK and America. The first show of its new series aired on June 15, 1958, featuring, among others, home-grown coffee-bar sensation Marty Wilde and blues-singing sometime Royal Court actress Beatrice Reading. *Six-Five Special* was a decent showcase for UK acts, but hardly a call to teenage revolution, although you would not necessarily have thought so if you listened to clergymen like Dr Donald Soper, the 'famous Methodist preacher and a man respected by all religious denominations' according to *Melody Maker*, who printed a lengthy interview with him in one of their regular attacks on rock'n'roll, under the non-controversial headline 'Artistic Suicide': 'I watch *Six-Five Special* sometimes – as a penance,' said Soper. 'I'm perplexed. I can't understand how intelligent people can derive any sort of satisfaction from something which is emotionally embarrassing and intellectually ridiculous.' The previous year, he had knocked popular music in general, saying that young people's supposed 'frustration' was 'the only explanation for rock'n'roll and the slush which is included in the average jazz song'.

Soper – raised to the House of Lords as a Labour peer in 1965 by Harold Wilson, who gave four rock'n'roll fans named the Beatles the MBE the same year – had already been lecturing the teenagers of the nation for several decades by this stage, and popular working-class entertainments of various kinds seem to have annoyed him. Back in 1938, he told an audience at a public meeting in London that: 'The good-time girl and the boy whose mind goes no further than the football pool and the cinema are representative of the age in which we live. Such habits as the reading of the Bible and being home by nine o'clock have passed away and with them the whole moral outlook.'

In the same week that Dr Soper's least favourite programme returned to the BBC, chart-topping Chelsea skiffler Chas McDevitt opened his own coffee bar at 44 Berwick Street, and unsurprisingly named it after his first hit, 'Freight Train'. By then, Chas was enough of a star that the film magazine *Photoplay* felt the need to interview his fan-club secretary, 21-year-old Christine Addy, for their July issue: 'I happened to be in a coffee bar in Chelsea where Chas was performing,' she told Raymond Hyams. 'Most of the group used to play there. When he finished his act we began talking in the informal way one does in these places and I soon became interested in skiffle and the exciting life of show business.'

British rockers might have been making headlines, but nothing quite like the kind that Jerry Lee Lewis was causing on his debut UK tour. The Killer hit the front page of the *Daily Mirror* on May 26, alongside his thirteen-year-old wife Myra, under the headline 'Police Check Up On Child Bride'. Many Teds will probably have noted the suave black drape jacket with fake leopard-skin trim and string tie which Lewis was wearing in the accompanying picture – here at last was a rocker who dressed like they did. On June 7, in his regular column for *Disc*, TV producer Jack Good reported on one of the Killer's shows at the Regal Cinema, Edmonton – one of only a handful which took place before the tour was cut short in a blizzard of angry headlines and questions asked in parliament – where similar sharp threads were on show: 'He dashed onto the stage in a bright pillar-box red suit with black velvet collar, cuffs and pockets.' As the original 1940s hipsters used to say, the man was a shape in a drape.

In the world of women's fashion, skirts had been growing progressively shorter for a while now – although they were still positively floor-length by sixties standards, and short in 1958 meant just below the knee – but *What's On in London*'s resident style guru Shirley Davenport was moved to predict in her 'Woman's World' column in the June 27 issue that the trend could not possibly last: 'In just a few short months our even shorter skirts will be thrown to the moths. I can already see them gathering on the horizon – or in the wardrobe – like a swarm of locusts sharpening up their mandibles for the banquet.'

However, at this stage, it is clear that she and other commentators assumed that the right to set the trend for skirt lengths or anything else in fashion lay pretty much exclusively with the Paris designers. Returning to the same theme in August, Shirley brought news that the French had declared that skirts would soon get longer: 'Another quick death sentence has been pronounced from Paris, and millions of women are holding their breaths waiting for the merciless guillotine to fall on Short Skirts.'

As it turned out, the woman who was eventually to have the final say in these matters was currently working away at her designs not far away in the King's Road, a street which was to make a huge contribution to the ending of decades of the French reputation for setting the worldwide fashion agenda.

Surrealist Rubbish!

While fashion commentators were arguing whether knees should be revealed, there was also a fair-sized argument brewing among theatre critics about the new developments in drama which had been seen on London stages in the past couple of years, some of which had found a sympathetic home at the Royal Court. Depending on which critic you happened to be reading, the likes of Osborne, Beckett, Ionesco, N. F. Simpson and Harold Pinter were either the leading lights of the avant-garde or a pack of charlatans. Chief among their defenders were Kenneth Tynan in the *Observer* and Harold Hobson at the *Sunday Times*, whereas Kenneth A. Hurren at *What's On in London* seems to have been finally pushed over the edge to declare war on the new tendency once and for all after having seen the Royal Court's Tony Richardson-directed Ionesco double bill of *The Chairs* and *The Lesson*, which opened on June 18.

Pausing briefly to dismiss Pinter's *The Birthday Party* as 'indefensible drivel', he went on to argue that 'the vogue for nonsense drama, for the theatre's equivalent of Action Painting, and for symbolism pushed to the point of obscurity, is getting right out of hand'. As for the two plays currently at the Court, he praised the acting while damning the content: 'Miss Plowright, who appears as a nonagenarian in the first play and as a seventeen-year-old student in the second, demonstrates a versatility no less awe-inspiring because the mental age of both characters is about six.'

The production was met with a fair amount of robust abuse in the theatre itself, where Devine and Plowright were fielding audience cries of 'Surrealist rubbish!' and the banging of chairs as patrons walked out mid-act. Largely enjoying such proceedings, the actors began incorporating these noises into their own dialogue.

Everyone, or so it seemed, had an opinion about the Angry Young Men, and a book-length appraisal of the situation appeared that summer in the form of Kenneth Allsop's *The Angry Decade* – a thoroughly entertaining dissection of the literary and dramatic upheavals of the preceding years. He was quick to state that many of these artistic innovations were irrelevant to much of the population: '*Waiting for Godot* may have caused palpitations of conjecture in the King's Road, but the argument did not penetrate much farther north than Hampstead Garden Suburb.' Interestingly, at a time when the film of *Look Back in Anger* was just about to go into production at Associated British Elstree Studios, Allsop held to the view that the impact of the play was already something of a spent force: 'When Jimmy Porter arrived there was a fair amount of fast identifying, but the suddenness with which that dropped away shows that, despite his trenchant turn of phrase which enlivened the ear, there was nothing of any size or depth to identify with.'

Despite such criticisms, Tony Richardson, having succeeded in annoying Kenneth A. Hurren with his Ionesco double bill, moved straight into work on the film adaptation of *Look Back in Anger*, which, although mostly to be shot at Elstree, would also feature London location work filmed at Stratford East, Dalston Junction and Deptford Market. Never having directed a feature film before, it is not surprising that the on-set interview Richardson gave to *Films and Filming* magazine suggests that he got off to a somewhat shaky start:

Tony Richardson, bright young theatre director, who shot to fame with *Look Back in Anger* and *The Entertainer*, at London's Royal Court Theatre, told me that the first day's shooting on the film version of John Osborne's 'angry' play was 'hell'. Richardson, however, began to recover his strength over a couple of vodka and tonics, and passed on the news that cinemagoers are unlikely to believe their ears when they go and see Nigel Kneale's film adaptation of the Angry Young Man saga. Said Richardson: 'The dialogue is going to be stronger.' I pointed out (tactfully) that I didn't think it could be much stronger than the play. To which Richardson replied: 'We're after an "X" certificate. If it isn't stronger, at least we are not going to make any concessions.'

Richardson also shocked some by commenting that he might even prefer directing films to directing plays, which sounded like heresy to many followers of the new drama. Screenwriter Nigel Kneale had been recommended to Woodfall by Kenneth Tynan. Kneale was best known to the public for his immensely successful science fiction stories *The Quatermass Experiment* and *Quatermass II*, which had been huge television successes and had then been filmed equally well for Hammer by one of their finest directors, Val Guest. Osborne himself seems to have been content to leave the adaptation of his work to someone else at this point, but his wife Mary Ure still played the role of Alison, which she had originated at the Royal Court. The major change was that the actor playing Jimmy Porter was to be Richard Burton, not Kenneth Haigh, which gave the low-budget film some much-needed star appeal. As Osborne recalled, Burton was 'a huge asset to our modest under-taking, which was regarded with general suspicion from Wardour Street'.

A Christ Figure Called Pilchard

While Richardson and Osborne were still making preparations for their film venture, the shooting of the cinema adaptation of John Braine's *Room at the Top* was already underway on location in Yorkshire that June, starring Laurence Harvey and Heather Sears, both of whom had previously appeared in English Stage Company productions at the Court. Braine was paid £5,000 for the film rights – a considerable sum in those days, enough to buy a fair-sized house in most parts of the country. Mind you, by the summer of 1958 it was estimated he had already earned a further £12,000 from sales of the novel. With rewards like that, some of the writers may have been young, but it would be interesting to see how angry they could remain under the circumstances, and it calls to mind the famous example of John Lennon asking his listeners to imagine 'no possessions' while singing the video in his Grade II listed Georgian mansion in 72 acres of grounds, which he sold in 1973 for the then colossal figure of £500,000.

Of course, Lennon in 1958 was still a teenage skiffle player up in Liverpool, covering songs made famous by the likes of Elvis, the Crickets, Lonnie Donegan and yes, the Chas McDevitt version of 'Freight Train'. As it was, the developing trend in British novels and cinema towards a more gritty, working-class and frequently northern subject matter helped pave the way for the eventual acceptance of a group from Liverpool at the end of 1962. Interestingly, Paul McCartney told Barry Miles that when he and Lennon first began songwriting in their Quarrymen days, they also tried to write a play 'involving a Christ figure called Pilchard' which seems to have been influenced by goings on at the Royal Court: 'We only got two pages but I can remember it quite clearly. There was the mother and the young daughter of the family sitting at home in a kind of John Osborne suburban parlour setting.'

In the short term, perhaps the key impact of *Room at the Top* – as well as heralding the start of the era when kitchen-sink subject matter was considered worthy of attention by the film industry – lay in the fact that it also largely escaped the hands of the censor, and in terms of sexual frankness was felt to be more in line with the kind of material which usually came from those apparently more liberated people across the Channel.

Working-class subject matter from a genuinely working-class writer surfaced at the Royal Court on July 14 when they presented Arnold Wesker's *Chicken Soup with Barley*, directed by John Dexter, after a short prior run at the newly opened Belgrade Theatre in Coventry. Ticket sales were relatively slow, but it was the start of another long association between a writer, a director and the Royal Court. Dexter was apparently not averse to saying to Wesker during rehearsals, 'Shut up, Arnold, or I'll direct this play as you wrote it.' With an ever-increasing number of new dramatists being drawn to the Court, George Devine established a Writer's Group that year, which met weekly in a former paint shop in Flood Street to discuss their aims and the current state of drama, and also improvise new scenes or pieces of business. However, a place on the bill at Sloane Square was not necessarily a guarantee of healthy ticket sales, as another new writer, John Arden, discovered, when his play *Live Like Pigs* opened on September 30 to a distinctly lukewarm welcome from the public.

Chelsea! We Bring You China!

On October 3 in the gossip column of the *NME*, 'Tail Pieces by the Alley Cat', activities in the King's Road received a namecheck in the run-up to that week's UK tour by Duke Ellington: '"Don't Get Around Much Anymore",

Duke Ellington's great composition, was brilliantly performed on the *Chelsea at Nine* TV show by Johnny Dankworth's orchestra on Tuesday.' Johnny's wife and singer, Cleo Laine had, of course, starred in *Flesh to a Tiger* at the Royal Court earlier in the year. A couple of weeks later one of Britain's home-grown rock outfits, Rory Blackwell and His Blackjacks also appeared live on *Chelsea at Nine*.

At the newly refurbished Classic Cinema on the King's Road, with its custom-made bronze door handles designed to match 'those very impressive ones on the Venice Film Festival Theatre', Mr Sinatra was stalking across the screen as Frankie Machine in a revival of the jazz-and-junk classic *The Man with the Golden Arm*, while across the street at the Chenil Galleries, from October 11, they were holding an exhibition of the Chelsea Art Society. Number 144 King's Road, a former fish shop, was now the South China Restaurant, whose proprietor was a young Chinese metallurgist from Sheffield by the name of Man Sung Wang, MSc, PhD. His adverts carried the snappy slogan 'Chelsea! We Bring You China!', regular customers included actors such as Sir John Gielgud and George Baker, and he told the press: 'When I was in London as a young student during the war, I was fascinated by Chelsea and spent many happy hours around the King's Road. Now I am very happy that my restaurant appears to have caught on.'

At Elstree, work was nearly finished on the film version of *Look Back in Anger*, and one of the last things to be shot was a sequence in which the Chris Barber Jazz Band, stars of Richardson's old Free Cinema short *Momma Don't Allow*, performed during a nightclub sequence. In the finished picture, the trumpet music played that day by Barber's sideman Pat Halcox would appear as the work of Richard Burton as Jimmy Porter.

As one Angry Young Man was immortalised on celluloid, another was making his debut in print that October. The novel *Saturday Night and Sunday Morning* by Alan Sillitoe told the story of Arthur Seaton, a 22-year-old Teddy boy working a lathe at a bicycle factory in Nottingham, whose behaviour, twenty years later, might have made Sid Vicious want to shake him by the hand. In the opening pages of the novel, Arthur gets himself heroically drunk in a local pub and throws up over a man by accident. Somewhat understandably, the man's wife objects:

> The woman stood a foot away from Arthur. 'Look at him,' she jeered into his face. 'He's senseless. He can't say a word. He can't even apologise. Why don't yer apologise, eh? *Can't* yer apologise? Dragged-up, I should think, getting drunk like this. Looks like one of them Teddy Boys, allus making trouble. Go on, apologise.'

Arthur's response is to throw up again, this time over the wife. *Saturday Night and Sunday Morning* is an immensely enjoyable novel, and when it was later adapted for the cinema by Osborne and Richardson's Woodfall Films with Albert Finney as Arthur, the result was a fine film which has stood the test of time better than many of the kitchen-sink productions of the era. It is hard, though, to reconcile the younger Sillitoe who wrote, 'you never knew when the Yanks were going to do something daft like dropping an H-bomb on Moscow. And if they did that you could say ta-ta to everybody, burn your football coupons and betting-slips, and ring up Billy Graham' with the Sillitoe in 2004 who wrote 'I was in favour of the war in Iraq [. . .] One can only congratulate the United States forces, and the soldiers of Great Britain.'

A Great Deal More Dirt

When Beckett's *Fin de partie* premiered in French in April 1957 by special agreement between the playwright and George Devine, it was also agreed that the English Stage Company would be allowed to have the work translated and then present it in English. This new production eventually opened on October 28, 1958 under the title *Endgame* as part of a Beckett double bill alongside *Krapp's Last Tape*, with Beckett himself supervising the last two weeks of rehearsals. It does not take an entire year and a half to translate a relatively short play: what had held things up was the inevitable struggle with the Victorian-minded censors at the Lord Chamberlain's office, who adopted a positively Orwellian doublethink in their attitude towards the text of *Endgame*. As a French-language text, it had been passed for public performance without difficulty the previous year. What now troubled the men of the Lord Chamberlain's office was their idea that any offending words must of necessity sound so much more *filthy* when spoken in English. Since January, Devine and Lord Harewood, who sat on the English Stage Company's governing body, had been holding negotiations with the Chamberlain's office, but the message did not seem to be getting through. Nicholas de Jongh quotes an internal letter from that office, written by a Brigadier Gwatkin, which shows what the Court was up against: 'I feel that the people erudite enough to go, understanding, to a French play, can take a great deal more dirt (I use the term broadly) than an average English audience seeing a direct translation in English. Quite apart from the fact that the French words sound more delicate than the English equivalent.'

This is the sort of twisted logic which would famously surface two years later during the *Lady Chatterley* trial, when the jury were asked by the prosecution whether it was the sort of book 'you would want your wives or your servants to read'.

The chief stumbling block with *Endgame* was the famous line about God, which said: 'The bastard – he doesn't exist.' After much haggling, this was finally altered to 'The swine,' presumably on the assumption that the Lord Chamberlain's office felt that it is better to be a farmyard animal than to be born out of wedlock, but if you have to call someone a bastard, you should at least have the decency to say it in French. George Devine's response to all this, according to Irving Wardle, was to tell Ann Jellicoe, 'You can get away with much more in French. Think what you could get away with in Japanese!'

Whatever language the cast were speaking, the critic Kenneth J. Hurren was not impressed. The Beckett double bill did, however, prompt him to offer the following reflection on the current state of English theatre:

> If the cat has kittens in the oven, remarked some sage of long ago, that doesn't make them biscuits; and I don't think there's a better way of saying that a lot of things are being dumped on the stage these days that aren't identifiable as plays. The current pieces at the Royal Court, in my view, are among them, and I urge you to inspect the litter. The chances are they will bore your ears off, but you can take no part in the most pressing theatrical debate of our time until you have decided for yourself whether they are kittens or biscuits. There is also the question of what's to be done about the cat . . .

In the event, several other reviewers who would normally have supported such a production were less than impressed with the final result, but Devine believed in Samuel Beckett one hundred per cent, and the playwright's association with the Royal Court would continue for decades.

In the sixties and seventies, the King's Road was not only a prime catwalk for the hip and the hopeful, but also became one of the places to drive your car, if you happened to have one that was likely to turn people's heads. In due course, this became known as the Chelsea Cruise, and vintage American fifties automobiles always played a big part in it. Diana Dors had loved to drive her powder-blue Cadillac up and down the street at the height of her fame, but in 1958, a style-conscious teenager who was later to have a huge effect on the look and sound of the sixties enjoyed travelling in style down the King's Road as a passenger in a friend's Lincoln Continental convertible after going to see Chelsea play on Saturday afternoons. All heads would turn in their direction as they passed by, and the young Andrew Loog Oldham loved every minute of it . . .

10

'An enormous Cadillac with built-in dancing girls'

War-Dance Music

Andrew Loog Oldham was not the only person who could see the attraction of a Detroit gas-guzzler in London: John Osborne, interviewed in the 'Motoring for Men' supplement of *Men Only* in June 1959 commented, 'I feel I'd love to have a really enormous Cadillac with built-in dancing girls.' The way things were going, he would certainly be able to afford one.

As the year started, Tony Richardson's film of *Look Back in Anger* – in the can but not released until the early summer – was already receiving the big build-up in the press. Peter Tipthorp in *Photoplay* wrote: 'I predict great things for John Osborne's *Look Back in Anger*. If any British picture can make more money at the box-office than the horrors this will be the one.' He also said that 'in *Room at the Top*, Romulus have what might be the surprise film of the year'. Straying away from the realm of cinema, Mr Tipthorp ventured a further prediction that 'some flashily dressed juvenile mad-cap, with a face like a monkey, will start bashing a guitar and screaming his head off – and suddenly he'll be earning £500 a week', and pursued this opinion elsewhere in the same issue of the magazine, in a three-page article entitled 'Rock'n'Roll Terror – Where Will it End?' He backed up his argument by consulting a conveniently anonymous gentleman identified only as 'one of our leading music authorities': 'Rock'n'Roll, he explained, matches the blood beat. "It stirs primeval things in almost everyone. It is war-dance music. Music of the drums that sent the African negroes wild when they were tribesmen – the sort of beat that prepared American Indians for their savage raids on white settlers."'

Having bolstered his claims with the aforementioned racist nonsense, he then consulted 'one of Britain's leading psychiatrists' – also nameless – who felt that 'in the course of the last fifty years we have swung from the extremely rigid society to a society where "anything goes". Our only hope of improving matters is to come back to the middle of the road'; all of which conjures up an irresistible image of the nation being saved by a diet of Max Bygraves records. Finally, Tipthorp sought the opinion of 'a London borough youth officer', who expressed himself in terms remarkably similar to those used in 1977 by Tory GLC member Bernard Brook-Partridge about the Sex Pistols. Mr Anonymous Youth Officer had apparently witnessed a 'rock'n'roll riot' and seemed to feel that a solid dose of the lash was called for: 'Although I think the hooligans who take part in this degenerate behaviour deserve a good whipping, I think there are certain people who deserve it even more. Those are the so-called stars who sing rock'n'roll. Every shake of the leg, twitch of the body is designed to stimulate the emotions of the youngsters in the audience.'

Having ended his article with a veiled threat of vigilante attacks against rockers by concerned citizens, the author probably had to go and lie down in a dark room for a while. Somehow, though, this picture of imminent rock'n'roll Armageddon did not scare off respectable organisations such as the British Macaroni Institute, the hosts of a large and defiantly spaghetti-themed fancy dress ball at the 15th-century Crosby Hall in Cheyne Walk, who invited Johnny Duncan and the Blue Grass Boys to provide the music. Tennessee-born Duncan – who made one of the only authentic British rockabilly-flavoured singles of the 1950s, 'Last Train to San Fernando' (1957) – provided the entertainment at this event billed as 'Britain's First Spaghetti Barbecue', while guests dressed as cowboys partied the night away with no sign of the rioting Tipthorp predicted. The occasion was organised to promote pasta-eating in London, and the location had been selected because, according to Jill Pound-Corner's report in the February 13, 1959 issue of *What's On in London*, 'here it was that Count Bonvisi served Britain's first macaroni meal four hundred years ago'. Among the illustrious guests there was even a future Time Lord: 'Jon Pertwee cut a dashing figure in a Red-Indian-type leather suede jacket and cowboy outfit. [. . .] And the British Spaghetti Queen, 19-year-old Geraldine Lynton, wore a costume made entirely of noodles! In the skirt alone, which was made from over half a mile of noodles, there was enough spaghetti to make 30 helpings.'

Highly Unsavoury and Dismally Uninteresting

In Sloane Square, the costumes owed more to battledress than Bolognese as Free Cinema film-maker Lindsay Anderson directed his first play for the London stage, Willis Hall's army drama *The Long and the Short and the Tall*, which opened at the Royal Court on January 7, having originally been performed at the Edinburgh Festival under the title *Disciplines of War*. Press adverts the following week quoted the *Sunday Graphic* ('Should run for ever'), and the fine cast included such future world stars as Peter O'Toole and Robert Shaw – and an understudy called Michael Caine, who eventually made it onto the stage when the production transferred to the Streatham Hill Theatre later in the year.

Anderson also directed a second play for the Court in February, which was a Sunday night without decor performance of *Progress to the Park*, a play by Alun Owen, who later wrote the script for the first Beatles film *A Hard Day's Night*. The play included the line, 'Tomorrow I'll get on that train, clutching in my hot sticky hand a second class ticket and brazen me way past Crewe in a first class seat and he can drop me off at Sloane Street any time at all, son, anytime at all.'

Meanwhile, Osborne and Richardson's Woodfall productions were reported to have paid £20,000 for the film rights to Shelagh Delaney's play *A Taste of Honey*, presumably not sharing the view of *What's On*'s book reviewer, J. Lillywhite Haffner, who was less than impressed when the playscript was published that spring:

> [It] may be a very good play when performed on the stage. I leave an assessment of that matter to another department. But I must say that it reads pretty poorly. The story of a sort of a prostitute, her daughter who becomes pregnant after an affaire with a Negro sailor, and the homosexual (one supposes) who lives with her, it is not only highly unsavoury but, I found, dismally uninteresting.

Despite some people's reservations about this kind of subject matter, the first of the kitchen-sink films, Jack Clayton's *Room at the Top*, was given a lavish charity premiere at the Plaza on January 22, and its realistic treatment of the love scenes was heralded as a daring advance into territory where only the Continentals had previously ventured. The *Monthly Film Bulletin* – while acknowledging the work as 'a rare departure in British film-making' – nevertheless noted 'its slightly self-conscious determination to bring sex to the British screen'. The first stirrings of the Permissive

Society were at hand, and Spike Milligan was certainly paying attention, as could be seen from the February 16 episode of *The Goon Show*, 'The Gold Plate Robbery':

BLUEBOTTLE: Oh ho hum.

ECCLES: What'd what'd the matter?

BLUEBOTTLE: I haven't had any sleep all night. You know that film *Room at the Top*?

ECCLES: Yer.

BLUEBOTTLE: Well, I'm in the room underneath 'em.

As if to confirm that the nation was about to embark on the slippery slope to sin and depravity, cheering merrily as it went, the film censor also passed a film called *Nudist Paradise*, directed by Charles Saunders. 'The First British Nudist Feature!' shrieked the adverts, just in case the title of the film was felt to be a little confusing.

In 1959 students were marching against the atom bomb, aristocratic British fascist Oswald Mosley – friend and near-neighbour of the former Edward VIII and Wallis Simpson – had crawled out from wherever he'd been hiding and was standing for election for the parliamentary seat of North Kensington, while somewhere in Middle England there was a schoolteacher named Mary Whitehouse who was getting ready to save the country from the threat of nudity in films and sex in general (or 'sex-and-violence', as she generally combined it, as if murder is the moral equivalent of most people's consensual bedroom activities). The new film censor John Trevelyan, who'd passed *Room at the Top* and *Nudist Paradise*, was a relatively liberal man compared to the reactionaries at the Lord Chamberlain's office – although that is setting the bar very low – and many of the cultural battles of the coming decade would be polarised between the likes of Mary Whitehouse and the Establishment on the one side, and the libertarians in the arts and entertainment on the other. The battle lines were being drawn, and *Look Back in Anger*, *Room at the Top* and rock'n'roll music were either a new dawn or the first warnings of Mary's legendary 'tidal wave of filth'.

Please Don't Talk About Me When I'm Gone

John Osborne's influence continued to make waves internationally. In February, British director Peter Cotes was responsible for a Dutch-language version of *Epitaph for George Dillon,* the early play John had co-written with Anthony Creighton, which opened in Rotterdam, while in America Gore Vidal wrote an article called *Love, Love, Love* examining theatre's kitchen-sink tendency, which appeared in the New York-based quarterly magazine *Partisan Review.* Founded in 1934 by the US Communist Party, by this time the publication was actually being financially propped up by the CIA via a front organisation in a covert bid to influence the direction of intellectual debate:

> A minor phenomenon of the theatre today is the milieu: kitchens in Kansas, cold-water flats, Bronx apartments, the lower-middle-class venue depicted in naturalistic terms by 'truthful' actors before an audience of expensively dressed, overfed burghers. [. . .] Is there a desire to know about things today? To be instructed by the narcissism of a John Osborne, who tells them: this is the way we are, young, angry, unique! And the burghers nod and belch softly, and some doze: it is the theatre of the Editorial and the Survey. [. . .] In England the Royal Court Theatre has offered hospitality to some of the good writers, but the plays so far produced have been disappointing.

If a US publication had noticed Sloane Square, the traffic worked both ways, and in February 1959 perhaps the greatest singer ever to emerge from America sang three songs in the old Chelsea Palace building on the King's Road for a national UK television audience. By July 17, she was dead, but not before she had been arrested in her hospital bed on drugs charges by New York's finest while lying there terminally ill. Who knows, maybe that particular week all the muggers and rapists had given up and gone home, so the police decided to arrest the dying Billie Holiday instead.

It was not very different from the way she had been treated by the authorities for most of her life, but back in the earlier part of the year, when she appeared on the *Chelsea at Nine* show in the King's Road, she was shown a great deal more of the respect that was her due. Bruce Grimes, working in the art department for Granada TV, told me his memories of the day that Billie appeared on the show:

I remember that one so vividly because really, when you saw her . . . she'd had a large bottle of scotch, and, er, something more than that, during the day. On the dress rehearsal she was helped onto the stage, and you felt sick, because she was a wreck, an absolute wreck, and she slumped against the piano and went through the motions . . . till the *show*. When the show was on, she walked out without any assistance, she didn't lean against the piano, she just put her hand gently on it, and she sang and the hairs just went straight up on the back of your neck. It was just *magic . . . wonderful . . .*

Billie sang 'Porgy', 'Please Don't Talk About Me When I'm Gone' and 'Strange Fruit'. She was accompanied by her piano player Mal Waldron, and on the first two numbers they were also joined by Peter Knight's Orchestra. For 'Strange Fruit', it was pretty much just her and Mal. She may not have been aware that she was singing right across the road from the place where Duke Ellington had cut some records back in 1933, the same year she had first sung in a studio herself. Luckily, by 1959, *Chelsea at Nine* was no longer broadcast live, and so the show was recorded. It went out in March, coincidentally the same month that the Classic Cinema along the road was showing an old film in rep entitled *Last Holiday*. Even though the Chelsea Palace has long since been pulled down by the developers, as long as they're running around putting up commemorative plaques on famous places, there is a fair-sized argument for something marking the spot where Billie sang at the corner of King's Road and Sydney Street.

Nympho-Dipsos and Cemetery Seductions

At the Royal Court, *Sugar in the Morning* by Donald Howarth opened on April 9. It had originally been one of the English Stage Company's Sunday night without decor plays. Among the cast was the actor Toke Townley, who had played the part of the chemist in Hammer's film of Nigel Kneale's *The Quatermass Experiment* (1955). Kneale had recently written the screen adaptation of Osborne's *Look Back in Anger*, which was shortly due in London cinemas, and in 1968 the little girl from *The Quatermass Experiment* would star at the Royal Court herself, as an adult, in a revival of *Look Back in Anger*. Her name was Jane Asher, and at the time of that revival, she had just split up from long-term boyfriend Paul McCartney, with whom she'd originally become friendly late one night over drinks at a house in the King's Road.

Next up at the Court was a Tennessee Williams play, *Orpheus Descending*, which arrived on May 15. The director was Tony Richardson, back in the theatre having directed the feature film of *Look Back in Anger*, which opened in cinemas in June. Ever since Williams's play *A Streetcar Named Desire* had been submitted to the closed minds at the Lord Chamberlain's office in 1949 and run into difficulties over its veiled homosexual references, staging his work in London had sometimes been a risky business. *Cat on a Hot Tin Roof* also ran into trouble in the mid-fifties, and was eventually presented as a private club performance at the Comedy Theatre in order to escape the Lord Chamberlain's ban. *Orpheus Descending*, however, was a different proposition, and was actually much more problematic for Williams than for the censors. It was a revised version of an early play of his from the 1940s called *Battle of Angels*, which he had rewritten five times over the years before its eventual US premiere in 1957. *Orpheus Descending* reached the Royal Court in the same year that Sidney Lumet made a film adaptation of it under the title *The Fugitive Kind*, which was memorably summed up by Leslie Halliwell as follows: 'doom-laden melodrama, almost a parody of the author's works, full of cancer patients, nympho-dipsos, and cemetery seductions; we are spared the final castration.' It is interesting to note that among the cast of Richardson's production was the actress Bessie Love, born in 1898, whose career stretched all the way back to include an appearance in D. W. Griffith's monumental 1916 film *Intolerance*.

If Tony Richardson and John Osborne chanced to read that summer's quarterly edition of *Sight and Sound* magazine, they were probably extremely pleased. The same issue which contained a lengthy feature about Truffaut, Godard and other leading lights of the *nouvelle vague* also found ample space to praise their own first venture into feature production. The editorial called *Look Back in Anger* 'outstanding among recent British films', and the magazine devoted further space to a script extract and a lengthy article about the film by David Robinson:

Look Back in Anger is a breakthrough – to a much greater extent, I believe, than *Room at the Top*, with which it must inevitably be compared. Here is a film which has something to say, and which says it without reference to conventional box-office values. [. . .] Can the breakthrough be maintained? We know our producers too well; and if *Look Back in Anger* makes money, they will be more inclined to produce disastrous imitations of the angry young man in the bedsitter. [. . .] The breakthrough will not be easily maintained by the series of films we can easily imagine, with Jack Hawkins as Porter or Dirk Bogarde as Porter or Kenneth More as Porter or John Mills as Porter.

In the film version, only Mary Ure remained from the original Royal Court cast, and scriptwriter Nigel Kneale had invented some extra characters, such as Johnny Kapoor, the Indian market trader, and old Mrs Tanner, played by Edith Evans. Arguments raged as to whether Richard Burton was too old to play the part of Jimmy Porter, but these days that is not the first question which springs to mind: mostly, it is just hard to see how this creaky, studio-bound film created such a fuss. Of course, this criticism could also be levelled at the original play, whose hideously twee bears-and-squirrels ending must have offended just as many people as Porter's diatribes ever did. Nevertheless, from the reviews, there is no denying the impact of Woodfall Films' first venture into the business, and its influence on the generation of British cinema that was to follow.

Sight and Sound also devoted part of that issue to an article by author Richard Hoggart about Free Cinema graduate Karel Reisz's South London Teddy boy documentary *We Are the Lambeth Boys*, while noting elsewhere that Harry Saltzman of Woodfall had struck a deal with another film company, Bryanston, in order to work on two upcoming Woodfall projects: an adaptation of Alan Sillitoe's novel *Saturday Night and Sunday Morning*, to be directed by Karel Reisz, and then a version of Colin MacInnes's novel *City of Spades*, to be filmed by Tony Richardson. All of a sudden, as Morecambe and Wise used to say, there seemed to be something hot on the kitchen table.

Peach Melba at the North Pole

The 1960s were now just around the corner – an era when perhaps the biggest insult that could be levelled at anything was to call it old-fashioned, and historic buildings were torn down across the nation to make way for concrete. The year 1959 had already seen the opening in Store Street, WC1, of what was advertised as the '70th birthday exhibition of the work of a universal genius' – the gentleman in question being Le Corbusier, whose influence on an entire generation of post-war architects can be seen in the crumbling 1960s high-rise rabbit hutches which were built all over Britain in imitation of the master's 'machine for living in'. As further proof of the way the wind was blowing, London County Council decided in their wisdom that the Luftwaffe hadn't destroyed enough of old Chelsea and that the beautiful Victorian construction known as the Albert Bridge should be demolished. They were eventually prevented from doing so by a campaign of public protest led by the poet John Betjeman, who went on to fight many such battles in the ensuing decades.

Mary Quant, Alexander Plunket Greene and Archie McNair had their flagship Bazaar on the King's Road, plus the Knightsbridge branch which they had opened in 1958, which was managed by Suzie Leggatt, who, as Mary recalled, 'had six, sometimes eight, girls working with her, mostly debs and ex-debs like herself. All these girls wore high black leather boots, black stockings and black leather coats.' At the end of each season, both branches would hold a sale, and girls would be sent out into the Chelsea streets wearing fairground-style Victorian-lettered sandwich boards which read 'Come to Bazaar. MAD Reductions'. Film star Kay Kendall once showed up at the King's Road shop wanting to try on a selection of dresses, and when Alexander took her downstairs into the restaurant below, which was closed for the afternoon, she peeled off her street clothes to reveal that, for her, underwear was apparently an alien concept. Such behaviour would be relatively common along the King's Road by the second half of the sixties, but in the late fifties, Bazaar's customers were clearly ahead of the pack. Philip Larkin famously reckoned sexual intercourse began in 1963, and if you lived in Hull, perhaps it did, but Chelsea in 1959 was a very different world.

Up the road in Sloane Square at the end of June, the critic Kenneth Tynan reportedly emerged from Arnold Wesker's new play, *Roots*, 'in a haze of emotion'. Directed by John Dexter and starring Joan Plowright, it was the second part of what was to be a trilogy, following on from *Chicken Soup with Barley*. (In September, Wesker's *The Kitchen* – unsuccessfully entered in the 1956 *Observer* play competition – would also be staged at the Royal Court.) *Roots* was followed on July 29 with a play that starred Scarlett O'Hara herself, Vivien Leigh, in a comedy called *Look After Lulu*, directed by Tony Richardson. This was a translation by Noel Coward of Feydeau's *Occupe-toi d'Amélie*, which it is said George Devine took on because it was likely to make money. In the event, it did not, because it played to packed houses at the Court but then ran into trouble after transferring to the New Theatre. Harold Hobson's verdict in the *Sunday Times* was as follows: 'If *Look After Lulu* is only half a success, the reasons are more than complimentary to everybody concerned. The trouble is that Mr Noel Coward is too witty and Miss Vivien Leigh too beautiful. For the kind of play that *Look After Lulu* is, beauty and wit are as unnecessary as a peach melba at the North pole.'

Tony Richardson, who seems to have been busier than a one-legged tap dancer during 1959, moved straight from directing Vivien Leigh at the Royal Court into directing her husband at Shepperton Studios. 'Laurence Olivier plays the role of the seedy music hall comic he made famous on the stage', *Films and Filming* announced to its readers in September, marking the start of principal photography on 'the long-awaited screen version of John Osborne's *The Entertainer*'. On the letters page, they also printed a note from a reader complaining that 'ribald laughter' had broken out at a screening he attended of *Look Back in Anger*, during 'the opening bedroom sequence'.

Ribald laughter would probably be the most common response these days if a magazine printed a review such as the one in *What's On in London* for Sean O'Casey's comedy *Cock a-Doodle Dandy*, which opened at the Court on September 17. With a choice of words recalling nothing so much as the opening season's production of *Lysistrata*, they described the play as an 'ebullient mixture of farce, satire and fantasy, set in an Irish village where the battle-lines are drawn between the kill-joy priest and a giant cock symbolising the unfettered joy of life.' Still, it was, as the *Daily Mail* assured its readers, a 'most stimulating theatrical evening'.

A Very Enterprising Child Indeed

In the country at large, there was an election to be fought, and it seems as if pretty much every nightclub in town organised a special election night party for October 8, having been granted extensions on their normal licenses. At Winston's Club in New Bond Street, where the current 'glamorous new extravaganza' featured drag artist Danny La Rue in a show called *Look Back and Laugh*, they were planning to project the results up on a screen. Over in Sloane Square, however, up above the theatre at Clement Freud's Royal Court Club, tickets were a hefty five guineas per couple for the night's entertainment, with the election results on television and radio, and a licensed bar till 3.30am. The extra drinking time would not necessarily make Harold Macmillan's government any easier to handle, but it was probably worth a try.

As the nation woke up the following day to a few more years of Mr 'You've never had it so good', *Picturegoer* had been working hard at their arithmetic, and were keen to give their readers the benefit of their calculations: 'Roger Livesey is aged fifty-three. Laurence Olivier is aged fifty-two. In *The Entertainer* Livesey plays Olivier's father. Which must have made him a very enterprising child indeed . . .'

In the evil, riot-provoking world of teenage beat music which had given Peter Tipthorp such sleepless nights, Tommy Steele was busy denying that he had given up recording rock'n'roll: 'That's not true,' he told *Picturegoer*'s John Edwardes. 'Lots of people have said this and I guess they got the idea after I did those two pantomimes. I've just made two records which bear a mighty close resemblance to rock.' Which two records those might have been, Steele did not specify, but he could hardly have meant his cloying new children's tune 'The Little White Bull' which hit the Top Ten in December, taken from his new film *Tommy the Toreador*. Strange to say, there were no newspaper reports of Teddy boys slashing the seats and causing mayhem at showings of the latter, but if they had, perhaps it would have just meant that they had given up gang war and taken up film criticism.

Tommy was turning deliberately into an old-school family entertainer, singing songs that would not have been out of place in the middle-of-the-road British singles charts of 1953. Lonnie Donegan, too, was heading away from his 'Rock Island Line' style towards music-hall comedy songs, having started the year with 'Does Your Chewing Gum Lose Its Flavour', and finishing 1959 by recording the chirpy cockney knees-up which would give him his first hit of the sixties, 'My Old Man's a Dustman'. Luckily, there was an influx of rockers to counterbalance this trend, and one of the greatest of them all, Gene Vincent, made his first visit to Britain that October, bringing with him the killer double-sided single, 'Wild Cat'/'Right Here on Earth'. Within a short time of landing, he had hooked up with *Oh Boy* and *Six-Five Special* producer Jack Good, who encouraged him to dress from head to foot in biker leathers for an appearance on his new show, *Boy Meets Girls*.

As it turned out, the first few years of the sixties in Britain were one of the very best times to see some of the original giants of rock'n'roll playing live, as Gene, Little Richard, Jerry Lee Lewis and Roy Orbison made repeated hugely successful tours of the UK, playing to packed halls when many of them could barely get arrested back in the States. Among those British audiences, and, increasingly, in supporting acts on the same bill, were a whole generation of young musicians who began by covering Jerry Lee, Chuck Berry or Elvis songs, and then wound up writing hit songs of their own, and then a year or so later formed the spearhead of the so-called British Invasion bands who made it big in America.

I Was Only Kidding, Dad

Just as Gene Vincent was flying in from the US to play that debut tour on a double bill with Eddie Cochran, a young English military conscript based in Anglesey who would catch their show early in the new year was preparing to move out to Texas. John Peel:

I saw the Gene Vincent and Eddie Cochran tour, four days before Eddie Cochran died . . . I was one of the last of the National Servicemen; if I'd been born two days later I wouldn't have had to go. My dad said to me when I was home on leave one time, 'cause he was worried about what I was going to do, as dads are, he said, 'I'll send you to the States, if you'll go.' And of course you think, 'Oh well, er . . . yeah, ok,' never expecting that he'd do it, and then when he did sort it out, it was too late to say, 'No, I was only kidding, Dad,' so off I went.

By the time John returned in 1967, London was allegedly 'swinging', and world pop culture had been turned upside down by events in the UK that few people could have imagined at the end of the fifties.

In the final months of that decade, the Royal Court presented a translation by Ann Jellicoe of Ibsen's *Rosmersholm*, starring Peggy Ashcroft, which proved to be their biggest hit of the year. They also staged a new work by John Arden which was a financial disaster, but was actually one of the finest works they had yet produced. This particular box-office disaster was *Serjeant Musgrave's Dance*, which opened on October 22 and lasted barely a month. George Devine believed in it as strongly as he had believed in the Beckett plays he had championed, and as Arden himself later wrote, 'It was a play which lost the theatre (I think) ten thousand pounds, but which [Devine] nevertheless had insisted upon presenting in the teeth of hostile critics and indifferent audiences until acceptance of its qualities was finally secured.'

Directed by Lindsay Anderson, *Serjeant Musgrave* had an excellent cast that included Ian Bannen, Frank Finlay, Colin Blakely and Stratford Johns, not to mention Freda Jackson, who in January would play a key role in one of the finest of Hammer's vampire films, *Brides of Dracula* (1960). Incidentally, the musical director for *Serjeant Musgrave's Dance* was a certain Dudley Moore, who the following August in the company of Peter Cook, Alan Bennett and Jonathan Miller would open at the Edinburgh Festival in a revue called *Beyond the Fringe*, thereby helping to ignite the entire sixties satire boom.

A few days after the premiere of Arden's play, *The Manchester Guardian* reported the inaugural meeting of the anti-nuclear Committee of 100, whose participants included several people with close ties to the Royal Court: 'The first disappointment is that there were not more well-known names present. Lindsay Anderson, Reg Butler, Alex Comfort, Doris Lessing, Christopher Logue, John Osborne and Arnold Wesker were there.' Public protest is often represented these days as a quintessentially sixties phenomenon, but many cultural figures had developed the habit during the second half of the fifties, and a fair few of them had their roots in the Chelsea scene of the day.

We'll All Have to Start Painting

On November 26, 1959, half a decade before her magnificent James Bond title-song recordings, Shirley Bassey topped the bill of that evening's *Chelsea at Nine* show singing 'Count on Me' and 'If You Love Me', live from the King's Road. Further down the cast was Joel Grey – who in 1966 would originate the role of the Master of Ceremonies in the Broadway musical *Cabaret*, famously reprising it for the film version in 1972 – and also Señor Wences, memorably described by Clifford Davis in that day's edition of the *Daily Mirror* as 'the world's greatest ventriloquist, he gave up bull fighting for show business'. A few weeks later, the programme showcased French Caribbean singer and comedian Henri Salvador, who was singled out for praise in trade paper *The Stage* by Guy Taylor: 'What a delightful artist he is. I have seen many times his "moron-ordering-a-meal-in-a-restaurant" and I have never failed to marvel at his exceptional timing.'

Meanwhile, the new teenage singing sensation Adam Faith hit the charts in December 1959 with his Buddy-Holly-by-numbers impersonation, 'What Do You Want?', prompting one angry Holly fan to write to the press and say, 'Your blood.'

Faith had made a very creditable stab at acting in the new film *Beat Girl*, with its ultra-suave soundtrack courtesy of the John Barry Seven, and an article in the December 4 issue of *NME* reported that 'Adam is now taking his acting seriously. He's about to start dramatic training at the Royal Court Theatre.' Years later, in his autobiography, *Acts of Faith*, Adam wrote that Lindsay Anderson had approached his manager, Eve Taylor, in 1960, wanting him to appear in a play at the Court. Apparently the director had been impressed with Adam's appearance in *Beat Girl*, and also on the TV interview programme *Face to Face* with John Freeman. Taylor, thinking it would be wrong for her client – probably because the money he might earn at the theatre would be only a fraction of what he could command for a live gig – turned Anderson down without even mentioning it to Faith, who only discovered the truth when talking to the director some time in the seventies. The English Stage Company went on to have a long history of involvement with figures from the music business, but this would have been a very early collision of the worlds of theatre and rock.

At the close of 1959, *Films and Filming* summed up the year in cinema: the top box office attraction in terms of admissions was *I'm All Right Jack* by the Boulting Brothers; their own critics' choice for Best British Film was Jack Clayton's *Room at the Top*; Tony Richardson was mentioned as having impressed them, along with three others, as a young director for *Look Back in Anger*, but the film failed to win any of their critics' awards. However, Dudley Carew of *The Times* named *Look Back in Anger* as his film of the year, as did Penelope Houston from *Sight and Sound* (along with *We Are the Lambeth Boys*), while John Waterman of the *Evening Standard* also concurred, saying, 'To me it was without doubt the most arresting film in the period, with style and content (even with *Room at the Top* in mind) of the utmost significance for the future of British feature films.'

Despite the fact that their debut production was in some ways outdated before it even hit the cinemas, Woodfall Films, a low-budget company put together by a couple of theatre people from one end of the King's Road, found themselves at the end of one decade setting an example which was to be followed by many of the new film-makers of the next.

Woody Allen once said, 'We'd better hurry up, or else the Renaissance will be here and we'll all have to start painting'; right now, 1959 was giving way to 1960, and, if you believed the hype, swinging was about to become pretty much compulsory . . .

Part Three

Granny Takes a Trip

11

'Dost thou dig that nightly jazz?'

Sex on the Screen

Whatever else people were about to get up to in this new decade called the sixties, *Photoplay* columnist Pip Evans seemed convinced of one thing – they would not be watching television. In a January 1960 article unambiguously entitled 'I Predict By the End of the Year the TV Cult Will Be Over', Evans told readers: 'The public are getting fed up with television. The "telly" cult is over.' Seen from the perspective of today, when it is possible to access hundreds of channels, twenty-four hours a day, it would seem to have been one of the less successful predictions of recent times. The reasoning behind Evans's argument was not that television had got worse, but that films had started to deliver something which the black-and-white box in the corner certainly did not: 'Towards the end of last year the British cinema saw a definite change. It became more daring, more adult. Spurred on, no doubt, by fine and frank films like *Room at the Top* and *Look Back in Anger*, the British Board of Film Censors decided to view in a completely new light the subject of sex on the screen.'

As it turned out, this was demonstrably untrue, since back in October 1957, little over a month after it had begun broadcasting to the nation, Granada's *Chelsea at Nine* show had beamed a notable UK television first direct from the King's Road into the homes of the nation: topless dancers, as Bruce Grimes explained to me: 'On *Chelsea at Nine* we were the first to show bare breasts on TV. Quite unexpectedly, and it caused panic in the control room! It was an African dance group – they wore bandana-type wraps during dress rehearsal, but not for the show . . .'

This was in the days when much of the output from Granada's King's Road studios was going out live, rather than pre-recorded as was common later. For the London stage, such exposure was considered daring, but not unique; for national television, it was unheard of. Bruce Grimes recalls:

> I was in the control room at the time and suddenly the cameras all kind of pointed at the floor or were wandering around on bits of scenery. The director was tearing his hair out, and the cameramen said, 'Well, they've got nothing on, they've got bare tits.' The producer was there, and the director just said, 'What do we do? Do you pull it, or what?' And the producer, you know, he had seconds to make up his mind, said, 'Well, we'll call it "ethnic". Go for it.' So the director said, 'Alright, lift the cameras up, show what's going on.' And it went out. There was a *hell* of a fuss, you know, it hit the press the next day, in a *big* way . . . The defence was that it was 'ethnic dancing', that that's the way it was. They did get away with it, but it was very tongue-in-cheek. But, shortly after that they had see-through dresses and everything, walking down the street.

On the front page of the following morning's edition of the *Daily Herald*, cunningly positioned directly below a large close-up smiling photo of Her Majesty Queen Elizabeth II on a state visit to Canada, the headline 'DUSKY BALLET BEAUTIES PRANCE NUDE ON TV' greeted the nation:

> Television finally did away with necklines altogether last night. Viewers goggled as dusky beauties of the African ballet cavorted nude from the waist up. It happened in ITV's 'Chelsea at Nine' show, during a dance version of jungle warfare entitled 'The Panthers and the Lions'. And right at the start three bare-top girls hurled themselves into the front of the picture. One spread herself on the floor right in front of the cameras and stayed there writhing and wriggling throughout. [. . .] And for the benefit of those who could not believe their eyes a Granada official said afterwards: 'Some of the girls were completely nude from the waist upwards. We decided to allow them to dance exactly as they do normally on the stage,' he explained. 'Actually, some of them find difficulty in dancing properly if they are made to wear surplus garments.' He added: 'We have had two calls from listeners [*sic*]. One was disgusted and the other thought it was "very nice".'

Practising the Wigan Brogue

The British attitude to this sort of thing had of course for many years been a standing joke among our more enlightened neighbours across the Channel. The expatriate Hungarian writer George Mikes, who moved to the UK in the 1930s, remarked in his 1946 book *How to Be an Alien*: 'Continental people have a sex life: the English have hot water bottles.' In 1960, he returned to the theme in his new book, *How to Be Inimitable*, and had this to say about his previous judgement: 'It has now become hopelessly out-of-date. How right was the kind (and to me unknown) lady who wrote to me in a letter: "You are really behind the times. In this field, too, things have changed and – this is the most important – techniques have advanced. We are using electric blankets nowadays."'

In the same book, Mikes identified another trend which was to reach epidemic proportions in the next few years – downward mobility:

> In the old days people used to aspire to higher classes. Since the angry young man literature has made its impact, quite a few people assert that they are of lower origin than they, in fact, are. (I am using here the word 'lower' in the worst snobbish sense.) The place of the upstart is being taken by the downstart. I know people who secretly visit evening elocution classes in order to pick up a cockney accent. Others are practising the Wigan brogue.

Someone with an authentic South London Elephant and Castle accent who now made it onto the stage of the Royal Court was Michael Caine, drafted in when Harold Pinter's *The Room* transferred there on March 8, after having premiered with a slightly different cast at the Hampstead Theatre Club in January. The working-class settings of some of the Court's plays, and of novels such as *Room at the Top* and *Saturday Night and Sunday Morning*, were certainly providing opportunities for the rising generation of young actors, some of whom then rose to fame appearing in the cinema adaptations of these stories. Conventional old-school RADA products with heroically posh accents that would have put the Queen to shame were soon to be elbowed out of the running by the likes of Albert Finney and Tom Courtenay. Karel Reisz – who cast Royal Court actress Rachel Roberts in a key role in that year's Woodfall film of *Saturday Night and Sunday Morning* – once told Alexander Walker of the struggle to find an actress who could manage the accent for this Nottingham-based working-class story: 'There seemed just no-one suitable in all of British theatre. We kept being sent

West End actresses who could "do" lower-class parts in a light-comedy way.' Diana Dors was at one time considered for the part that eventually went to Rachel, which might well have put a different slant on the film, although Diana had already proved herself a fine actress in a straight role in *Yield to the Night* (1956).

The male star of *Saturday Night and Sunday Morning*, of course, was Albert Finney; a perfect choice, being not only a superb actor, but also, as *Picturegoer* pointed out, the 'twenty-two year old son of a Manchester bookmaker' and something of an old Teddy boy at heart, just like the character he was playing. Finney had been impressed with director Karel Reisz after catching a showing of his documentary *We Are the Lambeth Boys*, largely because it did not resort to the usual tabloid clichés when depicting the rock'n'roll generation. 'I was knocked out by his understanding,' Finney told Bill Edwards, recalling the documentary while shooting *Saturday Night and Sunday Morning*. 'Reisz didn't emphasise for effect, he didn't exaggerate for sensation.' Edwards, who declared that Finney was 'as contemporary as a coffee bar', began his article with the actor's thoughts on the class struggle: 'When we let off steam, we're Teddy Boys, hooligans, louts, or something worse. When the society set does the same thing they're just high-spirited youngsters.'

Finney had started the year onstage at the Court in a play called *The Lily White Boys*, directed by Lindsay Anderson, whose cast also included Shirley Anne Field. She then appeared with Finney in *Saturday Night and Sunday Morning*, which began shooting in April. Finney was due to have made an appearance in Sloane Square a year earlier in the original cast of *The Long and the Short and the Tall*, but lost the role due to appendicitis, giving Peter O'Toole the chance to step in.

By the time that *Saturday Night and Sunday Morning* opened in London that autumn, Finney's working-class hero credentials were already being established onstage every night at the Cambridge Theatre, where he had opened on September 13 in the title role of Keith Waterhouse and Willis Hall's hugely popular new play *Billy Liar*, directed by Lindsay Anderson. The play was based on a novel of the same title by Waterhouse, and on the title page of the playscript there appears a one-line description, just below the cast list, which could almost stand as a blueprint for all the kitchen-sink films then emerging: 'The play is set in Stradhoughton, an industrial town in the North of England, today.'

Of course, when they came to film the play a couple of years later, the lead role went to Tom Courtenay, not Finney, and the director was John Schlesinger, not Anderson. Lindsay eventually got his crack at directing with *This Sporting Life*, which starred *Saturday Night and Sunday Morning*'s

Rachel Roberts. Tom Courtenay, meanwhile, also starred in *The Loneliness of the Long Distance Runner*, which was directed by Tony Richardson, based on a short story by Alan Sillitoe, the author of *Saturday Night and Sunday Morning*. The film of *Saturday Night and Sunday Morning* was directed by Karel Reisz, who'd started out co-directing back in 1956 with Tony Richardson, and Tony's new film *The Entertainer*, which opened in April 1960, also featured Albert Finney, who, let's not forget, starred in *Saturday Night and Sunday Morning*. If Britain's cinemas seemed full of kitchen sinks at the start of the sixties, audiences could also have been forgiven for thinking that the dishes were always being washed by the same collection of people, a significant number of whom had connections to the Royal Court.

Rock'n'Roll Tailors

Someone who had spent a fair amount of time watching the work of the Free Cinema directors and the French *nouvelle vague* from the vantage point of a seat in the stalls at the Everyman, Hampstead, was the teenage Andrew Loog Oldham, last seen heading down the King's Road in his friend's Lincoln Continental.

Andrew later credited the sense of style embodied in those films with shaping some of his strategies for marketing the Rolling Stones. In 1960, though, he was knocking on a door in Chelsea, looking for a job with Mary Quant's company. Oldham later wrote that the reason he wanted to work for her was because she was the 'one true manifestation of pop in the years between the archetypal rock'n'roll of the mid-50s and its eventual second coming with the Beatles in the mid-60s'. He wanted to be where the action was, and, as far as he was concerned, in 1960 that meant Bazaar, 138a King's Road. Mary Quant told me: 'Andrew Oldham insisted on working for me as a dogsbody helper – anything, he said. I think he was still supposed to be at school.'

Having made a few enquiries, he found out the address of their offices in Ives Street, announced that he was looking for employment, and was soon helping with a variety of jobs in both branches of Bazaar, from clothing deliveries to window dressing and even walking the dogs of the models. Oldham also had his first lessons in dealing with journalists, which stood him in good stead once managing the Stones. On top of this, he was simultaneously working nights at Ronnie Scott's Club, which gave him access to some of the finest music being played in town, and he would sometimes ring up Mary Quant and Alexander Plunket Greene to tip them off if anyone particularly worth seeing was playing there, so that they could jump in a taxi and come and catch the show.

After about six months, Andrew decided that he'd learnt all he could at
Bazaar and headed for the Continent for a change of scene. Mary Quant:
'When he left he wrote from the boat to France resigning, saying he could
now do any of our jobs standing on his head. He more or less proved it
by managing the Rolling Stones.'

Apart from the attractions of Bazaar, Oldham had a least one other
reason for coming to the King's Road that year – the men's fashions at a
shop called John Michael, owned, logically enough, by a man named John
Michael Ingram, which catered to the newly emerging modernists looking
for the styles they had been seeing in Italian films or on jazz album covers.
Sharp suits, narrow ties, thin lapels – it's a suave look, and although it was
later swept away by a hippie avalanche of kaftans, bells and other items
of essential goat-herding chic, it has since been revived many times in the
intervening decades. Some of those in the know had already been achieving
the required look by hunting out sympathetic tailors and having clothes
made to measure, as Mick Farren told me:

> When I was a young lad, there were two things going on: you know I
> was at St Martin's, so you saw girls who were doing fashion and got
> them to make you shirts, based on things that you'd seen; and then
> there was also the mod thing – the second-generation mods, but not
> many people knew about the modernists, listening to Miles Davis records,
> shooting down the East End and getting some old tailor to knock you
> up a jacket exactly like, you know, this picture of Buddy Holly, please
> guv, with the short lapels and the three buttons. That was it – old
> rock'n'roll tailors who had Brooks Brothers patterns and stuff like that.

With the advent of shops like John Michael in the King's Road, and
John Stephen in Carnaby Street, it was finally becoming possible to buy
some of these kinds of items off the peg, which drew in young, clothes-
conscious people like Andrew Oldham.

Bonnie Bell the Ding Dong Gal

The future Rolling Stones manager was not the only person attracted to the
area in 1960. Thriller writer Dennis Wheatley moved into number 60
Cadogan Square that year, becoming friendly with a new neighbour,
Christopher Lee, whom he soon met when giving a book reading up the
road at Harrods of his new novel *The Satanist*. Lee was to star in two of
Hammer's film adaptations of Wheatley novels, *The Devil Rides Out* (1968)

and *To the Devil a Daughter* (1976), after several years of trying to persuade the film company to consider Wheatley's work. Round about the time Wheatley was moving in, a gentleman who made his money from other methods took up residence in a top-floor Chelsea flat – Ronnie Kray, becoming for a while, in the words of John Pearson, the King's Road's 'gangster in residence'. Although the Kray brothers' main sphere of influence was generally further east, it did not prevent them from occasionally becoming involved in matters elsewhere, and Ron's brother Reg was apparently quite busy collecting protection money from various Chelsea nightclubs. In one of his prison memoirs, *Villains We Have Known* (1993), Reg Kray recalled being invited by crime boss Billy Hill to a meeting at a Belgravia pub called the Star to meet Charles Desilva, known as 'The King of the Con Men'. Desilva wanted to pay protection to Ron and Reg in return for their help in keeping another criminal off his back. 'Bill told us that Charlie Mitchell had been taking liberties with Charles Desilva, by blagging money off him,' recalled Reg, 'and he also said that Desilva would prefer to pay Ron and me money regularly rather than let Mitchell blag him, so would we mind him.'

Joseph Borras, proprietor of the Sa Tarragona restaurant on the King's Road, might perhaps have also benefited from some protection that year when he was attacked and held down by two intruders while having an afternoon nap at his restaurant, as was later explained in court to the magistrates at Marlborough Street:

> A cushion was pushed over his mouth, his wrists and ankles were tied with serviettes and another serviette was tied round his mouth. The men searched him all over, but failed to find his wallet, which had fallen from his pocket during the struggle. Then they ran out. After being treated at hospital he found that about £38 2s. had been taken from the till.

London's nightlife was attracting all sorts of people, and there were clearly significant amounts of money to be made, since the number of nightclubs and restaurants and bars in the entertainment listings of *What's On in London* had increased dramatically in the past two or three years. Strip shows, in particular, became a serious force to be reckoned with. Of course, there had long been the Windmill Theatre in Soho, which since the thirties had been presenting variety shows incorporating stationary tableaux of naked models who were forbidden by law from moving a muscle, but by 1960 things were much less restricted. The lavish adverts for the new shows tell their own story: at the Club Panama – 'We present the SEXIEST SAUCIEST STRIPTEASE SHOW'; Freddie's Peeperama – 'NEW FRENCH STRIP REVUE with

TWELVE International STRIPTEASE STARS and FRENCH FILMS'; the Geisha Theatre Club – 'NON-STOP STRIPTEASE REVUE'; The Keyhole Theatre Club – 'INTERNATIONAL STRIPTEASE Introducing the original and scintillating FLUFFLES THE TASSLER'; the Raymond Revuebar – 'INTERNATIONAL STRIPTEASE SPECTACULAR – Bonnie Bell The Ding Dong Gal, Les Batix – The Whip Sensation of the Century' plus, for some reason, 'the Roberts Bros CHIMPANZEES'. Then, of course, there was the Paint Box – 'Where You Can Lunch, Dine and Drink While Some of London's Most Lovely Models Are Being Painted'.

Anyone today still advancing the opinion that London was an uptight, sexless 'How Much is That Doggie in the Window'-singing mass of inhibitions until the Beatles came along in 1963 and taught it to swing would probably be roundly contradicted by Fluffles the Tassler or Bonnie Bell the Ding Dong Gal, were they available for comment. As for the Roberts Bros Chimpanzees, they're saying nothing . . .

Thrusting Close-Ups

Members of the public searching for something a little less revealing in the way of entertainment were being enticed to a place just north of the King's Road called the Café des Artistes, at 266 Fulham Road, by means of mock-Shakespearean adverts which read:

ROMEO: Dost thou dig that Nightly Jazz in Chelsea?

JULIET: Crazy

As it happened, some of the finest Shakespearean actors around were in the King's Road that year, but not generally speaking the words of the Bard. Alec Guinness had made a film of Graham Greene's *Our Man in Havana*, directed by Chelsea resident Carol Reed, which premiered in London in January 1960, breaking the box-office records at the Odeon Leicester Square. Guinness, however, later remembered the reviews as having been appalling, and wrote in his 1985 memoir, *Blessings in Disguise*, of an afternoon at Reed's house on the King's Road when the two of them watched small children passing by on the pavement outside and the director said, 'At least they can't read.' Meanwhile, Guinness's frequent partner in Shakespeare, Laurence Olivier, was much in the news that April, since the publicity build-up for Tony Richardson's film of Osborne's *The Entertainer* had begun, although it would not reach the cinemas till July, and Olivier at present was appearing onstage at the Royal Court in a production of *Rhinoceros* by Ionesco. As if the most famous stage actor in the world were not enough to ensure attention, the play itself was both produced and directed by none other than Orson Welles. As can be imagined, tickets were at a premium.

Credit: author's collection

> **ROYAL COURT**
> Sloane Square, S.W.1.   SLOane 1745.
> Evgs. 7.30. S. 5 & 8.15. Thurs., 2.30.
> **LAURENCE OLIVIER**
> Joan Plowright, Alan Webb,
> Duncan Macrae, Miles Malleson in
> Ionesco's **RHINOCEROS**
> Produced by Orson Welles

Welles directs Olivier at the Royal Court, April 1960

Rhinoceros had first been produced in Paris in January by Jean-Louis Barrault at the Odéon, but Welles's April incarnation, in a translation by Derek Prouse, was its British debut. The cast included the future Lady Olivier, Joan Plowright, future *Last of the Summer Wine* regular Peter Sallis, and one of the best-loved members of Hammer Film Productions' informal repertory company, Miles Malleson, who the previous year had given a virtuoso performance as the Bishop in their definitive version of Conan Doyle's *The Hound of the Baskervilles*, and had just completed filming *Brides of Dracula*, due out in July. Given the viciousness with which the 'serious' film critics regularly attacked Hammer at the time, it is worth noting that as well as employing first-class technicians, writers and directors, they also regularly gave work to some of the finest actors in the country, who were happy to move easily between their productions and the supposedly more 'respectable' theatre productions at the Court.

While Olivier was on the stage in Sloane Square dodging an outbreak of horned mammals, his performance as Archie Rice in *The Entertainer* was already being shown to the press. For some reason, following these spring 1960 screenings, the film was taken away and then substantially re-cut. Hence, although *Films and Filming* published a review in their May edition, the following month they ran a news item explaining that things had now changed, and in one month they went from this:

> The thrusting close-ups are as strident as Archie's home life or the backstage quarrels of 'Stars and Strips'. [. . .] *The Entertainer* is in the highest degree an actor's picture and another triumphant sign of renaissance in the realistic British cinema.

To this:

The production company was not happy about some of the technical quality. [. . .] There is a lesson to be learnt here by the young film-makers. Technique is *not* expendable. It is too easy to drift into films from university, the art theatre or television and talk a lot about new waves but overlook old techniques. For instance, one of the most irritating things for me about *The Entertainer* (both versions!) was some of the odd camera angles. They simply prevented the actors' performances getting close to the audience: they were quite without reason.

And perhaps too many 'thrusting close-ups'. Margaret Hinxman's review in *Picturegoer* – which seems to have been written after having seen the first version – praised the acting but blamed the script, written by John Osborne and Nigel Kneale, concluding that, 'in the end, the film is suspended in a limbo as hopeless as that in which the hero resides – neither great human drama nor a great social document.'

Olivier was not the only cast member attracting press attention; others a little further down the bill were also in the spotlight, as the June edition of *Photoplay* proved:

In *The Entertainer* a shapely blonde appears as a showgirl in several scenes with Sir Laurence Olivier. Her name is Jackie Fortune and she is now working at the Revue Club, one of London's strip theatres for £18-a-week. 'I hate stripping,' she says. 'I've lost my self respect. Appearing in a film with Sir Laurence was much more fun.'

When the film finally opened at the Odeon, Marble Arch, on July 28, despite its having been selected, as *Kine Weekly* reported, to be 'this year's official British entry at the Karlovy Vary Festival', many of the critics got their knives out, with the result that the distributors eventually ran adverts listing some of the bad quotes as well as the good: 'Like opening a dustbin' – *Daily Express*; 'Leering, shameful bawdiness' – *News of the World*; 'Deadly blasphemy' – *Sunday Express*; 'Vulgar' – *Daily Mirror;* all of which makes it sound a lot more entertaining than it actually was.

A couple of months before the *Daily Express* began opening their dustbins, Woodfall's usually silent partner, Harry Saltzman, had explained a little of the new company's philosophy in an article he wrote for *Films and Filming*, stressing their refusal to have story content altered to suit the demands of financial backers:

We may be bankrupt and out of business tomorrow, but we're going to give it a go. [. . .] Tony [Richardson] today is one of the most promising directors in the world market. *The Entertainer* will prove it definitely, and he will direct *A Taste of Honey* for us. He's been inundated with offers by some of the same people who turned him down as director for *Look Back in Anger*.

Excellent Menu, Personal Supervision

While half the film studios in and around town were filled with the sound of carpenters and set designers rigging up state-of-the-art facsimiles of working-class slum interiors – usually on the instructions of ex-public school and Oxbridge directors – Chelsea itself was gaining fashionable restaurants seemingly by the week, and there was also an outbreak of shops offering all the essentials for decorating that swinging, James Bond-style *pied-à-terre*.

Mannheim, at 305 King's Road, advertised their 'large selection of modern stainless steel, glass, enamel, pottery and wooden accessories for the home. Original Danish theatre posters by Bjorn Wimblad'. The good life, it would seem, had arrived, and shame on you if were so uncool that you'd never heard of Mr Wimblad. As for dining out, Mario was still offering to welcome you at the Pheasantry, but in a sign of the times, a former coffee bar, the Orrery, at 355 King's Road, had now been replaced with the presumably more profitable Patna Garden Indian Restaurant, while another Indian restaurant, the New Assam, had opened up at number 438. A little further east, on the ground floor of the thirties apartment building Chelsea Cloisters in Sloane Avenue, the Shorthorn Restaurant had just opened, run by Ezio Franks and David Corrigall, who reported that regular customers in 1960 included Milton Shulman and the actor Michael Medwin. In Sydney Street, the road running north up the side of the former Chelsea Palace, the 'newly opened' Scholar Gypsy Restaurant at number 119 was offering 'Soft lights, Felix Osa with his Guitar, Excellent menu, Personal supervision'. Personal supervision? For some reason this conjures up images of fork-holding lessons, barked instructions and points deducted for any items left uneaten, but it is probably unwise to speculate further.

On May 5, 1960, a small item in *Kine Weekly* announced that 'John Profumo, Minister of State for Foreign Affairs, will attend the world premiere of *Oscar Wilde* [. . .] at the Carlton, Haymarket.' Within three years, Profumo's name would be as notorious in the public mind as Wilde's had been at the height of his trial, and the words 'foreign affair' would likely have conjured up quite another meaning. Had he attended the House of Commons on May 16,

1960, Profumo would have had a chance to express his opinion when MPs debated the introduction of legal measures to control Teddy boys. It is comforting to know that just two years before Russia and America almost blew up the world with nuclear warheads, the British parliament had identified the real danger and was taking solemn steps to try to protect the public from a few teenage rock'n'roll fans with velvet collars.

Making film news in May was actress and 'top London photographic model, 21-year-old Sarah Branch', currently starring in *Sands of the Desert* with Charlie Drake, and who had also just made two pictures for Hammer, the classic crime drama *Hell Is a City* and the Robin Hood film *Sword of Sherwood Forest*, in which she played Maid Marian. As *Picture Show and TV Mirror* informed its readers: 'She is not married – in fact she has just broken off her engagement – and lives in a flat in Chelsea, loves decorating, reading, sewing, and film-going.'

Over at the Royal Court, they had recovered from the rhinoceros stampede and the stage was clear for John Dexter's production of Arnold Wesker's *Trilogy*, consisting of *Chicken Soup with Barley*, *Roots*, and *I'm Talking About Jerusalem*. Up the road at the Classic, you could catch Andrzej Wajda's *Kanal* (1957), also part of a trilogy (along with *A Generation* (1954) and *Ashes and Diamonds* (1958)), but if none of this appealed to you, there was still hope: somewhere in Regent Street there was an exhibition celebrating – don't all rush at once – the 150th Anniversary of Canned Foods, organised by the Tin Research Institute. Who said London wasn't swinging?

Sink Your Last Sixpence

The new British cinema which had developed from the 'angry' movement of the fifties continued to make the news: director Leslie 'father of Barry' Norman was pictured talking to Laurence Harvey on the set of the film adaptation of Willis Hall's 1959 Royal Court hit *The Long and the Short and the Tall* at Elstree, while *Kine Weekly* reported that 'the Motion Picture Critics and Commentators of America have voted *Room at the Top* sixth in the ten best films of 1959.' Of course, while it might have played well with the critics, out in the wider America, as John Peel told me, if, like him, you were living in Texas, the new British cinema meant almost less than nothing to most people, and signs of any impending cultural invasion were distinctly thin on the ground:

> *Saturday Night and Sunday Morning*? Yeah, things like that were shown, but they would have been shown anyway. I mean, you can imagine the sort of art people in Dallas, people who were genuinely interested, people

who acquire famous paintings as an investment and so on, but the actual number of people in Dallas at that time – and very likely now – who would be interested in what was going on anywhere other than in Texas was pretty limited, I mean, measured in hundreds, tens possibly even . . .

The King's Road kitchen-sink revolution may have fallen at the first hurdle in the town where men wore Stetsons and presidents would have been well advised to wear all-over body armour, but if Chelsea was not yet reaching out to some parts of America, at least the American woman with the ruby slippers was making the journey across the pond and coming to SW3. In the summer of 1960, Judy Garland rented Carol Reed's house on the King's Road and set up home there with her husband Sid Luft and children Liza, Lorna and Joey. She also gave a show at the London Palladium on August 28, and this would not be the last time that she was to live in the area.

Judy's current home was just a short walk from Alexander's restaurant at 138a King's Road, below Bazaar – 'Dine by Candlelight in Chelsea's Most Romantic Italian Restaurant' – which Mary Quant and Alexander Plunket Greene had eventually sold to the staff in order to concentrate on their ever-expanding fashion business. Even closer at hand was the Magic Carpet Inn, which was still, as the adverts noted, 'Personally directed by LGH Brampton (ex F/Lt. RAF)', also listing praise from various sources, including Egon Ronay: 'The Magic Carpet set Chelsea on the gastronomic road. Charming, warm, entertaining place to dine in.'

Meanwhile, further north, up at the Edinburgh Festival, four ex-students opened at the Lyceum Theatre in a revue called *Beyond the Fringe*, but it would be another year before this show starring Peter Cook, Dudley Moore, Alan Bennett and Jonathan Miller transferred to London and created a national and then an international sensation.

As the summer ended, Woodfall's film of *Saturday Night and Sunday Morning* starring Albert Finney finally opened in a London which was already queueing up to see him on stage as *Billy Liar* at the Cambridge Theatre. John Osborne later said that this was the first of Woodfall's films to turn a profit, and in the run-up to its release, Alexander Walker gave the new company an encouraging write-up in the *Evening Standard*: 'Woodfall is *British*. The brains behind it belong to John Osborne and Tony Richardson, men who are willing to sink their last sixpence – and their hearts – into the films they make. When rebellion is in the air, Osborne is pretty sure to be in on the act.'

As the box-office takings were to prove, it was not looking likely that Osborne would be down to his last sixpence at any time in the foreseeable future.

Something Silky and Ruffled

While Finney was packing them in both at cinemas and at the Cambridge Theatre, over at the Royal Court, John Arden's new play *The Happy Haven* was steadily losing money, just as *Serjeant Musgrave's Dance* had done the year before. To his credit, George Devine backed Arden to the hilt, and apparently joked about the losses, showing him a pile of reviews and saying, 'Well, boy, they're even worse than *Serjeant Musgrave*.' Arden had written *The Happy Haven* after being inspired by sessions of the Royal Court's weekly Writers' Group in Flood Street, and among the cast was Rachel Roberts, also to be seen at cinemas in *Saturday Night and Sunday Morning*. Rachel had a part in the next production to come to the Royal Court, whose box-office takings were in stark contrast to those of *The Happy Haven*. This was an early and less well-known Chekhov play called *Platonov*, for which George Devine had decided to bring in a high-powered star name in order to boost its chances of pulling a crowd. Since Olivier had proved by means of his appearances in *The Entertainer* and *Rhinoceros* that a major film star could also play effectively in Sloane Square, it is not surprising that Rex Harrison – then a considerable force in the cinema – was keen to sign up for the Chekhov. Originally, the play was to have been directed by Lindsay Anderson, who had Ian Bannen in mind for the role, but when Anderson was moved over to the task of directing Christopher Logue's *Trials by Logue* (due to follow *Platonov*), Devine took over the Chekhov and brought in the man known to the tabloids as Sexy Rexy.

Rex Harrison, who was living just near the Royal Court in Eaton Square, had been married to uninhibited Bazaar customer Kay Kendall, but she had tragically died of leukaemia the previous year. As it turned out, in the same way that Laurence Olivier got to know his future wife Joan Plowright while working together at the Royal Court, Harrison met his new wife Rachel Roberts while co-starring with her in *Platonov*. However, things were not quite as simple as might be imagined, because Roberts was still married to fellow Royal Court actor Alan Dobie, but during the production she and Harrison began the affair which would eventually result in their ten-year marriage. In Alexander Walker's biography of Rachel Roberts, *No Bells on Sunday*, he quotes from her journal in which she recalled this production:

> Rex cut such a dash. There was something Edwardian about him, something silky and ruffled. He liked his luncheons to be at a now long-forgotten and pulled-down, but then well-established little French restaurant off Sloane Square. *The Queen's* restaurant, it was called. Waiters were *waiters* there – long experienced in the trade and in the tooth. The

food was good classic bourgeois fare, the napkins were white, the glasses polished, the maître d' greatly impressed to have Rex as his customer. [. . .] I know that, for Rex, I represented the 'new blood' of the London theatre. The Royal Court was at its zenith. Our *Platonov* was eulogised by the critics, both the play and the actor.

While Rachel Roberts was acquiring a new lover, Lady Chatterley's old one from 1928 was causing something of a fuss in the courts, as a result of the obscenity case which had been brought against Penguin Books in an effort to protect the great unwashed from exposure to several English words of which, of course, were it not for D. H. Lawrence, they would never have heard. Although the book dated from 1928, it had never before been printed in its unexpurgated form in the UK. Following a parade of distinguished witnesses for the defence, including Richard Hoggart and even a selection of relatively liberal members of the clergy, *Lady Chatterley's Lover* was cleared of the charge of obscenity on November 2, which prompted the *Guardian* to write the following day that 'the jury's verdict on *Lady Chatterley's Lover* is a triumph of common sense – and the more pleasing because it was unexpected.' Both that paper and the *Observer* went on to print the work *fuck* in full, thus breaking a long taboo on such things in the media, but before we run away with the idea that the Chatterley trial was a clear example of how much more relaxed things had become as the century progressed, it is worth pointing out that the 1932 edition of D. H. Lawrence's *Collected Poems* contained the word *cunt* (in the poem 'Whether or Not') and yet had not been prosecuted. Similarly, if the Chatterley trial heralded a brave new dawn, no-one presumably saw fit to inform old-school judges such as Justice Michael Argyle, who a decade later would preside over the *Oz* magazine obscenity trial with thinly disguised prudishness, and whose judgments would later be overturned on appeal on the grounds that he had seriously misdirected the jury. It was alright to print Lawrence, because he was 'literature' – and most importantly, he was safely dead – but when it came to the actions of the younger generation who might be around at the moment and prone to stir things up, as the sixties and seventies would go on to show, there was still a lot of room left for the 'hang them and flog them' brigade to waste taxpayers' money with obscenity prosecutions.

Corsets and What Have You

In the ever-glamorous world of film, Dick Richards of *Picture Show* magazine was introducing his readers to an up-and-coming young actress from the King's Road area:

It was her first Press party. Susan Hampshire, ex-debutante and one of the Chelsea set, was going into business as a film star. Susan, a wide-eyed blonde whose only previous experience has been in a West End musical [. . .] has just been picked by 27-year-old Canadian director Sidney Furie to star in his film *During One Night*. [. . .] Young Miss Hampshire was holding court at her first Press party and she wasn't wearing shoes. *Footnote*: Miss Hampshire has very nice feet.

If Susan Hampshire was just starting out on the road to fame that autumn, two film actors who already had worldwide reputations – Sophia Loren and Peter Sellers – called in at the Chelsea Palace TV studio to appear on *Chelsea at Nine*. In an article about a court case published in *The Times* when Granada was involved in a dispute about the precise nature of its business in that building, the testimony offered by the company gave an insight into the daily routine the pair would have experienced:

When artists came on to the premises it was not for rehearsal to improve performance, but to ensure success in the process of transmission. The artists were concerned with three operations termed the 'stagger through', the 'run through', and the 'dress rehearsal'. The first two were purely informal in so far as the actors were concerned; they did not dress, they smoked, and the only objective was to get them in the proper position for the camera.

The Millionairess on release in London, 1960

Loren and Sellers had just finished shooting a film called *The Millionairess* at Elstree, whose posters showed Loren in fishnet stockings and a basque, and their comedy song from the film, *Goodness Gracious Me*, would hit the charts in November, rising to number four, undoubtedly helped by the fact that they performed it on the Granada show. Bruce Grimes, who designed the sets for their appearance and still lived around the corner in Flood Street, told me:

'We did the *Doctor I'm in Trouble* sketch. You know that famous thing of her in corsets and what have you? Well, I had a life-size cut-out of that, and I remember walking down the King's Road with it, because I took it down to my room which I had down there, with her tucked under my arm.'

While residents of cosmopolitan Chelsea might have been accustomed to seeing life-size cut-outs of half-naked Italian film stars being carried down the street, a renowned countryman of hers, himself a film director, chose that moment to deplore the smut that was apparently afflicting society. Michelangelo Antonioni, whose new film *L'Avventura* had just won the Special Jury Prize at Cannes, wrote an article for the December 1960 edition of *Films and Filming* called 'Eroticism – The Disease of Our Age', a title which arch-prude Mary Whitehouse could scarcely have bettered. 'Why are literature and the entertainment arts so thick with eroticism today?' asked Antonioni. 'It is the more obvious symptom of an emotional sickness. There would not be this eroticism if Eros were still in good health.' Interesting sentiments from a man who, six years later, shot a film called *Blow-Up* in newly 'swinging' London – partly in the King's Road area – which became known, among other things, for featuring mainstream UK cinema's first glimpse of pubic hair. Meanwhile, in the daily papers of 1960, reports were appearing of the development of a product, not yet on sale in Britain, which would come to be known simply as 'The Pill'.

This Vague Picture of Naked Ladies Sittin' Around

The English Stage Company's year rounded out with Christopher Logue's *Trials by Logue* – a double bill of two short plays, *Antigone* and *Cob and Leach*, directed by Lindsay Anderson, but taken off a week earlier than scheduled – and then a new play by Shelagh Delaney called *The Lion in Love*. Delaney was by now something of a household name, having been profiled in 1960 by Ken Russell in a short documentary for BBC TV's *Monitor* programme entitled *Shelagh Delaney's Salford*, in which the playwright was filmed revisiting her hometown, while Woodfall were about to begin shooting their cinema adaptation of her first play, *A Taste of Honey*, in spring 1961. Also moving into the public consciousness in 1960 was the writer David Storey with his debut novel *This Sporting Life*, which would be filmed in 1962 by Lindsay Anderson. Storey later became a successful playwright with a string of successes at the Royal Court, where he also served as Assistant Artistic Director from 1972 to 1974.

Newly enrolled at the Chelsea Art School in Manresa Road was a young woman called Virginia Ironside, whose mother Janey was Professor of Fashion at the Royal College of Art, with offices in Ennismore Gardens, not far from the V&A. In the previous couple of years Janey had largely done away with the traditional bias in favour of fashion students from privileged backgrounds, and many of the coming sixties generation of influential young designers were studying under her. As Virginia later wrote in her memoir of her mother, *Janey and Me*:

> People from the North in those days were considered beyond the pale and were never given a chance, but my mother welcomed the likes of Anthony Price, a farmer's boy from Yorkshire, and Ossie Clark from Salford and gave them an opportunity to use the College as a showcase. Then she persuaded leaders of the fashion industry to hire them.

As for Virginia's own entry into Chelsea College of Art, it was deceptively easy: 'You didn't need a portfolio; you wandered in and signed on. Unfortunately, art schools had just decided that teaching people to draw was old hat. The plaster casts and *écorchés* figures were chucked out of the cast rooms, and life drawing was despised.' Despite these drawbacks, in a couple of years, she was able to put her experiences of her King's Road student days to good use.

A certain Keith Richards had been at Sidcup Art College since the previous year, having joined in similarly casual circumstances on the recommendation of his headmaster, as he later told Victor Bockris: 'You're about sixteen or sixteen and you don't even know what the fuck they do in art school. You have this vague picture of naked ladies sittin' around. Drawing them . . . "Well, I'll try that."' Significant numbers of future UK rock musicians were also thinking along the same lines.

Looking back on 1960, *Films and Filming*'s annual survey of the critics revealed that, for all the kitchen-sink excitement, in terms of box-office receipts, the biggest money-spinner had in fact been *Hercules Unchained*, a sword-and-sandal beefcake extravaganza starring Steve Reeves, made in Italy with American money. Clearly, as far as the public were concerned, gritty northern dramas were all very well, but show them a muscle-bound gent in a skirt pushing some masonry over and they'd line up around the block. Several films were listed in the magazine's 'Most over-rated by the critics' category, including Tony Richardson's *The Entertainer*, but many reviewers had liked *Saturday Night and Sunday Morning*, including Alexander Walker of the *Evening Standard*, 'because it produced the year's only new star, Albert Finney, and this is the first film since the war to show the articulate working class lad in his own habitat'.

Finally, for Americans who had yet to be informed that London was 'swinging', the magazine *Esquire* had a few words of advice for those brave souls thinking of crossing the Atlantic, published in book form that year as *Esquire's Europe in Style*. Among the information generally aimed at the rich, male traveller – apart from where to pick up a mink for the mistress at the knock-down price of $10,000 – were the following cautionary words: 'Here's a random list, by no means complete, of things you'll have a hard time finding, or look for in vain: baked beans . . . cake mix . . . crabs . . . ginger snaps . . . baked potatoes . . . lollipops . . . marshmallows . . . peanut butter . . . pralines . . . salted peanuts . . . scallops . . . sliced bread . . .'

It is hard to imagine what kind of research produced these extremely strange statements, but just a few years later, many column inches were to be expended in the quest to describe sixties London, and Americans would no longer have to think of England as some sort of primitive wasteland where marshmallows were an unknown pleasure and people were starving to death in the street for want of a baked potato.

12

'A taste of money'

Flash Gordon Scenery and Prompt Corner Dialogue

By 1961, the Angry generation and the kitchen-sink dramas they provoked had made audiences in many parts of the world familiar with the back-streets and side-alleys of working-class England, or at any rate, the celluloid facsimile of them displayed in films such as *Room at the Top*, *Look Back in Anger* and *Saturday Night and Sunday Morning*. As with rock'n'roll in 1956, or later with Merseybeat or mid-seventies punk, once the cash registers started ringing, there was a horde of unlikely fellow travellers desperately trying to hitch a ride on the bandwagon. Tony Richardson, in an article written for *Films and Filming* as part of the publicity for his new film, *A Taste of Honey*, recalled that in his theatre experience, as in his film career, he had seen numerous attempts at cheap copies in the wake of any popular hit:

> Unfortunately, in the business as it is at present the success of films like *Saturday Night* will lead to copies. Anything that is immediately successful is copied. There may be good copies which are influenced by them which produce something new and interesting, something similar but which generally has its own truth and vitality: but there will also be many bad copies. It is exactly the same situation as we encountered at the Royal Court Theatre after we had a success. [. . .] Already Warwick has filed the title *Every Night and Every Morning*, and somebody else is making a film called *A Taste of Money*.

Certainly, the idea of taking plays which had appeared at the Royal Court and adapting them for the cinema was by now an established trend, even though one reader was moved to complain in that same issue of *Films and Filming* about the quality of some of the product; namely, a picture which had opened at the Plaza, Piccadilly on February 16: 'If *The Long and the Short and the Tall*, with its Flash Gordon scenery and prompt corner dialogue, reflects the direction in which Britain's "new wave" is headed then heaven help *Saturday Night and Sunday Morning* for pulling the trigger!'

Since kitchen-sink dramas from the Royal Court were a source of alleg-edly sure-fire box-office material, it is not surprising that someone got around to filming one of Arnold Wesker's dramas that year. You want a kitchen? Well, how about *The Kitchen*? Wesker's play, set among the ovens and dishes behind the scenes in a restaurant, and based upon his own three-year experience of working in the catering trade, had been presented two years previously at the Court as a Sunday night without decor pres-entation. It was brought to the cinema by an unlikely source, the film technicians union ACT (now the ACTT), venturing into film production for the first time, but bankrolled in this instance almost entirely by the National Film Finance Corporation. Starring German actor Carl Mohner, it began shooting in January 1961 at Shepperton, with Wesker in constant attendance. It was directed by James Hill, who was to have a major inter-national hit four years later with a rather less studio-bound subject, *Born Free*. Hill's *The Kitchen* may not have been a box-office sensation along the lines of *Saturday Night and Sunday Morning*, but it seems to have encouraged the English Stage Company to give the play a proper presentation at last, opening at the Royal Court on June 27 with a cast which included Tony Richardson's new discovery from *A Taste of Honey*, Rita Tushingham, as well as future Likely Lad James Bolam, who had also appeared in James Hill's film version.

While the cameras were rolling at Shepperton filming a kitchen which had first seen the light of day onstage in Sloane Square, a man who ran a real kitchen a little further down the King's Road – and whose food was regularly eaten by the actors from the Royal Court – was being profiled in *What's On in London*. His name was Murray Radin, and for the past five years he had been in charge of a restaurant called Au Père de Nico at 10 Lincoln Street, a few hundred yards down the King's Road, opposite the Duke of York's barracks. 'His relaxation is still the theatre,' said the article, 'He has a friendly association with the Royal Court theatre; and he was pleased when John Osborne chose his restaurant for his wedding reception.'

Injurious to Morality or Offensive to Public Feeling

Osborne had just completed a new play, *Luther*, which would come to the Royal Court later in the year. For the lead role, they chose an actor who, at the start of 1961, seemed to be the man who was making all the headlines: 'A new world star, Albert Finney', said the *Daily Express*, and they were right. 'Suddenly – It's Finney', ran the title of an article in the February edition of *ABC Film Review*, bolstering the actor's street credentials by pointing out that he had shown up to his own *Saturday Night and Sunday Morning* premiere 'casually dressed in flat cap, corduroy coat and tieless shirt'. In the immediate pre-Rolling Stones world, where dinner jackets were the norm for such occasions, this was considered pretty radical stuff. The interviewer, Elizabeth Hardie, asked Finney, 'Is there anything in the British way of life that makes you really angry?', to which he replied, 'Yes, the sort of person who writes to a national newspaper to complain that he's tired of film heroes in overalls.' Hardly had the bandwagon started rolling and people were already trying to saw the wheels off. Still, dissenting voices were few and far between, and the film certainly struck a chord with its new type of 'hero' a world away from the stiff-upper-lip brigade of previous years, as *What's On in London*'s handy plot summary makes clear:

> [. . .] set against a background of the worst kind of industrial North, its factories and its slums, [it] tells, quite brilliantly, the story of a lower-class Angry Young Man whose life ideal is complete self indulgence, who in line with his unmoral concepts, seduces his mate's wife, makes her pregnant, dodges the consequences and otherwise behaves oafishly throughout; a truly outstanding screen debut by Albert Finney.

Saturday Night and Sunday Morning's portrayal of working-class English life was chosen as the opening film for that year's Moscow Film Festival, and, to judge from David Robinson's report in *Sight and Sound*, seems to have been somewhat problematic for the Soviet officials: 'The energetic and attractive Minister of Culture', a certain Mrs Furtseva, 'was full of admiration for the film, but rather shocked. Whether it was with a woman's eye or that of an arbiter of socialist morality that she looked at the film, she said that she felt that it was not the sort of work that should be shown to the larger public.'

Mrs Furtseva evidently shared an attitude of mind common to moral guardians in many places – the ever-popular belief that such things are not dangerous when viewed by privileged people like themselves, but were quite unsuitable for everybody else, especially the lower orders. It was not just the land of the KGB and the Gulags which felt that way about Finney's debut feature – anyone unlucky enough to be living in Warwickshire in those days was also subject to the whims of a group of people who thought the film unsuitable for showing to 'the larger public'. Indeed, they were banning films left, right and centre that year in that county, as the February 9, 1961 edition of *Kine Weekly* reported:

> Warwickshire Cinematograph Licensing Committee, who recently banned *Saturday Night and Sunday Morning* have just banned *Beat Girl*, *The Green Mare's Nest, Sins of Youth* and *Peeping Tom*. The committee has also asked for private screenings of *Desire in the Dust, Night Heat, A Passionate Affair* and *Private Property* because it thinks that the synopses suggest that these pictures may be injurious to morality or offensive to public feeling.

Such a heavy reliance on film titles and printed synopses when engaged in the unending search for imaginary smut can lead to problems, and a quick glance at some film magazines of that year suggests that the scissor-happy censors of Warwickshire must have hardly known which way to turn: currently on release were *Go Naked in the World, Girls for the Summer, Breath of Scandal, Love and the Frenchwoman, Web of Passion, Shadow of Adultery* – indeed, there was even a Josh Logan film called *Fanny*. The picture captions in *Films and Filming* probably got the Licensing Committee hot under the collar as well: 'Cornelius and Tansy employ a bizarre way of sharing a banana while camping in Scotland, in this scene from Ralph Thomas' *No My Darling Daughter*.' For the record, the films in question were all on general release, and *No My Darling Daughter* was a U-certificate family comedy, but why let the facts get in the way of a moral panic?

This is a Letter of Hate

Of course, the floodgates had already opened as far as the watchdogs were concerned, because on January 30, 1961, the Pill had gone on sale in Britain for the first time.

Tony Richardson was preparing to shoot Woodfall's new film, *A Taste of Honey*, whose subject matter contained several elements which might also have given the moral re-armament faction cause for concern. The character of Jo, played by newcomer Rita Tushingham – a '£1 a week student stage manager at Liverpool Rep. [. . .] chosen from 2,000 applicants' according

Credit: author's collection

A Taste of Honey, set in the north, but partially shot in Chelsea

to *Kine Weekly* – does not appear to have been making use of the Pill, but, as an unmarried mother with a black lover and an openly gay man friend, her character was as different in her own way as Finney's in *Saturday Night and Sunday Morning*. Richardson had been disappointed with the feel of the studio work in *Look Back in Anger*, and for this picture he decided to shoot entirely on location, as a result of which decision, a significant part of the film's costs were down to the fact that they bought a house in Chelsea in which to film. As *Sight and Sound* reported: 'The unusual thing is that no filming whatsoever has taken place in a studio; the film has been shot on location in Manchester and Salford, in a Chelsea house taken over as combined studio and offices, and elsewhere in London.' One of the locations 'elsewhere in London' was the Royal Court's scenic workshop in Park Walk, World's End, which appeared in the film as Rita Tushingham's flat, while its exterior yard served for the firework scene. As Richardson himself wrote in *Films and Filming*:

> It was my decision to do *A Taste of Honey* independent of a studio [i.e. completely on location] because I think you get an authenticity that you can never get in a studio, because there you tend to become more conventional in every way. [. . .] In *A Taste of Honey* I wanted to force a much rougher style on the film, and to force myself to shoot in, I hope, a freer way.

Filming took place in the spring of 1961, just as the press were given previews of a picture which Tony Richardson had made after *The Entertainer*, and not in England, but in Hollywood for 20th Century Fox. *Sanctuary*, starring Lee Remick and Yves Montand, was based on William Faulkner's play *Requiem for a Nun*, which Richardson had directed at the Royal Court in 1957. Reviews were mixed, but many blamed the source material rather than the director, and it was certainly seen as a hopeful sign that someone who had come up so quickly from the 16mm documentary days of Free Cinema was now over there mixing it with the major studios in California.

While one English Stage Company mainstay was making inroads into Hollywood, its most famous writer was on holiday on the continent, firing off angry messages to the British press: 'This is a letter of hate,' wrote John Osborne from Valbonne in France, via the correspondence pages of *Tribune* magazine on August 18:

> It is for you, my countrymen. I mean those men of my country who have defiled it. [. . .] My favourite fantasy is four minutes or so non-commercial viewing as you fry in your democratically elected hot seats in Westminster, preferably with your condoning constituents. [. . .] Till then, damn you England. You're rotting now, and quite soon you'll disappear.

Osborne had obviously misplaced his no-doubt well-thumbed copy of *How to Win Friends and Influence People*, and the press reaction was predictably fierce, but it cannot have done much harm to the ticket sales for his new play at the Court, *Luther*, which had opened on July 27, but then, as Albert Finney's first stage role since *Billy Liar*, it was hardly likely to have been sparsely attended.

To judge from film projects being announced in the press, it was clear that as far as British cinema was concerned, the kitchen was showing no sign of sinking. Producer Joseph Janni had acquired the rights to *Billy Liar*, and its authors Keith Waterhouse and Willis Hall were working on the script, while at the same time the film rights to Robin Maugham's novel *The Servant* had gone to director Michael Anderson, whose *Around the World in 80 Days* had been celebrated with a launch party in Battersea Park some years back. However, on May 16, 1961, another film-related event in the park unwittingly attracted serious police attention. *Quatermass Experiment* director Val Guest, last seen putting coffee-bar sensation Cliff Richard through his paces in *Expresso Bongo*, had written a taut science-fiction script called *The Day the Earth Caught Fire*, set in a London in which the temperature was inexorably rising. On the opening day of shooting, the scene called for the Battersea Park Fun Fair and the river between Chelsea and Battersea to be covered in a mysterious creeping fog, generated by smoke machines. While they were filming, having turned a clear summer's day into something resembling a Jack the Ripper setting with fog swirling around the Chelsea Bridge, the crew received an urgent visit from the constabulary. It turned out that the wind had been blowing their mysterious mist a little to the north, where Her Majesty the Queen was slowly disappearing from view while attempting to declare that year's Chelsea Flower Show open to the public. Appearing in the film in an uncredited role as a policeman with dialogue advising characters that most of Chelsea has been blocked off was a Royal Court actor named Michael Caine, who would graduate to much more high-profile parts in the coming years.

Crap!

As the influence of the theatre on Sloane Square spread out around the world via the medium of film, Mary Quant's King's Road fashion designs were reaching out internationally, and in 1961 she and Plunket Greene and McNair formed Mary Quant Limited, in order to be able to begin manu-facturing clothes in quantity. This was a direct result of a trip they had recently made to New York, carrying with them a couple of suitcases full of designs, where, after enduring the brief but pungent opinion of the influen-tial woman from the *Herald Tribune* – 'Crap!' – they were championed first by *Women's Wear Daily*, then by Sally Kirkland at *LIFE* magazine. On returning to Chelsea, Alexander suggested that if they were about to receive national US publicity of that kind in future, then it might be an idea to have the manufacturing capacity to cope with the orders which would probably result. The days of one sewing machine in the Oakley Street bedsit and rolls of material bought over the counter at Harrods were long gone.

While Mary was making inroads into the American market, over in West Germany a young schoolboy called Wolfgang Doebeling was learning English as fast as he could by the very effective method of reading three of the London music papers from cover to cover each week: *NME*, *Melody Maker* and *Disc* (or *Disc and Music Echo*, to give it its full title). Now a senior writer at German *Rolling Stone*, and long-time Berlin radio DJ, Wolfgang's growing conviction – shared by many other young people over the next few years – that London was becoming the hip centre of the world had absolutely nothing to do with visions of Beefeaters, bowler hats, or a deep and abiding admiration for the policies of Harold Macmillan or Harold Wilson. It was music and pop culture that was driving this particular revolution, as he explained to me:

I started reading the music weeklies in 1960 or '61. I didn't have any money, so it was actually my grandma who bought me the magazines, and she did it because she knew that I was learning English at school. She thought she was doing me a huge favour, which of course she did. They cost two marks twenty at the time, all three of them together. Stuttgart, where I come from, was still bombed-out, basically, and that was a lot of money in 1960 – I got one mark pocket money a month at the time. It was brilliant, and my grandma and my parents supported me: 'Wolfgang, he can read *English* . . .' At the time, that was totally unheard of, really. English was something that you learned like Biology or something, you know, everybody hated it more or less, whereas I had a good reason for wanting to learn, and I was driven by that.

When he was a little older, but still at school, Wolfgang would save up his money all year in order to make one trip each summer to London, where the action was.

For now, in 1961, anyone walking down the King's Road would have seen yet more new restaurants opening up along a stretch of road which had over the course of the past ten years developed into one of the finest areas for dining out in the capital. In March, the Marco Polo opened at 95 King's Road, offering 'Splendid Chinese Food in Elegant Surroundings', modestly described by the owners as 'The New Rendezvous of the Music and Theatre World'. That being the case, presumably some of the music world would have been confused about where to go for the evening, since in June another place opened up at 257 Fulham Road calling itself Cafe le Jazzhot, whose introductory adverts urged people to 'visit the new meeting place for jazz fans, musicians, painters, and writers, set in the heart of Chelsea'. Then again, music fans could always give both places a miss and head for the Six Bells pub at 197 King's Road instead, the former drinking home of Rossetti and Swinburne, which was now a regular trad jazz venue offering live groups every Monday and Friday. Failing that, there was always the London School of Bridge, at 38 King's Road.

Knife Wound, Eh? Teddy Boy, Is He?

Future Chelsea resident Mick Jagger was commuting most days into town from Dartford in Kent, but his destination was the London School of Economics, not Bridge. For all the opportunities on offer in the metropolis, Jagger actually made the most important meeting of his life a short distance from his home in the suburbs when he ran into an old primary school acquaintance, Keith Richards, as they were both waiting at Dartford railway station. As has been lovingly documented many times over the years, the future Sir Mick attracted Keith's attention because he was carrying two US-import albums on the Chess label, *The Best of Muddy Waters* and Chuck Berry's *Rockin' at the Hops*, which Jagger had ordered by post from Chicago. Suave choices, and all but unobtainable in the Britain of those days, according to legend, but when I mentioned the story to Mick Farren, he had this to say: [adopts world-weary accent] 'Well that's *not strictly true* . . . I mean all that was kind of covered by Dobells [the central London jazz shop] and a couple of other specialist jazz-through-folk-through-blues shops.'

Jagger and Richards did not live in Chelsea yet – that would come the following year – but a politician called George Ward did, an ex-Secretary of State for Air who was friends with current government minister John Profumo. One day in the summer of 1961, John turned up at Ward's door with his new girlfriend, Christine Keeler, whom he'd met at a country house party of the Astors'. Between them and the press, they would eventually bring the government to the brink of collapse, but these were strange days for politicians, as Tony Hancock's character pointed out in the most famous episode of his television show *The Blood Donor*, which was broadcast that year: 'There's Adam Faith earning ten times as much as the prime minister. Is that right? (*Emphatically*) Is that right? Mind you, I suppose it depends on whether you like Adam Faith and what your politics are.'

That particular episode ends with Hancock being admitted to hospital having accidentally cut himself while making a sandwich (Doctor: 'Knife wound, eh? Teddy Boy, is he?'), while another 1961 episode, entitled *Hancock Alone*, opens with a camera panning around Tony's room, showing some books on his table, including *Das Kapital*, Colin Wilson's *The Outsider* and Osborne's *Look Back in Anger*, among others. The Angry Young Men, and also the Teds, were still on the cultural agenda, but fading a little around the edges.

A Beatnik Working in a Bra Factory

For the Royal Court, it was a varied year, as ever. They began 1961 with a one-man show featuring Micheál Mac Liammóir (born Alfred Willmore in Willesden) entitled *The Importance of Being Oscar*, which consisted of the actor talking about Oscar Wilde and reading from his works – a further sign, coming hot on the heels of two different film biographies of Wilde, that one of Chelsea's most famous former residents was no longer the unmentionable pariah which hypocritical late-Victorian society had made him. March brought the first of a season of French plays to the Royal Court, including another work by Ionesco, *Jacques*, directed by R. D. Smith, who, like Tony Richardson, had a background in television. The same month saw Mary Ure returning to Sloane Square to appear in Middleton and Rowley's Jacobean tragedy *The Changeling* as part of a fine cast which included Robert Shaw and Jeremy Brett. The French season continued with a translation of Jean-Paul Sartre's *Altona*, starring Claire Bloom, Nigel Stock, Diane Cilento and the original Jimmy Porter himself, Kenneth Haigh, and concluded with a production of Jean Genet's *The Blacks*.

What with these and also Wesker's *The Kitchen* and Osborne's *Luther*, the English Stage Company were backing up their aim to present a writers' theatre, rather than fall back on an easy West End-style diet of knockabout farce and musicals. However, *Beyond the Fringe*, the revue from the previous year's Edinburgh Festival opened in London at the Fortune Theatre on May 10 and was packing them in. Written by and starring Peter Cook, Dudley Moore, Jonathan Miller and Alan Bennett, it pointed the way forward towards a different type of entertainment, and ran in one form or another until September 1966. On the other hand, Agatha Christie's *The Mousetrap* was still going strong at the Ambassador's, where it had been for considerably longer than the entire life of the English Stage Company (and it is still running now, some seventy years after it opened, despite a pause in 2020–21 due to pandemic restrictions).

Space was regularly being rented in those days at the Duke of York's Barracks on the King's Road by TV companies for rehearsals, and former *Six-Five Special* presenter and radio DJ Pete Murray spent part of 1961 there working on a new show for ABC TV with his co-star Dora Bryan. The series was called *Happily Ever After*, and following each week's rehearsals in Chelsea, they would then catch a train up to Manchester for the actual filming. Murray returned to the area shortly afterwards when appearing in a low-budget feature film entitled *Fashion for Loving* (aka *Design for Loving*) in which he played 'a beatnik working in a bra factory'. The script required him to walk out into the King's Road and stop the traffic, and, having missed the correct car driven by a stuntman, he was ordered by the cheapskate producers to go ahead anyway and flag down real traffic, nearly causing a multiple collision.

Ian Fleming published another in his hugely popular James Bond series of novels – this year's entry was *Thunderball* – and plans were underway to turn his Chelsea-dwelling espionage hero into a film star, which would come to fruition the following year. The wedding of a real-life film star with strong connections to the area took place on March 17, 1961, at St Michael's Chester

Square, just behind the Royal Court, as Christopher Lee married Gitte
Kroencke, and after a few years of living abroad, they would return to set
up a permanent home just north of the King's Road in the mid-sixties.

Pleasure Wear and Leisure Wear

At the Royal Court Club above the theatre, cabaret performances started
every night at midnight, but in ordinary pubs, as Eric Idle later remarked,
the laws were still such that they had to 'close every time you wanted a
drink'. Anthony Shields and Robert Gaddes, who regularly wrote the 'Night
Life' column in *What's On in London*, commented on the fact that on June
16 MPs had been debating the licensing laws in parliament:

> These learned people, their fingers right on the pulse of the public,
> took up such vital questions as the alcoholic content of liqueur
> chocolates and whether confectioners should be specially licensed
> to sell them! [. . .] how hypocritical! For in answer to our enquiry
> the office of the Government Chief Whip had to admit that when
> Parliament is sitting, *the bar of the House of Commons is open all night*!

Clearly, the House of Commons was the place to go for all-night drinking,
but failing that, from June 1961 you could try your luck at a new nightclub
which opened up above a furniture store in Ilford. Perhaps inevitably, the
place was called the *Room at the Top*. Among the opening acts announced
was Petula Clark, and the management were hoping to book Diana Dors
and Mel Tormé. However, perhaps the club's main claim to fame these
days is that it was here the following year that TV producer Ned Sherrin,
searching for a Harold Macmillan impersonator – as you do – chanced to
be in Ilford one night when William Rushton was appearing there in a
revue along with Richard Ingrams, John Wells and Barbara Windsor.
Rushton did his impression of prime minister Macmillan, and was duly
offered a place in the pilot for Sherrin's new satirical show, *That Was the
Week That Was*.

In the world of London fashion, the word 'boutique' was spreading like
an epidemic that year, although many still discreetly aimed their advertising
at the gay market which had supported Vince Man's Shop since the fifties.
At number 20 Brompton Road the Continental Boutique Limited had
opened up, offering 'The Loveliest Continental Fashions in Suede and
Leather', while over in Soho there was Domino Male at 47 Carnaby Street
('London's Boutique For Men'), Marc Adam, Boutique for Men was at 41

Great Pulteney Street ('For Pleasure Wear and Leisure Wear'), and the Anglo Continental Men's Boutique was now in business at 75 Brewer Street. These days, when some people can manage to keep a straight face while describing their business as a 'boutique hotel' or a 'boutique law firm' – presumably 'boutique undertakers' are out there somewhere – the word is in danger of losing all meaning, but at the start of the sixties, it still had the benefit of novelty.

As a result of the new Betting and Gaming Act which came into force at the start of 1961, people could now also gamble legally at betting shops and casinos, and one of the first of the latter to open was the Cauldron Club, a short walk north of the King's Road near South Kensington Station at 47 Harrington Road, which promptly took out an advert for its upcoming 'Chemin de Fer Party'. The easing of restrictions on gambling would make sixties London a haven for all sorts of international interests, including, it was said, the US mafia. London was starting to swing, and many people of all stripes wanted a piece of it.

A Strain of Public Insult and Personal Vilification

At the Royal Court, the stars of *Platonov*, Rex Harrison and Rachel Roberts, returned in September in a new Nigel Dennis play, *August for the People*, having previously taken it to the Edinburgh Festival. It did not meet with good reviews at Edinburgh, and at the Court it turned into a shambles, because Harrison – who had just been offered the role of Caesar in 20th Century Fox's wildly overspending film *Cleopatra* – abandoned the Court production two weeks into the run, assuming that money would compensate them for the loss of their star in a production which was already attracting large audiences. Playwright Dennis felt that the show must go on, and asked that George Devine should step into the role, and when Devine understandably refused, it caused a major rift between them, despite their many years of friendship. Shortly afterwards, George Devine had a serious nervous breakdown.

The opening night of *August for the People* had been notable not just for the crowds but also for the sight of Lindsay Anderson and others holding up banners protesting about the jailing of various Royal Court writers who had been arrested in the company of over a thousand other people at a CND rally in Trafalgar Square on September 17. Anderson himself had been arrested, along with other members of the Committee of 100, including Bertrand Russell. An ITN news crew interviewed Russell during the Trafalgar Square sit-down demonstration, and he told them: 'Well the case is quite simple. We think the policy which is being pursued by the Western Powers is one which is bound to end in the extermination of the human race, and some of us think that that might be rather a pity.'

Also taken into custody that day were John Osborne, George Melly and Vanessa Redgrave, and the headline on the following morning's *Daily Express* said: '1,140 Arrested Including John Osborne, Fenner Brockway, Vanessa Redgrave, Shelagh Delaney and Canon Collins Too'.

There were other signs that criticism of those in power was becoming more permissible and increasingly regarded as a healthy alternative to the more deferential attitudes of earlier decades. October 1961 saw the opening of Peter Cook's satirical nightclub, The Establishment, at 18 Greek Street, Soho, on the site of a former strip club, with a new interior by regular Royal Court designer Sean Kenny. Shortly prior to the opening, an article had appeared in the *Observer* entitled 'Can English Satire Draw Blood?', giving Cook some high-profile publicity. The author was not entirely unknown to him, since it was Jonathan Miller, currently appearing each night onstage with Peter in *Beyond the Fringe*. Then, on October 25, the first issue of *Private Eye* magazine appeared, put together in William Rushton's bedroom in a house in Kensington. In the words of its long-time editor Richard Ingrams, 'Everyone lived in Kensington, Knightsbridge or Chelsea, and the early *Private Eyes* have a flavour of that world.' Initially, their distribution was virtually non-existent, being limited to various coffee bars and other likely places, as the magazine's initial editor, Christopher Booker, later wrote, recalling the launch of *Private Eye* and the success of The Establishment club:

> The first amateurish, yellow-paper copies of the magazine *Private Eye* were beginning to circulate in the bistros of Kensington and Chelsea. Between them they were to bring back into English life a strain of public insult and personal vilification which, although foreshadowed in the late Fifties by such things as Bernard Levin's Taper column and some of Peter Sellers' sketches, it had not known for many years.

When not writing angry letters to the *Tribune* or getting himself arrested in Trafalgar Square, John Osborne had become involved with Penelope Gilliatt, the film critic of the *Observer*, who lived just up the road from the Royal Court in Lowndes Square. He was also planning on branching out into television production, according to a report in the December edition of *Films and Filming*:

John Osborne and Tony Richardson have decided to take the plunge into TV. They have taken on as their aides Lord and Lady Marley. So, Woodfall, the company which made *Saturday Night*, *The Entertainer*, and *A Taste of Honey*, now plunges into the realms of *Wagon Train* and *Wyatt Earp*. Say Richardson and Osborne: 'The company will only accept subjects to which the directors feel they can bring an original and feature film approach.' Why so modest? We know they're after the lolly, and why not?

On November 30, a short item in Rex North's gossip column in the *Daily Mirror* took note of a retail development that even then would have been met with cynical reactions from more worldly readers, and a year or so later would have probably merited a police raid: 'New headquarters of the beatnik set – a pub off King's-road, Chelsea – has four machines for dispensing pills. Three are for aspirin. The fourth – for deodorants.'

Finally, as the winter nights drew in and 1961 sailed off into the sunset, the good folk at the *Melody Maker* were warning of a new horror soon to hit the UK from across the pond – a dance craze currently packing them in at the Peppermint Lounge on 45th Street in New York, which most people called the Twist, but which the paper's headline reckoned was 'The Most Vulgar Dance Invented'. Down in Aldershot, however, on December 9, a beat combo from the north of England were playing their first ever show in the south, in front of eighteen people who had been lured in from nearby coffee bars with the promise of a free gig, while the promoter moved among the few punters trying to encourage them to spread out a little and make the place look more crowded. History does not record whether any of the audience were tempted to engage in 'the most vulgar dance invented' that evening, but at least they could tell their kids they had been dragged in to see the Beatles for nothing.

13

'Introverts, extroverts and perverts'

Simple Honest Dirt

In 1962, it seemed in some quarters that if that filthy new dance the Twist
was not about to lead the entire country down the slippery slope to hell,
then the TV companies probably would. A report in the January 5 edition
of the *Guardian* about the Catholic Teachers' Federation Conference quoted
our old friend, the unnamed 'expert', who asserted that one of the most
popular programmes on the box was corrupting the youth of the nation
and that it was 'a matter for regret that the BBC should have made this
sudden dive in sexual psychopathology. [. . .] Clinic files bear witness to
the large number of sexual difficulties that arise from the sexuality of
adolescents and pre-adolescence being conditioned to aberrations presented
in this fashion.'

What, then, was this perverted programme that the psychologist found
so disturbing, having written about it originally in the *Catholic Teachers'
Journal?* An adaptation from de Sade, perhaps, or an illustrated version
of the Kinsey Report? No, it was *Z Cars*, the popular police series in
which the boys in blue drive around in flash motors solving crimes to
the accompaniment of a chirpy little theme tune. With the benefit of
more than half a century's hindsight, it now appears that teachers would
have been better off looking a little closer to home for signs of depravity,
given the very large number of cases that have since come to light
involving the repeated sexual abuse of children in their care perpetrated
over many years by the staff at Catholic schools in that era, and covered
up by the Church itself.

One of the supposed exercises in 'sexual psychopathology' contained in *Z Cars* was the showing of 'a woman in bed with a man other than her husband'. Naturally, such things never happen in real life, or if they do, presumably it is better to pretend that they don't – in fact, why not spare everyone's blushes and have a crime programme in which every character involved is behaving absolutely impeccably? In the event, someone admitted to the Chelsea Hospital for Women in Dovehouse Street on January 20 wound up there indirectly as a result of sharing a bed with 'a man other than her husband'. Her name was Christine Keeler, and she later wrote in her autobiography that she had been taken to hospital, seriously ill, after a backstreet abortion – the only kind available at the time since they were not yet legal in Britain. The father, she wrote, was government minister John Profumo.

Still, if reality was allegedly too disturbing to be portrayed on television, in British films its depiction seemed to be becoming compulsory. One review written by editor Peter G. Baker in *Films and Filming* that year began: 'It is not too difficult to make a British film with "social significance" these days if it has illegitimate kids or abortions, flirtations with "spades" or simple, honest "dirt".'

Paying no heed to such criticisms, Lindsay Anderson was keen to follow the likes of Tony Richardson in making the transition from Royal Court theatre director to feature director, and in January 1961 was busy casting for his debut project, an adaptation of David Storey's novel *This Sporting Life* – a gritty northern tale of rugby-playing folk and strained relationships, with Karel Reisz as producer. Anderson himself wrote an article for *Films and Filming*, shortly before the film was released, in which he recalled his journey from directing *The Long and the Short and the Tall* at the Royal Court to being allowed a shot at the movies:

> It was a success, and I enjoyed doing it. I was asked to do more plays. So I stayed in the theatre. I was not offered the film of *The Long and the Short and the Tall*. At that time in the British cinema no-one who was not already experienced in features could hope to be considered as a feature director. Richard Harris, who played in the film version of *The Long and the Short and the Tall*, told me recently that he had suggested at the time that the best way to film it was to give it to the original cast and director, but ABPC [the production company] had said, 'Oh well, you know Anderson, he's very long-haired.' But there really has been a revolution since then, starting I suppose with *Look Back in Anger* (which Tony Richardson only directed

because John Osborne had the right to insist), but clinched finally
by *Saturday Night and Sunday Morning*. Karel's immense success changed
the mentality of the producers overnight. Now new directors and
unknown actors seemed to be all they were looking for.

Anderson chose Rachel Roberts for one of the leading roles in *This
Sporting Life*, partly because of her performance in *Saturday Night and Sunday
Morning*, but also for the quality of her work at the Royal Court.

Casting was taking place that spring for the next film Tony Richardson
was to direct for Woodfall: an adaptation of Alan Sillitoe's story, *The Loneliness
of the Long Distance Runner*. The lead role went to Tom Courtenay, who had
been much in the news recently after taking over Albert Finney's part in the
stage production of *Billy Liar*, and Royal Court actor James Bolam also landed
a part in Richardson's film. Simultaneously limbering up on the starting block
was John Schlesinger's film version of Stan Barstow's novel *A Kind of Loving*,
with a screenplay written by Keith Waterhouse and Willis Hall (who had a
play due at the Court later in the year), which starred one of the original
stage cast of *Look Back in Anger*, Alan Bates. All things considered, London
theatre success was still proving to be a reliable route into British films.

Buttered Yak's Hide on Charcoal

Mary Quant's business took off in a spectacular way in 1962 when the
giant US chain J. C. Penney placed an initial order with the company for
6,235 of their garments, and almost overnight, King's Road fashion began
to have a truly international influence. The effect on Mary Quant's lifestyle
was also dramatic, as she told me: 'From 1962 I started to design clothes
and underwear for J. C. Penney – as well as my own Mary Quant collection. I also designed the Mary Quant Ginger Group collection creating a
"ready to wear" to retail world wide. I was commuting to New York once
a month, which I loved.'

The Penney order apparently came about as a result of US press coverage
such as Sally Kirkland's *LIFE* feature and a picture spread in *Seventeen* magazine, in which various girls had been photographed by Joe Santoro modelling
Quant clothes in a variety of locations around London and also on the beach
at Brighton, helping to drive home the idea that England could also be a
source of new developments in fashion. At home, Mary's designs received a
very high-profile endorsement on February 4, 1962, when the UK's first ever
Sunday newspaper supplement, the *Sunday Times Colour Magazine*, was
launched. One of Mary's dresses was on the front cover, modelled by Jean

Shrimpton and photographed by David Bailey. Inside that same issue, Mary herself and Alexander Plunket Greene were profiled, as was pop artist Peter Blake, and the supplement also included a James Bond short story by Ian Fleming. It would be hard to find a more definitive early artefact of the coming sixties revolution, and the editor of this ground-breaking new magazine was Mark Boxer, who had once edited the Cambridge student magazine *Granta*, as a result of which he had been thrown out of college for blasphemy in 1953, just as Shelley had been in 1811. As for how one of Mary Quant's dresses came to be on that front cover, she told me, 'It was all Mark Boxer's idea, I believe. He was a very exciting man and friend.'

In the same week that the *Sunday Times Colour Magazine* first appeared, issue number four of *Private Eye* became the first in which they employed their classic cover device of using speech bubbles on a photograph, which since that time has enabled them to put rather more entertaining words into the mouths of politicians, clergy and other notables than the people concerned would have been likely to have used in real life. The cover star that week was Queen Victoria, commenting on supposed plans to turn the Albert Memorial into Britain's first space rocket, whose speech bubble read, 'Ho Ho Very Satirical'.

Private Eye also included a parody magazine layout for something called *About*, 'for pseuds', which looked suspiciously like *About Town*. This featured fashion photos with captions poking thinly disguised fun at King's Road designers – 'striped shirt from Jean Michal, 28gns' or 'sweater in pearl pearl from Relaxiknit of Chelsea at £32:19:11½'. Among the alleged contributors was the defiantly working-class Harry Gash (a send-up of *Fing's Ain't Wot They Used T'Be* writer Frank Norman), whose play *Arnty's Froat's So Bleeding Tuff it Blunt Me Razer* was claimed to have been running in the West End for over a year; there was a parody of a film column entitled *Vaguely Nouveau*, namechecking Lindsay Anderson; and the fake restaurant reviews alleged that Sean Kenny, the Royal Court designer, had outfitted a posh restaurant to look like 'a "fish and chip shop" in the North of England'. The other restaurant review read as follows:

If you want to impress your friends with a knowledge of fashionable Tibetan delicacies, I strongly recommend the Bistro Lhasa which has just opened in the King's Road. The House speciality is Buttered Yak's Hide on Charcoal which really ought to be eaten with a flagon of snow-washed Potala betel-juice (very intoxicating!). Your host who is most amusingly dressed as the Dalai Lama was in fact until last month Victor Emmanuel of the Terazza Via Appia in Frith Street.

A Real Log Fire for Your Comfort

In the real world of Chelsea restaurants, there were yet more new developments: Buzzy's Bistro had opened up at 11 King's Road, offering 'Interesting Dishes at Low Prices', while down at World's End, a place called The Place, at 11 Langton Street, was advertising itself with the words, 'You May Bring Your Own Wine', although whether they were granting permission or hazarding a guess is open to debate. In the basement below Bazaar, Alexander's restaurant, lately under the ownership of Camillo Foglia, was pleased to announce: 'Now a real log fire for your comfort'. A short walk along the King's Road at the Pheasantry, after many years of running the same advert, it was no longer claimed that Mario Cazzini would be pleased to meet you, but he remained there nevertheless, and potential customers were assured that it was 'Chelsea's famous haunt of film and theatrical personalities, artists, writers and the Bohemian set. Please write to the Secretary for Brochure and details of Membership.'

On February 24, 1962, up on the outskirts of Liverpool, a gig was taking place at the local YMCA in Hoylake, but the band probably enjoyed it somewhat less than a certain disco hit of the seventies would have predicted, since they were booed offstage at the end of the show. Still, they now had a proper manager, who had persuaded them to ditch the Gene Vincent-inspired leather outfits they had been wearing in favour of tailored suits, and he seemed to be booking them plenty of shows, so maybe this would turn out to be the Beatles' year after all.

Meanwhile 'The Most Vulgar Dance Invented' was proving a big hit in Chelsea, as it was elsewhere, and a venue devoted to the new craze had opened up at 271 King's Road: 'The best of Chelsea Twists at the St Tropez Twist, Coffee Club, Nightly 9pm – 3am.' As for what to wear for an evening at the St Tropez, readers of the 'Women's World' section of the March 9 edition of *What's On in London* were treated to an article about the new 'Twist' skirts, accompanied by a photo of a woman demonstrating – for the benefit of anyone who'd been living in a cave for the last few months – how to dance in such apparel.

The landed gentry also appeared to be getting in on the act that year, since in June it was announced that Baron Ian de Fresnes and Gordon Eden-Wheen had opened a London branch of New York's Twist mecca the Peppermint Lounge just near Trafalgar Square. That same month, the Isley Brothers were climbing up the US charts with their own composition, 'Twist and Shout', but, like many American releases at that time, it was not a hit in the UK owing to lack of distribution, where two or three major labels had a stranglehold on product. This would leave the field clear for the Beatles to record a carbon copy version in February the following year, having spent the second half of 1962 performing it onstage, along with a version of Joey Dee and the Starliters' 'Peppermint Twist' and their own Lennon/McCartney song, 'Pinwheel Twist'. Incidentally, although mods were certainly patronising clubs in London by this time, the adverts for a Beatles show in Gloucester in March still felt the need to declare: 'At the request of the Council – No Teddy Boys and Ladies please do not wear stiletto heels.'

Drivellingly Preoccupied with the Sex Urge

At the Royal Court, another key work of 'swinging' sixties London made its Sloane Square debut on March 27, 1962: Ann Jellicoe's play *The Knack*, later to be filmed in 1965 by a post-*Hard Day's Night* Richard Lester under the title *The Knack – and How to Get It*. It was performed on stage at the Court in front of a set which featured a giant action painting by Alan Tagg, by a cast that included Rita Tushingham, Philip Locke, James Bolam and Julian Glover, and the *Daily Sketch* for one, found it funny: 'Very funny,' they said, 'Outrageously funny.' Nevertheless, perhaps predictably, it failed to impress Kenneth A. Hurren at *What's On in London*: 'My distastes this week are nothing if not catholic and easily encompass, too, Ann Jellicoe's grubby little Royal Court exhibit, *The Knack*, which is drivellingly pre-occupied with the sex urge ('the knack' is facility in seduction) to a spectacular and tiresome degree.'

Kenneth was on good form that year, objecting strenuously to several other Royal Court productions, such as the Tennessee Williams play *A Period of Adjustment* – a 'pitifully platitudinous piece' in which 'Mr Williams allows his preoccupation with the castration complex a bit of rein in some arch references to women so painfully repelled by sex as to favour "cutting it off".' Later in the year came *Happy Days*, the Beckett play in which the heroine conducts a virtual monologue whilst partially buried in a pile of earth, which must have been to Hurren somewhat akin to the proverbial red rag to the bull: 'Obscuration is the last refuge of the charlatan: in the arts it is the spastic offering of the hermaphrodite union of obvious thinking and arrogant mediocrity. [. . .] Mr Beckett's tragedy is not so much that he is misunderstood but that so much of him is understood only too well.'

Still, if some people did not care for the English Stage Company's productions, there was always the Royal Court Club upstairs, where the late-night patrons in April were being treated to Trader Faulkner and his Flamenco group, as well as 'Ian Hamilton, late of the Cambridge Footlights, offering satirical comedy' – a not entirely surprising choice, given those other ex-Footlights performers who were currently packing them in across town at the Fortune Theatre with *Beyond the Fringe.*

In a world newly obsessed with satire and the Twist, 'Angry Young' John Braine announced in the spring of 1962 that, contrary to his previous denials that such a thing would ever happen, he had now written a follow-up to his enormously successful 1957 novel *Room at the Top*, understandably entitled *Life at the Top*. By this stage Braine was forty years old, had a large house up north and was gradually moving politically more to the right – a drift which would see him coming out publicly in favour of America's war in Vietnam in 1967. Since *Room at the Top*, he had published one further novel, *The Vodi*, which had significantly failed to set the best-seller lists alight, perhaps because it concerned itself less with the struggle of the proletariat and more with 'a race of malevolent beings called the Vodi, ruled by a hideous ogress called Nelly', as the *Times Literary Supplement* phrased it. Still, fair play to him for at least trying to branch out, and already in July 1962, people were wondering whether the kitchen-sink trend in recent cinema was about to be replaced by something less monochrome, as Barrie Pattison asked in an article for *Films and Filming* called 'Taking in the Garbage':

> The success of *A Kind of Loving* means that the realist cycle is still with us. It will take a really large-scale flop (*The Entertainer* was too early in the event to be decisive) to tell whether these films represent a perma-nent advance to a more adult British cinema or whether succeeding films will just try to replace the quarterdeck with the bedroom and the village post office with the industrial street covered with real garbage.

A Kind of Loving – 'Replacing the quarterdeck with the bedroom', May 1962

John Schlesinger's *A Kind of Loving* had indeed opened to fine reviews which were then proudly displayed in the press advertising: 'Touching, shocking, daring, beautifully acted' – *Daily Sketch*; 'Humour, feeling and a dozen very good performances' – *Observer*; 'I could not take my eyes from the screen' – *Daily Express*, although the latter comment is hardly the most extravagant praise, given that there are not many other directions in which to look when sitting in a cinema. When Schlesinger's film opened, Lindsay Anderson was wading through acres of authentically grimy mud up in Wakefield shooting *This Sporting Life*, and Joan Littlewood from the Theatre Royal Stratford East was preparing to film the Cockney caper *Sparrers Can't Sing* in the bomb-damaged East End (written by Stephen Lewis, aka Blakey from *On the Buses*). On the other hand, one of the directors who had pioneered the trend, Tony Richardson, announced that Woodfall's new film would be a period drama, shot in the pastoral splendours of the West Country, in *colour*. Lined up for the starring roles were Albert Finney and a new young actress, Susannah York.

The Spy Who Ran Off to the Cold

As the Royal Court graduates continued to make waves in the British film industry, a writer who had submitted a play he had written in 1961 called *The Visit* that was eventually turned down by the English Stage Company was now in the newspapers for elaborately defacing library books in Islington. Joe Orton – arrested in April 1962 along with his boyfriend Kenneth Halliwell – was still two years away from his huge theatrical success, and in a move presumably designed to prevent a tidal wave of unrest in which rampaging gangs of malcontents laid waste to the libraries of the nation, they were both sentenced to six months in prison for the offence.

While these two people were exchanging their bedsitter in Islington for prison cells, a Chelsea resident who had been living in much grander style fifty yards from the King's Road at 18 Carlyle Square also opted for a change of scene and defected to Moscow. Kim Philby, who until then had worked for MI6, was part of the circle of wealthy former Cambridge students whose affection for Stalin and the Soviet Union was such that they happily supplied UK state secrets to the Russians over many years, regardless of the many deaths of British agents directly resulting from such behaviour. Somehow, he was allowed to leave the country, but maybe police resources were too thinly stretched on account of the elaborate manhunt for library offenders in Islington.

Philby may have run away from Chelsea that year – who knows, perhaps the constant noise from all those nightly dance sessions down the road at the St Tropez Twist was playing havoc with his radio transmitter – but just as a real spy was quitting the area, a fictional one who worked for the opposite team was getting ready to break into films. James Bond, a character who lived, like Philby, in a quiet Chelsea square just off the King's Road, was created by sometime Chelsea resident Ian Fleming and was about to be played onscreen by another sometime Chelsea resident, Sean Connery. *Dr No* – which turned out to be the first in a series which has now been running longer than much of its current audience has been alive – was in production and being readied for an autumn 1962 release, and like Richardson's upcoming *Tom Jones*, it had precious little to do with grimy backstreets, kitchen sinks or factory lathes.

However, these past few years of working-class settings and regional accents had done much to pave the way for the emergence of a new generation of actors, of artists like David Hockney, photographers like David Bailey, and in particular, the autumn 1962 chart debut of four blokes from Liverpool. Without the previous five or six years of irreverent, sarcastic, downwardly mobile characters which followed on from that first appearance of the character of Jimmy Porter at the Royal Court in 1956, regional accents and a mildly bolshie attitude would have been much harder to put across in the media in 1962, dominated then as now by people who had been educated at public schools and Oxbridge. As it was, the press were well conditioned to young working-class types by the time that the Beatles showed up on their radar, and by comparison with Osborne's 1957 state-ment that the Royal Family was 'a gold filling in a mouthful of decay', John Lennon's November 4 ,1963 comments in front of the Queen Mother and Princess Margaret asking them to 'rattle your jewellery' were pretty mild, and agreeing to play at a Royal Command Performance isn't exactly anti-establishment in the first place. By way of a contrast, try to imagine the Sex Pistols or the Clash performing at one of those in 1977, or, even more unlikely, imagine the relevant authorities asking them to.

Pop Goes the Easel

On May 22, 1962, a man who still divided his days between drinking in Soho and painting pictures in a defiantly cluttered studio near South Kensington tube station was given a retrospective exhibition at the Tate Gallery – a rare honour for a living artist, but then, Francis Bacon was hardly your everyday painter. As far as the art world in general was concerned, these were fast-changing times. Down on the King's Road, the Chenil Galleries may have been continuing in much the same fashion as ever – 'First London Exhibition, Arthur Forbes-Dalrymple, Oil Paintings and Watercolours, April 6–14' – but that same week, on April 10, a new gallery opened in Duke Street, in Mayfair, run by an Old Etonian who had recently returned from working in the US. Soon, the Robert Fraser Gallery would become one of the most important showplaces for new art in the country, and Fraser himself an integral part of the social circle surrounding London's new rock aristocracy.

Modern art was increasingly being covered by the mainstream media that year. Not only was Peter Blake mentioned in the first issue of the *Sunday Times Colour Magazine*, he was also featured – alongside three other young pop artists, Derek Boshier, Peter Phillips and Pauline Boty – in a fine documentary called *Pop Goes the Easel* directed by Ken Russell for BBC TV's *Monitor* programme, with a soundtrack of contemporary rock music. Blake and Boshier would both have exhibitions at the Robert Fraser Gallery in the next two years, while Fraser's face eventually wound up in a painting in the Tate, ducking the cameras and handcuffed to Mick Jagger in a work by Richard Hamilton titled *Swingeing London*. The boundary lines between the different arts were certainly becoming blurred.

Arnold Wesker found himself with a genuine hit on his hands with his latest play at the Royal Court, *Chips with Everything*, starring Martin Boddey, Frank Finlay and John Kelland, which had opened on April 27 and drew in consistently large enough crowds to merit a transfer to the Vaudeville Theatre on June 12. Described in *What's On in London* as 'A play by Arnold Wesker set on a RAF Station where the relations between officers and rankers symbolise the author's view of the class war in general', it wound up being one of the Court's most profitable productions of the year. Wesker's play, with its patronising call for the working class to reject supposedly inferior popular music in the charts and return to folk songs, and to abandon eating chips into the bargain, came just as he was about to embark upon a lengthy struggle to establish his Centre 42 arts centre – the chosen site for which was the Roundhouse in Chalk Farm. Given *Chips with Everything*'s anti-rock music bias, it is a nice irony that when the Roundhouse did eventually succeed in attracting large working-class audiences in the second half of the decade, it was largely as a rock venue, which it remains to this day.

I Say, I Say, Harold Macmillan

At The Establishment club in Soho, satire was packing them in nightly, and US comedian Lenny Bruce had made such an impression there that now they were thinking of booking Frankie Howerd. London's *original* satire club, the Satire Club – which, in recent years, didn't seem to have presented much actual satire at all – had closed earlier in the year, but was now reopening under the less-than-snappy name of Brad's. However, even though *Private Eye* was still only available in a very small part of London – their adverts at the time stated that 'the reactionary attitude of the distributive trades makes *Private Eye* very hard to get outside the area in which we can deliver direct to non reactionary newsagents' – satire was definitely in the air, and so Ned Sherrin had been charged with the business of putting together the weekly BBC TV show to be called *That Was the Week That Was*. Having made his fateful trip to the *Room at the Top* club in Ilford that summer, Sherrin found his Harold Macmillan impersonator in the shape of *Private Eye*'s William Rushton, and the rest of the team for the show was gradually coming together.

Making sarcastic remarks about the government of the day had not been a regular feature of British television up until that point, so the sheer shock value of a less-than-deferential attitude was considerable. As future Goodie Bill Oddie remarked to Roger Wilmut about this shift in the permissible subject matter for television humour: 'Instead of doing "I say, I say, my mother-in-law", you could do "I say, I say, Harold Macmillan", and it could be the same joke – and very often *was* the same joke.'

After a couple of pilot programmes shot in the late summer, *That Was the Week That Was* made its debut on BBC TV on November 24, 1962, and its producer Ned Sherrin later linked its origins directly back to the Royal Court when interviewed for David Pearson's 1982 television series *The Sixties*:

> You can trace the whole of *Armchair Theatre*, you can trace a lot of qualities about *That Was the Week . . .*, you can trace a lot of the different attitude of interviewing on news and current affairs programmes all to that revolution that John Osborne brought about as a one-man-band at the Royal Court, 1956, and that production at the Royal Court is *the* point which began to advertise and condition the change in the theatre and television and in a lot more of life. [. . .] *That Was the Week* was sort of the bastard child – it was by *Tonight* out of *Private Eye*.

It Was Filthy! It Was Disgusting!

As the BBC was limbering up to give its viewers a weekly dose of satire, an outfit which the Riverpark Ballroom in Chester had recently described as 'The North's No. 1 Rock Combo – They're Terrific – You Must See Them!' released their first single, entitled 'Love Me Do'. It hit the shops on October 5, 1962, the same month that various members of a scruffy R&B band who had been calling themselves the Rollin' Stones moved into even scruffier living quarters down at the tatty end of the King's Road in a side street called Edith Grove. While it is fair to say that Beatlemania didn't really start to break out until the release of their second single, 'Please Please Me', at least 'Love Me Do' made a quick showing on the *Record Retailer* charts the following week, although according to Mark Lewisohn's definitive reference work, *The Complete Beatles Chronicle*, their debut single's initial progress may have been due to some distinctly old-fashioned behind-the-scenes methods:

> There was a strong suspicion in Liverpool and in the record industry as a whole, hotly denied by Brian Epstein, that he hyped the disc by buying up 10,000 copies between October and December 1962. Certainly the single led an unusually erratic, up and down chart career. (Before it peaked at 17 on 27 December it showed at 49, 46, 32, 37, 29, 23, 21, 26, 19 and 22.)

While Brian Epstein was allegedly shelling out serious money to assist the Beatles' debut disc in sliding up and down the charts, in a second-floor flat at 102 Edith Grove, Brian Jones, Keith Richards and Mick Jagger were generally struggling to find a few pence to feed the gas meter during the coldest winter England had seen since 1947, often staying in bed all day just to keep warm. Several other people stayed there as well to share the rent, and conditions were not helped by the Stones' somewhat lax attitude to such things as hygiene and housekeeping. 'It was filthy! It was disgusting!' Keith told Victor Bockris, 'Mould growing on the walls!'

If the place was half-slum to begin with, the band were hardly likely to win a mention at the Ideal Home Exhibition by spitting at the walls, or wiring up the lavatory for sound so that people's private moments of contemplation could be recorded for posterity, and their most notorious flatmate, the legendary Jimmy Phelge, also enjoyed nailing up the toilet door with the occupant inside. Still, it was home to most of the band for over a year, during which time they lived in each other's pockets and rehearsed their guitar playing constantly, if only simply to keep warm or have something to do.

The band also took to rehearsing at the pub just around the corner at 500 King's Road, the Wetherby Arms, which is where they auditioned Bill Wyman for the post of bass player, and it was while Jagger was standing in a phone box in the same street that they were first offered a gig at the

Crawdaddy Club in Richmond by the promoter Giorgio Gomelsky. During the year that the flat was their home they first encountered Andrew Loog Oldham, and even Charlie Watts moved in there for a while. If anywhere can be said to be the birthplace of the Stones, then 102 Edith Grove has a better claim than most.

An Unattractive Display of Moral Squalor

The worsening weather that October was actually just what Tony Richardson claimed to be looking for. Out on location in the West Country shooting his next feature, he felt that it was giving his footage an added realism, as *Films and Filming* reported: 'Tony Richardson wants his version of Fielding's *Tom Jones* to have the authentic smack of England. Every day the colour cameras have been loaded and Richardson has uttered the previously unheard words, head poised skywards: "OK the sun's going in. Now roll 'em.'''

While Richardson was capturing shots of convincingly 18th-century-style mud on location, his depiction of 20th-century mud could be seen in cinemas that autumn as his latest film for Woodfall, *The Loneliness of the Long Distance Runner*, reached the cinemas, with Tom Courtenay wearing the grime-splattered boots in Alan Sillitoe's story of a Borstal boy. It appeared the same month as Kubrick's *Lolita*, Corman's *The Premature Burial*, and the first Bond film, *Dr No* – the latter would cause a huge sensation in British cinema and probably did more to let the plug out of the kitchen sink than most.

Over at the Pheasantry in November, the management had 'pleasure in announcing that the licence has been extended to 2am', and in a new restaurant at 312 King's Road, the Chelsea Grill & Cellar Lounge, they were offering 'Classic dishes prepared at your table by Manager Peter'. Meanwhile the ever-popular Magic Carpet Inn at number 124 now boasted regular entertainment supplied by Tommy Rogan and His Music, not to mention 'Inimitable Food – Top Service – Gay Atmosphere'.

Those willing to make the short walk north to the Albert Hall on November 15 could have witnessed a celebration of forty years of BBC music broadcasting, billed under the title 'The Twenties to the Twist'. The all-encompassing line-up was not so much eclectic as positively schizophrenic, including bowler-hatted trad jazz chart-topper Acker Bilk, Forces Sweetheart Vera Lynn, yodelling heart-throb Frank Ifield, the future Alvin Stardust Shane Fenton (and the Fentones), old-school organ soloist Reginald Dixon, play-in-a-day guitar maestro Bert Weedon and Latin American bandleader Edmundo Ros.

Somewhere on the bill they also found space for the Temperance Seven, who had formed in 1955 just across the road while attending the Royal College of Art, and had recently made an eye-catching appearance in Richard Lester's new film *It's Trad, Dad* (released across the pond under the title *Ring-a-Ding Rhythm*, for the benefit of US audiences for whom the UK's early sixties trad jazz boom meant absolutely nothing).

The bill at the Albert Hall paints a deceptively cosy picture of nightlife in London that November, and yet, just at that moment, director Guy Hamilton was shooting a feature film in the King's Road area called *The Party's Over* which would depict a group of Chelsea youth as 'introverts, extroverts and perverts', in the immortal words of Peter Cowie's location report ('The Amoral Ones', *Films and Filming*, December 1962). Hamilton was a former assistant to Carol Reed and had previously directed films such as *The Colditz Story* (1954). He later hit the big time in 1964 with *Goldfinger*, then *Funeral in Berlin* (1966), *Battle of Britain* (1970), *Live and Let Die* (1972) and *The Man with the Golden Gun* (1973), but his 1962 film had something that these others did not, which caused its release to be delayed until 1965, and meant that it rarely surfaced over the next four decades. *Goldfinger* had Bond, a gadget-laden Aston Martin and Pussy Galore; *Funeral in Berlin* had Michael Caine, authentic Cold War locations and a cracking Len Deighton source novel; *The Party's Over* had necrophilia. Mind you, it also had Oliver Reed, one of the finest young actors in the country, who at that stage was mostly known for his appearances in Hammer films such as *Curse of the Werewolf* (1960) and *The Pirates of Blood River* (1962), in which he had successfully buckled his swash with Christopher Lee. In *The Party's Over*, as Peter Cowie's article reported, 'Oliver Reed heads the cast as the swarthy, surly Moise (French for Moses), one of an amoral pack of Bohemians who absorb Melina (Louise Sorel) into their muddled life and indirectly cause her death.' The latter phrase only hints at what Leslie Halliwell was happy to spell out in a 1980s edition of his *Film Guide*: 'An American girl joins a group of Chelsea beatniks and dies in a fall from a balcony; her father investigates. Tasteless and boring swinging London trash which became notorious when its producers (Rank) disowned it because it features a party at which a man makes love to a dead girl. An unattractive display of moral squalor.'

Guy Hamilton directed the picture that autumn for Tricastle Films, a production company he himself ran in conjunction with Jules Buck, Jack Hawkins and Peter O'Toole. As Tony Richardson had done the previous year with *A Taste of Honey*, Hamilton was using real locations rather than studio sets, and had rented a large Victorian house just north of the King's

Road in Elm Park Gardens for the party scenes. 'Thanks to doing it this way, I've been able to put all my money on the screen,' Hamilton told Cowie, while 'standing in the picturesque garden of a house in King's Road, Chelsea'. One of the more widely distributed production stills from the film shows Reed and his 'pack' walking across the Albert Bridge, while at another point in the film, actress Catherine Woodville can be seen walking home along the King's Road after an all-night party in suitably bohemian gear comprising 'fishnet stockings, patent leather shoes and a bowler hat'.

Credit: author's collection

Oliver Reed (centre, rear) and his gang crossing the Albert Bridge

Ironically enough, this depiction of Chelsea youth engaging in an 'unattractive display of moral squalor' was originally set in Paris, a city familiar to the director and also to the film's American-born, French-resident screenwriter Marc Behm. Moving the story to London for financial reasons, they opted for the King's Road as the nearest equivalent location for some suitably Left Bank bohemian shenanigans. Little did they know that various members of the Rolling Stones were living just a short distance away from their party house in Elm Park Gardens, and that one of them would later star in a similarly controversial film called *Performance*, many of the interiors for which were shot just the other side of Sloane Street in a rented house in Lowndes Square.

The Pope's Wedding

As the supposed lifestyles of Chelsea beatniks were being documented down in London, John Schlesinger was in Bradford doing location shooting for his adaptation of Keith Waterhouse and Willis Hall's *Billy Liar*, while a double bill of new plays from the latter writing team opened at the Royal Court on December 18. The stage version of *Billy Liar* may have been one of the great successes of recent years, but these two works, *Squat Betty* and *The Sponge Room* – both starring George Cole, Jill Bennett (later Mrs John Osborne) and Robert Stephens – were something else entirely, and ticket sales so disappointing that they were withdrawn three weeks earlier than planned. Shortly before that double bill had opened, the debut play by a writer who was to be responsible for one of the Royal Court's best-known and most controversial productions was presented in a Sunday night without decor performance on December 9. The author was Edward Bond, but George Devine was not a fan of this particular play, *The Pope's Wedding*, and it would be another three years before Bond's next work, *Saved*, brought him international attention.

John Braine's novel *Life at the Top* was number one in the best-seller lists, the Beatles were zig-zagging around the music charts and beginning to show up on BBC radio (*The Talent Spot*, December 4) and Welsh television (*Discs a Gogo*, December 3, a show set in what was billed as 'the gayest coffee bar in town'), while Doris Richards was occasionally calling into the house in Edith Grove where her son Keith was now living to help out with the laundry – seemingly a little-known concept among the Rolling Stones. While all this was going on, Francis Boyd in the *Guardian* had been studying a new government report on social conditions in Britain, which he summed up for his readers in a December 19 article entitled 'Verdict on the Bingo Age'. The government's experts had seen the future of the 1960s, and it looked like this: 'More people will want to move into an outer suburban life, buy cars, educate their children longer, suffer their surgical illnesses in private rooms of hospitals, spend evenings staring at television, spend more, gamble more, buy more washing machines on hire purchase, take holidays in Italy, lay their own parquet floors, and so on.'

The year 1962 was all but over, and Beatlemania was knocking at the door – could parquet flooring be far behind?

14

'Trend or tripe?'

The Sound of Sixty-Three

As 1963 slithered into view, *Melody Maker* readers were given the lowdown on the new musical trends likely to set their feet tapping in the next twelve months. One man with the answer was bearded television star and future convict Rolf Harris, who had been appearing in the hit parade since 1960 with singles such as 'Sun Arise' and 'Tie Me Kangaroo Down, Sport', and was proud to announce that he had invented a new instrument during a routine visit to the lavatory: 'Rolf discovered that if he clonked the top of the cistern it juddered away like a cross between a motorbike starting and a penny settling on a table. "This could be the sound of '63," said Rolf.'

On another page of that same January 5, 1963 issue of *Melody Maker*, a different contender for the new sound was being discussed: 'Trend or Tripe? – Chris Roberts Sums Up the R&B Boom' ran the headline, in which the writer asked whether the likes of Cyril Davies or Alexis Korner were ever likely to make the Top Fifty. Towards the end of the piece, he gave a welcome plug to the singer of an up-and-coming young R&B outfit, currently living in World's End in conditions of heroic squalor:

> From one of the newer faces on the scene, Mick Jagger, singer with the Rolling Stones, came a thought-provoking suggestion: 'It has got to move out of London,' he said. 'Only two or three clubs are making any money at the moment, and it has to spread to live. That's the only way it can become popular, and retain its form at the same time.'

The band were currently playing a short residency at Wardour Street's Flamingo club, holding down the worst slot of the week, Monday night, whilst the more popular weekend fixtures went to the likes of Alexis Korner or the Flamingo's house band, Georgie Fame and the Blue Flames. John Gunnell – who compèred the shows each night in between selling shots of under-the-counter whiskey disguised in orange juice to beat the lack of a drinks licence – once told me that he sacked the Stones after they'd played a couple of their Monday night fixtures because they were only pulling about seventeen people. He and his brother Rik saw many of the future key figures of the beat boom pass through their door in the first couple of years of the sixties, as John explained to me:

> Over Christmas '61 the Twist thing took off. For about six months you couldn't lose, and during that time Georgie Fame and the Blue Flames became our regular band for the all-nighters. Early in '63 we tried putting on the Rolling Stones on Monday nights for a fee of £2, but they didn't pull anyone at all. Andrew Loog Oldham had formerly been our bottle collector at the Flamingo, and Mick and Brian always came down to the club a lot. Keith Moon always came down – his band the Beachcombers played at the Flamingo, and I think he made up his mind to split from them when one of the members decided he couldn't make our Christmas Eve gig because he had to go to midnight mass.

The fledgling Rolling Stones were also gigging on January 10, 1963 at the Marquee club, 165 Oxford Street, supporting the Cyril Davies All-Star R&B Group ('Members 4 shillings, Guests 5 shillings'). Until recently, the club had been solidly a jazz venue, but was now giving ground to the R&B trend. This kind of shift also seemed to be taking place at the King's Road's regular trad jazz venue the Six Bells, whose adverts that same week offered the following:

SIX BELLS, KING'S ROAD, CHELSEA
Jan 4th TONY COE QUINTET
Jan 5th BRUCE TURNER JUMP BAND
Jan 7th FAT JOHN GUEST NIGHT
Jan 9th DAVE HUNT RHYTHM & BLUES BAND

In the event, the pub was to mostly remain a solid jazz venue throughout the decade, with Humphrey Lyttelton in particular a regular mainstay. However, a different kind of event which took place two months after these listings, on March 6, resulted in considerable damage and the constabulary being summoned, as the *Daily Herald* reported under the headline 'Drink-Pub-Dry Students Clash With Police'. Two of those present were arrested after a pint of beer was poured over a policeman's head:

> Five hundred students from London University had gone to the Six Bells public house in King's Road, Chelsea. They planned to drink the pub's stock of draught beer – 2,742 pints – by closing time. [. . .] Said one: 'We were collecting for a good cause. It was not just a riot.' Pub landlord Mr Jim Brady said: 'The students did quite a lot of damage. Two tables and three chairs were smashed and I reckon I lost about 100 glasses.'

Anyone loitering in the general vicinity of Sloane Square that year might possibly have noticed the regular visits of a small group of Liverpudlians who would check into the Royal Court Hotel (these days renamed the Sloane Square Hotel) for a few days while conducting various pieces of business in the capital. On 19 January 1963, a pre-recorded Beatles performance was shown on the *Thank Your Lucky Stars* programme, their first time on national TV, which greatly increased their profile. The band had not yet moved down to London permanently – although the way things were shaping up, that day was certainly coming – and so the hotel on Sloane Square provided a useful base for their trips down south. Looking after them one day in a PR and publicity capacity was a certain ex-employee of Mary Quant Limited, Andrew Oldham, who would shortly begin co-managing the Rolling Stones. Just then, Oldham was working in the office of manager and PR man Eric Easton, and handling a certain amount of press duties for Beatles manager Brian Epstein. As Oldham later wrote: 'Down in the Smoke, Brian Epstein was rather snotty about the press and so I got to be "manager for a day" when the attractively scattered moptops came to London to squeeze in some radio shows and press interviews. [. . .] The Beatles greeted me in the lobby of a small hotel facing Smith's.'

They had a new single just out, called 'Please Please Me', which was being praised by Janice Nicholls, the 'Oi'll give it foive' girl from ITV television show *Thank Your Lucky Stars*: 'A lot of people don't like it, but I do.' As for what the Beatles themselves liked, it was all there in the February 16 edition of the *NME:* 'John: favourite foods – curry and jelly; likes – blondes, leather; personal ambition – to write musicals. Paul: favourite drink – milk; dislikes – shaving; personal ambition – to have my picture in the *Dandy.*'

Five Hundred 'I-Speak-Your-Weight' Machines Sing the *Hallelujah Chorus*

At the cinema, it began as a year of blockbusters, and Peter O'Toole – who had appeared in the Royal Court's 1959 production *The Long and the Short and the Tall* – was now packing them in at the Odeon Leicester Square in the 70mm first-run presentation of David Lean's *Lawrence of Arabia*. However, following on from *Lawrence* at the Odeon came Lindsay Anderson's down-beat tale of northern rugby-playing folk, *This Sporting Life*, starring Richard Harris and Rachel Roberts, which opened on February 7. As is clear from Anderson's article for that month's edition of *Films and Filming*, he was not exactly trying to compete with the big-budget epics: 'I don't think any of us are likely to forget those gruelling, claustrophobic weeks on the tiny kitchen set at Beaconsfield, the whole atmosphere somehow infected with the tense, grinding emotionalism of the situation the actors had to play.'

The theatrical origins of such methods of film-making are fairly obvious, and elsewhere in the same magazine, in an article making predictions for the coming year, Peter Cowie acknowledged the influence of the Royal Court on many recent British films:

> John Osborne remains, probably, our one outspoken writer of spas-modic genius, and his adaptation of Fielding's *Tom Jones*, which was produced and directed by Tony Richardson, will be a severe test of his capabilities and of his respect for a literary masterpiece. Certainly Osborne has outlived his notoriety. One can clearly see now that it was he who made the decisive breakthrough – with *Look Back in Anger*. And to this extent the British cinema is indebted to the theatre for its abrupt change of attitude.

As if to reinforce this argument, it was announced in the January 3 edition of *Kine Weekly* that the dramatist N. F. Simpson had formed a film production company called Pen Films with producer Michael Deeley and director Peter Yates to make a cinema version of Simpson's 1959 Royal Court play *One Way Pendulum*, in which a man attempts to teach 500 'I-speak-your-weight' machines to sing the *Hallelujah Chorus*. It was even-tually filmed by the aforementioned team, starring Eric Sykes, George Cole and Peggy Mount, but under the Woodfall banner, reaching the cinemas in January 1965. However, at a time when Tom Courtenay on the set of *Billy Liar* was already telling the press 'I do want to get away from my Northern accent in future', and the *Monthly Film Bulletin*'s review of *This Sporting Life* had pointed out that 'the familiarity of the Northern setting [was] already a legitimate target for *That Was the Week That Was*', another item announced in *Kine Weekly* in the same week perhaps gave a truer indication of the way in which British cinema was heading in the wake of Sean Connery's huge success as James Bond: 'Film rights to *The Ipcress File*, the new spy thriller by Len Deighton, have been acquired by Harry Saltzman. Deighton will write the screenplay for the film which is projected for production in the spring. Saltzman, of course, partners Cubby Broccoli in Eon, which filmed *Dr No*.'

Harry Saltzman was also the man who joined together in the late fifties with John Osborne and Tony Richardson to found Woodfall Films, so he had certainly been doing an excellent job of sensing upcoming trends in British film-making over the previous half-decade.

Rhymes with 'Wank'

Another British film mogul, Nat Cohen – the man behind the early *Carry On* films – returned from the US that spring saying that US distributors had been complaining about the cockney and northern accents in recent British films, ordering changes to the dialogue in *Billy Liar* so that it would not suffer in the same way that *A Kind of Loving* had recently done in America. Little did he know that a generation was growing up in the US for whom such accents and turns of speech would soon be the ultimate status symbol. John Peel – living in Texas at the time that news of the Beatles' success first filtered through – owed his start in radio to the fact that his accent was Liverpudlian. He was allowed on air at station WRR in Dallas during Jim Lowe and Bob 'Hoss' Carroll's *Kats Karavan* show having rung them up about some blues albums in his possession, as he told me:

> They put me on the air to talk about these things, I think, probably, because of my accent, rather than because of my extraordinary knowledge of the music. I've got a recording somewhere of the very first one that I did – only a portion of it – and I do sound like a minor member of the Royal Family [adopts upper-class twit voice] 'terribly high-pitched . . . Hello! My name's John . . .' and they must have thought '*What* have we got here . . .' But I did this for a while, until I had the impertinence to ask them to pay me for it, and then they sent me on my way. But I'd been bitten by the bug then.

While John was in Texas, up near the northern border of America, British accents were also proving fascinating to a Chicago schoolgirl, later famous under the name Cynthia Plaster Caster, who interpreted a teacher's advice to 'go out and make a plaster cast of something' to mean that whatever her favourite rock musician had hidden down the front of their trousers was fair game for being immortalised in three dimensions. When news of the Beatles reached Chicago, but before the first of the British Invasion bands showed up in town, a group of expatriate English musicians were pulling large crowds, mostly on account of their country of origin. As Cynthia told me, they gave her an invaluable introduction to the mysteries of cockney rhyming slang:

> They were called the Robin Hood Clan. Nobody I know has ever heard of them, from anywhere, but anyway, they came from Britain. They were slightly older guys that resided somewhere in Chicago. I seem to remember seeing them play in the suburbs. They had a big following because of their accents, just like John Peel. They taught us 'charver', 'barclay's bank' – rhymes with 'wank' – and 'hampton wick'. Those were the three, and that's all I needed . . .

The *Melody Maker*, however, seemed a little confused about recent developments, devoting four-fifths of its front page on March 23, 1963 to a large photo of the Beatles, with a headline that posed the question 'Is Liverpool Britain's Nashville?' The success of the Beatles meant that their home city became known around the world, but from 1963 onwards, if you actually wanted to run into a member of the band, you were much more likely to do so by hanging around in the vicinity of the King's Road than on the banks of the Mersey.

Ful Semyly Hir Wympul Pynched Was

For those confused about the modern pop scene, chart singer Kenny Lynch – who appeared on bills with the Beatles on a number of occasions – gave a lecture to students at Chelsea College of Science and Technology on February 16, explaining some of the pitfalls of the business. Both Kenny and the Beatles were part of a varied line-up alongside George Melly and, indeed, the king of the musical cistern, Rolf Harris, for a big show up the road at the Albert Hall on April 18 billed as 'Swinging Sound 63'. Interviewing the Beatles on behalf of the *Radio Times* was a teenager who regularly appeared on the TV show *Juke Box Jury*, Jane Asher. They had seen her on television, but this was the first time they had met Jane, and the band then invited her back to their hotel in Sloane Square, as Paul McCartney told Miles:

> We ended up back at the Royal Court Hotel where we were staying. We went to a journalist, Chris Hutchins' apartment on the King's Road. It was all very civilised and we were all there. But at the end of all that, I ended up with Jane. [. . .] I probably just sort of mentioned, 'Ful semyly hir wympul pynched was.' My only Chaucer line! Probably that did it!

A few days earlier, on April 14, after miming to 'From Me to You' on ABC TV's *Thank Your Lucky Stars*, the Beatles went off to check out the competition from Edith Grove for the first time. The Rolling Stones were playing at the Crawdaddy in Richmond, which was run by Giorgio Gomelsky and Hamish Grimes – brother of Bruce Grimes, the art director from the Chelsea Palace. It was Hamish who also later designed the famous band logo for the Yardbirds, and can be heard introducing the band at the start of their legendary 1964 LP *Five Live Yardbirds*. Bruce and Hamish used to hang out in the King's Road pubs with various members of the Stones back in their Edith Grove days, as he told me:

> My younger brother was the road manager for the Stones, the Yardbirds and Eric Clapton, so we used to meet up with them. In the pubs down there we all used to have jam sessions – the Six Bells and what have you. Giorgio Gomelsky was their manager, and my brother, Hamish is his name, actually found the Yardbirds, and took Giorgio to them, and he signed them up. They used to run the Crawdaddy Club out in Richmond. My brother used to run that, and then he came into town and used to do record covers, as a designer, so he did all that, the Cream, Yardbirds, the Stones . . .

As Bruce and his brother were drinking with the Stones, Peter Sellers was a short stroll away down at World's End in the middle of filming *Dr Strangelove* for Stanley Kubrick, in which he was playing several different parts. One day in March 1960, Kubrick was told that Sellers had fallen over in the King's Road outside a restaurant and broken his ankle, as a result of which he relinquished one of his roles, that of the Texan, Major Kong. The part was then played by Slim Pickens, but Sellers' biographer Roger Lewis casts doubt on whether the injury was genuine, or merely an excuse to avoid having to deliver a convincing Texan accent. It is perhaps not surprising that the King's Road features in this story, since Peter Sellers was spending a lot of time there that year, having begun a relationship with the actress Janette Scott, who told Lewis: 'He moved me into a flat at the top of the King's Road, which he said his company owned. He installed a record player, Stan Getz records and a (school of) Picasso painting. [. . .] the vast majority of evenings it was just the two of us in the flat off the King's Road.'

Just Out of Bed and Fuck You

While Peter Sellers may or may not have been tripping over in the King's Road to avoid a part in one film, Dirk Bogarde and James Fox were down the street shooting another – Joseph Losey's *The Servant* – at 30 Royal Avenue, just off the King's Road, opposite the real-life residence of W. Somerset Maugham. A certain amount of the picture was shot at Shepperton, but the exterior of the house can be seen to good effect at various points in the film, and the opening title sequence also affords a fine view of the premises of Thomas Crapper, Sanitary Engineer, at 120 King's Road.

On May 14, 1963, *Carry On* film star Bernard Bresslaw – who had worked regularly at the Chelsea Palace in the late fifties as one of the cast of *The Army Game* TV show – opened alongside Angela Baddeley at the Royal Court in *Day of the Prince*, a new comedy by Frank Hilton, and interestingly, it was advertised that most performances would be 'preceded by half an hour of jazz'.

For those in search of more music, the Pheasantry was now stressing in capital letters on its adverts that it offered 'DANCING NIGHTLY', while the proliferation of restaurants in the area continued, with new arrivals such as the Studio Restaurant and Candlelight Cellar at 342 King's Road, offering 'Spanish and Portuguese Specialities'. As the King's Road became increasingly known as a centre for clothes shopping, dining out and enter-tainment, the small area around Carnaby Street also began attracting attention, although when *What's On in London* ran a special feature about the latter on May 17 under the title 'Carnaby Street Village', a fair number of the businesses they highlighted had no links to the fashion industry: Inderwicks, 45 Carnaby Street, 'England's Oldest Pipemaker's Briar, Meerschaum and Calabash Manufacturers'; Stevo Typewriter Co., 47a Carnaby Street, 'Typewriters, Adding Machines, Tape Recorders'; Detroit Cleaners, 40 Carnaby Street, 'Same Day Dry Cleaning'. By 1966 it would be a very different picture indeed, and boutique owner John Stephen, the King of Carnaby Street, would own no fewer than six shops there.

May 22, 1963, was the first of the public days of the Royal Horticultural Society's annual Chelsea Flower Show, but if you were looking for the Duke of Edinburgh, he was up at the Albert Hall, attending an evening of wrestling. On June 5, the Secretary of State for War, John Profumo, admitted that he had lied to the House of Commons about his relationship with Christine Keeler, while the same week's *Melody Maker* was moved to assert that 'the inferiority complex that British popsters have had about American music is already starting to disappear. Because the new wave have shown that they can beat America at its own national music game.' The King's Road's own contribution to that wave, the Rolling Stones, had their debut single, 'Come On', reviewed in the same paper a week later in the ever-popular 'Blind Date' section, where a guest celebrity was played a selection of tunes while blindfolded and then asked to comment. This week it was '21-year-old singer Craig Douglas – a highly successful singer with 17 hits to his credit'. His verdict on the Stones single?: 'Very, very ordinary. Can't hear a word they're saying and I don't know what this is all about. If there was a Liverpool accent it might get somewhere, but this is definitely no hit. I dislike it, I'm afraid. Take it off!'

Luckily, the band picked up some better publicity in *Melody Maker* on June 29 in a short article by Chris Roberts entitled 'Rolling Stones Gather Speed':

Mick, a London School of Economics student, Brian, and guitarist Keith Richard [*sic*] all sport giant urchin haircuts which prompts people's comparison to the highly scrutinized Beatles. 'In fact, art students and college people have had these haircuts for years,' said Mick. 'They were around when the Beatles were using Brylcreem.'

Despite the misgivings of Craig Douglas, the Stones' first single hit the charts on July 25, 1963, eventually reaching number twenty-one, and the Beatles sent a card to them at Edith Grove which read: 'Well done, you'll be up here with us soon.' As bona fide hitmakers, Mick and the boys now needed proper promotional photographs, which were taken down by the river, a short walk south from their Chelsea home, as Andrew Oldham later recalled:

I made my first visit to the infamously rank and scummy Edith Grove flat to prepare the band for the Embankment snaps. The worn, dirty lino in the kitchen and the gas meter in the hall appalled me. There was no telephone and the place smelt like a never-ending fry-up. [. . .] Down at the Embankment I put the Stones, minus Ian Stewart, up against a grim looking wall near the river. [. . .] That look, that 'just out of bed and fuck you' look – the river, the bricks, the industrial location – was the beginning of the image that would define and divine them.

Credit: Mark and Colleen Hayward/ Redferns/Getty Images

'Just out of bed and fuck you' – the Rolling Stones' first official photo shoot, Chelsea Embankment, 4 May 1963

Britain Has Some Pretty Kinky Families

As one group of Chelsea bohemians were making the news, the fictional set in Guy Hamilton's film *The Party's Over* were running into well-publicised censorship problems. A news item in the August 1963 issue of *Films and Filming* said, 'Anthony Perry, who produced the film, told me that in his opinion the censors dislike the film because it attacks the weaknesses of middle class morality.' Chief censor John Trevelyan remembered the reasons somewhat differently in his memoirs, however: 'The idea of necrophilia – making love to a dead woman – did not seem to us attractive, and we felt that cinema-goers would probably agree with us.'

Another fictional group of young people could be seen onstage at the Royal Court every night that August, appearing in the play *Skyvers* by Barry Reckord, which was set among sixteen-year-old boys in a comprehensive school. This, too, had done battle with the theatrical censor over swearwords in the original script, and the programme notes included a piece by George Devine explaining that they were only able to present a 'watered-down version' due to the demands of the Lord Chamberlain's office. The play's director was Royal Court writer Ann Jellicoe, and among the cast of mostly unknown teenagers was a young David Hemmings, who would return three years later to the King's Road when filming *Blow-Up*.

The regular satirical 'Tell Me If It Hurts' page of the *Daily Herald* took aim on August 3 at the district's restaurants with a description in its 'Your Bad Food Guide' of a fictitious SW3 eatery:

> PHILOMELA, King's Road, Chelsea. This fashionable restaurant has been 'tarted up a treat' since our last issue. Run by Phil Dulcimer and Melvyn Dragge, two part-time actors, it offers a wide range of exotic-sounding and uneatable food. Prices stratospheric, but someone has to pay for the atrocious décor: bullfight murals, hanging guitars, draped fish-nets, sawdust on the floor – the lot. Spanish wine (75 shillings half-bottle). Keep off the *paella de toros* (bull's ear stew). Cover charge: 17s 6d. Recommended by Sodium Bicarb Inc., and all leading chemists.

On August 3, Stephen Ward, one of the key figures in the Profumo scandal, died in St Stephen's Hospital, Chelsea, having taken an overdose of Nembutal. Plans were already underway to try to make a film entitled *The Christine Keeler Story* – a project organised by Nicholas Luard, Peter Cook's partner in The Establishment club and *Private Eye*. Meanwhile the 3rd National Jazz Festival – which in later years mutated into the Reading Festival – was held on August 10 and 11 at the Athletic Association Grounds, Richmond, Surrey, headlined by British jazz stalwarts such as Chris Barber, Humphrey Lyttelton and Acker Bilk, and also featuring, at the foot of the list, the World's End's own Rolling Stones. Weekend tickets cost £1.

Lord Denning's report into the Profumo scandal was published on September 26, 1963, and predictably concluded that most people involved had behaved impeccably, which was then equally predictably denounced as a whitewash. As the older generation were getting hot under the collar buying the thoughts of Chairman Denning, many of the younger set were tuning in to a new music TV show which began broadcasting that September from a studio in Kingsway. *Ready Steady Go!* was fast, sharp and exciting, with pop art sets and celebrity interviews mixed in among the bands, and the hip crowd of teenagers who could be seen dancing each week on the show also gave the rest of the country a chance to check out what the London kids were wearing.

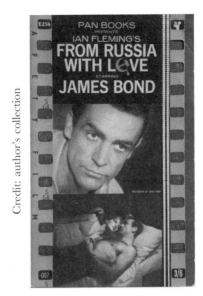

Credit: author's collection

A 1963 movie edition of Fleming's 1957 novel

The second James Bond film, *From Russia with Love*, premiered at the Odeon Leicester Square on October 10 – prompting Peter Baker in *Films and Filming* to comment: 'If Odeon cinemas really think the new Bond film is nice clean fun for all the family, then Britain has some pretty kinky families' – but the nation was clearly not listening, and Fleming's book sold 183,000 copies in the UK in October alone. Total Bond sales that year were estimated by Pan Books at four million, President Kennedy was reported to have had each new Bond book delivered to him directly on publication, and Lee Harvey Oswald is also said to have borrowed several Bond books from the Dallas Public Library. The smooth-talking spy from the King's Road, although largely a creation of the 1950s, was becoming one of the iconic figures of the new decade.

Knocked Up on the King's Road

It was not only Bond who was making the news over in America. On October 18, 1963, distinguished photographer Norman Parkinson assembled a group of up-and-coming London fashion designers down by the Thames by Cheyne Walk for *LIFE* magazine, the original caption of which read:

Young designers clamber on Chelsea Embankment. First row from left to right: Mary Quant, 29, and her husband Alexander Plunket Greene, moustachioed Kenneth Sweet, 34. Behind are Jean Muir, 29, of Jane and Jane, Gerald McCann, 29, Kiki Byrne, 26, and David Sassoon, 29. Hanging from lamp-post Sally Tuffin, 25, Marion Foale, 24, and milliner James Wedge.

A decade earlier, the idea that a mainstream American audience would have been interested in the work of a selection of young London fashion designers would probably have been laughed at, but times were changing fast. Harold Macmillan finally stood down as prime minister that month, nominating Sir Alec Douglas Home as his successor, while Labour leader Harold Wilson had clearly been watching a selection of kitchen-sink films and was playing up the 'working-class man-in-the-street' image as much as he could, and seemingly embracing all things modern, making ill-defined speeches about 'the white heat of a second industrial revolution'. Within a couple of years he would be desperately arranging photo opportunities for himself with the Beatles in an effort to buy off the youth vote, but the kids themselves in 1963 were being given a fair hearing for once by a couple of writers called Charles Hamblett and Jane Deverson, who were interviewing a wide range of young people for a forthcoming book, published in 1964. It was called *Generation X*, from which the 1977 UK punk band derived their name (not to be confused with the 1990s book which hijacked the title). One of the young people interviewed was 'Sally', a working-class girl from Shepherd's Bush who had become a 'Society Tart' and who offered some views on the rich women she had encountered in the class-crossing world of early sixties London:

> Call themselves ladies? They get themselves knocked up on the King's Road, Chelsea, and in Fulham and Soho and Belgravia with scummy little fortune hunters and degenerates I wouldn't give the drippings off my nose to. It's a vicious circle, really. While Nigel and Cecil and Julian and Ethelbert are screwing me, and girls like me, these society chicks are being screwed by Spades and film stunt men and Cockney property speculators. Perhaps that's one of the laws of nature, who knows?

On November 12, 1963, the BBC seemingly lost its appetite for satire and pulled the plug on *That Was the Week That Was*, announcing that it would be finishing three months earlier than scheduled. James Bond fan John F. Kennedy was assassinated in Dallas on November 22, 1963, and when fellow Bond enthusiast Lee Harvey Oswald was gunned down shortly afterwards at a police station, one of the curious onlookers a few feet away was John Peel, who had gone along because they announced on the radio what time Oswald would be being brought out. One of the many results of the assassination turned out to be that the London premiere of Kubrick's *Dr Strangelove* was postponed from December to January, for fear of somehow giving offence.

Eyes Shone, Teeth Flashed and Thighs Gleamed

As Christmas 1963 approached, the Royal Court was presenting a revival of J. P. Donleavy's play *The Ginger Man*, 'about a shiftless American student in Dublin, much preoccupied with gin and sex', starring Nicol Williamson and Susan Hampshire, which the good folk at the *Daily Sketch* found 'outrageously funny . . . a four star must'. It was also being announced in the press that the lead role in a new film called *The Collector* would go to a young actor called Terence Stamp – currently sharing a two-bedroom flat with Michael Caine in Ebury Street, a short walk east from the King's Road. Caine later wrote in his autobiography that Christine Keeler had come knocking on their door that year, followed a while later by the security services, after the Profumo case had developed. The two young actors became familiar faces in the Chelsea area from that time onwards, as Caine later wrote:

All at once it seemed that every pretty girl with no tits was modelling clothes and every pretty girl with big tits was modelling those. Mary Quant invented the mini skirt and every girl, pretty or not, was modelling legs. Brassières were discarded as breasts jiggled under blouses, but panties were retained as skirts rose higher to prove it. Eyes shone, teeth flashed and thighs gleamed. Cafés started opening up on the King's Road in Chelsea and we watched the weekend parade as we sat at our tables out on the pavement for the first time in London. The sixties were here at last – and the sun seemed to shine on London for the first time since the end of the war.

15

'Girls' haircuts and old-fashioned coats'

Wholesome Family Entertainment

As 1964 began, the BBC launched its new weekly TV programme, *Top of the Pops*, a rival to the other channel's hugely successful *Ready Steady Go!* show, which was doing well enough to merit the cover of *TV Times* in January. The Rolling Stones were also moving up the ladder, co-starring with the Ronettes on a UK tour called 'Group Scene 64', which drew a live review from the *NME* headlined 'Girls Scream at Stones: Boys at Ronettes!'

The Beatles, of course, were still the biggest thing in town, and were planning to head for America soon, to see if they could drum up the same response as they had in Britain. However, Pamela Zuck from the *Liverpool Daily Post* had been over there on a fact-finding mission, and reported: 'The boys and girls I met were not in the least impressed by the Beatles because, as they put it, "They have girls' haircuts and old-fashioned coats."'

Meanwhile, Tony Richardson's film version of *Tom Jones* had proved so successful, both at home and internationally, that Faber and Faber issued a book version of John Osborne's screenplay. Not everyone had been so impressed – *What's On in London* had called the film a 'large, lavish and sometimes laboured two-hour jape [. . .] directed with tiring technical tricks by Tony Richardson' – but if Tony himself had moved away from the kitchen-sink settings, much of TV drama was now being accused of being relentlessly glued to the draining board. Mary Crozier, TV critic of the *Guardian*, was quoted in the *TV Times* of January 19 saying, 'I think it is high time the device of making the viewer almost a recorder of what is going on in the kitchen was given a rest,' and over in Birmingham that same month a certain Mary Whitehouse and others launched the Women of Britain Clean-Up TV Campaign (later to become the Men and Women of Britain Clean-Up TV Campaign, then the Viewers' and Listeners' Association, then the National Viewers' and Listeners' Association). Mrs Whitehouse complained that, in the autumn of 1963, 'the BBC launched [. . .] into what have come to be known as the "kitchen sink" plays reaching a level of depravity not seen before or – with some notable exceptions – since.' She published a manifesto which stated that:

> [. . .] in particular we object to the propaganda of disbelief, doubt and dirt that the BBC projects into millions of homes through the television screen. Crime, violence, illegitimacy and venereal disease are steadily increasing, yet the BBC employs people whose ideas and advice pander to the lowest in human nature and accompany this with a stream of suggestive and erotic plays which present promiscuity, infidelity and drinking as normal and inevitable.

Although kitchen-sink-style drama seems to have been the focus of her main objections, if she had been serious about looking for genuine depravity at the BBC, she would have been better off simply knocking on the office door of the man who fronted both the first and very last episodes of *Top of the Pops* – in 1964 and 2006 respectively – Jimmy Savile, a serial abuser the corporation was happy to employ in multiple roles for over four decades despite the blizzard of rumours which swirled around him throughout those years. In the event, however, Whitehouse and her National Viewers' and Listeners' Association gave Jimmy an award in 1977 for what they called his 'wholesome family entertainment'.

All the Best Legs Come to London

Probably much to the disgust of Mrs Whitehouse and her friends, women's skirts had been getting progressively shorter each year, until something which came to be known as the mini-skirt began to be seen down the King's Road. Exactly where it came from, and who was responsible, has been a subject of discussion ever since. Mary Quant told me:

> There was no one day when the mini first happened. I made the skirts shorter and shorter all the time and Chelsea girls loved to wear them because all the best legs come to London. The King's Road became a catwalk for the mini. Many people disapproved of the mini-skirt

but after Courrèges also designed a mini-skirt collection it became
perfectly proper except in Italy when there was uproar about the mini
and a riot in Rome on our visit to collect the Piavolo D'Oro fashion
award in 1966.

While Mary had been establishing Bazaar internationally, a young man
named John Pearse was training as a tailor in Savile Row during the day
while also leading the mod lifestyle, with an interest in Italian suits and
American R&B. In a year's time, he would go on to open one of the most
iconic boutiques on the King's Road, Granny Takes a Trip. Recalling his
mod days, John told me:

> I was a sharp little dude, you could say. We used to hang out in the
> Scene club, and there was that Guy Stevens, who was the DJ there.
> He then started the Sue label, so that's what we were listening to.
> Georgie Fame was at the Flamingo, there was that show *Ready Steady
> Go!*, and there was a dancer on that show who I was at school with,
> who married one of those Faces boys.

In with the 'In' Crowd

Sixties London seemed to be becoming an enclosed world where – at least
among the 'In' crowd – it could seem as if everyone knew everyone else,
visited the same shops, clubs and restaurants, and lived around the corner
from each other, many of them in Chelsea.

The phenomenal success of the Beatles' first US trip, which took place
from February 7–22, only served to focus even more attention back onto
the city where they now lived and worked. Creative people from other
countries were also beginning to move to London, especially from the film
world, since economic and tax reasons meant that it was now frequently
cheaper to shoot in London and its surrounding ring of studios than in
Hollywood or parts of mainland Europe.

One such new arrival was Polish director Roman Polanski, then best
known for his art-house hit *Knife in the Water*, which had been nominated for
an Oscar in the best foreign film category. Roman was temporarily living
around the corner from the Royal Court at the house of his friend and
business partner Gene Gutowski in Eaton Place while preparing to make
his first English-language feature, *Repulsion*, most of the exteriors for which
would be shot a short distance away in the area around South Kensington
tube station. Polanski's move to London made him a near neighbour of

Peter Sellers, at that time living at 25 Eaton Place. Sellers married Britt Ekland on February 19, 1964, while Roman himself was to marry another Eaton Place resident whom he met the following year, Sharon Tate.

Diana Dors returned from Hollywood to live in Chelsea that year, renting a house in Elystan Place, just north of the King's Road, where she quickly became involved with a good-looking singer from the band Troy Dante and the Infernos, who all mostly wound up living there as well. Meanwhile seventeen-year-old Marianne Faithfull had come to London and moved into a flat that year in Lennox Gardens, just north of the King's Road, with her boyfriend John Dunbar. At a party in March 1964, she was introduced to the Rolling Stones and their manager, Andrew Loog Oldham; by August, her first single was in the charts – 'As Tears Go By', written by Mick and Keith.

A month after the hysteria of the Beatles' debut US trip, Brian Epstein found himself a permanent London residence on William Mews, just near Harrods, while the two rising stars of the film world, Michael Caine and Terence Stamp – still sharing a much less expensive flat in Ebury Street – were both in the press. Stamp, already known from playing the title role in the film *Billy Budd*, was currently filming *The Collector*, and Caine was nicely featured in one of the hit films of the spring, *Zulu*, whose musical score was written by a friend of his who lived around the corner in Cadogan Square, John Barry. Already riding a wave of success which had seen his theme tune to *From Russia with Love* hit the charts the previous November, Barry released a single tied in with the new film, entitled 'The Zulu Stamp'. A month or so later, having moved out of the Ebury Street flat, Michael Caine stayed for a while at John Barry's Cadogan Square apartment, and later recalled being kept awake all night when Barry was composing a new tune in the other room.

> I went out into the living room and found him slumped exhausted over the piano. He had obviously finally finished the one tune that he had been slaving on all night. I made him some coffee and he played it for me as the sun came up and warmed the room. Not only was I the first person to hear this tune, I heard it and heard it all night long. 'What's it called?' I asked him when he finished playing. 'It's "Goldfinger",' he replied – and fell fast asleep at the piano.

Thus, not only did the fictional Bond live just off the King's Road – as had the author of the books themselves for an important period of his life, and Sean Connery likewise – but also some of the finest music associated with those films was written right there in the area as well.

The Most Luxurious Pad I'd Ever Occupied

Alongside adverts for Beatles guitars for 59 shillings and sixpence ('with portrait of Beatles & signatures: you'll have them doing the Shake to the Mersey Sound!!'), or a Genuine Ringo Starr Snare Drum, a snip at four pounds, nineteen shillings and six ('Beat out that rhythm, Ringo style!'), the March 14 issue of the *Record Mirror* also carried the following one from a clothing shop called Adlers, based at 141 King's Road, on the corner of Flood Street:

MARKET FOR MODS
Twin Tab Double Cuff SHIRTS at lowest prices
from 29/6 upwards
PLAIN COLOURS WITH WHITE COLLARS AND CUFFS,
GINGHAM CHECK, PAISLEY, POLKA DOTS, TARTAN. WE
HOLD THE BIGGEST AND MOST COMPREHENSIVE
RANGE FOR MILES.
ALL BRANDS, HARDY AMIES, PRIME FIT, HOOKWAY, LE
ROI, AND MANY OTHERS. ALSO ALL PULLOVERS,
V-NECK, CREW-NECK, ROLL-NECK, AND AS WORN BY
ALL LEADING GROUPS
SEE OUR BASEMENT DEPT. FOR HIPSTER JEANS,
TROUSERS AND LATEST JACKETS. CORDUROY,
LEATHER, SUEDE, BEATLES, PIERRE CARDIN, AND LEVIS

However, there was bad news for such outlets, if you could believe the opinion of one of the young mods canvassed by *Rave* magazine in May for a feature called 'Way-Outspoken': 'I stopped being Mod two months ago because it was getting played out,' said Margaret McFadyen, described as a seventeen-year-old clerk-typist from Chelsea. 'Manufacturers started to put out trash to youngsters of 12, telling them it was Mod. I don't want to look the same as a lot of little kids in mass-produced gear.'

Having survived nearly being torn to shreds by fans in America, where their debut *Ed Sullivan Show* performance reached a record-breaking 73 million viewers, the Beatles showed up in Flood Street just a few yards south of the King's Road on April 18 and 25 to rehearse for Jack Good's upcoming Rediffusion TV special, *Around the Beatles*, to be broadcast on May 6, 1964. They spent these two days rehearsing in a building called the Hall of Remembrance in the company of the other acts on the bill: Long John Baldry, the Vernons Girls, Millie, P. J. Proby, Cilla Black and Sounds Incorporated, many of whom were also signed to Brian Epstein's

NEMS company. One day prior to the first of these rehearsals, the Rolling Stones' first LP went on sale, and by the following week it had knocked the Beatles' own *With the Beatles* album off the number one spot. By this stage, the band were no longer living in their two-room crash pad in Edith Grove, and when Jagger and Richards returned to live in Chelsea later that decade, they would find themselves in somewhat more expensive surroundings.

Credit: Daily Herald/Mirrorpix

Paul McCartney and John Lennon rehearsing for the
Around The Beatles TV special, April 1964

In May, Roman Polanski flew back to London from Paris, where he'd been finishing the script of *Repulsion*, and moved into his own London apartment in Eaton Place, just a few doors down from the home of his friend Gene Gutowski in which he'd stayed a few months before. 'It was the most luxurious pad I'd ever occupied,' he recalled in his autobiography, 'three well-furnished rooms in a typical Georgian house with a colonnaded portico, half a dozen steps leading down to the sidewalk, and a facade thick with glossy white paint.' Sometimes it seemed half of Chelsea was either in the music business or in films, one of the latest examples being Albert Finney's co-star from the new Karel Reisz feature, *Night Must Fall*. She was 23-year-old actress Susan Hampshire, also currently to be seen playing opposite Cliff Richard in *Wonderful Life*, and profiled in the June edition of *ABC Film Review:* 'Susan lives in a small apartment in Chelsea and is romantically unattached (at the moment).' Another arrival attracting even more press attention was Judy Garland, who came to live in the area again from July to December 1964, renting a house in the Boltons, South Kensington, she met the Beatles at a party thrown by singer Alma Cogan, and hung out with the Kray twins in the East End.

On June 10 and 11, the newly successful Rolling Stones, in America for the first time, spent a couple of days in Chicago recording at the legendary Chess Studio. Waiting for them at their hotel, along with a tiny handful of other fans, was schoolgirl Cynthia Plaster Caster, who had read in the papers about this latest group from England, as she told me:

> That fateful day in June, in front of the Watertower Hotel, there were maybe five of us, including me and my friend. Unbelievable. And maybe only a week before that I was aware of the Rolling Stones. They were number nineteen on the pop charts in Chicago with 'Not Fade Away', on the WLS Silver Dollar Survey. When the Stones came back just a few months later, oh my God, there were hundreds of girls, trying to get up to the rock'n'roll floor. Everything happened really fast, and every time a different British Invasion band would come to Chicago – they would be maybe a few months apart – there would be twice as many girls.

On that first occasion, when practically no-one was around, Cynthia spotted the band arriving, and made the acquaintance of a man who turned out to be Andrew Loog Oldham in the hotel lobby:

> He was walking in, in front of the Stones, with the sunglasses, and I just grabbed the first person that walked through the door, without looking too hard, and said 'Are you one of the Stones?' and he says 'Yeah' and starts making out with me, and starts putting his tongue in my ear, which was unheard of, to me. I couldn't hear or feel anything, except this snog . . . I'd barely snogged a local boy before this . . . this . . . sexy man who, you know, shaved, with this tight-fitting light-blue suit – I don't think it was seersucker – it was just a really cool, light blue suit, with the crotch kind of showing . . .

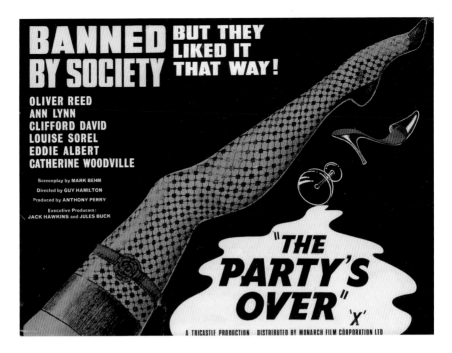

'The sad, sad little story about a group of Chelsea layabouts' – Monarch's 1965 press book for the belated cinema release of Guy Hamilton's tale of necrophilia in SW3. AUTHOR'S COLLECTION

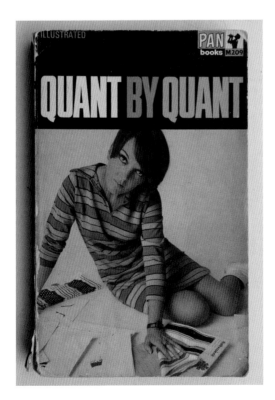

A 1967 paperback edition of Mary Quant's 1965 autobiography.
AUTHOR'S COLLECTION

Advance publicity in December 1958 for Tony Richardson's film of John Osborne's Royal Court Theatre success, *Look Back in Anger*. AUTHOR'S COLLECTION

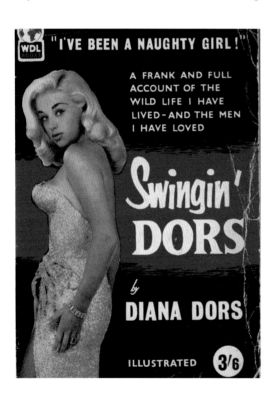

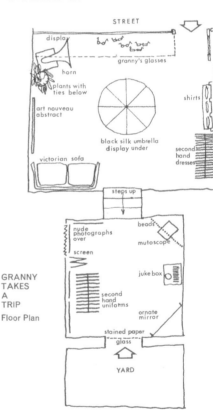

'Chelsea in those days, just after the war, was much wilder than it is today' – Diana Dors lifts the lid on the King's Road bohemian life in her 1960 autobiography. She first moved to the area in 1949. AUTHOR'S COLLECTION

Floorplan of Granny Takes a Trip, 488 King's Road, from the *London Magazine*, October 1966. AUTHOR'S COLLECTION

Some King's Road shopping tips from the April 1966 issue of *Rave* magazine.

AUTHOR'S COLLECTION

Antonioni's *Blow Up* on the cover of Films & Filming magazine, March 1967. Its party scene was filmed in Chelsea at a house in Cheyne Walk. AUTHOR'S COLLECTION

A specially-posed 1969 promotional still from the outer space Hammer Film *Moon Zero Two*, showing its stars James Olson and Catherine Schell inspecting a range of Mary Quant beauty products. AUTHOR'S COLLECTION

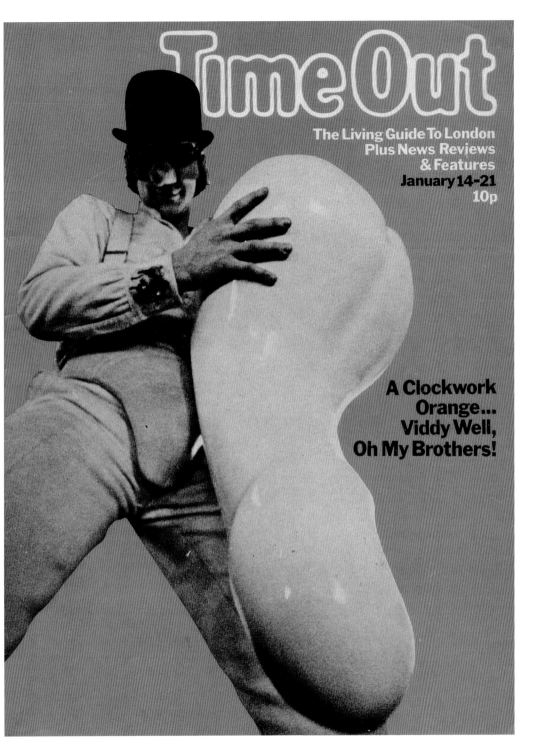

Kubrick's *A Clockwork Orange* hits London, January 1972. Key scenes were filmed at the Chelsea Drug Store (49 King's Road), and in the underpass at the northern end of the Albert Bridge. AUTHOR'S COLLECTION

The King's Road's most wanted on the cover of one of the best magazines of the era in June 1977, helping the Queen celebrate the Jubilee. AUTHOR'S COLLECTION

Johnson's – The Modern Outfitters, the last great King's Road rock'n'roll tailors, located at number 406 where World's End begins, pictured in August 1984. PHOTO BY THE AUTHOR

Above – The Pheasantry, 152 King's Road, pictured in 2022.
Below – The former dairy at 46a, Old Church Street which housed Joe Boyd's Sound Techniques Studio, pictured in 2022.
PHOTOS BY THE AUTHOR

430 King's Road, pictured in 2022, still Vivienne Westwood's shop more than 50 years after she and Malcom McLaren first opened for business there. PHOTO BY THE AUTHOR

'The "in" group wouldn't have been seen dead in Carnaby Street by 1966. Chelsea, after a period of decline, reasserted its role as the stage of fashion, and so it has remained ever since.' Long-time Chelsea resident George Melly's fine 1970 survey of recent cultural upheavals, with a cover by Peter Blake. AUTHOR'S COLLECTION

So That's What Goes On in Chelsea

Back in the UK, the first Beatles film *A Hard Day's Night* premiered at the London Pavilion on July 6, 1964, but David Bailey had plans to star the Rolling Stones in a film version of Anthony Burgess's novel *A Clockwork Orange*, in conjunction with Andy Warhol. Bailey approached Andrew Loog Oldham, and Oldham managed to announce it to the press before the idea was dropped, since the film rights were not available.

As these tentative plans to dress Mick and the boys up as droogs were falling through, Woodfall Films announced that they would be adapting yet another Royal Court theatrical success for the screen. This time it was the turn of Ionesco's *Rhinoceros*, with Tony Hancock starring in the Olivier role, to be directed by Alexander Mackendrick – a nice idea but it evidently ran onto the rocks somewhere further down the line. Meanwhile, the August edition of *Films and Filming* reported that John Schlesinger would be directing a film called *Darling* in the autumn, and made sarcastic noises about Polanski having learnt English in order to shoot *Repulsion* – 'Now how about persuading a Japanese to make a film in Siberia? That would be real progress' – and also informed readers that Lance Comfort was currently in the King's Road area directing *Devils of Darkness*, 'a black magic story, including Diana Decker as the owner of an antique shop which acts as a cover for the cult. So that's what goes on in Chelsea.'

Tony Richardson's worldwide success with *Tom Jones* had bought him another ticket to Hollywood, where he was about to shoot an adaptation of Evelyn Waugh's *The Loved One* – advertised as 'The Motion Picture With Something to Offend Everybody' – but in between he returned to the English Stage Company to direct the play *St Joan of the Stockyards* (according to John Fuegi largely the work of Emil Burri and Elisabeth Hauptman, but credited to Brecht). However, the English Stage Company was temporarily no longer in Sloane Square, the theatre having closed for renovations and repairs for a six-month period from March to September 1964, during which time they occupied the Queen's Theatre in the West End. More serious changes were underway, however, due to the fact that the company's pioneering artistic director had suffered a heart attack in the autumn of 1963, and was only slowly recovering.

On August 12, 1964, a little over a month before the premiere of the third James Bond film, *Goldfinger*, Ian Fleming died. When the film opened at the Odeon Leicester Square on September 17, the *Guardian*'s reviewer Ian Wright grudgingly admitted that 'whatever else, Fleming could tell a good story', but was relatively lukewarm about the film: 'It is all excitement and heavily self-mocking good humour, but how much better was Harold Lloyd at the same sort of thing. All that glitters?' Over at *Films and Filming*, *Goldfinger* was reviewed by Mike Sarne, the man who had a number one record in 1962 duetting with future *EastEnders* star Wendy Richard, and he reckoned that the character of Bond was 'a relatively recent hero in the grand fascistic tradition [. . .] played by the Glaswegian Sean Connery, who invariably sounds as if he is saying his lines with a mouthful of marbles while drowning in the middle of the Atlantic.'

The English Stage Company returned to their rightful home at the Royal Court on September 9, and the production which reopened the theatre, fittingly enough, was John Osborne's new play, *Inadmissible Evidence*, starring Nicol Williamson and Arthur Lowe, and directed by Anthony Page. In her memoirs, Marianne Faithfull reports that Page offered her a part in this play, but that her manager Tony Calder wouldn't let her do it, since she was earning considerably more from playing gigs than she would receive at the Court. As it turned out, the play was one of the hits of the season, and Williamson won the *Evening Standard*'s award for Best Actor of the Year, but Faithfull had to wait a couple more years before she too acted at the Royal Court.

Stuck With Four Lousy Haircuts

It was reported in *What's On in London* that sometime Court actor Albert Finney was now 'a *very, very* rich young man' as a result of his percentage deal in the profits of Woodfall's *Tom Jones*. Then – as if to confirm that it was a year in which it was almost impossible to avoid 007 – the same magazine also noted that 'N. F. Simpson has written an original screenplay, *MI99*, a spoof on the Bond thrillers, which Peter Yates will direct.' Indeed, there was already a revue running in London at the Poor Millionaire, Bishopsgate, called *From Rush-Hour With Love*.

If it wasn't Bond, it was the Beatles, and everyone had an opinion. Over in the US, according to the *NME*, fifties hitmaker Paul Anka commented: 'If the rock craze ever ends, the Beatles will be stuck with four lousy haircuts.' Even so, they had managed to display those haircuts on the cover of the August 28, 1964 issue of *LIFE* magazine, and in Chicago, Cynthia Plaster Caster, was looking for clues as to how the mod girls from London were dressing, as she told me:

> I started seeing some photos of what the girls that the Beatles liked looked like over there, and I didn't know it yet, but I wanted to have sex with a Beatle or marry a Beatle, [that] was what we all wanted. The

south side of Chicago was really a challenge, growing up, trying to be mod. We really were a one-horse town, period, and the south side was the squarest part of Chicago for fashion. Then I heard about the *NME*. I could get that in downtown Chicago. Because I was still living with my mother, who was really opposed to this – I'd call my mother the Warden – and one of the things she did was to throw away everything Beatlesque, or anything to do with the British Invasion, into the garbage.

As the British Invasion built up a head of steam over in America – and worldwide – the cuisines of much of the globe had succeeded in invading Chelsea, as Peter Noble acknowledged in his restaurant column in the October 23 edition of *What's On in London*: 'Along the King's Road, Chelsea, you will encounter every type of eating house and every nationality. Without moving from the district in and around the King's Road you can eat Chinese, French, Italian, Japanese, Filipino – or even English!'

It was becoming such a well-known stretch of road for dining out that a restaurant opened up that year simply named 235 Kings, relying on its potential customers to figure out that it would be at 235 King's Road. Run by Walter Storey and Jonathan Hansen, it was billed as the place to 'relax in a dilapidated atmosphere'.

At the Royal Court, Osborne's *Inadmissible Evidence* finished its run, and then on October 22 the playwright himself showed up in his occasional role as an actor, appearing there in a Ben Travers farce called *A Cuckoo in the Nest*, alongside Arthur Lowe, Nicol Williamson and *Beyond the Fringe* graduate Alan Bennett. During the run of that play, on November 3, the former Royal Court Club upstairs reopened under new management and a different name as a club called the Rehearsal Room, run by Nigel Corbett.

We Like Sex

Roman Polanski had been working hard shooting *Repulsion*, employing cinematographer Gil Taylor, whose work on *Dr Strangelove* and *A Hard Day's Night* had greatly impressed him. They shot exteriors in the streets around South Kensington tube station, including the pub the Hoop and Toy. Catherine Deneuve and John Fraser were filmed eating fish and chips at Dino's, just by the station, while 31 Thurloe Place posed as Madame Denise's Beauty Parlour. Another film with a local connection which was being shown to the press that autumn was *The Third Secret*, directed by Charles Crichton, described as a 'psychological suspense story set in Chelsea', starring Stephen Boyd as 'an American TV celebrity in London'. The *Monthly*

Film Bulletin, for one, was less than impressed: 'An unappealing and irritatingly muddled scribble of a film, thoroughly lacking in suspense, veracity and justification.'

As if to counterbalance Mrs Whitehouse and her happy band of puritans, Raymond Revuebar owner Paul Raymond founded his own monthly magazine called *King*, the first issue of which, dated Winter 1964, carried an editorial from the publisher:

> *King* is financed in part by the money sophisticated men have spent at the Raymond Revuebar and Celebrité. [. . .] Let me declare my philosophy now: We like sex. A bald statement maybe, but it needs saying today as much as ever. Happily a more liberal and broadminded attitude is developing in Britain. I believe the arts will benefit from it immeasurably and so will people. Especially me, but then that's another matter.

That first issue carried a short story written by Keith Waterhouse called *Duffy Rampant*: 'Wendy, for all her blue denim skirts, was not completely the sophisticate that Duffy had taken her for. [. . .] She had been unable to make a clean break from her environment, and after several months had secured only the most tentative foothold on the King's Road way of life.' Also featured in that issue of the magazine were nude photographs of Christine Keeler, an article *by* her, and an article *about* her by Colin MacInnes. This was a year when everyone seemed to be curious about Christine, as she later recalled: 'They all wanted to know me. The only two people in the world who wouldn't take my phone calls were the Pope and Marlon Brando. I tried.' *King*'s calendar girl that month was Cynthia Polegate, aged twenty-two: 'Her friends love the Pretty Things, the Rolling Stones, and of course the B*****s. Cynthia, we rather regret to say, loves Shakespeare. "For me," she says, "Will swings."'

Anyone else looking for clues to the swinging life in 1964 would have done well to pick up the debut novel by twenty-year-old former Chelsea Art School student Virginia Ironside. Set in a thinly disguised version of the King's Road scene circa 1963, the book came about as a result of an article she had written for *About Town* magazine, commissioned by Michael Parkinson. Secker & Warburg saw the piece and wrote to her asking if she had ever thought of writing a book. As it turned out, Virginia had just finished writing an autobiographical novel based on her recent experiences and current social life, so she posted them the manuscript. The resulting novel, *Chelsea Bird*, caused quite a stir in the press. As Virginia later recalled:

'What appeared to fascinate the media about *Chelsea Bird* was that it was about this brand-new, affluent, emancipated species known as "Young People". I was one of them, and I was spilling the beans.'

The new author's first promotional photos were taken – just like the Rolling Stones' – down on the Chelsea Embankment, by a defiantly grumpy Jeffrey Bernard. Thereafter, as Virginia says: 'I was photographed in almost every glossy magazine and every paper – in my mini-skirt, on top of ladders, walking down the King's Road in high boots, in black fishnet stockings, cross-legged in studios.' In the novel, the bird of the title is Harriet Bennett, who appears to be a thinly fictionalised version of the author. Characters all drink in the King's Road – coffee at a place called the Brazil (i.e. the Kenco), or a pub called the Chelsea Weaver (the Chelsea Potter). It is a world where being seen with the latest copy of *Private Eye* is a status symbol, and people strenuously cultivate working-class accents: '*Saturday Night and Sunday Morning, This Sporting Life*, Albert Finney, Terence Stamp all contributed to the movement. [. . .] As soon as people had seen the latest Tony Richardson movie, and read the latest Colin McInnes, their one idea was to get more lower class than anyone else.'

The heroine sews her own home-made imitations of Mary Quant's clothes, wishing she could afford to buy the real thing at Bazaar, and goes window-shopping late at night with her friend: 'We stumbled up the King's Road back home. We looked, as usual, in Sportique and Kiki Byrne and said how pretty the clothes were, and was Kiki Byrne better than Bazaar.'

Trendy boys have 'long hair', the police are the 'fuzz', anything admirable is 'with-it' or 'super' and the permissive society has well and truly knocked at the door, with arty blokes whose idea of a smooth chat-up line is, 'Come on. Let's go to bed. I'm not too keen on the preliminaries.' As an evocation of the King's Road scene at that time the novel has a real ring of truth about it, and a heroine who eventually sees through all the phonies and the coffee-bar cowboys, but concludes: 'Well, I'm just a super birdie still.'

16

'A group of Chelsea layabouts'

That Sort of Thing

Captain Edward Molyneux, seventy years old and sometime dressmaker to the Royal Family, announced at the start 1965 that he was making his comeback into the world of fashion after an absence of thirteen years. Naturally, there had been a fair amount of changes while he had been away – indeed, Mary Quant's whole career to date had happened in the interim – but the January 25, 1965 fashion pages of the *Daily Telegraph* confidently reported that Molyneux was the man of the hour, and that all this nonsense about mini-skirts would soon be a thing of the past. 'The wheels of fashion are turning fast – backwards,' they predicted. 'Look at the influence *My Fair Lady* clothes have already had. Luck is with the Captain. [. . .] He couldn't have returned at a more propitious moment.' The man himself had this to say: 'I detest very short skirts. Mine will cover the knees and more. I loathe the sight of a woman in trousers, except on very informal occasions. It will be no good coming to me for that sort of thing.'

By a strange coincidence, back in 1961, the seventeen-year-old Andrew Loog Oldham had for a time been employed by Molyneux's nephew, Peter Hope Lumley, who ran a model agency – called, with admirable logic, Model Agency – in Brompton Road, opposite Mary Quant's Knightsbridge branch of Bazaar. Oldham had come a long way since those days, and was currently having questions asked about his work in the House of Lords, in relation to the *Clockwork Orange*-inspired sleeve notes he had written for the back of the new Rolling Stones album, which urged fans to mug blind people in order to get the cash together to buy the record. Meanwhile, another section of the establishment, in the form of the Lord Chamberlain's office, expressed displeasure about the text of John Osborne's new play, *A Patriot for Me*, and on January 5 flatly refused to sanction its performance in its current condition.

Getting Some Blues Riff and Adding a Few Fucking Lyrics

The film crews were busy again around the Chelsea area – this time it was for Martin Ritts' adaptation of John Le Carré's *The Spy Who Came in from the Cold*. In the book, the character of Smiley lives just off the King's Road in Bywater Street, so in the film version Richard Burton can be seen crossing the road outside South Kensington tube station before visiting Smiley's house in a row of white Georgian buildings.

Burton might be able to walk around the King's Road, but it was becoming increasingly difficult for the Beatles to do likewise, although they sometimes managed to find ways around this, as Mary Quant told me:

> All the Beatles came to our shop Bazaar. Lennon also bought his cap and other things. Paul McCartney came to our garage/studio, because it was too difficult to go to Bazaar and be mobbed by King's Road customers. One of the girls working for me in the garage/studio passed out with shock and cracked her head open.

Newly famous Michael Caine – who had been sleeping on John Barry's sofa in Cadogan Square after making *Zulu* – was running around London and Berlin shooting a film version of Len Deighton's *The Ipcress File*, while someone else who had played a small role in *Zulu*, Peter Gill, had also been working as an assistant director at the Royal Court since June 1964, and now his own play *The Sleeper's Den* premiered at the Royal Court in a production without decor on February 28, 1965. *Happy End*, the musical by Kurt Weill, Elisabeth Hauptmann and Bertolt Brecht, opened at the Court on March 10, but the behind-the-scenes struggle over John Osborne's *A Patriot for Me* continued, and the Lord Chamberlain's office rejected the play yet again on March 26. Osborne and the English Stage Company refused to make the required cuts, and they decided that when it opened in the summer, the Royal Court would temporarily transform itself into a private members' club in order to circumvent the ban. If none of the aforementioned appealed to the London public, there was always Profumo scandal veteran Mandy Rice-Davies, currently drawing packed houses in cabaret over in Charing Cross Road at Freddie Mills Nite Spot in March, the same month that *Nova*, one of the best magazines of the sixties, made its debut on the newsstands.

Eaton Place was proving to be something of a magnet for people in the news. Roman Polanski – pictured in April's *Films and Filming* dressed up in a kilt and sporran, for reasons best known to himself – was happily ensconced there, and now his neighbours included the offices of the Who's management company, New Action, run by Kit Lambert and Chris Stamp, whose brother Terence had lived just down the road and was now doing very nicely thank you in the film business. Just to make the area even more rock'n'roll, Pete Townshend himself moved into a flat above those offices with a couple of Revox tape machines, where he would proceed to write some of the key hit songs of the sixties. The classic posters for the Who at the Marquee may have famously carried the slogan 'Maximum R&B', but, as Chris Stamp recalled in Andrew Loog Oldham's book *2 Stoned*, they knew that the future lay in original material, not covers:

> We religiously stuck with what Pete Townshend would come up with rather than go getting some blues riff and adding a few fucking lyrics. We totally understood what everyone was up to from day one; all the other wankers were doing was let's go and find a few black riffs that may be in the public domain and add a few Chelsea-type lyrics to them.

This was a pretty far-thinking strategy for early 1965, when a large number of the British beat boom acts had so far based a fair slice of their careers on covering US performances which had themselves often been denied a proper UK release or promotion. This resulted in the bizarre state of affairs that many fans in America then wound up buying the British cover version under the impression that it had been their own composition, unaware that the original artist might be scraping a living in clubs just down the road in Detroit or New Orleans. A good example would be the Swinging Blue Jeans, almost the whole of whose chart career consisted of covers of US recordings, but other acts such as Manfred Mann, the Moody Blues, Cilla Black, Herman's Hermits, the Searchers and the Nashville Teens all had Top Ten UK hits with cover versions of US singles which in virtually every case were pale copies of the originals.

Just as Pete Townshend set up home in SW3, in March 1965 one of the former residents of Edith Grove returned to the neighbourhood, this time with a lot more money in his pocket, and was happy to give Sue Mautner a guided tour for the benefit of readers of the *New Musical Express*:

TIME – 7pm . . . Destination – a mews cottage set in the heart of Chelsea . . . Motive – to interview Brian Jones in his new pad. [. . .] Brian answered the door, casually clad in white polo-necked sweater and grey slacks, with a cigar in one hand and a tall glass of Scotch and coke in the other. 'You'll have to excuse the mess,' he said, as we entered the richly furnished lounge-cum-dining room, with its long velvet curtains and Regency-styled furniture, 'but the cleaning woman didn't turn up.'

As for Mick Jagger, his current girlfriend, Chrissie Shrimpton, provided the lowdown on a typical London evening out for the two of them in a feature entitled 'The Girls Behind the Pop Boys' which appeared in the March edition of *Rave* magazine: 'They eat at places like The Casserole in the King's Road, Chelsea, and then go on to the Ad Lib Club in Soho. They enjoy a super good time.'

The Most Coolly Elegant City in the World

All across America in April 1965 you could see the wholesome grins of Herman's Hermits, who had broken through into that market the previous autumn with their bigger-selling but pedestrian cover of Earl-Jean's exquisite 'I'm into Something Good', and were now staring down from the US number one spot with a song called 'Mrs Brown You've Got a Lovely Daughter'. Over in England, an American journalist called John Crosby wrote an article called 'London – The Most Exciting City' for the *Weekend Telegraph,* all about how it was fast becoming the with-it capital of the world: 'Suddenly, the young own the town,' declared Crosby. It was now the place 'where the action is, the gayest, most uninhibited – and in a wholly new, very modern sense – the most coolly elegant city in the world'.

Another American journalist who visited London that year was *TIME* magazine's Piri Halasz, who in April 1966 was to write the most famous Swinging London article of them all. This was her first return visit to the city since 1949, and she was very much struck by all the changes which had taken place. *TIME*'s editorial – 'A Letter from the Publisher' – the following year made reference to her 1965 trip, and said that she had bought 'a pair of bell-bottom slacks by Foale & Tuffin' at a place in the King's Road, but Piri told me that this was not quite true:

'A Letter from the Publisher' said that I'd bought those trousers in the King's Road. It must have been a flight of fancy on the part of the editor who wrote that section, as the trousers were purchased in

Knightsbridge, I believe at either Maryon or Chanelle in the Brompton Road. I bought a dress by Gerald McCann at the same time. I never got any comments on the trousers, though I loved them (they were ladylike, not flashy). Michael Demarest, an editor on *TIME*, complimented me on the dress, and recognised it as having come from London. He had been raised in England, and in '64 had been back visiting for some time, so he knew what was going on there, both in fashion and politics.

While American journalists were checking out the London scene, British journalists were observing an American arrival, Bob Dylan, who came to the city for two shows at the Albert Hall in May as part of a UK tour, closely followed by film-maker D. A. Pennebaker, who immortalised the events in possibly the finest rock documentary ever made, *Don't Look Back*. For his pains, Bob was also interviewed by former *Melody Maker* writer Laurie Henshaw, now writing for *Disc*. Rock'n'roll-hating Henshaw had relentlessly written off Elvis, Gene Vincent and the rest back in 1956, but in 1965 he ran into a stone wall, interviewing someone who just did not want to play the game, and he floundered around asking Dylan for fashion tips:

> HENSHAW: Let's talk about you. Your clothes for instance. Are your tastes in clothes changing at all?
>
> DYLAN: I like clothes. I don't have any particular interests at all. I like to wear drapes, umbrellas, hats.
>
> HENSHAW: You're not going to tell me you carry an umbrella.
>
> DYLAN: I most certainly do carry an umbrella. Where I come from everybody carries an umbrella. Have you ever been to South Dakota? Well, I come from South Dakota, and in South Dakota people carry umbrellas.

Oddly enough, anyone looking at the front cover of the May edition of *Films and Filming* – which was in the shops while Dylan was being recorded – would have seen a photo of the assembled King's Road beatniks from Guy Hamilton's censorship-troubled film *The Party's Over* walking across the Albert Bridge, being led by actress Catherine Woodville, carrying an umbrella. Perhaps Bob was onto something after all.

Beatniks Should Be Made to Grow Up

Guy Hamilton's film was finally being released after three years of sitting on the shelf, but the decision probably had quite a lot to do with the fact that he had since directed one of the biggest-grossing pictures of the decade – a little-known thing called *Goldfinger* – and even *The Party's Over*'s scriptwriter, Marc Behm, had completed a recent script called *Help!*, which would also enjoy a tolerable amount of success in 1965. Even so, the film's original distributor, Rank, wanted nothing to do with the picture, therefore *The Party's Over* was released by a much smaller outfit called Monarch Films and was given a premiere by the Jacey cinema chain, whose repertoire for 1965 also included such delights as *Nude Las Vegas* and *How to Undress in Public Without Undue Embarrassment*. F. Maurice Speed, reviewing the film in the May 7 edition of *What's On in London*, hardly seemed to think it had been worth the wait: '[. . .] the sad, sad little story about a group of Chelsea layabouts and a zombie-like American girl who joins them. [. . .] The obvious and very commendable moral to be drawn from all this appears to be that all beatniks should either be made to grow up or buried with ironic honours.'

One notable irony lay in the fact that a 1962 fictional depiction of some Chelsea beatniks should surface in the cinema just as some genuine San Francisco beat poets arrived in town. During their visit, they appeared onstage at the Albert Hall for the June 11 performance, which is widely regarded as London's first mass countercultural event and was preserved on film in Peter Whitehead's documentary, *Wholly Communion*. It came about after Allen Ginsberg had done a poetry reading at Better Books in the Charing Cross Road, organised by Barry Miles, which had been a great success, and had also been attended by Warhol and members of his Factory, as Miles explained to me: 'Andy and Edie Sedgwick and Gerard Malanga were all at the Allen Ginsberg poetry reading that I put on at Better Books in '65, just before the Albert Hall reading. That was when I first met them.'

Several days later, Ginsberg had pointed out to Miles and his wife Sue and their friend Barbara Rudin that Lawrence Ferlinghetti was due in town in a few days, and that Gregory Corso was nearby in Paris at the time. Discussing it among themselves, they hit upon the idea of hiring the Albert Hall for a group reading, and Rudin duly picked up the phone and made the booking. Corso and Ferlinghetti stayed for a while in Chelsea at the Old Church Street home of the singer Julie Felix, and when Ginsberg and Miles went round there for dinner some days after the big event, as Miles later recalled, Corso attacked Ginsberg for 'being a drunken slob at the Albert Hall reading and of "letting down the ideals of the Beat Generation".'

The King's Road Was Becoming Notorious

George Harrison, part of a different beat generation, went into the night-club business that June, having shares in a place called Sibylla's, just off Piccadilly. One of Harrison's other partners in the venture was DJ Alan 'Fluff' Freeman, the latter of whom could be seen that year alongside Peter Cushing and Christopher Lee in the excellent *Dr Terror's House of Horrors*, engaged in a life-and-death struggle with a man-eating plant. Of course, if Sibylla's was a little out of your price range, the London Hilton had now converted its second floor into a club called the 007 Room, where they offered vodka martinis prepared as Fleming ordered, and you could 'dance to the international beat of the Bondsmen'.

Christopher Lee, meanwhile, had just returned from living in Switzerland to set up home in Chelsea, in Cadogan Square, a short walk from Lower Belgrave Street, where he was born. He recalled the move in his autobiography:

> We fled to a flat in a quiet London square, within a mile of the places where I'd been born, married and had Christina named. It was on the level of the tops of the plane trees. Not for the first time, the nearby King's Road was becoming notorious, but we hardly felt the vibrations of that. It was very peaceful. Our immediate neigh-bour was the delightful, soothing Boris Karloff. In the mews behind lived an owl.

As Christopher explained to me, he found some of the changes in London definitely not to his taste: 'Now, everything became "permissive". *Do what you want.* In the sixties we had the Permissive Society and the message seemed to be: "Do what you want, without any fear of retaliation." The late Roy Jenkins made one of the most asinine comments I have ever heard; he said: "A permissive society is a civilized society."'

Over at the Royal Court, it had been an interesting year so far. Back in April, they had given Chelsea a taste of pre-First World War Germany with *Spring Awakening* by Frank Wedekind, whose works provided the basis for Pabst's 1929 film masterpiece *Pandora's Box*. Among the cast were a couple of actors who went on to quite different careers in show business: Derek Fowlds, who became a TV star partnering glove puppet Basil Brush; and Barry Evans, who was a leading man in seventies softcore romps such as *Under the Doctor* and *The Adventures of a Taxi Driver*. June at the Royal Court saw a production of Charles Wood's *Meals on Wheels* (aka *Muck on a Truck*), which was given such a rough reception by the preview audience that for the opening night, expecting disaster, stars Roy Kinnear and Lee Montague rented a TV so that they could at least watch West Ham's European Cup match in their dressing room during odd moments offstage.

Following *Meals on Wheels*, the Royal Court turned into a members' club for the presentation of John Osborne's *A Patriot for Me*, which opened on June 30, much to the disgust of the Lord Chamberlain's office, which was allergic to its depiction of homosexuality. One of their private memos read: 'This play looks to me like the Pansies Charter of Freedom and is bound to be a *cause célèbre*.' If its path to the stage had been rocky, the run itself was marked by an event that was far worse. George Devine, the driving force of the English Stage Company since its opening season in 1956, had taken a role in Osborne's play alongside a distinguished cast which also included Maximilian Schell, Edward Fox and Jill Bennett, but on August 8, 1965, he collapsed during a performance at the Royal Court and was rushed to hospital, seriously ill. He never fully recovered from this last illness and was to die in January 1966.

Sex Perverts and Pinkos, Tennis-Shoe Wearers and All

On June 12, the Beatles were awarded the MBE, prompting a certain number of previous recipients to return their medals in protest. *Private Eye*'s front cover of June 25 made its own comment on the Wilson government's desperate attempts to play the trendy youth card, running one of Harold's photo opportunities with the band on the cover under the headline 'Beatles To Go On Vietnam Peace Mission'. The prime minister's speech bubble read: 'Good Evening Mao Tse Tung: May I introduce my Commonwealth colleagues.' Meanwhile *Help!* premiered at the London Pavilion on July 29, and Michael Caine, having completed filming *The Ipcress File*, was back on location in London doing a week's shooting for his new picture, *Alfie*, at the Victoria Children's Hospital in Chelsea.

Just to prove that it was now becoming difficult to make a film in 1965 without setting at least part of the action within spitting distance of the King's Road, another picture opened that month which seemed to have all the classic ingredients. This was called *The Pleasure Girls*, produced by the same company that had backed Polanski's *Repulsion*, with Ian McShane as a David Bailey-style photographer (a full year before Antonioni made *Blow-Up*) and a house full of King's Road dolly birds including Francesca Annis and Suzanna Leigh. Even Klaus Kinski was wandering around there somewhere. *Films and Filming* summed it up as follows: 'Sally Feathers comes to London to start work in a Model School and shares a large flat in Chelsea with Angela, Dee, Marion, an Australian girl named Cobber and Dee's homosexual brother Paddy.'

Richard Lester's film of Ann Jellicoe's Royal Court play *The Knack* also hit the cinemas that summer, and was duly praised in most quarters, including the pages of *Playboy* magazine, which concluded that '*The Knack* is a knockout.' The review appeared in the same issue (August 1965) as a lengthy interview with Robert Shelton, Imperial Wizard of the Ku Klux Klan, who took a moment to criticise the dress sense of the 'misfits' among the white race who had been getting involved in the civil rights movement: 'these sex perverts and pinkos, tennis-shoe wearers and all . . .'

If tennis shoes could get him that worked up, there is no telling what Mr Shelton might have made of the goings-on in a flat in Pont Street, just off Sloane Street, that year, although *Playboy*'s own Victor Lownes – Hugh Hefner's business partner who was preparing to open up the London Playboy Club in 1966 – could probably have given him some clues. That particular apartment became home to the World Psychedelic Centre, run by US acid evangelist Michael Hollingshead, whose autobiography was quite understandably entitled *The Man Who Turned On the World*. During its few brief months of existence, in the last era when LSD was still legal in the UK, the Centre attracted visitors such as Paul McCartney, Julie Felix, Robert Fraser, Eric Clapton, William Burroughs, Roman Polanski, Roland Penrose, Donovan, Alex Trocchi and others. As befitted a high priest of the new consciousness, Hollingshead was soon persuaded to dress in a suitably groovy fashion, as his autobiography revealed:

> Shortly after I moved into the Pont Street apartment, a couple of my friends took me aside and suggested that I get some new clothes, costumes of the Chelsea of the mid-sixties – Edwardian jackets, embroidered in gold and silver, and silk shirts with huge collars, velvet pants and blue suede shoes, and so forth . . . Accordingly, I let myself be persuaded to exchange my jeans and sweat shirt for a new wardrobe, and Michael Rainey's shop 'Hung On You' sent round a huge pile of fashionable clothes and a bill for £600. There were about five of us staying at the apartment and we divided the clothes between us. I ended up with a pair of flared pin-stripe trousers with an enormous belt and silver buckle, several silk shirts and ties, and a couple of hand-embroidered jackets. Now I was at one with the fashion of my times. The only problem was a psychological

one – I was embarrassed to be seen in them and consequently I stayed indoors, ignoring all invitations and gradually reverted back to my jeans and sweat shirt much to the chagrin of those for whom clothes had great significance. There was also the additional factor of the cheque, which bounced, and I felt somehow uncomfortable wearing these expensive clothes as a result.

The Pest Houses Are Now Everywhere

Hung On You, Michael Rainey's shop at Chelsea Green where Hollingshead bounced his cheque, had a name inspired by the title of a Spector/Goffin/King song on the B-side of the Righteous Brothers' summer 1965 hit, 'Unchained Melody'. One of the key boutiques of the era, it would relocate a year later to 430 King's Road, a site which was to change hands several times over the coming decade, and house some of the most important designers of them all. Rainey himself, part of the old money, upper-class Chelsea set, would be pictured in the following year's *TIME* magazine feature 'London: The Swinging City', attending an opening at the Robert Fraser Gallery, chatting to his girlfriend Lady Jane Orsmby-Gore, and his shop was one of the places where the emerging rock aristocracy mixed with the old-school aristocracy. The fact that Rainey chose to move his shop to what was then very much the unfashionable end of the King's Road, where Granny Takes a Trip would also open in the autumn of 1965, helped establish World's End as a focal point of the emerging counter-culture. Mick Farren told me:

> Well, in the King's Road up until say the mid-seventies there was a wealth of difference between Sloane Square and World's End, a real wealth of difference, you know [laughs] . . . Heading west, you kind of got to the Town Hall and the Fire Station, but after that there wasn't very much going on until you reached these almost kind of circled wagons at World's End. Rainey was an aristocrat, he was a lord. So you had all that – the sort of dispossessed Lord Alfred Douglas kind of characters, then you move over one step and you've got Quentin Crisp through to *The Rocky Horror Show*, then you move over three more steps and you've got the socialite end of the Krays and the Richardsons like Johnny Bindon. [Chelsea] was fun when it was sort of crumbling, even though there were people who lived off weekly cheques from Daddy or whatever . . .

It was a world where everyone seemed to know everyone else – or more to the point, it may have seemed that way to the public when reading about the lives of everyone under a certain age who was involved in the arts. For instance, photographer David Bailey got married in August 1965 to actress Catherine Deneuve – a couple of months after having been introduced to her by film director Roman Polanski – with rock singer Mick Jagger acting as best man. Bailey had first met Jagger because he was going out with Jean Shrimpton and Mick was going out with her sister Chrissie. Polanski, who had met Deneuve when she starred in *Repulsion*, returned to the area that summer from location shooting for his new film *Cul-de-Sac*, and he bought his first London home, at 95 West Eaton Place Mews, off Eaton Square. Meanwhile Bailey himself had been the photographer at another high-profile wedding of 1965 – that between Frances Shea and Reg Kray in the East End on April 20.

If you wanted to see the numerous examples of this new breed of 'swinging' Londoner, then Chelsea was certainly the place to go, and *Private Eye* in August 1965 was happy to satirise the bright young things who had colonised the area:

> Journal of Ye Plague Yeer Nineteen Hundred and Sixty Five – being some extracts from ye diary of Sam. Peeps esq. I walked this day in the village of Chelsea, where I did for the first time see many in the streets afflicted with the sicknesse and for the first time did also see the houses where plague had struck, marked out by blue-painted doors, wrought iron work, carriage lamps, bowls of geraniums hung from windows and the like . . . Much talk of the nature of the sicknesse and of how those affected soon begin to gibber strange sounds, 'with-it', 'dynamic', and the like, and attire themselves in shoddy materials, transported into some marvellous ecstasy . . . The pest houses are now everywhere, some called boutiques, some trattorias, some bistros, where the unfortunate sufferers may gather to find comfort in each other being like afflicted. It is a particularly sad sight to see the young girls, their faces pale and drawn with the plague, their skirts risen above the knee as a sign that they are stricken.

Dig One, You're Bound to Dig the Other

The papers seemed full of the King's Road that year, and the magazine *Tatler and Bystander* was relaunched with a view to covering cultural events in the capital under the name *London Life*, a title last used some decades before by an upmarket gentleman's porn publication. In a spirit of investigative journalism, one of the first things they covered was Michael Hollingshead's World Psychedelic Centre: 'LSD – the drug that could turn on London. Read the exclusive story in next week's *London Life*.'

While the visitors to Pont Street were quietly frying their brains before the drug squad moved in, over at the Railway Hotel in Harrow – scene of early triumphs by the Rolling Stones in their Edith Grove days – the hat-check woman, Vivienne, whose soon-to-be-ex-husband Derek was running the place, met a man with a seriously pale complexion named Malcolm Edwards. Later in 1965 she would move into a shared house in Clapham rented by her brother, and Edwards lived there as well, using talcum powder on his face to achieve his distinctive white effect, hence his nickname, 'Talcy Malcy'. Her name was Westwood, he later changed his from Edwards to McLaren, and the King's Road would be hearing from them shortly.

In New York, British fashion designers were giving a series of shows that were profiled in the September 10 issue of *TIME* magazine, highlighting the way in which the worlds of fashion and rock music increasingly crossed over. The report mentioned a Mary Quant fashion show held on the roof of Best & Co. in Manhattan, to the accompaniment of a rock band called the Skunks:

[. . .] and the biggest surprise of all is that the whole gas of a package had not been dreamed up in the pop-happy U.S. but in austere old England. As a matter of fact, the package had been tied up and delivered by Mary Quant, who at 31 is the dean of Britain's new-wave designers. Says she: 'The music and the new clothes are inseparable.' At Manhattan's Arnold Constable, the show belonged to Caroline Charles, one of the dozen young designers of the 'Chelsea Revolution', whose presumptuous styles have forced even the London fog to lift. [. . .] Said Caroline, to the rhythmic sounds of amplified guitars: 'Dig one, you're bound to dig the other.'

On September 1, 1965, the seriously ill George Devine officially retired as artistic director of the Royal Court, and Bill Gaskill took over. The theatre itself was such an established part of the social landscape by now that one of the newer restaurants, the Canova at 61–63 Lower Sloane Street, was taking out adverts in the press showing a route map of how to walk there from the Royal Court, and urging potential customers to try one of the specialities of the house, 'Sole in a Paper Bag'. Up above the Royal Court, the club called the Rehearsal Room was playing a small but

266

King's Road

important part in British comedy history, since it was here that David Frost came to check out a poorly attended revue staged there for a week by some Oxford graduates. Frost was one of the only people in the audience, but he saw something that he liked in the work of two of the performers, Michael Palin and Terry Jones, and offered them a job writing for a TV series he was putting together called *The Frost Report*, first broadcast on March 10, 1966. Since the other writers on the show included John Cleese, Graham Chapman and Eric Idle – in a stellar line-up which also featured Marty Feldman, Barry Took, Keith Waterhouse, Willis Hall, Dennis Norden, Barry Cryer and David Nobbs – this was the first occasion on which the future members of the Monty Python team worked together.

Pathetic, Tragic, Trapped, Drugs, Drink, Sex. Do You Want a Cigar?

In the cinemas, audiences could see Julie Christie in John Schlesinger's *Darling*, described by George Angell in the October 1965 issue of *Films and Filming* as 'the auto-biography of Diana, a girl from the Chelsea upper crust – a bright, beautiful, sexy, unstable amoral girl who drifts from man to man, and from one lover's bed to another'. Marrying into royalty, Christie's character becomes *Princess* Diana and appears on the newsreels visiting the sick, before finding out – surprise, surprise – that the swinging life is not all it is cracked up to be. Scriptwriter Frederick Raphael gave a fictionalised account of how he came to write this in his 1976 TV series, *The Glittering Prizes*, in which the sleazy film producer sums up the plot of the *Darling*-esque film they are making as follows: 'Pathetic. Tragic. Trapped. Drugs. Drink. Sex. Do you want a cigar?'

That autumn various members of the supposed 'In' crowd found themselves depicted in Bailey's photo collection, *David Bailey's Box of Pin-Ups*, which consisted of thirty-six full-page portraits with text written by Francis Wyndham printed on their reverse sides, all contained in a white cardboard box with photographs also printed on the sides. Celebrities pictured included Michael Caine, the Kray brothers, Lord Snowdon and various leading lights of the modelling, film, photography and rock worlds. Michael Frayn, writing in his column in the *Observer*, commented on the ironic distance he perceived in the portraits:

> They're offered complete with a fertile ambiguity of attitude on the management's part, which goes roughly: 'You can think these are pretty people if you like, or if you don't think they're pretty how

about thinking they're amusing? And if that doesn't appeal to you, what we're trying to say is how amusing it is that some people might think they're pretty, only don't quote us on that, because what we really mean is that it's finding them amusing that's really so amusing, so the laugh's on you, and anyway we have other irons in the fire.'

In 2005, when I was writing the original edition of this book, a copy of Bailey's *Pin-Ups* was being offered for sale by a London book dealer for £5,000. In 2022, another London book dealer had a copy listed for £20,000, while a US book dealer was asking $35,000 for a copy signed by David Bailey. The 1965 retail price was £10. To put that in context, for the same money that year you could buy a Philishave electric razor, two concrete household coal bunkers from an advert in the back of the *Sunday Mirror*, or around forty packets of cigarettes, but it is debatable whether any of these would have turned out to be quite such a good investment.

On November 3, several things happened which would provoke controversy both in the press and among the newly vigilant members of Mary Whitehouse's self-appointed National Viewers' and Listeners' Association. The first was the broadcast on the BBC of a play called *Up the Junction*, written by well-to-do Chelsea writer Nell Dunn, based on her research conducted across the river in the poorer sections of Battersea, to where she then relocated. On the same day, Edward Bond's *Saved* opened at the Royal Court as a members-only performance, whose scene of a baby being stoned to death in its pram on a South London estate made it instantly a matter of huge media controversy. In an author's note about *Saved*, published in 1966, Edward Bond wrote: 'Clearly the stoning to death of a baby in a London park is a typical English understatement. Compared to the "strategic" bombing of German towns it is a negligible atrocity, compared to the cultural and emotional deprivation of most of our children its consequences are insignificant.'

For that section of the Chelsea community for whom the words 'getting stoned' meant something else again entirely, the name of a new boutique which opened up for business in November at 488 King's Road would certainly have raised a smile. Granny Takes a Trip, started by John Pearse, Nigel Waymouth and Sheila Cohen, was an immediate success, catering to the rock elite and the emerging foot soldiers of the counterculture. John Pearse, who had taken time off after his Savile Row days – 'I'd been travelling in St Tropez, and Spain, so I was a kind of *gigolo* . . .' – told me that they attracted customers from the rock world 'the day we opened. Because we were kind of in it, in a way'. As for the original idea behind the shop:

'We were dealing in vintage clothes. What appealed to us was Aubrey Beardsley and the Victorians, *Against Nature* by Huysmans. So we were all doomed Romantics at that time. Not New Romantics, *doomed* Romantics. So that was the influence – art nouveau.'

Things Fall Apart; The Trousers Cannot Hold

Beardsley was certainly in the air that year – posters of his illustrations were becoming available and found their way onto many a student wall, the Victoria and Albert Museum just up the road was in the throes of organising the largest Beardsley exhibition ever seen, before or since, which opened in 1966, while a new biography by Stanley Weintraub was also in the works, which would surface in 1967. At Granny Takes a Trip, velvet was very much the order of the day, as Mick Farren explained to me: 'Granny's had a line in velvet trousers that we all lived in. They were pretty good, except that one of the seams on the fly always went . . . They were the sort of more foppish alternative to Levi's.'

When asked about the reputation which some King's Road clothes had for falling apart shortly after purchase, John Pearse says:

Well, actually, certain trousers that we made *did* fall to bits as well, very quickly, but nobody ever complained about it, because that was part of the thing. It was velvet, and you'd become like some tattered troubadour the next day, you know. Some things did fall apart, and everything had to be so tight, that seams could burst, especially on velvet. Flimsy cloth . . .

While Granny's was establishing itself at World's End, another iconic sixties boutique run by James Wedge and Pat Booth had opened further down towards Sloane Square at 135a King's Road: Top Gear, a tiny space near Cafe Picasso, with a black interior which had been painted by Albert Finney and his friends. As Pat Booth told Marnie Fogg: 'The shop was a meeting place every single Saturday. For the first time shopping became a social event. John Lennon used to sit on the window sill and put 78s on the old record player. Mick Jagger had an account with us for all his girlfriends.'

Miles, who had a lot of contact with the Beatles in those days, had this to say to me about Lennon in the Top Gear window: 'He was probably sort of in disguise, with an old mackintosh and so on, so no one would have thought it was him. I mean, I don't suppose he did it more than once, let's face it, they were pretty busy people . . .'

Credit: Eric Piper/Mirrorpix

14 November 1965: Kenneth Tynan (centre) at the Royal Court
debating censorship, the night after saying 'fuck' on television

Everyone seemed to be busy that autumn: at the Royal Court, babies
were still being stoned in their prams – although Joe Orton wrote to his
agent, Peggy Ramsey, after seeing it, calling it a 'remarkably sissy play'
– but there was also N. F. Simpson's spy parody *The Cresta Run*, which
disappointed *What's On in London's* reviewer ('Most of the jokes we get here
have a primitive lack of sophistication that might dismay admirers of Ken
Dodd'), as did Ann Jellicoe's new play *Shelley* ('damaged rather wilfully by
Miss Jellicoe's sporadic use of primitive Brechtian devices'); Ken Tynan
was giving Mary Whitehouse a heart attack on November 13 by saying
the word 'fuck' on live television, while in *Rave* magazine, Gary from the
Walker Brothers was explaining that Scott had bought a jeep from an
army surplus store: 'You should see us cruising Chelsea in this thing with
all the sides open – I wish he'd got a tank or something. Oh, I wish I
hadn't said that!'

Meanwhile *London Life* carried the following item about the arrival of
another boutique in the area, coming to a quiet location just south of the
Chelsea Potter:

Quorum are moving from their small shop in Ansdell Street, W8, to
52 Radnor Walk, SW3. Opening on Friday 19 November. As well as
stocking the full range of Quorum clothes, they will sell separates

designed exclusively for them by Alice Pollock, a 23-year-old director of Quorum. They will also sell gift vouchers for 1 guinea and 5 guineas. Open for retail and wholesale customers.

Also moving, but a little further away, was US singer P. J. Proby, who told Chris Hutchins of the *New Musical Express* in December that he was giving up his current home at 5 Cheltenham Terrace – just off the King's Road, near the Duke of York's Barracks – and heading for the somewhat less rock'n'roll environs of Wembley. He had gained something of a wild reputation locally during the previous year, and this announcement came only a month or so after a Chelsea electrical shop sent round three muscular gentlemen to repossess P. J.'s TV set and record player, resorting to force when denied entry: 'The next thing I know there's an almighty crash as they kick the front door down and it's obvious that I've got to come out of hiding. I grab one of my antique guns off the wall as I dash into the hall and hold 'em there until the police arrive to take care of the matter.'

Finally, in that last autumn before *TIME* magazine announced to the world that London was officially 'swinging', an ex-mod from Stoke Newington released his first single on November 15 under his new name of Marc Bolan, with a Decca press release that said: 'His writings mirror his experiences with mentionings of the magician's pact with the great god Pan. In London, walking down King's Road, Chelsea in the dead of night, he chanced to meet a girl named Lo-og who gave him a magic cat.'

In the Chelsea of late 1965, this would hardly have raised an eyebrow . . .

17

'Thigh-high skirts for dolly-looking birds'

Death of a Kitchen Sink Director

At the start of 1966, it seemed as if half the world wanted to be in London, and half the film world were there already: Truffaut was in town shooting *Fahrenheit 451* with Oskar Werner and Julie Christie; Charlie Chaplin, who would turn seventy-seven in April, was making his final comeback at Pinewood directing *A Countess From Hong Kong* with Marlon Brando and Sophia Loren; Michael Caine, Peter Sellers, Tony Hancock, Peter Cook and Dudley Moore were filming *The Wrong Box* at Shepperton, with music by John Barry; Stanley Kubrick was taking over four whole sound stages at Elstree while making *2001: A Space Odyssey*, amid reports in the press that he had asked Lloyds of London to insure his film against 'the discovery of extra-terrestrial beings prior to its 1967 opening'. Even Otto Preminger had decided that the Smoke was the place to be for his new thriller *Bunny Lake Is Missing*, and to prove how with-it he was he had signed up the Zombies for a guest appearance in the film, and was ill-advisedly photographed posing on-set with them while wearing a plastic Beatle wig.

Small wonder that Michelangelo Antonioni was planning to come to London in the spring to make his first ever English-language picture, *Blow-Up* – the only real surprise was that there was any studio space left for him to rent.

However, not quite everything was swinging on the King's Road at the start of that year. On January 19, 1966, George Devine, the founding artistic director and driving force behind the English Stage Company's remarkable theatrical breakthrough at the Royal Court, finally died, having never really recovered his health following his collapse the previous August while appearing in a production of *A Patriot for Me*. In a tribute to him published a few days later in the *Observer*, John Osborne wrote, 'It is a bleak week for English theatre. [. . .] I can imagine his special, amused shrug at the crass newspaper headlines which described him last week as a "kitchen sink director".' At the Royal Court, Edward Bond's *Saved* was still running as a members-only presentation, and would finally be successfully prosecuted by the Lord Chamberlain in April, thus closing off that particular legal loophole. However, the writing was on the wall for UK theatre censorship itself, and in a House of Lords debate on the subject on February 17, Lord Annan said, 'In my view, the serious author must be given freedom of choice as to what to say and how to say it. I am afraid this means that the language or the theme or the treatment may very well shock.'

Further up the King's Road on January 22, Immediate label recording artist Chris Farlowe played a show at Chelsea College – he was hanging around in the lower end of the Top Fifty with a song called 'Think', and still six months away from his number one single, 'Out of Time'. A reader's letter to *ABC Film Review* reckoned that the Beatles in *Help!* were well on their way to rivalling the Marx Brothers as a comedy outfit, while another in *Films and Filming* was allegedly cancelling his subscription because of a different Richard Lester film: 'Now we must part. To choose rubbish such as *The Knack* as best film [of 1965 in *Films and Filming*'s awards], just because the In set at Chelsea says it is, lowers your standards beyond excuse.'

Meanwhile time was running out for those among the Chelsea In set who had been visiting Michael Hollingshead's World Psychedelic Centre, as the local drug squad became ever-more suspicious of anyone in the area who looked particularly 'groovy'. John Pearse from Granny Takes a Trip remembers the hazards during those last days before LSD was criminalised, as he told me:

Oh yes, the Psychedelic Centre . . . Of course, it was all perfectly legal, nobody knew what it was, and the police again just tried to make scapegoats of us. It became quite unpleasant at that time. You were kind of on the spot all the time, the police would harass you, around the King's Road. Your hair was long, so you'd get stopped all the time.

As for the Chelsea drug squad themselves, John says, 'Well I think they were in the heart of things, anyway, so they were Star Drug Squad Men, and we were Star Druggies, and it all worked out . . .'

In those days, LSD was still an unknown quantity in many quarters, and books like John Cashman's *The LSD Story*, published in America in 1966, did not necessarily help to clarify matters: 'Impressive evidence of LSD's effectiveness in the treatment of alcoholics, homosexuals and frigid women has been recorded,' claimed Cashman, before describing the following senseless piece of animal abuse:

> Three researchers gave a massive dose of LSD to a fourteen-year-old bull elephant named Tusko at the Lincoln Park Zoo in Oklahoma City. After an intramuscular injection of 297 milligrams of LSD, Tusko staggered around for a while, then keeled over and died an hour and forty minutes after the injection. Tusko is the only known death directly attributable to the administration of a dose of LSD.

Cashman noted that LSD was almost entirely 'an American obsession', but added that 'only in London, which is fast becoming the hippest city in the world, has there been even a ripple concerning the illicit use of LSD.'

Squirm to the Music

On March 4, 1966, the London *Evening Standard* printed an interview with John Lennon which eventually resulted in bonfires of Beatles records in the Deep South of America because of his statement that 'Christianity will go. It will shrink and vanish. We're more popular than Jesus now.'

It was obviously the right month for offending people, because then, on March 25, 1966, all four of the Beatles showed up at Robert Whitaker's photographic studio at No. 1, The Vale, SW3 – which runs north from King's Road, just near the Roebuck pub – and had their pictures taken grinning happily in white lab coats while adorned with dismembered plastic babies, false teeth and bloody offcuts of raw meat. The resulting shots appeared on the notorious and hastily withdrawn US Capitol *Yesterday and Today* 'butcher cover' album sleeve. Evidently, the whole business of being 'four loveable moptops' had long since started to pall.

Oddly enough, the very same week that the Beatles were doing their best to leave behind their safe image of a year or so earlier, the *Saturday Evening Post* ran an article called 'Russia at the Crossroads', which featured a photo captioned 'Young Russians squirm to the music of the Beatle-like "Christmas Stars" in a Moscow night spot'. The band in question wore textbook Beatle haircuts and collarless imitation 1963 Beatle grey jackets. Even behind the Iron Curtain they were now attempting to copy London fashions.

In early April, one of the strangest events of the year occurred, as a
BBC film crew organised by freelance producer Jack Bond held a party at
Christopher Gibbs' house in Cheyne Walk and gave out free LSD to all
those present, for the purposes of filming the results. The drug was still
just legal at this point, but clearly, this was not the sort of programme-
making likely to impress Mary Whitehouse, and they had certainly not
learnt the lesson of Tusko's experiences in the Lincoln Park Zoo. In the
event, the *Sunday People* raised a predictable fuss, as Miles reported later in
April in the pages of a very short-lived underground newspaper called the
Global Moon-edition Long Hair Times:

> One Saturday, early in April, there was a scene in Chelsea where the
> BBC TV bought free acid for everyone and filmed a mass turn on
> with about 100 people present. The Sunday papers got the story and
> splashed it all over the front pages and the guys at the BBC who made
> it look like getting the boot. On the film are Hoppy, Steve Stollman,
> Ewan, Kate Heliczer, Pete the Rat and so on. There were a number
> of police photographers present taking pictures of people all the time.

The party received so much retrospective publicity that it even helped
John Pearse out of a local difficulty with a magistrate, as he told me:
'Unfortunately I had a run-in with the law, on the day that LSD was made
illegal, so my mitigation in court was that I'd been to the BBC party where
they were handing out the acid, and being a good boy I put it in my pocket
and forgot about it and put it on my shelf at home and never took it, Your
Honour . . .' And did John get away with it? 'Yeah . . .'

A Dionysiac Frenzy in the Works Canteen

Granny Takes a Trip was one of several King's Road locations profiled in
the April edition of *Rave* magazine, essential reading for would-be groovers
on several continents wishing to keep up to date with the London scene:
'One of the latest additions is called Granny Takes a Trip – in King's Road,
dealing with the Victorian look. New clothes on Victorian lines, men's frock
coats, girls' dresses with lace trim. Prices from 5 to 10gns.'

They also recommended 'The Chelsea Kitchen – 74 King's Road. A
coffee bar/restaurant popular with the Chelsea crowd. Specialise in all
dishes. Another great meet-up place', and then – for decorating that James
Bond or Emma Peel bijou apartment – there was the 'Chelsea Antique
Market – 245a King's Road. Anything and everything, probably even the

kitchen sink, provided it's Victorian! Plumes, combs, birds in gilded cages, paintings and really old 78 records. Anything from about £2 upwards.'

In April, the English Stage Company was duly fined 50 guineas costs and conditionally discharged when the Lord Chamberlain's prosecution of *Saved* went through, and Michael Frayn's column in the *Observer* made gentle fun of the Royal Court's regular audience and its playwrights: 'We are under a further categorical imperative to see Fred Umble's new play (Christopher will get us the tickets) about a group of workers in an expanded polystyrene factory who ritually beat the tea-girl to death with plastic spoons, and eat her for lunch in a Dionysiac frenzy in the works canteen.'

LIFE magazine, meanwhile, ran a lengthy feature about Britain's general election, which had taken place at the end of March, and had seen Harold Wilson returned for another term, during which, instead of getting himself photographed standing next to the Beatles, he would shortly try to hog the limelight by standing on the same balcony with England's victorious 1966 World Cup-winning football squad. 'Though at 50 he is the youngest Prime Minister since 1894,' said *LIFE*'s article, 'he is hailed as "Good old Mister Wilson".' By whom, they didn't specify. Perhaps it was Mrs Wilson. Meanwhile, proving that the Tories could be just as crass in their attempts to be 'with-it' and 'switched-on', opposition leader Edward Heath (born 1916) was photographed for the same issue attempting to ride a skateboard – in those days, an item rarely seen outside of California.

This, then, was the world into which *TIME* magazine's 'London: The Swinging City' cover feature was to emerge on April 15, 1966. As it happened, it arrived just one day after the launch of another landmark sixties document, Mary Quant's autobiography, *Quant by Quant*, published by Cassell at 25 shillings. Carole d'Albiac, reviewing the book for the new edition of *London Life* which appeared two days later, hailed it as one of two 'feminist books' published that week: 'The girl who restated women's fashion in this country, starting (in a way that has only since become traditional for young designers) with a workroom in a bedsitter in Oakley Street, scotch under the counter to fortify her and her helpers against their first customers.' Soon, it was being serialised in the press, and Mary, who had also been highlighted in *TIME*'s cover feature, was more than ever a focus of media attention, as she explained to me:

I do remember being in a state of shock after seeing an enormous blown-up photograph of myself on Fleet Street, when the *Sunday Mirror* newspaper bought a chunk of *Quant by Quant* to publish. We used to go every Saturday night to discuss the photographs etc. with the editor and put the paper to bed. The *Sunday Mirror* was the best visually edited newspaper at that time.

Quite simply, Mary and her designs had helped put the King's Road firmly on the international map, in a way which would have been incomprehensible a decade earlier. In *Quant by Quant* she had this to say:

Chelsea suddenly became Britain's San Francisco, Greenwich Village and the Left Bank. The press publicised its cellars, its beat joints, its girls and its clothes. Chelsea ceased to be a small part of London; it became international; its name interpreted a way of living and a way of dressing far more than a geographical area. The Chelsea girl, the original leather-booted, black-stockinged girl who came out of the King's Road looking like some contemporary counterpart of a gay musketeer, began to be copied by the rest of London and watched with interest by others all over the country. Soon the 'look' was to be copied internationally.

Kinky, Wobble-As-You-Walk Celluloid Eyelids

Mary Quant would already have been familiar to a certain proportion of *TIME* readers by that stage, but other figures profiled in their cover feature were less used to this kind of transatlantic high-profile treatment, like Screamin' Lord Sutch, who was pictured on election day having run against the prime minister on behalf of his own National Teenage Party. 'Harold Wilson, at 50 the youngest P.M. of the century, is referred to as "good old 'arold",' *TIME*'s readers were assured, and it was no more convincing than when *LIFE* had said it a few weeks earlier, but when Sutch had leaned over on the platform to light Wilson's cigar, his photo wound up on the front page of the *New York Times*, and now here he was a few weeks later with his picture in *TIME*. Sutch told Michael Wale in 1972: 'My record company in New York were amazed. They'd tried to get stars on the front page of the *New York Times* for years.' Other people with their picture in *TIME*'s feature were Jane Ormsby-Gore and Michael Rainey, 'owner of a Chelsea men's shop he calls Hung On You', while a London street scene was captioned: 'Companiably suited, a mixed mod twosome browses past a shop in King's Road, Chelsea.' Readers were also given some practical advice about the new trend in women's clothing: 'Miniskirts are for dancing, walking and girl watching. Sitting in them takes practice.' As if all this wasn't enough to send the curious visitor off to look up the King's Road in their guidebook, there was also the following account of a gathering of the 'In' crowd:

> Saturday afternoon in Chelsea, at Le Reve restaurant. Wolfing down a quick lunch are some of the most switched-on young men in town: Actor Terence Stamp, 26, star of *The Collector* and steady date of model Jean Shrimpton; actor Michael Caine, 33, the Mozart-loving spy in *The Ipcress File*; hairdresser Sassoon, 38, whose cut can be seen both at Courrèges in Paris and on Princess Meg; Ace photographer David Bailey, 27, professional associate of Antony Armstrong-Jones; and Doug Hayward, 28, Chelsea's 'innest' private tailor.

All this was once again almost immediately parodied by Michael Frayn in the *Observer*, in a fine piece entitled 'At Bay in Gear Street':

> I was practically knocked down by a stampede of perspiring corre-spondents as I stepped out of Galt's toyshop the other day holding a doll I'd bought for the children. 'Holy heaven, it's Actor Terry Stamp, 26, in mini-wig and PVC spectacles!' screamed the reporter from *TIME* magazine. 'And he's squiring diminutive dolly Cathy McGowan, 22, in an eight-inches-above-the-knee, Campari-red skirtlet, spectre-pale make-up, and kinky, wobble-as-you-walk celluloid eyelids!' 'Leave it to me!' shouted *TIME* magazine. 'I know these people's patois.' He turned to me and the doll. 'Greetings, British bird and British Beatle!' he said very slowly, waving his hands about. 'You – with it, yes? You – making scene, no?'

Flicking through the rest of that issue of *TIME* magazine, Len Deighton's novel *Billion Dollar Brain* was at number seven in the best-seller lists, the Royal Shakespeare Company were on Broadway with Peter Brook's produc-tion of the *Marat/Sade*, and Karel Reisz's new film *Morgan: A Suitable Case for Treatment* – a title shortened in the US but given a perky little exclama-tion mark to read *Morgan!*, presumably in imitation of that of the most recent Beatles film – was being very favourably reviewed. Best of all, though, was an item about a fortunate young chap with the best toy in the world:

> Britain's bonny Prince Andrew, 6, last week took delivery of a little number from Aston-Martin. It does 6mph flat out and can stop on a lollipop. The automaker's $11,000 gift is a scaled-down model of that

piece of incredibilia James Bond drove in *Goldfinger*. Tooling around the playgrounds, Andrew can be in constant contact by two-way radio with headquarters at either Windsor Castle or Buckingham Palace. There is also a radar warning system with a three-mile radius, a protective bulletproof shield, and the punch of a button can send up a giant smoke screen or fire streams of water from the two rear reflectors. So cool it, nanny.

Sheepdog Hair and Chalk-On-Blackboard Voices

If *TIME* magazine had plenty for the Anglophiles to sink their teeth into, the listings in the edition of the *New Yorker* published the following day offered much the same: John Arden's *Serjeant Musgrave's Dance* was playing Off Broadway at the Theatre de Lys, while at the El Morocco nightclub at 307 E 54th St., 'the password in this fashionable watering hole is Rule Britannia'. Then there was a club called Downtown, in Sheridan Square 'a plain-spoken but pleasant pavilion whose guests are mostly angelic Mods and Rockers.' As for the film listings, there was *The Knack* ('The time is spring, the theme is spring, the place is London'), *The Leather Boys* ('Shot in and about London . . .'), and *Morgan!* ('A troubled young man tears London apart . . .'). If the eager cinemagoer hadn't quite had their fill of celluloid London by this stage, what the hell, there was always a Michael Winner film:

> *The Girl Getters* is still another study of the tribal rites of passage of contemporary lower-middle-class English youth, and I won't be surprised if you feel that you have been over much of the ground before. These squalid young men, with their sheepdog hair and chalk-on-blackboard voices, would seem to indicate that the future of England will depend more on the playing fields of Borstal than on those of Eton.

As it happened, *The Girl Getters* was a two-year-old film from the UK, originally titled *The System*, which featured David Hemmings some way down the cast list, shortly to be doing his finest David Bailey impression for Antonioni in various parts of London as they filmed *Blow-Up*, including in the very same Cheyne Walk house owned by Christopher Gibbs at which the BBC had recently been handing out LSD.

If *TIME* and the *New Yorker* seemed full of the London influences, one of the other national US magazines, *LOOK*, was keen to tell people that they had been there first, as their adverts that April testified:

What made Mod the mode? Perhaps the millions who saw it first in *LOOK*. The first American shop selling Mod fashions opened last year at Dayton's, Minneapolis. *LOOK* ran an article on it in the November 30, 1965 issue. It was the first story on Mod to appear in any major magazine in this country. Since the *LOOK* preview, the British style import has swept America. Everyone seems to be going Mod.

Of course, to US teenagers, there remained the problem of finding out exactly what 'mod' consisted of in the first place. It certainly had very little to do with GS scooters and punch-ups at Margate or Brighton. Cynthia Plaster Caster had been hot on the trail since seeing the Beatles' 1964 *Ed Sullivan Show* appearance, as she told me:

I have a vague memory at that time of knowing what a mod dress looked like; they were about the same length as normal, but they just had that distinctive collar – like a gigantic Peter Pan collar – and lots of black, you know, a lot of monochrome. All I wanted to do was trim my hair into a nice mod bob, and I went to the trendiest hair salon in my neighbourhood, but they cut all my fuckin' hair off back like it was before, and wasted about six months of hair growth.

The Art of Japanese Bed Wrestling

With America seemingly awash with London influences, it was perhaps only fair that the traffic worked both ways a little. Hollywood superstar George Raft showed up in town fronting a casino called the Colony in Berkeley Square, while the Playboy organisation announced that they would be opening their first Playboy Club outside the US in London in June. Currently recruiting Bunnies, according to the April 16 edition of *London Life*, was 25-year-old Cindy Bury, who was also planning to marry the dentist in charge of manufacturing fangs for Roman Polanski's *Dance of the Vampires*, starring Roman's new girlfriend and Eaton Place resident, Sharon Tate.

On the King's Road, restaurant chain boss Peter Evans – whose Chelsea branch was at number 65 – announced plans to open up a nightclub in the basement below his own King's Road flat, but denied reports that it was going to be called the Ant Heap. Adverts for his restaurants appearing in the press in May began as follows:

THE ART OF JAPANESE BED WRESTLING is best studied after an appetisingly simple meal and an honest, friendly bottle of wine at your nearest Peter Evans Eating House. There is a state of lazometric euphoria – the most difficult ontological problems seem to vanish into a fourth dimension and you feel ready for anything.

If that did not appeal, you could always try Don Luigi, an Italian restaurant at 33c King's Road, run by Luigi Paglierani. According to *London Life*, 'your fellow munchers may include Sean Connery, Lance Percival and his gang, various types from the Royal Court, Mr Ambler and his Swedish Princess. [. . .] Expect to pay around £3 15 s for two.' The same issue of the magazine also gave the lowdown on jazz nights at the Six Bells, 197 King's Road: 'Probably the last stronghold of the long-haired Chelsea lads who claimed to qualify as beatniks. Weekly jazz sessions.' However, Miles from the Indica Bookshop does not reckon that the Six Bells would have been much of a hip hangout at that time, as he told me: 'It was probably all guardsmen, you know? Chukka boots and cavalry twills and stuff. We went to clubs like Cafe le Jazzhot [in the Fulham Road]. They were all places where you danced.'

The Royal Court crowd may have been eating at Don Luigi's, but just for the moment they were unlikely to include Joe Orton, whose agent Peggy Ramsey was negotiating in May with both William Gaskill at the Court and also the National Theatre with a view to staging the newly revised version of his play *Loot*. In the event, though, it went to neither of them, and premiered at the Jeanetta Cochrane Theatre on September 27, 1966. However, another of Orton's plays, *The Ruffian on the Stair*, was given a single performance without decor on August 21, directed by Peter Gill, and with 'wheelchair kindly loaned by Red Cross, Chelsea', according to the programme. Joe would probably have been amused that year to see that *LIFE* magazine was still commenting on the fact that in Chelsea these days it was hard to sort out the boys from the girls:

Thigh-high skirts for 'dolly-looking birds': What with the present boys' hair styles, it was only a matter of time before girls' slacks would have to go OUT and thigh-high skirts would have to come IN, if only to help Londoners tell girl from boy. [. . .] The new heights in skirts attract at least passing masculine attention, as any new fashion should. And they permit a certain freedom of movement for the more athletic indoor pastimes such as shooting pool at Chelsea Sunday brunches. 'In this modern age,' says one of the dolly-birds, 'they're the only thing to wear.'

As *LIFE* discussed King's Road hemlines, another US magazine, *Town and Country*, put the Rolling Stones on the cover of their 'debutante' issue, photographed in New York by David Bailey. The band posed with deb Alexandra E. Chase for the shoot, and were also namechecked the same month in an article in the *Saturday Evening Post*, which described a 'pot party' among some American college students, after which the journalist presumably had to go and lie down for a while in a darkened room to recover: 'You return to the room. They are playing the Rolling Stones. The Stones are part of your pot party, because they seem to fit into the room. They sing with their fingers. They seem to be doing exciting things to every song – they are raping the lyrics, word by word.'

Still, for perhaps the most dramatic instance of English culture invading American consciousness that summer, look no further than an advert in the August 1966 edition of *Playboy* for a new cologne by Revlon, called, believe it or not, *PUB For Men*, which came in a barrel-shaped bottle. Had they lost their minds?

Rich, Ripe, Randy

Michael Caine's new film, *Alfie*, appeared to glowing reviews ('A rave' – Felicity Green, *Daily Mirror*, 'Rich, ripe, randy' – Margaret Hinxman, *Sunday Telegraph*); Lee Marvin and the cast of *The Dirty Dozen* were in town on a day off and were filmed walking up the King's Road checking out the groovy people and dining in one of its restaurants; and Honor Blackman, fresh from *The Avengers* and *Goldfinger*, published her *Book of Self Defence*: 'If you find yourself grabbed and slammed hard against the railings or banister of a staircase, with no one else in sight, you might well feel fairly helpless – unless you know about the . . . *Nasal pressure and interior leg throw.*'

Bob Dylan might well have appreciated such advice, given the attitude of some of the people who turned up to gigs on his current UK tour, during which some armchair critic yelled 'Judas!' at him, for reasons best known to their psychiatrist. Dylan played two shows at the Albert Hall on May 26 and 27, and Mick Farren later described the look of those crowds in *Give the Anarchist a Cigarette*: 'Arrayed in thrift-shop capes, spray-painted wellington boots, Edwardian dresses and Victorian military jackets, they presented a DIY version of what, in twelve months, would be hawked on Carnaby Street and the King's Road as flower power.'

As for Chelsea's most famous designer, Mary Quant, on June 10 she was awarded the OBE. She was having a busy year, not only publishing her autobiography but also launching a range of cosmetics, designing clothes for the Albert Finney/Audrey Hepburn picture *Two for the Road* and for the film *Georgy Girl*, not to mention the clothes for George Harrison and Pattie Boyd's wedding. 'Pattie Boyd modelled for us,' says Mary; she was one of a couple of 'great models with fantastic legs who modelled for us and Tuffin and Foale on trips across the States.'

The July 1966 edition of *Films and Filming* carried a news item stating that Italian director Michelangelo Antonioni was filming something called *The Blow Up* [*sic*] 'completely on location. For this he took over a photographer's studio in West London for his main interior shots – the story centres around a photographer and his models – and built an exterior set in a park near Woolwich plus painting the road because it was not black enough.' For the lengthy drug party scene, he used Christopher Gibbs' house in Cheyne Walk, which he seems to have tried to film in the same kind of *cinéma-vérité* manner employed by the BBC documentary in April. As Keiran Fogarty recalled in Jonathan Green's *Days in the Life*: 'I was flung into this bedroom in Cheyne Walk, hair parted, purple shirt with paisley motifs, black knitted Jaeger tie, square ended, black jacket. Plonked on the front of this bed with about another nine people on it and Antonioni tossed a couple of kilo-bags of grass on the bed and said "Right, get on with it".'

For the gig scene, it is said that Antonioni had wanted the Who, having seen news photos of Townshend smashing guitars, but did not know how to contact them. Running into Yardbirds' manager Simon Napier-Bell at the Scotch of St James's, he was persuaded to use them instead, but insisted that Jeff Beck be filmed destroying his guitar. In the resulting sequence, the band play to a self-consciously blank audience who appear to have been recently embalmed, and Beck winds up smashing his guitar simply because it is malfunctioning, rather than as a pop art statement like Townshend. At long last, the lobotomised shop window dummies in the audience finally dissolve into screaming mayhem when Beck throws the guitar's broken headstock to them, despite having watched him slowly destroy the instrument without reacting at all. The real irony, though, in this supposed iconic mod film, is that the song they are playing is a direct steal from one of the finest rockabilly discs of the mid-fifties, Johnny Burnette and the Rock'n'Roll Trio's scorching definitive version of 'The Train Kept A-Rollin'' – here renamed 'Stroll On', for no discernible reason.

Antonioni seems to have been wandering around 'Swinging London' looking for things to put in his film, and John Pearse remembers him coming in to Granny Takes a Trip one day, which is how one of their garments wound up on one of the most famous film posters of the era:

'There's a poster for *Blow-Up*, with Veruschka on the floor in a beaded dress. He came into the shop, and I didn't really know who he was at that time – or, I think I did – anyway, he just bought that frock for Veruschka to wear.'

It is not recorded whether the director ventured into the King's Road's largest and most established shop, Peter Jones, during his search for with-it dresses, but the manager of that venerable establishment announced in July that they would no longer permit mini-skirts to be worn by their sales assistants, although they would continue to stock such items. Manager Dennis Turner said, 'We sell bathing costumes and wedding dresses, but we don't expect the staff to turn up for work in them. [. . .] Some of the short skirts which are beginning to appear in the branch are not in my view suitable for business.'

Turned Into a Stuffed Flunkey

While Antonioni was chasing the zeitgeist, at the Royal Court, even though George Devine was no longer there, continuity was being preserved. Arnold Wesker's new play *Their Very Own and Golden City* had been running since May 19, directed by William Gaskill and starring Ian McKellen, which was followed on July 21 by a production of Alfred Jarry's *Ubu Roi* with future Stiff Records recording artist Max Wall in the title role, and sets designed by David Hockney. Paul McCartney and Jane Asher went along to see it with Miles, who told me that they had problems at the box office because no-one could remember which false name they had made the bookings under:

Well Jane always booked it under somebody else's name, because of the paparazzi. The Beatles couldn't just walk around – it was just impossible to go anywhere with them . . . Through Jane, Paul was seeing all the first nights and meeting all the playwrights and hanging out, talking to Arnold Wesker and Harold Pinter and all the people doing stuff, and then through Robert Fraser he was very involved in all the art movements, and he knew Peter Blake and David Hockney and Richard Hamilton . . .

In America, many past Royal Court successes were being highlighted with the publication of two linked articles in the June 13 edition of *LIFE*, trailed by the cover headline 'Britain's Stage – A Lusty, Shock-filled New Elizabethan Era'. A photograph by Lord Snowdon of the baby-stoning scene in Edward Bond's *Saved* was printed across two whole pages, and the text claimed that 'the scene in *Saved* on pages 38, 39 sent some playgoers fleeing the theatre, hands cupped over mouths'. The first article, titled 'Gale of Shock Rips Across the British Stage', gave much of the credit for the current renaissance to the English Stage Company: 'Dramatic revolt began at the Royal Court Theatre in London and continues there with actors who flourish on the gruelling demands of repertory. [. . .] Repertory at the Royal Court has produced famous stars like Peter O'Toole, Rita Tushingham, Albert Finney.'

This was followed by an article written by John Osborne's wife, Penelope Gilliatt, which also drove home the importance of events in Sloane Square, and explained the link between the Royal Court's productions and the rise of English cinema in the early sixties: 'Before the historic opening of the English Stage Company at the Royal Court Theatre in April 1956, the country with the greatest body of dramatic literature in the world possessed a theatre that had turned into a stuffed flunkey. At that time there wasn't a contemporary English play worth discussing.'

After a decade of ever-increasing activity, a powerful cross-section of international media attention now seemed to be focused on the creative community of Chelsea.

Sighing for the Stone Age Man

On July 22, photographer Michael Cooper opened his own studio — funded by gallery owner Robert Fraser — at Studio 4, Chelsea Manor Studios, 1–11 Flood Street, running south of King's Road, which would shortly earn its place in history. At the same time, two King's Road landmarks changed hands after having remained constant for many years. Mario Cazzini of the Pheasantry had died, and by the summer, the club's regular weekly adverts in the press ceased. The next few years at the Pheasantry would prove to be somewhat more rock'n'roll. Just up the road at number 124, the Magic Carpet Inn with its 'provocative decor', which had been run by George Brampton since the forties, closed its doors and then reopened in the autumn under new management as Alvaro's, which would in its turn become one of the legendary King's Road watering holes. So popular was Alvaro Maccioni's new restaurant that it very quickly went ex-directory and acquired a clientele to match, as *Town* magazine's restaurant reviewer William Beaufitz noted in November: 'The service was excellent. Quick, friendly and unobtrusive. We did not see the Stones ("they have an account here"), Bailey, Quant or Shrimpton but we survived.'

During August, Rediffusion film cameras followed Yardbirds' manager Simon Napier-Bell around town for a few weeks, shooting a TV documentary about – yes, you've guessed it – swinging London, which included the desperately original ploy of renting a house in Chelsea for a 'wild' party. Meanwhile the actor who had played the leader of the Chelsea bohemians in *The Party's Over* was being profiled in the September edition of *Photoplay*: 'Oliver Reed has a theory about the mod, switched-on girl of 1966. He thinks she is sighing for the Stone Age Man! He could be right. Maybe that's why Oliver finds himself popular with feminine moviegoers because there's a trace of the neolithic about him.'

King's Road shoppers also found themselves stepping out of the way of yet another film crew that month, as Joe McGrath directed Dudley Moore and Suzy Kendall in a feature film called *30 Is a Dangerous Age, Cynthia*, which saw Dudley wandering around Chelsea in a morning suit being followed by a flock of young women in matching brides' outfits.

Credit: author's collection

Dudley Moore leads his many brides past number
33 King's Road in the film *30 is a Dangerous Age, Cynthia*

Michael Rainey's Hung On You boutique made the move from Chelsea Green to 430 King's Road, just past the turn at World's End, while on October 4, 1966, another Chelsea boutique, Dandie Fashions, was incorporated. Guinness heir Tara Browne was one of the people behind the latter, a few short months before his December 18 death in a car crash in Redcliffe Gardens, just north of the King's Road. Originally owned by John Crittle,

Miles recalls that Dandie Fashions later came under the control of the Beatles themselves: 'Tara Browne was one of the directors. He was a good friend of the Beatles, and he, indeed, blew his mind out in a car. Now Dandie Fashions was decorated by Binder, Edwards and Vaughan, and then later on I think Apple bought into it, but it was already in existence.'

The Next Step After the Topless Look

Miles himself was already running the Indica Bookshop and Gallery, one of the key counterculture locations, and was now involved in setting up the scene's first proper underground newspaper, *International Times*, commonly known as *IT*. The first issue appeared on October 14, 1966, and in the short list of addresses printed inside at which potential customers could expect to find *IT*, several were from the King's Road, including Granny Takes a Trip. Just to make sure that they were not missing out on any potential sales, Jim Haynes from *IT* rounded up some high-class transport and headed for where the action was, as he recalled in his autobiography, *Thanks for Coming!*: 'Then my actor friend Tutte Lemkow, who had two old vintage Rolls, would drive me around London, down the King's Road on Saturday afternoon, the back of the car stacked with papers, and I would sell in the street and deliver the papers. [. . .] That was the launch of *IT*.'

Issue number one had drug news ('Pusher named Nigel in Chelsea area reportedly being supplied with anything he wants by the fuzz, in order to set people up. Has red hair'); a pin-up on page three ('Unfortunately, we cannot give address and telephone number for our girl, but you can see her at the *IT* party, Saturday October 15, in the Round House Chalk Farm'); a review of the recent Stones show at the Albert Hall ('[Jagger] looked more like a gymnast in fancy dress than he ever did'); and a preview of an upcoming 'one man show' by Yoko Ono at the Indica Gallery ('on exhibit and sale for the first time in this country will be *Bag Wear*, a style of clothing that completely envelops the body covering head to foot – said to be the next step after the topless look'). It was here at Indica on November 8, the day before her exhibition opened to the public, that Yoko first met John Lennon.

The Royal Court rounded up a year which had begun with the death of their founding father by presenting a mixture of the old and the new. October 20 saw the heavy-duty box-office firepower brought to bear with a cast including Alec Guinness and Simone Signoret in a production of Shakespeare's *Macbeth*. By contrast, there was new Nigerian drama with Wole Soyinka's *The Lion and the Jewel*, which opened on December 12, and in between *A Provincial Life* by Peter Gill, based on a Chekhov story called

My Life, with a young Anthony Hopkins in the relatively minor part of 'Boris Ivanov Blagovo, a doctor'. The National Youth Theatre also came in to present two plays at the Royal Court: *Bartholomew Fair* by Ben Johnson, and a new play, *Little Malcolm and his Struggle Against the Eunuchs* by David Halliwell, the latter starring future James Bond Timothy Dalton as Malcolm.

That autumn, Weidenfeld & Nicolson published a debut novel called *Leftovers* which – like Virginia Ironside's *Chelsea Bird* two years earlier – had also been written by a representative of the younger generation. Its author was a nineteen-year-old Oxford University student, and the book told the story of some swingers who perhaps had more to worry about than whether Hung On You were running short of the latest trendy clobber, as the back cover of the paperback explained:

> A brief bout of biochemical warfare leaves the Earth depopulated – except for a group of free-living, free-loving hippies and a suburban couple isolated on an Underground train at the time of the attack. At first the hippies run wild in the deserted ruins of a world. They raid delicatessens for food, set up residence in Buckingham Palace and the Hilton, drive sports cars wildly all over the country – and make love with barely-subdued desperation.

The character Laura lives in World's End, another named Ben says things like 'Bloody raves. Make me sick,' while at one point Anna takes a drive through a deserted Chelsea, apparently in search of something that was no longer there: 'She reached South Kensington and drove down Sydney Street to the King's Road, down Oakley Street to the Embankment, and then left along the river to Cheyne Walk.'

Queen magazine called the book 'very cool', and *The Times* judged it to be 'a groovy romp'. With reviews like that, it might have seemed that a career as a novelist was in prospect, but thus far it has been Polly Toynbee's only one.

Girls, Are You Switched On?

If you believed everything you read in the papers, 1966 had been a far-out, happening year of compulsory swinging, in which even genuinely ground-breaking music venues like the Flamingo in Wardour Street were now advertising themselves with the tired slogan 'The Swinging Club of Swinging London', and a mainstream popcorn magazine like *ABC Film Review* was running a readers' competition which asked: 'Girls, Are You

Switched On? – If you are really switched-on and have a way-out wardrobe to prove it, why not enter the Switched-On Girls Contest being run
at your local ABC Theatre?'

This was printed next to a photo of two previous winners, one of whom
appeared to have won some kind of diseased Sonny Bono lookalike contest
by showing up seemingly dressed as a yak. If this was how 1967 was shaping
up, then all bets were off.

The final word, though, should probably go to Godfrey Hodgson in the
November issue of *Town* magazine, suggesting that Chelsea might supposedly be way-out, but most people were still struggling to find the way in:

> [. . .] the pubs still shut at eleven, for heaven's sake. If you're lucky
> enough not to be somewhere where they shut at half-past ten. [. . .]
> The new fashions may be fun, and within the reach of most people.
> The theatre may be going through a real Elizabethan age. But the
> plumbing is still Victorian, and nobody seems to know how to repair
> it. The food in restaurants has got better. But the service still makes
> one feel that the customer is resented as an over-privileged snob, and
> serve him right if the toad's *off*, dear. Swinging is all very well for
> Twiggy and the tourists in the King's Road. What strikes me as far
> more urgent is to get away from all the small Puritanisms, the patient
> acceptance of small miseries. If only our everyday *vita* were just a
> little more *dolce*.

18

'Turn on, tune in, drop dead'

Let's All Make Love in London

On one of the last days of the old year, a new club called UFO had opened up in the basement of the Berkeley Cinema, 31 Tottenham Court Road. Plenty of the Chelsea groovers who would also form part of *IT*'s readership would come here to dance and to watch the bands – you could even place orders there for clothes from King's Road boutiques like Hung On You and Granny Takes a Trip.

Then, on January 11, 1967, one of the bands who played at UFO and had also appeared at the *IT* launch party at the Roundhouse on October 15 walked into a Chelsea recording studio called Sound Techniques at 46a Old Church Street, just down the side of the Essoldo Cinema on the King's Road. The studio was run by a man named Joe Boyd, who had produced a debut album there for the Incredible String Band the previous year. The group in Sound Techniques were being recorded and filmed by Peter Whitehead, the man who had already made a documentary of the 1965 *Wholly Communion* poetry reading at the Albert Hall, and then one about the 1965 Rolling Stones' Irish tour called *Charlie Is My Darling*. Now he was shooting a new film about the scene which had exploded in the capital since 1966, called *Tonite Let's All Make Love in London*. The band in Sound Techniques that day were playing a song named 'Interstellar Overdrive', and at that point still called themselves The Pink Floyd. The following day, there was a different band at Sound Techniques, who were also to be firm favourites with the crowd at the UFO club. Their name was the Purple Gang, and the single which Joe Boyd cut with them that day was entitled 'Granny Takes a Trip'.

The Purple Gang were a psychedelic jug band whose singer Pete Walker was a full-on Satanist and a member of the Alderley Edge Coven, with a tattoo of the Goat of Mendes on his arm. They duly had themselves photographed standing outside the Granny Takes a Trip shop at 488 King's Road. Granny's would change their frontage every so often, but the results were usually designed to intimidate the casual passer-by. At that time, their window was painted with a large mural of Mae West's face, and was almost entirely opaque, except for one detail, as John Pearse told me: 'You could look through her lips. That was painted on glass, on the original window. Sadly, that was smashed in by the away team at Stamford Bridge, so after that we just put a board over it.'

Mickey Finn, later to join up with ex-mod-turned-bopping-elf Marc Bolan in T. Rex, helped out with some painting at Granny's, including the Mae West window, says John Pearse: 'He didn't do very much, I hasten to add, but he was around, you know. Like that Mae West thing, it was chalked out so maybe he got the red segment. He wasn't an artist, [laughs] not even a conceptualist . . .'

This, then, was the window that the Purple Gang were photographed against. According to John Pearse, Joe Boyd, who was also managing the band, was a friend of Granny's co-owner Nigel Waymouth. The band apparently asked permission to use the shop's name as a song title. John Pearse wasn't particularly bothered either way: 'I didn't pay much attention. I didn't much even like the song, I have to say. Thought it was twee.'

The Gardeners, Noted for Their Planting

By 1967, the 'underground' was well on its way to the surface, so the long-haired brigade and the new rock aristocracy were easily visible targets for the coming backlash. The Chelsea drug squad – with the notorious Sergeant Pilcher, of 'semolina pilchard' fame – had begun raiding King's Road boutiques the previous August, and were more than happy to oblige, as Mick Farren says: 'Well they were the worst, the drug squad, yeah. I mean, they were the gardeners, you know, they were the fit-up artists, noted for their planting . . . I don't know if anybody ever *needed* planting . . .'

So many musicians were targeted that year by the squad that former Pretty Things drummer Viv Prince was heard to remark, referencing the hip London after-hours club favoured by off-duty rock stars, 'Chelsea Police Station gets more like the Speakeasy every day . . .'

On February 12, 1967, various key figures of the new glitterati were busted for drugs down at Keith Richards' house, Redlands in West Sussex –

Mick Jagger, Marianne Faithfull, Robert Fraser, Chelsea antique dealer Christopher Gibbs and Flood Street photographer Michael Cooper. Just under a month later, it was the turn of the *IT* offices in Mason's Yard, beneath the Indica bookshop. Suddenly, it seemed like open season on the freaks. Meanwhile, in *The Times* on February 17, Malcolm Muggeridge was preaching Armageddon, claiming that 'the so-called "permissive" morality of our time' would bring about an era . . .

> [. . .] when birth pills are handed out with free orange juice, and consenting adults wear special ties and blazers, and abortion and divorce – these two contemporary panaceas for all matrimonial ills – are freely available on the public health, then at last, with the suicide rate up to Scandinavian proportions and the psychiatric wards bursting at the seams, it will be realized that this path, even from the shallow point of view of the pursuit of happiness, is a disastrous cul-de-sac.

This is the same concerned moralist who in a 1964 dialogue about pornography with Len Deighton, published in issue number one of *King* magazine, came to the following utterly indefensible conclusion:

> MUGGERIDGE: If you know that a particular book will induce little boys to masturbate excessively then you can't really say that the book ought to be published. Can you?

> DEIGHTON: Not unless the little boys would otherwise go off and rape little girls.

> MUGGERIDGE: It might be better for them if they did.

With the forces of reaction on the warpath, the spring of 1967 might not seem like the ideal time to launch a new underground publication, but nevertheless, February saw the first issue of something called *OZ* magazine. It was the work of a group of ex-pat Australians, led by Richard Neville, who had arrived at Dover the previous September and asked the lorry driver when hitching a lift to take him to 'Swinging London'. Issue number one was heavily in thrall to *Private Eye*, and tried to make up for this by attacking that magazine straight away, printing a mock interview with *Eye* editor Richard Ingrams which said: 'We've always taken a point of view. *Look Back in Anger* gave us that point of view and for six long years we've done little else. That we have been boring and repetitive is of course another issue. Often was the next issue.'

OZ also included a photo-collage story called 'Turn On, Tune in, Drop Dead', in which the hero, Frisco Ferlinghetti, stages a happening in the King's Road outside the Chelsea Pet Stores by drinking enormous amounts of milk: 'I sat in King's Road and drank pinta afta pinta (kindly assisted by Bradley Martin). Failing to reach the climaxic regurgitation expected. Nevertheless it was cold + wet and no-one took the slightest interest. It was, however, a functionally valid "happening", although actually nothing happened.'

The King's Road was naturally one of the first locations in which they attempted to sell copies of the new magazine, and many of the people who produced *OZ* lived around there, including Martin Sharp, the psychedelic illustrator who was to give the magazine its distinctive look. He already had a studio in Chelsea, but in 1967 moved into a flat at the Pheasantry, 152 King's Road, which he shared with Eric Clapton, in a year when what had formerly been one of the area's fashionable members' clubs turned into something of an arts commune, with writers, designers and photographers all occupying space in the now crumbling building. Sharp and Clapton collaborated on the song 'Tales of Brave Ulysses', the B-side of Cream's June 1967 single 'Strange Brew', and Sharp then designed the cover for their album, *Disraeli Gears*. Germaine Greer moved in, as did David Litvinoff, who the following year would be the dialogue coach and technical adviser for the film *Performance*, and even John Peel's brother lived there for a time. Mick Farren, who was going out with Germaine Greer for a while, remembers the Pheasantry well at this time, as he told me:

> It was falling down. It had sort of gone through its popular phase, but no money had been put back into it to fix the roof and stuff, and the roofs were leaking and everything was kind of coming apart and Martin Sharp was moving in and all that was left behind were a few sort of upper-class junkies who couldn't move when the party moved on.

In the basement downstairs, there was a club, and anyone who lived upstairs could hear the sounds coming up through the floorboards, but there were always problems, as Mick says:

> It would be an R&B club for a bit, and then everybody would get fed up with the noise, or the parking or the cops or something, and then it'd become a gay club for a while, and there'd be Lindsay Kemp

in there doing whatever Lindsay Kemp sort of did. The Pheasantry always seemed to be always hosting various floating crap games, some of which were R&B, some of which were folk music and some of which were gay. I think also it had a back room where the doors were closed and people went on drinking, and I think there were gangsters involved.

Miles remembers the Pheasantry as a place where the likelihood of having your drink spiked with acid was pretty high. He also has vivid memories of its residents, in particular the man whose response to the Rolling Stones being busted at Redlands was to jump off a bus in the middle of the King's Road yelling 'The revolution starts here!':

Nicky Kramer was living there as well. You see him on certain album sleeves, he was one of those typical King's Road freaks, with his hair completely frizzed out. At one point he had a rabbit that he dyed bright green, that committed suicide by leaping off the roof. I think he used to give it acid. He was a fucking mad idiot. I mean, there were a lot of people like that, particularly at the Pheasantry, it was really filled with them.

This Latest Antonioni Put-On

The Pheasantry might have been the place to find the green rabbit, but if you were looking for The Pink Floyd, they were back in Joe Boyd's Sound Techniques studio in Old Church Street on February 27, recording their debut single, 'Arnold Layne'. It was released on March 11, backed by the other song they recorded that day, 'Candy and a Currant Bun', and on April 6, the single gained them their first *Top of the Pops* appearance. The band then signed to EMI, which meant a new producer and a move to Abbey Road studios, but in those outsize rooms built to accommodate the recording of dance orchestras, they struggled to recapture the sound achieved on 'Arnold Layne', and they had to return to the more compact Sound Techniques on May 23 to record 'See Emily Play'. By the time of their final show at the UFO club in the summer, the Floyd's Syd Barrett had taken so much acid that to Joe Boyd he looked almost like a different person. In the September issue of *Beat Instrumental* magazine, Rick Wright from the Floyd spoke about how they had achieved what were described as 'the weird sounds on "Emily"':

'It was in the "Sound Technique" [sic] studios in Chelsea,' said Rick. 'Although it sounds a bit gimmicky, hardly any special effects were used. Take that "Hawaiian" bit at the end of each verse. That was just Syd (Barratt) using a bottleneck through echo. The part that sounds speeded-up, John Woods, the engineer just upped the whole thing about an octave. On stage we have cut that particular bit out.'

According to the March 3 cover of *Private Eye*, it was not just Syd who had been at the substances: 'DRUGS – THE GHASTLY EFFECTS' said the headline, with speech-bubbled pictures of Harold Wilson ('Hello! I've gone to pot'), the Queen ('Well Philip keeps going off on trips'), Pope Paul VI ('Freak out, Bambino!') and Marianne Faithfull ('Is this a Jagger that I see before me?').

Antonioni's *Blow-Up* premiered in London on March 16, then won Best Picture at Cannes, where the French branch of MGM organised a 'mod' party, while David Hemmings was photographed at the New York launch after-show shindig dancing with Françoise Hardy. So far, so groovy. It went on general release in the UK on May 14, to a barrage of publicity, some favourable, some not. Robin Bean in *Films and Filming* called it 'a painfully true representation of youth today', and added 'it is very, very erotic'. *What's On in London* found the picture 'a slow fascinating crime thriller given depth and significance', but Sidney Skolsky in *Photoplay* dismissed it as 'this latest Antonioni put-on', and *ABC Film Review* printed a letter from a reader in Glasgow who seemed personally offended by the experience: 'It is the worst film I have ever seen. The picture of with-it life in London was positively revolting and I'm sure completely misleading and untrue.'

Nobody seemed to want to point out the basic flaw in the central plot device, which is that you will not uncover much more in a huge photographic print than you can see by looking directly at the 35mm negative with a decent magnifying glass in the first place, but hey, why would filmmakers know anything about celluloid?

Most letters in film magazines about *Blow-Up* over the next few months simply complained that significant amounts of the nudity had been removed at provincial showings compared to the version which premiered in London, owing to the well-known habit of projectionists snipping out frames for their private collections. *Blow-Up* was the first mainstream film in Britain to show a glimpse of pubic hair, and it was perhaps this, rather than its paper-thin crime story, which was attracting the crowds.

Just as David Hemmings was on screen portraying a fictional London photographer, it was reported in the *Marylebone Mercury* on June 16 that a real-life one who lived in Tedworth Square, Chelsea, John Bignell, had three of his cameras worth £400 stolen while at a Chinese restaurant in the King's Road. He spent much of the 1960s taking candid street pictures in and around the area, and published a book of them in 1983 entitled *Chelsea Photographer*.

That's a Nice Dog, Did You Knit It Yourself?

Towards the end of March, an exhibition of collages by Kenneth Halliwell – Joe Orton's lover and future murderer – opened in the basement of an antiques shop called Anno Domini on the King's Road, near World's End. The owner, Freddie Bartman, had noticed Halliwell's work when visiting Orton's agent, Peggy Ramsey. The exhibition failed to attract the crowds, which came as no surprise to Halliwell, who had said: 'As if anybody will go and see the pictures stuck away at the wrong end of the King's Road.' By contrast, Orton himself was very much in demand. Back in January, Brian Epstein's office had contacted him to enquire whether he would be interested in rewriting the screenplay for the new Beatles film, which led to a meeting with Epstein and McCartney. Orton noted in his diary that McCartney had played the new Beatles single to him: '"Penny Lane". I liked it very much. Then he played the other side – "Strawberry" something. I didn't like this as much.' Orton produced a screenplay entitled *Up Against It*, but by March the Beatles and Epstein were no longer taking his phone calls and the project was allowed to die, for which Orton blamed Epstein, 'a thoroughly weak, flaccid type'. The script was returned with no comment on April 4.

On March 30, the four musicians who would not now be starring in *Up Against It* arrived at Michael Cooper's Chelsea Manor Photographic Studios in Flood Street to stand in front of an assemblage of hardboard figures designed by Peter Blake and his wife Jann Howarth, depicting various celebrities, alive and dead, including former Chelsea residents such as Oscar Wilde, Aleister Crowley and Karl Marx, although Elvis, Hitler and Jesus failed to make the shortlist. Donning some cartoon approximations of Victorian uniforms, they stood behind a floral display and were photographed by Michael Cooper for the front cover of an album they were currently recording, called *Sgt. Pepper's Lonely Hearts Club Band*. Following the photo session, they headed for Abbey Road Studio 2 to work on overdubs for the song 'With a Little Help from My Friends'. The sleeve became one of the most famous in rock music history. Blake and Howarth were paid a flat fee of £200.

For the April edition of *Town* magazine, Jeffrey Bernard wrote a feature on 'how to chat up the birds' – billed on the cover with the fine strapline 'That's a nice dog you've got there, did you knit it yourself?' – in which, as King's Road lotharios could not have failed to notice, he listed among his current top places to pick up girls 'the au pair's pram parking lot at Peter Jones'.

Across the road from that department store at the Royal Court, so far that year, despite their reputation for championing new plays, they had presented Restoration drama from 1680 in the form of *The Soldier's Fortune* by Thomas Otway – with music composed by Johnny Dankworth – a 1913 D. H. Lawrence play called *The Daughter-in-Law*, and then on April 18 opened up with a Chekhov play written in the year 1900, *Three Sisters*, starring Avril Elgar, Glenda Jackson and Marianne Faithfull. Marianne was by now Mick Jagger's girlfriend, which meant that – in contrast to the last time she'd been offered a part at the Court, which her manager had turned down because of the low wages – the pay was no longer necessarily a consideration. As she put it in her autobiography, *Faithfull*: 'Once I became Mick's girlfriend, I no longer had to work, not for the money anyway. I could do *The Three Sisters* for just £18 a week and not give a damn.'

While one woman linked to the Stones was appearing at the Royal Court, another, Anita Pallenberg, was signing up at the English Boy Model Agency, founded that year by Mark Palmer and based above the Quorum boutique at 52 Radnor Walk, although she did not stay on their books for long. Someone else who joined English Boy that year was Christine Keeler, who around this time also rented a three-bedroom house in Shawfield Street, just off the King's Road.

Heaven on Earth for Leg Men

One of the regular opinion columns in *LIFE* magazine in those days was entitled 'The View From Here', written by Loudon Wainwright Jr., father of Loudon Wainwright III, and grandfather of Rufus and Martha Wainwright, among others. In May 1967, he devoted a whole page to one particular aspect of women's fashion under the heading 'Mini-looking in London', in which he admitted that he had always suffered from a 'ridiculous inability to be stealthy enough to take more than the slightest peek' at women's legs:

[. . .] but a few days of lovely spring weather in London have abolished it forever. The balmy sunshine there brought out the miniskirts in mind-reeling profusion. The town was positively atwinkle with thighs, and I discovered the joys of looking as long as I pleased. [. . .] The key to wearing the skirts is, of course, confidence, and the young lady who showed me around some of London's better mini emporiums used the word 'freedom', which I guess means that she feels liberated by the style. [. . .] But the lack of such assurance is distinctly notice-able in some novice wearers. They tread gingerly among the hordes in Saturday parade along the King's Road, their hands at the ready for a sudden gust, anxious looks on their faces, like girls in a carnival fun house waiting in dread for something awful to happen.

Fellow American Frank Sinatra was also in town, shooting a film called *The Naked Runner*, but the hippie explosion which had taken place in the last couple of years turned his stomach, and he did not stay long. While he was there, however, he made the most of it, as his valet George Jacobs recalled:

> The first few weeks in London on *The Naked Runner* were like a running bachelor party. 'Swinging London' was in high gear. There were countless Mia-like waifs in their Biba miniskirts and Mary Quant tights strutting their great stuff on the King's Road. This was heaven on earth for leg men. [. . .] People in England worshipped him. It was amazing going into some trendy restaurant with him, like Trattoria in Soho or Alvaro's in Chelsea. The waters would part. He liked the scene, but he didn't like the food.

Twiggy in the middle of the King's Road, 13 June 1966

A place like Alvaro's could become famous even though it took out no adverts in the papers and had gone ex-directory. Word of mouth was one thing, but there was also another factor – a new generation of guide books had started to arrive, keen to advise all those who might be wandering around town in search of the 'scene'. Mr *Ipcress File* himself edited a 1967 volume called *Len Deighton's London Dossier*, which came complete with a cover shot of the woman of the moment, Twiggy, taken by photographer Adrian Flowers in his Chelsea studio in Tite Street. Len himself would often eat at Alvaro's, in the company of people like Bond film set designer Ken Adam, and was happy to give his readers the lowdown on that particular restaurant, including the elusive phone number: 'Alvaro's is in Chelsea at 124 King's Road, and gets so crowded that unlike most London restaurants there is no menu outside nor any clue except the word Alvaro, and what's more, his phone number is ex-directory. It is KEN 6296.'

From Len's guide, potential visitors could also learn that 'the landlord of the Chelsea Potter in the King's Road, Chelsea, claims to have the largest variety of aperitifs and spirits in London, including such exotica as tequila and saké, and keeps forty different wines to serve by the glass', or that 'the swinging variety of bird is to be found concentrated in the King's Road, Chelsea, on a Saturday afternoon. [. . .] Flocks of these creatures occur welded to the folded hoods of vintage and modern open cars.' Readers were informed that the Casserole, at World's End, was a superior bistro – '*very* superior since Nureyev started coming', but warned that the Gigolo club downstairs was 'exclusively male, so don't go down there if you like women'. The potential King's Road clothes shopper was offered the following advice:

> Boutiques have proliferated [. . .] and include, at this moment, Top Gear, Countdown, The Shop, Granny Takes a Trip, Hung On You (men), Susan Locke Boutique and 430. The success of boutiques depends on the originality of their stock and their relaxed atmosphere. Not only is there no hard sell, it is sometimes difficult to get any attention at all. The girls who work in them are invariably depressingly pretty, and manage to look always as if they are doing someone a favour by just holding the fort for an hour or two. They sit at the back somewhere reading magazines, entertaining their friends, or telephoning interminably about special autumn orders of astrakhan mini-spats.

Competing for space in the bookshops and in tourists' eager hands was a similar volume written by Karl Dallas entitled *Swinging London – A Guide to Where the Action Is,* which arrived complete with a suitably sceptical introduction from Barry Fantoni, who understood that this was already an age full of 'Fleet Street hacks who when hung up for two thousand words take a taxi into Carnaby Street or King's Road and write a fab load of switched-on rubbish that gets subbed down to a caption for a photo of some swinging dolly with her skirt up over her knickers'. As he and a fair number of other writers were pointing out at the time, 'London has been swinging for ages, it's just that *TIME* magazine and the supplements hadn't noticed it.' Dallas's guide gave a useful idea of some of the prices being charged that year in the King's Road boutiques, for example:

> Count Down, 137 King's Road. 2gns to 60gns, James Wedge, Pat Booth Quorum, 52 Radnor Walk. Underwear £1–£3. Clothes £3–£30. Alice Pollock Susan Locke, 414 King's Road. Shirts £3. Trouser suits £20. Susan Locke Unique, 56b King's Road. Dresses 3gns–15gns, Eric Shemilt Vanessa Frye, 6f Sloane Street. £2.10s–£35. Vanessa Denza, Madeleine Frye

Karl – born into a communist family and named after former Chelsea resident Marx – also had this to say about the essential difference between Carnaby Street and the King's Road, as things stood in 1967: 'Carnaby Street customers are (to use an unfashionable expression) working class. While they think nothing of spending a week's wages on a complete outfit, the class that shop on King's Road will spend that sort of money on a *shirt*.'

When I'm Stoned, There's No Vietnam and No Bomb, Man

Another person who had been asked to write a guidebook was Piri Halasz, the author of the April 1966 *TIME* magazine cover story, whose book *A Swinger's Guide to London* was published by Coward McCann in 1967. To that end, Piri had revisited London in June 1966, staying with friends in Eaton Place, and then in the Carlton Tower. This is something she was happy to write, as she explained to me:

> I don't think anybody expected that the cover story would stimulate as much discussion as it did. I know I certainly didn't. Not surprisingly, I was happiest with the readers who liked what we'd written, and less happy with the complaints, though I was well aware that the cover hadn't been perfect. I didn't like tacky details like the mention of the exotic dancer who did her act with a cheetah, and I was quite prepared to admit that not all of London was swinging, the way that the cover implied it was. One reason I wanted to write my own book was so that I could correct these mis-impressions and give my ideas about Swinging London, not those of *TIME* magazine.

On May 10, it seemed that Swinging London was fast turning into Swingeing London, as the events which led to Richard Hamilton's famous painting of that name unfolded. Mick Jagger, Keith Richards and Robert Fraser were brought to court that day on charges arising from the impromptu police house party at Keith's place back in February, and remanded on bail awaiting trial. On the same day, Brian Jones was busted at his Courtfield Road flat along with his friend Stash (Stanislaus Klossowski de Rola, son of the painter Balthus) by future jailbird Sergeant Pilcher of the drug squad, who took them to Chelsea Police Station. As Andrew Loog Oldham recalled in *2 Stoned*: 'The next day, 11 May, Brian and the Prince, known as "Stash" to his intimates, were remanded on £250 bail for a 2 June trial. The following day, Brian would be spotted on a shopping spree at the Chelsea Antique Market.'

Chelsea Antique Market advert from *OZ* magazine, October 1967

A week later, the BBC decided in one of its regular fits of curtain-twitching prudishness to protect the public from itself by banning the Beatles song 'A Day in the Life' on the grounds that part of the lyric might have a sexual or drug connotation, a form of blanket censorship they had been indulging in since the early 1930s. During that time, the corporation, with its radio broadcasting monopoly, had also sternly protected the delicate listener from hearing certain songs by a wide variety of dangerously subversive artists including Bing Crosby, Deanna Durbin, Ken Dodd, Billie Holiday, Liberace, Elvis Presley, Ella Fitzgerald, George Formby, Eartha Kitt, Perry Como, Bessie Smith, Frank Sinatra, Petula Clark, Bobby Darin, Alma Cogan, Louis Armstrong, Connie Francis, the Andrews Sisters, the Beverley Sisters, Gene Vincent and Lonnie Donegan, to name just a few.

Based on that showing, arch BBC critic Mrs Whitehouse ought to have been cheering the organisation from the rooftops rather than campaigning against it.

On the same day that the BBC banned the song, the ever-active Chelsea police raided Dandie Fashions in the King's Road, searching all the customers for drugs. The recently deceased Guinness heir Tara Browne supposedly alluded to in the lyrics of 'A Day in the Life' had owned shares in the business, and it would later become the Beatles' own boutique, Apple Tailoring. This event gave the *Daily Mirror* an excuse to use a large bikini-clad picture of a person they identified as 'strip-dancer Peki D'Oslo, 23, [who] was taken in tears to Chelsea police station and later freed on bail'. According to owner John Crittle, 'ten plain-clothes police, including a woman and with a dog, barged in'. Given that there were only nine customers present at the time, this seems like an excessive use of resources.

As the Summer of Love kicked off, and all the young people across America were allegedly heading for a sight of the Golden Gate Bridge and wearing flowers in their hair – or at least, those of them who hadn't been drafted and sent to Vietnam – a few artefacts from the Haight-Ashbury scene were already available to shoppers at one of Chelsea's hippest boutiques, as the *Melody Maker*'s weekly gossip column by The Raver noted on May 27: 'Dandie Fashion, in London's King's Road, Chelsea, selling Fillmore Auditorium posters from San Francisco.'

This was just one week after the Beatles had previewed *Sgt. Pepper* to the press at Brian Epstein's home, 24 Chapel Street, off Belgrave Square, an event covered in a special report by Jack Hutton on the same page of that issue of the paper, a fair amount of which was devoted to the band's clothing choices, rather than their music:

> The 'boys', as they are affectionately known by their management, were in fine fettle. Lennon won the sartorial stakes with a green, flower-patterned shirt, red cord trousers, yellow socks and what looked like cord shoes. His ensemble was completed by a sporran. With his bushy sideboards and National Health specs he resembled an animated Victorian watchmaker. Paul McCartney, sans moustache, wore a loose-ly-tied scarf over a shirt, a striped double breasted jacket and looked like someone out a Scott Fitzgerald novel.

A Joe Orton double bill of *The Ruffian on the Stair* and *The Erpingham Camp* opened at the Royal Court on June 6 under the title *Crimes of Passion*. Orton himself went to the first night, and recorded the event in his diary:

'Everybody enthusiastic. Had a drink in the club of the Court. I left early as I wanted a bit of sex.' Three days later the House of Commons held a debate on the question of theatre censorship, and a certain Sir Cyril Osborne, MP, closed his mind and opened his mouth to say: 'I am rather tired of democracy being made safe for pimps and prostitutes, the spivs and the queers.' Presumably much to Sir Cyril's disgust, the passage on July 27 of the Sexual Offences Act 1967 saw the legalisation of homosexual acts between men over the age of twenty-one. Things may now have been safe for all sorts of people, even MPs, but sadly not for Joe Orton, beaten to death in his sleep on August 9 by Kenneth Halliwell, who then killed himself with an overdose. At Joe's funeral on August 18, they played the song which the BBC had banned, 'A Day in the Life', written and recorded by the group who hadn't bothered to get back to him about the script they had commissioned.

Richard Hamilton's *Swingeing London* series of pictures, showing Mick Jagger and Robert Fraser handcuffed on their way to court at Chichester, was displayed for the first time on June 10, 1967, at the Robert Fraser Gallery, while in the *Guardian* on June 24, Charles Marowitz argued that some of those in the counterculture were simply drugging themselves into mindless oblivion: 'Many of London's hippies are not only "drop outs" (people who have rejected any form of social or political activism) but "cop-outs" – people who equate mind-erasure with the dissolution of social problems. ("When I'm stoned, there's no Vietnam and no Bomb, man, it's groovy.")'

Still, at least some of Chelsea's young people were able to stay up late doing something other than lying around in a crash-pad, as *The Times* showed in a large photograph they printed that month under the headline 'King's Road Goes "Pop" In The Night', recording the passing of a venerable slice of the street's history, accompanied by the following caption: 'Students of the Royal College of Art and the Chelsea School of Art taking part in an all-night painting session in King's Road, Chelsea. Their murals cover two 100ft sections of hoarding on the site of the former Granada Theatre, now being redeveloped.'

Like Scarves That Have Slipped Down a Bit

Having banned a Beatles song in May, the BBC decided in its wisdom to broadcast another of their songs on June 25 to the largest worldwide television audience yet seen. This was the performance from Studio One of Abbey Road of 'All You Need Is Love', and the reporter presenting that segment of the show was none other than Steve Race, the man who had denounced rock music in 1956 as a 'monstrous threat' in the pages of *Melody Maker*. During the broadcast, the band were surrounded by various members of other bands such as the Stones, the Who and the Small Faces, the latter of whom, according to Miles, were all attired in brand-new clothes from Granny Takes a Trip. John Pearse confirms that they were regular customers, as were a lot of people who were in the studio that day: 'Yeah, they had a lot of stuff, and the Beatles, and the other lot . . .' He told me that famous Granny's customers also included 'Brigitte Bardot, Monica Vitti, Stamp, Warhol, everybody . . .'

Meanwhile, over at the Cinephone on Oxford Street in May they were showing a Japanese film called *The Pornographer*, supported by a twenty-two-minute short film by Desmond Marshall entitled *Where Once Kings Road*, depicting 'young Londoners in the King's Road', set to music provided by the Spencer Davis Group. The following month a low-budget 'Swinging London' film called *Mini Weekend*, about a man obsessed with mini-skirts, was given a 'mini premiere', at which all girls wearing such clothing were admitted free, while the women's pages of *What's On in London* commented that 'most mini-skirts these days look like scarves that have slipped down a bit'.

This kind of clothing was also provoking thoughtful exchanges on the letters pages of *Mayfair* magazine that month: 'Today I followed a girl upstairs in the bus. She was wearing a mini-skirt but no knickers. [. . .] Is this the latest trend among the hippies? I think it is shocking to go out in public knicker-less,' said E. K. of Leeds, who was presumably so shocked he just had to sit down and write to a soft-porn magazine about it. C. F. of Bolton, however, was all in favour of them, for slightly different reasons: 'I hope this new fashion for male mini-skirts catches on. I for one have very good legs and see no reason why men, just as much as women, should not show them off.' That month's Miss Mayfair was Honey, 'the nineteen-year-old with the saucy smile', who had apparently turned down a promising career as a vet because 'Swinging London was too much of an attraction'. Hence, inevitably, 'she moved into Chelsea'.

David Storey, the author of the novel *This Sporting Life*, began a long association with the Royal Court when his play *The Restoration of Arnold Middleton* opened there on July 4. It won the *Evening Standard* Drama Award for Most Promising Playwright, and was the first of a string of his works to be presented at the Court over the next decade. Storey's play was followed on July 18 by the superbly named *Ogodiveleftthegason* by Donald Howarth. As all this was occurring, several Court luminaries were engaged elsewhere, making a film called *The Charge of the Light Brigade*. Tony Richardson was directing, from a script written by two English Stage Company playwrights, John Osborne and Charles Wood, while the film starred David Hemmings and Vanessa Redgrave, both fresh from *Blow-Up*. Director Anthony Page, meanwhile, was about to start shooting a film version of *Inadmissible Evidence*, from John Osborne's screenplay, starring Nicol Williamson and Jill Bennett.

Gaily Dressed and Very Matey

On July 10, Christopher Gibbs held a party at his Cheyne Walk house, which Miles experienced under the influence of some extremely strong hash cakes, and recalled in his memoir, *In the Sixties*:

> The plan was that after dinner we were all to go on to another house where Princess Margaret was dining and we would all have a royal time. [. . .] I have only fragmented memories of the party: a long talk with Michael Cooper about his photographs of the Beatles and the Stones and the possibility of an exhibition at Indica. Michael Rainey in Sherwood green. Tall, grinning as always, stoned, talking about UFOs. Mick Jagger and Marianne Faithfull: Marianne wearing a skimpy dress that showed her breasts from all angles except the front. [. . .] Allen Ginsberg arrived, straight off the plane from Italy . . .

Private Eye got into the swing of things with its August 18 Flower Power cover, accompanied by a masthead that now read 'All You Need Is *Private Eye*' and a photo showing three extremely elderly bearded 'hippies', whose speech bubbles said 'Turn On', 'Freak Out' and 'Piss Off'.

The newly emerging hippie capitalists continued in their ceaseless quest to monetise this thing known as Swinging London. Readers of the music press were treated to an advert which appeared in late summer, featuring the obligatory photo of a switched-on dolly – in this case TV pop personality and model Samantha Juste, shortly to marry Mickey Dolenz of the Monkees – advertising something called the Carnaby Card, the outdated name of which alone should have rung alarm bells:

HEY THERE! CRASH IN ON THE HIPPEST SCENES EVER. Be a member of CARNABY CARD – the new swinging idea for the swinging new generation – and you've made it! Right away, you become a member of dozens upon dozens of clubs like the Marquee, like the Pink Flamingo. [. . .] What's more, you get the red carpet treatment in all the jazziest boutiques right across the country.

And the address of this organisation which thought that Carnaby Street was still the epicentre of all things groovy, making no mention whatever of the King's Road in their advert? Number 1, Chelsea Manor Studios, Flood Street, Chelsea – the very same building that housed Michael Cooper's photographic studio, where six months earlier he had photographed the cover picture for the *Sgt. Pepper* LP.

On September 30, the Wilson government's designed legislation to close down the offshore pirate radio stations, the Marine Broadcasting Offences Act was passed, overseen and championed by former Postmaster General and now Minister of Technology Anthony Wedgwood Benn (formerly Viscount Stansgate, later simply Tony Benn). The BBC then launched Radio One, and staffed it by promptly hiring most of the former pirate DJs, including John Peel, who had been running a show on the pirate Radio London since returning from seven years in the USA earlier in 1967. Anne Duchene, writing in the *Guardian* on September 11, managed to sound suitably patronising about the impending pop station:

It must in fact be a fairly arduous aspect of public service, catering for so much sustained mindlessness, and Mr Robin Scott, the new programme's director, who told the press last week it would be 'a top gear type of forward-looking programme' has plainly been working hard at bridging the discrepancy between the programme's demands and his own BBC urbanity. The former pirates, gaily dressed and very matey, were a disarming crew. They each have an eight-week contract, will earn at the least not less than before, and are grateful for the refuge.

John Peel, with his Liverpool accent, had enjoyed a fair amount of celebrity already as a DJ over in the US, when anyone who could claim some kind of kinship with the British Invasion bands was at a premium. He had arrived over there in 1960, and as he told me:

Nothing happened for about three years or so, until the Beatles came along, and then it just went mad. I mean, I got mobbed in a department store in Dallas. I'd done a few programmes with a man called Russ Knight, 'The Weird Beard', and he'd been talking about Liverpool

– talking bollocks, basically – and I'd phoned him up, tried to correct him, and he said, 'Are you from Liverpool?', and I said, 'Well yeah, near enough, you know.' So he put me on the air to talk about Liverpool, and then the following weekend asked me if I'd go down to a department store in Dallas where they were having a giveaway: some Beatles LPs. They'd imagined sort of fifty or sixty people would turn up, but in fact there were several thousand girls in there, and they just ripped the store to pieces.

During his time in the States, John worked as a DJ in Oklahoma City, and then in LA, making friends with classic mid-sixties garage bands like the Seeds and the Misunderstood (whose demos he also produced), once even acting as onstage security for a Rolling Stones gig. He had never been back to England during the whole time, and while he was in Texas, his life had resembled something out of a film:

You'd go to a drive-in movie, which was the only place where you could be alone in the dark, and they used to come round, and if the windows were misted up then security would rap on the windows. You'd just drive round, you know, see people that you knew, and you'd kind of race between traffic lights and all that kind of *American Graffiti* stuff. At the weekends I used to drive out to places with funny names. There was a place called Bug Tussle, Texas, and so you'd drive 150 miles, just to say you'd been to a place called Bug Tussle. Jot 'Em Down was another one.

John returned in 1967 to find himself in the middle of a London that was determinedly swinging, and almost immediately wound up at the centre of things, on the radio, having a huge effect on popular taste, where he remained for the next four decades. As for his impressions of the newly 'swinging' city and its groovy clothes: 'I'd not been back, 'cause I couldn't really afford to, and I don't like flying, anyway. You'd heard so much about it, and taken it all, obviously, with a pinch of salt, so it didn't seem that strange or remarkable a place when I got back.'

Tight Pink Trousers and Matching Floral Shirt

In America at that time, the readers of the *Saturday Evening Post* were being invited to find out more about this new race of strangely dressed people, with a cover headline in the September 23 issue that promised: 'The Hippie

Cult: Who They Are. What They Want. Why They Act That Way'. Inside was Joan Didion's landmark article 'The Hippies: Slouching Towards Bethlehem', in which she described visiting San Francisco to check out the scene: 'The five year old's name is Susan, and she tells me she is in High Kindergarten. [. . .] For a year now her mother has given her both acid and peyote.' Next to this, Nicky Kramer dosing his rabbit at the Pheasantry starts to look like normal behaviour.

At Sound Techniques recording studio in Old Church Street, the Incredible String Band had now recorded another album, *The 5000 Spirits or the Layers of the Onion*. Then, in the autumn of 1967, Fairport Convention came in to make their debut album, *Fairport Convention*, with Joe Boyd and Tod Lloyd producing, and in the coming years some of the key folk records of the sixties and seventies would be made there. Robin Williamson of the Incredible String Band recalled working with Joe Boyd at that time in an interview with Richie Unterberger:

> He didn't interfere, really. He was more of an enabler than a director. He used to just sort of get you in there. And if you said to him, 'Well, I would like such and such,' he would get it for you. But otherwise, just let you get on with it. And I think it's impossible to underestimate the contribution of John Wood, the engineer, who had a lot to do with developing some of those early techniques in the studio called Sound Techniques. He was one of the first guys to have all the modern multi-tracking facilities in Britain that I know of. In fact, my impression was that he developed and invented some of that stuff.

Eighteen-year-old Martin Amis, then still living at home in the Fulham Road, spent a lot of his time, as he later wrote, 'mincing up and down the King's Road in skintight velves and grimy silk scarves and haunting a coffee bar called the Picasso, and smoking hash (then £8 an ounce) and trying to pick up girls.'

As if proof were needed that the King's Road was truly where it was at for an aspiring literary type, the October edition of *Town* magazine ran an interview with Adam Diment, 23-year-old author of a James Bond-imitation youth-orientated novel *The Dolly Dolly Spy*, which stated that he was 'hoping to move from his Fulham Road flat to trendy King's Road, where his tight pink trousers and matching floral shirt will be more appreciated'. *The Dolly Dolly Spy* itself featured detailed descriptions of a character called Veronica, the hero's main love interest:

She always wears the minimum of clothes. [. . .] She is also switched on, tuned in, right on the ball, with it (wherever that may be) and pretty near beat out when I met her. [. . .] She was wearing her latest acquisition, bought in a boutique in King's Road which is a cross between an Eastern bazaar and a rugger scrum. It was very short and covered with overlapping blue and yellow flowers. Over her heart, which was almost visible because it was as low at the breast as it was short at the thigh, was a bright pink heart. She'd had her hair done during the afternoon but it still looked like a chaotic tangle of black hay – as she was so brown she'd given up wearing stockings. She was about as naked as you can get these days without being nicked for indecency.

That same edition of *Town* magazine featured a guide to London's 'Young Pubs', and recommended a couple of King's Road hostelries: the Chelsea Potter, 'the heartland of Chelsea', and the Markham Arms, next door to Bazaar, which was allegedly 'full of talent'.

The tragic case of a young female regular at the Chelsea Potter made front-page news in September, prompting headlines such as 'Model Is Murdered In Chelsea Flat' and the speculatively judgemental 'Mini-Skirt May Have Led To Murder'. Eighteen-year-old Claudie Delbarre, who modelled under the name Claudie Danielle, was found dead in her £8-a-week bedsit in Walpole Street, off the King's Road, and it was reported that she had been given some advice by a constable a couple of days earlier on account of the shortness of her leather mini-skirt: 'The policeman spoke to her outside the Chelsea Potter pub in King's-road, the haunt of swinging chicks, hippies and flower children. Barman Bill Webster, 21, said last night: "Claudie always wore these fantastically short skirts. She told me she was warned by a policeman to wear something longer for her own protection."'

In the event, a 37-year-old American property dealer named Robert Lipman was convicted of the killing, whose defence QC told the court Lipman had taken LSD at the time and had gone on a trip 'to the centre of the earth'.

This was one of roughly 400 homicides in England and Wales that year, but the vast majority were not ascribed by the press to a particular choice of clothing, nor accompanied, as in this instance, by bikini-clad photos of the victim.

By contrast, Bazaar's leading light, Mary Quant, was currently appearing in the *Guardian* as part of a series they were running entitled *The Permissive Society*. She was interviewed by Alison Adburgham for a piece which ran in the paper on October 10, and said:

This is a very balanced generation, and the crotch is the most natural erogenous zone. Clothes are designed to lead the eye to it. The way girls model clothes is all doing the same thing. It's not 'come hither', but it's provocative. She's standing there defiantly with her legs apart saying 'I'm very sexy, I enjoy sex, I feel provocative, but you're going to have a job to get me. You've got to excite me and you've got to be jolly marvellous to attract me.' Now that there is the pill, women are the sex in charge.

A selection of this kind of people were pictured in a new book of photographs by John D. Green, entitled *Birds of Britain*, featuring '55 of Britain's most attractive women', which was previewed in the December edition of *King* magazine. They explained that the subjects had been photographed in 'poses that owe everything to Green's fertile imagination and leave very little to the imagination of everyone else'. These included model and Top Gear and Count Down boutique proprietor Pat Booth, who was covered in double-sided Sellotape and then had the contents of a feather pillow case emptied over her: 'It is a tribute to her delicacy that she makes sums of money out of modelling other people's clothes, and it is a tribute to her competence that she now makes even more out of the boutiques through which she sells her own.'

In case the general public was not heartily sick of hearing about what a wonderful time young people were supposedly having in SW3, November brought a new single release by a fine singer in the Dusty Springfield mould, Truly Smith, who was originally from Warrington. It was a lovelorn beat ballad called 'The Boy From Chelsea', in which the title character works in a trendy coffee shop in the area, and was reviewed by the appropriately named journalist Peter Jones on the singles page of the *Record Mirror*, where it was up against such varied competition as the superb 'The Intro and The Outro' by the Bonzo Dog Doo-Dah Band, the King's Road's Nancy Whiskey with a re-recording of her skiffle hit 'Freight Train', and also a Liverpool band who were reckoned to have a fair chance of a hit with something called 'Hello Goodbye'/'I Am the Walrus'.

Just to prove that, in a street overflowing with boutiques, there was still money to be made launching yet another one, a custom-designed stainless-steel space-age variant fitted out at a cost of £30,000 opened its doors on the King's Road on November 28 under the name Just Looking, designed by the team that had created the nightclubs of Cunard's new liner, the *QE2*. It was described by *The Times* as 'a shiny silver nail in the coffin of the amateur shop owner'.

Credit: Julian Brown/Daily Mirror /Mirrorpix

Models Vicky Wise, Jenny Skelton, Jane London and Diana Reeves
pictured at the opening of Just Looking boutique

For those in search of spiritual guidance, Michael Rainey of Hung On You announced to the press in October that Merlin the Magician was alive and living in Somerset, flying saucers did indeed exist and he had seen one the previous week in Wales, and that all human beings were reincarnated.

In other news, journalist Bob Dawbarn, who had been with the *Melody Maker* since the mid-fifties dawn of the first British rockers – when he memorably told readers, 'If you want Willy to earn lots of lovely lolly, provide for Mum in her old age, become the idol of British girlhood and star at the Palladium, then teach the lad to Rock'n'Roll' – wrote a spoof almanac in the last issue of the year containing predictions for the coming 1968. These included 'Scott Walker says he is giving up music to explore the Amazon. The Amazon says she is delighted', 'Somebody writes a jazz novel without mentioning drugs', and 'A 98-year-old Chelsea Pensioner wins *Opportunity Knocks* by reciting "Eskimo Nell" while riding a Pennyfarthing in the nude'. No surprises there then.

The year 1967 had been the one in which the hippie dream went public, and the King's Road scene showed up in all the guide books. As Len Deighton advised the curious tourist: 'If you haven't had enough models, mods and minis then take your cab to King's Road. When you see a *dense* crowd – tear your way through it to find the Guys n' Dolls coffee bar. From now on you are on your own . . .'

19

'Mister Freedom, Sister George'

Incredibly Overpriced and Really Shabby

Granny Takes a Trip had a well-deserved reputation for intimidating potential customers. As McLaren and Westwood's variously titled King's Road shop would also do in the seventies, the frontage acted more as a statement of identity and a barrier than an encouragement. It is hardly surprising; after all, a shop that within months of opening had people like the Beatles and the Stones as customers – who went on to wear some of those clothes on their album sleeves, out in public and also on television – hardly needed much in the way of passing trade. Nigel Waymouth told the writer Paul Gorman that Gram Parsons used to sleep on the floor of the shop because he liked it so much, while other star names who wore their gear included Pink Floyd, the Animals, the Who and even Barbra Streisand. As for John Peel, he told me that there was a lot of pressure to be seen dressed in a fashionable way:

> We used to walk past Granny Takes a Trip and look longingly into the windows. I've never really had the figure for trying to be fashionable, or the inclination. I tend, really, to prefer to dress in kind of mud colours that enable me to blend into my natural surroundings, but there used to be a couple of kind of hippie shops in Kingly Street, that runs parallel to Carnaby Street, where I used to go and buy hippie gear. I wore it when I went to that 14 Hour Technicolor Dream, or whatever it was, and I wore it for the Stones in the Park, and Pink Floyd in the Park, and stuff like that, and I used to wear it when I went to UFO, but, you know, I was very much of a kind of weekend

hippie as far as dress went. The hippie stuff was amazingly badly made, too. Incredibly overpriced and really shabby stuff. What it came down to, it was all to do with sex, really. You'd kind of walk around, hoping that you'd see some hippie chick, as they were being described at the time, who'd empathise with you, but I never felt at all convincing, and dressed like that as seldom as possible, really, 'cause I just felt uncomfortable and vulnerable and rather faintly laughable.

Anyone wanting to observe a gathering of seriously trendy celebrities in their fashionable best would merely have had to walk down the King's Road on January 20, 1968, and loiter in the general vicinity of Chelsea Registry Office as friends such as Peter Sellers showed up for the wedding of Roman Polanski and Sharon Tate, which was followed by a star-studded party at the Playboy Club. As a couple, they had already been in the habit of entertaining the likes of Warren Beatty, Laurence Harvey and Yul Brynner at their home just past Sloane Square, and for the stag night the previous evening, guests had included Michael Caine and Terence Stamp. On the day, according to Polanski's account, media interest was such that the photographers outnumbered the guests, and as for the wedding couple's clothes: 'Sharon wore a cream-coloured taffeta minidress, and I sported an olive-green Edwardian jacket – a tribute to some hard selling by Jack Vernon, a Hollywood boutique owner. We were a grotesque sight.'

Credit: David Housden and Harry Fox/ Sunday Mirror/Mirrorpix

Roman Polanski and Sharon Tate's King's Road wedding

Other sights of a similar nature featured in a couple of fashion-related items with a Chelsea connection which appeared in that month's edition of *Rave* magazine. Firstly, in their 'Rave at the Flicks' film section, came news of the following motion picture: '"The Mini Mob", set in and around the King's Road, Chelsea, London, takes a light-hearted look at some swinging dollies who decide to kidnap their boyfriends. One of the men on their list is jazz man Georgie Hart, played by Georgie Fame.'

In the event, the picture – with Willie Rushton as the Chancellor of the Exchequer, and also featuring Madeline Smith, Clive Dunn and Roy Kinnear – was released under the slightly different title *The Mini-Affair*. Then, in the magazine's heartbreaking serial love story, *Ronny, Diary of a Rave Girl*, a *ménage à trois* flat share hits the rocks: 'So now I'm waiting for him to come back from buying some ciggies and we're going over to Guys and Dolls in the King's Road to have some lunch and a talk. Although I can't face up to it, I just know that one of us will have to move out, or all split up.'

One relationship which had definitely turned sour that spring was that of a wealthy American woman who lived at Whitelands House opposite the Duke of York's Barracks and her estranged husband, to the extent that the High Court banned the latter from within a mile of her home, as the *Daily Mirror* reported under the headline 'JUDGE BARS A HUSBAND FROM THE KING'S ROAD': 'King's Road, Chelsea, one of the places where "Swinging London" all began, was put out of bounds yesterday to the husband of an American heiress. He was warned that if he goes to the road – world famous for its Saturday morning parade of mini-skirted girls and dedicated male followers of fashion – he will be arrested and jailed.'

Ram it in the Punters' Faces

The Beatles themselves had recently gone into the rag trade, opening the Apple boutique in Baker Street in November 1967, and were now planning to open a second outlet on the King's Road. To this end, the former Beatles road manager Neil Aspinall, who was now MD of Apple, became a director of Dandie Fashions on February 2. This was a preparatory move to the establishment of Apple Tailoring, the King's Road outlet which would be unveiled in May.

OZ magazine was now being marketed in Chelsea by a new young street seller called Felix Dennis, whose sales tactic involved rounding up some girls to help him and dressing them in the shortest mini-skirts available, which enabled him to shift a hundred copies a day, as he told Richard Neville: 'I set myself up in King's Road with three chicks in short skirts and ram it in the punters' faces.'

Short skirts were not the only things confronting the punters of the district, according to a trend highlighted in April in the regular *Daily Mirror* column, 'Felicity Green on the Fashion Scene', for something called the show-through, which were a more expensive Chelsea variation on the pasties worn by strippers in burlesque shows:

> Like night following day, like summer following spring, so the See-through is being followed by the Show-through. [. . .] Made for the kind of trade that's briskest in the King's-road, it was designed by James Wedge, who runs the very successful Top Gear and Count Down boutiques. James Wedge said he had the See-through idea about three years ago but it never caught on until St Laurent did it in Paris earlier this year – which tends to prove that there's still nothing like a spot of haute couture for making a tarty idea seem respectable.

Film director Robert Aldrich was also walking down the King's Road in the spring of 1968. Two years after the cast of his film *The Dirty Dozen* had been photographed there checking out the Chelsea sights, the director himself was in the area because he wanted to shoot part of his new film in the longest-established lesbian club in Europe, the Gateways, in Bramerton Gardens, just off the King's Road. The picture was called *The Killing of Sister George*, based on a play by Frank Marcus which had run very success-fully in the West End in the mid-sixties. A key sequence of the film was set at the Gateways, in which Beryl Reid and Susannah York dress up as Laurel and Hardy for a night out, and these scenes were filmed in the spring of 1968, with a full complement of the club's regular clientele onscreen instead of extras, before Aldrich then went to LA in May to shoot the rest of the film's interiors. This eventually led to the club being given some national publicity in the *Daily Mirror*, just ahead of the film's release:

> In the King's Road basement Aldrich set up his cameras and found willing extras among Gateways members. Women and girls with cropped hair, tweeds, pipes, trousers (even stiff white collars) stepped smartly into the glare. Social barriers barely exist between members, who include shopgirls, secretaries, actresses and schoolteachers. Any night in the Gateways, scores of women (and a few men) will be in passionate, animated conversation, supping spirits and pints of beer. Handholding couples cluster round a juke-box while others dance, sometimes gently, sometimes in aggressive embrace.

At the Royal Court, meanwhile, there'd been a D. H. Lawrence season in February, consisting of three plays, *A Collier's Friday Night* (1906–7), *The Daughter-in-Law* (1912) and *The Widowing of Mrs Holroyd* (1914), the latter featuring 'Oil Lamps by Christopher Wray's Lighting Emporium', according to the programme, showing that the Court could still turn to local shops in time of need.

Following on from these three plays written before the First World War, the English Stage Company then presented a new work by the man who created such a stir with *Saved*, Edward Bond. It was called *Early Morning*, and opened at the Royal Court on March 31, directed by William Gaskill, with a cast that included future *Minder* star Dennis Waterman and future *Withnail and I* director Bruce Robinson. It also starred Marianne Faithfull as Florence Nightingale, who is raped by Queen Victoria, then opens a brothel and has a threesome with Disraeli and Gladstone. Victoria and her family were depicted as cannibals, and – although apparently set in the 19th century – one character makes reference to the BBC's new station, Radio One. The published edition of the text carried the following note on the title page: 'The events of this play are true.'

Len Deighton was continuing to give travel advice about London, this time in the pages of *Playboy*'s May edition, where in its 'Capsule Guide to Urban Europe', he recommended that visitors should try Alvaro's ('daily Mod lunch-in; Italian flavour'), and also 'stroll along King's Road, where boutiques and dollies abound'. Deighton was careful, though, to downplay the idea that all of the city's thoroughfares were crammed with swingers: 'London isn't Carnaby Street and King's Road and never was. [. . .] As in most major cities of the world, there are indeed certain areas of London that swing wildly, but you must know the right people, be able to get in the right places and have plenty of pounds to spend.'

While Deighton was advising *Playboy* readers, Mary Quant was telling *TIME* magazine on May 17 that she still believed in mini-skirts, despite the trend for longer styles: 'It's not that the mini is out. It has such freedom of movement that I'll always use it. But why should I get hung up on one particular hemline? I had hoped that by now people understood that we can have the mini, the midi and the maxi.'

We Decided to Chop it in Half

On the same day Mary's views were published in *TIME*, the London film-trade news-sheet the *Daily Cinema* printed a snappily titled article called 'The Corporate Structure of the Apple Corps Ltd', which gave a breakdown of the various wings of the new company the Beatles had set up. That particular newspaper's readers would mostly have been interested to hear of Apple's new film division, which was announcing plans to film a script by Royal Court dramatist Edward Bond called *Walkabout*, to be directed by Nicolas Roeg. However, the article also said that the company would have a retail arm, known as Apple Merchandising: 'The retail division at Apple at present embraces two shops in the West End of London. The one in Baker Street, opened last November, the other, Apple Tailoring at 161 King's Road, is undergoing alterations and will be opened later this month.' On May 22, a party to celebrate the launch of the grandly titled Apple Tailoring (Civil and Theatrical) was duly held at Club Dell'Aretusa, 107 King's Road, attended by George and Pattie Harrison, and – supposedly for the first time in public – John Lennon and Yoko Ono. The latter pair were then photographed in the King's Road as they made their way to the new shop at number 161. Two weeks later, *Disc and Music Echo* ran an article about the new shop, and interviewed 25-year-old John Crittle, who was both its manager and designer, and had owned and run the place under its previous incarnation, Dandie Fashions: 'We won't get teenyboppers here, because prices will be too high for them. [. . .] We're catering mainly for pop groups, personalities and turned-on swingers. The teenagers seem too frightened to come in, even though they know this is the Beatles' place. Maybe it's because the place is too elegant and too expensive.'

Given that their made-to-measure suits started at 30 guineas (£31.50), he probably had a point. A guinea was 21 shillings, and there were 20 shillings to the pound. A can of Heinz beans at Tesco that year cost one shilling, and today, at the time of writing, the same supermarket offers them for £1 each, which would mean that the made-to-measure suit would now be £630. On the other hand, beans are considerably cheaper these days in real terms than they used to be. If you measure it in terms of cigarette prices, a pack of twenty Player's No. 6 cigarettes cost three shillings and sixpence, so you could get 5.7 packs for a pound. The average cost of a pack of 20 cigarettes in the UK now is around £12, and the same number of packs would cost you a little over £68, bringing the equivalent price of the Apple Tailoring suit to a bracing £2,142. Cheaper, perhaps, for a teenage Beatle fan to try to steal one, but they would then probably wind up making the acquaintance of a selection of prison officers, whose 1968 starting salary in London was £14 a week.

Just as the Beatles were getting into the boutique business – and music publishing, and merchandising, and films, and an arts foundation, and electronic inventions courtesy of 'Magic' Alex Mardas, a man whose talents would have been better employed selling fridges to the Eskimos – the original team at Granny Takes a Trip decided to call it a day. Admittedly, they had been mighty busy these past couple of years. Nigel Waymouth and his friend Michael English were also a graphic design team called Hapshash and the Coloured Coat, and then Waymouth and Pearse made an album for producer Guy Stevens under the Hapshash name. Added to that, Pearse was also on the books of the English Boy model agency at Radnor Walk, and had little affection for the increasingly hippified turn which men's fashions were taking, such as the ubiquitous Afghan coat and the seemingly obligatory bells worn round the neck. John Peel told me that even he felt obliged to have a bell at one point, while John Gunnell, who ran the Flamingo and Bag O'Nails clubs, explained to me that he had to put a sign up at the entrance to the latter forbidding bells because the deafening sound of a roomful of hippies clanking about the place was getting to be a serious annoyance: 'The Flamingo started to peter out, to my mind, round about 1966. The whole R&B thing had changed, and after that the scene gradually became robes and bells and hippy shit. We'd opened the Ram Jam Club in Brixton that year and put on Otis Redding and I concentrated more on developing that place.'

At Granny Takes a Trip, one day it was suddenly just all too much, and tempers boiled over. In keeping with their policy of changing the look of the place, they had recently installed the front end of a 1947 Dodge motor car in the front window, as if it was breaking out of the shop into the street. When asked where he had managed to get hold of half of a 1947 Dodge, John Pearse told me:

> I had a *whole* of a 1947 Dodge, which broke down in Notting Hill in 1968, and that was it, we decided to chop it in half. I think we'd seen the Claes Oldenburg *Lovers in the Back Seat of a Dodge*, and that was its fate. It was very dark green. Beautiful upholstery, and glowing green dials, but a real packet of trouble, I should never have bought it.

Credit: author's collection

488, Kings Road; Chelsea; London. S.W.IO./304,E 62nd. N.Y.C. U.S.A.

'A real packet of trouble': The Dodge at Granny's

It has been said that the arrival of the Dodge in the window of Granny's was the last straw for the local council, who objected strenuously to this latest addition to the sights of old Chelsea, but this was not all, as John says:

> It was also the last straw for me, as well. I walked out. That was my closing monument to Granny Takes a Trip. Tempers were fraught between me and my partner [Nigel Waymouth], about who was going to write songs for the band that we had, about what the backdrop was going to be of this car, and he wanted the cosmos and I wanted skyscrapers, and I think we were just sort of leaning across the bonnet throwing punches. 'Right, I'll have the band and you can have the shop.' Neither of us did any good after that . . .

This was not, however, to be the end of Granny Takes a Trip, and it would soon pass into other hands and survive into the seventies, when for a while it co-existed with McLaren and Westwood's shop a short distance down the street. For the moment, the Tremeloes were happy to give them a namecheck in response to a reader's enquiry from Barry Morse in Gloucester in the *Melody Maker* on July 13, who wrote: 'You recently printed a photo of the Tremeloes wearing heavily embroidered coats. Where can these be obtained?' The band's bass player Chip Hawkes responded with the following helpful advice: 'We bought some of the coats in Scandinavia, but others came from Granny Takes a Trip, in King's Road, Chelsea. Another source of supply is Afghanistan Carpets in the Edgware Road.'

Street-Fighting Mannerisms

A regular customer at the hipper Chelsea boutiques was sitting in his King's Road flat on May 21, 1968, when he received a phone call telling him that the local drug squad were about to raid his home. Convinced that he had nothing to hide, Brian Jones nevertheless refused to answer the door, which resulted in the boys in blue crawling in through the window and miraculously discovering some hashish.

As one of the band was being busted, another one was written up the following day in the ever-informative film trade newspaper the *Daily Cinema*, which carried the announcement that a major Hollywood studio was prepared to cast the first Stone:

> Mick Jagger, lead singer of the Rolling Stones, has been signed to make the picture *The Performers* [*sic*], it is announced by Kenneth

Hyman, executive vice president of Warner Bros-Seven Arts in charge of world-wide productions. Jagger will star opposite James Fox in the colour and wide screen production which will be directed by Donald Cammell and Nicolas Roeg, from an original screenplay by Cammell. While his role in *The Performers* is a straight dramatic portrayal, Jagger will sing one song within the framework of the story and is writing the musical score for the picture. Principal photography will begin in mid-July in and around London locations.

Jagger and Marianne Faithfull had moved into a fine house at 48 Cheyne Walk – a relatively short walk from Mick's old 1962 lodgings in Edith Grove, but with considerable differences in decor and amenities. Christopher Gibbs, rather than Jimmy Phelge, was hired as interior decorator, and Marianne also made her contribution, spending £6,000 of Mick's money on a 17th-century chandelier for the drawing room, which would have been more than enough to buy a house in most parts of the country at that time. As it turned out, many of the interiors for Mick's new picture would be filmed not far away in Lowndes Square, just off Sloane Street. This building served as the inside of Mick Jagger's house in the film. The exteriors for that house were shot in Notting Hill, in Powis Square, but that was about it, as Mick Farren recalls: 'I knew a bunch of people who lived in that house, and the interior isn't like that at all.' By June 12, it was being announced that the name of the picture had changed slightly: '*Performance* is the new title for the contemporary drama starring James Fox and Mick Jagger which was originally called *The Performers*. Due to begin shooting on 29 July.'

At that point Mick and the Stones were in the middle of making the album *Beggar's Banquet* with producer Jimmy Miller at Olympic Studios out in Barnes. Before he would play his role in *Performance*, Jagger would be involved in another feature film, as Jean-Luc Godard dropped in to the studio for two days in June in order to shoot footage of the band working on the song 'Sympathy for the Devil'. This would form the centrepiece of his new film, *One Plus One*, sandwiched in between a selection of trendy revolutionary chic in which humourless types waving machine guns stood around in a scrapyard by the Thames yelling stuff like 'Long Live Mao!' and 'The major enemy is whitey!' Jean-Luc himself was later quoted in issue 14 of *OZ* magazine saying, 'I thought it would be nice to go to the most conservative country in the movie-making world to see how it is.'

Mao was incredibly popular with the students that summer; indeed, there had been a giant photo of him swimming the Yangtse on the wall in Hung On You the previous year, although there were a few million people cluttering up the cemeteries of China who would have told another story, had the Great Leap Forward not leapt all over them.

Cheyne Walk home-owning resident Mick Jagger was singing about a 'Street Fighting Man', and May had seen the Paris student riots, at which, as *TIME* magazine helpfully informed its readers, 'there were Maoists, Trotskyites, ordinary Communists, anarchists and "situationists" – a tag for those without preconceived ideologies who judge each proposition as it arises'. One of those in Paris was Fred Vermorel, who sent letters back to his student friends Jamie Reid and Malcolm Edwards (shortly to become McLaren). Over in Paris, the graffiti proclaimed messages like 'It's forbidden to forbid,' and 'Humanity will not be happy until the last capitalist is hanged with the entrails of the last bureaucrat.' With one foot on the barricades and a sharp eye on possible careers as sociology lecturers, the shock troops of the new revolution were out in the streets. *Private Eye*'s cover on June 7 had the headline 'Revolting Students', featuring a photo of De Gaulle and his wife driving away in a car, with her speech bubble reading 'Let them smoke pot.' Sadly, Malcolm and Jamie were not in Paris, so they did the next best thing and occupied Croydon College of Art and Design with a group of students, issuing a series of situationist demands. Seven years later, they would bring their situationist slogans to the King's Road, and paint them on the inside walls of number 430.

On July 8, the Chelsea Drug Store opened in a blaze of publicity, even meriting a large article entitled 'Vive "Le Drug" De Londres!' in that day's edition of *The Times*, who were usually above noticing such things:

> [It] consists of two bars, a restaurant, a soda fountain and ten stalls selling everything from sweets to sweaters, hit records to hair brushes. It will trade for 16 hours, seven days a week, opening for breakfast at 8a.m. and closing at midnight. [. . .] The complex includes a pharmacy that will stay open until 11p.m. at night and a 'flying squad' delivery service for foods, wines and papers, operated by cat-suited girls on motor cycles.

The Drug Store was a purpose-built hip hangout designed to attract the beautiful people, constructed on the corner of Royal Avenue at 49 King's Road. A fine old Victorian pub called the White Hart used to stand on this site (and can be glimpsed in the 1963 film *The Servant*), but the self-consciously trendy design of this new cafe/bar/shopping outlet never quite attracted the cognoscenti in the way it was supposed to. True, it would be namechecked the following year by the Stones in the lyrics to 'You Can't Always Get What You Want', but although it lasted under that name into the eighties, these days it is a branch of McDonald's.

Nude Sculptures Out of Patent Leather

As the paving stones were being torn up in Paris, back in Sloane Square they were staging two new plays by former fifties revolutionary John Osborne at the Royal Court: the first, *Time Present*, opened on May 23, starring Jill Bennett, who had recently married Osborne; two months later, on July 3, came the second, *The Hotel in Amsterdam*, starring Paul Scofield, who had recently won great acclaim appearing as sometime Chelsea resident Sir Thomas More in the film *A Man for All Seasons*. Further down towards World's End, near the site of Henry VIII's old manor house, a rock group who would single-handedly attempt to revive one of the former king's favourite sartorial embellishments, the codpiece, entered Joe Boyd's Sound Techniques studio in Old Church Street on June 13 to begin recording their debut album, *This Was*, for Island Records. Sessions lasted until August 23, and the album was released on October 25, 1968. The band named themselves Jethro Tull, after the 17th-century Berkshire agriculturalist who invented the seed drill, and embarked upon a singular career of standing on one leg and playing the flute which continues to this day. Mixed in with the Tull sessions, Sound Techniques also played host to another artist who began recording his debut album that July. This was Nick Drake, the album *Five Leaves Left*, with production by Joe Boyd, and it would be released in 1969. In keeping with the acoustic mood, a new folk club opened in Chelsea at the end of May. It was called La Fiesta, 168 Fulham Road, and the support act on its first night was an up-and-coming singer called Ralph McTell, who would score a worldwide hit four years later with his much-covered song 'Streets of London'. Jean Aitchison, reviewing the gig for *Melody Maker*, described his appearance that evening as follows: 'Perched like an elf on a high stool in this candle-light [*sic*] basement, he seemed at first to merge with the shadows then he sprang to life with a scintillating and unflurried guitar technique which enchanted everybody.'

Over the next three months that basement played host to the Strawbs, Stefan Grossman, John Martyn, Sandy Denny, and many other key names of the folk world. One of the biggest of them at that time, Julie Felix, had been living in the area for several years, while making many television appearances on *The Frost Report*, and had recently finished a run of her own TV series, *Once More with Felix*. Her King's Road flat featured heavily in an interview she did with the *Melody Maker*'s Tony Wilson, entitled 'Chelsea Swings Below, But Julie Keeps On Working', which began as follows: 'KING'S ROAD, Chelsea, is one of the main arteries for the life blood of Swinging London. With its colourful shop-fronts, pubs and restaurants, it is a parade ground for fashion where people go to look and be looked at. Julie Felix lives in King's Road, in a white-painted flat that looks down onto the Swingers Parade.'

Of course, there's swinging in the *LIFE* magazine sense, and then there's swinging of a slightly different kind, and the district's longstanding reputation in the rest of the country as a place where all manner of lewd things were supposedly on offer for the jaded benefit of the fashion-conscious groovers was reinforced by journalist David Cumming in his regular weekly column for the *Record Mirror*, who came up with this fake advert in June for an imaginary SW3 nightspot: 'HURRY! HURRY! New club opens Tuesday. SUNDAY'S JOINT, King's Road, Chelsea. Hurry! Hurry! Opens Tuesday. Rock'n'Roll played by topless girl group. Hurry! Hurry! Closes Wednesday.'

Back in the world of film, principal photography had begun on *Performance*, and trade paper the *Daily Cinema* dropped by to write a lengthy on-set report on August 14, although the future Sir Mick had not yet filmed any of his scenes. The newspaper was published from offices right in the heart of the film trade at 142–150 Wardour Street, but they spared no expense to track down the *Performance* location unit, picking a day when they were filming some scenes in a room above a restaurant in, well, Wardour Street. Having first of all established that the two co-directors did not in fact have chairs with 'Donald Cammell' and 'Nicolas Roeg' written on the backs, it fell to Roeg to explain their joint working methods: 'Of course on the set only one can say do this or do that, this or that way, so that is Donald's part, while I concentrate on the camera lighting.' As for the areas of London where shooting was taking place, the article stated:

> In order to reflect and capture the kaleidoscopic moods of the London of the story, the team is filming entirely on location both in the streets of the city and in houses specifically taken over for the purpose. The two residences utilised by the cameras – and which will appear as a single entity on the screen in the shape of the house occupied by Jagger – are in the smart Chelsea district of Lowndes Square, and the high-priced, tree-lined environs of Hyde Park Gate, a thoroughfare already etched firmly into Britain's history as the home of the late Sir Winston Churchill.

George Harrison's wife Pattie went into the retail business herself, opening a stall at Chelsea Antique Market on the King's Road at the end of July, which she co-ran with her sister, Jenny Boyd. This was not destined to remain a low-key venture for very long, since *Disc and Music Echo* devoted a half-page article by Caroline Boucher to the event the following week, published under the self-explanatory title 'Beatle Wife Pattie Sets Up Shop':

'George doesn't mind at all,' Pattie told *Disc* as she sat wedged in her tiny stall, behind the so far scant array of antiques. 'Jenny and I are learning as we go along.' [. . .] One of the attractions of the market for pop stars and young people is the clothes stall, which has been the main source of ruffled shirts, velvet trousers and jackets and caftans for some time. Regular customers include Mick Jagger and Marianne Faithfull.

Any seasoned King's Road celebrity-watchers who happened to be in the neighbourhood on August 30, 1968 would have had the chance to see Paul McCartney and Ringo and Maureen Starr arrive at Chelsea Registry Office to attend a wedding on what also happened to be the release date of the new Beatles single, 'Hey Jude'/'Revolution'. The happy couple were Susie Ornstein and Apple MD Neil Aspinall, who was taking time out from dodging the avalanche of poverty-stricken artists, freeloaders, con-merchants and hippie deadbeats who were descending on his offices in droves looking for a handout, following announcements in the press that the Beatles would be funding cultural projects. Richard DiLello, Apple's 'House Hippie', recalled some of the results in his memoir, *The Longest Cocktail Party*:

'That girl is in reception.'
'What girl?'
'The one from Wigmore Street who wants financial backing to make nude sculptures out of patent leather covered in oil to simulate . . .'
'Tactile delight?'
'That's the one!'
'Send her up!'

Apple Merchandising was already starting to unravel, and the troubled Baker Street boutique had been closed down in July on John Lennon's orders, with the remaining stock given away free amid scenes of utter chaos. Whatever the crowds of bargain-hunters were imagining that day, 'no possessions' didn't appear to be part of it.

Real Fucking Psycho Thugs

Over in Lowndes Square, they were shooting *Performance*, which was putting a severe strain on relationships within the Rolling Stones, since Mick Jagger had started an affair with co-star Anita Pallenberg, who also happened to be Keith Richards' girlfriend, while Mick's other half, Marianne Faithfull, was at that time pregnant and temporarily living over in Ireland. Added to the mixture were a cast of genuine East End hard men, some of whom also liked to hang around at the Pheasantry, where David Litvinoff, the film's dialogue coach and technical adviser, was living. Mick Farren told me that there was some kind of illegal late-night drinking club in the Pheasantry at that time, which may have been part of the attraction:

> There was a thing with the Pheasantry – which makes me think it was also an after-hours drinker in the back or something – because there was those sort of Chelsea hoods like Johnny Bindon, I mean real fucking psycho thugs, who generally came up via the movie industry, or being you know, Jimmy Page's minder or something. *Performance* brought a bunch of them into circulation, they just sort of surfaced with Cammell. There were other places not quite on the King's Road; if you go up to the Earls Court intersection with Fulham Road, there was a basement place down some steps, it was open all night. Me and Lemmy used to go down there when we were speeding and the place was full of, you know, South African mercenaries waiting for a job, Mad Mike Hoare's mob. Certain gangsters would come in and I know they were going on down to the Pheasantry. The moment the after-hours drinking started, the mobsters and some really strange mercenaries and Australians and drag queens wandered down from Earls Court, you know, a very odd mixture.

Lovable old Sergeant Pilcher from the drug squad was also taking an interest in the residents of the Pheasantry that summer, but, true to form, it was celebrity rock musicians he was scalp-hunting, rather than genuine criminals. In his tireless campaign to protect the public from rich guitar players with frizzed-out white-boy Afros and a serious Granny Takes a Trip habit, Pilcher came knocking at the Pheasantry in September looking for Eric Clapton. What he found was Martin Sharp from *OZ*, so, in a spirit of improvisation, he nicked him instead. If it was rock stars with a drug problem that he was looking for, he should have walked down the King's Road a few hundred feet, where, as Mick Farren recalled, 'Jim Morrison could be encountered drinking in the Chelsea Potter and swallowing hashish by the quarter-ounce lump while in London for the Doors gigs at the Roundhouse.'

Should Pilcher and his associates have wanted to blend in more effectively when infiltrating the scene, *Daily Mirror* columnist Christopher Ward offered some sage words of advice in August for anyone desperate to speak the very latest King's Road lingo:

> Everyone likes to think he is more In than the next man, of course, and nowhere is this more marked than in Chelsea, that well-known launching pad for freaks, fads and fetishes. [. . .] Hairdressers are now known as crimpers and crimpers are considered to be very 'together cats' just now. No finer honour can be bestowed on a man down the King's Road than to be called a together cat. Are you a together cat? Together cats don't buy records, they buy *sounds*, and they never blow their cool. [. . .] If someone is funny, a together cat will say: 'It's a gas, man', not to be confused with 'It's *the* gas man', who is the bloke who calls to cut off the supply.

Down at the Royal Court, since August 21 they'd been presenting a play called *Trixie and Babs* by former Chelsea Palace *Army Game* scriptwriter John Antrobus – whose previous works also included the perkily titled *You'll Come to Love Your Sperm Test*, and co-writing *The Bed Sitting Room* with Spike Milligan – and then on September 11, it was followed by a Christopher Hampton play, *Total Eclipse*, starring Nigel Hawthorne. At long last, on September 26, the Theatres Act became law, abolishing the centuries-old right of the Lord Chamberlain's office to interfere with the writing and performance of plays, and so, as David Tribe wrote in *Questions of Censorship*, 'the theatre was now free and almost at once celebrated with the nude scene in *Hair*, though such was the lighting that only owls could have been stimulated or shocked'. The Royal Court contented itself with David Cregan's play *The Houses by the Green*, with a small cast including Bob Grant, soon to star in the UK's highest-rating TV programme *On the Buses* alongside Stephen Lewis, who had been treading the boards at Sloane Square himself two months previously in the play *Trixie and Babs*. Another future mainstay of seventies cult TV showed up in a Court production on October 29: Martin Shaw, later of *The Professionals*. The play in question was a revival of John Osborne's *Look Back in Anger*, and in the Mary Ure role was Jane Asher, who had recently become the ex-girlfriend of Paul McCartney.

Who Needs a Record?

As one Beatle couple split up, so had another. John Lennon's marriage to Cynthia was now firmly a thing of the past since John and Yoko had not merely been photographed together walking down the King's Road, but had just been pictured nude on the cover of their latest LP, *Two Virgins*. When asked what the album was like, Apple's press officer apparently commented, 'With a cover like that, who needs a record?' *Private Eye* used the picture on their October 25 cover, with Lennon's crotch covered by a small sign reading 'Member of the British Empire', and a speech bubble coming from his mouth which said, 'It's no good, officer. It won't stand up in court.'

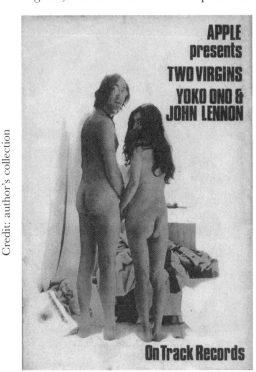

'With a cover like that, who needs a record?'

In case eager pop fans might have concluded from all this that John spent most of his time walking around naked, there was reassuring news in the regular 'Clothes Line' section of weekly music paper *Disc and Music Echo* on November 2 – the key spot for finding out where your favourite stars had been shopping and having beauty treatments, which suggests that some of the staff working in such Chelsea establishments were earning regular backhanders for supplying the details:

Mind boggles at John Lennon in a jump suit. But he bought a black one last week from 'John Crittle's' in Chelsea's King's Road (formerly 'Apple Tailoring') for 10 gns. Dave Clark paid weekly visits to the hairdresser's – Leslie Cavendish – in Chelsea King's Road, London.

Dave just had a shampoo, hand-drier and manicure (£1 5s 6d), but group organist, Mike Smith, had his hair cut, besides shampoo, drying and manicure (£2 12s).

In *Photoplay* magazine, Michael Caine, now the proud owner of a Mayfair apartment with eight rooms, four bathrooms, and twenty-four telephone extensions, described a typical day for the benefit of readers: 'We'll go to somewhere like Alvaro's Club [*sic*] in King's Road and stay there eating and talking until about 1.00am. Then we'll go on to Dolly's, the Speakeasy or Sibylla's and have a dance or two and wind the evening up. That's a usual day for me when I'm not working.'

Meanwhile, a typical day for Malcolm Edwards at that time involved being a student at Goldsmiths College, taking courses in film and photography, while Vivienne Westwood was studying there too, training to become a primary school teacher. However, Michael Rainey – the man who was then occupying the shop premises at number 430 King's Road which were later to become the launch pad from which Westwood and McLaren would unleash the Sex Pistols on an unsuspecting world – decided that autumn that he was tired of running Hung On You, and word began to circulate that the location might be up for grabs. The people who struck a deal to take it over were Tommy Roberts and Trevor Miles, who promptly opened up one of the other great Chelsea stores, Mr Freedom. The choice of name was probably not entirely unconnected with the American film director William Klein's French-made anti-US imperialist feature *Mr Freedom*, with a varied cast including Serge Gainsbourg. It was shot in 1968 and was already being listed in UK film magazines by the summer of that year, and double-page adverts featuring a photo of some of the cast appeared in the press in January 1969, around the time when Roberts and Miles opened their boutique. The film concerns the exploits of a gung-ho superhero character who manages to destroy most of France while attempting to save it from the evils of communism. He, and many of the cast, are given to dressing in cartoon-like costumes in bright, primary colours based on American sports clothing and decorated with stars and stripes, not unlike some of the styles which Mr Freedom was to sell in the boutique.

Better for Rolling Joints On

At 402 King's Road, a few feet away from the shop which Roberts and Miles had just acquired, was one of the other prime outlets that made World's End a favourite destination in those days: Town Records, a shop with a commendable reputation for stocking albums which most other shops had not yet discovered. As Miles recalls, it was situated 'just as the road made that turn, a record shop everyone used to go to'. As for what it was that made it such a good shop, Mick Farren is in no doubt:

> It was because of the import section. That was it, absolutely, one hundred per cent. They'd have them in really fast, you know – *Ruben & the Jets*, or whatever. I mean, it was ridiculous – the first Country Joe album took, I think, thirteen months to come out in England, and they didn't sell one, because everybody had got an import by then. And everybody liked American imports apart from anything else because they didn't have Clarifoil on, they were brighter, they were better for rolling joints on and a million other things.

John Peel would shop for imports at Town Records, and also at the prime West End outlet, One Stop Records in South Molton Street, and he also told me a story about that Country Joe album:

> My favourite LP of that era, really, was and remains Country Joe & the Fish's *Electric Music for the Mind and Body*, and I couldn't understand why it wasn't in the charts, 'cause everybody I knew had a copy of it. But, of course, it was actually that everybody who had a copy of it was somebody that I knew. Several hundred copies had been sold, but I knew everybody who'd got one . . .

On November 4, 1968, a little bit of San Francisco's counterculture came to the Royal Court in the shape of Michael McLure's play *The Beard*, directed by Hollywood actor Rip Torn. As it turned out, this was just a prelude to a visit in December from two other members of the Haight-Ashbury scene: Frisco Pete and Billy Tumbleweed from the San Francisco chapter of the Hell's Angels. George Harrison had invited these visiting representatives to drop by at Apple HQ for a few days and make themselves at home, and for a time, Frisco Pete stayed at Mick Farren's place. Mick told me of his experiences of taking his guest sightseeing in search of Swinging London, and riding down the King's Road on the back of Pete's motorbike: 'It was great fun. He'd pretty much seen the King's Road because of Haight Street. He could appreciate the slight cultural difference, but basically it was another strip. The mind-blowing thing for him was the Houses of Parliament and the tourist stuff, the old stuff. He liked that.'

Mick had been spending a fair amount of time in the King's Road himself that year, recording a debut album with his band, the Deviants, at Sound Techniques in Old Church Street, using £700 fronted by Chelsea heir Nigel Samuel, who lived near Sloane Street. The record was called *Ptooff!* and was engineered by a man called Victor, who liked to be known as 'Sister George'. Also floating about the area that year was a young singer called David Bowie, who lived not far from South Kensington tube in Clareville Grove, where he taped demos of ten songs in 1968 for Chrysalis Music, including a version of the future number one 'Space Oddity', and many of the tunes which were later to be recorded for his album of the same name.

Back in the world of film, Kenneth Hyman, the executive vice president of Warner Bros/Seven Arts in charge of worldwide productions – the man who gave Peckinpah the go-ahead to film *The Wild Bunch* at a time when no-one else in town wanted to know – returned to London from Hollywood and saw some of the footage which Donald Cammell and Nicolas Roeg had been shooting for *Performance*. As he told me in an interview in 1995: 'Yes, we started that, and killed it. I actually axed the movie. I axed it on a trip over here when I saw what had been shot. I saw enough that I didn't like what I saw and had to take a tough decision.'

Cammell and Roeg's film would live to fight another day, eventually emerging in 1970, but although the latter date is the one always ascribed to it in the textbooks, it is actually a picture of how things were in the summer of 1968, for a select few in the counterculture, as Marianne Faithfull wrote: 'The film was truly our *Picture of Dorian Gray*. An allegory of libertine Chelsea life in the late 60s, with its baronial rock stars, wayward jeunesse dorée, drugs, sex and decadence – it preserves the whole era under glass.'

20

'Give booze a chance'

Ticket Stubs to the Chemical Gardens

On January 27, 1969, as the last year of the sixties began, the House of Commons was debating the possible legalisation of cannabis, and *OZ* magazine was reviewing the MC5's new album. The Wootton Committee had delivered a report on cannabis use in the UK, which estimated the number of users at up to a million and recommended legalisation, prompting James Callaghan, the Labour home secretary and future prime minister, to express a desire 'to call a halt to the rising tide of permissiveness'. *OZ* magazine's reviewer was Graham Charnock, and he had a slightly different message for his readers: 'Stoned? Got the album on? Can you get more volume? Hit it. KICK OUT THE JAMS.'

It is hard to be sure what politicians get up to in their leisure time, but it is probably fair to assume that Mr Callaghan was unlikely to have been first in the queue at Town Records in the King's Road for a copy of the album. As it happened, the same issue of *OZ* carried a review of the particular Mothers of Invention album to which Mick Farren had referred, *Cruising With Ruben & The Jets*, but it gave strong hints that writer Bryan Willis might perhaps have been smoking certain substances of which Jim Callaghan disapproved: 'So where are the ticket stubs to the chemical gardens for rusty shit people? Are the ashen faced heroes of all the grooves sitting on the birdshit spattered fence and whistling for true love through the bars of the 7th cage on the left?'

While pondering these and other vital questions of the day, the magazine's readers could also check out the small ads: 'TWO Virgins wish to make contact – Phone/write 3 Savile Row, London W1 01 734 8232. John / Yoko'; and just below that, 'Eight First Class Photos Of Young Men At Play And

In a Relaxed, "Informal" Mood for Only 16/- [. . .] Five Superb Female Models'. The address listed for the company offering the latter enticements was a regular location for all kinds of dodgy outfits: Dryden Chambers, Oxford Street, which coincidentally would later be the home of Glitterbest, the Sex Pistols' management company, proprietor M. McLaren, esq.

We're Not in Kansas Any More

Chelsea police took time off in February from the relentless pursuit of drugged-up rock stars to nail some hardened teenage criminals, who then pleaded guilty at Marlborough Street Magistrates Court to stealing a plastic sauce bottle from the Old Kentucky Restaurant in the King's Road, as the *Kensington News and West London Times* reported: 'PC Laing said that shortly before midnight in King's Road he saw the youths. Murphy had the container and was squeezing the contents at a shop window. Dineen admitted that he had actually taken it from the restaurant.'

This particular restaurant seems to have inadvertently inspired some sort of mini crimewave that year, but once again, the eagle-eyed constabulary were on hand to protect the public in June when a 24-year-old – who lived in Carlyle Square, Chelsea – was seen taking milk from a crate outside the Old Kentucky Restaurant. The case came to the same court, and was detailed in the *Kensington Post* under the heading 'PINTA THIEF WAS THIRSTY': 'Imposing a fine of £5 on a young student who admitted stealing a bottle of milk, Mr Edward Robery the Marlborough Street magistrate commented, "On the face of it this doesn't seem very serious, but so many people are doing it all over the place that the police have to take action."'

In other news, the February 1969 edition of *Films and Filming* printed an advance photo from Tony Richardson's new film of Vladimir Nabokov's novel *Laughter in the Dark* – a Woodfall picture, with an Edward Bond screenplay and, among the cast, a certain John Pearse, formerly of Granny Takes a Trip: 'I was in a film with Anna Karina and Nicole Williamson, Nabokov story . . . It was shot in a house on Holland Park. I was an extra in this thing anyway. I think I'd been in Italy, become interested in cinema . . .'

This meeting with Tony Richardson led directly to the offer of a job at the Royal Court, where they had just opened up the Theatre Upstairs, occupying the space where the old Royal Court Club and Rehearsal Room nightspot used to be. John Pearse, however, was working down in the main theatre with Tony Richardson: 'He gave me a job as his assistant; I was an assistant director on a Chekhov production of *Uncle Vanya*, with Paul Scofield.' Asked whether this then resulted in further work at the Court, Pearse laughs:

No, I got fired . . . I think I felt rather restricted. I felt my talents were not being used to their full ability. What I should have been thinking about was working in the Court Upstairs. Sam Shepard had just started his work there, and that kind of theatre, and the Living Theatre, that was more my metier than Chekhov at that time. Lindsay Anderson was the artistic director there, and you'd be assigned to go and see plays and write a precis and give a report on what you'd seen, and I would never go to anything. Or I would go and write about *Flesh* by Andy Warhol, or a Pink Floyd gig at the Albert Hall, so they kind of tolerated me there, if that, but you know, the idea of Nottingham Rep and bleak Northern towns . . . No, I couldn't hack it at all. I'd come from La Dolce Vita, and I didn't want to go to Nottingham Rep. So I quit, or not, and never had a job again, properly.

Another production still which found its way into the February edition of *Films and Filming* was one showing a naked Anita Pallenberg and Michele Breton having a bath in *Performance*, which was at that time a full year away from securing a release, and it may be that the supplying of some photos to the press was one way of trying to generate some momentum or financial backing to get the thing finished. The policy continued the following month, when a naked and trussed-up James Fox was shown on the same magazine's front cover in the process of being tortured – the excuse being an article inside about 'violence in the cinema'. Also included within were a further three pages of stills from *Performance*, with the film credited to Donald Cammell and that previously unknown female director Nicola Roeg. It might have been struggling to secure a release, but it certainly wasn't lacking in exposure.

Judy Garland and Mickey Deans
in the King's Road arriving for their wedding.

Judy Garland, who had lived in Chelsea at various times earlier in the decade, was now back in town, and chose not only to settle in the area, but also to get married right on the King's Road at Chelsea Registry Office on March 15. To be specific, Judy and her new husband Mickey Deans had already been through a service on January 9 at Marylebone Parish Church, but they were not legally married until they had completed the Chelsea Registry Office ceremony, at which time they also moved into a cottage they had rented at 4 Cadogan Lane, Chelsea. Sadly, it proved to be Judy's last ever address, and she died there a few months later on June 22 of an accidental overdose of sleeping tablets.

No Beating About the Bush

Alan Bates, one of the original 1956 cast of *Look Back in Anger*, was back at the Royal Court, starring in a play by David Storey called *In Celebration*, which opened on April 24. Lindsay Anderson directed, and among the cast were two actors who would be household faces on 1970s TV: James Bolam in the *Likely Lads*, and Fulton Mackay in *Porridge*. (Another *Porridge* mainstay, Richard Beckinsale, would soon appear at the Court on July 18, in the restoration drama *The Double Dealer*.) Anderson at that time. had recently scored one of his biggest critical successes in the cinema, *If . . .*, starring Malcolm McDowell, while Bates had just finished shooting *Women in Love*, directed by Ken Russell, which would be released later in the year.

Meanwhile *The Killing of Sister George*, Robert Aldrich's film made in 1968, with location shooting at the Gateways in Chelsea, was now hitting the cinemas, in various states of repair. The cause of all the controversy was the lesbian sex scene towards the end of the film involving Susannah York and Coral Browne, and it did a fair job of showing up the UK's haphazard censorship system for the unworkable mess that it was. Chris Jones in *Films and Filming* – who identified the Gateways by name in his review and told readers that it was off the King's Road – was encouraged by the film's frankness, although he might perhaps have chosen his words more carefully: 'There is no beating about the bush . . . these women do have sex with each other, and what's more we see them having it.' British Board of Film Censors head John Trevelyan, who usually liked to pose as a libertarian, had a simple solution to this portion of the film, as he explained in his memoirs: 'This scene was easily removable since there was no backing of dialogue or music, so we removed it.' Very simple, four minutes chopped off the running time, and he probably couldn't see why anyone complained, but then, this was the same man who, as David McGillivray once pointed out, saw no problem with chopping Russ Meyer's *Vixen* down from 71 to 47 minutes. The bizarre thing about *The Killing of Sister George* was that the GLC gave it a certificate just for London which deleted only forty seconds, while the local censor in Berkshire passed the film with no cuts at all. So, in answer to the time-honoured question, 'Must we fling this filth at our kids?', the reply would appear to have been, 'Well, it depends where they live.' As for the film's subject matter itself, Chris Jones concluded: 'It will, for many, remain a twilight world of mainly SW3, but Robert Aldrich in bringing *Sister George* to the screen has paved the way for a lot more broad-mindedness on the screen in particular, and in the arts in general.'

On May 7, middle-of-the-road singer Des O'Connor's new single entered the UK charts, entitled 'Dick-a-Dum-Dum (King's Road)', and would eventually reach number fourteen. The song was written for him by former 1950s rock'n'roll singer turned *Carry On* film star Jim Dale, and as the review of the single in the *NME* explained, 'the verse tells of Des's intention to stroll around Chelsea looking for a girl to pick up'. If Des getting frisky raised a few eyebrows, much more disturbing in hindsight was an item in that month's edition of *Rave* magazine, in which Dennis Wilson of the Beach Boys explained to writer Keith Altham about one or two things he found scary: 'Sometimes the Wizard frightens me – Charlie Manson who is another friend of mine who says he is God and the devil! He sings, plays and writes poetry and may be another artist for Brother Records.'

A month later, a new King's Road boutique opened for business – in those days a relatively commonplace event – but the owners and designer behind Stop the Shop had ensured that it would attract national publicity for one reason alone: it revolved, as Clarissa Burden reported in the *Daily Mirror*:

> The main sales floor is circular and rotates with its load of clothes. As you walk in, you step straight onto this roundabout and relax while it carries you around. The idea was thought out by architect Tony Cloughley. The centre floor turns anti-clockwise, going full circle once in one and a half minutes. At night, after the shop closes, the turntable will be speeded up so that there is a continuous rotating display.

Cloughley was also the architect responsible for designing the nearby Chelsea Drug Store and the 1967 King's Road boutique Just Looking.

On July 3, one of the King's Road's dedicated setters of fashion, Brian Jones, died in the swimming pool at his new home, Cotchford Farm. That same day, a launch party was held for the Plastic Ono Band's new single 'Give Peace a Chance' at Chelsea Town Hall, which had been recorded live in John and Yoko's hotel room in Montreal on June 1 during one of their 'bed-ins'. Lennon had talked about these events during a UK television interview he gave on June 15, signally failing to impress one viewer, the *Carry On* star Kenneth Williams, who noted in his diary:

> That Beatle who is married to an Asiatic lady was on the Frost Programme. The man is long haired & unprepossessing, with tin spectacles and this curious nasal Liverpudlian delivery: the appearance is either grotesque or quaint & the overall impression is one of great foolishness. He and his wife are often 'interviewed' from inside *bags* in order to achieve 'objectivity' and they have 'lie-ins' whereby they stay in bed for long periods & allow a certain number of people into the room. I think this man's name is Ringo Starr or something . . .

A short while later, on July 1, John and Yoko were involved in a car crash in Scotland, and so could not make it to the King's Road launch party for 'Give Peace a Chance', which was instead presided over by Ringo and his wife Maureen. The single reached number two in the charts, and was swiftly parodied by the Bonzo Dog Doo-Dah Band in a version called 'Give Booze a Chance', which they recorded in December 1969 for a BBC live session.

Keith Richards and Anita Pallenberg moved into their new home that summer, 3 Cheyne Walk, next door to the house where George Eliot had died, and a short walk from Mick Jagger and Marianne Faithfull's place at number 48, which must have been very convenient for Sergeant Pilcher and the local drug squad when they were doing their rounds. Keith bought the place for £50,000 from a member of the Tory government, and the bed which he and Anita slept in was the one which had been used during the filming of *Performance* for the love scenes between Anita and Mick.

Nudes on the Stage

The current state of the supposed Permissive Society, both in the UK and in America, was summarised in the results of a Gallup Poll, and reported in the *Daily Telegraph* of July 21, 1969 as follows:

> The survey, and a similar one made by Gallup in the United States in May, showed the British as considerably more permissive. While 71 per cent of Britons said they would not find pictures of nudes in magazines objectionable, 73 per cent of Americans said they would. Nudity on the stage has more opponents than supporters on both

sides of the Atlantic, but here again, the British are less censorious. Only 59 per cent of Britons would object, compared with 81 per cent of Americans. American disapproval applied almost equally throughout all levels of society. But in Britain 52 per cent of men and 62 per cent of young people did not object to nudes on the stage.

If that was how permissiveness was viewed across the UK generally, in Chelsea, so the popular wisdom went, things were much more relaxed. As if to confirm this impression, 1969 saw the publication of an interesting large-format photo book called *Young London: Permissive Paradise*, with pictures by Frank Habicht, and 'Views on the Scene' written by Heather Cremonesi (in favour) and Robert Bruce (very much against). There were ninety-one full-page pictures, each with an ironic or whimsical caption, drawn from 250 rolls of film shot over seven months, and of those printed, fifteen were views of the action in the King's Road. Clearly, if you were looking for that elusive thing called 'permissiveness', this was supposed to be a good place to start. Mary Quant's Bazaar was pictured, as was the Chelsea Student Carnival, with shots of stripping students in the King's Road. Heather Cremonesi's introductory essay traced the rise of Swinging London back to: '[. . .] an older generation of "rebels with causes", of Angry Young Man vintage, the Dick Lesters, the John Michaels, the John Stephens, the Mary Quants, the Time-Lifers, the record company boys of greying eminence.'

Some parts of the King's Road area were still a relatively cheap option for young people seeking accommodation, as is clear from Cremonesi's reference to 'the Chelsea-Kensington-King's Road shopping secretary in her bed-sit and share-a-flat', and it was also one of the best places to observe the late-sixties all-purpose freak lifestyle as it was lived and marketed:

Flower power, flower people, love people, hippies bearing flowers and love buttons, heralding their presence with prayer-bells, incense and mirth, bask in the reflected glory of the bright windows down the King's Road boutiques, in the yellows and blues of 'Count-Down', the cool 'thirties silverings of Drug Store, the Bauhaus shell of Just Looking.

The contrary position in *Young London: Permissive Paradise* was set out by Robert Bruce, who pointed out quite usefully that when the mini-skirt had first become accepted in London, it would still have been a rare sight indeed in surrounding towns a mere hour's train journey away, but that by the time of writing it had become international: 'But now, finally, it has arrived everywhere, even apparently to the north coast of Iceland. London sets the pace not only for Britain but sometimes for the whole of the Western World.' As for the wider question of whether London's permissiveness was a benefit or a curse, he felt that it was probably the latter:

The new freedoms have become a burden in themselves. The relaxation of the old rules and boundaries has left many people feeling insecure, and some of us actually frightened. [. . .] Describing the work of Andy Warhol, the pop artist, someone once wrote that his talent was for 'photographing depravity and calling it the truth'. Frank Habicht has photographed the truth – and it wouldn't be hard to call it depraved. Paradise? More like a vision of hell.

Down in Cornwall, according to the *Telegraph*, some local residents were equally unimpressed with the beautiful people, although they seemed to be under the strange impression that the bongo-banging days of the late fifties had not ended, and that the place was supposedly awash with disciples of Kerouac: 'A petition signed by 2,321 residents and holidaymakers at St. Ives, Cornwall, was handed to the Mayor, Ald. Archie Knight, during the weekend. It calls for tighter vagrancy laws to rid the town of beatniks. [. . .] Mr Eric Kemp, one of the petition organisers, said yesterday that the problem of beatniks was "a national sickness".'

Play My Fucking Record

There may or may not have been beatniks in Cornwall, but on British TV that July, there seemed to be virtually nothing whatever to watch except endless programmes about the Apollo moon landings, as the normal television schedules were swept aside to accommodate hours of grainy live broadcasts accompanied by the crackling sound of NASA technicians in Houston talking to themselves. Still, at least they served to introduce to British viewers the song which David Bowie had demoed in his bedroom in South Kensington the previous year, 'Space Oddity'. It gave him his first hit, reaching number five in the charts in September. Bowie also made a half-hour promotional film called *Love You Till Tuesday*, and sang the song wearing his silver Major Tom suit made by Dandie Fashions in the King's Road. Jonathan King had theoretically managed to go one better by getting a tape of his song 'Everyone's Gone to the Moon' on board Apollo 11 itself. The trouble was, the astronauts never played it on air, as King told Michael Wale in a 1972 interview: 'I managed to get it onto the actual spaceship on the tape that was going to the moon. [. . .] They went up there and stood on the fucking thing, and as he got off and said one giant step for mankind and all that crap I thought, "Don't come with all these awful truisms, play my fucking record, I want a plug." And they never did.'

King may have regarded the Apollo missions as just a ruinously expensive failed promotional device for plugging a four-year-old record, but other people were a little more enthusiastic, including one of the contributors to *Mayfair* magazine's August 1969 issue, sci-fi writer and Chelsea resident Roland Winchester, who was described as follows: 'A 32-year-old bachelor and confirmed space-travel addict. [. . .] He lives in Chelsea, "within a mini-skirt's flip from the King's Road", and drives a decrepit Alfa. [. . .] "I am presently engaged on a story about the Langevin paradox," he tells us airily. "The hardest part is making it sexy as well."'

It is possible that Roland might have run into a woman called Nikki, that month's Miss Mayfair, as readers were assured that they could 'see her in the King's Road any Saturday morning, shopping for her favourite outfits. [. . .] She has a preference for lush, dark fabrics and the tiniest of mini-skirts'. On the other hand, the two of them might both have encountered a Japanese film crew that summer who had come to the King's Road to shoot a picture called *Hi Hi London*, telling the story of a pop group from Japan 'who sell their souls to the devil in order to visit the Mecca of pop'. While the latter may have been fiction, the documentary makers were still busy down Chelsea way, and August saw the cinema release of a forty-eight-minute documentary by Norman Cohen called *The London Nobody Knows*, which inevitably included some footage of a part which almost everyone by now seemed to know – the King's Road.

We Got Conned

On August 9, 1969, Roman Polanski received a phone call at his London home, 95 West Eaton Place Mews, telling him that his wife Sharon Tate had been murdered, along with several of their friends, at his Los Angeles house in Benedict Canyon by the Manson Family. In the September 15 edition of *LIFE* magazine – whose cover article was devoted to 'The Phenomenal Woodstock Happening' – Polanski himself, understandably still completely dazed and under incredible stress, was interviewed by Thomas Thompson sitting on the porch of the Benedict Canyon house, next to its white front door which still showed the signs of the word 'Pig' that had been written in the blood of one of the victims, Voityck Frokowski. Thompson's article felt the need to point out that Sharon 'had the legs that mini-skirts were created for' and that she was 'buried in a Pucci print mini'.

Later that month, also in *LIFE* magazine, a two-page advert for ITT highlighted the fact that the UK's most famous new passenger ship relied upon the company's satellite guidance systems for navigation, and began with the words: 'The great new Cunard liner, Queen Elizabeth II, is as bright, mod and advanced as anything Britain can offer except, maybe, King's Road, Chelsea, in London.'

John Lennon, meanwhile, was being interviewed by Miles on September 23 and 24 for an upcoming *OZ* magazine feature, talking about another part of the hippie dream that had turned sour:

> Apple was a manifestation of Beatle naiveté, collective naiveté, and we said we're going to do this and help everybody and all that. And we got conned just on the subtlest and the most grossest level. We didn't really get approached by the best artists, or any of the recording thing, we got all the bums from everywhere – they'd been thrown out from everywhere else.

Someone else who was expressing reservations – this time in a much more pronounced and extended fashion – was Christopher Booker, *Private Eye*'s first editor, who published a book called *The Neophiliacs* in October 1969 which took a hammer to many of the prized concepts of the sixties generation. The title was a word of his own coinage, meaning people who were obsessed with anything new. In an introduction which Booker wrote for a 1992 edition of the book, he recalled that many reviewers treated it harshly on first publication: 'In the *Sunday Times* Cyril Connolly expressed lofty astonishment that I had dared to question the significance of so many cultural icons of the age. "Would we have been any happier (or wiser if you like)," he asked, "without Tynan, Frost, Satire, *Queen*, the colour supplements and the Beatles? Certainly not."'

The Neophiliacs provided a fascinating alternative view of the sixties revolution, written by someone who had started out as a leading light of the satire boom but then revised his opinions radically somewhere around the middle of the decade. However, it also consigned much that was good to the dustbin, and had a little of the flavour of books by people who have found a new religion and want everyone else to see the light. It is not surprising that Booker goes on to say that it was not only championed by Malcolm Muggeridge but also that part of the book had been written while the author was staying at Muggeridge's house.

In the same month that *The Neophiliacs* was published, the ubiquitous Mr Muggeridge and a regular Sunday night religious discussion programme which he chaired were moved out of the way to make space for a new television comedy show, *Monty Python's Flying Circus*, which was first broadcast on October 5. When news of this change to the schedules was first announced back in August, the *Daily Telegraph* weighed in with a pre-emptive attack on a programme they had not yet seen: 'Is this [the pursuit of ratings] a sufficient reason for dropping that programme with glee, and substituting comedy shows which the BBC announces as "Nutty, zany and oddball"?'

Muggeridge, when not chairing religious discussions, had not only expressed the opinion that rape might be preferable to the publication of smutty books back in 1964, but in 1968 had resigned as rector of Edinburgh University in protest at the student requests that the campus health centre prescribe contraceptive pills, saying that he would feel more sympathy for them if they blew up Edinburgh cathedral. The *Daily Telegraph* might have been better occupied asking what a man like that was doing with a high-profile TV chat show in the first place. Some parts of UK society might have been described as permissive in 1969, but there were definite battle lines being drawn, and the coming decade would see many a conflict in that area.

Hippie Atrocities

Back in the King's Road, you could go and see Hawkwind playing a gig in the basement of the Pheasantry on October 18, the noise of which would presumably have filtered up through the floorboards while Germaine Greer was upstairs in her room, attempting to write her new book, *The Female Eunuch*. While she was working on that, elsewhere Tim Rice and Andrew Lloyd Webber were writing something called *Jesus Christ Superstar*, for which they would eventually need a woman to sing the part of Mary Magdalene. Yvonne Elliman turned out to fit the bill, and she was discovered one night by Lloyd Webber, singing at the Pheasantry.

In November there was the new edition of *OZ* magazine, with a front cover that could have been purpose-built to enrage Mr Muggeridge, featuring a photo showing various half-naked freaks skinning up and a headline which read:

HIPPIE ATROCITIES
MOTHERS – WHERE IS YOUR DAUGHTER TONIGHT?
THE FULL *SHOCK STORY* FROM SIBERIA TO
SCUNTHORPE

As it turned out, *The Times* reported that someone's eighteen-year-old – the 'daughter of rich parents', as their article phrased it – was at the

Central Criminal Court that month being prosecuted on trafficking charges alongside two men friends. The accompanying headline, 'Teenage Girl In "Gigantic Drug Plot"', sounded more like the kind of thing a scandal rag like the *News of the World* might have come up with, and indeed, the language used at the trial by Sir Harold Cassel defending one of the male accused was equally lurid, claiming that his client had been 'deflected by the delights of "Sin Street", namely the King's Road'.

At the Royal Court, they planned to see out the decade with a Christmas show called *The Three Musketeers Ride Again.* One of the stars was Rachel Roberts, who had met her husband Rex Harrison at the Court back at the start of the decade when they were both appearing in a Chekhov play. Now, in the middle of rehearsals on December 19, and without warning her, Harrison instructed his lawyers to issue the following statement: 'In view of certain rumours that have begun to circulate about his marriage to Rachel Roberts, Rex Harrison has authorised me to announce that he and his wife are living separately and apart.' Royal Court director Anthony Page met her shortly afterwards in the foyer of the Royal Court Hotel on Sloane Square, and thought that she looked very ill. Rachel told him she had just swallowed fifty aspirins, but astonishingly, claimed that she was alright and did not need a doctor. Later that night, Page received a phone call from Lindsay Anderson, saying that Roberts was in hospital.

I Got Stoned and I Missed It

New in the shops for Christmas was a pop annual aimed at Radio Luxembourg listeners, called *FAB 208 1970*, in which there was an interview, presumably conducted sometime in the summer, with the man who had most recently appeared onstage with his band at Altamont on December 6. Asked by journalist John King whether the Stones would be following the Beatles' lead and forming an organisation like Apple, Mick Jagger replied, 'I'm not interested in being a shopkeeper.' As for the prospect of growing old, the 25-year-old singer offered the following useful health advice: 'If you can stop your body falling apart physically you have won half the battle. If you eat any old rubbish like lots of potatoes and take no exercise, then you end up looking like a potato – all knobbly knees and bloated.'

Altamont, of course, is usually held up as the point at which the rot set in for the swinging sixties dream, but in fairness, Woodstock has a lot to answer for as well. The latter event was thrown together by organisers who thought that you could invite almost half a million people to sit in a sea of mud for three days with just a handful of toilets, totally inadequate washing and catering facilities, and roads jammed for miles around, watching a selection of celebrities moving around on a stage in the far distance playing through a sound system which these days would be considered pathetically small for a festival. As a journalist in the *NME* once tellingly remarked about Woodstock half a decade later, 'When the wind changed, you could smell the shit of half a million people.'

Rock'n'roll had started out in the clubs and halls, where the live experience hits you right between the eyes, and, with luck, you might even be able to see the facial expressions of the people playing the music. Woodstock was not the first big outdoor festival, but the huge publicity it generated – especially on account of the success of the documentary film of it that followed – helped encourage a movement of music out into huge arenas and fields, in which the bands onstage rarely even get a soundcheck, and the main objective seems to be to cram in as many thousands of people as possible, forming a captive audience to which you can then sell overpriced beer and burgers. Years later all of the assembled then have the pleasure of desperately trying to recall a single one of the bands supposedly present that day, while perhaps idly humming to themselves Shel Silverstein's immortal song from 1972, 'I Got Stoned and I Missed It'.

Still, let's give the last word about the swinging sixties to Frank Norman, the ex-convict author of the excellent Soho clubland memoir *Stand On Me* and the book of the musical *Fings Ain't What They Used to Be*, who had been affectionately sent up in the 1962 *Private Eye* parody of *About Town* magazine as the alleged writer of *Arnty's Froat's So Bleeding Tuff it Blunt Me Razer*. In 1969, Norman published a very fine, idiosyncratic book about London, called, with admirable directness, *Norman's London*, in which he wrote the following:

> Of late I have taken to visiting King's Road Chelsea, of a Saturday morning, to drink of course at the Markham Arms and ogle the stunning mini-skirted girls as they parade up and down without destination in the company of their narcissistic boy friends, with lank medusa hair, frilly shirts and gormless expressions. I feel old, ugly, fat and lonely. I long to speak to them but lack the courage. I am inhibited by my thoughts and their appearance. [. . .] Since that wildly inaccurate article in *TIME* magazine about 'Swinging London' I have searched for it ceaselessly as though it were the Holy Grail, but have found little evidence of it. [. . .] There is a good deal of verbiage – talked and written – these days about the permissive society and the amoral younger generation. When, I should like to know, were young people not amoral and permissive?

Part Four

Oh Bondage Up Yours

21

'Raking around in the gutter'

That One Which Goes 'Yeah, Yeah, Yeah'

As the new decade began, if you were looking to pitch new drama ideas at the BBC, there were certain subjects which it was best to avoid, according to some advice from Andrew Osborn, the corporation's 'Head of Series, television drama', published in *The Writer's Guide 1970*:

> A word about some of the things in which we are definitely not interested: The 'Kitchen Sink', sex, drugs, politics, the 'Permissive Society', militant students, foul language, violence, offence against existing tastes, blasphemy, denigration of existing societies, sects, groups or institutions, and so on. In other words, there is endless drama without raking around in the gutter.

All of which begs the question what exactly they *were* looking for, since if you believed what people like Mary Whitehouse had been saying, their entire output since about 1962 had consisted of virtually nothing but items drawn from the above list. In fact, in terms of 'permissiveness' in the media and arts generally, the sixties were mild compared to the first half of the seventies, as numerous film-makers and magazine and book publishers woke up to the fact that they could now depict things which even three or four years previously would have landed them in court.

The King's Road had its Mr Freedom boutique, but in March on a visit to America, the Archbishop of Canterbury gave a press conference in which he claimed that teenagers were being led to damnation by permissiveness and pop culture generally, and the King's Road in particular, as *The Times* reported under the headline 'The False Freedom': 'The Archbishop of Canterbury, Dr Ramsey, said in New York today that there had been a breakdown in the moral values of young people in England and other Western countries. Young people, he said, enjoyed a false freedom of doing only what they liked. This freedom was typified by such things as the fashions of King's Road, Chelsea.'

All of which, coming from a man who habitually wore a dress in public, showed a distinct lack of self-awareness. David Bowie tried wearing one that year on the UK cover of his new LP *The Man Who Sold the World*, and his American record company were so uptight about the image that they replaced it with a cartoon. As it happened, what Bowie called his man-dress was by London designer Michael Fish, who had made the androgynous white outfit Mick Jagger wore for the 1969 Rolling Stones Hyde Park concert, and was also responsible for Sean Connery's dress shirts in *Dr No*. It was purchased not in the King's Road but from the designer's own Mr Fish boutique in Clifford Street, near the more traditional home of British tailoring, Savile Row.

And what of Antonioni, the man who had come to London to check out the groovy people, and delivered a film called *Blow-Up*, containing some brief full-frontal nudity? In January 1970, people were still trying to figure out what his 1969 film *Zabriskie Point* might actually mean. He told *LOOK* magazine, 'America has changed me [. . .] I have even changed my view of sexual love. In my other films, I looked upon sex as a disease of love,' which may have helped clarify things, but probably just added to the confusion.

Christopher Lee, still living in Cadogan Square, north of the King's Road, was certainly no fan of the permissive society, as he explained to me: 'For somebody like me, this was the beginning of a lowering of standards.' As it happened, he had a new film in the cinemas in the spring of 1970 which had brought him into contact with some of the leading lights of the sixties music revolution. *The Magic Christian*, based on a novel by Terry Southern, featured a varied cast of celebrities including Peter Sellers, Ringo Starr, Raquel Welch and Spike Milligan. As a result, Christopher Lee told me, he encountered the Beatles:

Yes, I met them during the shooting of *The Magic Christian* at Twickenham Studios. I believe that was the only time I ever met them. It may sound incredible, but I don't recall being very aware of their music during the 1960s. I assume I must have heard them. The only one I remember hearing is that one which goes 'Yeah, yeah, yeah'. I never followed the careers of those kinds of musicians. I wasn't aware of the Rolling Stones. In fact, the only rock musician I saw was David Bowie. He gave a concert in Los Angeles, sometime in the mid-seventies, and he invited me and my family along. I'd met him a few years earlier with a view to making a record together some time. The only problem was that we could never quite decide what kind of music it ought to be. That would have been some time in the early seventies. He was charming. I liked him very much.

As it turned out, following on from Christopher's appearance that year for Hammer in *Scars of Dracula*, the company would then start planning the Count's next appearance – in a modern-day setting this time – which resulted in a screenplay being written in 1971 by Don Houghton for a self-consciously groovy vampire film tentatively titled *Dracula Today*, based in the King's Road. Houghton later went on to create the long-running Scottish TV soap opera *Take the High Road*.

Only Sold Through Ironmonger's Shops

The Beatles themselves were in the process of disintegrating as 1970 began, with Paul McCartney secretly working on a solo album, and producer Phil Spector at Abbey Road sifting through the tapes for the upcoming *Let It Be* album – editing, overdubbing and splicing in order to create the version which would eventually be issued in the UK on May 8. John Peel told me what it was like running into the Beatles around that time:

John Peel receives *Melody Maker*'s 'Best Disc Jockey' award, 18 September 1969

We used to know John and Yoko, before they went off to New York. Obviously, your relationship with them was compromised by the fact that he was a Beatle. You couldn't say, 'Come up to our house,' or 'Let's go to the match on Saturday.' Couldn't be done. And you think, 'What a life . . .' Obviously, lovely to have the money and so forth, but the rest of it, a nightmare, really. It was really interesting talking to him, because one of the last Beatles LPs had just been released, and he'd sent somebody out from Apple to go and buy the weekly music papers, and I said, 'Well why do you need to do that?' and he said, 'Look, you couldn't stop the record selling, even if you only sold it through ironmonger's shops, it would still go to the top of the charts, but I like to read the critics, because that way I find out what my songs are about . . .' Again, it was the era of Richard Williams and people like that, who could see far more in these records than the people who'd actually made them. It was Richard Williams who famously reviewed the tone on the B-side of a single-sided white label, maybe it was the John and Yoko album . . .

As the Beatles were splitting up, someone whose showbusiness career went back to the late forties was onstage at the Royal Court, making something of a comeback. Diana Dors was starring, together with her husband Alan Lake, in a comedy by Donald Howarth called *Three Months Gone*. This role brought her some of the best reviews of her career, not to mention flattering visits from Laurence Olivier backstage, prompting Diana to comment, as Damon Wise reports, 'When you've done a lifetime of cheese-cake, the status you get from a well-done kiss from Olivier is something.' Her triumph was more than slightly marred, however, by husband Alan getting into a vicious pub brawl in the company of singer Leapy Lee Graham midway through the run, which eventually led to him being jailed for eighteen months.

On March 15, Hawkwind were back in the area, gigging at Chelsea College this time, while a former mod from Stoke Newington who had recently shortened the name of his band from sixteen letters to a more manageable four was talking to Pete Frame of *Zigzag* magazine in March, and had clearly been shopping on the King's Road: 'I've been playing on David Bowie's new record, because I really dig David. We have a very good head thing but we don't make love. I wear chicks' shoes, because they look nice, and because you can't get men's in green and silver and purple.'

His last single, 'King of the Rumbling Spires', had managed one week at number forty-four in the charts, but in October 1970, Marc Bolan and his band T. Rex released a song called 'Ride a White Swan', ushering in the glam rock revolution, at which point the King's Road would be seeing an awful lot more of him. World's End was the place where Marc and many of the early seventies rock stars went to find the clothes they might wear on that week's *Top of the Pops*, or onstage. As styles gradually made the transition from hippie chic to glam flash with plenty of silk and satin, the likes of Mr Freedom, Alkasura and Granny Takes a Trip were ready to supply the goods. However, there was also another strand of fashion which Tommy Roberts at Mr Freedom had been developing, which would prove to be the initial inspiration for McLaren and Westwood when they would eventually become King's Road shop traders themselves the following year: Teddy boy clothing. A little over a decade after it had last been hitting the headlines – after years in which kaftans and bells were considered in some quarters to be essential items of a gentleman's wardrobe – fingertip drape jackets, velvet collars, narrow trousers and brothel-creepers now looked positively revolutionary. Tommy Roberts explained to Paul Gorman the effect his fifties styles had at that time:

> We got a lot of publicity because it was sexy, it was new, it was bright. There'd be Peter Sellers coming in taking photographs, Marc and June Bolan buying stuff, and Mick Jagger used to drop by every Saturday just to hang out. At the time, the Stones weren't doing very much and it looked like it all might be over, so he seemed like he was at a loose end. He just used to come in and talk about what he was going to do.

Another customer was singer Nick Drake, who had been back at the Sound Techniques studio in Old Church Street recording his next album *Bryter Later*, the sessions for which also featured members of Fairport Convention and John Cale. 1970 was quite a year at Sound Techniques: Fairport Convention cut their LP *Full House*, with Joe Boyd producing; Steeleye Span recorded their debut album, *Hark! The Village Wait*, produced by their manager, Sandy Robertson; Elton John and Linda Peters (who later became Linda Thompson) sang vocal on eleven demos for Joe Boyd's Witchseason Music Publishers, consisting of songs written by Nick Drake, John Martyn, Beverly Martyn, Ed Carter and Mike Heron; and John and Beverly Martyn recorded their LP *The Road to Ruin*, produced by Joe Boyd. The latter album sessions were not a particularly happy experience, according to John Martyn's later recollections – he had memories of Boyd reading newspapers during them – but, as can be seen, the selection of talent passing through that one studio that year was remarkable.

Mick Jagger Thought It Was Rubbish

While the singer of the Rolling Stones was browsing the clothes at Mr Freedom, the film he had shot with Tony Richardson out in Australia, *Ned Kelly*, for which he unwisely sported a beard, was being given its first press previews. Filming had not been a happy experience, what with initial Australian resentment at an Englishman playing their national hero, followed swiftly by the terrible shock of Marianne Faithfull's attempted suicide. To cap it all, the press did not really like the film, and neither did he, as was made clear later in the year by a much-mocked advertising campaign run by the *Guardian* newspaper, designed to establish the independence of their critical views: 'Mick Jagger Thought It Was Rubbish,' said the adverts. 'The Guardian Thought It Was Great.' Mick was right.

Michael Caine, meanwhile, appeared in the March edition of *Photoplay* expressing his views on that very sixties class of people, the swingers: 'Caine says: "If my daughter showed signs of becoming a swinger like some of the girls I've seen around, I'd clamp down so hard she'd hardly get out of the house!" And believe us, Mike Caine has seen plenty of those swingers.'

Caine's old flatmate, Terence Stamp, also issued a press release that month, predicting a turn away from permissiveness: 'A new Victorian era is about to hit Britain. There will soon be a return to puritanical living and behaviour in this country, and its influence will spread worldwide. It must happen, today's permissive society allows anything. I know I get bored watching all the non-stop battering of sex during plays and in some films.'

Round about the time when Caine's comments were hitting the news-agents, the *OZ* street sellers in the King's Road were touting copies of issue number 26, which carried the following message on the cover that the law courts would later claim was designed to corrupt all sorts of people's sons and daughters: 'Want to edit *OZ*? Are you under 18? See page 46.' This was the innocent offer to let a selection of schoolchildren help edit an issue of the magazine, and it eventually landed three of the *OZ* team in the dock at the Old Bailey. For the moment they were unaware of the trouble looming, and in issue 27, *Acid OZ* – the one where they spread the rumour that if you chewed the corner of a certain page you'd get high – the magazine ran the following update: 'Any teenybopper readers who missed the historic meeting and would like to help create *OZ*, please telephone our office. The shared ambition of those schoolboys who turned up was to "clean up *OZ*", with the exception of one 12-year-old who planned to include "more gay news".'

Here One Day and Gone the Next

On April 18, the ever-active Hawkwind were back playing at the Pheasantry again, while in Chelsea Town Hall a Quorum fashion show was taking place, with the likes of Amanda Lear modelling Ossie Clark designs, and one girl needing to be dragged off the catwalk because she apparently could not bear to step back out of the limelight. The Automobile Association published their new edition of the *AA London Guide*, which – along with their customary information about garages, car parks and parking meters – also contained some words of advice about the merits of the King's Road as a tourist destination. Ballroom dancing was listed as a regular attraction at the Chelsea Town Hall, and the Chelsea Potter was described as follows: 'Popular modernized pub associated with the nearby Chelsea potteries. Young clientele. A wide and unusual range of spirits. Snacks. Watneys.'

As for boutiques, the guide listed Count Down, Top Gear and Granny Takes a Trip, but made no particular comment about them, seeming to regard this type of shop as something only slightly more permanent than traffic jams or buskers: 'The problem about recommending particular ones arises from the very nature of the boutiques themselves, i.e. that they are quite literally here one day and gone the next.' It was as if by this stage, everyone had heard of this thing called Swinging London and therefore felt the need to mention it – a road sign for the by now terminally unhip Carnaby Street was prominently displayed on the cover of the guide – but people were still not necessarily sure where to find it.

Granny Takes a Trip was hardly 'here one day and gone the next' – by 1970 it had already been trading for half a decade – but the original trio that had founded the shop in 1965 had fragmented when John Pearse left in '68, and now Nigel Waymouth and Sheila Cohen decided to call it a day, signing over the shop and the name to Freddie Horninck, who brought in Gene Krell and his partner Marty to run it, as Nigel Waymouth explained to Paul Gorman:

> They were very nice guys, but I didn't go in there again because they never changed it. Also, I was pissed off because the local council told them to take the car down, and instead of making a scene about it, like we would have done, they just complied. I thought, 'Oh, you've lost it.' Of course, by then smack had moved in and it plodded on.

Giving Pornography a Dirty Name

Down at the Royal Court, starting on June 17, director Lindsay Anderson rounded up some serious theatrical muscle with a cast which included John Gielgud and Ralph Richardson in a production of *Home* by David Storey. It also featured Dandy Nichols, most famous for playing the long-suffering wife of Warren Mitchell's Alf Garnett in the sitcom *Till Death Us Do Part* alongside Mr 'Randy Scouse Git' himself, Tony Booth. A slightly different kind of theatrical presentation was being rehearsed that month just along the King's Road in the gymnasium of the Duke of York's regiment, which might have been more to the taste of Booth's onscreen alter ego. In those quiet surroundings cast members were busily honing their acts for the long-awaited London opening of Ken Tynan's erotic revue, *Oh! Calcutta!*, having already been turned out of a previous rehearsal space after the hall's management expressed fears that by accepting rent they might be liable to charges of living off immoral earnings. Now, in their new King's Road home with the Ministry of Defence as their landlord, rehearsals went ahead as planned and the review, which one New York critic described as 'the kind of show to give pornography a dirty name', finally opened at the Roundhouse in July. Mary Whitehouse's National Viewers' and Listeners' Association predictably attempted to bring an obscenity prosecution against it, but the DPP refused to press charges, whereupon Lady Birdwood from the NVALA wrote to MPs asking for their help, describing this filth in some detail. Labour MP Tom Driberg wrote back with fine sarcasm, saying that his secretary had been 'at first shocked and then fascinated by your description of *Oh! Calcutta!* [. . .] Please send me six more copies [. . .] as I know that some of my friends and constituents would be pleased to have them.'

Gerald Hamilton, said to be Christopher Isherwood's inspiration for the title character of the novel *Mr Norris Changes Trains*, died on June 9, and his obituary in *The Times* noted that he had been a resident of Chelsea: 'In his last years, Hamilton lived something less than the *dolce vita* in a bedsittter above the Good Earth restaurant in the King's Road, Chelsea. "Better to be above the good earth than below it," he said.'

The film of *Woodstock*, co-edited by a certain Martin Scorsese, hit the London cinemas that summer, with pompous adverts that declared: 'This time the young people opened the eyes of the older people and perhaps for the very first time, made them see what was happening. This time the earth was strangely consecrated by the boys and girls who came from all over the USA.'

Mostly, according to onsite medical officers, the ground was being 'strangely consecrated' by broken glass, jagged empty tins and anything else that the boys and girls could throw away, so that, as *LIFE* reported, 'cut feet were the major medical problem'. *Woodstock* was not the only cinema representation of the US hippie lifestyle doing the rounds in London just then – *Alice's Restaurant*, Arthur Penn's film based on a song by Arlo Guthrie, had arrived a month or so earlier, prompting the film's distributors to organise a series of tie-in competitions at various cinemas, at which people were invited to show up in their finest 'mod gear'. Hence the September issue of *ABC Film Review* carried an article headlined 'Two Trendy Triumphs', complete with a photo of the lucky pair of winners of the contest held just across the river in Battersea Pleasure Gardens standing next to a sign saying 'Hi There!! Groovy People'. The three celebrity judges – film stars Pamela Franklin and Ron Moody, and Radio One DJ Tony Blackburn – understandably look like they would rather be somewhere else.

Can You Spare Some Cutter, Me Brother?

On September 8, 1970, the Chelsea home of the Attorney General, Sir Peter Rawlinson, was bombed by the Angry Brigade, an attack apparently subjected to something of a news blackout in the press. Following their normal habit, the Brigade then issued a statement, called Communiqué 5, which referred to this and other recent attacks: 'We are not mercenaries. We attack property not people. Carr, Rawlinson, Waldron would all be dead if we had wished.' Six years later the King's Road would become famous for a song about anarchy, but this was something else entirely.

Another person stirring up a certain amount of violence – albeit on the cinema screen – was Stanley Kubrick, whose last film, *2001: A Space Odyssey*, had been a nice quiet film for the counterculture to sit back and drop acid to. This time, however, he was intent on realising Andrew Loog Oldham and David Bailey's mid-sixties dream of filming the Anthony Burgess novel, *A Clockwork Orange*. News items appeared in the press in October to the effect that this would be his next project, and by November 1970 shooting had begun, with a couple of key location scenes taking place in the vicinity of the King's Road. The 'Musik Bootick' where Alex picks up two girls who are eating ice creams before inviting them to his home for a high-speed orgy is actually the Chelsea Drug Store. Then, in the latter part of the film, when Alex has been let out of prison, supposedly cured of his addiction to ultraviolence, he is walking along the Chelsea Embankment just by the Albert Bridge when he meets a tramp who asks him, 'Can you spare

some cutter, me brother?' This turns out to be the same tramp that Alex
and his droogs attacked at the start of the film. When the old man recog-
nises him, he drags Alex off to be set upon by his mates, who are waiting
in the pedestrian tunnel which runs under the northern end of the bridge.
As Alex's voice-over says: 'Then there was like a sea of dirty smelly old
men, trying to get at your Humble Narrator, with their feeble rookers and
horny old claws.'

Alex is seen being given a thorough pasting, right underneath the spot
where Oliver Reed and his beatniks were standing a decade earlier in the
most famous still from the film *The Party's Over*.

Just to prove that cinema in the seventies was determined to be a much
grittier proposition – at least until Spielberg and Lucas got hold of it in the
second half of the decade and made a fortune pitching films at eight-year-olds
– Michael Caine was up in Newcastle shooting a film adaptation of Ted
Lewis's British pulp masterpiece *Jack's Return Home*, which would be released
the following year under the title *Get Carter*. By way of research, Caine conducted
lengthy taped interviews with a genuine London gangster, edited highlights
of which had appeared earlier in the year in an article in *Club* magazine called
'Inside the Mind of a Villain'. Having questioned the man about violence,
jail, and methods of earning money ('my pension is my jukeboxes'), Caine
then asks his anonymous role model if he has ever been married: 'Do me a
favour, Mickey. No, I've got a smashing flat, near the King's Road, and pull
fantastic birds. Not any old slags. It's got to be a bit special. I think I've had
birds of every nationality – and I've never been abroad.'

Given that Caine's research had consisted of interviewing a King's Road
villain, it is perhaps appropriate that when filming commitments prevented
him from attending *Get Carter*'s 1971 Newcastle premiere, he shot a special
message to be shown to that audience, while standing on a pavement in
Chelsea as the number 11 bus went past, its front decked out with posters
for the film: 'Hello ladies and gentlemen,' said Caine. 'I'm speaking to you
from the King's Road in Chelsea, London, and down here on all the buses
it says "CAINE IS CARTER" . . .'

Fuck That Drab Shit, Lets Get This On

In November 1970, after four years of living at the Pheasantry and providing
psychedelic illustrations for *OZ* and for countless thousands of student bedsit
walls, illustrator Martin Sharp decided to pack up and head back home to
Australia. Richard Neville described sitting in Cafe Picasso on the King's
Road with him, and Sharp's feelings that the scene was not the same any

more: "'King's Road has turned into Carnaby Street. The musicians, poets, graphic designers . . . all gone." Eric Clapton had fled to his new house in the country, in his new Bentley. "It's all show and no substance . . ."'

Another resident of the Pheasantry was currently doing publicity for the book she had written while living there. The November 1970 edition of *Penthouse* magazine contained an interview with Germaine Greer, discussing some of the ideas presented in *The Female Eunuch*, and providing a few insights into life on the King's Road: 'I live among musicians who are supposed to be the prophets of the new agenda and their sexual prejudice is just so vile you wouldn't believe it. A chick digs someone enough to want to ball him and before she knows it she's considered to be the property of the group.'

As the winter drew in, Adam Faith – whose manager had once turned down an offer from Lindsay Anderson of a role at the Royal Court without even telling him – was now finally about to establish himself in the public consciousness as an actor rather than a singer. He therefore found himself rehearsing at a place in the King's Road for a new television drama series written by the *Billy Liar* team of Keith Waterhouse and Willis Hall. Originally the show was called *The Loser*, but the title was later changed to *Budgie* when its production company, London Weekend Television, was taken over by Rupert Murdoch, who thought that the original was not commercial enough. In his autobiography, *Acts of Faith*, Adam said that his friend, photographer Terry O'Neill, provided the inspiration for how to play the title character: 'It can sometimes be a very small thing that gives you the key to the personality of a character. [. . .] For me, the trigger was walking along the King's Road watching Tel's shoulders shrugging. The cheekiness of it was the essence of Budgie. On that short walk, Tel had given me my character.'

It had been a transitional year, with Alex the droog, Jack Carter and Budgie making their way down the King's Road, signalling that the seventies were shaping up to be a very different proposition to the decade that had just passed, with little sign of the 'return to puritanical living and behaviour' that Terence Stamp predicted. As Christmas approached, Marc Bolan was riding high in the charts, and, as Mick Farren remarks, power-to-the-people-style combat fatigues were getting to be a drag, and something far more glamorous was coming down the road for 1971: 'I mean, twelve months earlier we would have been in our Che Guevara outfits . . . Fuck that drab shit, let's get this on . . .'

22

'The Female Eunuch Meets Tarzan'

Bored with Che Guevara

If the mid-point of the sixties was when one generation of classic King's
Road boutiques came into prominence – Hung On You, Granny Takes a
Trip, Quorum, selling velvets and frills and *fin de siècle* dandyism – then
1971 marked the rise of a different sensibility based on full-on, glammed-up,
stack-heeled seventies flash, courtesy of shops like John Lloyd's Alkasura,
the new-look Granny's and whoever happened to be running the shop at
430 King's Road that week. As Mick Farren says:

> There was a real marker between the sixties and the seventies . . .
> 1970, '71 . . . everybody got a bit bored with Che Guevara, you know?
> The girls started wearing high heels again, the radicals started dressing
> up a bit decadent, and although it was still the same underground, it
> was looking a little bit different. It was a weird little era, that's almost
> sort of forgotten.

Kubrick continued shooting *A Clockwork Orange* all through that spring,
which, when released, certainly prompted various skinhead gangs down
in Portsmouth where I was living at the time to go out in white boiler
suits, bowler hats and canes looking for some ultraviolence of their own.
While glam rock would not fully kick in across the board until the
following year, the key event happened in February 1971 when Marc
Bolan appeared with glitter on his cheeks on *Top of the Pops*, promoting
the first number one T. Rex single, 'Hot Love'. A generation of early

teenage kids – many of whom would later form the first wave of punk rockers – saw that the future of rock'n'roll held something slightly more exciting than sitting around stoned in hippie crash pads mumbling about the Tibetan Book of the Dead.

Bolan spent a lot of time on British television that year, often wearing suitably flash clothes from Granny Takes a Trip or Alkasura. Glam rock, as it soon came to be called, was generally utterly reviled by the slightly older generation of fans and music critics, most of whom never seemed to be able to forgive Bolan's transition from the subtle acoustic duo sounds he had been making in the last two years of the sixties with Tyrannosaurus Rex to the amped-up three-chord foot-stomping rock'n'roll of his seventies chart hits. Understandable, perhaps, but it completely ignores the fact that he had also done time in the very fine garage band John's Children in 1967, cranking up his electric guitar and whipping it with a selection of chains when onstage, helping to stir up serious enough riots in Germany to get them thrown off a tour. As John Peel points out, as a young kid, Bolan had 'carried Eddie Cochran's guitar', and a rocking electric Marc was really nothing new.

While Bolan was inventing glam, Frank Zappa was at Pinewood Studios making the film *200 Motels*, shooting and editing the whole thing on video, rather than celluloid, which accounts for the less-than-pin-sharp picture quality, since this was very early days for such an attempt. He flew over various members of the girl band the GTOs to appear in the film, and also paid for Cynthia Plaster Caster to make her first ever visit to the city which had fascinated her ever since she had seen the Beatles on the *Ed Sullivan Show* back in February 1964. This gave her the opportunity to check out the fashions, as she told me.

> The first week I was staying in Windsor at this hotel that Pamela Des Barres and Janet Ferguson and Lucy GTO were staying in that was not too far from Pinewood Studios, and then after that I went to London for about a month. I was on the set of *200 Motels* for about a week . . . I saw Keith Moon there, I saw Theodore Bikel. Frank had two weeks in which to do this filming, and he told me he would try to write some sort of teaser moment for me to be in the film somehow, but he just didn't have the time. But I did go to Biba. I'd go down there on Saturday mornings and it would just be a madhouse. I grabbed up a pair of boots that didn't even fit me . . . [laughs] a pair of knee-high, suede lavender beautiful go-go boots that cost, I think, under ten dollars, which was unbelievable

back then. But I did get a really cute dress. The few cool people that I saw on the street looked definitely not American – I mean, even the normal day-worker looked extremely groovy, had longer hair than any self-respecting American would have, pants that fit really nice, and the hair was really long, but it was really nicely cut. I saw people with total outfits . . .

All the Sales Girls in the Flash Boutiques

Number 430 King's Road – the premises which for the first four decades of the 20th century housed a pawnbroker's shop, and in the fifties was selling jellied eels and a wide variety of working men's grub under the name Café Eden before being part of the mid-sixties boutique revolution as Hung On You – had briefly abandoned clothes and returned to food, reopening as an Italian restaurant named Osteria 430, advertising themselves as 'open for dinners only, 6.30pm to 11.30pm, Monday to Saturday, Fully Licensed', but they would not last the year.

The cast of *Oh! Calcutta!* may have moved on from their King's Road rehearsal room, but, according to his diary, the show's guiding force, Ken Tynan, was certainly spending a lot of time in the Chelsea area in 1971. On February 25, he passed the evening at the house of Peter Sellers in Cheyne Gardens, discussing with George Harrison a forthcoming musical at the National Theatre based on William Blake's poem *The Tyger*, only to eventually discover that George had not only never heard of the poem, but also had no idea who Blake might have been either. On March 4, Ken and his wife Kathleen were back again, cruising the neighbourhood in some style:

> We consider and finally abandon the idea of buying a 1955 Cadillac hearse, recently offered for sale in the King's Road. The owner, a young American, asks only £500 for it, since superstition deters many potential buyers, and I'm attracted by the brass buckles and knobs on it, which light up at night. [. . .] Taken for a spin in the sepulchral flivver, we are pleased by the eagerness with which other traffic gives way for us, but disturbed by a tendency on the part of hospitals to flag us in as we drive past.

What with driving around in hearses, chatting to one of the Beatles, and also smoking dope with *Paint Your Wagon* film director Josh Logan – now a Chelsea resident – Ken Tynan also managed to visit the Royal Court now and then. Since they had the main auditorium and the Theatre Upstairs running simultaneously, the choice of programmes on offer was very broad. Sometimes, the same actors would be appearing in productions both upstairs and down at the same time. A case in point would be *Man is Man* by Brecht, which opened on March 1, with a cast that included Bob Hoskins and a pre-*Rocky Horror* Tim Curry, both of whom had also been appearing since February 9 at the Theatre Upstairs in another Brecht play, *The Baby Elephant*. The Court served up Jacobean revenge tragedy in January in the shape of Peter Gill's production of *The Duchess of Malfi*, starring Judy Parfitt, while in April came a Dennis Cannan play called *One at Night*, and also a play by Michael Almaz with a title which might have appealed to some of the future Seditionaries customers a few years hence – *Anarchist*. Preparations were also underway for the production later that year of a new John Osborne play, *West of Suez*, but in the spring of 1971, the Royal Court's original bad boy was reaching the public in a different way, giving an excellent onscreen performance as the sinister northern Mr Big, Cyril Kinnear, in the finest British crime film of them all, *Get Carter*.

Lord Longford – an unelected hereditary peer whose ancestor Kitty Pakenham had been the wife of the 1st Duke of Wellington – continued in his self-appointed role as a guardian of the nation's morals when addressing his fellow members of the House of Lords on April 21, complaining about *Oh! Calcutta!* and adding that 'pornography, in my conviction, has increased, is increasing and ought to be diminished.' Even so, the public were still queueing up for Ken Tynan's revue in record numbers, and also for a rival entertainment running at the Duchess Theatre, WC2, called *The Dirtiest Show in Town*, written and directed by Tom Eyen, advertised with a quote from the US TV network NBC: 'Dirty can be beautiful.'

On the cover of David Bowie's new album, *The Man Who Sold the World*, he was seen reclining in his 'man-dress' – an ankle-length blue and pale green silk creation by Mr Fish, which he had also worn on a promotional visit to the States, where he informed reporters that he used to be 'a shaven-headed transvestite'. Bowie might have been pioneering new fashions for men, but the Angry Brigade – having apparently run out of cabinet ministers to attack – were now taking a stern view of boutiques and everything that went with them, setting off a bomb at Biba's in Kensington High Street on May 1, and issuing Communiqué 8, which parodied Bob Dylan and also took a swipe at the Chelsea Drug Store:

'If you're not busy being born you're busy buying.' All the sales girls in the flash boutiques are made to dress the same and have the same make-up, representing the 1940s. In fashion as in everything else, capitalism can only go backwards – they've nowhere to go – they're dead. The future is ours. Life is so boring there is nothing to do except spend your wages on the latest skirt or shirt. Brothers and Sisters, what are your real desires? Sit in the drugstore, look distant, empty, bored, drinking some tasteless coffee? Or perhaps BLOW IT UP OR BURN IT DOWN. The only thing you can do with modern slave-houses – called boutiques – IS WRECK THEM. You can't reform profit capitalism and inhumanity. Just kick it till it breaks.

Revolution.

Communiqué 8, The Angry Brigade.

Meanwhile, a large crowd of celebrities who presumably had a different view of 'modern slave-houses' was arriving that month at the Royal Court for a fashion show held there by Ossie Clark of Quorum. The programmes for the show were designed by David Hockney, and the models' outlandishly high platform shoes by Manolo Blahnik, who had only just given up the idea of being a stage designer and was collaborating here for the first time with a fashion designer. Those attending included Pattie Boyd, Penelope Tree, David Bailey, Alice Ormsby-Gore, and Paul and Linda McCartney.

A Good Stone's Throw from the Albert Bridge

A more low-key event at the Royal Court was the opening at the sixty-capacity Theatre Upstairs on May 17 of a play called *Corunna* by Keith Dewhurst, directed by Bill Bryden, featuring among the cast some musicians who were no strangers to the King's Road, being regulars at Joe Boyd's Sound Techniques studio. The band were Steeleye Span, who not only acted in the play alongside the likes of Brian Glover but provided the music as well. These songs wound up on that year's Steeleye Span album *Please to See the King* and its follow-up, *Ten Man Mop or Mr Reservoir Butler Rides Again*. Keith Dewhurst had written the play especially for Steeleye Span as a follow-up to a previous one-night performance they had given at the Court of his play *Pirates*, inspired in its turn by an October 1970 gig that the band had done at the theatre. Richard Dacre, who in the punk days would work at the Other Cinema in Tottenham Street, hosting events featuring the likes of the Sex Pistols and the Slits, went along to see *Corunna* during its one-week run at the Royal Court. He told me:

I was heavily into folk music at the time. I didn't really even know where the Royal Court was, I just saw that Steeleye Span were playing.

I was beginning to get left wing and political, and I'd heard that this was a radical reinterpretation of British history through the songs of 'the ordinary people'. It was done in costume. I don't think Steeleye Span were really known at the time. The attraction for me would have been Tim Hart and Maddy Prior. I went to folk clubs most nights, all over London, and I'd also go to Chelsea Arts Club to see Jo Ann Kelly and Dave Kelly there.

Back in the expensive part of the neighbourhood, Ken Ferguson from *Photoplay* magazine was being ushered into the presence of Peter Sellers, whose most recent film, *There's a Girl in My Soup*, had included scenes of him driving down the King's Road:

> To enter his world you speak your name through a grille at the front door of a house in Cheyne Gardens, a good stone's throw from the Albert Bridge under which flows the River Thames. If your name fits, then the doors to Sellers' London residence (which he rents) is opened by his attractive secretary. She shows you into a spacious lounge dominated by two very large white stereo loudspeakers which stand on the floor in front of the French windows which lead out to a paved garden.

As for his choice of location, Sellers told Ferguson: 'Actually, I live here because it is useful and it is a part of London I like.'

Sorry You Missed It

In July, glossy American magazine *New York* ran an article by Caroline Seebohm which recalled how the popular perception of London women had altered a few years earlier:

> It was not until the early sixties that the English girl changed dramatically from the ugly duckling of Europe into the swan, or more precisely, bird, and was subsequently immortalized in the pop culture of that decade. The words 'King's Road, Chelsea' summoned up, like Proust's *petite madeleine*, an endless frieze of mini-skirted, booted, fair-haired angular angels, each one inviting with her eyes and her smiles the flash-popping tourist to wrest her from her pedestal and trap her for eternity between the sheets . . . of the photograph album.

OZ magazine, meanwhile, was in serious trouble as a result of the publication the previous year of issue number 28, *Schoolkids OZ*, as could be seen from the front cover of its new edition, which featured a cartoon farmyard animal in a police helmet with the headline 'Special Pig Issue', below which it said:

STOP PRESS: OZ OBSCENITY TRIAL
JUNE 22 OLD BAILEY

In order to raise money to help meet their legal costs, various celebrities had donated artworks which had been exhibited in the King's Road and then sold there at auction to raise money. These pictures included David Hockney's three nude drawings of the defendants, Richard Neville, Felix Dennis and Jim Anderson. The exhibition and auction were held at 271 King's Road, which was then a fashionable art gallery called Clytie Jessop, but in 1962 had been the St Tropez Twist 'coffee club'. An article inside the new edition of *OZ* listed the roster of heavy-duty counterculture names who had come forward to help:

> Objets d'Art, an exhibition of fine art and artefacts such as the Cunt
> Power bikini, which ran for two weeks at Clytie Jessop's gallery in
> King's Road, is over. Sorry you missed it. All proceeds from the exhi-
> bition have been donated by the contributors listed below to the Oz
> Obscenity Fund. Thanks to Alan Aldridge, David Bailey, Lyn Barnes,
> Ed Belchamber, David Boyd, Richard Dunn, Andy Dudzinski, Michael
> English, Terry Gillian [*sic*], Adrian George, Germaine Greer, Anthony
> Haden-Guest, David Hockney, Richard Hamilton, Marsha Herskovitz,
> Leonard Hessing, John Lennon, Jim Leon, Mike McInnerney, Philip
> Mora, David Nutter, Yoko Ono, Bob Owen, Patrick Procter, William
> Rankin, Gerald Scarfe, Ralph Steadman, Martin Sharp, Joe Tilson,
> Peter Till, Felix [*sic*] Topolski, Andy Warhol, Heathcote Williams and
> Ray Walker and everyone else who helped to make it a success.
> Particularly, of course, auctioneer George Melly, who skilfully drew
> large sums of money from the opening night crowd of people who
> consisted of penurious friends and unscrupulous dealers rather than
> wealthy left-wing art collectors.

The *OZ* trial lasted until August 4, with many defence witnesses called, such as George Melly, Caroline Coon of Release and Edward de Bono. John Peel also appeared for the defence, and was given a demonstration that the peculiar worldview of some prosecutors had not advanced one inch from the days of the 1960 *Lady Chatterley* trial ('Is this a book you would wish your wives or your servants to read?'), when he was subjected to offensively irrelevant questions such as 'Have you ever had a venereal disease, Mr Peel?' The underlying message of the whole prosecution was simple – these people are dirty, did not go to the right schools, and they should be punished. All of which was best answered by Keith Richards at his 1967 trial: 'We are not old men. We are not worried about petty morals.' At the *OZ* trial, Jim Anderson was sentenced to twelve months in prison, Felix Dennis to nine months, and Richard Neville got fifteen months. Down in the cells a few minutes later, Neville met another prisoner who asked him what sentence he'd received, and was then told: 'That's terrible. I got the same – and I tried to murder my wife.' Outside the Old Bailey, they were burning an effigy of trial judge Justice Michael Argyle in the street, while a naked caricature of him by Ralph Steadman appeared on the cover of the August 13 edition of *Private Eye*, under the headline 'This Justice Should Be Seen To Be Done'.

Bottomless Hot-Pants

Later that month, John Osborne's new play, *West of Suez*, opened at the Royal Court, starring Ralph Richardson, Nigel Hawthorne and Osborne's wife, Jill Bennett. Ken Tynan, in his diary entry for August 13, noted that he had been out for dinner with Laurence Olivier and Joan Plowright, and had spent much of the time discussing Osborne, including the assertion that he and Tony Richardson had once considered hiring a thug to beat up Tynan and Laurence Olivier. As for Osborne's new play: 'Larry [Olivier] derides JO's repeated assertions to the press of unswerving loyalty to the Royal Court, his artistic cradle, spiritual home, etc, it's pure balls – he's only doing the new play there because every West End management turned it down. Anthony Page, the director, dislikes the play and has only staged it out of loyalty.'

The Angry Young Man was at the Royal Court, and the Angry Brigade were apparently just down the road, as a bomb attributed to them was detonated on one of the supports of the Chelsea Bridge on September 20, probably because of its proximity to Chelsea Barracks. During 1971 many army locations were bombed in protest at events in Ulster, and at this time several alleged members of the Angry Brigade were on trial.

At Goldsmiths College, the student formerly known as Malcolm Edwards had now graduated and had changed his name by deed poll to Malcolm McLaren, taking the surname of his father, who had abandoned the family when he was eighteen months old. Malcolm was spending more and more time in the King's Road, and seemed to have designs on the shop which was now at number 430 named Paradise Garage, currently owned by Tommy Roberts's old partner from Mr Freedom, Trevor Miles.

An address a little further east, at 203 King's Road, right next door to the Six Bells pub, was offering a musical service via the classified adverts pages of the *Record Mirror* that September:

EXCHANGE TAPES with 'The Recording Kittens' the UK's top female tapesponding team and all the other members of 'The Great Britain Tapesponding Club'. Details from G.B.T.C., 203 King's Road, Chelsea, London SW3

History does not record whether Warren Beatty encountered the Recording Kittens on his travels, but he was certainly in Chelsea, getting himself namechecked in Ronnie Cowan's gossip column in the film trade newspaper *Today's Cinema* on September 24, partying at a favourite King's Road club: 'Almost didn't recognise Warren Beatty without his beard. He was at the Aretusa with a nameless girl wearing what looked like bottomless Hot-Pants. All I could see was a huge belt with cuffs . . .'

Edward Bond – who had written the script for Nicolas Roeg's rightly praised current film, *Walkabout* – had a new play opening at the Royal Court on September 29 called *Lear*, directed by William Gaskill. Its large cast included Harry Andrews, Bob Hoskins, and, somewhere further down the cast list, Gareth Hunt, who was to rise to television fame five years hence as Gambit in the *New Avengers*, in which Joanna Lumley would occasionally wear clothes from Quorum.

A different kind of show was taking place that September at the Roundhouse, as a selection of Warhol's glitter-smeared Factory-hands turned up to appear in *Pork*, and on one of their days off, they made a point of catching David Bowie's act, who was half a year away from his 1972 glam breakthrough with the single 'Starman', and whose dress sense failed to impress the New Yorkers: 'Oh dear, what a disappointment. How boring. He was wearing yellow bell-bottom pants and a big hat.'

King's Road shoppers out for a quiet afternoon that summer might have chanced upon Keith Moon from the Who and Viv Stanshall from the Bonzo Dog Doo-Dah Band driving up and down the street in a pre-war staff car dressed in Nazi uniforms, jumping out onto the pavement and then enthusiastically '*Sieg Heil*-ing' confused passers-by. Andy Powell from Wishbone Ash, who had just toured the US supporting the Who, later recalled: 'I was travelling up the Kings Rd, Chelsea in a black cab and saw

Moon and Vivian Stanshall from the Bonzos, in full SS Officer's uniform goose-stepping down the street just to outrage people (talk about politically incorrect – doesn't even come close to it).'

Delete the Word 'Kinky'

Also in the news at that time was a long-time resident of Cadogan Square, whose upcoming feature film used the King's Road itself as an integral part of the story. The September edition of *Films and Filming* announced that 'Peter Cushing and Christopher Lee are to appear in *Dracula Chelsea 72* which will be directed by Alan Gibson and produced by Josephine Douglas.' The intention was to make a Dracula film set in the present day, with a cast of groovy King's Road swingers, and the Count himself holed up in a deconsecrated church down near the Albert Bridge. Shooting began on September 27, by which time the film's title had been changed to *Dracula Today*, but Christopher Lee was appalled by the thought of a modern-day King's Road update of Bram Stoker's tale, as he explained to me:

> I thought that was a dreadful idea. I said to them, 'Why don't you do his book?' Actually, I turned down the last four films I did for them. I said, 'This is nonsense.' I used to get hysterical phone calls saying, 'You've got to do it because we've already sold it to the Americans.' And then, which was an even worse thing to say, 'Think of all the people you'll be putting out of work if you don't do it.' I made no secret of the fact that I strongly disapproved of the content. The only reason why people even know about those films these days is because of video and DVD, or the occasional late-night television showing.

Johnny Alucard and his Chelsea vampire groovers crash
Stephanie Beacham's party in *Dracula AD 1972*

The film's producer was Josephine Douglas, who many years before had been a mainstay of the rock TV show *Six-Five Special*, but when it was eventually released under the title *Dracula AD 1972*, all its pop culture references seemed also to belong to a bygone era. The main problem was that the script written by Don Houghton – then in his early forties – featured a selection of with-it swinging mods and dollies who could have stepped right out of 1965 or '66. Even the switched-on hangout where they all gather to plot their black masses is called The Cavern – in reality an Italian restaurant at 372 King's Road called La Bersagliera, which occupies the same site today. One character description from the screenplay read as follows: 'LAURA, SEXY, nubile, giggly, down-to-earth, daring in her dress and ultra-broadminded, dances with a MOD in really way-out gear. They jerk and contort to the music.'

In a series of script amendments dated October 1, various items of supposedly groovy dialogue were added ('There's a "happening" at Ailsa Morris's place tonight. She says the sky's the limit and she has a new batch of discs for the stereo'), but some restraint was apparently also being shown ('Scene 57. Delete: The word "kinky" from Jessica's 1st speech'). Houghton's original September screenplay also carries evidence of an interesting piece of casting for the film's upmarket Chelsea party sequence, in which a rock band are playing at the home of a rich teenager who is celebrating his birthday. When filmed in the autumn, the band they used was Stoneground, an American act led by Sal Valentino (formerly of San Francisco garage kings the Beau Brummels), but they were a replacement for a British band who were to hit the charts for the first time in December with a single called 'Stay with Me'. As the party spirals out of control, with would-be vampire Johnny Alucard and his mates wrecking the place and go-go dancers writhing on top of the piano, the mother of the birthday boy demands an explanation:

MATRON: Charles, I asked you to invite one or two of your friends, but . . .

CHARLES: (indignantly) These are not my friends, mother. I've never seen them before in my life! All I did was invite the Faces . . .

Introducing Eddy and the Falcons

Rod Stewart's band may have missed out on their chance to star in a Hammer film that autumn, but the Faces would prove to be a prime inspiration for Steve Jones and Paul Cook, who were drawn to the King's Road having heard that the band were customers of Granny Takes a Trip. In doing so, they would encounter the couple who had staked their claim at 430 King's Road in October 1971 with a shop called Let it Rock.

Malcolm McLaren in Ted gear outside 430 King's Road, 14 March 1972

It is nice to think of Malcolm McLaren in his Teddy boy gear walking down the King's Road in the direction of World's End that month, past the Essoldo Cinema at number 279 outside which the Hammer crew shot footage of Peter Cushing interrogating a frightened member of Johnny Alucard's group, then La Bersagliera at 372 done up as The Cavern, before rounding the turn and halting outside Paradise Garage at number 430. Trevor Miles, the owner, was out of the country at the time, but McLaren struck a deal with the manager, Bradley Mendelssohn, which enabled him and Vivienne Westwood to set up their gear in the back half of the shop and put a sign out on the pavement advertising Let it Rock. The final, most notorious, stage of the King's Road story had begun.

Paradise Garage was not in great shape anyway, and the day after McLaren and Westwood moved into the rear half, Mendelssohn failed to show up to take care of the front, a situation which continued until the owner Trevor Miles returned some days later, demanding money. Things turned confrontational, and one day the Let it Rock pair turned up to find

all their stock had been dumped out in the street, at which point they
sought the help of a lawyer whom Tommy Roberts had recommended.
The upshot was that the whole of number 430 became theirs, and McLaren
and Westwood set about turning it into a complete homage to the late
fifties British rock'n'roll era of Teddy boys and British bikers – a land where
Gene Vincent was god and Billy Fury something like the second coming.
Vintage 45s were available, many of them supplied by Ted Carroll – who
would go on to form Rock On, Chiswick Records and then Ace Records
– while Oliver Reed and his gang of ton-up kids from the classic 1963
Hammer Films biker flick *The Damned* stared down from the walls of the
shop, a film whose nihilistic title song would have been a perfect soundtrack
for the shop's early days.

I spoke to Ted Carroll about his memories of the early days of Let it Rock:

> There was a shop called Paradise Garage. They were doing OK, because
> they were selling second-hand denims and overalls and things, and then
> somebody else opened a shop further up King's Road selling the same
> shit, so they started not doing so well, and then Malcolm and Vivienne
> got a little corner in there you know, and started selling some of their
> weird shit and gradually took over. The interesting story – I don't know
> if you've heard it – is that Malcolm, when he was at film school, for his
> degree show, wanted to make a film about Billy Fury, and in the course
> of his researches he went up to Northampton and Leicester, places like
> that, to see if he could get authentic, original clothes for the extras, and
> discovered all these old shoe factories with loads of old shoes.

While Malcolm was locating potential sources of vintage fifties wear,
Ted himself had been building up contacts in America over the previous
couple of years from which he could obtain hard-to-find original US 45rpm
singles from the same era, which also helped to make Let it Rock a prime
destination for rock'n'roll aficionados, as he told me:

> I got to know Malcolm pretty well at that stage. I did quite a bit of
> business with him – this was probably about '72, I guess – and I'd sussed
> out a wholesaler in New Jersey I could buy oldies from, 45s. I started
> importing thousands at a time, all these different artists, a huge catalogue.
> They were cheap; landed I think they cost me about 32p each. I Xeroxed
> the listing after removing the address and gave it to Malcolm, and
> Malcolm would order loads of records, and then when they arrived I'd
> pay on delivery, pay the shipping company. I'd go out to the airport on

my scooter – thousands of 45s on the back of my scooter – and then I'd drop 500 of them to Malcolm, charging him about 60p or something. So, you know, he was paying for the whole shipment, basically, and then he was selling them for two quid, three quid each.

McLaren had been photographed by the *Daily Mirror*, standing out in the King's Road in front of number 430 a couple of months after they opened, wearing full Teddy boy gear. Whatever else was on the agenda at the close of 1971, it had little to do with a peace-and-love, flowers-and-bells hippie vibe.

Like Granny Takes a Trip half a decade before, the new shop did not have to wait long before the press started running enthusiastic articles. In truth, the fifties look had been making a comeback for some while already. There had been high-profile rock'n'roll revival shows in the USA at the end of the sixties, and cartoon greaser band Sha Na Na had even played a much-publicised slot at the Woodstock Festival. The original black leather rebel, Gene Vincent – who died on October 12, 1971, just as Let it Rock was about to open – had been met at London airport by a posse of Teds on his last visit. Glam rock, which was seriously starting to kick in by now, would often have a vintage rock'n'roll element, with bands such as Wizzard and Mud appearing on *Top of the Pops* in full Teddy boy gear, Roxy Music pillaging key sections of the look of that era, and the likes of the Rubettes releasing songs such as *Juke Box Jive*. Mungo Jerry, who had a fine piano player from the Jerry Lee Lewis two-fists-and-one-boot-heel school of piano pounding, even put out a song called 'Too Fast to Live, Too Young to Die', a title which would replace Let it Rock above the door of number 430 in a couple of years' time. Wizzard went even further, recording a criminally underrated album called *Introducing Eddy and the Falcons*, for which Roy Wood wrote excellent songs in the style of different fifties artists – an Elvis Sun impersonation, an Eddie Cochran, a Del Shannon and so on – while the cover showed the band draped up and menacing in a greasy transport cafe, with a torn poster for *Rebel Without a Cause* on the walls. A solid helping of fifties flash was very much the coming thing at that time, but McLaren and Westwood took it and ran with it, eventually twisting their inspiration into something else entirely. Sharp-eyed readers of Waxie Maxie's (Max Needham's) regular fifties rock'n'roll column in *Record Mirror* on December 25 will have spotted the following short news item in the 'Waxie's Bop Flakes' section at the foot of the page beneath his main article about Duane Eddy: 'Hey! Wow! Teddy Boy gear is selling fast at the new "Let It Rock" shop (formerly Paradise Garage) at 430 King's Road, Chelsea, SW3 –

nobody can expect otherwise with drapes (£25), bootlace ties (50p), winkle-pickers (£4.50), and suede shoes with fat crepe soles (£6.50) . . .'

Biggles Flies Undone

The Monty Python team had their first film in the cinemas that autumn, *And Now for Something Completely Different*, which was advertised with the slogan: 'With All the Beauty of Shakespeare's Sonnets, Solomon's Song and Mrs Whitehouse's Letters to *The Times*'. They had also published their *Big Red Book*, which included photos of various theatrical productions by the Batley Ladies Townswomen's Guild rolling about in mud in the local vicar's field, hitting each other with handbags: '1965: *The Marquis de Sade's Memoirs*, 1966: *Look Back in Anger*, 1968: *Camp on Blood Island*. [. . .] Next Year: *Groupie*.' The book also contained an offer of 'classic' works from the Python Literary Guild ('Dear Mailman, please rush me my 26 copies of the entire philosophy of the world in pictures with nude photographs of girls on the cover . . .'), which included *Biggles Flies Undone*, *Mary Queen of Bolton*, *Five Go a Wife-swapping* and that King's Road favourite, *The Female Eunuch Meets Tarzan*.

Nick Drake returned to Sound Techniques in Old Church Street towards the end of the year to record his third album, *Pink Moon*. Joe Boyd had moved to the US by this stage, and the LP was produced by his regular engineer, John Wood, who recalled that the album was recorded in one long after-midnight stretch, followed by another single evening session, and that was the lot: 'It took hardly any time to mix since it was only his song and guitar, with one overdub only.'

Nick's records have certainly stood the test of time, although his sales in those days would hardly have been cause for celebration in any record company boardroom. By contrast, the new king of glam had stirred up something which by Christmas 1971 the papers would call 'T Rextasy'. As Michael Wale wrote in his 1972 book, *Vox Pop – Profiles of the Pop Process*:

> By mid-winter *Jackie* magazine, which sells over 600,000 copies a week, reported that they were receiving 800 letters a week about Bolan as well as having to deny ugly rumours that the star was dying of a rare blood disease, an occurrence unknown in the fan-mag world of pop since rumours of Paul McCartney's death after the Abbey Road album.

Weekly singles sales were huge in the early seventies, dwarfing the pathetic amounts needed to get the average identikit pop act to the top of the charts these days, and the system managed to support no fewer than five weekly music papers, any one of whose sales figures would make those of the *NME* in its last days of being a physical title charging a cover price look like those of a badly distributed fanzine. Wale quotes some sales statistics for an average copy of those papers for the close of 1971: 'Three of the papers, the three major ones, *Melody Maker* (winter sales 1971 154,000), *New Musical Express* (winter sales 1971 147,000) and *Disc* (no ABC sales given) are owned by the giant IPC conglomerate . . . The other regular music papers in London are the *Record Mirror* and *Sounds*.'

For comparison, when it was the last surviving weekly music paper, the *NME*'s paid-for circulation in 2015 before turning into a free title decorating the floors of tube trains was a mere 15,000, and the print edition finally ceased publication altogether three years later.

Add to the above titles other popular early 1970s magazines like *Zig Zag, Disco 45, Jackie, Popswop* and *Fab 208*, to name but a few, and it is clear that there was a huge audience out there for music. What Bolan or Bowie wore on *Top of the Pops* one day would be copied the next in towns up and down the country, and also abroad through exposure on mid-European television shows with colossal viewing figures such as Germany's *Musikladen*.

Glam got the kids used to foot-stomping, three-chord, rabble-rousing dance music, and also accustomed them to tinted hair, *loud* make-up, outrageous clothes and being slagged off by the hippies. It was the first part of a one-two punch in which punk then came along and delivered the follow-through. Even today, scratch a dyed-in-the-Afghan hippie or a prog rock enthusiast, and a surprisingly high percentage still hate glam and punk, and display a tedious compulsion to say so repeatedly in the comments sections below music articles on national newspaper websites. The whole business of putting out singles was considered frivolous and demeaning by some of the supposedly more 'serious' bands of the early seventies, something which could be left to the despised 'teeny-bopper' groups, as John Peel explained to me:

Of course, by that time music had subdivided, you know, which really started with people like Hendrix. Because prior to that, it wouldn't have been regarded odd to have gone out and bought a Doris Day record and a Gene Vincent record, 'cause I did it, you know, but the only bands that got signed up – and this was in an era when bands didn't do singles – were bands that contained at least one member of a previously successful band that had broken up. And almost the only new band that came through during the whole of that time was Roxy Music, so that's why when punk came along, it was such a welcome breath of foul air, because you hadn't realised how bored you'd been . . .

23

'Cobblers to the world'

A Downright Redneck Novel

As 1972 began, Marc Bolan and T. Rex were riding into the year on the back of a pre-Christmas number two hit, 'Jeepster', and just a couple of weeks away from scoring their third number one with 'Telegram Sam'. David Bowie had not troubled the charts since his one-off hit, 'Space Oddity', back in 1969, but in January 1972, he decided to raise the stakes of the game during a much-publicised interview with *Melody Maker*: 'I'm gay, and I always have been,' he told them, 'even when I was David Jones.' Mick Ronson later recalled the effect of this sort of announcement on his family back home in Hull: 'I think it used to be a bit difficult when all the Ziggy thing was going on. I know people used to stop my sister in the street and say "Is that Mick of yours really a pouf?"'

People were certainly sending out ambiguous signals. Malcolm McDowell was on the front cover of a fair few magazines that January, wearing prominent false eyelashes on one eye, matched with heavy boots, some sort of a large armoured codpiece and a bowler hat, accompanied by a serious milk habit and a fondness for Beethoven. A little further down the line, Kubrick would withdraw *A Clockwork Orange* from British cinemas – a ban that lasted the rest of the century – but for now, starting on January 13 at the Warner West End, the crowds were lining up. *Time Out* put the film on its cover that week, with an article by Verina Glaessner, who seemed intent on making it out to be *2001: A Space Odyssey Part Two* while slagging off the source novel: 'Kubrick has taken Burgess's politically questionable, if not downright redneck novel (published in the early sixties), and virtually turned it inside out.' In the music section of that same edition of *Time Out*, there was also 'The Other LP Chart', which was 'compiled from listings from the following record shops: Town Records, King's Road, SW10, Musicland, Portobello Road, W10 and Berwick Street W1, One Stop Records, South Molton Street, W1, Virgin Records, Oxford Street, W1 and Notting Hill Gate, Harlequin Records, Oxford Street, W1.' Interestingly, the two groups who were considered by Hammer for a part in *Dracula AD 1972* were both selling strongly in these shops: *A Nod's as Good as a Wink* by the Faces was at number one, while 'bubbling under' were *Zero Time* by Tonto's Expanding Headband and *Family Album* by Stoneground.

Second-hand clothes store El Cheapo at 507 King's Road was featured in the magazine's 'Sell Out' section, also giving notice that another Chelsea landmark had closed: 'When I visited the shop they were selling beautiful Ossie Clark dresses at about half price (incidentally now that Quorum has closed down, El Cheapo is being supplied with the left-over stock, which they will sell at two-thirds the original price).' At the other end of the King's Road from Town Records, the Royal Court Theatre Upstairs was presenting *Sylveste* 'by, with and from the Ken Campbell Roadshow'. *Time Out*'s anonymous reviewer seemed mildly impressed:

> It's a jolly rollicking fairground show, but would have been much better if the group had erupted into your local or got going on an Underground platform or somewhere like that. They get their responses by shock tactics, by needling the balloon of conventional behaviour, and in the Theatre Upstairs full-frontal male nudity doesn't even constitute a prick.

Also at the Theatre Upstairs, on January 30, but presumably not losing their laundry, were Georgie Fame and Alan Price, playing a benefit concert, while downstairs in the main theatre from January 26, Rachel Roberts and Albert Finney, two stars of the film *Saturday Night and Sunday Morning*, were reunited yet again in a play called *Alpha Beta* by E. A. Whitehead. Roberts, who had appeared at the Court a couple of years previously just as her ten-year marriage to Rex Harrison was falling apart, was now cast in this play as one half of a couple whose twelve-year marriage was falling apart. It proved a huge success during its limited run of thirty-two shows, and Roberts eventually won the *Evening Standard* Best Actress Award for her performance.

Partake Freely of All White Starchy Vegetables

Over in New York, Barry Miles was reviewing a February 11 gig at the Mercer Arts Centre featuring the New York Dolls and Wayne County:

> They are representative of a new wave of New York groups who have picked up on Marc Bolan, Slade, Elton John, David Bowie in a big way and combined them with such historical figures as The Fugs, the early Mothers and the very much present-day Lou Reed. [. . .] It's a fact that LA soft-rock has been stomped on by glittering lurid day-glo platform shoes worn by a female-impersonating posturing hard-rock singer. [. . .] The audience could well have been in the group, a woman with black lipstick looked dead, very weird scene, many men wore full drag, a man near me with a full beard also disported a floor length red ball gown and ethereal smile. Some couples wore uni-sex makeup and were hard to distinguish from each other in the welter of day-glo, lurex, tinsel, glitter dust on flesh, and clothes, studs, satin, silk and leather, lurid reds, pink angora tops, green boas, totally transparent blouses and of course every one had gained at least 3" in their multi-coloured platforms.

Andy Warhol's *Interview* magazine attempted somewhat unsuccessfully to clarify the situation: 'The Dolls are the visual epitomes of this semi-transvestite style in their girl's shoes and makeup. They represent a new sexuality which is neither heterosexual nor homosexual, nor is it necessarily bi-sexual.'

Other people visiting Manhattan at that time were two of the recently released *OZ* defendants, who took some flak in the April 6 edition of *IT* as a result, in an item entitled *Free Who-Was-It-Again Dept*:

> Getting away from rock for a minute, Felix Dennis and Richard Neville are in New York for the opening of the play of the *OZ* trial and the casting of the musical of the play. If we had known that we were making the world safe for Broadway spectaculars when we rallied to the cause last summer, we probably would have stayed in bed!

Still, aside from inter-magazine sniping, *IT* also carried the following astrologically orientated cookery and diet advice for those who believed – like Kenneth Williams's radio comedy character Arthur Fallowfield – that the answer lies in the soil: 'Aquarius: The colours are indigo and white.

The foods largely the white fruits and vegetables. Celery, asparagus, parsnips, potatoes and pears are especially good. All air signs can partake freely of all white starchy vegetables. Aquarians require less food than any of the other 12 signs.'

At the Royal Court, perhaps recklessly unaware of the effects of their respective star signs on their white starchy vegetable requirements, John Gielgud and John Mills were appearing in a Charles Wood play called *Veterans*, in a cast which also included *Upstairs, Downstairs* mainstay Gordon Jackson, as well as Bob Hoskins and James Bolam. Then, on May 24, a play by John Antrobus opened at the Court entitled *Crete and Sergeant Pepper*, with the character of Pepper played by Bill Maynard, although what if anything this may have had to do with the album whose cover had been photographed just down the road five years previously is hard to say. The Beatles were long gone by now, and a different kind of musician was in the area, as Mick Farren remembers:

Lou and David and Iggy all kind of turned up, from Berlin or wherever [laughs]. They were wandering around doing things, and there was some talk of getting at least Paul Rudolph and maybe the rest of the Pink Fairies in to work on what would eventually be *Raw Power*. But then Iggy decided he'd be more comfortable with bringing the Stooges over, but this was all kind of circulating really in the same dimension.

Iggy Pop had come into the orbit of David Bowie and was in town trying to make an LP, while David's manager, Tony DeFries, had set up an organisation called MainMan, based just off the King's Road in Gunter Grove, which for a while would handle both artists' affairs. Nick Kent described Bowie's manager in *Creem* magazine the following year: 'You can sometimes see DeFries standing at the back of the hall while Bowie is performing. You can't miss him: debauched East End Italian face, big nose and an even bigger cigar fixed between his lips. The clothes are tastefully trendy, while his features only hint at the constant motion of the whiz-kid brain.'

Once the rest of the current line-up of the Stooges had come over to join Iggy – Ron Asheton, Scott Asheton and James Williamson – they rehearsed for the coming album sessions in a room around the corner from the MainMan office. Mick Rock visited them in May 1972 to take photographs of Iggy, and recalled the event in *Mojo* magazine: 'This was the place that he called "The Hole". It was on Seymour Walk, off Fulham Road, where they were rehearsing – the cheapest, dirtiest place, fucking crap everywhere, a real Stooge-Hole! He was very at home and specifically said how happy he was there.'

An Electric Age Nightmare

Here is a brief sample of some of the things that were happening on the radio during one random week while the Stooges were rehearsing, according to the May 26 issue of *Time Out*: in session on John Peel's Radio One *Sounds of the Seventies* show on the evening of May 26 were Slade, Paladin, the Johnstons and Stone the Crows; John Antrobus was appearing on Radio London's *Festival Time* show to talk about his Royal Court play, *Crete and Sergeant Pepper*; finally, on Radio London's 'rock magazine' show *Breakthrough with Steve Bradshaw*:

> This week, Mick Jagger on the new Stones double album *Exile on Main Street*, Lou Reed on his new solo album and also talking about the Velvet Underground; particularly the third album, which he will be commenting on track by track; and John Cage on his current work which involves experiments in vocal music based on Navajo Indian chants.

Also, if you wanted to rent somewhere quiet in which you could make your own vocal experiments based on Navajo Indian chants, someone in the small ads was looking for a 'Girl to share friendly modern King's Road flat. £30 p.m. inc.'

In June, David Bowie released his new album, *The Rise and Fall of Ziggy Stardust and the Spiders from Mars*. It was called 'an electric age nightmare' by *Cashbox* magazine in the US, and the man himself said: 'I like to keep my band always well dressed. I'm out all the time to entertain. I'm the last person to pretend I'm a radio. I'd rather go out and be a colour television set.' On June 24 his new single, 'Starman', entered the charts, and with one classic appearance on *Top of the Pops*, Bowie established himself as a very big deal indeed. TV Smith, who a few years later would front one of the first and best of the UK punk bands, the Adverts, told me that he caught the Ziggy tour down in the West Country:

> I saw Bowie at Torquay Town Hall, Ziggy Stardust period – blew my mind. It was just astounding, you know. I'd never seen anything like that. I'd seen a couple of gigs already, but that gig really . . . to see such brilliant songwriting and showmanship and playing, in Torquay

Town Hall, you know what I mean? I thought, God, what's going on? That was one of the rare occasions that someone who really impressed me came to the West Country. I think the only other people I saw that I liked down there were the Heavy Metal Kids and the Doctors of Madness. They put on a show, and they had their own image, and those were the bands we were looking out for . . . So, no way were the Sex Pistols ground zero, and you're not gonna tell me that they weren't informed by the Dolls and Iggy and the Small Faces as well . . .

In July, Bowie brought Lou Reed out onstage for the encore at the Royal Festival Hall to do three Velvet Underground numbers. Lou was in town to start recording the *Transformer* album, with Bowie producing. Onstage a week later in King's Cross, Reed wore 'black eye makeup, black lipstick and a black velvet suit with rhinestone trimmings'. In the August 19 edition of the *NME*, Charles Shaar Murray referred to a track on the new Pink Fairies album, *What a Bunch of Sweeties*, as 'classic British punk rock', and in the same issue, 24-year-old Marc Bolan was talking to Keith Altham, who wrote that 'he does not believe he has too long to live, which ought to be the silliest thing to make the papers world-wide since Paul McCartney hid in Scotland and everyone presumed he was dead'. As it turned out, Bolan had just five years left. That summer, Marc also did an interview at a King's Road restaurant called Newton's, explaining that he had bought 'quite a few' of his clothes at Alkasura and at Granny Takes a Trip.

A new shop of which Bolan would certainly have approved opened that year down the King's Road selling shoes featuring towering platforms and wedges – Terry de Havilland's magnificently titled emporium Cobblers to the World. As Terry's website later explained: 'It was the first of its kind – a vision of peach mirror glass walls, a tented ceiling featuring an oversized chandelier and purple velvet banquette seats, described – memorably – at the time as a Venetian Bordello!' Customers would include Britt Ekland, Bianca Jagger, Rod Stewart, Anita Pallenberg and Angie and David Bowie. As de Havilland – formerly Terry Higgins of the East End – told Clare Coulson in the *Daily Telegraph*: 'Everyone came to the shop. I was hanging out with Led Zeppelin, photographers, models and all the rock star wives – it was a crazy time.'

What's Long and Hard and Comes Out This Week?

August 1972 saw a huge rock'n'roll festival at Wembley Stadium, headlined by Bill Haley, Chuck Berry and Little Richard. Much further down the bill was music of a slightly different kind, courtesy of the MC5. McLaren and

Westwood from Let it Rock printed up plenty of T-shirts saying 'Vive Le Rock' and rented a stall at the show, assisted by Ted Carroll, but sales to the fifties fans were disappointing. Mick Farren was also a Let it Rock customer back in those days:

> I think we called them up and borrowed a couple of gold Elvis jackets for the Personality Ball, because you know we were the heroes of the revolution at the time . . . At the same time Iggy turns up with no shirt and silver jeans, which I think were starting to smell somewhat, and a furry handbag, and he's come up to see Wayne Kramer and the MC5, because Rob [Tyner] had gone home . . . and this shit just went around, the orbits intersected – there weren't *that* many people.

Actress Susan George, fresh from appearing in Peckinpah's *Straw Dogs*, told *Photoplay* in September that she had recently stopped living with her parents out near Windsor, bought 'a pretty little Alfa Romeo sports car' and then moved into a flat of her own just off the King's Road. She also thought that her nude scenes in *Straw Dogs* were perfectly justified, which is something that Lord Longford would probably have claimed to have been shocked by. His thorough, some would say obsessive, report into pornography had just been published, which duly earned him a place on the cover of *Private Eye*. He was pictured standing next to a member of the Salvation Army, with appropriate speech bubbles – Longford: 'What's long and hard and comes out this week?' Salvationist: 'Ask me another!'

In September, it was announced that director Anthony Page planned to shoot a film adaptation with Albert Finney and Rachel Roberts of their Royal Court success from earlier in the year, *Alpha Beta*, while elsewhere, Roberts was among a selection of regular Court actors including Ralph Richardson and Arthur Lowe who were spending the summer being filmed at great length by Lindsay Anderson for his new film, *O Lucky Man*. Meanwhile, Chelsea itself was making a showing in the cinemas that month. Val Guest, who memorably blanked out the opening ceremonies of the Chelsea Flower Show a decade earlier when filming *The Day the Earth Caught Fire*, had now directed a sex comedy called *Au Pair Girls*. As was explained in *Photoplay*, the film featured various young women who arrived in London to work as au pairs, including one called Christa from Germany: 'Young Carol Fairfax, amazed to find Christa is a virgin, decides to alter this by taking her to a club in Chelsea's King's Road.' *Films and Filming*'s reviewer Alex Stuart was not so convinced about all this: 'She is "dollified" by Carol [. . .] and taken to a disco – Groovers (any disco with a corny name like that would be laughed all the way to the bankruptcy court) – to meet turned on, tuned in pop singer, Ricky Strange.'

It was definitely the month for unconvincing King's Road discos on the silver screen, because on September 28, cinemagoers were finally treated to the sight of Johnny Alucard and his swinging collection of outdated mods and chicks hanging out at The Cavern in Hammer's *Dracula AD 1972*. Advance publicity for some strange reason had begun as far back as January, when *Photoplay* ran an article entitled 'Dracula Drops in on the Mod Scene' – 'For the first time the famed Count leaves his Transylvanian setting to stalk the trendy King's Road in Chelsea!' – and most of the film magazines enjoyed printing the publicity shots of Christopher Lee surrounded by a selection of naked women, which had precious little to do with anything that would appear in the finished film. Oddly enough, after many years of sneering at pretty much any film originating from the Hammer studios, *Films and Filming* chose this moment to start handing out the praise, and, even more surprisingly, gave a bouquet to the scriptwriter: 'Dracula in the King's Road works very well indeed. [. . .] Don Houghton's screenplay deserves a medal for having success- fully uprooted the old vampire from the overworked domain of Transylvania.'

Chelsea must have been well used to the sight of film crews by now, and at the end of that summer, Douglas Hickox showed up with another one, shooting the hugely enjoyable horror film *Theatre of Blood*, in which Vincent Price plays a disillusioned actor who sets about murdering his critics in the manner of various of Shakespeare's tragedies. For the section based on Othello, he tricks one of them into smothering his wife to death in her bed: the wife was played by Diana Dors; the house where this took place was very convincingly played by number 16 Cheyne Walk, Dante Gabriel Rossetti's former home.

A Bucket of Urine

The record reviews section of the October edition of *Film Review* magazine carried a slightly belated appraisal of the Ziggy Stardust album ('David Bowie continues to sweep all before him with his own particular brand of camp-rock'), just as the American band who had performed at the Mercer Arts Centre in full drag earlier in the year arrived in Britain for the first time. The New York Dolls had been invited over by the Faces, which is interesting, since those were later to be the two biggest influences on the sound of the Sex Pistols. They were scheduled to play in Birmingham with Lou Reed, London with the Faces, and Manchester with Roxy Music. Nick Kent reviewed the October 29 Faces Wembley show in the *NME*:

What was the *Daily Express* doing putting on probably the finest rock'n'roll concert I've witnessed so far this year? What were the three pillars of rock outrage: Ladbroke Grove's red peril – the Pink Fairies, 42nd Street's own version of Satyricon – the New York Dolls and the rockin' rooster plus his bunch of gang-busters, doing performing under the banner of one of the more conservative daily journals in England's green and pleasant land? I dunno.

After the gig that night, the Dolls went to the Speakeasy, and later in the evening their 21-year-old drummer, Billy Murcia, tragically died during attempts to revive him after he had passed out.

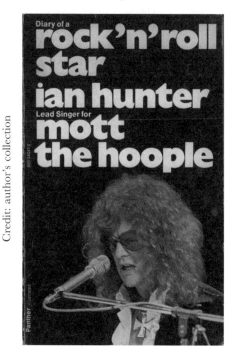

Ian Hunter's classic tour memoir, 1974

As one of the great US bands was coming to London, one of Britain's finest were flying out for a US tour, and their lead singer decided to record it for posterity in a book. The band was Mott the Hoople, who were being handled by the Chelsea office of MainMan and had scored their first chart hit back in August with 'All the Young Dudes'. Ian Hunter's resulting tour memoir, published under the title *Diary of a Rock'n'Roll Star*, remains one of the most entertaining insider accounts of the business. Before they set off, there were clothes to be bought:

Now we've got to look groovy so our manager, Tony DeFries, gives us all £100 to buy clothes. That's OK, but the clothes are all shit – Carnaby Street, Ken Market, King's Road – ridiculous prices for rubbish that doesn't last five minutes; oh, and I saw Julie Christie on King's Road, smaller than I expected but that jaw does something to me.

Meanwhile, Roxy Music's Bryan Ferry was considering his new-found success in the *NME*: 'We're not a singles group. I certainly don't want to go down that Slade/T. Rex corridor of horror.' As for Eno, 'He's planning to shave the top of his head till it's short and stubbly like grass. Then he's going to lay a crazy paving path up the middle, leading to a little cottage at the top.' Eno had been busy recording an album with Robert Fripp called *No Pussyfooting*, which featured a track named 'Swastika Girls', some four years before some misguided factions of the punk scene got excited about this sort of thing. Roxy Music's first album, wittily entitled *Roxy Music*, featured a cover partly styled by designer Anthony Price, after Ferry had rung him up from a phone box in the King's Road in order to ask him if he would like to do it.

On October 1, 1972, at the Royal Court's sixty-seat Theatre Upstairs, they presented *England's Ireland*, a play which seemingly attempted to outnumber the audience with authors, it being the work of Tony Bicat, Howard Brenton, Brian Clark, David Edgar, Francis Fuchs, David Hare and Snoo Wilson. Directed by Hare and Wilson, its cast included Tim Curry. The Irish theme continued in the main Royal Court auditorium on November 2 with Edna O'Brien's *A Pagan Place*, directed by Ronald Eyre. This opened on the same night that Lou Reed and his excellent touring band the Tots played just down the road at the Pheasantry as part of a series of UK gigs to promote the *Transformer* album (the previous evening they had played in Mile End). Four days later the Pheasantry hosted another band down in the basement, and this gig would convince the owners of Trident Studios to sign them up and set about finding them a record deal. The singer was a Kensington Market stallholder who called himself Freddie Mercury, and the band were Queen, who were, as the *NME* memorably pointed out in 1974, 'later described in the press by Roxy Music's Paul Thompson as "too contrived" and by Nick Kent as "a bucket of urine".'

You Don't Have to Pretend to Be American

While the Pheasantry was seeing some action, down towards World's End at Sound Techniques, Steeleye Span had been in again recording another album, *Below the Salt*, with engineer Jerry Boys – their first for a major record label. At the Royal Court, the year ended with another John Osborne play, *A Sense of Detachment*, starring Nigel Hawthorne and Rachel Kempson – the mother of Vanessa Redgrave, while in the world of film, Hammer were encouraged enough by the performance of *Dracula AD 1972* to announce in December that they would soon be filming another modern-day vampire film under the title *Dracula is Dead . . . and Well and Living in London* (eventually produced under the title *The Satanic Rites of Dracula*). After a year on release in the cinemas, *A Clockwork Orange* was still provoking angry discussions in the media. *Films and Filming* voted it 'Most Over-Rated Film of the Year', yet gave Malcolm McDowell's Alex an award for 'Best Male Performance'.

In the field of popular music, the new generation were on their way up, taking inspiration from a few of the English bands who didn't feel the need to sing in a Mick Jagger fake delta blues accent. One such was Eric Goulden, eventually to emerge on Stiff Records in 1977 as Wreckless Eric, who told me:

> I always remember 1972, right, it was the year I left school, and of course as I left school, *School's Out* by Alice Cooper came out – that's a great album – but also the other record that was hugely important, that I related to hugely, was 'All the Young Dudes' by Mott the Hoople. Of course it was a Bowie song. The whole Bowie thing was somehow from an English perspective, but it was not ever apparent to my consciousness until I saw the Kilburns and I thought 'You can do it, and be English, you don't have to pretend to be American,' because the assumption had been up to then that you had to be kind of an American. Before that, when Ray Davies did his really English thing, it never really occurred to me. 'Dedicated Follower of Fashion', that was very English, but it was a bit gimmicky, it was a bit novelty, and this was English without novelty. The Who, as well – the Who got more and more English.

Kilburn and the High Roads – who formed in 1973, fronted by another future Stiff recording artist, Ian Dury – never quite made the big time, but certainly helped mark out the territory for much of what was to follow. Glam would still be massive that year, but something much tougher was stirring out there in the pubs and tatty clubs . . .

24

'Liberal dollops of sex and space travel'

Bombarded by Real Live Sweaty Rock'n'Roll

At the height of the media-and-McLaren-generated hysteria about the Sex Pistols, venues were cancelling their shows, radio stations pulling their records from the schedules and the tabloids printing scare stories about this new breed of degenerates out to drag the nation down into the gutter. Somehow though, in January 1973, none of this kind of fuss accompanied a different band who had many thousands of impressionable early-teenage fans, but managed to go on *Top of the Pops* to promote their new single with the bass player dressed up in a spiked German helmet, Nazi armband, painted-on Hitler moustache, lipstick, eyeshadow and silver platform boots, winking at the camera.

McLaren and Westwood would later use swastikas on their 'Destroy' and 'Karl Marx Anarchy' shirt designs, and SEX shop assistant Jordan wore a Nazi armband at the side of the stage when the Pistols made their debut 1976 TV appearance on Tony Wilson's *So it Goes* show, but Steve Priest from the Sweet got there first, in front of a TV audience of millions, while shrieking 'W-w-w we just haven't got a clue, *what* to do . . .' as they performed 'Blockbuster'. Context is everything: if you are just having a laugh, then that's one thing – but as Andrew Loog Oldham had already proved in the early days of the Rolling Stones – if you say that you're a dirty filthy menace to society, then society may well believe you.

Other parts of the coming revolution were also firmly in the public eye by that stage, such as the famous 'Tits' T-shirt design, which Seditionaries would introduce in 1977 and claim as one of their own creations. Yet

Alice Cooper had already worn one on the front cover of the *NME* on February 10, 1973, and it was being offered for sale as 'The No-Bra Look' in the pages of the ultra-trendy *Evergreen Review* as far back as 1971 by a San Francisco company with the less-than-subtle name of Jizz Inc. before McLaren and Westwood even started.

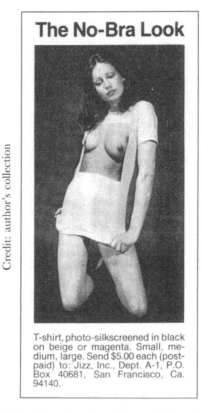

US t-shirt advert from *Evergreen Review*, 1971

Further clues that overblown stadium gigs or 400,000 people sitting in the mud at a festival weren't necessarily the answer to everything were provided in an *NME* article by Tony Stewart:

Want to hear nothing more than a gang of promising adolescents fighting for air in a smoke-sodden room with Vox AC30s? [. . .] In London there's the famous Marquee and Speakeasy. Or the Fulham Greyhound – a helluva boozer – or the Torrington, Finchley. If you like, Upstairs At Ronnies or the Pheasantry, King's Road. Plus a couple of seedy little hops where you'll be near squashed to death and bombarded by real live sweaty rock'n'roll.

In January, Donovan was telling the press that 'the seventies are finally emerging as a very theatrical music scene'. Perhaps he had been watching the Sweet on *Top of the Pops*, but whatever the reason, an actor called Richard O'Brien – currently playing the part of Willie the Space Freak at the Royal Court in a production of Sam Shepard's *The Unseen Hand* – was about to help make the music scene even more theatrical. He had been writing something of his own, and showed it to the director of *The Unseen Hand*, Jim Sharman. At that stage, it was provisionally titled *They Came From Denton High*, and then *The Rock Horroar Show*, but would premiere under its final name *The Rocky Horror Show* later that year at the Theatre Upstairs on June 19. Downstairs at the Court starting on February 27 was a play directed by Albert Finney, *Freedom of the City* by Brian Friel, with a young Stephen Rea among the cast.

The ever-active Steeleye Span had been back in Sound Techniques at the start of the year recording yet another album, this one titled *Parcel of Rogues*, and it is a measure of how much more quickly the music business could move in those days that it was due for release on March 30.

In February, Elton John made a promotional appearance for his new LP, *Don't Shoot Me I'm Only the Piano Player*, at a record shop called Sloane, at the eastern end of the King's Road, hosted by Radio One DJ and future Mr Blobby overlord Noel Edmonds, at which the singer was reported to have signed 'records, boots, bare skin and possibly blank cheques'. That same month, fellow radio DJ Tony Blackburn was defending the new T. Rex film *Born to Boogie* in the pages of *Melanie* magazine – 'Let's face it, pop films are for you to enjoy, they're not made to keep the oldies happy!' – and then in April, Bolan helpfully informed *Melody Maker* readers that 'Glam Rock is dead.' Meanwhile, onstage at a gig in Buffalo, New York State, Lou Reed was bitten on the buttocks by a fan screaming 'Leather!', and in the *NME*, said to Nick Kent: 'Maybe I'll do a song called "Get Back in the Closet, You Fucking Queers". I got bored with wearing all that makeup: pancake, green lipstick, y'know. I gave it up because it wasn't me. All that glamour scene will run its course. The only one who'll come out fully intact will be Bowie.'

As for Iggy and the album which he had been working on in that rehearsal room off the Fulham Road, Roy Carr reviewed *Raw Power* in the *NME*, calling it 'the first real rock album of the seventies'.

I'd Like to See More Filth on Television

The Monty Python team took over *Time Out* for a special issue of the magazine on May 4, in which Michael Palin talked more sense about the permissive society than Lord Longford had managed in the whole of his career:

We're not a nation of prudes whatever anyone thinks. It's only when you come on television you're led to believe the people of Britain are very delicate flowers who must be nurtured and not offended. Unfortunately, the people who dislike us or who are critical of the BBC are very vocal and well-organised, viz. Mary Whitehouse. She says, 'I have 800,000 people who all agree with me, this is obscene.' But it's nothing against the 18 million people who actually enjoy *Till Death Us Do Part*. They don't actually fill in questionnaires and say, 'Yes, I'd like to see more filth on television.'

Among the many parodies of listings and small ads written by the Python team for that issue was a fake accommodation advert which read, 'Couple wanted to share Couple in Chelsea. No hip injuries please. Photos essential', and the following restaurant review:

Carmello's, 261 Cheyney [*sic*] Walk. Really fantastic! They have food! And what's more they give you this food if you pay them! [. . .] And the sweets are out of this world! Something in something else for 85p was unbelievable, and one of us had something else with something or other all over it for 90p which was just so far out I had to go to the toilet! Boy! Was that a good evening! Great! Just wait till I write it up! Hey! All those things on the wall! Too much! Those colours, man! Did you see those colours! . . . (The rest of this review has been deleted and submitted as evidence – Ed.)

At Granny Takes a Trip, Gene Krell had become friendly with Malcolm McLaren and Vivienne Westwood down at number 430, who that year changed the name of their shop from Let it Rock to Too Fast To Live Too Young To Die. Granny's was still very popular with the rock star crowd, not necessarily just for shopping. Marianne Faithfull recalled an encounter at the shop around this time with her former boyfriend, which took place three years after their relationship ended:

In front of Granny Takes a Trip I ran into Mick, who embraced me passionately as if we had just been reunited after a brief separation. We held hands and looked into each other's eyes. When he began to caress my back, I realized he wanted to have sex with me. He asked the owner if we could use the room upstairs. We went upstairs and made love. Afterwards we got dressed, kissed goodbye and went our separate ways.

A few doors along at Vivienne and Malcolm's shop, a fifteen-year-old schoolboy customer wandered in one day looking to buy a pair of brothel-creepers. He also asked McLaren if they needed any extra help at weekends, since he had recently lost his Saturday job at Whiteleys department store, and Malcolm duly hired him. The successful applicant's name was Glen Matlock, who recalled that occasion in his autobiography, *I Was a Teenage Sex Pistol*:

> Let It Rock it was called. Or maybe Too Fast To Live, Too Young To Die. It had signs up for both so I could never work out which it was. [. . .] The bonus for me was that the money was so much better than Whiteleys. Instead of getting 36 bob for Thursday evening and all day Saturday, Malcolm paid me three pounds ten shillings – almost twice as much – for the Saturday only. Plus, while I had to get up at eight for Whiteleys, I didn't have to get into Let It Rock until 11. So I was well happy.

Sharing some of the same customers and having its own distinctive identity was another King's Road clothing outlet which was to play a significant role in the punk revolution. From a stall at the rear of the Antiquarius Market at 135–141 King's Road, John Krevine and Steph Raynor sold a mixture of old furniture, jukeboxes, shoes, and new and vintage clothing, mostly with a forties and fifties look. They traded under the name Acme Attractions, and their stall was managed by future Roxy club DJ Don Letts, who had previously worked at Jean Machine in the King's Road. By the end of 1973, they had relocated to premises downstairs at Antiquarius, where there was more space and they could turn the jukebox up louder.

Also selling clothes to the cognoscenti from two branches on the King's Road were a couple of shops named after a Neil Young song called the Emperor of Wyoming, who could do a decent job of fitting out any would-be urban cowboys, with adverts that said: 'Western Clothing Stores, 404 King's Road and 196 King's Road, Boots, Saddles, Western Shirts, Jeans.' McLaren and Westwood were not selling leather themselves yet, but it was only a matter of time.

Mutants, Transvestites and Various Other Goodies

Down at the opposite end of the King's Road from import specialist Town Records, former teenage budgerigar seller Richard Branson – who in 2021 would spend an estimated $841 million blasting himself into the earth's upper atmosphere for roughly fifteen minutes, representing a bargain rate of a mere $934,444 per second – had opened up a record shop called Virgin Imports at 2b Symons Street, just off Sloane Square, which would have been competing to a certain extent for a share of those customers who were looking for the latest albums from the US. Just across the square from that shop, over at the Royal Court, Christopher Hampton's new play *Savages* was examining the plight of Brazilian Indians and the destruction of the rainforests, which did not particularly impress *Time Out*'s reviewer: 'Definition of liberal didactic theatre: first choose a harrowing and insoluble problem which is a long way from home and on which there is a large potential basis for agreement; then author and audience celebrate shared feeling of impotent anger.'

As an alternative, Chelsea theatregoers could also check out another new John Antrobus play at the Theatre Upstairs, *Captain Oates' Left Sock*, although what the sometime Oakley Street resident Scott of the Antarctic might have made of it was anybody's guess. Still, for anyone wanting to move to the neighbourhood, there were apparently plenty of opportunities in the small ads of the magazine for the right applicant, such as: 'GUY, 27, SEPARATED, seeks beautiful, sexy chick to share his luxury Chelsea house. Photo appreciated.'

Marc Bolan was back in the area, being interviewed there by Roy Carr for an article published in the June 16 edition of the *NME*, accompanied by a photograph showing him 'languishing amidst the flowers and weather-worn statues on the terrace of a chic Chelsea beanery situated at the unfashionable end of the King's Road'. Returning to a theme he had explored a month or so earlier in *Melody Maker*, he told Roy: 'Glam Rock is now as dead as a doornail to the point where it has become very boring. *Born to Boogie* got slated to shit, but despite that it's now about the third biggest grossing picture in England.'

On May 18, *Give the Gaffers Time to Love You* by Barry Reckord received a Sunday night presentation at the Royal Court Theatre Upstairs, directed by Pam Brighton, with Tim Curry among the cast. Curry had been a regular at the Court ever since 1970, when he had appeared in a revival of *The Sport of My Mad Mother*, but it was his next role at the Theatre Upstairs which was to bring him international fame. Richard O'Brien's *The Rocky Horror Show* had its world premiere there on June 19, directed by Jim Sharman, with Tim as Frank-N-Furter, who landed the part after singing a version of 'Tutti Frutti'. O'Brien himself played Riff Raff (looking not unlike Brian Eno, who was then preparing to leave Roxy Music), Julie Covington was Janet, Patricia Quinn played Magenta and Little Nell appeared as Columbia. Jonathan Adams, who took the role of the narrator and went on to play Dr Everett V. Scott in the 1975 film version, had studied painting at Chelsea College of Art. Lighting design was by Rory Dempster, who had begun his career in the sixties doing lights for Jimi Hendrix and worked on many classic Royal Court productions, surrounded – as David Hare has pointed out – by the asbestos commonly used in those days, exposure to which in various workplaces eventually caused the meso-thelioma which killed Rory in February 2005.

The Rocky Horror Show began to draw crowds – or at least, as near as you could get to a crowd in a sixty-seat theatre space – so that when the run finished, arrangements were made for it to transfer a short distance along the King's Road to the Classic Cinema at number 148, where it opened on August 11. The gig guide in that week's *NME* previewed the event as follows: 'It is the first live show ever staged at this venue. [. . .] We are promised monsters, mutants, transvestites and various other goodies – laced with a generous helping of rock, plus liberal dollops of sex and space travel.'

Eventually it would move even further down the King's Road to a more permanent home at another cinema, the Essoldo, at number 279, which ceased being a cinema at that point and was renamed the King's Road Theatre.

Doing the 'Time Warp' every night on the King's Road

Snake Guitar and Lizard Girls

Bob Marley and the Wailers came to town in the early summer of 1973 to record their album *Burnin'* in Studio 2 at Island's Basing Street facility, working on rhythm tracks that they had already laid down at Harry J's studio in Jamaica. The record label provided Bob and the band with a house on the King's Road to live in for the duration of their stay, to which regular supplies of vegetables and plaice were delivered as part of their Rastafarian diet. Upstairs in the larger Studio 1 at Basing Street, the Rolling Stones were recording, one of whom received an unscheduled early-morning alarm call from the boys in blue on June 26. Keith Richards and Anita Pallenberg were at home asleep at number 3 Cheyne Walk when it happened, as Keith recalled: 'To actually wake up and find the drugs squad in your bedroom, that's something that's indelibly printed on your brain.' Charged with possession of drugs and guns, they were eventually fined and given probation.

On the same day that Keith and Anita were getting busted, Ken Tynan went down to the Royal Court to check out Howard Brenton's new play, *Magnificence*, recording in his diary that it was 'about the possibility of revolution in England, which, like many similar plays, spends 90 per cent of its time explaining how neurotic, paranoiac and ineffective revolutionaries are, and only 10 per cent demonstrating why revolution is necessary'. Another famous theatrical diarist, Peter Hall, saw the same show on July 11, and came away feeling a little more positive: 'Brenton is a writer worth watching. He is also very funny. He deals in caricature, but his voice is assured.'

Brian Eno finally announced at the end of July that it was all over with him and Roxy Music, telling Nick Kent: 'I'm leaving to pursue a partially defined direction – probably involving further investigations into bio-electronics, snake guitar, the Human Voice and Lizard Girls.' The following week he added: 'Actually the real truth is that Bryan Ferry and I are secretly breaking away and we're going to form a duo called the Singing Brians.'

On July 21, 1973, the punk word showed up again in the *NME*, spread across several pages this time in a feature devoted to classic sixties garage bands such as the Standells, the Sonics and the Seeds, with the magnificent headline 'Warning: This Page Has Bad Breath'. The first contemporary band to have described themselves with this term were the genuinely ground-breaking New York outfit Suicide, who placed an advert in the *Village Voice* back in 1970 for their October 10 show at 729 Broadway which simply said 'PUNK MUSIC BY SUICIDE'. In this, as in many other respects, they were years ahead of their time.

If the term punk rock was understood to mean anything specific by 1973, it was not a million miles away from an image of snotty adolescents with cheap guitars and badly earthed amps attempting to play the collected works of Them at high volume through a broken fuzz pedal. Lenny Kaye's hugely influential *Nuggets* compilation was out there spreading the good word, and the likes of the Dolls and the Stooges were still blazing a trail which rightly valued attitude over technique. Nick Kent also wrote a subsidiary piece on the same page titled 'Let Us Now Praise Famous Punks', in which he specifically used the term 'punk bands', while elsewhere in the same paper, reviewing a John Lee Hooker album, Charles Shaar Murray remarked that

'*NME*'s own 20th Century Punkoid Ham, Nick Kent, makes the fascinating point that Hooker could be the world's only punk blues guitarist.' Meanwhile, just to prove that the whole music business had by no means gone punk crazy by 1973, prog rock titans Yes were trying to make an album by means of the time-honoured tradition of 'getting it together in the country'. Having failed to find a suitable rural studio, the *NME* reported that they wound up in one on Willesden High Road surrounded by 'potted plants and a multitude of greenery' provided by the band's management, who then went that crucial extra mile: 'to ensure greater realism, two papier-mâché cows, replete with nodding heads and tails, were also installed.'

TV Smith had this to say to me about the punk-referencing articles which pointed the way in those days:

I used to read *NME* faithfully, you know. *Sounds* as well, when that came a little bit later. But then of course you'd read about this stuff and it all sounded fantastically interesting, but then you couldn't hear it, you know? You know, every now and then you'd risk ordering a record, not having heard it, but the only way you were gonna hear any of this stuff was on Peel's show, and that was it . . .

Having a Fucking Knees-Up

Back at Westwood and McLaren's shop at 430 King's Road, the predominant theme was still fifties-inspired clothing, and they were offering a made-to-measure service, turning out Teddy boy drapes, and also forties and fifties double-breasted suits reminiscent of the kind seen in classic film noir. Kilburn and the High Roads, the new band fronted by Ian Dury, came in to get themselves fitted out. As Wreckless Eric told me: 'One of the things that was terribly important was Kilburn and the High Roads, and seeing Kilburn and the High Roads was like, they were doing rock'n'roll, but they were really, really, really English.' Two other people who also turned out to be pretty good at playing English rock'n'roll started visiting number 430 as well, as Glen Matlock recalled:

This is where I was first introduced to Paul Cook and Steve Jones, both of whom were regulars in the shop. They'd get off the bus from West London there because they were such big Faces fans and Malcolm's shop was right next door to the home of the dandy fashion shop Granny Takes a Trip – a shop which had a Cadillac [*sic*] sticking out of its window – where the Faces and the Stones bought their clothes.

Spider Stacy, who went on to form the Pogues with Shane MacGowan, was thirteen years old in 1973 and living in Golders Green. His elder sister had moved out in 1970 and left him a stash of 200 albums including the MC5, Dylan, the Doors and many more, and he'd gone out and bought the first Velvet Underground album aged eleven, soon followed by the first Stooges album, which had shown up miraculously in a Hampstead newsagents among a stack of budget-label Music For Pleasure LPs. As Spider told me, 'It's like it was put there for me to find, because what the *fuck* was it doing in this shop? I had to go round to one of my friends' houses and borrow 50 pence off his dad to get the record.' Like Steve Jones and Paul Cook, he was a fan of the Faces, and his own style at that time reflected that. 'Not so much the glam sort of thing, more the sort of boot-boy look. Layered hair, probably taking it more from the sort of Rod end of the market, as opposed to the Bowie, Bryan Ferry kind of thing.' The Faces played the Reading Festival in 1973, and Spider and his two mates blagged their way in:

> We had this scam, we only had one ticket, but one of us went in the river with his jeans on, with the ticket in his pocket, came out and we had a very wet ticket and basically that meant that all three of us were able to get in: 'Our tickets have disintegrated, we've just got this congealed mass . . .' The Faces were on the Saturday night, and Genesis were on Sunday, and the Faces were absolutely fucking brilliant. A complete mess. Pissed, out of tune, more interested really in kicking a football around and just having a fucking knees-up, you know. And actually, the funny thing was that the bad atmosphere, and the tension and the violence actually happened when Genesis were playing, because they didn't come back for an encore, and the stage just got a real serious bombardment of bottles . . .

Although the 1976 British punk movement owed a huge debt to the likes of Iggy, the Dolls and the Ramones, the cranked-up ramshackle exuberance of bands like the Faces or Mott the Hoople and the rising generation of pub rock bands, and especially the stripped-down Canvey R&B of the razor-sharp Dr Feelgood, were also a serious inspiration.

Mock Rock

In the world of the theatre, Ken Tynan was spending a fair amount of his diary entry for August 19 explaining to himself why he *wouldn't* be going to the Royal Court to see David Storey's new play *Cromwell*, due to open on August 23, starring Albert Finney. Tynan's entry then turned into a more general expression of dissatisfaction with the whole artistic policy of the English Stage Company:

> If only there were a dash of verve, colour, panache at the Court: it is nowhere to go for anything but a twisted smile, instantly to be wiped off the face. But I expect that to people like Lindsay A, showmanship is deeply suspect and colours like magenta are downright sinful. This sort of grimness was inherent in the Court right from the start, though in those days it was tempered by the occasional flamboyance of people like Tony Richardson and (verbally at least) the early Osborne.

Oddly enough, the new director of the National Theatre, Peter Hall, was also casting doubts on the Court's policies in his own diary on August 28, contrasting their normal output with that of Alan Ayckbourn: 'I think that Ayckbourn is much more likely to be in the repertoire of the National Theatre in fifty years' time than most of the current Royal Court dramatists.' As it was, the Court's programme for the remainder of the year was much as ever, with Lindsay Anderson directing another David Storey play, *The Farm*, which opened on October 18, and then on November 11 an adaptation by Peter Gill of D. H. Lawrence's *The Merry Go Round*. By way of a change, on December 2 the Court presented an appearance by George Melly.

The New York Dolls returned to the UK on November 20, and there to meet them at their South Kensington hotel were Malcolm McLaren and Vivienne Westwood, together with Ian Dury and also Chrissie Hynde, who was working then for the *NME* and was also to work at Too Fast To Live Too Young To Die – a shop which the Dolls proceeded to investigate. Nina Antonia reports that the band were originally scheduled to make an appearance on the Monty Python TV show, which would certainly have been something to see. As it was, they wound up performing 'Jet Boy' and 'Looking for a Kiss' on the *Old Grey Whistle Test*, after which presenter Bob Harris gave a foretaste of the sneering distain which most of the hippie media would display towards the punks in a couple of years' time. Staring at the camera like a kind of sarcastic geography teacher he uttered the words 'mock rock', before moving swiftly along. Whispering Bob might not have liked it, but the Dolls had put themselves across on television, and the message was getting through to where it was needed the most.

Also on that trip, the New York Dolls played at Biba's in Kensington High Street, and Malcolm and Vivienne went along. The costume which Vivienne wore to that gig was displayed at the 2004 Westwood retrospective exhibition at the V&A, and it shows that even as early as 1973, when the shop was still basically catering to a fifties clientele, she could already put together a look which would completely set the wearer apart from the crowd. TV Smith was still down in the West Country, but the word had spread: 'I heard about the New York Dolls playing Biba's and I wanted to come up, you know, but I was too young, I wasn't allowed to come up [laughs].'

One part of the late sixties counterculture dream sailed off into the sunset that autumn as the final edition of *OZ* was published, with a cover featuring some nude hippies against a background of numerous mugshots of Richard Nixon. This was *OZ* number 48, labelled 'The Last Issue – Winter 1973' and costing 30p. In its heyday, it had been a monthly magazine, but the previous edition, *OZ* 47, had appeared back in April, and had only cost 25p. Times were tough, and not just for Tricky Dick Nixon.

It was the end of another year, with another Monty Python publication in the shops, *The Brand New Monty Python Bok*, which included the following parody of Philip Jenkinson, presenter of BBC TV's *Film Night* programme:

Hello there. One or two apologies to readers, first of all to the film buff who wrote in to correct me about something I said in my exhausting analysis of Von Sternberg and his impact on the cinema. Well I have checked, and yes you're quite right, you *can* still buy that wash-and-wear fabric for shirts at 'Guy's an' Dave's', King's Road. Secondly, there are so many films to look at this week that I'm afraid that the knitting pattern I promised you in the Michelangelo Antonioni profile will have to be held over until next time.

25

'Everything we had was either home-made or stolen'

The Politics of Flash

Chelsea in 1974 was showing many signs that it had moved on from the 'swinging' days of the mid-sixties, and was already light years removed from its situation in the early fifties, when there were only a handful of restaurants, and most of them did not even have a drinks licence. Although the London Museum in W8 were holding an exhibition that spring entitled *Mary Quant's London*, and listings magazine *What's On in London* still had a section labelled 'Discotheques and Swinging Clubs' – which included 'Francoise, 23 King's Road. Open 8.30pm–3.00am. Membership £6. Entrance fee £1' – much had altered in the previous ten years. Novelist John Le Carré knew the area well, and his long-running series character George Smiley lived in Bywater Street, a quiet spot running north off the King's Road. In 1974, Le Carré published a new novel called *Tinker, Tailor, Soldier, Spy* in which George pondered the changes that had taken place in the district:

> Smiley arrived at the King's Road, where he paused on the pavement as if waiting to cross. To either side, festive boutiques. Before him, his own Bywater Street, a cul-de-sac exactly one hundred and seventeen of his own paces long. When he had first come to live here these Georgian cottages had a modest, down-at-heel charm, with young couples making do on fifteen pounds a week and a tax-free lodger hidden in the basement. Now steel screens protected their lower windows and for each house three cars jammed the curb.

Admittedly, Smiley's character was based in the wealthier part of the King's Road towards Sloane Square, whereas down at World's End, many things were still reliably tatty, and cheap accommodation could still sometimes be found. The local council had been building the World's End Estate for the last four years, and it would take in its first tenants in 1975, including Christine Keeler, but the general trend was inevitably towards gentrification, and the suppliers of steel window screens would be kept very busy over the coming years.

Journalist Wilfred De'Ath, profiling Poet Laureate and Radnor Walk resident Sir John Betjeman for the *Illustrated London News*, expressed his surprise at the start of his article to find him 'living in Chelsea, a mere pebble's throw from that sewer of trendiness, the King's Road'.

At the Royal Court, they began the year with a South African season, comprising a triple bill of plays, *The Island, Sizwe Bansi is Dead* and *Statements After an Arrest Under the Immorality Act*, with playwright Athol Fugard also directing. In February, Sam Shepard directed a production of his own play, *Geography of a Horse Dreamer*, with a cast that included Stephen Rea. Meanwhile, a former Royal Court success from the previous year was going from strength to strength. *The Rocky Horror Show*, which had begun at the Theatre Upstairs and had then transferred to the Classic Cinema further down the King's Road, was now moving to the newly converted Essoldo, renamed the King's Road Theatre. Peter Noble's column in the March 8 edition of *What's On in London* announced that plans were also underway for the Classic, revealing that one of the men behind this was none other than the man known to the newspapers as Mr Parnes Shillings and Pence – Britain's prime rock'n'roll manager of the fifties, and one of the major inspirations for Malcolm McLaren: 'Larry Parnes and Laurie Marsh have done a deal to turn three cinemas into Theatres. They are the Cameo-Poly, to be known as the Regent; the Essoldo, Kilburn, to open as the Broadway; and the Classic in King's Road. All will be opening with plays or musicals later this year under the Parnes-Marsh banner.'

McLaren himself was to feature in a ground-breaking article written by Nick Kent for the *NME*, published on April 6, 1974, under the title 'The Politics of Flash'. A lengthy examination of various fashion designers who were currently making clothes for rock musicians, it featured the likes of Gene Krell and Marty Breslau at Granny Takes a Trip ('among customers: Ronnie Wood'), Annie Reavy ('clothes custom-built for Elton John'), Roxy Music favourite Anthony Price ('designs for B Ferrari') and the Rock Taylor crew ('thread-weavers by appointment to Sweet'). It is no surprise that Kent included 430 King's Road in such a line-up. Aside from the shop's obvious qualifications, the *NME*'s Chrissie Hynde was working there, and she in turn was going out with Kent for a while.

Malcolm duly got his picture in the paper, standing on one leg dressed up in fifties-styled pegged trousers and some sort of moulting furry sweater which made him look as if he was being eaten alive by chinchillas. It was a photo which the *NME* would gleefully dig out of the archives at the height of the Sex Pistols notoriety and caption 'We are flying down to Rio'. The shop at 430 was still called Too Fast To Live Too Young To Die at this stage, and McLaren lost no time putting the boot into the competition: 'Granny's is really nothing more than a theatrical costumiers now. It's all right for what it is but . . .' He also told Kent that 'Mick Jagger stood outside the shop for half-an-hour once and never came in. Ringo Starr was the only one who dared to actually come in on a Saturday.'

Considering that Let it Rock had been commissioned to make Teddy boy clothing for Ringo to wear in the film *That'll Be the Day*, it is hardly surprising that he might pay a visit for a fitting. 'I don't know why half these rock stars come in here in the first place,' said McLaren, having spent the entire interview carefully identifying as customers half the musicians in the charts at that time, including Roy Wood, Bryan Ferry and Andy Mackay from Roxy Music, Alice Cooper, the New York Dolls, David Bowie and Elkie Brooks. Interestingly, though, the one name which is mentioned absolutely nowhere in this lengthy article is that of Vivienne Westwood, least of all by McLaren, who is presented throughout as the sole force behind the shop. When the article appeared, Too Fast To Live Too Young To Die's days as a fifties outlet were numbered. They had already started selling the T-shirts which featured real chicken bones ('I get 'em from the cafe across the road'), and although a new name had not yet been settled on, it was decided that the shop's design would 'change into something more like a gymnasium'.

You Can Get Laid a Lot Working in a Shop Like This

Gene Krell and Marty Breslau at Granny's were profiled in the same article as suppliers of clothes to the surviving sixties rock hierarchy; the former apparently could 'often be seen on the King's Road carrying a copy of Rimbaud's complete works' while the latter 'resembles a wasted-looking Warren Beatty with long hair'. Krell and Breslau were happy to have a go at rival Chelsea store Alkasura, run by John Lloyd: 'I tell ya, if we started selling milk in the shop, Alkasura would buy up a herd of cows.' Much was made of the fact that they regularly supplied clothes to the Rolling Stones, and in a final quote, Krell showed that it wasn't just McLaren who was intent on shoe-horning references to various philosophers into the fashion business:

'Like,' Krell free-associates, 'I'd have loved to design a suit for Friedrich Nietzsche. Man, could you imagine it – Zarathustra coming down from the mountain in a Granny's rhinestoned suit!' 'Yeah,' mutters Breslau, 'You should also mention that you can get laid a lot working in a shop like this.'

For Granny's, this was actually almost the end of the road, as hardcore drugs had seemingly become more important than clothes at that stage, and some parts of the World's End were very much the worse for wear. Paul Gorman, whose book *The Look* chronicles the history of rock and pop fashion, was a fourteen-year-old regular visitor to the King's Road at the time, and he told me:

> Granny's by then was completely drug-ridden. 1971 was the Faces look and Keith Richards, but they were dealing out of there, and by '73 it was really open. I had to walk past it to get the bus. In '74 it was still there, but it was just completely druggy. It was really quite scary for a fourteen-year-old, because it just had this really horrible vibe to it. Gene Krell says that there was one shop down the King's Road where they'd bought a lion cub at Harrods. They had it in the shop. It was then that you started to realise that things were out of control down there. When I started going down there it was so tatty . . .

There certainly appeared to be a sharp increase in the amount of hard drugs in the neighbourhood during the early part of the decade, and according to a 1972 report in *The Times*, 'The CURE centre in King's Road, Chelsea, had coped with double the number of Chinese heroin addicts [by which they meant people addicted to Chinese heroin] in the past year than it had done in the previous year.'

Some people, however, did not even bother going as far as Harrods when looking for big cats, such as whoever stole one of a pair of two-foot-high porcelain Chinese lions from outside the Ming Yuan restaurant in the King's Road in December 1973. It was reportedly valued at £1,000, which rather suggests that it might have been a relatively optimistic decision leaving it out in the street in the first place.

For a shop like 430 to be selling Teddy boy gear or straight jeans in those days was relatively unusual, but even so, the classified adverts pages at the back of the *NME* in the early seventies showed many clothing firms obviously doing a thriving mail-order business, and at least some of them catered for what were then minority tastes. While most advertisers simply offered the

standard late-hippie fare of split-knee loons, Afghans and platform-soled
Maltese Cross-emblazoned clogs, straight jeans were being manufactured
for the boot-boy trade by a firm in Birkenhead ('Original Skinners – Parallel
Jeans'), while a company called Orpheus – which operated from the concrete
splendours of 'Britain's ugliest building', the Tricorn Centre in Portsmouth
(lovingly demolished in 2004) – sold a complete mail-order range of Teddy
boy gear from drapes to creepers to bootlace ties via their weekly ads in the
back of the *NME*. It is interesting to note that a week or two after Too Fast
To Live Too Young To Die was profiled in the paper, Orpheus were advertising their range under the title Too Young To Die. Even Zeppelin's Robert
Plant was getting in on the act, confusing the crowd at a February 14 Roy
Harper gig when he walked onstage in a leopardskin drape with hair greased
back into a DA, the result, he said afterwards, of having 'been playing too
many Ral Donner records'.

Chelsea resident David Bowie, March 1974

All the same, despite the market out there for drapes and straight jeans,
someone who set up home in Chelsea that year was offering the teenage
readers of *Mirabelle* magazine an alternative vision of men's clothing: 'When
I first started wearing dresses there was a big outcry about them, which I
really couldn't understand. There doesn't seem to be anything wrong to me
in any guy wearing something which is both comfortable and fashionable.'

The man in question was David Bowie, but admittedly by June he was telling the press that he favoured 'French and Italian well-made suits'. He had moved with his wife Angie into a five-storey Georgian house off the King's Road in Oakley Street, near the Albert Bridge. Visitors chez Bowie would include Mick Jagger (who lived round the corner at 48 Cheyne Walk), Twiggy with Justin de Villeneuve, Ron Wood, Marianne Faithfull, Dana Gillespie, Elliot Gould and Ryan O'Neal. Bryan Ferry, whose career was handled by EG management in the King's Road, lived a short distance away from the Bowies over in Battersea, and would sometimes sleep on their sofa. Angie later wrote that she had come home one day to find David and Mick Jagger upstairs in bed together.

Bin There, Done That

While Mick and David were apparently keeping warm in Chelsea, somewhat further north the future Wreckless Eric was laying the groundwork for his own DIY renaissance, forming a group which had all the essential ingredients memorably later spelled out in the immortal words of the Desperate Bicycles, 'It was easy, it was cheap, go and do it,' as he told me:

> I had this band in the art school up in Hull, and we were called Addis & The Flip-Tops, which was named after the Addis Flip-Top bin . . . 'Cause when we started practising we didn't even have a drum kit, and we'd had this Addis Flip-Top bin that was in the guitar-player's kitchen and the drummer played that. And we said, 'All we need now is a name,' and someone said, 'Well the name's on the front of the bin . . .' We always said that everything we had was either home-made or stolen.

At the same time that Steve Jones down in London was busy nicking much of the gear which would get the Sex Pistols started, Eric's band were adopting a similar approach up in Hull:

> We had the art school's PA system. There were two Echolette columns on the wall, a Selmer PA amplifier in the back of the main hall, a microphone stand and a ribbon microphone. They never used it, so we went in there one night and fuckin' had it all away. We had to borrow a handcart – 'The getaway vehicle was a handcart . . .' We'd had to get a ladder, fucking unbolt the columns from the wall, and there was a patch of paler paintwork where the columns had been – it was there until I left, you know . . .

Art school also came to the Royal Court that April, or at least, one aspect of it, in the subject matter of David Storey's play *Life Class*, directed by Lindsay Anderson and starring Alan Bates, who first appeared at the Court back in 1956 in the original cast of *Look Back in Anger*. Bates starred opposite Rosemary Martin, who played the nude model in an art class, and he later recalled that 'there was no exhibitionism, no paranoia about taking her clothes off – she just did it – calmly, easily and beautifully, and played the part itself so superbly that Harold Hobson wrote about it for five Sundays afterwards.' The poster for the play used on the Underground survived the censorship of the London Transport's Advertisement Selection Committee, which was the first time that they had approved a nude image.

Lou Reed had been seen around Chelsea for a couple of years at this stage, but now another founding member of the Velvet Underground, John Cale, came to live and record in the area. Cale's current partner was Miss Cindy, an ex-member of Frank Zappa's girl band, the GTOs. Together, they relocated from America to London, as he recalled in his autobiography, *What's Welsh for Zen*:

We moved at first into a two-storey house on Britannia Road near Chelsea football ground. Cindy had many old friends living and working on the King's Road. I had no friends there. [. . .] The Carnaby Street scene was over, but Malcolm McLaren was a permanent character among those featured on the King's Road. We eyed each other warily across the street, and one day I found him in the bank queue ahead of me in a great pair of pants with tassels down the sides. I never met him formally, but was aware of him over time, after I left, when the Pistols were coming up.

Cale was in Chelsea recording his new album, *Fear* – recorded both at Sound Techniques in Old Church Street and also at Olympic Studios in Barnes – and Mick Gold from the *Melody Maker* dropped by the former location for an article which was published on July 27:

In the studio located a few yards from London's King's Road, John Cale, Eno and Phil Manzanera are huddled around the mixing desk with the engineer, adding, overdubbing, arguing about each note. [. . .] The evening is rapidly mutating into a John Cale song. Cale is still leaping up and down screaming at the mike; everyone else is slumped in the control booth. The engineer rolls some more tape and a very beautiful, ethereal track with organ and 12-string guitar starts playing.

Light Years Ahead

Mick Farren – at that time one of the chief writers on the *NME* – would sometimes call in at Sound Techniques, which now had *The Rocky Horror Show* right on its doorstep at the King's Road Theatre a few yards away, pulling big crowds having won Best Musical in the *Evening Standard* Drama Awards, as he told me:

> We used to do a lot of recording down the side of that theatre in Sound Techniques, which was originally Joe Boyd's studio, but a lot of people used it. You'd find yourself mixing with the Rocky Horror people in the same pubs around there. A number of times a year you'd be down there visiting somebody, saying, 'Oh look there's Tim Curry,' you know. I don't think I was doing anything at the time, but there were people you'd go down there and see – I think the Pink Fairies were down there at one time . . .

On June 29, a Mick Farren live review appeared in the *NME* of a band he had seen at Dingwalls in Camden Town: 'It's not often that the jaded, booze-soaked crowd that throng Dingwalls dance hall bring an almost unknown band back for three encores. [. . .] In some ways it's like being transported back to an early Yardbirds gig, except that the band are technically light years ahead of anything that went on at the Crawdaddy.'

The band was Dr Feelgood, in the original line-up featuring Wilko Johnson on guitar, who had short hair, a black suit without flares and a black telecaster. If anything was pointing the way forward in the eighteen months immediately prior to the first Ramones album and the rise of the Pistols, it was these people. As Farren wrote: 'They are almost anti-rock, with their haircuts, ties, and uncompromising approach. On Sunday they played Wandsworth Prison, and it's a far cry from the pseudo-faggot glitzies or urban cowhands who seem to be the current norm in rock and roll.'

Glam, however, despite Marc Bolan's attempts at burying it, was still very much on the television screens and in the charts that year, which saw the launch of a new children's TV programme called *Tiswas* that hosted many of the big-name glam acts. Presenter Sally James spent a lot of time shopping for clothes in the King's Road, and a particular favourite of hers was the shop Ace, which started out at 185 King's Road and then moved to number 193. Silk, satin, lurex and sequins was the name of the game on that show, although visiting bands such as Slade or the Sweet would tend to leave their good clothes at home before appearing on *Tiswas*, since guests had a habit of being drenched with water and covered in slime.

There was a new Edward Bond play called *Bingo* at the Royal Court, opening on August 14, which saw English Stage Company regulars John Gielgud and Arthur Lowe back at Sloane Square, directed by Jane Howell. Peter Hall called in to see the production on August 20, and found it 'an excellent evening, intellectual and mandarin and very elliptical'.

As an alternative, he could have tried heading up to one of the many attempts to recapture the Woodstock vibe that summer, this time in the shape of the Buxton music festival, one of whose audience then wrote to the papers claiming to be recuperating from 'severe exposure, frost-bite, dysentery, food poisoning, pneumonia and solidified mud'. Entertainment comes in many forms. Meanwhile the gossip column in the *NME* provided a cautionary story about the dangers of attempting to go shopping at Granny's while out of your brain on Class A drugs: 'The following tale concerns Keith Richards and a visit by our punk hero to a King's Road clothing establishment to purchase a pair of trousers. [. . .] "Yeah," drawls the lad, examining them at suitably protracted length, "Yeah, I'll try these, man . . . Where'sa changin' room?" "Er, you're *in* it, Keith."'

After attempting unsuccessfully for several minutes to undo his own trousers in order to try on the new ones, he apparently abandoned the attempt, saying 'Oh, lissen, man . . . I carn 'andle this. I'll take the fings on spec.'

Sex Symbol

Somewhere due south of one man's heroic struggle with the consumer society, a rock band called the Guildford Stranglers were registering their name for business purposes on September 11, which they would later shorten before becoming one of the first of the British punk bands to reach the charts. Out in the West Country, TV Smith formed a band called Sleaze, under the influence of Iggy and the New York Dolls. However, the conditions were not yet ideal, as he says:

> The only bands you got down in Devon were bands that were doing cover versions of Free stuff, you know, unless you were doing that it was really hard to get a gig. I put on a couple of gigs and I was doing all stuff that I'd written myself and people were just standing there going 'What the fuck is this? This is horrible . . .' I knew I was on

the track of something – it wasn't very good back then, before the Adverts. The previous bands were probably actually pretty shit, but at least I was doing my own thing, you know?

As TV was giving the public Sleaze, Malcolm and Vivienne at 430 had decided they were going to give them SEX. To that end, the shop had been closed for several months during the summer of 1974, reopening under the new name in September, with a large padded PVC sign spelling out SEX above the window, presumably much to the delight of the members of the local Conservative Association next door. Glen Matlock, who had been thrown out of his steady Saturday job by the closure, appealed to McLaren for help and was put to work helping out with the refit and putting up the new sign, as he later wrote: 'I helped do the SEX sign and put all this foam rubber on the walls which were then decorated with spray can graffiti from the '68 Paris student revolt. Slogans like "Under the paving stone lies a beach", and *"prenez-vous ça que vous désire pour la réalité".'*

Malcolm, who missed the Paris uprising by two months back in 1968, finally had the chance to bring some late sixties situationism to the King's Road shoppers. The mood of the place was now very different from its Teddy boy beginnings, owing more to fetish clubs, existing specialist rubber-gear outfits like She-An-Me – who would become one of SEX's suppliers – and the kind of leather outfitters who catered to the gay S&M trade. Billy Fury had nothing to do with it: from this point forward, the aim was to shock. Purely by coincidence, a couple of weeks before SEX opened, million-selling prog-rock titans Emerson, Lake and Palmer released a triple live album.

Yet despite the makeover, it appears that there was still a fair amount of leftover Ted-related stock being sold at the shop for a while. An article about the favourite shops and designers used by several current pop stars including Gary Glitter and Alvin Stardust, which appeared in the *Record Mirror* on November 9, had this to say in the section about 430 King's Road, written in the breathless style of a teenybopper magazine:

London has a famous 50s shop which is always changing its name and is about to do so now. However, if you walk right down King's Road (catch a bus, it's quite a walk) almost to World's End you will hit Let It Rock or whatever it's called! You can't miss it. Why can't you miss it? Simply because the window and inside is packed with Ted shoes, brothel creepers around £10, two-tone shoes, ones worn by Eddie Cochran and the 50s singers and those long, pointed winklepickers. There is a goodly selection of Slim Jim bootlaces and for girls and crazy guys the real and original torture cinch belts for around £2. Plenty of studs for jackets are available and for girls with nerve, some incredible mini studded leather skirts and shirts studded and shaped to draw attention to you know what. There are some super white t-shirts and for girls the real authentic eye-catching (unless you wear trousers!) fishnet stocking for just over £2. The drainpipe trousers cost in the region of £8 and jackets £30 plus. And look out for some super mohair jumpers.

As the new generation limbered up, one of the leading lights of the 1967 psychedelic explosion who started his recording career at Sound Techniques returned to live in the area. Chelsea Cloisters, the thirties block of flats on Sloane Avenue which in three years' time would for a while be home to John Lydon and Sid Vicious, now became the last London address of Syd Barrett prior to his move back to Cambridge. While at the Cloisters, it is said that he had seven TV sets in one room which he watched simultaneously.

Lady Clarissa Minge-Water's Coming Out Ball

Back on the King's Road, Richard and Linda Thompson were at Sound Techniques recording their third LP, *Hokey Pokey*, continuing the remarkable run of significant folk albums which had been cut there. Next door to the studio was the theatre where the stage version of *The Rocky Horror Show* was still packing in the crowds, and 20 miles west of Chelsea in the run-up to Christmas, Jim Sharman was shooting a big-screen adaptation of the musical, not surprisingly opting for the title *The Rocky Horror Picture Show*.

The filming took place at Bray Studios out near Windsor, an appropriate choice, since it was for many years the home of Hammer Film Productions, and the gothic mansion used in the film, Oakley Court, can also be seen in many of the Hammer classics of the fifties and sixties. By any standards, for a show to have gone from opening in front of sixty people in the Theatre Upstairs at the Royal Court to being turned into a hugely successful feature film in the space of little over a year was a remarkable achievement. It was a show and a film which soon began inspiring audiences to dress up in costume when attending, a new trend which was also happening with some rock bands. The October 19 edition of the *NME* devoted a double-page spread to an article which examined the motivations of people who had turned up to see a Roxy Music gig at the Rainbow. Printing a photo of

Bryan Ferry in his full gaucho gear next to lots of shots of the glammed-up punters, they ran a speech bubble out of Ferry's mouth which said, 'If you think I look a prune – get a load of this lot . . .' As Charles Shaar Murray wrote, 'most of these people are around eighteen or nineteen, they all like Bowie and Roxy and Lou Reed and they always dress up for concerts'. As for Roy Carr, he didn't like the look of it at all:

> There were droves of flat-chested *femmes fatales* and their frail skinny hipped chaperones, heavy-boobed waterfront B girls with scarlet slashes for mouths and pug-nosed palookas for protectors, sixth-formers fresh from raiding their grandma's wardrobe, and fresh-faced fops in white tie and tails who looked like they'd be more at home throwing champers over each other at Lady Clarissa Minge-Water's Coming Out Ball than washing down Jamaica Patties with Brown Ale. But then, Finsbury Park has never been the hub of cafe society . . .

Clearly, there was a generation coming up that was looking for something else to wear other than the obligatory denim or cheesecloth shirts. Whether they were up for the all-over inflatable rubber suits and nipple-clamps look which McLaren and Westwood were currently heading towards is a good question, but the DIY clothing explosion seen at early punk gigs in '76 before the tiresome identikit punk uniform set in would certainly give a lot of these kids a chance to dress up and feel different.

Right now, though, as the year closed, Teddy boy drape-wearing glam outfit Mud were at number one in the charts with 'Lonely This Christmas', and singer Les Gray did his finest Elvis impersonation while the rest of the band stood on a stepladder and sprinkled fake glitter-snow on his head. As all this was going on, Malcolm McLaren had temporarily deserted the King's Road for New York, heading over there in November in an attempt to revive the flagging career of the New York Dolls. In the event, the solution was already on his doorstep, and the following year would see the first gigs by the Sex Pistols, but it would also witness number one hits by the likes of Telly Savalas, Typically Tropical and Art Garfunkel, not to mention Windsor Davies and Don Estelle . . .

26

'Machine Bubble Disco'

Do the Strand

January 1975: at 430 King's Road they were having SEX. Future Roxy club owner Andy Czezowski was acting as the shop's accountant, and future Clash manager Bernie Rhodes was helping out with various stratagems while Malcolm McLaren was currently sidetracked by his quixotic US attempt to keep the New York Dolls together by dressing them up as happy little Communists. Down in the basement below Antiquarius, future Roxy DJ Don Letts was cranking up the reggae sound system while selling a selection of vintage demob suits and reconditioned jukeboxes at Acme Attractions to a mixed crowd who'd soon be part of the punk scene, while at Beaufort Market just off the King's Road future Sex Pistols tour manager Nils Stevenson was flogging 'leather jackets, drainpipes, pegs, winkle-pickers and drapes' and getting friendly with Westwood and McLaren. Punk rock was a high-speed collision just waiting to happen.

So what are upcoming eighties heavy metal stadium rockers Judas Priest doing playing a show right there on the King's Road on January 5? These were transitional times . . .

As it happens, although *The Rocky Horror Show* would continue its run very successfully at the King's Road Theatre for another couple of years, in early 1975 there seems to have been a regular policy of giving over Sunday evenings at the venue to live rock gigs. The Judas Priest show mentioned above must have gone well, because they were back again on April 20. Less successful was the show by the Winkies on January 26, according to a February 11 news item in the *NME* (headed *The Winkies Go Wonky?*) which claimed their gig had been such a mess that the band had split almost immediately after-wards, with singer Phil Rambow and guitarist Guy Humphries arriving at what was euphemistically termed 'a conversational impasse'.

Still, if that particular performance had been a disappointment, there was always regular attraction George Adair just down the road at the Nose Wine Bar. However, in early February, one of the key bands of the pub rock scene, Ducks Deluxe, appeared at the King's Road Theatre, featuring Sean Tyler, whose next band the Tyla Gang would release the fourth ever single on the new Stiff record label the following year. Also in Ducks Deluxe was Martin Belmont, soon to become part of Graham Parker and the Rumour. That night on the King's Road they played versions of Sonny Curtis's much-covered anthem 'I Fought the Law' and also the Flamin' Groovies song 'Teenage Head'. The place was half-empty, but the band certainly had the right idea.

A much less publicised musical performance took place a few hundred yards further down the King's Road that spring, when Steve Jones, Paul Cook, Glen Matlock and Wally Nightingale played the only show of their career as the Strand. The occasion was a party above Tom Salter's Cafe at 205 King's Road, and the band managed three whole songs, with Jones on vocals, including Sam Cooke's 'Twisting the Night Away', a choice which probably owed a lot to the fact that Rod Stewart had recently covered it. Nightingale was sacked shortly afterwards – a move instigated by McLaren on his return in May.

Before he had headed off to New York, Malcolm, together with Vivienne and Bernie Rhodes, had drawn up a list of 'Hates' and 'Loves' which were then printed on one of their most famous T-shirts, which began 'You're gonna wake up one morning and know which side of the bed you've been lying on!' Not only did these two lists mention 'Kutie Jones and his SEX PISTOLS' – in the 'Loves' column, unsurprisingly – but it also namechecked a few Chelsea people of one type or another. Included in the 'Hates' were Nigel Waymouth, Michael Caine, George Melly, John Osborne, Ossie Clark and 'ANTIQUARIUS and all it stands for'. Among the 'Loves' the district didn't score too highly, with only Christine Keeler and Marianne Faithfull flying the flag, although people with memories of the Fantasie back in the late fifties might wish to include 'Coffee Bars that sell whiskey under the counter'. The overwhelming impression of most of the 'Loves' and 'Hates' is of how rooted in the sixties so many of them were; your average rebellious teenager would have been way too young to have even heard of a fair proportion of the list and probably wouldn't have given a monkeys about David Frost, John Dunbar or failed murderer Valerie Solanas. It was halfway through a new decade, but like the sixties situationist graffiti reproduced on the walls of SEX, it sometimes smacked of someone trying to re-fight the student battles of an earlier era.

Arthur Burned My Wallet

In Oakley Street, between the King's Road and the Albert Bridge, Angie Bowie was giving an interview to Ray Fox Cumming of the *Record Mirror*, and shared some touching domestic details from the house in which she and David had been living for the past two years:

> While her husband and son are away, Angie has reluctantly acquired for company a dog called Marcus. 'A friend left him here,' she explains. 'He's a Dobermann Pinscher and a very fine one,' she says to his face, 'perfect in every respect except he's only got one ball.' [. . .] Marcus also has a chronic and somewhat unfortunate wind problem, which results in him frequently being banished from the living room at very short notice.

At the Royal Court in March you could see *Don's Party*, a new play by David Williamson, starring Ray Barrett and directed by Michael Blakemore, or else at the Theatre Upstairs, as *Time Out* noted on March 14, there were:

> John Burrows, John Harding and Peter Skellern in their new show *Loud Reports*, the memoirs of Colonel Ian Corfe-Prater, VC, DSO, MC. Directed by Mark Wing-Davey. [. . .] It's a kind of an alternative Young Winston. Peter Skellern adds some interesting songs and also plays most of the fall guys surprisingly well. The spare, economical style, the deadpan, controlled performances and some ironic scenes make this sophisticated agitprop well worth a visit.

After charting in 1972 with 'You're a Lady', Skellern had not had a hit since, but then on March 29 – just two weeks after this review – he made it into the Top Twenty again with 'Hold On To Love', which peaked at number fourteen. Meanwhile, Rachel Roberts arrived in London to appear in John Osborne's new play at Greenwich, *The End of Me Old Cigar*, and stayed with John's wife Jill Bennett at her home just off the King's Road for the duration. Sadly, luck finally ran out one day that spring for one of John's former wives, Mary Ure – who played the original female lead in the 1956 production of *Look Back in Anger* and was now married to Robert Shaw – as Peter Hall recorded in his diary on April 3: 'Desperate news late this afternoon. Mary

Ure opened in a play in London last night and this morning she was discovered dead in her bed. The rumour is that she had been drinking and took sleeping pills. She choked to death. Poor Bob Shaw. And the eight children.'

In the country at large, Labour prime minister Harold Wilson had made the surprise announcement that he was resigning on March 16, and in the words of Kenneth O. Morgan, 'unemployment and inflation both rose to record post-war levels and the government seemed to travel in the wake of events. [. . .] [Wilson's] reputation, however, was further sullied by a final honours list which, in Lloyd George style, honoured old cronies.' Harold was replaced by Jim Callaghan, who now faced across the floor of the Commons a female Leader of the Opposition named Margaret Thatcher, currently living in a house in Flood Street, just off the King's Road. On March 21, she made her first appearance on the cover of *Private Eye*, with a speech bubble that read: 'Isn't it about time I was on the cover of *Private Eye*?' It certainly wouldn't be the last time.

Credit: Tom King/Daily Mirror/Mirrorpix

Margaret Thatcher sweeping the front path of her Flood Street home, south of the King's Road, for the benefit of the press, 2 February 1975

Malcolm McLaren arrived back from his US sojourn in May, having witnessed the New York CBGB scene at first hand, fully aware of what people like the Ramones, Richard Hell and Television were up to. That same month, Rick Wakeman from Yes was preparing to appear at the Empire Pool Wembley in support of his new solo album. Not that Rick was planning to hold the fort entirely alone, as the adverts made clear:

RICK WAKEMAN
IN
THE MYTHS AND LEGENDS OF KING ARTHUR
A PAGEANT ON ICE
FEATURING
THE ENGLISH ROCK ENSEMBLE
THE NEW WORLD SYMPHONY ORCHESTRA
THE ENGLISH CHAMBER CHOIR
THE NOTTINGHAM FESTIVAL CHOIR
NARRATION BY TERRY TAPLIN
PLUS A HOST OF ICE STARS

In the event, it appeared that London wasn't ready for King Arthur and his ice-skating musical Knights of the Round Table, and the financial consequences were dire, as subsequent headlines revealed:

ARTHUR BURNS WAKEMAN WALLET
'I LOST MY SHIRT' SAYS SHAKEN RICK

Waterskiing Nude on Lake Geneva

Just as Wakeman's warriors were doggedly skating around Wembley, Nick Kent published a three-page history of Iggy and the Stooges in the *NME*, accompanied by Richard Creamer's photo of a bleeding Iggy being held up by Ron Asheton, who was wearing one of his favourite SS uniforms with a swastika armband. Ever since the film *Cabaret* had been a big hit a couple of years previously, there had been a certain amount of Nazi chic floating about in London, and in the mail-order pages near the back of the *NME* in April 28, 1973, you could find an advert headed *Achtung!*, illustrated with a drawing of a man wearing a Nazi helmet, and offering nickel swastikas for 55p, Iron Crosses (with ribbons) also 55p, swastika rings, Luftwaffe eagles, swastika cap badges and so on.

Ron Asheton was well known for his Nazi memorabilia, but McLaren and Westwood would later use a large swastika as part of one of their most famous designs, the 'Destroy' shirt, combined with an upside-down crucifix for maximum offence potential. It was all part of a policy – along with pictures of Karl Marx, pornographic cartoons of Snow White having sex with all seven dwarves, and Cambridge Rapist T-shirts – to stir up as much trouble as possible. Anything taboo was fair game. Back in the 1850s, when the first printing of Baudelaire's *Les Fleurs du Mal* had been confiscated and burnt on the orders of the French government, Gustave Flaubert wrote him a letter saying, 'Congratulations, society has bestowed on you the only compliment that it can offer an artist, it has banned your work.' McLaren and Westwood were also looking to get banned: that was the prize.

On June 7, Lisa Robinson wrote a lengthy article for the *NME* about the thriving new music scene at a Bowery club called CBGB in New York, complete with numerous pictures, helping to ensure that people like Television, Wayne County, Debbie Harry, the Dictators, the Heartbreakers and the Ramones would very soon be much more well known nationally in the UK than they were in the US. By the time the likes of the Ramones hit London the following year, their debut British gigs took place in front of considerably bigger crowds than they were used to in New York, while outside that scene back home they were lucky to get any publicity at all. At Acme Attractions in the basement of the same Antiquarius market which the 'Love/Hate' SEX T-shirt so despised, they had for some time dealt in vintage jukeboxes. Now in June 1975, Acme's John Krevine branched out by holding a sale exhibition in Maddox Street of numerous examples of them, with individual machines costing up to £2,000 for a Wurlitzer 1015. At those kinds of prices, it is not surprising that the buyers were mostly rich rock stars: Jimmy Page of Led Zeppelin – whose management offices were in the King's Road – bought a Filber model, and Bryan Ferry was reported to have shown an interest. Keith Emerson from ELP – another band who made the 'Hate' column on the SEX T-shirt – was elsewhere that summer, however, being photographed waterskiing in the nude on Lake Geneva, for reasons best known to himself.

During the summer of 1975, a new venture was launched by Ted Carroll, the man who had been supplying rare records to Malcolm at 430 King's Road ever since the start of Let it Rock – some of which were bought by a young Charles Saatchi, whose company later helped a certain Flood Street resident become prime minister in 1979. Carroll was branching out from selling records at his Rock On market stall to also making them by starting Chiswick Records, which was essentially the first of the UK punk indie labels. Helping Ted set up the label was Roger Armstrong, and the two of them were looking for the right band with which to launch it. The perfect recording studio for their purposes, Pathway in Islington, had been recommended to them by Jake Riviera from the Hope and Anchor, who was soon to start that other great pioneering indie label, Stiff Records. The pattern was set which produced much of the great music of the next two years – a fine live band used to playing in sweaty smoky pubs, recorded cheaply at high speed in a tiny studio. Roger Armstrong told me:

> I was working for Ted on the market stall down in Soho. We recorded the Count Bishops in August '75, the *Speedball* EP. We went and bought *Melody Maker* one night. They were called Chrome at the time, and they were at the Lord Nelson in Holloway Road, and we thought, that's a good rock'n'roll sounding name, let's go and see them. Jake had told us about Pathway, and we went in in August, and it was one of those summers . . . At about 10 o'clock at night, Ted wandered in, and we'd had a couple of beers, but nobody was out of it in any way whatsoever, and Ted comes in with a huge box full of beers and a bottle of whiskey and a chunk of dope, and everybody got stuck in. We'd recorded a lot of stuff, so we were playing it all back, and everybody got really inspired, and by about midnight we got back onto it again and recorded more till about two in the morning. We got an EP out of that. 120 quid, it cost. I remember finding the bill.

Skiffle – Part Two

Of course, this is the polar opposite of the approach which Malcolm McLaren and Bernie Rhodes would follow with the Pistols and the Clash, where the aim was to sign to a major label for as much money as possible, and the big-budget studios used generally had much larger rooms and a correspondingly much higher bill to pay at the end of the session. Malcolm's dream owed more to Larry Parnes, Andrew Loog Oldham and even the fraudulent 'Colonel' Tom Parker than it did to Sam Phillips in his living-room-sized studio at Sun records. Much of the coming punk explosion, though, was smaller-scale, low-budget and flexible. As Wreckless Eric told me, 'It was really Skiffle – Part Two.'

The same month that the founders of Chiswick Records were sitting in the tiny Pathway studio recording the Count Bishops, Malcolm McLaren went for a drink one evening in the Roebuck pub on the King's Road, to meet up with the people he had been trying to mould into a rock band. Also along for the ride was a potential new member of the group and sometime SEX customer John Lydon, recently seen walking around the area in his home-customised T-shirt. As Lydon recalled in his first autobiography:

> The punk thing started pretty much nonmusically. Bernie Rhodes spotted me wearing my 'I Hate Pink Floyd' T-shirt on King's Road and asked me to come back that night and meet Malcolm, Steve Jones and Paul Cook in the Roebuck pub on the King's Road. I wasn't going to go alone. I could have gone with Wobble, but I brought John Gray. Fuck this, it sounded like a setup to me.

The Roebuck in those days was a heroically tatty King's Road pub, of a kind which has virtually been wiped out these days owing to the corporate brewing industry's ceaseless attempts to make the world safe for middle management execs looking for an overpriced microwaved lunch in carefully neutered surroundings. It stood on the corner of King's Road and Beaufort Street, and was the regular watering hole for the people from SEX. As Mick Farren told me:

> Yeah the Roebuck was always good. *That* was a pub . . . you could not only run into Gene October, you could run into George Melly and Peter O'Toole, you know. It had a lot of bars, as I recall. See, that was the sort of flagship boozer for the other end of the King's Road. You know, there was the Chelsea Potter and the Six Bells, and if you went further west, that was the next watering hole, and after that, it was kind of the Stamford Bridge pubs . . .

Someone else who was with Malcolm McLaren in the Roebuck on the night of John Lydon's Pistols 'audition' was the writer Paul Gorman, at that time a fifteen-year-old enjoying a spot of underage drinking with his elder brother Timothy who worked nearby at a boutique called Domidium, in the Blue Bird Garage, and was friendly with McLaren. Paul and his brother had been painting a house up the road, and knocked off for a pint after work:

> It was probably opening time, half past five, by the time we got in there, and the evening just went on and on and on. The Pistols were in there quite early and I remember McLaren was wearing this uncomfortable looking garment, incredibly tight . . . He knew Tim

because they'd met each other a lot, literally in the bank, queueing up with Jordan, her in a complete rubber outfit, just cashing the takings. They were minting it. It was very, very expensive stuff, and I think it was part of the whole plan, to really fuck people off. OK, they'd become trendy, but God, you'd make them pay for it. So Malcolm was just nicking my brother's Senior Service, and we were chatting, talking about straight jeans – my brother said, 'Oh, you've always stocked them,' and now there were a couple of other places who'd started to; I think the Emperor of Wyoming had them. Malcolm was sitting with his back to these others. You could see Lydon's face, and he just had that fucking great haircut . . . I don't remember green hair, and I think I would do actually. There was also this bloke who I thought was Freddie Mercury, who I really didn't like, but I reckon it was John Cale. He was sat at one table, and we were at the one in between and the Pistols and their lot were at the next one. I got absolutely hammered . . .

As history records, Lydon and the others then walked along the road to SEX where he mimed along to Alice Cooper's 'I'm Eighteen' on the shop jukebox, and the bargain was sealed. Rick Wakeman may have been treating the country to King Arthur on ice, but rock's own version of Richard III was now about to make his public debut.

And just what had Joe Strummer been up to that summer?

Harlequin Record Store 97/99 Dean Street W1
presents for your comfort
Live on Saturday 18th July 1pm
THE 101'ers
Free Admission

Some Snotty Little Band Throwing Chairs Around

The Sex Pistols played their first gig at St Martin's School of Art – where Glen Matlock was a student – on November 6, 1975, but you would have needed luck to have been there, because you were not likely to have read about it in the press, as Paul Cook recalled:

We used to turn up at college gigs opening up for hippie bands. We weren't booked at a lot of those gigs because they wouldn't have us on. We would play unannounced at places like Holborn and the

Central School of Art and Design. [. . .] These were just learning gigs around Christmastime of 1975. The strange thing was that people latched onto us straight away. We got a reaction wherever we went; a lot of it was positive.

On the same night as the first Pistols show, if you had been wandering around London looking for entertainment, there was the Tyla Gang at the Golden Lion in Fulham, another chance to see the 101ers at the Elgin in W11, or the very wonderful Viv Stanshall's Vivarium at the Nashville. These, in the main, however were not what the country was grooving to: the Bay City Rollers were in the Top Five of the charts with 'Money Honey', and Queen – nine years before they broke the UN cultural boycott of Apartheid South Africa by playing a string of shows at Sun City, and ten years before being retrospectively canonised by the media following their appearance at Live Aid – had just released 'Bohemian Rhapsody', whose video would appear on *Top of the Pops* seemingly on an interminable tape loop for the next month or so. Virgin Records, meanwhile, had recently spent large amounts of money taking out double-page adverts in the press just to announce that you could hear the new Mike Oldfield album, *Ommadawn*, premiered on the John Peel show in its entirety on October 24, and that seventeen other radio programmes nationwide would be following suit. This, then, was the world into which the Sex Pistols ventured that November. A year later, they would be front-page news in all the tabloids, and their gigs regularly cancelled by concerned moralists and petty little attention-seeking minor officials across the land.

On December 5, 1975, the front page of the local paper, the *Chelsea News*, greeted its readers with the cheery headline 'Residents Tell Of Early Morning Bottle Fights'. The accompanying story detailed the proceedings of a public hearing in which objections had been raised to an application for a late licence by the Nose Wine Bar on the King's Road, quoting a witness who said: 'There was one fight which was really violent. Some people came out stinking drunk. They broke the tops off their wine bottles and began to attack each other. One girl looked really bad, she was covered in blood. Then the police arrived.'

To make matters worse, the wine bar had sometimes also presented live music, but this had been discontinued due to previous complaints.

Inside the paper, there was a small advert placed by the Beaufort Antiques Centre, 374–399 King's Road – just near where McLaren and Westwood had recently marketed Ted gear – who were selling 'Clothes of Yesteryear – A wild flight from the Gay 20s to the Fabulous 50s'. In the classified ads section towards the back, someone was offering a 'framed print of decorative balloon made for Napoleon's coronation' for £1.50, another seller had flared jeans for £7.50, whereas if you threw caution to the winds and spent an extra couple of pounds, £9.50 would secure a highly desirable tea trolley – '2 tiers, Melamine, teak finish trays, gold anodised aluminium frame, packs flat for easy carriage, as new'. Finally, in what may have been a sign of the times having moved away from the more exotic hippie styles of a few years earlier, there was also the following: 'TURKISH Kaftan, long, green velvet with gold embroidery, medium size, never worn, half cost price at £8'.

For the moment, however, on the day that this particular paper was published, you could still catch a performance of the long-running *Rocky Horror Show* at the King's Road Theatre, or else a mere 40p would get you a ticket to see the 'Sex Pistols + Machine Bubble Disco' at Chelsea College of Art ('Chelsea Students 20p') if you happened to wander down the King's Road to check out their fifth ever gig. At those prices, the band's fee would not have amounted to much, and it would certainly be a while before they would have been able to consider asking John Krevine if he had any more jukeboxes for sale. Still, maybe a tea trolley was on the cards . . .

The Pistols were emerging onto a London gig circuit that autumn which also included the likes of the Stranglers, Eddie and the Hot Rods, the Count Bishops, Roogalator, Kilburn and the High Roads, the 101ers and Flip City (featuring a man who was soon to call himself Elvis Costello), while Dr Feelgood were already front-page headline news, having just completed a thirty-date UK tour. Once the Pistols became huge, press attention naturally concentrated on them as if they were the blueprint for everything that followed, but the original scene from which they came was considerably more diverse than that. As TV Smith says:

> I mean, part of the Pistols schtick was – not just Malcolm, Rotten as well – they tried to make out that it was only him and that was all that there was to it, and everyone else was copying. But you know, this kind of self-aggrandisement is all right, it's funny, but it's not really the way it was. It was definitely a *team* of people – a lot of whom were inspired, certainly, by early Pistols concerts. I mean, I was actually thrilled to see in *NME* that some snotty little band was throwing chairs around, you know, it was definitely one of the reasons why I came up to London, but it does annoy me when people say, 'Oh, you formed a band because of the Pistols,' because it's absolutely not true. I already had a band in Devon.

Similarly, Nikki Sudden and his brother Epic Soundtracks were from the Midlands, and had formed their band the Swell Maps back in 1974. When Nikki first saw the Sex Pistols in April 1976 at the Nashville supporting the 101ers, he had a similar sense that here was another group who were doing the same sort of thing which he and Epic had been trying to do. Nikki was in London in the autumn of 1975, and he told me: 'I remember going to see *Cabaret* at the cinema, and walking out thinking that London then was like Berlin at that time – I had this really strong sense that something was about to happen, but I didn't know what it was. Then the punk thing did happen, that kind of all came together.'

Just as the winter was setting in, Charles Shaar Murray wrote an article for the *NME* which printed the first large pictures of the Ramones to be seen in the paper, together with glowing reports of their gigs at CBGB. Under a headline which asked 'Are You Alive to the Jive of the Sound of 76?', Murray made the following entirely sensible recommendation: 'The Ramones [. . .] are a band that the London rock scene could really use.'

27

'It's the buzz, cock'

Daylight Rubbery

Like 1966 and 1956, 1976 was a year that put the King's Road back on all the front pages. Twenty years earlier, the cause of all the fuss had been the Angry Young Men. Then it had been Mary Quant, Granny's and the whole Swinging London mythology; this time around, it would be Anarchy in the UK.

That would also turn out to be the last time, because by 1986 the slow gentrification of the area had advanced to such a stage that only people who had already made it could afford to be there. A mid-eighties version of McLaren and Westwood would not have had a hope of setting up for business down the King's Road in the same zero-budget, ramshackle way that they managed it at the start of the seventies. A measure of how the street was fast becoming a no-go area for poverty-stricken creative types can be seen from the way that the even the very cheapest accommodation was going up in price just as punk began. Here is an advert from the Temporary Accommodation classifieds in *Time Out* for March 12–18, 1976:

CHELSEA B&B from £9.75 pw, colour TV, cooking facilities, no curfew. 352 0555

By August 1977, a year and a half later, the same B&B had gone up a staggering 50 per cent, although now it was claiming to be the *best*:

CHELSEA'S BEST B&B – £16 pw – £3 pn. Colour TV, cooking, keys. No curfew. 01–352–0555

To have an idea what those prices mean, in 1976 a new LP was going to set you back roughly £2, the average T-shirt (complete with 'witty' slogan) would be £1.50 to £2, an ordinary pair of jeans around £6, a ticket for a gig at Hammersmith Odeon £2 or a show at the Marquee in the region of 75p. While we are on the subject of filthy lucre, let's have a look at the prices of goods being sold by our friendly neighbour-hood anarchist emporium, SEX: 'All in one rubber suit £40, Rubber stockings £12, Rubber mini-skirts £7, Leather corset £35, Silver shoes £15, See-through T-shirts £5, Wet-look trousers £15, Leather bra £14, Leather skirt £25, Wet-look T-shirt £7.'

Although these prices might look relatively cheap to modern eyes, their see-through T-shirts would set you back almost seven times as much as a ticket for a show at the Marquee. If a London club gig might cost roughly £12 these days, then you're talking the modern-day equivalent of £80 for the see-through T-shirt, £400 for the leather skirt and £600 for the rubber suit. No wonder most of the punks I knew used to make their own clothes.

The prices quoted for the above selection of SEX merchandise come from a fashion spread which appeared in issue number one of a short-lived upmarket paper called *Bailey and Lichfield's Ritz*, which appeared to be an attempt by the two well-known photographers – David Bailey and Patrick Anson, 5th Earl of Lichfield – to launch a publication to compete with Andy Warhol's *Interview*, which was unlikely to be mistaken for a photo-copied-and-stapled punk fanzine by even the most comatose of teenage glue-sniffers. In among the adverts for Chanel No. 5, Rive Gauche by Yves Saint Laurent or the Zapata shoe store in Old Church Street, there was an interview with Jordan from McLaren and Westwood's shop, together with photos of her with David Bailey's wife, Marie Helvin, both modelling the above-listed clothes from SEX. The article was interesting in that it actually gave credit to Vivienne Westwood for a change, rather than to Malcolm, even if they still couldn't seem to manage to spell her name correctly. Jordan was asked about the clothes she was wearing, which had even caused her problems on home territory like the Roebuck:

This outfit? The only outfit I have that really has much meaning to it and really gets me into a hundred per cent trouble every time. It's got Nazi stuff all over it. I get thrown out of pubs wearing this outfit.

No joke, the last time I went to the Roebuck all these old fogies wanted to throw beer all over me. The guy that runs the pub said, 'Please don't come in here again wearing that outfit otherwise I'll be forced to throw you out.' So I just said 'Piss off.'

Elsewhere in the same paper, there was a two-page fashion spread devoted to another cutting-edge King's Road emporium, Acme Attractions, where the focus was still very much on the sixties retro look. The picture spread was titled 'Mini Skirts', and the female model was wearing a 'black PVC and fur fabric animal print mini skirt and matching zip-up top £22.50 from Acme Attractions (Antiquarious [*sic*]). Mary Quant plastic rain shoes "Quant Afoot" £8 from Acme (with original Mary Quant plastic carrier bag).' The male model wore an old Moss Bros suit, shoes, shirt and tie, all from Acme Attractions. Some kind of explanation for all this can be found in a short piece about Acme which had appeared in the *NME* back in December 1975, which claimed to be able to predict the new fashion which would be gripping the youth of the nation in 1976:

The Beatles look, of course. A merry wheeze indeed to don the velvet-lapelled suits of yore, the tab-collared shirts and elastic-sided Chelsea boots with cuban heels that had them rockin' at the Cavern. Remember plastic wigs? Cilla Black? Hamburg? No, neither do I but at Acme Attractions King's Road Emporium, Donovan Letts and his friendly staff bring 1963 back to life with every conceivable accessory necessary to become a Fab Four lookalike once more. Apparently Beatlemania phase two will soon be sweeping the country and nostalgia doesn't enter into it. Sez Don: 'Our first grade trend setters are looking for something different and fashions are moving towards the Beatles again. There'll be a big mod revival next year without a doubt. See these things may be old fashioned but to a nineteen-year-old like me or the kids it's obviously new.'

On the other hand, at the *NME*'s annual Christmas bash at Dingwalls, Kilburn and the High Roads singer Ian Dury had shown up wearing a safety pin as an earring, so there were obviously a variety of options on offer. Indeed, just because McLaren and Westwood were selling fetish gear to the cognoscenti down at 430, and the Sex Pistols were now out there annoying art students who had come along to see some other headlining band, the King's Road was hardly a seething mass of anarchist rebellion at the start of 1976. Flared trousers, long hair and beards were still very much the order of the day and the clothes shops still had their fair share of thirty-inch high-waist baggies, satin bomber jackets, cotton drill loons, Roger Dean posters and 'Keep On Truckin' T-shirts. Sissors Hairdressers at 46 King's Road had just opened another branch at number 69, and from the look of their adverts, it would seem that attempting to look like a member of Manhattan Transfer or one of the blokes from Abba was an extremely popular option that year. Meanwhile the Top Ten of the album charts featured *The Very Best of Slim Whitman* and Manuel and His Music of the Mountains – actually the Geoff Love Orchestra in disguise, giving Latin-themed renditions of 'The Way We Were', the 'Peanut Vendor' and 'Moon River' – while also making a surprise comeback in the singles charts thirty years after his death was none other than Glen Miller.

Utterly Self-Pitying Smugness

At the King's Road Theatre, *The Rocky Horror Show* continued its very successful run, having been playing at one end of the street or the other since 1973, while at its first home, the Royal Court, Jane Asher returned to co-star with James Bolam in a play called *Treats* by Christopher Hampton, which *Time Out* greeted as follows:

> Hampton, at present a moderate talent, works with a kind of world-weary wit and a good deal of irony, sometimes heavy, sometimes so intricate that it hardly has any resonance at all. There is at least one moment of superb theatre – James Bolam sitting alone listening to Dylan's 'I Threw It All Away' with an expression of utterly self-pitying smugness.

The Sex Pistols had been playing shows since November 1975, but mostly these had been under the radar, and if you were relying on the music papers for information, you would have been lucky to see any mention of them. The 'Teasers' gossip column in the back of the *NME* for January 31 did, however, carry the following cryptic in-joke: 'Lookout Blast Furnace: Kursaal Flyers currently enthusing about East End rock band Shadbolt and their ace guitarist Sid Vicious.'

This was partly a reference to *NME* writer and ex-*OZ* magazine schoolkid Charles Shaar Murray, who had recently formed a band playing Feelgood-style R&B under the name Blast Furnace and the Heatwaves. As for Sid, he would not be part of the Pistols for another year, but would have been known to various writers on the paper like Nick Kent, and the idea of anyone describing him as an 'ace guitarist' would certainly have raised a smile. On February 12, the Sex Pistols received their first proper namecheck in the *NME*, but this was just a case of them being listed in the weekly gig guide for an upcoming show supporting Eddie and the Hot Rods at the Marquee. In the venue's own display advert, the band were not mentioned: it just said 'plus support'. In the event, it was this show which was to bring them much attention, as the *NME*'s Neil Spencer – who seems to have come down to see the Hot Rods – arrived in time to catch the last few numbers of the Pistols' set, and wrote a live review for the February 21 edition which carried a fine close-up photo of the Rotten onstage sneer and a headline which McLaren could have written himself:

DON'T LOOK OVER YOUR SHOULDER, BUT THE SEX PISTOLS ARE COMING

If the headline was good, the article was better. After an intro which started with 'Hurry up, they're having an orgy onstage', Spencer described them as 'a quarter [*sic*] of spiky teenage misfits from the wrong end of various London roads, playing 60s styled white punk rock as unself-consciously as it's possible to play it these days i.e. self-consciously.' It contained vivid descriptions of Rotten throwing chairs around and chatting to his mates, along with classic quotes such as 'No-one asked for an encore but they did one anyway' and 'Actually, we're not into music, we're into chaos.'

It was reported the following week that the Pistols had been thrown off the Rods tour after that one show, but although they had other support slots ahead of them and were still half a year away from a record deal, the band who first met up together at the Roebuck the previous August were finding an audience. For the moment, though, it remained a small exclusive club, and they had a chance to develop organically in a way that would be very difficult today. As Dave Barbarossa – the original drummer for Adam and the Ants, who then played in full Vivienne Westwood pirate gear in the McLaren-managed Bow Wow Wow – explained to me:

Today, if there's a scene, if there's a celebrity, you've fucking got that big promotional thing pushing it out, from the *Daily Mirror* to the *Guardian* to MTV to fucking *Newsnight*. In those days the idea was to

keep it secret and small and nobody would encroach on our scene.
Punk rock was so exclusive, so chic, that nobody knew about it until
months after, and I think that's a very profound difference between
those days and today . . .

Dave says that before getting involved in punk, 'I'd come out of Hackney,
the Tottenham Royal, Southgate Royalty, James Brown, you know, Prince
Buster, Blue Beat, that was my thing, although I was also very heavily into
Roxy and Marc Bolan and David Bowie and so on.' As for the clothes he'd
have been wearing before joining Adam Ant:

It would have been almost bordering on the Oxford bags and platform
shoes, high waist buttons, high waisters, tank tops, penny collars . . .
I sort of looked like somebody from Slade more than anything else,
and I think before that came out I was like suedehead – crombie,
Levi's Sta-Press, Dr Martens, Ben Sherman, short hair – but I never
had *really* short hair, I always had this wild sprouting Afro situation.
It was a good look . . . unlike Bow Wow Wow . . . we looked like a
bowl of fucking fruit [laughs].

Arms, Fingers, Groin, Knees

Some of the original 1960s King's Road boutiques were still in business,
but not everyone was a fan, especially the people who lived above the
1967-vintage Just Looking, whose justifiable antagonism resulted in a court
case which was reported as follows by *The Times* on February 10:

For the second time within a year an alarm bell that caused annoyance
by ringing during the night has been kicked off the wall. Denis Kelly,
aged 30, a labourer, admitted at Horseferry Road Magistrates' Court,
Westminster, yesterday, smashing the alarm bell above the Just Looking
Shop in King's Road Chelsea. When it started ringing at two in the
morning he climbed out of the window and kicked it off the wall. He
was conditionally discharged.

At the Chelsea Drug Store – designed by the same architect as its alarming
neighbour – radio DJ Emperor Rosko did a show on February 3, while
another DJ, Peter Powell, told the teenage readers of *Fab 208* magazine that
he bought his shoes from Kickers in the King's Road, and many of his
clothes from another shop in the same street called the Common Market.

Marc Bolan had rented a three-storey house at 25 Holmead Road, just off the King's Road, outside which fans would sometimes gather, and Nikki Sudden of the Swell Maps told me:

> I went to Holmead Road once, and he saw us waiting. It was raining, and we were sheltering under this ledge of the house opposite, and he came out and said hello and had photos taken with us. He'd just been to the hairdressers, got his kind of Valentino Bolan haircut that day, and my friend Karen said, 'I'll never like him again,' because she didn't like the new haircut. That was around the time of 'I Love to Boogie'. I got this photo taken, and my mum said, 'Who's this girl you're with?' I thought, 'He doesn't look like a very attractive girl . . .' He was wearing a blue boiler suit. Didn't look very cool at all. Just came out because he liked talking to fans. He was the first star I'd ever met, and he lived up to all my expectations of what a star should be – always really friendly, always had time for the fans.

When not door-stepping Marc Bolan, Nikki was also reading the *NME*, and he had seen Neil Spencer's February 21 live review of the Sex Pistols and decided to go and check them out:

> The first time I saw the Pistols they were supporting the 101ers in April '76, at the Nashville. I'd read about the Pistols in the *NME*, so I went to see them, and that's the day that Jordan and Vivienne had the fight. I took a photo of the gig. The 101ers were so, kind of, sad, compared to the Pistols, they looked like a bunch of old gits, and they sounded like it as well. Their time had been and gone. The Pistols were so vibrant, they had so much energy, and they were so fresh – it was just kind of the way rock'n'roll *should* be. There were a lot of their friends in the audience, obviously. I met Rotten at the Patti Smith gig at the Roundhouse a couple of weeks later, May '76. I asked Rotten for his autograph, and he said, 'No-one's ever asked me that before.' I got him to autograph my copy of *Biggles – Air Commodore*. He said, 'Oh, I used to read those when I was a kid.' I said, 'You should still read them, they're really good.'

Just as the band from SEX was on its way up, a new TV series appeared purporting to tell the story of one band's struggles in the down-and-dirty world of the music business. It was written by Howard Schuman, who saddled it with the unappealing title *Rock Follies*, and equally unappealing fictional band name the Little Ladies, but it at least had the advantage of songs written by Roxy Music's Andy Mackay. However, a small part of its dialogue managed to inspire the name of one of the finest punk bands of them all – a line from the show which was picked out and used as the headline for a preview in the February 20–26 edition of *Time Out*:

IT'S THE BUZZ, COCK!

It's the buzz, cock. When you sing rock music you get this buzz – it starts in your chest, maybe it's to do with the amplifiers or the microphones, I don't know, it's something electric, something about energy, I don't know, anyway it starts in your chest and spreads from there, like when you toss a pebble in a pond, I mean it ripples only not gently, in great energy waves, arms, fingers, groin, knees, toes, throat, mouth, head, loud, terrifically loud head buzz and when the gig's over . . . you can't just turn it off . . . you have to move, dance, break things, make love . . .

Those keen on the visual arts could visit the Nigel Greenwood gallery that spring, at 41 Sloane Gardens, where there was an exhibition of sculpture by Nicholas Pope. As *Time Out*'s reviewer pithily commented, 'If you like to see large pieces of chalk supported by twigs, this is the man to see'. Failing that, 60p in advance or 70p on the door would have secured entry to the March 13 show at Chelsea College of Art by Kilburn and the High Roads. Oddly enough, it was a photograph apparently taken at the Sex Pistols' December 1975 show at Chelsea College of Art which was used to accompany the *NME*'s April 17 review of their show at the Nashville supporting the 101ers – headlined 'Punks' Progress Report' – in which the words Machine Bubble Disco were clearly visible on the posters behind Johnny's head. Lydon was wearing one of SEX's Cambridge Rapist T-shirts, while Steve Jones modelled the ever-popular Two Cowboys design. Reviewer Geoff Hutt called their songs 'intelligent punk rock'.

The day before that *NME* piece about the Pistols gig was published – which was still six months before the release of their debut single – an LP review by N. Menhenick in the local London paper the *Harrow Observer* hailed the great Chris Spedding's self-titled new record as 'an album of pure, delightful "punk rock".' A week later the same writer profiled Ian Dury and the Kilburns – formerly known as Kilburn and the High Roads, commenting that Dury was 'a punk through and through', and that the band 'play sleazy punk rock like no-one else', and quoted Ian's belief that 'the world revolved around parallel legged trousers'.

King's Road Avant Leather, Rubber and Bondage

March at the Royal Court saw a play called *Parcel Post* by Yemi Ajibade, directed by Donald Howarth, the story of 'a Nigerian household in Islington where the family nervously await the arrival of the virgin bride. When she arrives, things do not turn out as expected.' This was followed by a production celebrating the seventieth birthday of one of the most famous playwrights of the age, as Samuel Beckett's *Waiting for Godot* was presented in German, directed by Beckett himself, in a transfer from the Schiller Theatre, Berlin. This formed part of a Beckett season that also included a revival of *Endgame*. Peter Hall saw the production on April 24, and wrote in his diary: 'This is a masterpiece. Absolute precision, clarity, hardness. No sentimentality, no indulgence, no pretension . . . It revived my shaken faith in the theatre.'

The Royal Court's Beckett season, April 1976

April 24 was also the day on which the Sex Pistols were the subject of a major feature in *Sounds* by Jonh [*sic*] Ingham, based around a show they had played at a Soho strip club called El Paradise, in which Ingham described the look of the band's followers:

> Flared jeans were out. Leather helped. All black was better. Folks in their late twenties, chopped and channelled teenagers, people who frequent Sex, King's Road avant leather, rubber and bondage clothing shop. People sick of nostalgia. People wanting forward motion. People wanting rock and roll that is relevant to 1976.

This is just one of the article's several references to SEX, and, once again, it is entirely seen as Malcolm's shop, with no mention of Vivienne, least of all from McLaren: 'I opened the shop because I wanted people to make a certain statement if they wore my clothes. The Sex Pistols are another extension of that.'

As for John, he was already quite capable of speaking for himself: 'I hate shit. I hate hippies and what they stand for. I hate long hair. I hate pub bands. I want to change it so there are rock bands like us.'

A month earlier in the *NME* gossip column 'Teasers', 'Malcolm of the Sex Shop (in trendy King's Road)' had claimed that he would be running regular gigs at the El Paradise to promote gigs by 'young off-the-wall bands who can't get gigs at regular venues'. Down at the bottom of that same page, there was also a poem mourning the demise of Nick Kent's two-tone Terry de Havilland boots, bought on the King's Road, accompanied by a photo of the deceased footwear.

Zigzag ran an article by Paul Kendall in May called 'Punk Rock Comes to Town', but this was about Eddie and the Hot Rods, and it seemed that the aftermath of the Pistols/Hot Rods February show at the Marquee had left some bitterness:

> Eddie and the Hot Rods are different, because they don't rely solely on effect. Unlike joke bands like the Sex Pistols (who, when granted the privilege of supporting the Rods at the Marquee recently repaid the favour by smashing up their gear, driving out their audience, and pelting them with bottles) they also deliver the musical dynamism which has to accompany any rock dream.

On May 15 and 16, the emerging punk audience had its first real chance to turn out in force, when the Patti Smith Group played two nights at the Roundhouse in Camden, supported by the Stranglers. The following day, the Sex Pistols played at the 100 Club in Oxford Street for the second time in a week. Meanwhile, EMI, the organisation whose record division would sign them by the end of the summer, announced in its in-house publication *EMI News* that one of its products, 'Bohemian Rhapsody' by Queen, had been the biggest-selling single of 1975. In June, the same publication noted another of their successes ('The UK's answer to American West Coast country rock – the Wurzels – shot up to number one in the Music Week/BBC charts last month with the single "Combine Harvester"'), while also detailing the summer shows being presented by EMI's theatre division, such as the *Black and White Minstrel Show* at Blackpool Opera House, the *Val*

Doonican Show at the Futurist, Scarborough, and comedian Dick Emery at the ABC Theatre, Blackpool. Within three months, much to the disgust of some of its own employees, EMI would release 'Anarchy in the UK'.

In the meantime, jet-setting couple Rod Stewart and Britt Ekland briefly touched down for a while in the King's Road area in June, according to a report in *Record Mirror* by Rosalind Russell: 'Whilst in London, they are staying in a small house in Chelsea (Rod declines to confirm that it belongs to a friend of Princess Margaret). They are returning to the States on Friday and frankly, Rod can't wait to get back.'

Sick and Tired of Fish Fingers and Spam Fritters for Tea

On July 8, *Small Change* – another play by long-time Royal Court associate Peter Gill – was presented at the theatre, prompting *The Times* to call it 'a beautiful product of uncompromising puritan imagination'. The product of a slightly different kind of imagination (aided by a £400 loan from Lee Brilleaux of Dr Feelgood) was a new indie label called Stiff Records, founded that month by Dave Robinson and Andrew 'Jake' Jakeman (aka Jake Riviera). By August 14, they released their first single, Nick Lowe's 'So it Goes'/'Heart of the City', recorded for the princely sum of £45, which at 430 King's Road that summer would have been just enough to buy an all-in-one rubber suit and a see-through T-shirt.

The rise of the Pistols continued, with a front cover of *Melody Maker* on August 7, accompanied by a favourable article by Caroline Coon, which again stressed the role of McLaren and the shop:

> The British punk rock garb is developing independently, too. It's an ingenious hodgepodge of jumble sale cast-offs, safety-pinned around one of the choice, risqué T-shirts especially made for the King's Road shop, Sex. Selling an intriguing line of arcane '50s cruise-ware, fantasy glamour ware and the odd rubber suit, this unique boutique is owned by Malcolm McLaren, ex-manager of the New York Dolls, now the Sex Pistols' manager. His shop has a mysterious atmosphere which made it the ideal meeting place for a loose crowd of truant, disaffected teenagers.

Melody Maker's Allan Jones, writing in the same issue, had a different view: 'It is this irresponsible emphasis on violence and mundane nihilism – perfectly expressed through the Sex Pistols' "Anarchy in the UK" – that is so objectionable.'

For most people inspired by the Sex Pistols, or the Ramones, whose pitch-perfect first album hit London that summer, it wasn't about nihilism, it was about limitless possibilities. Wreckless Eric would shortly sign to the new Stiff Records. As he told me, in one of the best expressions of the 1976 impulse I've ever encountered:

> It was in the process of becoming something that was called punk. We didn't know if it was punk, and people used to ask us stupid questions like, 'Are you punk or new wave?', and we didn't know. And Nick Lowe said 'Don't ever call me punk. Punk means that you haven't got any style and class, and I've got loads of style and class.' The thing that I related it all to was Dada, where 'Dada' became a word that they used instead of 'art' so if they wanted to call it 'punk' instead of 'art', fine with me, but I wasn't really interested in punk. I liked the Sex Pistols but I wasn't really interested in having a Marshall and a Les Paul and that and going 'Aaaaaaggghhhh . . . grunge, grunge . . .' you know, because that was the old order. Well, the media got hold of it, the businessmen got hold of it, and the old guard came in, the old guard always come back . . . I'll tell you what, we were sick and tired of fish fingers and spam fritters for tea, and *Blue Peter*, and O levels and A levels and last buses . . . [laughs] and just all that kind of shit, really . . . The thing is, we were constantly being told, 'When we were your age, there was a war going on . . .', and I'd go, 'I wasn't even here, it's not my fucking fault, I didn't *start* it . . . it's not my fucking fault there was a war on . . .' There's always that line I always think of 'Don't know what I want, but I know how to get it . . .' But really it's 'Anyway, anyhow, anywhere . . .', 'Can't explain – got a feelin' inside, can't *explain* . . .'

More Camp Rubbish Left Over from the Late Sixties

The man behind the phenomenally successful *Rocky Horror Show*, Richard O'Brien, was back at the Royal Court on August 10 with his follow-up play, co-written with Richard Hartley, called *T. Zee and the Lost Race*. J. W. Lambert in the *Sunday Times* of August 15 called it: '[. . .] a curiously decorous, quite jolly mish-mash of yet more camp rubbish left over from the late sixties. Comical to hear a Royal Court audience, long-haired, bejeaned, bangled and presumably as liberated as all get out, tittering with self-conscious glee at the ever-so-naughty word "shitty".'

Running at the Theatre Upstairs at the same time was something with a much more sombre theme, *The Only Way Out* by George Thatcher, as

Time Out explained: 'In 1962, George Thatcher spent three weeks in the condemned cell for a murder he insists he did not commit. His sentence was commuted to life imprisonment and his play was smuggled out while he continued it. In David Halliwell's moving but stark production a man fights for raw dignity and justice.'

John Peel's show for one sample week in August 1976 displayed a distinct sixties bias: 'The Stones are tonight's featured group, followed by Cream, Soft Machine, the Faces and the Yardbirds.' Within a few months, his programming would change drastically as he embraced the music of the new punk bands and thereby annoyed the hell out of many of his old listeners, as he explained to me:

> There was a chap called Johnny at the Virgin branch in Marble Arch, he used to let me take records out on approval, and I took the first Ramones LP out, just 'cause it looked interesting – the idea of tracks that were a minute and twenty seconds long – 'What?' You know, having spent the last two or three years trying to avoid listening to Genesis and Yes and all that kind of stuff, it was just so refreshing, but the average age of the audience dropped by about ten years in the space of a couple of months . . . The hippies were saying 'You must not play this,' because they wanted us to go on playing Grateful Dead LP tracks for the rest of their lives – playing their record collections, effectively. A lot of people are happy to do that, but I really didn't want to do that. So it was incredibly exciting, and it was nice to feel that you were – 'cause, you know, I was an old bloke even then – it was kind of nice to feel that you were kind of part of it, you know. You'd go to gigs and things, you didn't feel as though, despite the fact that you were old and not punky looking or anything at all, that you were not part of this . . .

King's Road shoppers now had another place where they could attempt to track down some of this music, when a new record shop opened up at 182a King's Road in August with the very 1966-sounding name of Les Discothèque: 'Just Opened . . . The most luxurious record shop in London. Late night trading. Open all day Saturday and Sunday. Personal attention . . . Imported records from US.'

Much further north, on September 20 the Buzzcocks and Eater played a show at Holdsworth Hall, Deansgate, Manchester, at which singer Howard Devoto wore a pair of Vivienne Westwood leather trousers from SEX. His band had recently been instrumental in bringing the Pistols to Manchester, and they had also supported them at the Screen on the Green in Islington on August 29. On the same night as the Buzzcocks' Manchester gig, the opening evening of the 100 Club's two-day Punk Festival took place back in London. Things were now moving at such a rate – when it was still common for bands on the London pub circuit to appear three or four times in the same week in different parts of town – that some fans took to attending several shows in the same evening, running from venue to venue in an attempt not to miss anything. As for what to wear to the shows, there were still no hard and fast rules. Marco Pirroni, guitarist for the Models and then for Adam and the Ants, recalled in John Lydon's autobiography:

> The 1976 punk look was a mixture of absolutely everything. A lot of ted, a lot of rocker, a lot of fetish stuff, transvestite sort of stuff, a bit of mod, and a lot of glam. That's what it was. People didn't wear leather motorcycle jackets in 1976. Mohicans didn't exist then either . . . The real impact of John Lydon's look was, 'Fuck, he's ripped everything up!'

Once again, it is worth stressing that this was still only a tiny handful of people, and that the general fashions of that autumn were somewhat different, to say the least. By way of a contrast, it is interesting to examine what *Esquire* magazine was holding up as the epitome of masculine style in their October 1976 issue. In a fashion spread headlined 'Wild & Woolly – C'Mon Let Yourself Go This Season!', they featured a freshly shampooed, bearded Barry Gibb clone, wearing a coat which cost more than the average family would have spent on food in the entire year:

> Finally, great furs for men! Real, manly furs reminiscent of wonderful old raccoon coats. His is coyote (about $3,800), he being Jacques Malignon, an international photographer reputed to be one of the world's greatest dressers. His Shetland sweater from Jaeger ($23.50) in a dazzling fuchsia could inspire you to try a new colour this fall.

While 'one of the world's greatest dressers' was appearing in the papers, the Sex Pistols finally signed to EMI, inking the deal on October 8. That association, unlike the First World War, would all be over by Christmas.

Rock Cult Filth

The front cover of *Private Eye* on October 15, 1976 showed US president Gerald Ford – the man who gave a full and unconditional pardon to his predecessor and former boss Richard Nixon, whose vice president he had been – with a speech bubble saying 'There Are No Russians In Russia', which the following year would be a punk song title by the Radio Stars, released on the Chiswick label. The singer of the band was Andy Ellison, who had been in John's Children with Marc Bolan in 1967, a group photographed that year posing outside the front window of Granny Takes a Trip. The two of them would meet up again by chance in 1977, when Bolan was being driven in his car down the King's Road and noticed Ellison walking along the street to a nearby rehearsal room. As a result of that chance meeting, Bolan invited the band onto his new TV show, *Marc*.

On October 22, the first true British punk single, 'New Rose' by the Damned, was released by Stiff Records, reportedly selling 4,000 copies in the first week. The band were named after the same British biker movie made by Hammer Films whose poster had adorned the walls of 430 King's Road back in its Let it Rock incarnation, and they made the front cover of *Sounds* on November 6, accompanied by the headline:

> DAMNED head for the charts. PISTOLS hit the road
> . . . Punk is on its way!

On the other hand, back on October 23, the very day after 'New Rose' appeared, the good folk at *Record Mirror* were already asking if the movement was over and done. In a fearless spirit of enquiry, they flagged down assorted young people in the King's Road, photographing them and canvassing their opinions on the subject:

> PUNK-ROCK may be the newest exciting thing for the media and record companies to get worked up about but apparently it has been going on long enough already for some people to be thoroughly fed-up with it. [. . .] Well, from the reactions RM got, it seems that the media and the record companies are once more making a mountain out of a molehill.

None of the eleven passers-by interviewed were wearing anything remotely like punk fashions, and their haircuts were similarly unremarkable for the era, yet a surprising number claimed to have already seen the Sex Pistols and other punk bands playing live. Caroline from Knightsbridge, aged nineteen, said that the Stranglers 'occasionally get me tapping me feet' but she was not especially impressed with any others: 'I've seen the Vibrators, the Sex Pistols and Eddie and the Hot Rods. It's good for a laugh, it's a good night out, entertaining. Not only can you laugh at the bands, you can laugh at the audience as well.'

Charles, also nineteen, was a fan of the new music, but he and his female companion Lindsay, seventeen, managed to give the impression that there was virtually only one type of place at which you could watch the bands live. 'I see them at the discos and gay clubs that they play like Bangs, the Sundown and Louise's,' said Charles, while Lindsay stated that she had not been to see any punk bands 'because I'm not gay so I don't go to gay clubs. I don't think it's all gay but that's where my friends go to see them play'. Nowhere else to watch them at all, apart from the 100 Club, the Nashville, the Marquee, the Red Cow, the Brecknock, Dingwalls, the Hope and Anchor and numerous other pubs and clubs across London which presented live music seven days a week where the early punk bands were already cutting their teeth.

As for seventeen-year-old Jay, he had seen the Sex Pistols and the Clash, and reckoned they did not know how to play. He had also been present at that summer's landmark July 4 Roundhouse show by the Flaming Groovies, Ramones and the Stranglers 'and they were awful too'. Jay concluded with some words of advice: 'I work around here and I see lots of fans that dress up like the groups, but I don't see how it can catch on because punk-rock hasn't got the same sort of appeal to middle-class housewives as the Beatles had.'

Quite what A&R man Nick Mobbs – the man who a week or so earlier had just signed the Pistols to EMI – might have made of all this can only be imagined.

For the moment, however, all was apparently well, and the December edition of EMI's in-house journal *EMI News* – published in late November – printed extracts from chairman Sir John Read's end of year statement, which made no mention whatever of the Sex Pistols, or, indeed, any other act on the label. It read, in full:

> In the United Kingdom music operations as a whole achieved even higher turnover and results, but there was evidence of a progressive decline in consumer expenditure due to the economic recession. EMI Records maintained its leading position, together with an increased share of the cassette market, and the company also secured a high volume of export business.

That was it for the music side of the company. A few days later, all hell broke loose in the wake of the Sex Pistols' appearance on the Bill Grundy TV show, which was not even a nationally broadcast programme, and stirred up a fuss far in excess of what the actual content merited. Paul Gorman was sixteen at the time:

I remember the Grundy thing. I watched it with my parents and my sisters. My mum walked out, and my dad, who was quite old by that point and had been in the army and things like that, he just said, 'Well, he deserved everything he got . . .' I mean, my dad wasn't posh by any means, and so he probably sided with Steve Jones, and I said, 'Well, I've met those people.' They said, 'What the hell are you talking about?'

The following day the tabloids had the band for breakfast, with the famous *Daily Mirror* headline 'TV FURY OVER ROCK CULT FILTH' reporting that a lorry driver called James Holmes 'kicked in the screen of his £380 TV' after seeing the Pistols' interview, a reaction a little like cutting your own throat in a restaurant because you object to the food. Even Mr Holmes seems to have regretted the move, as the article stated:

'It blew up and I was knocked backwards,' he said. 'But I was so angry and disgusted with this filth that I took a swing with my boot. I can swear as well as anyone, but I don't want this sort of muck coming into my home at teatime. It's the stupidest thing I've ever done. I dread to think what my wife will do when she finds out about it.'

The majority of the front-page article – which somehow took three journalists to write – consisted of a word-for-word transcript of the short interview, with the swearing blanked out. Across the top of the front page was another smaller headline which said 'THE PUNK ROCK HORROR SHOW', making a link in some Londoners' minds with the former Royal Court musical still running at the King's Road Theatre. Inside the paper itself there was another full page devoted to the Pistols, entitled 'KINGS OF THE PUNK CULT', which was essentially an advert for the group engineered by McLaren, designed to publicise their upcoming Anarchy tour. Malcolm himself was interviewed for the piece, and seemed determined to make sure that blood would flow:

'It is very likely there will be violence at some of the gigs,' says tour organiser Malcolm McClaren [*sic*] 'because it is violent music. We don't necessarily think violence is a bad thing because you have to destroy to create.' McClaren, 28, is the owner of a Chelsea boutique called Sex which specialises in punk gear – ripped T-shirts, dresses made from plastic rubbish bags, moth-eaten sweaters and 'Cambridge Rapist' leather masks with zips across the mouth.

All of which helped stir up trouble for countless teenagers across the land whenever they left the house in punk gear and had to spend most of their time dodging aggression from local meatheads. Four years later during the mod revival, kids painted bullseye targets on their parkas, but right from the early days of the Pistols, with statements like this McLaren was deliberately attaching targets to anyone wearing punk clothing and stirring things up so that it was open season on them. Still, someone was making money out of all this.

There's Nothing Wrong with Being Nasty or Rude

The gig listings for the upcoming Anarchy shows were also helpfully included elsewhere in that same issue of the *Daily Mirror*, in their regular 'WOW – What's On Where' section, compiled by the ubiquitous Laurie Henshaw, twenty years after his *Melody Maker* article denouncing rock'n'roll that approvingly quoted a vicar who called the music 'a revival of devil-dancing . . . the same sort of thing that is done in the black magic ritual'.

The Pistols embarked on the Anarchy tour the following day – the gig listings having been printed only to find that the likes of Frank Thistlethwaite, Vice Chancellor of the University of East Anglia, had now appointed themselves music critics and were banning concerts, untroubled by the fact that they had never heard a note of the music or seen the London region-only Grundy show. Lancaster Students' Union president was quoted on the front page of the *Daily Mirror* on December 3, saying they had cancelled the show 'because the movement was "sexist"', demonstrating that student organisations then as now could be as censorship-happy and draconian as any local council or religious pressure group. Inside the paper, publicity-shy McLaren was interviewed yet again, along with most of the Pistols, and also Vivienne Westwood. Yet again reusing the tag line 'THE PUNK ROCK HORROR SHOW' in the banner above the article, John Jackson wrote:

> The centre of Britain's notorious new pop cult is a boutique called 'Sex' in trendy King's Road, Chelsea. Its owner, Vivienne Westwood is the girlfriend of the Sex Pistols manager Malcolm McLaren. They have lived together for ten years and have a nine-year-old son. 'There's nothing wrong with being nasty or rude,' said 35-year-old Miss Westwood.

The article was accompanied by a couple of sidebars labelled 'Yuk! Yuk!', presenting a mirth-free selection of one-liners seemingly cooked up by newsroom hacks with a whole five minutes to spare before heading for the pub:

> WHICH is Britain's dirtiest railway station? St Punkras.

> WHAT name do you give someone who fried rotten potatoes?
> A chip-punk.

> Send your punk jokes to: 'Punk', *Daily Mirror*,
> London EC1PDQ.
> The prize for the best jokes will be a Sex Pistol record. The worst
> ones will win TWO Sex Pistol records.

On the same day, the *Guardian* attempted to explain this new phenomenon to their readers, in the process also giving yet more publicity to Malcolm McLaren and the shop at 430 King's Road, which seems to have been the result of the man himself feeding the journalist handy snippets of information designed to drum up controversy:

> To visit a Sex Pistols performance is to look in on an expanding new youth culture that has no time for drugs and long hair, frowns on flared jeans, thinks the Rolling Stones are Establishment, and has outright contempt for philosophies of love and peace. Most of the young punks are between seventeen and nineteen. To be in your twenties is to be old. [. . .] Punks are from the generation to whom pornography is just another comic book. They were nine or ten when *Penthouse* first went pubic. They picked up on fashion portrayed in *Club International* and *Forum* which were sold at a King's Road boutique called Sex (now renamed 'Seditionaries') run by the Sex Pistols' manager, a twenty-eight-year-old called Malcolm McLaren. They came out with leather T-shirts, swastika armbands, bondage outfits and a variety of rubber-wear and T-shirts designed to shock. One of the boutique's best-sellers is a shirt portraying the Cambridge rapist. Another, featuring two homosexual cowboys, caused an arrest last year.

All the shock horror publicity – not to mention the solid but brief injection of EMI's promotional muscle, which would also have played a part in securing the band's Grundy appearance on Thames TV, a company

50 per cent owned by EMI – at least served to position the band right
in the mainstream music news sections the week their single was launched.
Take, for instance, regional paper the *Stamford Mercury* for December 3,
the opening day of the Anarchy tour, whose singles review column dealt
with only five 45s out of all the available releases that week, the first three
of which read as follows:

Abba, 'Money, Money, Money' (Epic): Once again Abba are gunning
for the top spot with another catchy, commercial number. This could
be their fourth No. 1 within the year.

Queen, 'Somebody to Love' (EMI): Hopefully this imaginative, tight,
little number will be riding high for weeks to come. It says everything
about Britain's most progressive band.

Sex Pistols, 'Anarchy in the UK' (EMI): There is little wholesome
about this eruption on the pop scene. But it will appeal to teenyboppers disillusioned with the smooth, safe groups. A calculated hit.

You Don't Make Your Statement Off a Coathanger

If one King's Road shop could launch a band, then why not another one?
Steph Raynor from Acme Attractions had been managing the singer Gene
October and his band Chelsea. The band's management was then taken
over by Vivienne Westwood's sometime accountant at SEX, Andy Czezowski,
at which point they changed their name to Generation X – taken from the
title of the very fine 1964 youth culture book by Charles Hamblett and
Jane Deverson. A member of the Sex Pistols' Bromley contingent of fans,
Billy Idol, was brought in on vocals, leaving October to form a new line-up
of Chelsea. However, Gene had tipped Czezowski off about a run-down
gay club in Covent Garden called Shageramas, in Neal Street, which Andy
then took over and turned into pioneering punk venue the Roxy, with
Generation X headlining the December 21 opening night. The new music
had found a home. Czezowski, knowing Don Letts from Acme Attractions,
invited him to come down and work at the club as the resident DJ.

While the former accountant from 430 King's Road and the manager
of Acme Attractions joined up to launch the first punk club, Bernie Rhodes,
who had been part of the scene at SEX, was now managing a new group
who were interviewed by Miles, formerly of *IT* and Indica, now back in
the UK after many years in America and working for the *NME*. The feature,

which ran on December 11, was headlined 'Eighteen Flight Rock . . . and the Sound of the Westway'. The band were the Clash, and their philosophy of clothing was directly at odds with the self-consciously expensive designer label ethos to which Vivienne Westwood aspired:

> Strummer paces the room nervously. He wears boots and a boilersuit painted with abstract expressionist slashes of colour. The group make their own clothes since they are too poor to buy any, transforming jumble sale shirts by painting on words and colours. Anyone can do it. [. . .] They talk about there being no clubs that stay open late, of how Britain has no Rock'n'Roll radio stations, of how there is nothing to do. They speak of how kids who like Clash will get beaten up because of how they look. Joe has even been thrown out of a pub full of hippies because he has short hair.

This was the other side of punk fashion – the DIY spirit. Don't buy it, make it. TV Smith, whose band the Adverts had just signed to Stiff Records and whose debut single 'One Chord Wonders' provided one of the most perfect summaries of the new liberating attitude, had this to say when I asked him if they ever wore clothing by Westwood and McLaren:

> No, absolutely no way, we couldn't afford stuff from Seditionaries . . . I mean, Gaye had a pair of Seditionaries trousers because Malcolm actually, in a rare moment of generosity, gave her a pair, probably because he thought it would be a good advert for their shop, but I mean, no-one else could. We got ours out of charity shops and fiddled about with it, you know. That was the whole fun, you were making something. The whole ethic – well, not the whole ethic, but certainly a good part of the ethic – was the do-it-yourself thing, whether it was clothes or records. It wasn't just because that was what you were *supposed* to do, you know, it's bloody good fun, it's creative. If you were wearing something you'd done just one thing to, then that's *your* thing, it's not the thing out of the shop any more, you've made it your own. You're making your statement, and I don't think you make your statement off a coathanger that you bought that someone else has made, the same as in music – you make your statement by what you write and the way you present yourself, you don't make it by copying other people's songs and image. To be an individual is what it's all about, and I think that's what punk rock was presenting.

John Lydon himself had a creative attitude to customising clothes, combining safety pins, strategic rips, the odd crucifix, syringes, chains and Oxfam jackets, mixed with a selection of items from Malcolm and Vivienne's shop. Sometimes, as he wrote in his autobiography, his own inventions would suddenly *become* items from the shop:

> A lot of the northern press would say we were just clothes horses and models for Malcolm's shop. Of course, Malcolm would not deny anything – even though Malcolm's shop was run by Vivienne and everything in it was done by her, the same way Malcolm thought he wrote Pistols songs. There was a lot of Viv selling stuff that she took from everything and everyone, particularly me. I was angry about that. I would put things together, and she'd have it in the fucking shop a couple of weeks later – mass-produced. There wouldn't be the slightest blinking or guilt about it.

Decency and Good Taste

The tabloid press were clearly rubbing their hands together with glee at the emergence of punk rock as a cheap sensation they could use to sell more papers. On November 28, the *Sunday People* devoted most of a page to an article by Jim Lawson about a long-haired new band from Birmingham called Rocks whose headline suggested that perhaps he was not necessarily approaching the subject with even-handed journalistic detachment – 'Puke Rock! – This New Band Makes Me Sick': 'YUK! That's the only word for Britain's vilest pop group. After the bizarre and distasteful Punk Rock Cult, this outfit specialises in PUKE Rock. Their lead singer vomits on stage, indulges in four-letter-word lyrics and slashes himself with a shattered whiskey bottle.'

Lawson then quoted the musings of various band members at considerable length, before rounding off his article with some heart-warming wishes for their future: 'What rubbish they talk. I for one wouldn't be sad if, entertainment-wise, they choked on their own vomit.'

Never mind, running down the right-hand side of the same page was a wholesome column written by a classic 'much-loved family entertainer', currently in the middle of a charity walking tour in Scotland in aid of various good causes: 'And how lucky we are when there's so many people who can't walk about for one reason or another. Weather permitting, we should take a few thousand quid today for colour tellies and food parcels for old folks.'

One way or another, Jimmy Savile always managed to keep himself in the news.

The basic lack of knowledge and condescension displayed by the journalists who were wheeled out by their editors to attack the new music was exemplified by the *Daily Mirror*'s lead book review written by George Thaw and published on December 9 under the non-judgemental headline 'Why Punk is Sunk': 'If you are worried about what Punk Rock will lead to, stop and think about Wet Willie and Dr John the Night Tripper. They specialised in outrage, violence, sex and obscenity and called it pop music. They failed . . . and are now vanished.'

This misinformed tripe was Thaw's opening paragraph to a review of Tony Palmer's spin-off book from the excellent TV series, *All You Need Is Love*. Southern boogie outfit Wet Willie – from Mobile Alabama – while hardly a household name in the UK, were a conventional chart act in America, have now been gigging in one form or another for the past fifty years, and at the time of writing are scheduled to play gigs in 2022; while the only thing that finally put a halt to the stellar sixty-five-year career of the great Dr John – one of the most important musicians ever to emerge from New Orleans – was his death in 2019.

As EMI recording stars, the Sex Pistols – whose name had probably been unknown to group chairman Sir John Read the previous month – now finally merited attention in the pages of the January issue of *EMI News*, published in the closing days of 1976. In addition to a letters page featuring angry protests from EMI employees about the Pistols, there was a front-page article in which Read himself addressed the question of the media storm which had been kicked up by the company's new signing:

Malcolm and the Pistols at an EMI press conference,
2 December 1976, the day before the Anarchy tour

POP DISCS: EMI WILL REVIEW GUIDELINES –
CHAIRMAN

The content of records, and EMI's attitude on this matter, was the subject of comment by EMI Group Chairman Sir John Read at the company's Annual General meeting on 7 December at EMI's New London Theatre. [. . .] 'Throughout its history as a recording company, EMI has always sought to behave within contemporary limits of decency and good taste. [. . .] The Sex Pistols incident, which started with a disgraceful interview given by this young group on Thames TV last week, has been followed by a vast amount of newspaper coverage in the last few days. Sex Pistols is a pop group devoted to a new form of music known as "punk rock". It was contracted for recording purposes by EMI Records Limited in October 1976 – an unknown group offering some promise, in the view of our recording executives.'

Next to this article on the same front page was a large photo captioned 'Trendy Tape Dresses Are An Eye-Opener', featuring two semi-nude models standing next to Frank O'Kane, a machine operator in EMI Tape's coating room. The women were wearing nothing but strips of EMI Tape 'to show the staff just how exciting EMI blank tape can look. The tape fashion show is part of the company's current promotion campaign' – undoubtedly 'within contemporary limits of decency and good taste', as Sir John would say.

When that issue of the paper went to press, the band were still on the label, but in a matter of weeks, they would be gone, leaving their former company to continue promoting the Black and White Minstrels.

At the start of 1976, Mick Farren had written a story for the *NME*, with a front cover photo showing a smashed-up bar with a broken jukebox and rubble everywhere, accompanied by the headline, 'Is Rock'n'Roll Ready For 1976? Is 1976 Ready For Rock'n'Roll?' It sang the praises of small studios, cheap recordings and a return to basics. Mick followed this up with a mid-year call to arms in the same paper entitled 'The Titanic Sails at Dawn'. Now it was the end of 1976, and a whole new generation of bands was out there. I asked him about the remarkable success of those predictions he'd made:

You want the truth? It was kind of like shooting fish in a barrel, really. Because what triggered it was a load of mail that had come into the *NME* about the Who at Charlton and the stuff at Earl's Court and

'Have we really got to put up with this?' And all I wrote was, 'No, you haven't, you can change it yourself, you can make it yourself, you can go look for it yourselves,' knowing damn well that the Pistols were already going, the Stranglers were already going, Dr Feelgood were in full flight, there were club acts coming up, the 101ers and the London SS had combined . . . So what I was really predicting was kind of for the kids in the suburbs in a way, because it wasn't any prediction, it was actually there. It was flourishing and it was signed to CBS almost . . . [laughs].

28

'Cheat, lie and dress to win'

No SEX Please, We're Seditionaries

January 1, 1977 – punk rock, anarchy, safety pins, gobbing . . . And who was on the cover of the *NME*? It was spiky-haired teenage tearaway Phil Collins and his mates from Genesis. Ah well, can't win 'em all . . .

Mind you, serial glue-sniffers with 15p burning a hole in their pockets at the local newsagents could simply have opted for a copy of *Sounds* that week instead, since their cover stars were an as-yet-unsigned beat combo called the Clash, wearing their home-stencilled, paint-splattered clothes, accompanied by the headline 'CLASH – Our Pick For '77'. It did not take long for this particular prediction of success to be tested out, since they signed to CBS on January 27, released their first single 'White Riot' on March 18, and by mid-April their debut album was done and dusted and being reviewed in the papers. It is interesting to note that from signing to release – including the creation of the finest UK punk album of them all in a matter of days – was just four months, which is roughly the same amount of time which your average seventies rock supergroup or pampered nineties Britpop band would have spent working on a few tambourine overdubs. Events were moving very fast in those days, having come round full circle to the recording strategies of fifteen years before, and the music was all the better for it. As John Peel told me:

> Well that's where it all went so wrong in the sixties. You'd read that
> – didn't matter if it was the Rolling Stones or whoever – that they'd
> take some studio somewhere for like three months, and you'd think,

'No, no, that's not what you should do at all.' You know, I still think that the first Rolling Stones LP was the best, and their best single, for me, and the only one that I can still enjoy listening to really, is 'Have You Seen Your Mother, Baby, Standing in the Shadow?', which most people have forgotten even existed, but it was the only one that seemed to me . . . it just seemed less contrived . . .

A band who certainly had the right idea were the Buzzcocks, who released their astonishingly assured *Spiral Scratch* EP on January 29, an object lesson and inspiration for all the DIY bands who followed, proving that you could do it fast, cheap and with style and humour. Three days later, singer Howard Devoto quit the band, which led to Pete Shelley fronting the Buzzcocks and Devoto forming Magazine, which is what is known as a win/win situation.

Malcolm McLaren's boys had opted for a major label rather than an indie like Stiff or Chiswick, and as the year began, they found themselves without a record deal when their new employers opted out. The January edition of *EMI News* covered this event with just a small item on the back page – with no picture – that simply said 'EMI and the Sex Pistols group last month mutually agreed to terminate their record contract' before going on to admit that the previous autumn's hysterical press outrage may perhaps have been exaggerated. In the meantime, McLaren's relentless quest for yet more manu-factured shock horror quotes in the papers scored another success with a mention in the Juicy Lucy gossip column in the January 15 issue of the *Record Mirror*, very likely based on information which he himself had supplied: 'On the shop front, I hear that "Sex", the King's Road store owned by Malcolm McLaren, manager of the Sex Pistols is being re-furnished and decorated in the style of Dresden after the bombing. How tasteful, no doubt they'll be including charred corpses to give extra authenticity.'

The shop at 430 had actually now changed its name from SEX to Seditionaries, and its range of clothing continued to move away from rubber and into bondage, with parachute-strap shirts, classic bondage trousers in black, red or white (£30 to you, guv'nor . . .) and muslin long-sleeved shirts with clips and D-rings (£6.50), and clothing labels which said 'for soldiers prostitutes dykes and punks'.

Acme Attractions also opted for a change of name, together with a change of location, moving up from the basement at Antiquarius to a shop a short distance away at 153 King's Road which was to be called BOY. Don Letts and Jeanette Lee (later of Public Image Limited) were managing the shop, and Don was holding down the regular DJ spot at the Roxy as well, in addition to filming the bands on Super 8. BOY sold a range of punk gear, but was felt by many to be the place to go if you couldn't afford the prices at 430 King's Road, and Letts told Paul Gorman: 'I personally felt we were copying Seditionaries, and the magic of Acme Attractions was lost.' It was in a far more exposed location than the old Acme had been, or even that of Seditionaries, and as such became a target during the punk/Ted violence which would erupt in the street that year, largely stoked by excessive media coverage during Jubilee week.

You Total Fucking Poser

For many, of course, actually *buying* off-the-peg punk clothing defeated the whole purpose of the exercise. Spider Stacy, who first met his future band-mate Shane MacGowan at a Ramones gig in April 1977, told me:

> If I saw someone wearing clothes from Malcolm's shop, I just thought, you total fucking poser. Poser was the biggest insult in those days, worse than boring old fart. The whole thing as I understood it was the home-made thing, do it yourself. If you have a pair of flares, hack them up or just fucking pin them together. I had this shirt that a friend made for me which was three white shirts that he'd just ripped up and sewn back together to make one shirt . . . fucking brilliant. And these army combat trousers, really shapeless baggy horrible things, and really old Doc Martens that were falling to bits. I also had a tail coat with a skunk's skin safety-pinned to it, which I was quite proud of . . .

On February 12 at Chelsea College of Art there was a gig by Plummet Airlines, who made the eighth single release on Stiff Records (the one right after 'Blank Generation' by Richard Hell and the Voidoids), but although the college had booked the Pistols back in 1975, most of their entertainment choices were the more typical student fare of those days, featuring bands who mostly wanted, in the parlance of the era, to 'lay down some goodtime boogie'. If you were looking for authentic punk rock action on the King's Road in the spring of 1977, then the place to go was the next pub along from the Roebuck, just on the bend at World's End where it curved around to Seditionaries. This was the Man in the Moon, at 392 King's Road, another landmark Chelsea watering hole which is now long gone. It was here you might encounter various members of the still-unsigned Siouxsie and the Banshees, managed by ex-Beaufort Street Market stallholder and sometime Pistols road manager Nils Stevenson. Another important early punk band who could be found there was X-Ray Spex, who made their debut appearance early in the year at the Roxy, and then in March began a regular Sunday night residency at the Man in the Moon, although you would have been lucky to find them listed in the gig guides. Nikki Sudden remembered going to their first gig there, as he told me:

> I saw X-Ray Spex at the Man in the Moon in the King's Road, and I ended up at a party with the band that night. I was hanging out with Michael Dempsey, the publisher who managed the Adverts. I used to go to the King's Road every week. I can't remember how I heard about that gig. There'd be flyers, or maybe I'd have bumped into one of the band. You just knew all the people then. I used to run into Subway Sect all over the place, I used to know Glen Matlock vaguely in those days. We all went to the same parties. The Damned would be there, and Johnny Thunders and all the Heartbreakers would wander in and disappear into the bathroom for two hours and come out later and leave . . .

One of the other classic 1977 punk bands who would play shows at the Man in the Moon was the original line-up of Adam and the Ants, with Dave Barbarossa on drums, sometimes supporting X-Ray Spex. Jordan from Seditionaries showed up to one of these gigs and got to know the Ants, prompting Adam to write a song about her called 'Letter to Jordan', whose lyrics namecheck the shop and also comment that, 'I didn't like the clothes there'. *Zigzag* journalist Alan Anger later described the scene at the Man in the Moon in a retrospective article called 'The Joy of Spex', published the following year:

> The dive bar was very tiny, without a stage, and the equipment was so shabby that it suited the surroundings. [. . .] The gigs were advertised by way of photocopied ads left lying around in 'specialist' shops such as Rough Trade or by word of mouth. The regular support acts for Spex at this time were the Unwanted and Adam and the Ants. This was where X-Ray Spex gained their regular following and when they stopped playing there, the place never really caught that atmosphere again (though small bands like Defiant and Local Operator did attempt to recreate it – to no avail).

The Unwanted, formed in March 1977, were fronted by singer Olli Wisdom, who had been working selling clothes on the King's Road, and, like X-Ray Spex and the Buzzcocks, would soon appear on the *Live at the Roxy* album which captured the scene at Andy Czezowski's club shortly before the building's owners forced him out in May.

The Brainpower of a Haddock

At the Pigeonhole gallery off the King's Road that March they were offering for sale limited edition sets of ten Andy Warhol prints of Mick Jagger for the bargain price of £3,700. However, for those who preferred their rock stars in the flesh rather than on paper, the two men who had pretty much single-handedly launched glam rock back at the start of the decade were putting on a free show for passers-by in the King's Road, as the *NME*'s gossip column 'Teasers' reported on March 12:

> David Bowie was in London last week for the Iggy tour. [. . .] On Wednesday last DB was taken to lunch at Toscanini's in the King's Road by cuddly Marc Bolan. After washing down their din-dins with a drop of nourishing wine, these two young men about town emerged onto the street and decided to present an impromptu performance of sound and vision to the nearest convenient audience – an open-topped bus full of schoolkids on a sightseeing trip. The young tourists, however, paid little attention to the ridiculous antics of the two cranks on the pavement. This provoked the Two B's into leaping up and down and squealing pathetically, 'I'm Marc Bolan,' or, alternatively, 'I'm David Bowie.' Wisely, the younger generation continued on to find more interesting sights on the other side of the road.

In March, *Melody Maker* found the Clash's debut single 'White Riot' 'catchy enough to sing in the bath', while a certain Mac Garry at *Zigzag* was doing a hatchet job on the Damned's debut album, managing to repeat the stupid lie which Malcolm McLaren later enthusiastically peddled about the Pistols, that none of these punk bands could play:

> Anybody with a brain bigger than a moorhen's egg knows they can't sing or play, but there are enough cretins about to make this a viable release, financially. [. . .] It would be preposterous to treat the Damned as musicians – I've heard ice cream vans with a better sense of melody – but you will be highly impressed with the music on this record. Especially if you happen to be a juvenile delinquent with a safety pin through your nipple and the brainpower of a haddock.

The Damned, meanwhile, were touring Britain supporting some-time King's Road resident and impromptu street performer Marc Bolan on his UK tour – a cracking double bill which came about after Bolan noticed a photo in the music press of Captain Sensible wearing a T. Rex T-shirt. Following that tour, the Damned went out round the country again, head-lining this time, with label mates the Adverts in support, giving rise to a fine Stiff advertising slogan accompanying the published dates:

THE DAMNED CAN NOW PLAY THREE CHORDS
THE ADVERTS CAN PLAY ONE
HEAR ALL FOUR OF THEM AT . . .

April saw the release of the Adverts' debut single, 'One Chord Wonders', which brilliantly caught the scene as it was in early '77 in much the same way as the Clash's first album. I asked TV Smith whether they first approached Stiff with a demo tape:

No, absolutely not. They came down to the gig – I mean, that's the thing, this was the sort of record company where the people came down to the Roxy club. This is what makes the difference, when people come and see a live gig. I mean, the majors, they probably wouldn't have even set *foot* in the Roxy, you know, no way. Same with Peel, you know, Peel used to regularly come down to the Vortex, which was the most violent club in London. If you were gonna choose a club not to go to, that'd be the one, because by then it was getting so violent, and such a horrible atmosphere down there, but he was sure enough there watching, checking out the bands and talking to people. You can tell who people are by what they do sometimes. It's the same with the record labels, you know, there was Jake Riviera from Stiff coming down and checking out the bands – came down with Nick Lowe and saw us and said, 'We like this' – obviously a great image with Gaye, and they liked the songs and they thought we had enough to do it.

No Time to Fuck-Arse About

As it happened, people such as the Adverts, X-Ray Spex, Ian Dury and the Blockheads and Wreckless Eric would be some of the last to come through the huge gap which punk had opened up. For a short while anything seemed possible, before inevitably the big money moved in, an identikit

punk uniform took over, and all sorts of older chancers like the Police who
had been around the block way too many times would cut their hair and
jump on the bandwagon, splintering it into pieces and making something
a thousand per cent less interesting out of the scraps.

Wreckless Eric's magnificent debut single 'Whole Wide World', released
by Stiff in August that year, was considered a punk song, and the punks
loved him, but he was light years away from the clichéd leather-jacket-
and-studs caricature with which the movement later became identified.
He told me:

> I think the big lie about punk is that it was working class. It was not
> working class, because working-class people who want to get anywhere
> have not got time to fuck-arse about with that kind of thing, to make
> clothes out of bin-liners . . . I had clothes made out of hotel
> bedspreads, stuff like that, a lot of the first Stiff tour stuff, you know.
> We had the time because we were middle class – I mean, I'd been to
> art school for four fucking years, you know, on a grant . . . I remember
> some newspaper writing about me and saying that 'Whole Wide World'
> was 'My mother said to me / There's only one girl in the world for
> you / and she probably lives in Tahiti.' And the writer said, 'The
> thing is, Eric's mother will never go to Tahiti, but maybe Eric will.'
> And I remember my mum reading that and saying, 'Who do these
> people think they are? How dare they, I could go to Tahiti tomorrow.'
> It was this assumption that we came out of the gutter, but we didn't
> come out of the gutter.

The trouble was, if you looked in the tabloids that year, the image that
they painted of punk rockers was of lower-grade violent morons who walked
around with safety pins 'through their noses', vomited almost continuously
and were never happier than when head-butting old ladies or mixing it
with the Teds down the King's Road on a Saturday afternoon. The *Evening
Standard* devoted a double-page spread to a pioneering piece of journalism
in which they rounded up a group of Teds – who were in their teens or
early twenties, rather than 1950s originals – and then followed them about
for the afternoon in the hope that they would chance upon some punks
and some violence would ensue. Naturally, they went down the King's
Road, with the reporter following somewhat in the manner of David
Attenborough on the track of an obscure and decidedly primitive tribe up
the Amazon. *The Times* reported such things in a more sober fashion, noting
the court appearances of a group of combatants on July 25: 'Thirteen

young men appeared at Horseferry Road Magistrates' Court, Westminster, yesterday after violent clashes between punk rockers and rival Teddy boys in King's Road, Chelsea at the weekend. [. . .] Nine youths including a Teddy boy who was said to have chased a punk rocker girl shouting death threats, were remanded on bail.'

Disporting in Linen Knickers

If the *Evening Standard* had been lucky, they might have even chanced upon John Lydon and Sid Vicious, because by then the two Pistols were sharing a flat which was small, cockroach-infested (according to John), and just a stone's throw from the King's Road. They were living in Chelsea Cloisters on Sloane Avenue, at a time when it was becoming increasingly dangerous to walk the streets in punk clothing. McLaren's policy of stirring up as much controversy as possible had left the band members out on the streets, often without enough money for a taxi, but with well-known faces and readily identifiable clothes – an easy target for the vigilantes. One of the great philosophical questions of the day was how the hell you were supposed to run away from the boneheads when your legs were tied together in a pair of bondage strides. I asked Mick Farren if he encountered any trouble on the street that year:

By the time punk came along I wasn't that old, but I was thirty-something . . . and very strange, you know. I mean, your average Nazi cab driver had *no idea* how to deal with me . . . and of course I'd been dealing with those arseholes for ten years. Well I was nearly killed quite a few times – 1967, '68, '69 – after that, I got very adept at avoiding that kind of thing, you know, taking tips from everyone from the Hell's Angels to Quentin Crisp . . .

As for the problems which the punks were having in Chelsea, compared with his own days in Ladbroke Grove a few years beforehand, Mick said:

When you talk about the King's Road, I mean, the punks were very exposed. Chelsea was always a bit dubious, because first of all down the road you had Stamford Bridge, then you had Fulham one way and the Putney Bridge Nazis in another . . . The worst problem we had up in the Grove was that me and Lemmy and Phil Lynott and Edward the cartoonist even, there was a while when we couldn't go out the door without getting arrested, frisked for drugs [laughs], but not anybody looking to go freak-bashing. I mean, let's face it, who the fuck is going to pick on me and Lemmy walking down the street, anyway? It was a bit of a different ballgame. No, but we were aware that Rotten was having a terrible time . . . Well, you know, if you give everybody the finger, somebody's going to take offence and punch you.

John Lydon, who was attacked elsewhere in London that summer by right-wing thugs, had this to say in his autobiography about the atmosphere in the King's Road:

When the Chelsea football club was at home, you'd get the Chelsea boot boys running down there after the away supporters. You'd get punks, Teds, away supporters, and football hooligans all together. You would see trouble, and because of the chaos, it was a very interesting place to be. [. . .] The violence was really severe, particularly when I got slashed outside the recording studio. Sid and I were living in Chelsea Cloisters. We weren't like Paul or Steve. We didn't have any permanent place to stay, so we were more open to being victimized. When I was slashed there was a problem at the hospital and they wouldn't treat me. Malcolm wouldn't even organize a cab to take us anywhere.

When not dodging angry vigilantes, the Sex Pistols were having a strange year. New member Sid Vicious had replaced Glen Matlock, who'd been forced out allegedly for 'liking the Beatles', according to the story which was carefully spread around the press at the time. The band signed to A&M Records on March 9 in a staged photo shoot in front of Buckingham Palace, and – with the ink barely dry – were promptly dropped by the label on March 16, putting paid to the projected release of their new single, 'God Save the Queen'. To give Sid something to do, John helped him secure a job at Seditionaries, thus continuing the policy of Sex Pistols bass players working at 430 King's Road. Hence, the few fans of the group who could afford the prices now had the chance to buy some of the merchandise from one of the stars who made the items famous in the first place. Indeed, anyone showing up on April 14 would have seen the entire band in the shop, doing a photo session for the German early-teenage music/fashion/relationships paper *Bravo*, with Lydon's hair combed like a Teddy boy.

Once again, though, it is worth remembering that there was an alternative to the Seditionaries range of 'Piss Marilyn' and 'Fuck Your Mother' T-shirts on offer for the discerning gent that year. *Esquire*'s fashion tips for men in March included a feature whose headline could easily have been sprayed across the walls of Seditionaries: 'How to Cheat, Lie and Dress to Win'. The mood, however, was closer to Jay Gatsby, 1926, than the Paris barricades, 1968: 'The bow tie this summer should be a narrow foulard (San Francisco $15). White buck shoes, Cole-Haan, $50; suede cap, Bob Posey for Byer-Rolnick, $18. Once upon a time, gentlemen disported in linen knickers like those opposite (Alexander Julian, $75).'

This Week, I Will Mostly Be Wearing Zips and Bits

Sid Vicious may have temporarily been working at Seditionaries, but long-time shop worker Jordan was fast becoming almost as famous as the place itself, having recently returned from New York, where she was fêted by the US media, and then on April 16 she was profiled in the *NME*, complete with pictures of her dressed in the new range of bondage gear:

> Jordan (real name Pamela) is something of a star. Although she's a shop assistant (in Seditionaries, the shop owned by Sex Pistols' manager Malcolm McLaren), there's little that is mere routine in her life. [. . .] I met Jordan at the shop, situated, ironically enough, next door to a Conservative Club, but there was little conservatism about her as she strode purposefully across the road, seemingly oblivious to the open-mouthed stares of Joe Public. [. . .] School was her pink period ('I had bright pink hair'), Harrods (yes, Harrods) was her green period. America? Well that was when she was into rubber. Spring 1977 finds her clad mostly in black. A black jacket resembling a straight-jacket, all zips and bits. Black trousers (more zips and bits), and black suede boots. The only break is vivid pink rouge and brightly coloured lipstick . . .

Once again, as in so many items in the media which deal with the shop, it is seen entirely as Malcolm's creation. However, at least in this feature, Vivienne is mentioned, albeit with her name mis-spelled, and it is clear that it was Jordan who brought her up in the interview:

> She adores working for Malcolm. 'I'm very involved in the shop and have great faith in the clothes. Vivian (McLaren's girlfriend) and Malcolm are the two most creative people around.' [. . .] Jordan sees

Seditionaries as 'the hub of the situation that young people are in'. And she adds: 'We get other bands in the shop to get the clothes that the Pistols wear. Mr Big even came in to buy vinyl trousers . . .'

While the shop was doing very good business selling T-shirts of Her Majesty with a safety pin through her lip, Malcolm was busily engaged in the search for a new label which could release the aborted second Sex Pistols single, 'God Save the Queen', and would soon strike a deal with Richard Branson's Virgin Records, who issued it in time to coincide with Elizabeth II's Silver Jubilee. As it turned out, the label which had put out the band's first single was also planning a release to celebrate the occasion. An item in the April 1977 edition of *EMI News* gave details of the EMI record division's own special response to the Queen's upcoming festivities – an album called *Sound of the Jubilee*, featuring Elgar's Coronation Ode and also his arrangement of the National Anthem. Whether this was recorded by an orchestra dressed entirely in costumes designed to show 'just how exciting EMI blank tape can look' remains a matter for conjecture.

Towards the end of May, a couple of the original CBGB bands from New York showed up in town as part of a tour of Britain, and found themselves playing considerably larger venues than they would have done back home. Television were headlining, whose *Marquee Moon* album had already seen some British chart action, while the support act was Blondie, who would have to wait until 1978 for their first hits. For band member Gary Valentine, author of songs such as 'X Offender' and '(I'm Always Touched by Your) Presence Dear', this was his first chance to visit the London he had been hearing about ever since the sixties, back when it was allegedly 'swinging'. Blondie's look and sound owed a lot to the mid-sixties British Invasion bands, and Gary told me about his memories of seeing those bands on TV and what it was like to arrive in town to play at Hammersmith Odeon just as the fuss around the Queen's Jubilee celebrations was about to kick off:

Back when I was about eight, on Friday afternoons the teacher let us bring in 45s, and we had these cardboard cut-out guitars and we would pretend to be whoever we were playing, so we were the Zombies, or the Animals or whoever. My mother liked the Beatles but she didn't like the Stones. They were the bad guys.

Anything coming from England was cool. I think the first film I remember seeing was *Doctor No*. Then *The Avengers* TV series, that whole pin stripe, umbrella thing. The aesthetic was very small, very neat.

Anything on TV that had London was just really, really cool – you'd watch these tiny little cars whipping around these narrow little streets someplace.

My first visit to England was in May of 1977. I was twenty-one. I was on tour with Blondie, and Blondie at that point was a sixties retro group, really, which is strange, because not even a decade had passed. I was still quite young and completely blown away by being here. All of my interests and expectations had been coloured by what I'd seen on TV when I was a kid, and trying to find those places. I mean, we walked down the King's Road hoping people would recognise us, you know . . . I don't know if they did [laughs]. I don't remember it being saturated with punks, put it that way. I remember you might see somebody – 'Oh God, look . . .' – it was more like when you went out to some club, obviously you saw it. *We* looked strange, that's the feeling I got. Mostly it was Clem Burke, Jimmy Destri and I, we were walking around as a group. Chris and Debbie had their own thing to do, but we walked around, we were the kids, and we dressed up like 'Hey, wow, this is it, we're in England, we're in London . . .' We got people coming up to us saying 'Are you guys in a band?' I don't remember any violent hostility, it was more like acceptance. It was like, these guys are wearing black suits, skinny ties, they must be doing something, you know? We wound up going to Anello & Davides to get Beatles boots and things like that, and I remember going to wherever Stiff Records' headquarters was at that time, and to Dingwalls and to the Music Machine. The London of one's imagination is in many ways a broader, richer place than the actual thing, but I was not disappointed, I have to say. I enjoyed it. I was ten years past the sell-by date of swinging London, but echoes of it were still there.

Dressed in What Looked Like a Plastic Table-Cloth

In July it seemed to be open season on the punks, with members of the Damned, the Boys, the Stranglers and the Boomtown Rats being attacked in separate incidents over the course of a few days, some of them while onstage, and the *NME* reported that someone had been at an X-Ray Spex gig in the Man in the Moon trying to stir up a group to go out and look for some Teds. They also said: 'Clashes between punks, Teds and boot boys have been rife in the Chelsea area ever since the Jubilee. Two people were arrested for threatening behaviour on Saturday afternoon at Beaufort Street's punk market, scene of other encounters. Local police force told *NME*: "It was the usual thing that happens on Saturday after-noon in the King's Road."'

Also in July, with the Roxy club having temporarily gone through an uncertain phase mixing fifties rock'n'roll nights and what was advertised as 'new wave' – the handy phrase at the time for people who were too frightened to call the music what it was – the other big London punk club of 1977 opened up for business, the Vortex, based at a disco called Crackers in Wardour Street. It was here, John Peel told me, that after having given so many of these groups their first exposure on the radio, he finally got to see his first live punk band:

> I think it could have been Generation X at the Vortex. Then I saw the Damned in a theatre in Victoria. I thought they'd probably just beat me up as soon as they saw me, but in fact they were actually rather sweet. I saw the Ramones at the Roundhouse. Never saw the Pistols, never saw the Clash. I saw more of those kind of post-punk bands, you know, and of course I was still doing gigs myself. It all tends to blur into one . . .

The same week that the Vortex opened for business, the Man in the Moon at 392 King's Road featured in the live reviews section of the *NME*. The occasion was an X-Ray Spex gig, and journalist Paul Rambali seemed fairly unimpressed with the venue and, indeed, the audience: 'a nondescript watering-hole with a high percentage of SW3 poseurs slumming it with the new wave'. As for the band:

> Poly Styrene is 19 years old and is the leader of a band called X-Ray Spex. She's been writing songs for two years now, and one of them, the succinctly titled 'Oh Bondage Up Yours', suffers the ignominy of being included on the *Live at the Roxy* album. [. . .] Poly, dressed in what looked like a plastic table-cloth, does a sort of mutated watusi and generally screams her head off – and I thought girls with braces were supposed to be shy.

Poly the singer had an instantly recognisable self-invented visual look, and had at one time run a stall on nearby Beaufort Market. X-Ray Spex went on to record a studio version of 'Oh Bondage Up Yours' which was released later that summer as their debut single, and in early September, they were filmed performing the song for a documentary being made by Wolfgang Büld entitled *Punk in London*, which was shot over the course of about ten days.

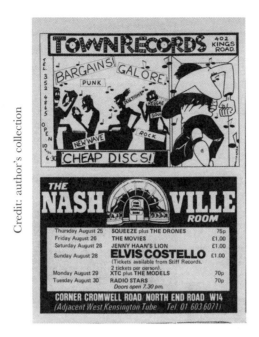

Town Records advert, and punk shows at
West London pub venue the Nashville, August 1977

Its mixture of performance and interview footage of bands such as Chelsea,
the Adverts, the Lurkers, Subway Sect, the Jam and others – together with
related interviews with some Teddy boys, a *Sounds* journalist and Geoff Travis
from the Rough Trade shop – combine to make it probably the best document of its kind. Don Letts had of course shot several hours of invaluable
Super 8 earlier in the year at the Roxy, but this was a different kind of film,
in which many of the protagonists – including a young Kevin Rowland
fronting the Killjoys – were invited to explain themselves on camera. Almost
inevitably, during the opening titles, there are shots of punks hanging around
in the King's Road outside Town Records, near Seditionaries. If you were
looking for punks that summer, this was supposed to be a good place to
start. Wolfgang Büld told me how he came to make the film:

> I was at the Munich Film School, and they asked me to do a docu-
> mentary so I said, 'If you pay for me to travel to London to take a look
> at this punk thing, maybe I can make something.' We went for research
> I think in August '77 and the shooting definitely was in the beginning
> of September. It was very easy at that time: you went to the clubs,
> looked at the bands and spoke to their managers, and the next day you
> got a call or somebody was waiting in front of your hotel offering you

another band. We made all these contacts within one week. We contacted the Clash and the Sex Pistols as the first bands, but the Sex Pistols were not available. They were trying to do this *Who Killed Bambi?* with Russ Meyer in Scotland, and were not in London at that time. With the Clash I met Bernie Rhodes nearly every day, and it was really horrible to work with him, because he never said no. Nearly every day I had an appointment with him and he asked me to come to places all over London – the most crowded and noisiest places – and was speaking the most complicated English to confuse me. The difficult thing for me was in this ten or twelve days we had for shooting to decide what to film, because if you looked at *Time Out* you would see that today are playing Siouxsie and the Banshees, Generation X and three other bands, you name it. You had to decide: do I go to the Marquee, to the Vortex? . . . The Roxy wasn't very good at that time . . .

Safety-Pin Stuck in My Art

While the Teddy boys were out in the King's Road looking for punks, any punks visiting the Royal Court that August to see *Once a Catholic* by Mary O'Malley would have found that there were Teddy boys up on stage, as *Time Out*'s reviewer noted: 'Set against a background of Elvis and Teds and neatly focused by Mike Ockrent's brisk production, this witty cracker should restore entertainment's good reputation to Sloane Square.' Meanwhile, down at the other end of the street, *The Rocky Horror Show* was *still* running at the King's Road Theatre, four years after opening upstairs at the Court.

In the music section of *Time Out*, Mick Houghton was deploring the increasing number of fake-punk bandwagon jumpers getting into the singles market:

> 'Let's Go' by Blitzkrieg Bop (Mortonsound) is the perfect example. The track is a banal rip-off of 'Let's Go to San Francisco' while the B-side features a totally inane one-minute song called 'Bugger Off'. A Newcastle area band, they sound horribly ill at ease in their new wave guise. The suitably blank expression on the sleeve photos and punk pseudonyms – Blank Frank, Mick Sick, Telly Sett – are a complete giveaway.

Five hundred copies of this were pressed and self-released, and in the intervening years the collectors' market for anything at all from those days produced in such small numbers has gone through the roof, where rarity determines value. In 2022, the Discogs record-dealing site listed the lowest price paid for a copy as £102.86, and the highest £400, and the musical content becomes almost irrelevant.

On the London live scene in the summer of 1977 there was hardly a lack of decent bands worth seeing. Indeed, one week's gigs at just one venue that August, the Nashville, offered the Count Bishops, the Adverts, Elvis Costello, London, XTC and the Radio Stars. Gig prices in those days at that venue ranged from free up to about a pound. On the other hand, you could always invest your money instead in a giant mirror-encrusted safety pin sculpture made by McLaren and Westwood's friend, the artist Andrew Logan. He was exhibiting it that August at the Whitechapel Art Gallery, and *Time Out* commented that 'Logan is the hip young thing of the moment, the foremost post-Roxy English pop artist. He's also being avidly collected by Arab art-fanciers, who, I'm told, are oblivious to the campy humour behind these gaudy contraptions.' An early Sex Pistols show had been a performance at Andrew Logan's Valentine's Day party in 1976, and Dave Barbarossa from Adam and the Ants remembers playing at another Logan bash at his place in Lots Road in Chelsea:

> It was just magical, stylish, it was like an eighties video in 1978, you know, people were just *sleek* . . . but it was all arty . . . I was in my own little world, like: 'Adam's God, wow, all these birds, all this booze . . .' I just couldn't believe that I'd landed, you know, out of Hackney, on the dole, didn't know where I was going, broken home, blah, blah, blah . . . into this amazing world of very white, pasty beautiful people . . . it was brilliant.

If the Chelsea art world represented one strand of the circle around 430 King's Road, another side of the scene showed itself at an event organised by the left-wing film centre the Other Cinema in Charlotte Street, which would show films, stage gigs and then hold political discussion afterwards. At an event on August 21 the theme of the evening was punk rock, under the heading 'The New Sound of the Streets?' It featured a gig by the Slits and Sham 69, followed by a discussion on the nature of punk, to which all four members of the Pistols showed up, and the assembled crowd witnessed a little-known sight, Sid Vicious – babysitter. Richard Dacre was working at the Other Cinema in those days, and at the end of each evening he and his friend, future Palace Pictures boss Steve Woolley, would close up the building and then head down to the Vortex to see the bands. He recalls the night when the Pistols arrived at the Other Cinema:

It was a phenomenally good gig, but what made it kind of exciting was that the Pistols came, they were in the audience. At that time Sham 69's singer and John Lydon had had a falling out, so there was lots of vibes going on. What made it such a terrific evening was that they all came to the discussion. They didn't just go home after the gig, so after the show we had Jimmy Pursey and John Lydon in the audience, having the argument, but actually within the context of having the argument, rather than a slanging match . . . The only one who didn't join in was Sid. Did the Slits have kids? There were three little kids there, anyway, and after the gig had finished and the auditorium was empty, they were sitting in the front row and Sid just looked after them and was entertaining them. I've got photographs of it . . .

Corrupted Reality

The work of Don Letts from BOY, Acme Attractions and the Roxy made the front cover of the August 26–September 1 edition of *Time Out*, under the headline: 'Punk's Home Movies – starring Johnny, Siouxie [*sic*], Dee, Palmolive, Joe, Billy, Shane, Jordan and the entire New Wave elite in Super 8 and glorious mono.' There was an interview with him inside, in which he spoke of how he'd come into contact with the punks from working at BOY. Alongside that was an article previewing a showing of some of Don's Roxy footage at the ICA, calling him the 'Pennebaker of Punk'. It also mentioned plans for other forthcoming punk movies, including the Pistols' Russ Meyer effort, and another which would turn out to be Derek Jarman's *Jubilee*, starring Jordan from Seditionaries. The article's writer, Dave Pirie, specifically raised the question of how the previous decade's Swinging London films had failed to capture the scene, and wondered if the proposed punk features would also miss the mark as badly:

> We all know what a bastardism and saccharine version of Swinging London eventually hit the screen. Most of the films were so bad that they effectively corrupted the reality altogether – with the result that now it's hardly possible to recall the real pulsating energy of that time without being poisoned by images of dolly girls in union jack dresses dancing down Carnaby Street. [. . .] Director Derek Jarman and producers Howard Malin and James Whaley seem to have contrived a wild pot-pourri of odds and sods including stars Jenny Runacre, Richard O'Brien, Jordan from Seditionaries, Little Nell (best known, like O'Brien himself, from *The Rocky Horror Show*)

and the Slits. Plot points so far leaked include time travel, Britain's degeneration, a rampaging female punk gang and at least some Latin speaking. It all sounds a bit like *Rocky Horror Picture Show* mixed with *Sebastiane*. Another film still at the planning stage is *Punks Rule OK* from producer Mark Forstadter who made a lot of money out of *Monty Python and the Holy Grail*. The last we heard his project was being revamped as a comedy.

In the event, *Jubilee* and *The Great Rock'n'Roll Swindle* proved every bit as disappointing as most of the swinging sixties films – although compared to Alex Cox's *Sid and Nancy* they were works of genius. The true spirit of that era was best captured via the documentary approach of Don Letts and Wolfgang Büld, or in the live footage from the Clash's *Rude Boy*. Punk was fast becoming a commodity to be bought and sold, just as Swinging London had been, and for many of the original fans it was already over. Wolfgang Büld told me how he had been struck by the number of people from the scene whom he had interviewed that September who spoke of London's punk movement as a thing that had already gone: 'It was surprising that at the end of '77 with most of the people involved, even with someone like Roadent [the Clash roadie], that punk was of the past already.'

While the scene was being shakily immortalised on film with varying degrees of success, it also found its way onto the stage of the Royal Court, a month after the Teds had been there for Mary O'Malley's play. The occasion was a show by Alberto Y Lost Trios Paranoias entitled *Sleak!*, which opened on September 12. The Albertos had an EP out on the Stiff label called *Snuff Rock*, whose piss-taking send-up of punk nihilism was so effectively done that it proved a big hit with the punk audience, in much the same way that Peter Sellers' send-ups of rock performers in the fifties were popular with the Teds. They made the front cover of *Time Out*'s September 9–15 issue, with the headline 'Every night in Sloane Square, this man dies in the name of rock'n'roll . . .', while the opening track on their EP, titled *Kill*, threw in a handful of existing punk clichés over a relatively convincing background of buzzsaw guitar. Roger Armstrong of Chiswick Records said to me:

They were a theatre group, really, weren't they. I didn't see that show. I mean, we sold the single in the Rock On shop, but, again, it's that thing of what punk was – it was beyond just punk, if you like. I mean, punk was the centre. What punk actually achieved was that it gave a voice to a lot of people with a lot of things to say who at that point in the business weren't getting a look-in, because the business was run by big management.

As *Time Out*'s article pointed out, the Albertos were less than pleased to have been described as 'the underground Barron Knights', but they were not the only people writing their own fake punk lyrics. A fourteen-year-old schoolboy called Gideon Sams published a novel – actually more of a short story – called *The Punk*, which was marketed with a real safety pin stuck through the cover. Sams, who seems to have relied on the tabloid press and television for a fair amount of information, was profiled as follows inside:

> He spent the last three years at Westminster City Grammar School, where he showed an obvious talent for languages. [. . .] He does almost all his homework at the Cadogan Pool Room in King's Road. An avid outdoor skate board enthusiast, his current project is designing a skate board he can 'pogo' on while travelling at high speeds.

The book itself told the torrid tale of one Adolph Sphitz, and his charming mates Sid Sick, Bill Migraine, Johnny Vomit and Vince Violence. ('None of these names were their born names, but punks like to have odd, and often depressing names, as in their nature.') Adolph's life revolves around visits to the King's Road, going to gigs at the Roxy, and getting into fights with Teds. Part of the problem is his star-crossed romance with a Teddy girl called Thelma, former girlfriend of a dangerous geezer called Ned the Ted. Somehow, readers may have been forgiven for suspecting that it would all end in tears. Still, at least Sams had a good idea of which pubs were the favourite punk hangouts:

> Thelma and Adolph got off the train at Sloane Square and walked down King's Road towards the Roebuck and the Man in the Moon. The Roebuck was one of Adolph's favourite pubs but the Man in the Moon had a lot of punk clientele. It was a bright Saturday afternoon. By the time Adolph and Thelma got to the King's Road Theatre they were pretty tired. They'd seen a lot of Teds on the way but surprisingly they hadn't been beaten up yet.

Inevitably, they are almost immediately given a thorough kicking by a group of Teds and then stabbed to death a few minutes later in the King's Road, but you can't help thinking, it is probably what Adolph would have wanted. As TV Smith says: 'Oh, brilliant scenario . . . how did he think up that one . . . [laughs]? That was just the way it got spoilt, really, people taking it second-hand and turning it into a cliché.'

We Went Down the Toilet

The *NME* decided to make fun of the more desperate aspects of the scene by reviewing a fake single by an imaginary band the Snivelling Shits, which prompted rival music paper *Sounds* to call their bluff and actually *form* a band of that name from among their own staff. Barry Myers (aka DJ Scratchy), who in 1977 was the house DJ at Dingwalls before later becoming the regular on-tour DJ for the Clash, had previously worked at the branch of Virgin Records off Sloane Square called Virgin Imports, at 2b Symons Street, and was then writing an 'Imports' column for *Sounds*. He wound up playing bass in the Snivelling Shits, as he explained to me:

> It was the *Sounds* house band, really. It started totally as a joke. When I joined we were gigging, we did a Peel Session [in June 1978], though we had to be called the Hits. We played a lot of gigs at the Speakeasy, we opened up for Thunders a couple of times. One night Sid Vicious wanted to borrow my bass, and I went 'Yeah, yeah sure . . .' and as soon as he was out of range I went 'God, is that the time?' and I was out the door [laughs]. There was no way I was gonna let Sid play my bass, I would never have seen it in one piece again. We were gonna sign to Island Records: there was us and Stiff Little Fingers, and then Chris Blackwell decided that he didn't want any more punk bands on his label. So Stiff Little Fingers went to Chrysalis, and we went down the toilet . . . [laughs].

Things were getting so self-referential that in the autumn one of the major labels, United Artists, released a single by a punk band called the Maniacs which was called 'Chelsea 77' – presumably a reference to the year, rather than a football result. It was reviewed by *Sniffin' Glue* magazine's Danny Baker in the December edition of *ZigZag*, which also contained the following sign of the times in the 'For Sale' section of its small ads: 'Longhair gets pnuk [*sic*] *OZ* 35 issues, *Ink 3* issues, *Zappa Live*. SAE box ZZ101.'

In Edinburgh that December, local punk band the Valves put out a single called 'Tarzan of the King's Road', complete with ape calls, but what were Chelsea's own four loveable moptops the Sex Pistols up to? Well, since their

Jubilee riverboat excursion on June 7, if you lived in London you could not actually see them do anything as conventional as playing a concert – you would have been better off in Middlesbrough, where they'd been appearing under the name Acne Rebble, or over in Holland, where they played a string of shows in early December. McLaren had worked very hard to ensure that one of the best live bands ever to emerge in the UK couldn't actually be seen by its audience, in much the same way that Tom Parker managed to deprive most Elvis fans outside the US of the chance to see the man in question. However, if you were in Chelsea that autumn, there was still a fair possibility of running into individual members of the band, and Lydon himself bought a house just off the King's Road in Gunter Grove, one street along from the squalid flat which the early Stones had occupied in 1962. In the event, he was to have no peace while he lived there, being bothered partly by fans but mostly by the constant attentions of the local police, who seemed to regard it as part of their job description to raid the house as often as possible.

Johnny and Sid from the Pistols were interviewed by John Tobler for Radio One that December, and Vicious took the opportunity to complain about the music press: 'They always lie about you. They said something about me picking at prawn cocktails in a King's Road restaurant and then driving away in a limo, where I'd actually just scraped the money together for egg'n'chips and left in a black cab!'

And while these two punk icons were talking to Radio One at the end of a year of anarchy, pogoing and youth rebellion, which record was currently superglued to the number one spot in the charts? The bagpipe-friendly sounds of Paul McCartney and Wings with 'Mull of Kintyre' . . .

Part Five

The Party's Over

29

'Where's Bill Grundy Now?'

Horrible Almost Beyond Contemplation

Two singles that appeared in 1978 summed it all up, more or less: the party was over, the revolution had packed up and gone.

Elvis Costello and the Attractions made the charts in March with a song called '(I Don't Want to Go to) Chelsea', with lyrics that pointedly referred to mini-skirts, photographers, model girls and getting 'your kicks in '66'. A gleeful burying of Swinging London and trendiness in general, its title also had a resonance for a lot of the original 1976 punk audience, who had just seen their own revolution bought and sold by the opportunists and the money men – many of the latter being classic hippie capitalists now in their thirties who had figured out in the interim how to sell the counter-culture back to the young at a tidy profit. It was perhaps no surprise that having burnt through two major label deals in the space of a few months, the Sex Pistols were then picked up and marketed to the nation by Richard Branson's Virgin Records.

The other 1978 single that served as a sign of the times was far from being a chart hit, but well known among the punk audience and on John Peel's show. It was an EP called *Where's Bill Grundy Now?* by the Television Personalities, released in November 1978 on the band's own label, King's Road Records, based at Flat 26, 355 King's Road, within spitting distance of Seditionaries. The new label was run by Dan Treacy and Ed Ball, both of whom grew up just off the King's Road. Dan's band was the Television Personalities; Ed's was called O Level. They also published their own fanzine, which was called – perhaps you're starting to see a pattern here – *King's Road*.

They'd written to the Desperate Bicycles to ask them for details about how to record and press your own single, and were hoping for airplay from John Peel, which duly occurred. The key track on this EP was a song called 'Part Time Punks', taking the piss out of the new breed of King's Road tourists who thought that they were being really daring by wearing a pair of straight jeans, but would only pogo in the privacy of their own bedrooms, 'when their mum's gone out'. The next release from the label was O Level's 'We Love Malcolm McLaren'. According to Ed Ball, the self-appointed arch provocateur McLaren warned of legal action over this, and also threatened to set Steve Jones on them.

Dan Treacy could actually see the Seditionaries shop from out of the window of his flat, as he told *Sounds* the following year: 'My mum used to do their dry cleaning. [. . .] You see all the stars up here. I must see Steve Jones five times a week. Gene October. They all go in there, Charlie Watts, Diana Dors, [TV newsreader] Reggie Bousanquet. I wrote a song about that, "I Saw Reggie Bousanquet Yesterday".'

As for the whereabouts of Bill Grundy, the man who conducted the infamous 1976 Sex Pistols TV interview, a book published in 1979 provided some clues: apparently he had been wandering around the city looking at the sights. Bill's guidebook, entitled *Grundy's London*, featured a dapper shot of the man himself on the cover, drink in hand, standing outside one of his favourite pubs. Indeed, he devoted a fair amount of space in the book to recommending decent hostelries across the capital, but he also had a few words to say about the street which gave rise to the Pistols:

Much of the bizarre quality which has overwhelmed the King's Road in the last decade or so is ugly in the extreme. Shoddiness is everywhere. King's Road may once have been a genteel thorough-fare [. . .] but today it is nothing of the sort. In many ways it resembles a very long Carnaby Street, which is an idea so horrible as to be almost beyond contemplation. The young people who frequent it do not seem to be much troubled by the need to earn a living. Whether that is because they have private means or live off public money I cannot say. I suppose they are enjoying themselves in their own way, although the need to keep up with every little change in fashion, and to be seen to be doing so, must surely be somewhat exhausting. Nevertheless the King's Road is worth a look at if only to prove the truth of the Lancashire saying, 'There's nowt so queer as folk.'

These One Night Stands Are Killing Me

When Grundy's book was published, it was not only the guys from King's Road Records who were living near Seditionaries – Joe Strummer was there as well, staying across the road in the World's End Estate. The Clash were busy recording their *London Calling* album, and when the title track was issued as a single, they came to that stretch of river just south of the King's Road, in the shadow of the Albert Bridge, to shoot the video in torrential rain on a pontoon anchored at the Battersea Park end. Don Letts from Acme and BOY directed the shoot. The Clash's road manager, Johnny Green, recalled in his hugely entertaining memoir of his days with the band how, when filming had finished, he took out his frustrations by picking up items of band equipment one by one and 'throwing mikes, amps and drums into the River Thames'.

It was a transitional time. After successive waves of music styles from fifties rock'n'roll to early sixties pop to R&B and Merseybeat to the tougher sounds of the mid-sixties to psychedelia to full-blown hippie music to prog rock and heavy metal and glam all the way up to punk, the UK music scene had thrown up something relatively new every couple of years, but 1979 saw not one but three revivals: ska, rockabilly and mod – the latter including a self-penned single by Squire entitled 'Walking Down the King's Road' – all competing for space backed by their own crop of new bands. The future had always stolen from the past, but now it was starting to look almost as if the future *had* passed and only the past was the future.

Punk was now everybody's property – something which had achieved such media saturation that it was hard to see what it was supposed to mean anymore. It seemed to be everywhere, but it was a caricature of itself. Comedy team the Goodies had already done a punk parody on their TV show back in 1977, while Alan Bennett recorded a conversation with Lindsay Anderson in his diary in 1978 in which the latter said to him, 'Have you heard there's a new punk rock group? They perform in Brady and Hindley masks and call themselves the Moors Murderers. That's why we can't have satire in England.' *Private Eye* meanwhile ran a photo making fun of Princess Margaret and her boyfriend Roddy Llewellyn on its cover for March 3, 1978, showing her standing next to a hospital skeleton, with the skeleton's speech bubble reading: 'These one night stands are killing me,' and Princess Margaret's speech bubble saying, 'Roddy's gone all punk.'

Joe Strummer may have moved into the area in 1979, but a very different kind of long-term resident was busy moving out that year. Margaret Thatcher – whose house in Flood Street, just south of the King's Road, had long been guarded by whichever members of local police could be spared from the pressing business up the road of kicking John Lydon's door down – shifted her belongings from there to Downing Street, having won the General Election in May 1979. On the steps of Number 10, she quoted St Francis of Assisi: 'Where there is discord, may we bring harmony.' In this, as in many other things, she failed miserably. It had been a punk cliché in 1977 to sing about life on the dole, but that was a golden age compared to what followed in the early 1980s, and by 1981 unemployment in the UK stood at 13.3 per cent, the highest in Western Europe. Inflation was running at 20 per cent, and eventually the number of unemployed rose to 3 million, which was double the 1977 figure, the sharpest rise since the days of the 1930s depression.

Of course, if you had already made your money and had a solid job, then life was good, and in particular, if you were lucky enough to have bought a house in Chelsea back in the sixties when they were still relatively affordable, then the Thatcher years would slowly begin to put you in the millionaire class. For the huge underclass of the jobless and the low-paid, it was another story, and the punks who were seen on the King's Road by 1983 were the identikit brigade, many of whom would have been at primary school in '76, but now came to the King's Road after the party had moved on, not to start anything new but to beg on the streets, hassling tourists for change in return for letting themselves be photographed, like something in a zoo. These adopted the leather-and-studs and Mohican look, some with tattooed faces and the words 'Punk's Not Dead' written on their jackets. As the joke at the time went: no, it ain't dead, it just smells funny.

Wreckless Eric: 'I never ever saw a Mohican, and a leather jacket with chains on it and "Anthrax" until I saw it on an early eighties King's Road postcard.'

TV Smith: 'The Teddy boys in those days did seem incredibly *retro*, you know, which was something we tried hard not to be . . . which is a bit of a joke now, when you see all the punk rockers now looking exactly the same as they did twenty-five years ago [laughs].'

The punks of 1976 wouldn't have been seen dead begging in the street – they had far too much self-respect for that. They wanted a riot of their own, not a handout.

This Big Clock Going Backwards

Following the break-up of the Sex Pistols in 1978, Malcolm McLaren had presided over the release of all manner of barrel-scraping material being put out under the group name, and the same few tracks were reissued again and again, at one point under the appropriate title *Flogging a Dead Horse*. The posthumous feature film, *The Great Rock'n'Roll Swindle*, in which he repeats as some kind of mantra the assertion that the group were useless and that the only reason for all the interest in them was because of his own brilliant situationist media strategies, has the distinction of being a film about the Pistols with hardly any footage of John Lydon, one of the most charismatic frontmen in the history of popular music. As such, it is an Elvis movie without Elvis.

Sid Vicious, like Che Guevara, was born to have his face on a T-shirt (although, unlike Che, at least Sid never sent hundreds of people without proper trial to be shot down by firing squads). Seditionaries duly obliged in the wake of Nancy's murder with a T-shirt – 'She's Dead, I'm Alive, I'm Yours' – but an image is only part of the story, and the Pistols without Lydon were a complete non-starter. Johnny, meanwhile, got sick of the constant harassment of the Chelsea police and eventually sold his house in Gunter Grove, moving to America, where he has remained ever since.

As for McLaren and Westwood themselves, they came to a parting of the ways, in which she kept the shop, now renamed World's End, with its distinctive backwards-spinning clock dial exterior, and he concentrated on building up his new group, Bow Wow Wow. Malcolm put them together using most of Adam and the Ants after having sacked Adam, who responded rather well to this by almost immediately becoming one of the biggest chart acts of the early eighties. Dave Barbarossa from Bow Wow Wow remembers McLaren's attempts to use the management and group-building strategies which he had employed on the Pistols in order to create the new group:

> Malcolm came along to this rehearsal room in Hackney and you know, we were awestruck – he looked brilliant, he was in this Dickensian, Georgian kit, you know, immaculately turned out, and we thought God, we're in the room with a legend, the guy that's basically designed our lives, you know. I think that Malcolm instantly liked the fact that we were three unsung heroes, the backing band, the sidemen, that were quite capable and relatively presentable, and obviously in awe of *him* so it was ideal, we were there for the picking. He made us listen to weird albums and aboriginal blokes just banging sticks together, African-style drumming, Latin . . . We just were steeped in this by Malcolm, weren't allowed to listen to anything vaguely western for about three or four months, and so this sound started appearing. He took away my hi-hat and snare drum and I had to sink or swim. He'd call you up at six o'clock in the morning

and ask you what you'd done, he'd be fucking merciless. What happened was, we got an advance from EMI, a really great record deal, and he upped our wages to like thirty quid a week [laughs] and then we turned up at his new shop and there was this big clock going backwards and all this new clothing, so we knew where our advance went . . . You know, fair enough, fair dos. What he gave me, Lee and Matt, money can't buy really, so fair enough, let him have it . . .

Perhaps the last of the great King's Road clothing stores was Johnson's, which opened in 1978 just around the corner from McLaren and Westwood, right on the turn of the road at World's End. It was owned and run by ex-mod Lloyd Johnson, who once had a stall on Beaufort Market with Pistols road manager Nils Stevenson, and whose stylish sixties and fifties-cut suits, jackets and shirts were to clothe a succession of bands for many years to come, upholding the flag of rock'n'roll tailoring in a street which was rapidly gentrifying its way towards mainstream fashion and posh designer labels.

The Sloane Square side of things gradually crept along in the direction of World's End as the eighties wore on, and with the exception of Johnson's and the rock'n'roll shoe and clothing store Robot, there were not many places left catering to potential new bands who might fancy themselves as the new thing. Sure, there were shops like Review at 81 King's Road at the start of the eighties which helped to outfit the likes of Boy George and Culture Club, and punk outlet BOY at 153 King's Road had done a licensing deal which enabled them to sell versions of the classic Seditionaries designs to the new generation of punks, but as the decade progressed it was club culture not Culture Club which would set the agenda, and the rising tide of sports clothing would eventually sweep all before it.

The Royal Court's archetypal rebel of 1956, John Osborne, wrote in 1981, 'I have no son and am unlikely to father one now but it is more than passing comfort not to have begotten a future Transport Minister, Golf Club Secretary or Royal Court actor.' The Court itself has survived as a much-respected writers' theatre, despite a financial crisis in the mid-seventies. Osborne, Tony Richardson, George Devine, Lindsay Anderson and many others who were the architects of the theatrical and cinema breakthrough which had its roots at the Royal Court are no longer alive, but they helped send out a remarkable number of shock waves around the world – no small achievement for a theatre company which at one point looked as if it would struggle to last out its opening season. Not everyone felt the same way though – Peter O'Toole, who trod the boards there in 1959 in *The Long and the Short and the Tall*, had a few words to say about the

Court in a March 2005 interview with the *Radio Times,* and not many of them were complimentary. Commenting that George Devine 'taught people how to do farts', he called Lindsay Anderson 'a poor untidy soul' and *Look Back in Anger* simply 'a good repertory play', adding: 'Books have been written about that so-called "renaissance" at the Royal Court Theatre. Bollocks. I watched this appalling bunch of strange young men creeping around, talking pompously . . .'

In 2000, the *Guardian* reported that Mary Quant was standing down from her directorship of Mary Quant Limited in response to a 'generous offer' from her Japanese licensees, saying:

> Quant was responsible for hot pants, the Lolita look, the slip dress, PVC raincoats, smoky eyes and sleek bob haircuts, but it was make-up that eventually made her company the most money. Her immediately iden- tifiable bottles of nail varnish and capsules of lipstick were licensed to be sold around the world. The current licence is held by Mary Quant Cosmetics Japan Ltd – there are now more than 200 Mary Quant Colour shops in Japan, generating around £95m a year, while there are just two in London. [. . .] She instigated a new era in style, one in which fashion was for any modern young working girl rather than just for rich ladies. Anyone could wear a Quant mini, if they had the legs.

Vivienne Westwood had a high-profile retrospective exhibition in 2004 at the Victoria and Albert Museum, just up the road from the place where in 1977 she had sold T-shirts depicting Victoria's great-granddaughter, Elizabeth, with a safety-pin through her lip. Designs which people had been arrested under the obscenity laws simply for wearing were displayed in dignified surroundings in one of the nation's most prestigious repositories of culture, with a video showing vintage footage shot inside 430 King's Road, and a soundtrack of music taken from the shop's jukebox selections back in the SEX days. Having lived much of the seventies in the shadow of Malcolm McLaren as far as the media were concerned, this was credit where credit was due.

Twenty-five years on from the Queen's Jubilee, in 2002, when Elizabeth was celebrating another one, Sotheby's auctioned a selection of Pistols- related artefacts: a pair of black SEX bondage trousers went for £1,200; a Seditionaries 'Destroy' muslin shirt for £1,100; and the original artwork for the *Never Mind the Bollocks* album sleeve for £2,600. These days, those prices would be a bargain.

* * *

The King's Road in the sixties and seventies meant many things to many people. Some hated it, seeing it as a shallow catwalk for fashion victims and debutantes or a haven for all kinds of depravity. For others, it was an inspirational place where you could find something of this allegedly new and exciting world which the newspapers and the television were talking about. If you did nothing but sit with a pint in a window seat in the Chelsea Potter and looked out at the passers-by during those years you could have seen a great many of those who directly affected the changes in popular music, film, fashion, photography, drama and art of the day: Stanley Kubrick, David Hockney, Marianne Faithfull, Michael Caine, Syd Barrett, Twiggy, David Bowie, Julie Christie, Samuel Beckett, Francis Bacon, Keith Richards, Siouxsie Sue, John Lennon, David Hemmings, Billie Holiday, Quentin Crisp, Jimi Hendrix or John Lydon. Some, like Jim Morrison, might have been sitting at the bar stool next to you. On the other hand, you'd probably have wound up too drunk to even notice.

For a short strip of pavement in a city which until the mid-fifties was most famous abroad for bowler hats, the Changing of the Guard and Sherlock Holmes, the King's Road in the two or three decades that followed played a major role in the popular culture of the Western world. Since the seventies, the area has pretty much been the preserve of those with a fair amount of money in their pockets, and the days of £9-a-week B&Bs are long gone, but people still come to the King's Road in search of the myth. Nearly fifty years on from Westwood and McLaren's punk clothing designs at SEX and Seditionaries, punk-oriented kids all over the world who want to dress up and look rebellious are still basically following the patterns that were set at 430 King's Road. Or if they are into the classic hippie/sixties dandy look, then like as not they're influenced by the clothes which the Stones or the Small Faces or Hendrix bought from Hung On You and Granny Takes a Trip. Films like *A Clockwork Orange*, *Blow-Up*, *Performance* and *Dracula AD 1972* all contain fragments of the now-vanished Chelsea scene of the sixties and seventies, whose traces can also be found in a multitude of television programmes and books of the day, and the King's Road remains one of the select few street names which are known around the globe, an integral part of the hip London of the imagination.

Acknowledgements to the 2005 edition

Firstly, a heartfelt thank you and a raised glass to my agent Lesley Thorne for all her support and advice and for having faith in me from the start, and to my editor Alan Samson for commissioning this book and for many extremely helpful comments on the manuscript. Thanks also to Leah Middleton and everyone at Gillon Aitken Associates, and to Kelly Falconer, Emma Finnigan, Tom Graves, John Gilkes, Carole Green and everyone at Weidenfeld & Nicolson.

It's been said far too many times that if you can remember the sixties then you weren't really there. On the other hand, a fair number of those who *can* remember the sixties (or indeed the early punk days) have been condemned to relive them for the benefit of interviewers many times over the years, and so I'm doubly grateful to the following for sparing the time to share their memories with me: Roger Armstrong, Dave Barbarossa, Wolfgang Büld, Richard Dacre, Wolfgang Doebeling, Mick Farren, Paul Gorman, Bruce Grimes, Piri Halasz, Kenneth Hyman, Christopher Lee, Miles, Barry Myres, John Pearse, John Peel, Cynthia Plaster Caster, Mary Quant, TV Smith, Spider Stacy, Nikki Sudden, Gary Valentine, Colin Wilson and Wreckless Eric. For their help and kindness during the writing of this book, I'd also like to thank Janey Bain, Joe Boyd, Bruce Brand, Jenny Bulley, Dominique at John Pearse, Margaret Duerden, Tom Gilbey, Martine Grimwood at Mary Quant Ltd, Oliver Huzly, Michael Hyman, Lea and Uli from Wild At Heart, Andrew Male, Maren Meinhardt, Claire Munro, Sheila Ravenscroft, Sally Riley, Mark Rubenstein, Neil Scaplehorn, Phil Shöenfelt, Sven Severin, Chris Sheward, Sylvie Simmons, Carl Stickley, Huck Whitney and Damon Wise.

Thanks are also due to the staff at the British Library at St Pancras and the JFK Library, Berlin. A tip of the hat to the Chelsea Potter, for resisting the temptation to go the way of the late lamented Roebuck or the Man in the Moon, and to the Cafc Picasso, another fine spot for sitting back and watching the life of the King's Road go by.

Finally, much love and thanks again to Katja Klier, without whom . . .

Max Décharné, Berlin, June 2005

Bibliography

Books

William Acton *Prostitution Considered in its Moral, Social, and Sanitary Aspects in London and Other Large Cities and Garrison Towns,* London: John Churchill & Sons, 1870 (first published 1857)

Martin Amis *Experience – A Memoir,* New York: Hyperion Books, 2000

Cecil Beaton (Richard Buckle, ed.) *Self Portrait with Friends – The Selected Diaries of Cecil Beaton,* London: Penguin Books, 1982 (first published 1979)

Victor Bockris *Keith Richards – The Biography,* London: Penguin Books, 1992 (revised 1993)

Edward Bond *Plays: 1,* London: Methuen, 1997 (first published 1977)

Angie Bowie (Don Short, ed.) *Free Spirit,* London: Mushroom Books, 1981

Angela Bowie with Patrick Carr *Backstage Passes – Life on the Wild Side with David Bowie,* London: Orion Books, 1994 (first published 1993)

Brian Boyd *Vladimir Nabokov – The Russian Years,* London: Chatto & Windus, 1990

Jane Boyd *Murder in the King's Road,* London: Harvill Press, 1953

John Braine *Room at the Top,* London: Eyre & Spottiswoode, 1959 (first published 1957); *Life at the Top,* London: Penguin Books, 1966 (first published 1962)

Richard Brown, ed. *The AA London Guide,* London: The Automobile Association, 1970

Hall Caine *My Story,* London: William Heinemann, 1908

Michael Caine *What's It All About?,* London: Arrow Books, 1992

Humphrey Carpenter *The Angry Young Men – A Literary Comedy of the 1950s*, London: Penguin Books, 2003 (first published 2002)

Gerald Clarke *Get Happy – The Life of Judy Garland*, London: Little, Brown & Company, 2000

Richard Clayton *Portrait of London*, London: Robert Hale, 1980

William Congreve *Love for Love – A Comedy*, London [no publisher given], 1710

Peter Cook (William Cook, ed.) *Tragically I Was an Only Twin*, London: Arrow Books, 2003 (first published 2002)

Aleister Crowley (John Symonds, Kenneth Grant, eds.) *The Confessions of Aleister Crowley – An Autohagiography*, London: Penguin Books, 1989 (first published 1969)

Karl Dallas and Barry Fantoni *Swinging London – A Guide to Where the Action Is*, London: Stanmore Press, 1967

Lionel Davidson *The Chelsea Murders*, London: Penguin Books, 1979 (first published 1978)

Len Deighton, ed. *Len Deighton's London Dossier*, London: Penguin Books, 1967

Charles Dickens *Dickens's Dictionary of London, 1879: An Unconventional Handbook*, London: Charles Dickens, 1889

Adam Diment *The Dolly Dolly Spy*, London: Michael Joseph, 1967

Diana Dors *Swingin' Dors*, London: WDL, 1960

Erica Echenberg and Mark P *And God Created Punk*, London: Virgin Books, 1996

Mick Farren *Give the Anarchist a Cigarette*, London: Jonathan Cape, 2001

Christopher Finch *Image as Language – Aspects of British Art 1950–1968*, London: Pelican Books, 1969

Ronald Firbank *Vainglory*, London: Grant Richards, 1915

Ronald Firbank (Osbert Sitwell, Intro.) *Five Novels*, London: Duckworth, 1949

Tony Fletcher *Dear Boy – The Life of Keith Moon*, London: Omnibus Press, 1998

Marnie Fogg *Boutique – A '60s Cultural Phenomenon*, London: Mitchell Beazley, 2003

Jean Overton Fuller *Swinburne – A Critical Biography*, London: Chatto & Windus, 1968

Jonathan Green *Days in the Life – Voices From the English Underground, 1961–1971*, London: Minerva Books, 1989 (first published 1988)

Germaine Greer *The Female Eunuch*, London: Paladin, 1976 (first published 1970)

Bill Grundy *Grundy's London*, London: Quartet Books, 1979

Frank Habicht, Heather Cremonesi and Robert Bruce *Young London – Permissive Paradise*, London: George G. Harrap & Co. Ltd, 1969

Peter Hall (John Goodwin, ed.) *Peter Hall's Diaries*, London: Hamish Hamilton, 1984 (first published 1983)

Leslie Halliwell *Halliwell's Film Guide: Fifth Edition*, London: Paladin, 1986 (first published 1977)

Charles Hamblett and Jane Deverson *Generation X*, London: Tandem Books, 1964

Reginald J. W. Hammond, ed. *London – Ward Lock's Red Guide*, London: Ward, Lock & Co. Ltd, 1967

Jim Haynes *Thanks for Coming!*, London: Faber & Faber, 1984

Bill Henkin *The Rocky Horror Picture Show Book*, New York: Hawthorn/ Dutton, 1979

Val Hennessy *In the Gutter*, London: Quartet Books, 1978

Adrian Henri, Roger McGough and Brian Patten *The Mersey Sound – Penguin Modern Poets 10*, London: Penguin Books, 1979 (revised and enlarged 1974, first published 1967)

Robert Hewison *Under Siege – Literary Life in London 1939–1945*, London: Methuen 1977 (revised 1988); *In Anger – Culture in the Cold War 1945–60*, London: Methuen 1981 (revised 1988)

Clinton Heylin *From the Velvets to the Voidoids*, London: Penguin Books, 1993

Vyvyan Holland *Oscar Wilde and His World*, London: Thames & Hudson, 1979 (first published 1960)

Don Houghton *Dracula Today*, unpublished screenplay, London: Hammer Film Productions, 1971

Ian Hunter *Diary of a Rock'n'Roll Star*, London: Panther Books, 1974

Richard Ingrams, ed. *The Life and Times of Private Eye, 1961–1971*, London: Penguin Books, 1971

Virginia Ironside *Chelsea Bird*, London: Secker & Warburg, 1964

George Jacobs and William Stadiem *Mr S – The Last Word on Frank Sinatra*, London: Sidgwick & Jackson, 2003

Clive James *Visions Before Midnight – TV Criticism from the Observer 1972–76*, London: Picador, 1981 (first published 1977)

Christine Keeler with Douglas Thompson *The Truth at Last – My Story*, London: Pan Books, revised edition, 2002, (first published 2001)

William Kent (revised Geoffrey Thompson) *London for Everyman*, London: J. M. Dent & Sons Ltd, revised edition 1969 (first published 1931)

John Lahr *Prick Up Your Ears – The Biography of Joe Orton*, London: Penguin Books, 1987 (first published 1978)

Sam Lambert, ed. *London Night and Day*, London: The Architectural Press, 1951

Bob Larson *Rock – For Those Who Listen to the Words and Don't Like What They Hear*, Wheaton, Illinois: Living Books, 1984 (first published 1980)

James Laver *Whistler*, London: White Lion Publishers Ltd, 1976 (first published 1930)

John Le Carré *Tinker, Tailor, Soldier, Spy*, London: Book Club Associates, 1974

Bernard Levin *The Pendulum Years – Britain and the Sixties*, London: Pan Books, revised edition 1977 (first published 1970)

Mark Lewisohn *The Complete Beatles Chronicle*, London: Chancellor Press, 2002 (first published 1992)

Frederick Locker-Lampson *My Confidences – An Autobiographical Sketch Addressed to My Descendants*, London: Smith, Elder & Co., 1896

Roger Longrigg *A High-Pitched Buzz*, London: Penguin Books, 1962 (first published 1956)

John Lydon with Keith and Kent Zimmerman *Rotten: No Irish, No Blacks, No Dogs*, New York: St Martin's Press, 1994

Jeremy Maas *The Victorian Art World in Photographs*, London: Barrie & Jenkins, 1984

Glen Matlock *I Was a Teenage Sex Pistol*, London: Omnibus, 1990

Henry Mayhew *London Labour and the London Poor: Cyclopædia of the Condition and Earnings of Those That Will Work, Those That Cannot Work, and Those That Will Not Work, Volume IV,* London: Griffin, Bohn & Company, 1862

Dave McAleer *Hit Parade Heroes – British Beat Before the Beatles*, London: Hamlyn, 1993

Chas McDevitt *Skiffle – The Definitive Inside Story*, London: Robson Books, 1997

Tony McGartland *Buzzcocks – The Complete History*, London: Independent Music Press, 1995

George Melly *Owning Up*, London: Futura, 1985 (first published 1965); *Revolt into Style – The Pop Arts in Britain*, London: Penguin Books, 1972 (first published 1970)

Kenneth O' Morgan *The People's Peace – British History 1945–1990*, Oxford: Oxford University Press, 1992 (first published 1990)

Bert Muirhead *Stiff – The Story of a Record Label*, Poole, Dorset: Blandford Press, 1983

Jane Mulvagh *Vivienne Westwood – An Unfashionable Life*, London: Harper Collins, revised edition 2003

Pete Murray with Jeremy Hornsby *One Day I'll Forget My Trousers*, London: Everest Books, 1976 (first published 1975)

Simon Napier-Bell *You Don't Have to Say You Love Me*, London: Ebury Press, revised edition 1998 (first published 1983)

Richard Neville *Playpower*, London: Paladin, 1972 (first published 1970)

Jeff Nuttall *Bomb Culture*, London: Paladin, 1970 (first published 1968)

'One of the Old Brigade' (Donald Shaw) *London in the Sixties*, London: Everett & Co., 1908

John Osborne *A Better Class of Person – An Autobiography. Vol. 1: 1929–1956*, London: Penguin Books, 1991 (first published 1981); *Almost a Gentleman – An Autobiography. Vol. II: 1955–1966*, London: Penguin Books, 1992 (first published 1991)

Tony Palmer *The Trials of Oz*, Manchester: Blond & Briggs, 1971

Mark Paytress *Twentieth Century Boy: The Marc Bolan Story*, London: Sidgwick & Jackson, 1993 (first published 1992)

John Pearson *The Profession of Violence – The Rise and Fall of the Kray Twins' Vicious Criminal Empire*, London: Panther Books, 1977 (first published 1973)

Mark Perry (Terry Rawlings, ed.) *Sniffin' Glue – The Essential Punk Accessory*, London: Sanctuary, 2000

Mary Quant *Quant by Quant*, London: Cassell, 1966

Oliver Reed *Reed All About Me*, London: W. H. Allen, 1979

John Richardson *The Chelsea Book – Past and Present*, London: Historical Publications, 2003

Rachel Roberts (Alexander Walker, ed.) *No Bells on Sunday*, London: Pavilion Books, 1984

Johnny Rogan *Starmakers & Svengalis – The History of British Pop Management*, London: Queen Anne Press, 1988

William Rothenstein *Men and Memories*, London: Faber & Faber, 1931

John Ruskin *Fors Clavigera, Letter the Seventy-ninth*, London, John Ruskin, July 2, 1877

Gideon Sams *The Punk*, London: Polytantric Press, 1977

Jon Savage *England's Dreaming – Sex Pistols and Punk Rock*, London: Faber & Faber, 1992 (first published 1991)

Anthony Scaduto *Mick Jagger*, St Albans: Mayflower Books, 1975 (first published 1974)

O. F. Snelling *Double O Seven, James Bond – A Report*, London: Panther Books, 1965 (first published 1964)

Tony Stewart, ed. *Cool Cats – 25 Years of Rock'n'Roll Style*, London: Eel Pie Publishing, 1981

Bram Stoker *Miss Betty*, London: C. Arthur Pearson, 1898

Paul Stump *Unknown Pleasures – A Cultural Biography of Roxy Music*, London: Quartet Books, 1998

Jonathan Swift *Gulliver's Travels*, London: Penguin Books, 1970 (first published 1726)

Kathleen Tynan *The Life of Kenneth Tynan*, London: Methuen, revised edition 1988 (first published 1987)

Kenneth Tynan (John Lahr, ed.) *The Diaries of Kenneth Tynan*, London: Bloomsbury, 2001

Fred and Judy Vermorel *Sex Pistols – The Inside Story*, London: Omnibus Press, 1987 (first published 1978)

Gore Vidal *United States: Essays 1952–1992*, London: Andre Deutsch, 1993

Harriet Vyner *Groovy Bob – The Life and Times of Robert Fraser*, London: Faber and Faber, 2001 (first published 1999)

Horace Walpole (Peter Cunningham, ed.) *The Letters of Horace Walpole, Earl of Orford, Volume 1*, London: Richard Bentley, 1857

Irving Wardle *The Theatres of George Devine*, London: Jonathan Cape, 1978

Keith Waterhouse and Willis Hall *Billy Liar*, London: Michael Joseph Ltd, 1960

Mary Whitehouse *Cleaning Up TV – From Protest to Participation*, London: Blandford Press, 1967

Kenneth Williams (Russell Davies, ed.) *The Kenneth Williams Diaries*, London: HarperCollins, 1994

Tim Willis *Madcap – The Half-life of Syd Barrett, Pink Floyd's Lost Genius*, London: Short Books, 2002

Joan Wyndham *Love Lessons – A Wartime Journal*, London: Flamingo, 1987 (first published 1985); *Love is Blue – A Wartime Diary*, London: Flamingo, 1987 (first published 1986)

Various authors *A Pictorial and Descriptive Guide to London*, London: Ward, Lock & Co., 1933; *The Yellow Book – An Illustrated Quarterly, Volume 1*, London: Elkin Mathews and John Lane, 1894

Articles, etc.

'13 Accused After Clashes', *The Times*, July 26, 1977

'Accordion Used On Society Dates', *New Musical Express*, August 22, 1952

Jean Aitchison, 'Noel Murphy', *Melody Maker*, June 1, 1968

'Alarm At Chelsea Shop Again Kicked Off Wall', *The Times*, February 10, 1976

Carole Alfred, 'Fashion Economy!', *What's On in London*, March 9, 1962

Kingsley Amis, Review of *The Outsider*, *The Spectator*, June 12, 1956

Lindsay Anderson, 'Sport, Life and Art', *Films & Filming*, February 1963

'Angry Young *Film*-man', *Films & Filming*, June 1957

'Angry Young Man', *Evening Standard*, July 7, 1956

Michelangelo Antonioni, 'Eroticism – The Disease of Our Age', *Films & Filming*, January 1961

'Armed "Teddy Boys" Hold Up Americans', *Oxford Mail*, September 26, 1955

Alfred G. Aronowitz, 'Pop Music: The Most, Or Just A Mess?', *Saturday Evening Post*, July 15, 1967

'Artificial Teeth', *Chelsea News & General Advertiser*, July 3, 1875

Bernhard M. Auer, 'A Letter From The Publisher', *TIME*, April 15, 1966

'Back Scratchers Unite', *Films & Filming*, February 1963

Peter Baker, Review of *The Loneliness of the Long Distance Runner*, *Films & Filming*, November 1962

_____, Review of *A Taste of Honey*, *Films & Filming*, November 1961

John Barber, 'Today's Angry Young Men And How They Differ From Shaw', *Daily Express*, July 26, 1956

'BBC Should Take A Tip From MM', *Melody Maker*, September 30, 1967

Jeffrey Bernard, 'The Line Shooters', *TOWN*, April 1967

Stephen Birnbaum, 'Getting Away – The Best Bits of Britain', *Esquire*, November 1977

Anthony Blond, 'Bistros and Bargains', *TOWN*, April 1967

Dirk Bogarde, Letter to the editor, *Films & Filming*, May 1961

Pat Boone, 'I Refuse To Offend Anybody', *Melody Maker*, December 22, 1956

'Boring Old Gits To Wed', *Daily Star*, February 11, 2005

Caroline Boucher, 'Beatle Wife Pattie Sets Up Shop', *Disc & Music Echo*, August 3, 1968

'Box Office Champions 1962', *Films & Filming*, January 1963

'A Boy Thug Talks', *Sunday Pictorial*, March 19, 1950

Francis Boyd, 'Verdict on the Bingo Age', *The Guardian*, December 19, 1962

Pat Brand, 'On the Beat', *Melody Maker*, July 21, 1956

_____, 'On The Beat', *Melody Maker*, August 4, 1956

'Britain in '63', *Films & Filming*, February 1963

Tony Brown, 'Elvis Presley', *Melody Maker*, July 21, 1956

_____, Review of *Rock Around the Clock*, *Melody Maker*, July 21, 1956

Clarissa Burden, 'The Revolving Shop', *Daily Mirror*, June 6, 1969

Maurice Burman, 'Radio', *Melody Maker*, September 29, 1956

'Cabarets', *London Life*, October 30 – November 5, 1965

'Café Eden', *West London Press*, September 22, 1950

'Cameras Stolen', *Marylebone Mercury*, June 16, 1967

Carnaby Card advert, *Record Mirror*, September 2, 1967

'Carnaby Street Village', *What's On in London*, May 17, 1963

Raymond Chandler, 'The Simple Art of Murder', *The Atlantic*, December 1944

'"Chelsea At 9" Is New TV Series', *West London Press*, September 13, 1957

'Chelsea Vestry', *Chelsea, Pimlico & Brompton Advertiser*, July 14, 1860

'Children's Moral Dangers Increasing', *St Pancras Gazette*, March 25, 1938

'Clothes Line', *Disc & Music Echo*, November 2, 1968

'Club, Disc Boom as Rock-and-Roll Craze Spreads', *Melody Maker*, July 14, 1956

'Come To Britain – Ancient & Mod', *Harper's*, April 1966

'Come to the Fair', *Films & Filming*, August 1957

Cyril Connolly, Review of *The Outsider*, *Sunday Times*, May 27, 1956

Peter Cowie, 'The Amoral Ones', *Films & Filming*, December 1962

_____, 'The Face of '63', *Films & Filming*, February 1963

'Crombie Forms Rock-and-Roll Unit', *Melody Maker*, August 4, 1956

'Crombie Rockets Net Palladium TV', *Melody Maker*, September 22, 1956

David Cumming, 'David Cumming Column', *Record Mirror*, June 8, 1968

Ray Fox Cumming, 'An Audience With Angie', *Record Mirror*, March 8, 1975

Shirley Davenport, 'Woman's World', *What's On in London*, June 27, 1958

Bill Davidson, 'The Hidden Evils of L.S.D.', *Saturday Evening Post*, August 12, 1967

Clifford Davis, 'The Busy Miss Bassey', *Daily Mirror*, November 26, 1959

Bob Dawbarn, 'The Scots-Born Irish Hill-Billy From London', *Melody Maker*, May 19, 1956

_____, 'Old Dawbarn's Almanack', *Melody Maker*, December 30, 1967

_____, 'Rock'n'Roll Pays Off', *Melody Maker*, December 8, 1956

Wilfred De'Ath, 'The Lonely Laureate', *Illustrated London News*, March 1, 1974

'December Highlights in all the Arts', *Films & Filming*, December 1962

'Des Bird Spotting In The King's Road', *New Musical Express*, April 19, 1969

'Diana Dors at Battersea Fun Fair', *Films & Filming*, July 1958

Joan Didion, 'The Hippies: Slouching Towards Bethlehem', *Saturday Evening Post*, September 23, 1967

'Dracula Drops In On The Mod Scene', *Photoplay*, January 1972

'Drink-Pub-Dry Students Clash With Police', *Daily Herald*, March 7, 1963

'Eastern Europe: Life Under A Relaxed Communism', *TIME*, March 18, 1966

'Electric Impulse Not An "Article"', *The Times*, October 10, 1961

Electrola advert, *Record Mirror*, February 12, 1952

'Elton Gets The Boot In With Noel', *Record Mirror*, February 3, 1973

'EMI Break With Sex Pistols', *EMI News*, February 1977

L'Epicure, 'Eating Out', *What's On in London*, June 28, 1957

Pip Evans, 'I Predict By the End of the Year the TV Cult Will Be Over', *Photoplay*, January 1960

'Face Up To The "Rough Stuff" Problem', *Kinematograph Weekly*, September 5, 1956

'The False Freedom', *The Times*, March 10, 1970

'A Few Days Since Was Executed At Chelmsford', *The World*, August 19, 1788

'Fifth Annual Chelsea Dance Band Contest', *Melody Maker*, October 1930

'First Day "Hell"', *Films & Filming*, November 1958

'For The Benefit Of A Public Useful Charity', *Public Advertiser*, June 26, 1764

'France Enragée: The Spreading Revolt', *TIME*, May 24, 1968

'Gateway To The Other World', *Daily Mirror*, December 18, 1968

Ken Gay, 'How Free Can We Be?', *Films & Filming*, September 1957

'The Girls Behind The Pop Boys', *RAVE*, March 1965

'A Golden March', *Films & Filming*, January 1960

'Gonella Forms R&R Outfit', *Melody Maker*, September 8, 1956

Gordon Gow, Review of *A Kind of Loving*, *Films & Filming*, June 1962

'Gospel Dynamite Will "Rock Reds"', *The Sunday Sun*, May 12, 1957

Felicity Green, 'After The See-Through: The Show-Through', *Daily Mirror*, April 15, 1968

Stuart Greig, Michael McCarthy and John Peacock, 'TV Fury Over Rock Cult Filth', *Daily Mirror*, December 2, 1976

Piri Halasz, 'London: The Swinging City', *TIME*, April 15, 1966

'Haley Comets to Tour With Lewis, Whittle', *Melody Maker*, September 22, 1956

'Hamp Slants Show on Rock'n'Roll', *Melody Maker*, October 6, 1956

June Harris, Review of *Rock Around the Clock*, *What's On in London*, July 27, 1956

Chris Hayes, 'Tremeloes Get Their Gear From Granny', *Melody Maker*, July 13, 1968

'Hello. This is She', *London Life*, October 30 – November 5, 1965

Laurie Henshaw, 'The Pop Discs', *Melody Maker*, May 26, 1956

————, 'The Pop Discs', *Melody Maker*, July 7, 1956

————, 'The Pop Discs', *Melody Maker*, July 21, 1956

————, 'The Pop Discs', *Melody Maker*, September 1, 1956

————, 'The Pop Discs', *Melody Maker*, September 22, 1956

————, 'Rock'n'Roll Swamps '56 Music Scene', *Melody Maker*, December 15, 1956

————, 'Mr Send Up', *Disc*, May 22, 1965

————, 'WOW – What's On Where', *Daily Mirror*, December 2, 1976

Godfrey Hodgson, 'Babylon '66', *TOWN*, November 1966

Philip Hope-Wallace, Review of *Waiting for Godot*, *Manchester Guardian*, August 5, 1955

'How To Cheat, Lie, & Dress To Win', *Esquire*, April, 1977

Dusty Hughes, Review of *Treats*, *Time Out*, February 20–26, 1976

Kenneth A. Hurren, 'Brendan Behan', *What's On in London*, July 27, 1956

————, Review of *The Chairs* and *The Lesson*, *What's On in London*, June 27, 1958

————, Review of *Endgame* and *Krapp's Last Tape*, *What's On in London*, November 7, 1958

————, Review of *The Good Woman of Setzuan*, *What's On in London*, November 9, 1956

————, Review of *Happy Days*, *What's On in London*, November 9, 1962

————, Review of *The Knack*, *What's On in London*, April 6, 1962

————, Review of *Lysistrata*, *What's On in London*, January 3, 1958

————, Review of *A Period Of Adjustment*, *What's On in London*, June 22, 1962

————, Review of *Shelley*, *What's On in London*, October 29, 1965

————, Review of *Uncertain Joy*, *What's On in London*, April 8, 1955

Chris Hutchins, 'Proby Vows: My Hell-Raising Days Are Over', *New Musical Express*, December 17, 1965

Jack Hutton, 'A Beatle Listen-In', *Melody Maker*, May 27, 1967

Raymond Hyams, 'She Worked For An M.P.', *Photoplay*, July 1958

'I Hate Stripping', *Photoplay*, June, 1960

'If You Must Rock'n'Roll – These Are the Best Discs', *Melody Maker*, September 22, 1956

'In Camera', *Films & Filming*, September 1959

'In The Botanic Garden', *The Standard*, August 8, 1827

'Intellectual Thriller', *TIME*, July 2, 1956

ITT Advert, *LIFE*, September 26, 1969

'Jack Clayton: Accepting the Challenge', *Films & Filming*, December 1961

John Jackson, 'Night of The Nasties', *Daily Mirror*, December 3, 1976

'John Schlesinger', *Films & Filming*, June 1962

Max Jones, 'Jazz at Wood Green', *Melody Maker*, April 7, 1956

_____, 'About Rock'n'Roll', *Melody Maker*, September 8, 1956

Peter Jones, 'Your Guide To This Week's New Singles', *Record Mirror*, November 25, 1967

'Joy Webster', *Photoplay*, May 1956

'Judge Bars A Husband From The King's Road', *Daily Mirror*, February 28, 1968

'Juicy Lucy', *Record Mirror*, January 15, 1977

'Jungle Music Cry At Randall US Show', *Melody Maker*, May 26, 1956

'Just For Fun', *Kensington News & West London Times*, February 14, 1969

'Karel Reisz: Free Czech', *Films & Filming*, February 1961

'King's Rd. Restaurant Owner "Gagged With Serviette"', *West London Press*, March 4, 1960

'King's Road Goes "Pop" In The Night', *The Times*, June 12, 1967

Alexis Korner, 'Skiffle or Piffle?', *Melody Maker*, July 28, 1956

'Lady Chatterley Acquitted', *The Guardian*, November 3, 1960

John Francis Lane, 'Franco Cristaldi: Golden Boy', *Films & Filming*, November 1958

Lewis H. Lapham, 'Miami Beach: Swinging In The City Of Illusion', *Saturday Evening Post*, February 26, 1966

Jim Lawson, 'Puke Rock!', *Sunday People*, November 28, 1976

'Learn To Dance Jive', *New Musical Express*, November 14, 1952

Letter to the editor, 'American B's', *Films & Filming*, October 1959

Letter to the editor, 'Heartened By Record Packers' Reaction', *EMI News*, January, 1977

Letter to the editor, 'Place for Credits', *Films & Filming*, January 1961

Letter to the editor, 'Pulling the Trigger', *Films & Filming*, June 1961

Letter to the editor, 'Rock-and-Roll', *Melody Maker*, May 12, 1956

Letter to the editor, 'The Sex Pistols Controversy', *EMI News*, January, 1977

Letter to the editor, 'A Social Document', *Films & Filming*, April 1959

Letter to the editor, 'Teeners' Hero', *TIME*, June 4, 1956

Letter to the editor, 'Walking For Monty', *New Musical Express*, January 29, 1954

David Lewin, 'Live – That's EMI Entertainment', *EMI News*, July 1976

'Little Miss Moffitt', *TOWN*, November 1966

'The London Scene, Eleven Variations', *London Life*, October 30 – November 5, 1965

'Longer, Lower, Wider, Faster, Swinger', *Evergreen Review*, March 1966

'A Major Writer – And He's 24', *Evening News*, May 26, 1956

'Man Of The Year – General Westmoreland', *TIME*, January 7, 1966
Roger Manvell, Review of *The Entertainer*, *Films & Filming*, May 1960
'Market For Mods', *Record Mirror*, March 14, 1964
Sue Mautner, 'Brian Jones' New Pad', *New Musical Express*, March 26, 1965
N. Menhinick, 'Record Reviews', *Harrow Observer*, April 16, 1976
_____, 'The High-Roadin' Kilburns', *Harrow Observer*, April 23, 1976
Suzie Menkes, 'Innocence and Decadence: Remembering Ossie Clark', *International Herald Tribune*, July 22, 2003
'Merrie, Merrie England', *TIME*, June 11, 1956
Russell Miller, 'Kings Of The Punk Cult', *Daily Mirror*, December 2, 1976
'Mine Host – Murray Radin', *What's On in London*, February 3, 1961
'Mini-Skirt Ban On Shopgirls', *Daily Mirror*, July 4, 1966
'More Particulars Of The Storm On Sunday', *The Porcupine*, November 13, 1800
'Mr J. E. Thorne', *West London Press & Chelsea News*, December 17, 1943
'Mulligan Forms Skiffle Group', *Melody Maker*, September 29, 1956
'Music Halls', *What's On in London*, October 17, 1952
'Necessary Technique', *Films & Filming*, June 1960
Max Needham, 'Waxie's Bop Flakes', *Record Mirror*, December 25, 1971
Kris Needs, 'Silver Jubilation', *Zigzag*, June 1977
Mike Nevard, 'Dusky Ballet Beauties Prance Nude On TV', *Daily Herald*, October 16, 1957
_____, 'Jazz in Danger', *Melody Maker*, June 30, 1956
'New Police', *The Standard*, October 1, 1829
'New Shop', *London Life*, October 30 – November 5, 1965
Andrew Nicholds, 'It's the Buzz, Cock!', *Time Out*, February 20–26, 1976
'Night Life' Cabaret Adverts, *What's On in London*, August 26, 1960
Peter Noble and Frederick Deeps, 'Show Talk', *What's On in London*, April 4, 1952
_____, 'Show Talk', *What's On in London*, November 9, 1956
_____, 'Show Talk', *What's On in London*, October 9, 1964
Rex North, 'Life In The Mirror', *Daily Mirror*, November 30, 1961
'November Highlights in all the Arts', *Films & Filming*, November 1962
'Now It's the Rock'n'Roll Sinners!', *Melody Maker*, September 29, 1956
'Now The Beatles' Fashions Invade Swinging Chelsea', *Disc & Music Echo*, June 8, 1968
'Osteria 430', *Chelsea News*, January 29, 1971
'Our Mysterious Children', *Saturday Evening Post*, September 23, 1967
'Ozone Whiskey', *Chelsea News & General Advertiser*, February 7, 1880
'Paints With Her Thumb', *West London Press*, January 12, 1951

'People', *TIME*, May 21, 1956

'People', *TIME*, July 2, 1956

'People', *TIME*, July 16, 1956

'People', *TIME*, May 17, 1968

'The Pheasantry', *What's On in London*, November 2, 1956

Hella Pick, 'Beatle Hysteria Hits US', *The Guardian*, February 8, 1964

'The Pink Floyd's Circus', *Beat Instrumental*, September 1967

'Pinta Thief Was Thirsty', *Kensington Post*, June 27, 1969

'Pistols Are Sent Packing', *Daily Mirror*, December 3, 1976

'Pop Discs: EMI Will Review Guidelines – Chairman', *EMI News*, January, 1977

'Pop Paraphernalia', *Record Mirror*, November 9

Jill Pound-Corner, 'Woman's World', *What's On in London*, February 13, 1959

'Punks? What Punks', *Record Mirror*, October 23, 1976

'QC Says Man Was On LSD "Trip"', *The Times*, October 8, 1968

Steve Race, 'Opinion', *Melody Maker*, May 5, 1956

Eric Random, 'I Call This Cult Dangerous', *Photoplay*, September 1956

'Ranelagh House, Chelsea', *Daily Post*, May 22, 1742

'Rapid Rise In Use Of Illegal Chinese Heroin', *The Times*, January 26, 1972

'Rave At The Flicks', *RAVE*, January 1968

'Recording Kittens Advert', *Record Mirror*, September 25, 1971

'Residents Tell Of Early Morning Bottle Fights', *Chelsea News*, December 5, 1975

'Restaurants', *What's On in London*, October 17, 1952

Review of *Chips With Everything*, *What's On in London*, June 22, 1962

Review of *Cock-a-Doodle-Dandy*, *What's On in London*, October 2, 1959

Review of *The Entertainer*, *What's On in London*, October 17, 1952

Review of *Look Back in Anger*, *TIME*, October 14, 1957

Review of *The Rocky Horror Show*, *Time Out*, February 20–26, 1976

Review of *Saturday Night And Sunday Morning*, *What's On in London*, February 3, 1961

Review of *Tom Jones*, *What's On in London*, January 17, 1964

Tony Richardson, 'The Two Worlds of Cinema', *Films & Filming*, June 1961

'Rock and Riot Boys Don't Worry Crombie', *Melody Maker*, September 8, 1956

'Rock-and-Rollers Nix the Basie Beat', *Melody Maker*, June 30, 1956

'Rock'n'Roll Bands at Jazz Weekend', *Melody Maker*, September 29, 1956

'Rock'n'Roll Riots Don't Scare Haley', *Melody Maker*, September 15, 1956

'Ronnie Harris for Rock'n'Roll Package', *Melody Maker*, October 13, 1956

'Ronny, Diary of a Rave Girl', *RAVE*, January 1968

Rosalind Russell, 'Wine, Women & Rod', *Record Mirror*, June 19, 1976

Harry Saltzman, 'New Wave Hits British Films', *Films & Filming*, April 1960

Jimmy Saville column, *Sunday People*, November 28, 1976

Caroline Seebohm, 'English Girls In New York', *New York*, July 19, 1971

Anthony Shields and Robert Gaddes, 'Night Life', *What's On in London*, November 22, 1957

_____, 'Night Life', *What's On in London*, June 16, 1961

'A Silver Submarine', *The Times*, November 27, 1967

'Singles Scene', *Stamford Mercury*, December 3, 1976

'Sir John Read's End Of Year Statement', *EMI News*, November/December, 1976

'Sound Of The Jubilee', *EMI News*, May 1977

Catherine Sparks, 'Shopping In London', *What's On in London*, March 10, 1967

F. Maurice Speed, 'Cinema', *What's On in London*, July 27, 1956

_____, Review of *The Party's Over*, *What's On in London*, May 7, 1965

Alan Stanbrook, Letter to the editor, 'Osborne and Love', *Films & Filming*, September 1959

Barry Stanley, 'Mini-Skirt May Have Led To Murder', *Daily Mirror*, September 21, 1967

'Star Time at Battersea', *Melody Maker*, May 19, 1956

'Sunless', *Films & Filming*, November 1962

'Taking the Plunge', *Films & Filming*, December 1961

Guy Taylor, 'Maybe This Is Why TV Gets Away With Murder', *The Stage & Television Today*, December 24, 1959

'A Teddy Boy – And He's At Red Circle!', *The Hotspur*, December 11,1954

'The Teds', *TIME*, September 24, 1956

'Teenage Girl In "Gigantic Drug Plot"', *The Times*, November 27, 1969

'Telepage', *Daily Mirror*, October 8, 1957

'These Names Make Noise!', *Record Mirror*, December 22, 1956

James Thomas, 'TV', *News Chronicle*, September 20, 1957

Peter Tipthorp, 'I Predict', *Photoplay*, January 1959

_____, 'Rock'n'Roll Terror – Where Will it End?', *Photoplay*, January 1959

'To Be Lett At Chelsea', *Daily Journal*, June 26, 1728

'To Be Sold By Auction', *Public Advertiser*, November 16, 1772

'Too Much Rockin' Says Nat Gonella', *Melody Maker*, December 15, 1956

'Top of the Pops', *Melody Maker*, April 7, 1956

Philip Toynbee, Review of *The Outsider*, *The Observer*, May 27, 1956

'Trendy Tapes Dresses Are An Eye-Opener', *EMI News*, January 1977

'A Two-Foot High Ornate Porcelain Chinese Lion', *Westminster & Pimlico News*, December 21, 1973

Kenneth Tynan, Review of *Look Back in Anger*, *The Observer*, May 13, 1956

'US Rock-and-Roll Show For London', *Melody Maker*, August 25, 1956

John Vincent, 'Films and Filming in Britain', *Films & Filming*, November 1958

————, 'Films and Filming in Britain', *Films & Filming*, October 1959

'Vive "Le Drug" De Londres!', *The Times*, July 8, 1968

Loudon Wainwright, Jr, 'Mini-Looking In London', *LIFE*, May 26,1967

Christopher Ward, 'The Meditations Of Michael', *Daily Mirror*, October 2, 1967

————, 'You Didn't Know That Pacey Has Danged Out Trendy?', *Daily Mirror*, August 27, 1968

Peter Warren, 'In Britain', *Films & Filming*, March 1961

————, 'In Britain', *Films & Filming*, May 1961

'Way-Outspoken', *RAVE*, May 1964

'The Week Ahead', *London Life*, October 30 – November 5, 1965

'What's Happening', *TOWN*, November 1966

'Wild & Woolly – C'Mon, Let Yourself Go This Season', *Esquire*, October, 1976

Tony Wilson, 'Chelsea Swings Below, But Julie Keeps On Working', *Melody Maker*, April 6, 1968

'Wrath At The Helm', *The Times*, May 26, 1956

David Wright, 'Dancer Charged After Drug Raid On A Boutique', *Daily Mirror*, May 20, 1967

Ian Wright, Review of *Goldfinger*, *The Guardian*, September 18, 1964

'The Year 1959', *Films & Filming*, January 1960

'The Year 1960', *Films & Filming*, January 1961

'Yeh-Heh-Heh-Hes, Baby', *TIME*, June 18, 1956

'Your Bad Food Guide', *Daily Herald*, August 3, 1963

'Z Cars 'May Harm Children'', *The Guardian*, January 5, 1962

INDEX

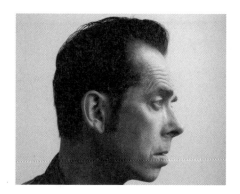

Max Décharné is a writer and musician from London. His other books include *Vulgar Tongues, Hardboiled Hollywood, Straight From The Fridge, Dad* and *A Rocket In My Pocket*. He has written about music for *MOJO* magazine since 1998 and his work has also appeared in the *Spectator,* the *Sunday Times Colour Magazine,* the *Observer,* the *Guardian* and the *TLS,* among others. Max was the drummer in Gallon Drunk, then the singer and principal song-writer with The Flaming Stars. In a long and varied career in the music business, he has recorded many albums and singles, nine John Peel Sessions and played shows all across the USA, Canada, Japan and virtually every country in Europe.

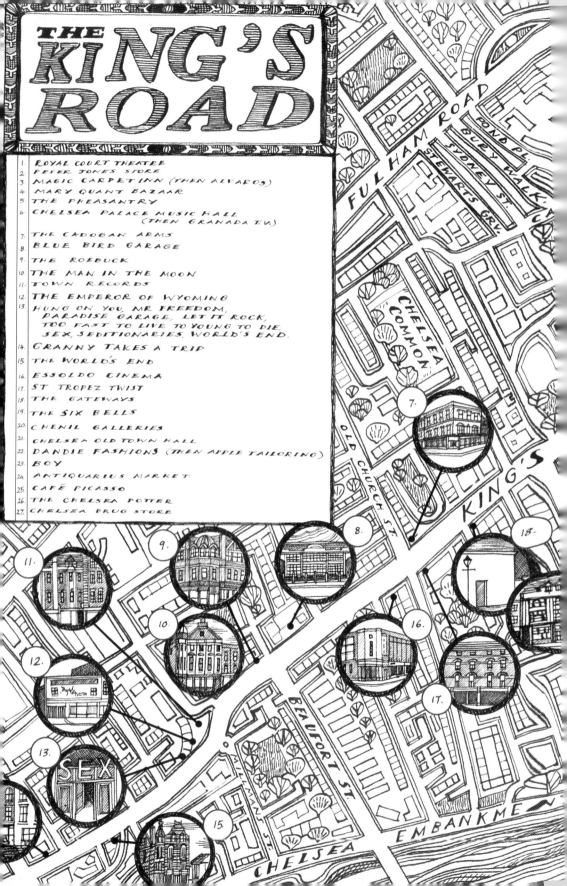

THE KING'S ROAD

1. ROYAL COURT THEATRE
2. PETER JONES STORE
3. MAGIC CARPET INN (THEN ALVAROS)
4. MARY QUANT BAZAAR
5. THE PHEASANTRY
6. CHELSEA PALACE MUSIC HALL
   (THEN GRANADA T.V.)
7. THE CADOGAN ARMS
8. BLUE BIRD GARAGE
9. THE ROEBUCK
10. THE MAN IN THE MOON
11. TOWN RECORDS
12. THE EMPEROR OF WYOMING
13. HUNG ON YOU, MR FREEDOM,
    PARADISE GARAGE, LET IT ROCK,
    TOO FAST TO LIVE TO YOUNG TO DIE,
    SEX, SEDITIONARIES, WORLD'S END.
14. GRANNY TAKES A TRIP
15. THE WORLD'S END
16. ESSOLDO CINEMA
17. ST TROPEZ TWIST
18. THE GATEWAYS
19. THE SIX BELLS
20. CHENIL GALLERIES
21. CHELSEA OLD TOWN HALL
22. DANDIE FASHIONS (THEN APPLE TAILORING)
23. BOY
24. ANTIQUARIUS MARKET
25. CAFÉ PICASSO
26. THE CHELSEA POTTER
27. CHELSEA DRUG STORE